CYBERLAW
HANDBOOK
FOR E-COMMERCE

John W. Bagby
The Pennsylvania State University

THOMSON

SOUTH-WESTERN
WEST

Australia · Canada · Mexico · Singapore · Spain · United Kingdom · United States

THOMSON
SOUTH-WESTERN
WEST

Cyberlaw Handbook for e-Commerce, 1e
John W. Bagby

Vice President/Editor-in-Chief
Jack W. Calhoun

Vice President/Team Director
Michael P. Roche

Sr. Acquisitions Editor
Rob Dewey

Sr. Developmental Editor
Susanna C. Smart

Marketing Managers
Nicole C. Moore
Steven Silverstein

Production Editor
Daniel C. Plofchan

Manufacturing Coordinators
Rhonda Utley
Doug Wilke

Sr. Design Project Manager
Michelle Kunkler

Cover and Internal Design
Ramsdell Design/
Craig Ramsdell, Cincinnati

Cover Images
©PhotoDisc, Inc.

Photo Researcher
Deanna Ettinger

Compositor
Trejo Production

Printer
Transcontinental Printing
Louiseville, PQ

Library of Congress
Control Number: 2002111609

ISBN 0-324-26028-8

CONTENTS

INTRODUCTION

Cyberlaw Handbook for E-Commerce Law was written to fulfill an emerging need for direction regarding technology law issues for both traditional commerce and emerging e-commerce. This handbook fully integrates both perspectives. Traditional commerce and electronic commerce are merging today, as evidenced by the number of business-to-business transactions accomplished with significant e-commerce components in payments, electronic data interchange, or electronic processing of documents. Transactions between businesses and consumers are following a similar pattern, evolving to include significant elements of electronic assent, transaction processing, and performances. For example, most new car purchases involve some Internet activity, businesses advertise through the Internet, and consumers use retailing, travel, and other services available on the Internet. In addition, sectors such as government utilize the Internet through interactive processes with citizens (taxes, licensing, information), as well as the procurement of goods and services from vendors. Electronic marketplaces are also changing the face of consumer-to-consumer transactions as electronic auction markets make secondhand resale markets more liquid. As business is no longer based only on the traditional economy, this handbook captures the evolution toward regulations applicable to both e-commerce and traditional methods of business.

The dot.com revolution of the late 1990s abruptly ended in a sobering realization that many aspects of traditional business models are still valid. The dot.com bubble economy misled venture capitalists, the securities markets, and a whole generation of entrepreneurs into believing that traditional measures of profitability and return on investment were inapplicable to Internet enterprises. Sole reliance on electronic commerce methods seems appropriate for only narrow sectors of the economy.

Yet smokestack industries that resisted the cyberspace revolution in the 1990s are increasingly involved in e-commerce. For example, traditional industries are progressively more involved in on-line business-to-business marketplaces. They are migrating their customer service networks to e-mail, electronic data interchange, and on-line customer information, including Web site catalogues, specification listings, and electronic contracting. Tremendous efficiencies are derived through the widespread use of electronic bill presentment and electronic payments, electronic commercial document processing, and enterprise software using computerized networks to connect multiple locations and customers and suppliers.

Since the burst of the dot.com bubble, it has become apparent that neither the traditional sector of the economy nor the e-commerce sector should be viewed in isolation. A few years ago, some commentators heralded the "new" economy, dubbing it "clicks" and predicting its superiority over the "old economy," the "bricks."

There was widespread speculation about a long, steady decline in the traditional economy. Others rejoiced at the burst of the dot.com bubble, claiming that e-commerce lacked any real substance. This position overlooks the rather substantial influence and ongoing growth of computerized telecommunications and information technology and its substantial influence on existing and emerging businesses. Increasingly, there is a recognition that most businesses in the future will converge on a hybrid of methods that must first retain the rigors of the traditional economy, including financial control, profitability requirements, disciplined management, and attention to supply chain efficiencies. At the same time, successful future businesses must implement effective information and communications technologies that were once considered the sole province of e-commerce companies: electronic communications, electronic data mining, electronic contract negotiation and formation, electronic transaction processing, electronic payments, and electronic performances.

The modernization of business techniques offered by e-commerce business models offers tangible productivity improvements, speeds the effectiveness of commercial interactions, and is replacing many paper-based and hand-operated business processes of the traditional economy. All this suggests that a convergence of traditional business models with information technology methods requires major redesign of business models and business processes in order to sustain competitive advantage. The laws facilitating this transition must be understood and respected for the timeless aspects of traditional public policies. Recognizing which laws must be updated—sometimes even replaced—reflects the changing reach and functionality of new technology. Business managers need an understanding of traditional legal problem areas such as tort, criminal law, and contract law, as well as for emerging problem areas such as privacy laws or intellectual property protection.

The study of e-commerce and information technology law will have enduring relevance applicable today and in the future. It is intended to provide understanding of the evolution and the integration of traditional and new legal principles to the evolving marketplace. The evolution to e-commerce is forcing all business and government managers to reevaluate their basic principles, develop new models and analytical tools, and then integrate them into traditional functions.

It is widely predicted that e-commerce practices will radically change traditional business and government methods as innovative methods are ever more frequently introduced. During such turbulence, a firm grounding in basic legal concepts is needed to understand potential legal pitfalls and to anticipate and forestall problems.

There are several reasons why decision makers need both an understanding of basic legal principles that have been applied to traditional methods and an understanding of e-commerce cyberlaw. First, the enforceability of contracts is essential to encourage use of, reliance upon, and investment in e-commerce. The risks of nonenforceability—and even the risks of higher transaction costs—are currently a significant barrier to faster growth in e-commerce. Second, many participants in cyberspace and many decision makers have been proceeding into e-commerce without the benefit of careful strategic review by legal counsel competent in cyberlaw. Considerable risk of loss is already well documented for such underinformed ventures. Third, many businesspeople and government workers are more experienced with traditional commercial practice than with the unique property rights problems of intellectual property. Continued unfamiliarity with copyright and trademark ownership, licensing, and infringement are already leading to extensive and costly litigation. This handbook enables decision makers to better understand the law's effect on both traditional and e-commerce-related practices.

John W. Bagby

This book is dedicated to my mother, Lucinda, and father, Emmett,
whose constant and steadfast encouragement keep me on track.
I am grateful for the patience and support of my wife, Robin.
Finally, I hope my children, Julia and Jack, are inspired by
the work effort needed to develop and execute large projects.

CHAPTER I
LAW IN E-BUSINESS

The impact of law and regulation is pervasive in business, the professions, and government and for most who work in nearly every endeavor. "Ignorance of the law is no excuse" is an old saying of increasing importance to decision makers in the traditional economy as well as in e-commerce. The study of law is complex, wide-ranging, yet deep. This handbook covers all these attributes for the new millennium. This first chapter provides a framework for the study of the legal and regulatory environment of traditional commerce and e-commerce. The 14 chapters of this handbook cover the major areas of importance: the legal system, intellectual property (IP) rights, commercial law, and regulation.

In the early days of the Internet, really just a decade ago for most people, law was rarely invoked. The Internet community was self-regulated, supplemented by contractual agreements among owners-operators of the communications and computing infrastructure. The U.S. government and the National Science Foundation (NSF) provided some seed money and nominal oversight to ensure the system functioned. Standardization emerged to "regulate" functionality, but the lack of a central control was the primary design objective to make the Internet robust and relatively immune to attack. This utopia was artificial; it could not be sustained after large sectors of the population discovered the Internet's power and utility. Through the 1990s, the many risks of such open architecture became apparent, one by one.

This handbook chronicles the progressive identification and resolution of these risks. It reviews how some solutions are destined to failure and how many traditional legal concepts adapt fairly well to cyberspace. Fences are going up in cyberspace; that is, property rights are protected, dependable commercial relations are emerging, and public order is being restored by legal and regulatory institutions in much the same way the Wild West frontier was made safe for civilization and commerce. The legal system discussed in this chapter establishes the processes used to impose the duties and vindicate the rights discussed in the remainder of this handbook.

THE NATURE OF LAW AND THE LEGAL SYSTEM

Law and regulation are the official implementations of political processes that govern society by controlling the behavior of people and institutions. Criminal law maintains order; tort law vindicates wrongs, property rights law grants incentives, constitutional law organizes society while limiting the influence of government, commercial law facilitates commerce and lowers transactions costs, and regulation corrects failures in the various markets. **Law** is what is published or known from constitutions, statutes, regulations, and cases. However, law is also the reality of customs and practices, the emphasis given to enforcement, and the departure from the positive law that occurs when the legal system gives selective emphasis or de-emphasis to particular matters. This section reviews a variety of key legal concepts used throughout the study of law.

CLASSIFICATION OF LAW

Law has been classified in various ways, so it is important to recognize some key terms used throughout. **Substantive law** sets the rules that regulate society's activities. It defines rights and duties and then sets the remedies or penalties—the corrective measures that restore rights and deter unlawful activities. **Procedural law** sets out the processes by which substantive rights or duties are vindicated or enforced. All legal systems have both substantive and procedural law, but they can differ greatly between legal systems.

American law is most fundamentally based on the **common law**, a legal system originated in medieval England. Common law is created from largely from precedents set as courts of law settle real disputes. Stare decisis, "let the decision stand," is a doctrine that encourages the common law. There are only vague duties of reasonable action until a dispute arises between parties. The resolution of their dispute sets a **precedent**, a binding judicial decision that becomes the standard for all later, similar, and analogous cases. Under the common law, the courts are the primary place where law is created, applied, and interpreted. The American colonists brought English common law to the New World, and common law became the basis for the Anglo-American legal system used in more than twenty nations, mostly of the former British Empire. Common law is flexible; precedents can be changed to reflect changing technologies and public policy. Common law permits maximum liberty until an actor acts unreasonably, as determined in an adversarial trial.

A different system developed on the European continent. **Civil law** originated with Babylonia's Hammurabi code of the seventeenth century B.C. but was also influenced by the Roman codes. Some codes were imposed by monarchs, but modern codes are written by legislatures. Civil law has the advantage of providing greater clarity, often called **transparency**, so society can know what is expected. More than sixty nations take the civil law approach. Islamic and Chinese systems are also influential. The United States is now a hybrid; elected bodies in all fifty states and many municipalities, as well as Congress, sit as legislatures—institutions that impose codelike statutes or regulations. Still, most laws in the United States are interpreted by the courts, which is the common law method.

There is a very different sense of the term *civil law* that distinguishes it from criminal law. In this other sense, civil law protects individuals. It opens the courts to private parties to vindicate their individual rights. These rights arise from breaches of duties to refrain from intentional aggression or to act carefully (the tort law). These rights also arise from duties voluntarily assumed (contracts and commercial relations). The objective of civil law is to compensate individual victims who suffer damage by the wrongs of other individuals. Of course, civil law both protects and obligates human individuals as well as institutions like business firms and even government units. Contrast civil law with the criminal law. **Criminal law** protects society as a whole from wrongdoers and uses punishment to deter and rehabilitate. Criminal prosecutions are sometimes initiated after an individual victim files a complaint. However, criminal cases are actually brought by prosecutors working for governments: the district attorney (DA) for a municipality, the attorney general (AG) for a state, or the U.S. attorney for the nation. Further distinctions between civil and criminal law are introduced in Chapter 3 and detailed in the e-commerce and IP chapters of this handbook.

Law, lawmaking, legal process, and regulatory process in the United States depend heavily on many important basic concepts of constitutional law, introduced in Chapter 2. The relative importance of constitutions, statutes, state laws, regulations, and local ordinances are discussed there as part of the structure of government. For example, these key concepts include **federalism**, the tension between the parallel governmental powers of the states and the federal government, as well as the **supremacy** of federal law; **separation of powers**, the way government powers are split among the executive, legislative, and judicial branches of government; and various fundamental constitutional rights such as due process, equal protection, and the Bill of Rights.

INTERNATIONAL LAW

The Internet did not single-handedly lower international barriers to global commerce. This process has been going on for centuries with oscillations between inwardness and outwardness. In some eras, some nations strive to be insular and seal themselves off from the influences of foreigners. At other times and in various places, nations become more open to trade and interaction with other nations and cultures. **Globalization**—the lowering of trade barriers and opening of markets— was well under way before the Internet became important. Of course, e-commerce could further fuel this trend. Therefore, the culture, customs, and laws in other nations are becoming very important to both traditional commerce and e-commerce. International law is very complex because many nations' laws are quite different from those in the United States. The **harmonization** of these differences is a major focus in international relations. It can be accomplished through treaties between nations and confederation among member nations of **affiliated trading groups**. This

The European Union (EU)
http://europa.eu.int

chapter provides a brief overview of some foreign legal systems. All other chapters focus on the most important international issues for both traditional commerce and e-commerce.

THE STUDY OF LAW

Legal study is enhanced greatly when students regularly use several well-developed study skills. The basics of these methods may already be familiar to many students. Indeed, many recent educational reforms are largely based on these methods. Nevertheless, most students of law benefit from additional depth and refinement in these techniques. This section assembles guidance on these skills so that the **pedagogy of law** can become more effective in legal studies. First, the methods of critical thinking are explored. Next, these tools are extended through Socratic dialogue into legal reasoning. Legal study is a well-established application of the **problem-based learning** approach. Finally, similar techniques are adapted using moral reasoning to enhance the analysis of ethical dilemmas.

CRITICAL THINKING

Critical thinking is the processing of information by using inquiry and logical analysis. It involves reasoning by acquiring and testing information to develop independent conclusions, to analyze advocacy representing points of view, to examine assumptions and test allegations of fact, and to reconcile inconsistencies between new information and existing personal beliefs. Critical thinkers must uncover bias that can affect the accuracy and persuasiveness of oral or written expression. Critical thinking permits you to evaluate evidence or advocacy, evaluate the quality of expression, support assertions or formulate effective rebuttals, write convincing essays, contribute to class discussions, evaluate public policy arguments, and test claims supported by empirical evidence. It encourages ferreting out and sorting sometimes conflicting information about both factual phenomena and normative, prescriptive, or policy choices.

CRITICAL THINKING INQUIRY

Critical thinkers consciously use several analytical steps to test the validity of argument. That is, as new information is developed, heard, read, or otherwise considered, critical thinkers test it for reasonableness and validity before they rely on it to make decisions. The steps in critical thinking analysis are used to probe into the reasons, logic, and weight of evidence used to support conclusions. Several, but not always all, of the process steps discussed next are repeatedly used in critical thinking analysis. Critical thinkers first determine the issue and conclusion; then they unearth the supporting reasons. Often doing so requires clarification of ambiguous terms, phrases, or concepts and may require uncovering the hidden values or descriptive assumptions of those who advocate the particular position. Factual evidence is evaluated by examining the quality of scientific evidence and statistical inference used. Alternative or rival explanations are developed. Analogies are tested, and reasoning errors or logical fallacies are uncovered.

Issue and Conclusion

The **issue** answers the question, "What is the subject?" The issue is the subject of the expression or controversy. An issue may be a factual, normative, or even strategic conclusion leading to decision. Forthright authors clearly state and often restate the issue. However, **sophists**, who practice devious argumentation, often try to hide the issue. Judges usually state the issue as a question to be decided in a court case.

The speaker, author, or advocate's answer to the issue is the **conclusion**. The conclusion is the end point of the logical **syllogisms** used in the progressive steps of an argument. Syllogisms are the chain of reasoning that starts from assumptions, proceeds through intermediate conclusions, and ultimately results in answers. Many such conclusions dictate outcomes. For example, the holding of a judge, the requirements of statutes and regulations, and the strategic decisions of senior managers are all conclusions. Conclusions follow indicator words such as *therefore*, *thus* or *as a result*. Critical thinking is futile without a clear understanding of the issue and the conclusion.

Evaluating Reasons and Evidence

Advocates or decision makers usually offer reasons to answer "why" and thereby support their conclusions. **Reasons** are the proof of the conclusion, using facts, examples, evidence, analogies, and sometimes values or beliefs. Reasons are indicated by words such as *because of* or *as a result of*. Some reasons are ambiguous, so critical thinkers should look for words or phrases susceptible to different meanings. For example, the technical terms in some professions have different meanings to a lay audience. Critical thinking considers how different meanings could change the conclusion.

Critical thinking must sometimes evaluate empirical evidence, those reasons gathered systematically through valid measures under the discipline of the scientific method. Empirical evidence is most often expressed as statistical measures. Critical thinkers evaluate it by examining the research model; they look for sampling bias and use the tools of statistical inference. Evaluating the logic used and uncovering fallacious reasoning are also important to critical thinking.

Law uses **analogical reasoning** by examining similar previous events and applying universal principles, called precedents, to similar situations. Analogies are strong when the situations compared share many similarities, but they are weak when there are too many differences. Too often, some of the reasons are hidden as presumptions, or they are not adequately tested when based on assumptions. Critical thinkers should ferret out such hidden or assumed reasons because they are often vulnerable to criticism.

Rival Hypotheses and Conclusions

Critical thinking also tests the method and outcome of reasoning by developing rival or alternative theories or explanations. A conclusion is weakened when another plausible explanation, hypothesis, or theory could result in the same conclusion. Similarly, conclusions are weakened when there are other reasons or evidence that could lead to the same conclusion. Experts in the profession or field in question are usually good at developing rival hypotheses or conclusions. However, sometimes critical thinkers from other fields, who are not burdened by the assumptions widely held by experts in that field, can become a good reality check.

IMPORTANCE OF CRITICAL THINKING

Critical thinking is important in all endeavors. In repetitive or deterministic decision making, it helps professionals adapt their existing knowledge and methods to new discoveries or changes in scientific facts. Critical thinking is also important in domains where decisions are more controversial, appear to have various possible approaches, or reflect opposing viewpoints. Law is the ideal environment to refine critical thinking because it represents a political compromise among varying and often opposing interests. Decisions are often made in law and regulation long before there is a consensus of scientific proof to guide decision makers.

Fundamental critical thinking skills can bridge the gap between specialized learning and higher-order reason and discovery. Business is an ideal environment for critical thinking because successful decision making in risky environments is also based on uncertainties and seemingly valid but varying viewpoints. Competitive decision makers go well beyond simple mastery of technical content. Critical analysis is the heart of imagination, creativity, and the avoidance of self-deception. Critical thinking skills are acquired through practice in using the methods discussed here. Critical thinking skills engender respect for the public forum as the place where public policy is formulated. Public policy continues to have a profound impact on business, making critical thinking skills a key factor in the success of business decision making.

LEGAL REASONING

Critical thinking is a major component of legal reasoning that is used throughout the study of law. Critical thinking is used by many who do advocacy: debaters, politicians, legislators, business decision makers, boardroom advisers, consultants, and lawyers. Lawyers use it in their preparation for and conduct of trials. Arguments are framed by anticipating and preparing for the opposition's rebuttal. Students are helped to develop these skills as questions are posed by instructors. Business law texts contribute by posing controversies and focusing attention on the various components of critical thinking. This further contributes to students' skills in anticipating business problems and preparing for business decisions that minimize adverse impacts on the firm.

Legal reasoning is fundamental to **stare decisis**, the common law form of law-making. Under the common law, legal rules are established in adversarial proceedings that apply and refine precedents created in prior similar cases to later similar cases. Precedents are strong and more compulsory when they are derived from many cases over long times. Precedents are weaker when few states follow them or they last for only short times. Adapting precedent to new situations is a good reason to use the Socratic method of instruction.

The Socratic Method

The Socratic method was traditionally used to teach philosophy and law. Today, the Socratic method is much more widely used as a critical thinking method in other fields. Among the forms of Socratic method are the debating exercises called dialectics. Typically, the instructor uses questioning, advocacy, and disputation. These were the methodical approaches to philosophical reasoning first developed by the ancient Greek philosophers. The Socratic method in law study pits the instructor and student into an interactive dialogue in which they explore a legal problem. Students must become proficient in quickly using several of the critical thinking inquiries discussed here. For example, hypothetical or real-world problems are dissected using logic. The instructor and sometimes other students force the reciting student to examine the assumptions used in a case. This process permits them to uncover omissions of critical information, fallacies, and other flaws in reasoning. The students' own biases are often revealed as they generate alternative hypotheses, analogies, and critique conclusions. The Socratic method provides students with well-motivated practice to refine their own chain-of-reasoning analysis and test the limits of applying concepts and rules.

MORAL REASONING

Another adaptation of the critical thinking method is analysis of ethical situations, using the moral reasoning approach. Ethics is a subset of philosophy that analyzes proposed or completed actions by applying moral principles. Moral principles apply varying conceptions of good, justice, and right to human behavior. **Moral reasoning** is an implementation of critical thinking that uses moral principles as premises, analyzes a problem through a logical chain of reasoning, and produces a moral judgment of a proposed action or of the best practice taken from a range of possible alternatives.

There are several sources for the basic moral principles used in moral reasoning, including philosophies, religious precepts, strong beliefs, and prophecies. For example, moral principles can originate from the Ten Commandments, Golden Rule, classic Greek philosophers such as Plato and Aristotle, the Qur'an of Islam, or the Hindu Veda. Contemporary economic and humanist movements are the source for additional moral principles, such as forthright truth, respect for persons, self-interest, or Pareto optimality. Like other forms of critical thinking, this ethical analysis uses ethical theories by asking questions, posing alternatives, and weighing outcomes to determine whether an action is acceptable or which action from among various choices might be best. Ethical analysts choose the theory dictated by their cultural or religious stimulus. Moral reasoning is sometimes criticized as "situational ethics" because many individuals seem to have wide choices to select the most compelling ethical principle from among various theories as they find it to be personally appropriate.

Two theories predominate: utilitarian and universal theories. **Utilitarian** theory judges an action by measuring its consequences. Actions are morally correct when they produce the most good for the most people, not on the inherent rightness of the decision or its process. Clearly there is controversy over defining what is good and how it is measured, but happiness and wealth are often used. Utilitarianism is a teleological theory because it focuses on consequences. Machiavellianism, "the ends justify the means," is unfortunately a commonly used justification for political actions. The other major theory is **universal** or **Kantian** theory, based on the eighteenth-century writings of Immanuel Kant, which focus on the means rather the ends. Kant insisted that there were **categorical imperatives**, timeless duties that must be universally followed, much like the Golden Rule or the Ten Commandments.

Logical Analysis

Philosophers have also contributed to the reasoning process by developing two major modes of reasoning: inductive and deductive reasoning. **Inductive reasoning** examines many specific situations or data observations to find generalizations. When common attributes are discovered, the analyst simplifies by restating the commonalities as an inductive conclusion. For example, legal reasoning using precedents is inductive because numerous cases are examined for commonalities and the rule taken from each is generalized to become the prevailing precedent. **Deductive reasoning** is just the opposite, in that general principles are applied to specific cases. For example, statutes or rules are general principles that are applied to particular cases by using deductive reasoning. Law uses both inductive and deductive reasoning, sometimes in rapid and close succession.

BUSINESS ETHICS AND CORPORATE SOCIAL RESPONSIBILITY

Business ethics may be viewed as an application of traditional moral reasoning to actions of managers making decisions in business contexts. A firm's ethics are determined by the corporate culture and by the collective personal ethical profile of the firm's employees. Of course, strong leaders can shape the culture to reflect the leader's vision. Reaction to a firm's business activities that public opinion views as unethical is a powerful force for reform. For example, the Enron bankruptcy and the complicity of some Arthur Andersen partners and employees has pressured Congress, various regulators, the states, and the European Union (EU) to react to perceived unethical business practices with reforms and stronger regulations. Managers are constrained by law, but when the law is unclear or undeveloped, business ethics can provide important guidance. Society continually views business firms as having responsibilities to avoid harming society. Ethical issues are noted throughout this text to present recurring moral dilemmas, heighten awareness of the pervasiveness of ethical issues, and sharpen moral reasoning skills.

There have been various stages in the development of the social responsibility of American business. Before the latter part of the nineteenth century, the corporate form was seldom used. Without the limited liability of the corporate form, business owners were personally liable for business debts. The discipline on business was felt directly by owners who had no shield from personal liability. As the limited liability concept became more widespread during the industrial revolution, a new stage of business responsibility developed. Passive investors were encouraged to provide the capital needed for industrial expansion. As the use of the corporate form widened, ownership and control of business were separated, creating new ethical dilemmas for managers in their relations with shareholders. Managers became more insulated from many of the consequences of their decisions. In recent years, managers have become more aware of the interest and power over corporate affairs that various groups can wield.

CORPORATE STAKEHOLDERS

In performing strategic planning, business should be aware of the diverse expectations of numerous groups. Business can actively identify its stakeholders and attempt to understand their reaction to and influence on corporate actions. **Corporate stakeholders** are groups or entities affected by the firm's activities. Society actively monitors the impact that business has on its stakeholders. For many of these stakeholders, there are significant measures of business performance other than the firm's profitability.

Numerous parties that have direct or indirect contact with business may consider themselves corporate stakeholders. Consumers, customers, wholesalers, employees, and retailers are the predominant stakeholders because they contract with the corporation. Participants in the distribution chain expect the corporation to act responsibly in satisfying their concerns. They evaluate the corporation's responsibility by the quality of its products or services, by its work environment, and by its honesty in describing products and services. Employees and suppliers expect fair dealing and prompt payments. These audiences usually receive considerable attention from firms.

The financial community is another audience that demands the firm's attention. It consists of shareholders, creditors, investment advisers and analysts, investment bankers, the financial press, and potential investors. Firms must provide sufficient and accurate information concerning their financial status and prospects. Contributors of capital may use the legal system to remedy a firm's irresponsible behaviors. If a firm's management becomes unresponsive, shareholders can take over the firm or use its proxy process to oust its management or change its policies.

Another audience is the local community near the firm's facilities. For example, nearby homeowners and businesses can pressure the firm through the legal system, deny needed zoning or operating permits, and influence the public with adverse publicity. Local communities can provide or deny access to tax-free industrial revenue bond funding for the firm to build new facilities. Firms should monitor the attitudes of their major audiences and modify their policies to avoid detrimental reactions by these stakeholders. Exhibit 1.1 suggests how these stakeholders interact with business.

Stakeholders' Expectations and Influence

Business is expected to refrain from having a negative impact on various stakeholders. Some stakeholders expect business to generate favorable benefits, sometimes

Exhibit 1.1 Corporate Stakeholder Interactions

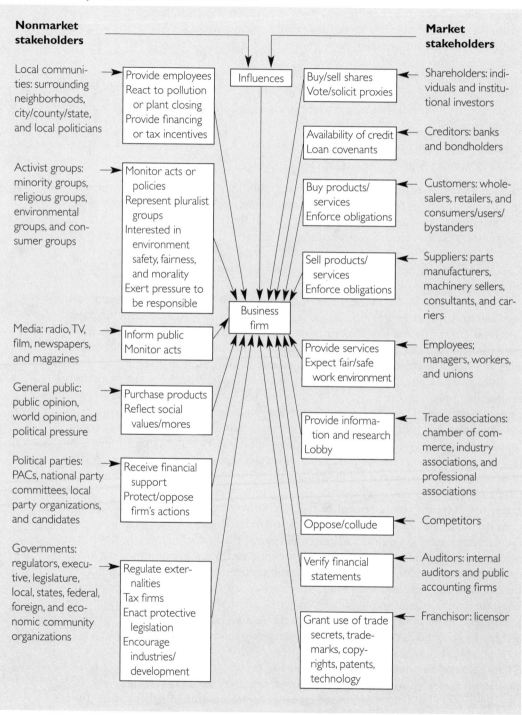

called **positive externalities**. For example, many consider corporate philanthropy, economic growth, freedom from pollution or industrial accidents, and beneficial research to be the responsibility of business. If some audiences of a firm have sufficient political or economic power to pressure it to act in a more "responsible" manner, then the firm must surely consider their influence in its decision making. To avert costly regulation, business managers must understand the complex power structure of government and the relationships among the participants in government who affect the social, legal, and regulatory environments of business.

CAMPAIGN FINANCE LAWS, POLITICAL ACTION COMMITTEES, AND REFORMS

Advocacy during political campaigns or referenda is a primary method by which business can exert political influence. Today, elections are often won by the candidates who spend the most. Political consultants and pollsters, television advertisements, and electioneering visits to voters are very costly. Many businesses are able to make large political contributions. Numerous observers argue that such contributions pervert the political process by making politicians beholden to business.

In the late nineteenth century, some businesses made large direct-money contributions in elections. Society believed that the political influence of these businesses was excessive, so in 1907 Congress passed the Tillman Act, which prohibited corporations from directly contributing to candidates in federal elections. Some states have similar laws. To bypass the Tillman Act, some business executives were paid large bonuses and expected to make political contributions. Corporate staff, facilities, and consultants are sometimes provided to candidates. In recent elections, some candidates have had their debts canceled or been given free rental cars or secret contributions.

Federal Election Campaign Act

In 1971, Congress reinforced the Tillman Act with the Federal Election Campaign Act (FECA), which established the Federal Election Commission (FEC) to administer the campaign finance laws. The FEC requires disclosure of political contributions, receipts, and expenditures by both contributors and candidates. The FECA permits the formation of political action committees to solicit campaign contributions from particular groups. The FECA limits individuals' political contributions to federal candidates, parties, and political action committees. Generally, there are no limits on an individual's personal campaign expenditures. Senator John McCain persevered to win campaign finance reform in 2002, following revelations of the political influence the Enron Corporation had with politicians, regulatory agencies, and the states. The constitutionality of new contribution limits of this law will probably be tested soon.

Political action committees (PACs) are groups formed by individuals, labor unions, corporations, trade associations, and other special interest groups. PACs must file regular financial reports with the FEC, identifying their contributors and recipients. PACs advocate policies favorable to their members. They channel contributions received from management, employees, stockholders, or others to the causes or candidates they believe support their best interests. The political campaign financing activities of PACs were severely limited by the 2002 legislation. For example, PACs were previously permitted to make unlimited "independent" expenditures called "soft money," in favor of particular candidates or causes if contributions were made without the candidate's cooperation. However, the PAC system came under continuing criticism for controlling legislation favorable to their industries' interests. The Enron crisis finally galvanized public opinion, so campaign finance reforms effective after the 2002 federal elections will drastically change campaigns if the constitutionality of the McCain-Feingold reform law is upheld. Chapter 2 discusses how the First Amendment's freedom of speech might invalidate portions of this new law.

THE DIVERGENT GOALS OF BUSINESS AND SOCIETY

Before the New Deal era, Supreme Court interpretations of the U.S. Constitution reinforced our historical preference for free market decision making. This philosophy was founded on the colonists' contempt for the British crown's authoritarian rule and the economic restraint imposed by British mercantilism. The framers included provisions in the Constitution and in the Bill of Rights pronouncing broad social, political, and economic freedoms to encourage **laissez-faire** free markets and other libertarian ideals. These principles limited the role of federal, state, and local governments in the economy and thereby minimized governments' intrusion on business. Today, U.S. economic freedom starkly contrasts with the intrusive government decision making throughout many developed and developing economies.

Laissez-faire capitalism is founded on freedom of contract. Contemporary implementation of this theory by a few economists like Milton Friedman argues that a corporation's sole social responsibility is strict adherence to the profit motive, which will result in the best allocation of goods and services. These economists insist that competition alone leads to the success of efficient firms and the failure of inefficient ones. The ideal of free choice is a primary driver in this theory because it determines the types and quantities of goods produced. Managers are motivated to succeed by heeding market signals.

The best-known statement of this traditional laissez-faire model is Adam Smith's 1776 publication, *The Wealth of Nations*. He predicted that the "invisible hand" of capitalism implemented through self-interested economic actors would "naturally" drive the market to optimize social welfare. Private property would provide incentives to take risks and innovate as long as actors were entitled to the profits of their effort. Competition would discipline participants to become efficient; new competitors would be attracted as abnormally high profits became available. The primary economic questions would be answered with *allocative efficiency*: what is produced, how is it produced, who receives that production, and how is production changed.

Adam Smith's model makes further assumptions, such as those underlying the **perfect competition model**: Markets must have numerous rational buyers and sellers, all market participants have perfect information, there are no barriers restricting new firms' entry into markets, only standardized products are sold, and no participant possesses market (monopoly) power. The market "clears" for quantities and at prices that form an *equilibrium*. Adam Smith believed there is only limited justification for government intervention in free markets because government intrusion is "unnatural." In his view, government has only three legitimate duties: (1) provide for national defense, (2) administer the justice system to preserve property rights and facilitate enforcement of transactions, and (3) establish public works or other public goods that are valuable throughout society but that private enterprise might neglect (e.g., roads, dams, parks). Does society agree that such conditions are sufficient control over aberrant business behavior? Much of this handbook discusses the social and political pressures for regulation.

Corporate Philanthropy

Many firms seek to act responsibly by giving educational or research grants or engaging in other philanthropic efforts. In some early court decisions, judges prohibited philanthropy and deemed it an improper corporate goal. Should corporate law permit firms to intentionally provide societal benefits? This is a vitally important question.

The judicial attitude toward corporate philanthropy has evolved since the early twentieth century. Today, many firms make charitable contributions. A firm's ultimate successes may be enhanced by its reputation for responsible acts. Philanthropy may actually be in a firm's best interests if it leads to favorable public impressions of the firm. In an early 1950s case, a group of stockholders alleged that a corporation's donation of $1,500 to Princeton University was beyond the corporation's powers.[1] Such gifts are clearly valid today because they can advance the corporation's interests.

Justification for Corporate Philanthropy

[I]ndividual stockholders' . . . interests rest entirely upon the well-being of the . . . corporation, [and these stockholders] ought not be permitted to close their eyes to [the corporation's] high obligation as a constituent of our modern social structure.

Universities provide educated employees and research discoveries that are used directly by business. However, philanthropic contributions are permissible even if business receives less direct benefits.

In *Schlensky v. Wrigley*,[2] a minority shareholder in the Chicago Cubs sued Philip K. Wrigley and the Cubs' corporate directors, claiming management was not maximizing shareholder wealth. Wrigley Field, the Cubs' home park, had no field lights, prohibiting lucrative night games that all other major league teams enjoyed to maximize attendance. Without night games, the Cubs' profitability was allegedly limited. The Illinois court sustained the board's decision, stating:

It appears to us that the effect on the surrounding neighborhood might well be considered by a director who was considering the patrons who would or would not

---

1. *A. P. Smith Mfg. Co. v. Barlow*, 98 A.2d 581 (N.J. 1953).
2. 237 N.E.2d 776 (Ill. 1968).

attend the games if the park were in a poor neighborhood. Furthermore, the long-run interest of the corporation in its property value at Wrigley Field might demand all efforts to keep the neighborhood from deteriorating.

ONLINE

Chicago Cubs and
Wrigley Field
**http://chicago.cubs.
mlb.com**

Of course, the lights now at Wrigley Field are further hastening the demise of baseball as a day sport, a fear voiced by Philip K. Wrigley. Today, modern constituency statutes would not even require that a board connect the firm's financial interests so directly to the condition of the surrounding community. The modern goal of the firm includes serving the interests of a variety of stakeholders in addition to shareholders. Over half the states, including Delaware, have adopted "corporate constituency" takeover legislation that permits corporate boards to consider the effect of its operations on surrounding communities, customers, suppliers, and others.

CODES OF RESPONSIBILITY AND ETHICS

Regulatory responses are often initiated when self-discipline is perceived as insufficient or nonexistent. Government initiates many of these responses, but there has also been a trend toward the imposition of **ethical codes** by firms or their industry associations. Although professional codes are not always laws, they may nevertheless become an issue in trials. The determination of professional malpractice liability often depends on professional standards. For example, it is often convincing evidence of malpractice if an auditor fails to follow generally accepted auditing standards (GAAS), a real estate agent violates the Realtor's code of ethics, or a lawyer violates the bar association's code of conduct.

Increasingly, industry groups have adopted and enforce codes of conduct. For example, many advertisers, broadcasters, many trade associations, and purchasing managers voluntarily abide by codes of conduct. Typically, these codes require professionals to be loyal to their clients' interests and to avoid conflicts of interest. The professional must exercise best efforts for every client. Confidential relationships with clients must be maintained, and due care exercised in all efforts made on behalf of clients. However, business in general has yet to develop a comprehensive and universal code of conduct for general application. Nevertheless, many firms have developed specific in-house codes with varying degrees of success.

In recent years, numerous corporations have instituted codes of ethics for their own employees. These codes are usually enforced with disciplinary sanctions and termination for serious violations. Typically, corporate codes of conduct prohibit employees from taking or making bribes or kickbacks. They usually prohibit conflicts of interest, illegal political contributions, and other general violations of the law. Other prohibitions that appear less frequently in such codes include misappropriation of inside information and insider trading, bribery, falsification of records, antitrust or FCPA violations, and work for other firms. Codes increasingly include limitations on the personal or inappropriate use of e-mail, the Internet, and the firm's computers or telecommunications systems. The Organization of Economic Cooperation and Development (OECD) has urged adoption of an international code of conduct for multinational corporations since 1976.

Two important factors help raise compliance with corporate codes of conduct. First, upper management must clearly endorse the code and appear to comply. This means that the "tone from the top" must signal a policy of commitment to ethical conduct in general and specifically to the firm's own code. Second, the system for investigating and punishing violations must be perceived as providing fair due process. It must also routinely punish violations. If many exceptions are made for guilty personnel, other employees lose respect for the code.

Legal Effect of Corporate Codes of Conduct

There is a strong trend toward the adoption and active enforcement of corporate codes of conduct. First, codes are sometimes adopted to appease regulators. For example, some defense contractors found guilty of overcharging the U.S. government have agreed to develop, implement, and strongly enforce codes of conduct in order to retain their defense contracting business. Alternatively, codes have been instituted under consent decrees made with various regulators. Second, codes probably improve the firm's public image. The proliferation of codes poses questions about their legal effect on the criminal, tort, and regulatory liability of both employers and employees. If strictly enforced, codes may sometimes reduce legal obligations.

Although codes generally parallel the law, they may actually trigger additional legal obligations. For example, in the insider trading context, a corporate code or other work rules that prohibit insider trading actually trigger the misappropriation theory. This means that employees who violate corporate codes prohibiting misappropriation of information may be liable for insider trading or for revealing confidential nonpublic information when making a tip to an outsider. Investment banking firms that enforce such codes may avoid some vicarious liability for their employees' insider trading. For example, the firm's liability is reduced if **Chinese wall** procedures are implemented to prevent the leak of inside information from the firm's underwriting division to its brokerage division. Other provisions of the securities laws eliminate liability for firms that have effective compliance programs and that act in good faith with no knowledge of the illegal activities of the person(s) they control (e.g., employees). Should judges or juries consider leniency for a firm that strictly enforces its code of conduct? This topic is covered in Chapter 3 where the U.S. sentencing guidelines are introduced.

THE COURT SYSTEM

Much of the focus of law and regulation is on deterring lawlessness and wrongful actions. With few exceptions, most civilizations show strong confidence that legal institutions largely work to order society. Nevertheless, disputes continue to arise, particularly as regulation is used to correct market failures. Legal systems define processes for the resolution of disputes, in the courts, in regulatory agencies, and through private or alternative dispute resolution methods. This section discusses the structure of the institutions of legal process or **litigation**—lawsuits brought in the courts of law. Criminal prosecution is detailed in Chapter 3.

Litigation is centered in the **judiciary**, one of the three branches of federal, state and local government that includes the courts of law. Courts create common law precedents when novel cases are presented, and they interpret constitutions, statutory codes and regulatory rules. The judicial systems of most states parallel the federal structure, although there are some significant differences that are only generalized here. Most regulatory agencies also have courtlike tribunals inside their agencies. The structure of these hearings is discussed later in this chapter in the section on administrative law. The court hearing a case must have jurisdiction or power to hear the dispute, also detailed later. Exhibit 1.2 depicts the structure of the court systems.

TRIAL COURTS

Most cases start out at the **trial court** level, where the courts have original jurisdiction to hear the controversy, make factual findings after the presentation of evidence, and apply the law, resulting in a ruling, verdict, or judgment. State and local trial courts that have jurisdiction over many types of cases go by different names, such as district court, county court, superior court, chancery court, and the court of common pleas. Many states have inferior courts below the general trial courts that handle limited matters, such as municipal courts,

Exhibit 1.2 State and Federal Court Systems

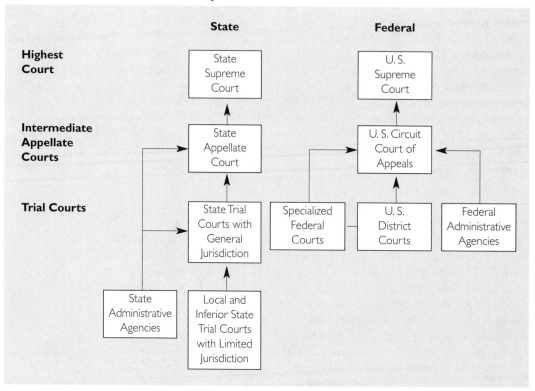

justices of the peace, and small claims courts. There are also specialized courts for particular problems, such as probate courts, family or domestic relations courts (divorce, custody), and juvenile courts. At the federal level, the **federal district courts** are empowered to hear criminal and civil matters. Specialized federal courts include bankruptcy courts, the court of claims, and the tax court. There are nearly 100 federal judicial districts operating in the 50 states that vary in geographical size to balance shifting populations and caseloads.

ONLINE

Links to the federal courts
http://www.uscourts. gov

INTERMEDIATE APPELLATE COURTS

Parties dissatisfied with an outcome from the trial court may appeal to an **intermediate appellate court**. Appellate courts typically do not reexamine witnesses or the evidence; instead, they judge whether there were errors made in the pretrial or trial process. For example, if the trial court judge applied the wrong law, the appellate court is primarily responsible to correct this mistake. State appellate courts may be called the court of appeals or even the supreme court. At the federal level there are the **circuit courts of appeal**, most of which encompass several districts from numerous states. Exhibit 1.3 shows the current boundaries of the 13 federal circuits.

Exhibit 1.3 Federal Judicial Circuit Courts

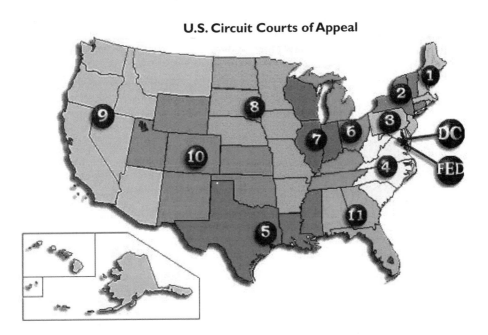

U.S. Circuit Courts of Appeal

Source: http://www.uscourts.gov/links.html.

SUPREME COURTS

Every state and the federal government have a "court of last resort," the highest court to hear appeals. These supreme courts announce the "law of the land," which is typically changed only by that court at a later time, by subsequent legislation, or by the U.S. Supreme Court. The state courts are typically called supreme courts, but a few states call them courts of appeal or supreme judicial court. Very few of the hundreds of thousands of cases going through the courts each year are ever accepted by the supreme courts. A few states have mandatory appeals, such as for crimes involving capital punishment. The U.S. Supreme Court's jurisdiction in most cases is discretionary. The nine justices review applications for appeal and grant a **writ of certiorari** and choose to accept only a few cases of great importance each term. The U.S. Supreme Court has original jurisdiction to sit as a trial court in limited circumstances, such as border disputes between the states, although this method is rarely used. The Supreme Court justices may issue a **certification** to settle disputed legal rules between the various circuit courts of appeal. Entry into the judicial system requires that the court targeted for the case being brought must have jurisdiction, discussed next.

ONLINE

U.S. Supreme Court
http://www.uscourts.gov

JURISDICTION

The various states and nations often have very different laws that reflect strongly felt cultural, religious, and moral norms. Many of these customs are unknown to outsiders; some are unknown even to its citizens. It has always been a daunting task to effectively navigate the contradictory laws of numerous governments. Good faith compliance with foreign laws has traditionally taken two forms. First, "when in Rome, do as the Romans do" is a practical adage that reminds foreign visitors of their duty to learn and comply with foreign law. Second, serious cross-border commercial activity must be carefully reviewed by legal counsel and for compliance with cultural norms. These are often costly but necessary steps in interstate or international trade.

Pressure from business, lawyers, and some governments has made many commercial laws relatively uniform. For example, the Uniform Commercial Code and international trade agreements have significantly reduced unexpected surprise or arbitrary enforcement of unknown foreign laws. However, the Internet complicates this considerably. Methods of regulating activities become less effective as individual and commercial activity migrates from the physical world into cyberspace. The rise of the Internet has catapulted the concept of jurisdiction into the limelight, making jurisdiction a most central concept in maintaining law and order in cyberspace.

WHAT IS JURISDICTION?

Jurisdiction is a term used in several related senses. First, it most generally refers to a political entity, the nation, state, or local subdivision, which is called a jurisdiction.

Second, jurisdiction is the power and authority of a government or subdivision to regulate activities of its citizens or businesses. Third, jurisdiction most narrowly refers to the constitutionally permissible exercise of governmental power by a tribunal (e.g., administrative agency, court) to render verdicts over particular matters. As discussed in Chapter 2, the Constitution may limit the reach of jurisdiction under due process when it affects the life, liberty, or property rights interests among the parties litigating before that **forum**—the particular court or tribunal.

IMPACT OF E-COMMERCE ON JURISDICTION

The law of jurisdiction has been fairly well settled for many years. However, the Internet may be making it much more likely that the activities of a person in one political subdivision would fall within the regulatory powers of another place. This could permit the exercise of court or regulatory jurisdiction to affect rights implicated by these activities. Jurisdiction generally exists over the citizens, businesses, and other activities conducted within a political subdivision. However, jurisdiction is not always possible over the activities of foreigners who reside outside a state or in another nation. Foreigners include individual citizens or businesses residing outside the jurisdiction in question and may also become a question about activities conducted outside that state or nation. The traditional concepts of jurisdiction must be reevaluated as the volume of interstate and international contacts grows on the Internet.

Consider how local authorities regulate obscenity, gambling, blasphemy, or privacy with some success in the physical world. The physical presence of persons, goods, rendition of services, and facilities permits the enforcement of individual rights, as well as criminal and regulatory law enforcement. However, with the advent of the Internet, it is understandable that these authorities are becoming anxious. Their citizens are bombarded on the Internet with content or interactivity from outside. Much of this activity may violate the jurisdiction's public policy, perhaps as obscenity, blasphemy, predation, or otherwise illegal acts with direct impact on their citizens. The traditional law of court and regulatory jurisdiction is beginning to evolve to address the impact of the Internet. Individuals and businesses engaged in cyberspace activities are becoming anxious about their potential liability under unfamiliar and conflicting laws, regulations, and interpretations by governments in other jurisdictions.

GENERAL PRINCIPLES OF JURISDICTION

Governments generally exercise police power through regulation to protect the health, safety, welfare, and morals of their citizens. In the United States, government regulation is limited by the due process clause of the Fifth and Fourteenth Amendments of the U.S. Constitution, as discussed in Chapter 2. The power to regulate or adjudicate must generally be based on some close connection, often called a **nexus**, between the political entity and the regulated entity. A physical presence in the state or nation clearly confers jurisdiction. However, other activities can be regulated if the exercise of jurisdiction would not "offend traditional notions of fair play and substantial justice." If a person or business against whom suit is brought has had some **minimum contacts** in the state, then jurisdiction may be valid.[3] Governments can regulate activities if the person or business has made a **purposeful availment**—that is, has taken the "privilege of conducting activities within the forum State, thus invoking the benefits and protections of its laws."[4] This means that because of their activities, a reasonable person would "anticipate being haled into court" in the foreign state or nation.[5] There is no jurisdiction over sporadic mail order or phone order business, conducted across state lines in a random, fortuitous, or attenuated manner.[6] However, activity directed at persons within the state confers jurisdiction on that state's courts.[7]

Types of Jurisdiction

The law of jurisdiction is complex. The most important forms are **personal jurisdiction,** power over the individual litigants; **specific jurisdiction,** power to entertain litigation arising out of particular activities within the state; and **general jurisdiction,** the power to entertain nearly all lawsuits involving the parties. General jurisdiction is justified when the defendant has systematic and continuous contacts within the state. Jurisdiction is nearly always assured over the activity of residents and businesses domiciled or doing business within the state. Most states and many nations have nonresident jurisdiction laws, often called **long-arm statutes,** which confer jurisdiction over nonresidents when their contacts in the state justify invoking jurisdiction.

THREE EMERGING MODELS OF JURISDICTION IN CYBERSPACE

In 1997, the American Bar Association (ABA) recognized that there are huge stakes at risk from unpredictable Internet jurisdiction. The ABA Jurisdiction Project is an interstate and international effort to balance these competing interests by creating a uniform model of jurisdictional power. Despite efforts to make the substantive law uniform between the various states and nations, key differences seem inevitable. Instead, the Jurisdiction Project is most concerned with making the application of foreign law more predictable and fair. This is the most complex of any ongoing ABA project ever initiated, involving consensus negotiations at the state, national, and international levels.[8]

Many Internet jurisdiction cases arose in the 1990s, and it is becoming possible to predict how the law of jurisdiction over Internet activity will apply going forward. *Zippo Mfg. Co. v. Zippo Dot Com, Inc.* is a leading case, decided by the federal

---

3. *International Shoe v. Washington*, 326 U.S. 310 (1945).
4. *Hanson v. Denckla*, 357 U.S. 235 (1958).
5. *World-wide Volkswagen Corp. v. Woodson*, 444 U.S. 286 (1980).
6. *Burger King Corp. v. Rudzewicz*, 471 U.S. 462 (1985).
7. *Keeton v. Hustler Magazine, Inc.* 465 U.S. 770 (1984).
8. See *Achieving Legal and Business Order in Cyberspace: A Report on Global Jurisdiction Issues Created by the Internet.* American Bar Association Global Cyberspace Jurisdiction Project (Am Bar Assn., 2000). http://www.abanet .org/buslaw/cyber/initiatives/draft.rtf.

district court for western Pennsylvania.[9] Zippo, the Bradford, Pennsylvania, manufacturer of classic tobacco lighters, sued Zippo Dot Com of Sunnyvale, California, for trademark dilution and infringement in using the Zippo.com domain name for Zippo Dot Com's Internet news service business. In finding that Pennsylvania jurisdiction was proper, the court categorized jurisdiction over three different types of Web sites, as discussed next.

Passive Web Sites

A passive Web site simply posts information that becomes accessible to anyone from nearly anywhere over the Internet. The content is generally informational or more like advertising. Many operators of such Web sites make no intentional decision to direct their content to particular jurisdictions. Much of the educational material on university Web sites is passive. Most cases hold that passive Web sites that have no or very limited interactivity generally do not trigger jurisdiction in a foreign state or nation. Nevertheless, European nations have sought to block their citizens from even seeing content posted on some passive Web sites when the content is banned under their laws. For example, Germany and France outlaw Nazi memorabilia and have pressured the local affiliates of U.S. Internet service providers (ISPs) to block their citizens' access. This reinforces an important point about international jurisdiction: When assets of foreign firms reside on another nation's soil, jurisdiction may be irrelevant because those assets could be seized, nationalized, or held for ransom until the firm relents to that nation's assertion of jurisdiction.

Highly Interactive or Commercial Web Sites

On the other end of the spectrum are Web sites that purposefully direct activity into a foreign jurisdiction. This highly interactive contact makes sufficient minimum contacts, and thereby the foreign firm purposefully avails itself of the foreign jurisdiction's protections. Highly interactive or commercial Web sites can be subjected to jurisdiction in the foreign state or nation. The foreign jurisdiction's long-arm statute could be validly used to subject the foreigner to regulation, liability for Web site activities, or judicial determination of their rights. Operators of highly interactive Web sites must carefully consider the risk exposure of conducting business in a foreign state or nation before directing activity to its citizens.

Interactive Web Sites

Between the two extremes of passive and highly interactive or commercial Web sites are broad ranges of activities that raise considerable uncertainty. Web sites occupying this middle ground risk some assertion of jurisdiction. Where the level of Web site interactivity is more than *de minimus* or passive accessibility, courts may be asked to exercise jurisdiction over the nonresidents operating these Web sites or e-commerce activity. The court must analyze numerous factors and thereby make an ad hoc decision on exerting jurisdiction.

---

9. 952 F.Supp. 1119 (W.D. Pa. 1997).

The cases cannot yet be narrowly generalized, but several factors are emerging. First, something more than mere passive accessibility is required to validly exert jurisdiction. A few cases confer jurisdiction with minimal Web site interactivity. Nevertheless, there must generally be a deliberate "availing" in the forum before jurisdiction is conferred. If there are substantial, non-Internet, ancillary activities in the state, these may combine with the online presence to trigger jurisdiction. Some states might find that activities that would not alone confer jurisdiction might do so when combined with interactive Web sites. For example, providing toll-free numbers, conducting isolated and sporadic contacts, or even a single completed sale could combine with Web site presence to confer jurisdiction. As the frequency of contacts in a state rises to become nearly continuous, this implicates jurisdiction. Repeated e-mail contacts may confer jurisdiction. Frequent commercial or profit-making activity is likely to confer jurisdiction. Jurisdiction over Web sites that are somewhat interactive are judged on a case-by-case basis.

Jurisdiction is a recurring theme throughout this handbook. For example, many of the questions posed in Chapter 14 about the taxation of electronic commerce are largely jurisdiction problems.

VENUE

Two or more courts may have valid jurisdiction over a particular controversy. Most **litigants**, the parties involved in litigation, have an incentive to find the court or other forum that is most likely to favor them. For example, some parties may find favor in courts close to home, in federal over state courts, or in courts inconvenient for the opposing party. This can be a zero-sum game because bias favoring one side in litigation generally disfavors the other party. The law of **civil procedure** includes procedural methods and constitutional protections that balance this favoritism among the parties.

Venue is the court in which a case is brought. One party may seek a change in venue to a more appropriate court with jurisdiction. A major consideration is a geographic nexus between the parties or the suit's subject matter and the court hearing the case. For example, the most appropriate venue for a suit over the boundary of land would usually be the court in that county. Under the doctrine of *forum non conveniens*, venue changes are sometimes appropriate if a plaintiff brings suit far away from the defendant's residence. Another justification to move the venue from the place where the case could have been filed to another venue is to assure a fair trial. For example, the criminal terrorism trials brought against the Oklahoma City bombers was moved to Denver to better ensure the defendants received a fair trial.

FEDERAL JURISDICTION

Federal courts were established for two broad reasons. First, the federal courts provide a forum for resolution of **federal questions**—matters involving the application or interpretation of the federal law from the Constitution, federal statute, treaty, or federal regulation. Second, the federal courts are available for non-federal questions, usually involving state law, if the parties are from different states (**diversity of citizenship**) and the amount in controversy exceeds $75,000. "Don't make a federal case out of it" is an old saying that captures the essence of this **federal diversity jurisdiction** because the federal courts are available venues only when the trial held in either party's different home might not provide unbiased fairness.

STANDING

The Constitution grants judicial review powers only when there is a **case or controversy**. This limits access to the courts to assure that parties have genuine adverse interests. The common law system assumes that only true adversaries have sufficient incentive to gather facts and fully argue the facts and law. Collusive suits between nonadversarial parties are likely to produce poorly reasoned precedent. Any person seeking judicial review must be a **real party in interest** to sufficiently identify their affected interest to the outcome of the litigation.

The modern test for standing requires the plaintiff to show that the agency's action caused injury in fact. Injuries may be economic, environmental, or aesthetic. In one case, the Sierra Club sought to halt the development of a ski resort, which would have cut through Sequoia National Forest. Threats to aesthetic, recreational, and environmental interests could confer sufficient standing to sue. However, the Sierra Club failed to allege any direct impact on its membership, so it was denied standing. The plaintiff must not only allege injury to protected interests but also be among those who are injured.

CONDUCT OF CIVIL TRIALS

Litigation is an **adversarial process**. The disputants expect a zero-sum outcome; losses by one party come primarily as gains for the other party. Each side investigates, researches the law, and presents arguments most favorable to their side and most damaging to the opposition. This adversariness often produces a spectacle at trial, when the differences in claims, counterclaims, and interrogation to determine "the truth" are observed by the judge and jury. Litigation is a costly and divisive method to settle disputes. Fortunately, despite reports of increased numbers of lawsuits and higher damage awards, the reality is that most disputes, more than 90%, are settled without going through trial. The threat of litigation probably serves as a strong incentive to avoid and settle disputes by using various methods of alternative dispute resolution (ADR) discussed later.

With the exception of a very few parties who hit the jackpot with huge verdicts, most parties are well advised to avoid litigation when possible. If disputes are anticipated, perhaps a different contract term should be used to prevent the problem or an ADR method considered. A willingness to be reasonable and work through difficulties with others nearly always goes a long way toward avoiding litigation. It is always best to understand the risks undertaken in any contracts before entering them. Well-designed administrative procedures also help avoid litigation or strengthen your case. For example, documents should be routinely retained, records prepared, and evidence regularly preserved, such as questioning eyewitnesses soon after an incident.

There are many similarities between the civil litigation process discussed here, the administrative hearing process discussed at the end of this chapter, and the trials of criminal prosecutions discussed in Chapter 3. However, make note of these key differences as these three forms of legal process are examined.

THE PRETRIAL PROCESS

With the exception of small claims and a few other ADR methods, most disputing parties are well advised to retain competent and experienced counsel to represent them. An **attorney at law** is a legal counsel, a lawyer licensed by the bar association in that state to represent clients in legal matters. Attorneys work in solo practice, in small or medium-sized "boutique" firms that specialize in particular areas, in large firms with hundreds of partners and nonpartnered associates, or directly as employees at firms. Many attorneys work for the government. Litigants generally need an attorney to represent them to prepare for litigation and to conduct the trial or appeal. Attorneys also negotiate deals for their clients, draft various documents, and provide counseling on the possible legal implications of strategic decisions. As discussed in Chapter 13, the attorney-client privilege prevents a breach of the confidentiality expected when the client communicates to the attorney in confidence. However, the privilege does not apply to all information revealed to lawyers working for a corporate client.[10]

Attorneys are "retained" under service contracts that can specify different forms of compensation. Many attorneys, including most defense attorneys, prefer to work at a **billable hourly rate** for the work performed in preparing documents, negotiating deals, or engaging in litigation. Some firms charge a flat fee for more routine services, such as preparing a will, a simple divorce, or a real estate closing. At larger firms and when the client's case involves unique and novel questions, several attorneys may provide services. The varying fees charged by senior and junior attorneys are typically blended into the final billing. Large corporate clients may place their primary law firm(s) on **retainer**, usually a minimum fee for a minimum amount of work that rises when the client becomes involved in big litigation or deals. Plaintiffs who cannot afford to pay billable hours if they lose their case may still be able to find a plaintiff's attorney to agree to a **contingency fee** arrangement. The attorney's compensation is then computed as a predefined percentage of the final judgment or settlement amount. Many states limit contingency fee to no more than 25%, 33%, or 40%. Increasingly, law firms are bidding on proposals for work packaged by corporate clients. Variations and mixtures of compensation packages are emerging.

---

10. *Upjohn v. U.S.*, 449 U.S. 383 (1981).

The Pleading Stage

Plaintiffs and experienced defendants typically hire counsel before the lawsuit is filed. Some inexperienced defendants hire an attorney only after they learn they have been sued. In either case, pleadings and investigation are iterative processes for most litigants. Trials are initiated by plaintiffs, who claim they have been wronged in a **civil complaint** filed in a court with jurisdiction over the parties and the subject matter. The complaint sets out details of the alleged wrong and the applicable law, "praying" for the court to grant the plaintiff relief (a remedy). The complaint must be delivered by an officer of the court to the defendant. This is the **service of process**, and it usually includes a **summons**, a court order notifying the defendant of the lawsuit and requiring a response. The defendant has a fixed time (e.g., 20 days) to prepare a response, called the **answer**, admitting or denying, point by point, the plaintiff's allegations of fact and interpretation of how the law applies. Many other types of pleadings and motions are often made before and during the trial.

Pretrial Discovery

The U.S. litigation system is based on truth and justice, both considered attainable only when dispute settlement decision makers have maximum access to all relevant facts. In the United States, both parties may access much of the same information, making litigation much less a game of concealment. The U.S. law encourages pretrial **discovery**, using investigatory techniques to acquire information in the hands of others: the opposing party, their consultants, employees, suppliers, or customers. **Depositions** are transcribed testimony under oath taken outside court to preserve testimony or determine how a witness is likely to testify. **Interrogatories** are written questions submitted to the opposing party, also under oath. **Examinations** are physical inspections or assessment of critical subject matter, such as a visit to premises or a medical or mental examination of the plaintiff to determine the extent of injuries.

Probably the most costly form of discovery is the **production of documents**. Copies of documents or computer files relevant to issues in the case must be given to the opposing party, including correspondence, notes, business records, and financial statements. Electronic discovery has become a treasure trove of damaging e-mails and hidden sets of alternate financial records. Indeed, even Microsoft's Bill Gates has been embarrassed when prosecutors and plaintiff's lawyers have confronted him with damaging e-mail messages at the various civil antitrust trials brought against Microsoft. As discussed in Chapter 13, only privileged testimony or documents are exempt from discovery. However, judges are empowered to place sensitive documents or transcripts **under seal** to maintain the confidentiality of trade secrets during trials.

Many courts conclude pretrial discovery with a **pretrial conference**—a meeting between the parties' lawyers and the judge to narrow the issues. Such conferences are usually successful in eliminating unnecessary, wasted trial time and effort on minor, tangential, or undisputed issues. Practical issues around the scheduling of witnesses and the order for presentation of the evidence are also resolved. Pretrial conferences often permit the attorneys to understand the futility of a costly trial, which can encourage settlement.

TRIALS

For the small percentage of disputes that are not settled and actually make it to trial, the law of civil procedure sets the sequence of events. An important initial question concerns decision makers at the tribunal. The judge invariably decides what law to apply to the facts, based on the judge's own knowledge and legal research and on the self-serving interpretation of the law the parties present in their pleadings. But what really happened between the parties? The trial produces evidence from eyewitnesses, expert witnesses, documents, direct and circumstantial evidence, demonstrative evidence (weapon), and other sources. The judge assesses these information sources to make the factual findings unless there is a jury. The U.S. Constitution's Seventh Amendment requires that juries be permitted if either party requests one in most civil cases. The parties may mutually agree to waive trial by jury. Factual questions not decided under the law, such as injunctions, which are heard **in equity**, are never decided by a jury. As discussed in detail in Chapter 3, jury selection, called **voir dire**, is often a critically important process to attempt to attain jurors' impartiality and demographic representation.

Typically, after jury selection, the parties may make **opening statements** that provide the judge and jury with an overview. Next the plaintiff presents its **case in main**, examining witnesses and other evidence. The defendant may **cross-examine** witnesses by interrogating them to reveal hidden inconsistencies in their testimony or their biases. After the plaintiff's case is presented, the defendant may then present the testimony of witnesses and other evidence, and the plaintiff's counsel can cross-examine defense witnesses. At the conclusion of evidence, each party provides a **summation** or closing statement. The judge or jury is then excused to deliberate over the case and returns with a **verdict**, the determination of fault, liability, or legal responsibility.

Not all evidence is admissible under the **rules of evidence**, which were traditionally common law doctrines but are now codified in most states and as the **federal rules of evidence**. The rules of evidence exclude testimony or other evidence unless it meets several tests of relevance, reliability, and objectivity. For example, documents and records must have been handled carefully to assure they are unaltered. The **hearsay rule** generally prohibits a witness from relating the word of another person unless there are exceptional circumstances (other person's dying declaration, habitually kept business records). The verdict is a judgment that weighs the evidence from each party to resolve the controversy. The "tipping point" to adjudicate in favor of one party or the other is the **burden of proof**, a legal standard as to the amount of proof needed to find liability. The civil standard is **preponderance of the evidence** in most cases or the **greater weight of the evidence** in some states or cases. These are much lighter burdens than the standard of **beyond a reasonable doubt** used in criminal cases.

POSTTRIAL ACTIVITIES

Following the verdict, the losing party may choose to capitulate and pay the judgment or drop the case. If the liable party refuses or is incapable of paying, the law provides various processes to enforce judgments. For example, the plaintiff might seek an execution or **attachment**, a court order directing the sheriff to seize the defendant's property for a **judicial sale**, with the proceeds used to satisfy the plaintiff's judgment. **Garnishment** is also available to take a portion of wages, salary, or bank accounts. However, if either or both parties genuinely believe they have a reasonable opportunity to prove the judge made errors, the judge applied the wrong law, or the law is somehow invalid, the party may appeal. Usually there is a very short limitation period, such as 60 days, to file for an appeal. Briefs are filed, arguing a particular interpretation of the law. Generally, no new evidence is presented; instead, the appellate judges use a transcript of the trial and other documents to determine whether there were irregularities in the evidence as admitted or excluded. If the appellate judgment holds that new evidence is needed, it may order a new trial, although this happens infrequently. Some appeals courts have several judges, often panels of three, but sometimes they sit **en banc** as several judges, like the nine sitting on the U.S. Supreme Court.

ALTERNATE DISPUTE RESOLUTION

The costs and difficulties of litigation have spawned strong pressures to settle disputes outside the courts. **Alternative dispute resolution (ADR)** refers to a range of different methods outside litigation to resolve conflicts. The most popular methods are discussed here: arbitration, mediation, and several ancillary techniques designed to encourage settlement through negotiation.

ARBITRATION

Probably the best-known and most actively used form of ADR is **arbitration**— hearings held before panels or individual arbitrators authorized to **award** a remedy to the winning party. Arbitration is generally conducted in a private tribunal, outside the courts of law, although **court annexed arbitration** is increasingly prevalent; for example, in California, courts can order litigating parties to submit to arbitration. Arbitration is the most common form of commercial dispute resolution in international trade. It is used extensively in labor and employment disputes and in disputes between brokers and their investor clients. It is commonly imposed on consumers in business-to-consumer (B2C) e-commerce transactions by click-wrap terms and conditions on commercial Web sites. Arbitrators are often more familiar with the subject matter than judges typically are. Arbitration is usually kept confidential, and it can be held anywhere and at any time without waiting through a backlogged court docket.

Several states and the federal government strongly encourage arbitration with statutes or case law that permits enforcement of arbitration agreements and awards. Parties generally voluntarily agree to submit their disputes to arbitration in a contract concluded before or after the dispute arises. The **American Arbitration Association** is often named in such contractual arbitration clauses because it specializes in providing arbitration services and competent arbitrators. Courts generally enforce arbitration, and there is usually no appeal from an award. Only limited appeal is possible, such as when the arbitrator is biased or went beyond the authority granted in the contract.

The **rent-a-judge** or private justice technique has been used with considerable success in California but has spread only slowly to other states. This technique resembles arbitration in that it is done outside the court system, can be scheduled at the parties' convenience, is confidential, and binds the parties if they agree to make it binding. However, rent-a-judge typically uses retired judges and applies the law.

MEDIATION

Two other forms of dispute resolution are frequently used: mediation and conciliation. **Mediation** uses an independent third-party **mediator** to examine the dispute. It permits the parties' cathartic release of emotional tension, and this may enable them to see the relative strength of both parties' positions. Sometimes the mediator communicates proposals and counterproposals between parties who may have trouble facing each other in the early sessions of the mediation. The mediator helps the parties find common ground, encourages settlement, and may propose compromises, such as graceful or face-saving concessions. **Conciliation** is similar, but the third-party conciliator is not expected to propose compromises or solutions. Unlike most arbitrators, mediators and conciliators have no binding decision-making authority. Both mediation and conciliation are popular in employment and union disputes.

OTHER ADR MECHANISMS

There are several other ADR techniques, most designed to encourage settlement through negotiations. **Minitrials** are generally staged affairs enacted in front of senior managers who need an understanding of the relative strengths of the parties' cases and the credibility of the evidence and witnesses. Minitrials are held privately, sometimes with dramatic presentations, including a mock jury chosen to be similar to the expected demographic profile of the real jury. The jury's explanation of how they would vote is often quite compelling. Similarly, an independent, expert adviser's opinions of the case's strength are influential. Like mediation, successful minitrials jolt the parties into reality with a better understanding of how a real trial would probably play out. Minitrials often trigger more serious settlement negotiations.

ADR mechanisms should become popular in e-commerce. Often the stakes are so small or the potential damages so speculative that certainty in risk management strongly suggests the avoidance of litigation. ADR is already quite prevalent. Indeed, most readers have likely agreed to Internet access license agreements that require arbitration, simply when they clicked "I agree" to access a site. Check out whether arbitration is required at one of your favorite sites, by clicking on the terms and conditions of use.

Some ADR methods actually use the Internet to file claims, submit evidence, make arguments, communicate with arbitrators, and render the award. For example, the resolution of domain name disputes by ICANN uses the on-line Uniform Domain Name Resolution Process (UDRP), discussed in Chapter 7. Such on-line ADR processes hold great promise to handle the growing number of disputes efficiently. However, they will remain controversial until adequately studied. Reasonable checks and balances must develop to counteract the unfairness, just like the ones that developed over centuries of experience with litigation. For example, on-line dispute resolution is likely to give advantages to already powerful players, compromise developed due process protections, and decrease the influence of democratic processes in developing the law.

ONLINE

CPR Institute for Dispute Resolution
http://www.cpradr.org

REGULATORY PROCESS BY ADMINISTRATIVE AGENCIES

The regulation of business is pervasive, a significant legal and economic development of the twentieth century. Administrative agencies at the local, state, and federal level enforce laws, promulgate (pass) regulations, and enforce the regulatory law covering most aspects of business activity. Regulation over e-commerce and other Internet activities is spreading rapidly. There has been a long-standing trend toward **deregulation**, the dismantling of regulatory programs and the reform of regulatory process. Nevertheless, regulation imposes significant constraints and will continue to do so for the foreseeable future. For business to effectively manage its regulatory environment, managers must understand the public policy pressures for reregulation, the substance of existing and proposed regulations, and the administrative processes agencies use. These matters, including the processes used by particular regulatory programs, are discussed throughout this handbook. This section focuses on **administrative law**, the processes that shape the regulation of business by local, state, and federal administrative agencies. The reasons for regulation are discussed in Chapter 14, and agencies' need for information from investigations is discussed as a privacy matter in Chapter 13.

NATURE OF ADMINISTRATIVE AGENCIES

Administrative agencies begin life in an **enabling statute**, a law passed by the legislature that creates the agency and then delegates certain powers to it. The most basic reason for agencies is that they must oversee subject matter that is too complex or technical for constant legislative oversight. Agencies acquire specialized talent by hiring scientific and other experts to conduct the regulatory program. Regulation must adjust as necessary to meet changing social and political needs and to reflect technical changes.

Agencies have three basic functions that parallel the three branches of government. **Executive powers** enable the agency to set policy, gather information, and then investigate or prosecute violations of statutes or regulations. **Legislative power** is delegated to agencies by the legislature but only within narrow guidelines. Finally, **judicial power** is used to adjudicate controversies. The three functions of government are separated to create checks and balances that are applicable to agencies, between agencies, and within agencies. The primary function of agencies today is the promulgation and enforcement of their own rules. Most agency law enforcement processes are defined by statute, executive order, or the agency's rules. Federal agencies generally have similar procedures because they are prescribed in the **Administrative Procedure Act** (APA).

Agencies are referred to by an acronym taken from the first letter of each word in the agency's official title. Although this practice seems like an esoteric exercise in alphabet soup, it is a good idea to become familiar with some of the better known agencies' acronyms. For example, several federal and some state agencies are important to matters discussed in this handbook. The Department of Justice (DOJ) prosecutes federal crimes; the Federal Trade Commission (FTC) is the primary regulator of privacy and shares antitrust enforcement with DOJ. The Patent and Trademark Office (PTO) and the Copyright Office of the Library of Congress (LOC) regulate intellectual property rights. The Federal Communications Commission (FCC) regulates communications systems integral to the Internet's operations. These are the predominant agencies discussed in this handbook, but other agencies are also mentioned, such as the Securities and Exchange Commission (SEC), which regulates the securities markets.

Each state has several administrative agencies, although their procedures vary considerably. Nevertheless, there are many similarities with federal administrative procedure law because most states have adopted procedural laws modeled on the federal APA. State administrative agencies commonly license professionals, regulate banking institutions, set utility rates, regulate insurance sales and claims processing, regulate land use (e.g., zoning), collect taxes, administer prisons, regulate environmental and labor matters, and support education.

CONTROL OF AGENCY ACTIONS

Administrative agencies have significant powers that can be abused. Some agencies are quasi-independent from direct political pressures so that politicians cannot misuse agencies. However, regulatory agencies left unchecked could become tyrannical, and so the public and the three branches of government have certain controls over agencies. Four types of controls are exercised over agencies by the checks and balances of democratic government.

Judicial controls may be the most important because the courts can stop agencies from abusing their powers through judicial review. This involvement begins with application of the **delegation doctrine,** which prohibits the legislature from abdicating its legislative responsibilities. The delegation is illegitimate when the legislature's grants of power are excessive. A delegation is excessive if the enabling act contains conflicting policies and the agency has no standards to operate narrowly or if it provides insufficient accountability or due process. The delegation doctrine requires the enabling act to provide both substantive and procedural controls to limit the overexercise of agency powers. Agencies may have broader powers where technical expertise is necessary or there are rapidly changing conditions in the regulated industry.

Legislative controls are imposed by the legislature. For example, Congress has initial control over federal agencies because the enabling legislation (1) creates the agency, (2) defines its policies and mission, (3) designs the agency's organization and structure, (4) provides for special procedures, (5) passes additional laws for the agency to enforce, and (6) gives the agency rule-making power. Some states and federal laws require automatic periodic review of agencies, called **sunset legislation**. Agencies are dissolved if the legislature does not renew them. This brinkmanship forces the legislature, regulated entities, and other constituencies to reexamine the agency's record and predict its future contributions. For example, the Commodity Futures Trading Commission (CFTC) is reviewed and must be renewed every five years or it would be automatically dissolved.

Funding of agency operations is an important control device. Typically, the legislature initially authorizes budget lines for each agency and then makes an annual appropriation of specific budget allotments. Particular agency activities can be supported with specific additional funds or extinguished by the removal of funding. For example, the SEC was given additional funding following the Enron bankruptcy and the crisis of financial disclosure in 2002. State governors and the president also have significant budgetary control. For example, the president's Office of Management and Budget (OMB) reviews budgets and can make changes. Certain annual expenditures for entitlement programs (e.g., Social Security, welfare) are fixed by statutory formulas and are not subject to the regular budgeting process.

The legislature also exercises indirect control through mechanisms such as Congressional oversight committees, many with watchdog authority, that can investigate agencies and hold public hearings. The threat of reform legislation, as well as the political and public pressure, often urges agencies to change their behavior. Studies by special Congressional agencies such as the General Accounting Office (GAO) also focus attention on the strengths and weaknesses of regulatory programs. Although the president usually selects department heads and regulatory commissioners, the legislature often approves these appointments under the power of **advice and consent**. The **civil service system** insulates the majority of state and federal employees in the bureaucracy from political pressures.

Executive controls are imposed by the president or state governors. Some observers call administrative agencies a **fourth branch of government** allegedly separate from the other three. However, most agencies operate under the executive branch because it typically has the clearest line of authority. Many agency heads are political appointees who are ideologically and directly responsible to the president's administration or the governor. The president has the ultimate law enforcement and policy-making responsibility because the U.S. Constitution requires the president to assure that the laws are "faithfully executed." This gives the president and many state governors an inherent managerial power to hire and fire administrative agents at will. The chairs of independent commissions are routinely appointed by the president. Subject to the civil service system and Senate approval, the president can control the attitudes, abilities, and political loyalties of the policy makers in most agencies. However, Congress and some state legislatures require some independence from the executive's domination. For example, the SEC, FTC, FCC, CFTC, Federal

Reserve Board, and all Congressional agencies (e.g., LOC) are quasi-independent. Their policies are protected from political pressure. Most quasi-independent agency heads or board members have fixed terms of office, political party balance, staggered terms, and protection from firing except "for cause" (e.g., inefficiency, neglect of duty, or malfeasance in office). Some state agencies are independent of the governor but are politically responsive if they are separately elected, as are public utility commissioners and judges in some states.

The president has control over the department-level agencies. For example, the president's control over the DOJ gives the presidential administration practical control over many regulatory programs because only the DOJ may prosecute regulatory crimes (e.g., insider trading, securities fraud). The DOJ is headed by the attorney general (AG), who is directly responsible to the president. Many agencies have separate powers to bring civil actions, seek injunctions and civil fines and damages, and issue binding orders.

Agencies may be reorganized by the president with Congressional consent. Under the Reorganization Act, the president may transfer functions and powers among existing agencies or to newly created agencies. Reorganization consolidates functions in the hands of experts, coordinates conflicting policies, and reduces the inefficient duplication of functions. For example, the Environmental Protection Agency (EPA) and the Federal Energy Regulatory Commission (FERC) were given powers held by other agencies.

Indirect public controls are also possible by various parties, such as pluralist interest groups, which often pressure agencies. For example, the Sierra Club often brings environmental problems to the EPA's attention. Lobbyists influence Congress and regulatory policy makers in similar ways. Publicity in the press about the public acceptance or rejection of the legitimacy of regulatory programs is also influential. For example, the press often mobilizes support for or pressure on administrative agencies, Congress, and the president's administration to pursue or change policies. Two statutes facilitate the indirect public control of agencies. The government in the **Sunshine Act** opens up to public scrutiny many of the meetings of the independent agencies. However, most staff-level meetings are not subject to the sunshine; instead, only the meetings in which official policy-making actions must be made public. The Freedom of Information Act (FOIA), sunshine laws, and state open meetings and open records laws are discussed in Chapter 13.

INFORMATION

Securing information is critical to the efficiency and effectiveness of the regulatory process. Agencies acquire information through (1) direct observation of regulated activities, (2) public complaints and comments, (3) inspections of private areas, (4) subpoenas directing witness testimony, and (5) subpoena duces tecum requiring the production of documents. The Constitution protects individuals and regulated entities from unreasonable searches and seizures in the Fourth Amendment and from self-incrimination in the Fifth Amendment. Constitutional and privacy constraints on agency information gathering are detailed in Chapters 2 and 13.

HEARINGS

The vast majority of administrative actions are processed informally, through negotiation, and without litigation of any kind. However, hearings are frequently used; they are a form of adjudication. Administrative hearings are not identical to court trials and assume many variations. The constitutional right of due process protects regulated business entities from unfair regulatory hearings. Due process lies at the heart of many regulatory processes. Chapter 2 discusses the Constitutional right of due process, which prohibits government from depriving a person of life, liberty, or property without due process of law. The individual or business must be given adequate notice, a meaningful opportunity to be heard, and fair trial procedures. However, because of the wide variation in administrative responsibilities and the liberty and property interests they affect, the precise type of due process protections can vary considerably.

The exact form for the administrative hearing may differ greatly among various agencies and between types of actions brought by a particular agency. Procedures may include adequate notice of the hearing, an impartial tribunal, preservation of the hearing record for appeal purposes, oral hearings, the right to cross-examine witnesses, presentation of evidence, representation by counsel, written decision of findings and conclusions, public or private hearing, procedural and evidentiary rules, other parties' participation, and the right to an appeal. The APA requires that "persons entitled to notice of an agency hearing shall be timely informed." This means "notice reasonably calculated to apprise interested parties of the pendency of the action and afford them an opportunity to present their objections."

Hearing Procedures

The typical order of a court trial is often followed in administrative hearings. The parties file pleadings or motions and may attend prehearing conferences to crystallize the issues. Counsel usually introduces exhibits, examines witnesses, and makes closing arguments. The parties also submit legal briefs and proposed findings to the **administrative law judge** (ALJ). The ALJs are hearing officers with specialized expertise in the regulated matter and who work for the agency. They are not part of the judiciary. When regulated entities are sued, the complainant, usually a lawyer working for the agency, acts like a civil prosecutor. The agency must usually satisfy the burden of proof by initially going forward with allegations and presenting convincing evidence. Most administrative cases are determined by the ALJ, using the preponderance of the evidence standard as the point of persuasion.

The form of evidence at administrative hearings is somewhat different than at a judicial trial. Although a witness's oral testimony is often taken, the APA provides that written statements may replace direct testimony if no prejudice results. Written affidavits, questions, and answers are often appropriate. Some agencies allow the parties to make brief oral summaries of written testimony. The judicial rules of evidence are often not applicable in administrative hearings. This means that rules concerning hearsay, privilege, or incompetence do not apply in administrative hearings. The APA allows agencies discretion in the admission of oral or documentary evidence and the power to exclude "irrelevant, immaterial or unduly repetitious evidence."

The Decision Process

In many agencies there are lower levels of review and determination before any formal hearing is held. For example, an Internal Revenue Service (IRS) agent often gathers evidence and makes an initial determination of tax liability. Most agencies have a formal, trial-like hearing in which the ALJ or hearing examiner determines facts and applies law and policy to the controversy. ALJs function like judges, but they are not passive referees as judges are; instead, they often actively question witnesses. ALJs are presiding officers independent of the agency's policy-making and political pressures to provide checks and balances. They are assigned cases by rotation.

ALJs issue initial decisions by applying law to the facts determined. This initial decision may become the agency's final decision unless it is appealed. Recommended decisions by ALJs are overseen by either the agency's intermediate appeal board or by the agency's head(s). Although ALJ's decisions typically carry great weight, sometimes their decisions are overturned. The ALJ's findings and conclusions are included in the record, a discipline that forces them to consider all the evidence and justify their conclusions. Review is more accurate if a complete written record is available.

It is illegal to bring improper influence on a decision at any agency level. These influences may come from outsiders or litigants, both from within and outside the agency, or from an ALJ's own personal biases. Investigators and prosecutors may not participate in hearing decisions except as witnesses or counsel. ALJs are free to have ideological and generalized views on law or policy. However, a fixed opinion concerning a particular litigant would be prejudicial and require disqualification of the ALJ. The test is whether prior exposure to the evidence makes it virtually impossible to sway the ALJ's mind. Clearly, an ALJ's financial stake or direct pecuniary interest in the outcome would make participation in the decision improper. For example, a state optometry board made up of sole practitioners was financially biased against optometrists working for corporations. The board members had a financial stake in restricting the entry of chain-store optometrists into the state and were illegally biased.

Improper influence could also be exerted from Congressional or executive pressures. Bias may be presumed where there are **ex parte contacts**—"oral or written communications not on the public record with respect to which reasonable prior notice to all parties is not given." Off-the-record communications from regulated entities and regulators are considered unsavory because they may exert political or financial pressure without an opportunity for the public or opposing parties to disprove them.

RULE-MAKING

Enabling legislation usually gives agencies substantive law to apply. However, many regulatory details require experience and expertise, so rule-making authority is often delegated to agencies. Rule-making is more advantageous than adjudication in several ways. Rules apply equally to all persons or businesses. They are a clearer and more legitimate source for policy making than are regulatory precedents. All affected parties have an opportunity to participate in rule-making. A single rule-making is often more efficient than a case-by-case or piecemeal approach to making policy. **Rules** are "the whole or part of an agency statement of general or particular applicability and future effect designed to implement, interpret, or prescribe law or policy." Regulations are similar to rules.

New regulations generally are published as a notice in the *Federal Register*, the chronological collection published every weekday that includes all agency proposals, rules, notices, and presidential proclamations. The *Federal Register* and most agency rules in force are now published on the Internet. Each year the newly published regulations are reorganized and added to the **Code of Federal Regulations** (CFR), which is organized by agency and by subject matter. Browse the Web sites of federal agencies discussed in this handbook to find their rules and regulations.

Rules may be interpretative or substantive. **Substantive rules** are legislative, with a substantial impact directly on affected parties. **Interpretive rules** are intended by the agency to explain the meaning of the terms and procedures it uses. Most regulations have the force of law, subject to invalidation by the courts if they conflict with the Constitution, a statute, or an executive order. There are three basic rule-making processes: exempted, formal, and informal or notice and comment rule-making. These processes vary in the type and amount of public participation afforded.

Exempted rule-making is permitted to agencies under the APA when public participation is not desirable in certain sensitive areas. For example, there is no requirement for notice and comment periods or for a hearing if the rule-making involves the military, foreign affairs, the agency's management or personnel, public property, loans, grants, benefits, contracts, interpretative rules, general statements of policy, or rules of agency organization, procedure, or practice, or otherwise where public procedures are impracticable, unnecessary, or contrary to the public interest.

Formal rule-making is more like adjudication than legislation. It is required when enabling statues envision the need for interactive participation by opposing constituencies. After notice of formal rule-making is made in the *Federal Register*, a formal hearing is held on the record. Trial-like proceedings allow testimony and cross-examination of witnesses. The agency issues its findings as a formal rule that can be judicially overturned if it is not supported by substantial evidence. Formal rule-making is extremely costly and time-consuming, sometimes generating thousands of pages of exhibits and testimony. The process is usually used in economic determinations, when licenses are granted or rate making occurs.

Informal rule-making is the predominant type of rule-making, using the public **notice and comment** form of participation. The agency must publish notice in the *Federal Register* of "either the terms or substance of the proposed rule or a description of the subjects and issues involved." The legal authority relied on must be stated, and the agency usually solicits comments from any interested persons. A contact person at the agency is provided to obtain further information. Most information submitted to the agency is placed in the public record and becomes available for public inspection. These items include the "submission of written data, views, or arguments with or without the opportunity for oral presentation."

After the agency has considered the comments of interested persons and has decided to issue a final rule, it must publish the final rule at least 30 days before it becomes effective. The publication of a final rule must include "a concise general statement of their basis and purpose." Agencies are not bound to follow comments, criticisms, or views submitted by the public. However, the agency must at least consider the "relevant matter presented." As a practical matter, comments often have impact on rule-making unless they are clearly self-interested or in conflict with the public interest.

Regulatory Reform and Modifications of the Rule-Making Process

In recent years the president and other executive offices have had an increasing impact on the mechanics of rule-making. Concern prompted regulatory reforms by several successive presidents: the Ford, Carter, Reagan, Clinton, and both Bush administrations. State legislatures and Congress have also modified regulatory policy making. There are two important reforms. First, Executive Order 12,291 issued by President Reagan requires that all nonindependent federal regulatory agencies analyze major new rules on a cost-benefit basis. **Major rules** are regulations likely to have a significant financial effect on the economy. OMB continues to have the greatest oversight powers in all phases of this economic justification process. Although the independent regulatory agencies are not bound to follow these procedures, they must comply with the second most important cost-benefit/analysis (C-B/A) requirements under the Regulatory Flexibility Act. Doing so requires estimation of the impact of new regulations on small firms and governmental units.

Regulatory reform generally requires agencies to consider five broad goals. First, agencies must consider adequate information in formulating rules. Second, an initial C-B/A must be performed on all rule proposals to determine whether a major rule is present. Third, regulatory objectives should maximize net benefits to society, and regulatory action should be taken only if societal benefits outweigh the costs. Fourth, alternative proposals must be considered. Fifth, all regulatory proposals should be correlated to reduce conflicts between agencies and with other rules. Each major rule is subjected to extensive C-B/A, and a regulatory impact analysis is prepared to justify the rule-making.

There are problems with the economic justification of regulation. First, ex parte contacts occur and are not usually recorded, making it difficult for other interested parties to adequately respond to the contact's arguments if they influence the agency to modify a rule or policy. Second, C-B/A cannot be appealed to the courts. The methodologies used to justify regulations are far less open to public scrutiny or effective expert criticism. Third, OMB has the most discretion to specify methods used in the C-B/A, and OMB is politically biased toward the presidential administration's regulatory priorities. This can slow or even halt rule-making required by law. Fourth, tangible or immediate costs are much easier to quantify than intangible or future costs or benefits. This reduces the accuracy of C-B/A. For these reasons, it is important for regulated entities and the public affected by rule proposals to participate in the process. For example, the submission of comments and the criticism of assumptions, methodologies, and projections could refine the impact analyses.

In the future, additional regulatory reform can be expected. The most honest and forthright form is through the legislative process that eliminates unneeded programs that have outlived their usefulness. Regulators who continue to spend tax money to maintain agencies but fail to regulate effectively subvert democracy while falsely mollifying the electorate. As of this writing, there is building a strong reaction to the losses of privacy rights that followed the September 11 terrorism events. Bills will likely go through Congress to reinstate privacy rights whenever regulations might change privacy rights. For example, a **privacy impact statement** might be required from all agencies, including the DOJ, similar to the C-B/A just discussed.

JUDICIAL REVIEW

Dissatisfaction with agency decisions may permit the courts to intervene. A group of technical issues may permit or prevent appeal, called **judicial review**. These are based on efficiency and on separation of powers. Jurisdiction is an initial issue in most tribunals at law or concerning regulatory action. The enabling legislation or a related statute may call for specific procedures. However, even if there is no specific statutory provision, the common law writs may give partial relief. For example, an injunction may be issued to stop an agency from causing irreparable harm by an unauthorized act. Declaratory judgments may pronounce whether an agency is authorized to take a particular action. A **writ of mandamus** orders an agency official to perform an action required under law or to exercise its discretion. **Statutory preclusion** is related to jurisdiction. In a few instances, a statute denies judicial review if the matter is totally committed to agency discretion. For example, if the Department of Veterans Affairs (DVA) denies particular benefits, this denial is precluded from review. Military draft and dishonorable discharge matters are generally precluded from review. When particular decisions are committed to agency discretion, they are generally nonreviewable because they involve political matters not appropriate for judicial review. Matters affecting national defense or foreign policy are generally unreviewable. **Standing** is another basis to deny judicial review. The APA provides standing to any person "adversely affected or aggrieved by agency action."

The **exhaustion of administrative remedies** appears to be the essence of administrative red tape. Judicial review is postponed until *all* administrative procedures are pursued completely. It prevents a plaintiff from short-circuiting the agency's internal process. In most cases, an agency's final order must be issued before judicial review is allowed. This rule permits full development of the facts and expertise from within the agency before the courts may step in. The agency may correct its own mistakes, eliminating unnecessary judicial review. Agency autonomy is undermined by excessive judicial review, so the courts initially defer until the agency's internal procedures have run their course. However, if the agency becomes deadlocked or further proceedings would be futile, then judicial review may be appropriate to interrupt the agency's process. Where agency actions are not authorized by statute or where constitutional questions arise, judicial review many precede an exhaustion of remedies.

Primary jurisdiction is a doctrine similar to exhaustion, but it recognizes that the agency has special expertise or competence. The courts may give varying interpretations to agency regulations, which can lead to inconsistent results. Agencies with specialized expertise are best suited to make certain factual and technical determinations. Primary jurisdiction does not apply if the matter is nontechnical or other legal issues predominate in the case. After a full record is compiled, the courts may then review the agency's exercise of its discretion for conformity with legal standards.

Ripeness of an issue for appeal focuses on the fitness of the issues themselves for judicial determination at the time the suit is brought. An issue is not ripe for review unless parties will suffer hardship if the agency's decision is not immediately reviewed. Issues that are factual, require expertise, or are policy determinations are usually unfit for judicial review. Where the potential harm to the parties is great, the court should consider the issue as ripe. Most ripeness cases arise when the agency has not yet taken any action. Instead, if the regulated entity suspects it might be affected by the agency's action sometime in the future, it may hope to stop the agency from taking any further action. Consider the example of an agency's decision to condemn private property. The agency's action is probably not ripe when it holds a hearing to determine which land it needs. By contrast, the agency's action is more likely to be ripe when its field staff orders a demolition crew to unload bulldozers onto the private property.

Sovereign immunity is an ancient concept derived from a quaint notion that rulers were of royal bloodline; often monarchs were considered divine. Clearly, no legal challenge could be brought against such perfect individuals, thus inspiring the saying "the king can do no wrong." The sovereign immunity doctrine prohibits suit against the government or its officials. Today, the fallibility of government is readily apparent, so there are different justifications to limit suits against government; for example, government liability could impose huge financial burdens on taxpayers, or the threat of suit hampers the discretion of leaders.

Generally, agencies are immune from suit for money damages if the suit arises out of discretionary policy actions of the federal or local governments. The Eleventh Amendment discussed in Chapter 2 assures the states sovereign immunity against federal law. Texas and Georgia still have strong sovereign immunity against many types of suits. However, there are cracks in sovereign immunity's armor. No immunity exists if government performs acts that a private person could be held liable for, the so-called proprietary functions of government. Additionally, many statutes and court decisions now expose most governments to negligence suits. For example, the Federal Tort Claims Act waives the sovereign immunity of the U.S. government. Private plaintiffs injured by federal conduct that is negligent or involves intentional assault, battery, false imprisonment, false arrest, or abuse of process may sue the federal government. The APA and some state administrative procedure laws allow suit against the government for court orders if money damages are not sought and the agency causes wrong to the private party.

Scope of Review

How should a court review an agency's action? There are two primary standards for the scope of review of agency decisions. The **substantial evidence** test is used to invalidate the agency's determinations of facts if they were unsupported by substantial evidence. Substantial evidence exists if a reasonable mind might accept it as adequate to support a conclusion. This is a very low threshold; there need only be at least some evidence supporting the agency's conclusion. This amount of evidence may be far less convincing than the evidence required for a criminal conviction (beyond a reasonable doubt), for significant deprivations of fundamental rights (clear and convincing evidence), or for civil damage judgments (preponderance of the evidence or greater weight of evidence). The court need find only that there is some evidence supporting the agency's decision and that the agency considered the evidence offered by both sides in the case.

A different standard applies when agencies dictate policy or exercise discretion, such as in informal rule-making, investigations, or prosecutions. Discretionary agency decisions are overturned on review only where they were **arbitrary, capricious, and an abuse of discretion**. A reviewing court may overturn an agency's discretionary decision if inappropriate factors were considered, appropriate factors were not considered, there were clear errors of judgment, or the decision makers were clearly biased. Although the two standards differ conceptually, they converge in practice as measures of reasonableness.

CHAPTER 2
CONSTITUTIONAL LAW

The U.S. Constitution establishes the basic framework for government, including the sphere of influence of various levels of government and the rights reserved to the people. It has always had a major impact on commerce. In early days it implemented the colonists' desire for free markets and self-determination. As the nation grew, the interpretation of several key constitutional provisions—the Commerce Clause, the Bill of Rights, and federalism—guided industrial development. More recently, as e-commerce evolves, the Constitution is again playing a major role. Governments and citizens are grappling with their evolving rights and duties that have been made much more complex by the Internet's borderless reach and the greater dependence on trade in intellectual property.

Nearly every major provision of the U.S. Constitution reflects a reaction to the tyrannical rule that the English crown exercised over the American colonies. To restrict the potential misuse of governmental powers by the central government, which the colonies experienced, the federal system spreads governmental powers among separate branches at each level of government and separates powers between the federal and local governments. The colonies first organized into a confederation to confine the central government's powers, but the **confederation** form of government did not coordinate the states' activities. The resulting protectionism and conflicting policies were finally seen as harmful to the whole country's strength. The Constitution became a compromise between the **Federalists**, who desired a strong central government, and the **Anti-Federalists**, who supported stronger states' rights. This federalism forms the basis for all American law and represents the foundation for power at all levels of government. As the supreme law of the land, the Constitution establishes the basic structure of the federal government, provides for the states' self-government, and limits government encroachment on business and personal activities. The structure of the U.S. Constitution is so well balanced that it has been widely imitated.

The courts have reinforced the federal government's pervasive power to regulate business and interstate commerce. Nevertheless, there are still disputes over the relative roles of the states in our federal system. Many cases hold that the federal powers to regulate business activities are so pervasive that they preempt any state interference with interstate commerce. By contrast, other cases have carved out pockets of states' rights to regulate local business activity. However, state laws that interfere excessively with the federal government's enumerated lawmaking powers are held unconstitutional under the supremacy clause. The **supremacy clause** of the U.S. Constitution makes federal law supreme and permits the Supreme Court to declare unconstitutional any conflicting state law. This is a major component of federalism, a theme throughout this chapter.

The successful growth of e-commerce depends on the U.S. Constitution to encourage free markets, balance libertarian incentives and privacy with security, protect intangible property rights, and maintain open access to the infrastructure of e-commerce. Indeed, because electronic communication is the very essence of e-commerce, the U.S. Constitution's protection of free speech is the key legal infrastructure supporting the Internet. This chapter examines this and other basic constitutional issues triggered by activities in both the traditional economy and cyberspace.

ONLINE

Further reading on constitutional law can be found at **http://www.law. cornell.edu/ constitution/ constitution.overview. html**

The constitutional bases for some of the emerging e-commerce issues—states rights, obscenity, and intellectual property rights—are covered here in depth. Other issues—due process and jurisdiction, defamation, taxation of e-commerce, and privacy—are detailed in other chapters. Many of the most complex challenges in accommodating the convergence of the traditional and Internet economies trigger constitutional questions. Therefore, a basic understanding of the U.S. Constitution is essential to any participation in the public policy debate over regulation.

THE BASIS FOR CONSTITUTIONAL POWERS

The Constitution has two major parts and several subparts. The first part contains the Preamble and seven substantive articles that establish and empower Congress, the executive branch, and the judiciary and then regulate relations among the states and authorize constitutional amendments. The second part contains amendments that were enacted after the founders' initial drafting. The first 10 amendments, the Bill of Rights, were ratified in 1791 to protect fundamental freedoms and liberties. Since then, thousands of amendments have been proposed, but only 18 have passed. They deal with liquor prohibition, taxation, the abolition of slavery and its effects, congressional pay, and election matters. Although 28 amendments have been passed, only 27 amendments are currently effective. In 1933, the Twenty-First Amendment repealed prohibition, the grand experiment, which was originally imposed by the Eighteenth Amendment in 1919.

Amendment proposals in recent years have sought to require equal rights for women, balance the federal government budget, outlaw desecration of the American flag, and establish the right to life for the unborn. The discussion in this chapter reorganizes this structure by first examining the historical context, next reviewing the basic powers of government, and then discussing the basic constitutional constraints on traditional and e-commerce activity.

THE HISTORICAL PERSPECTIVE

Conflict over the separation of powers has dominated the history of U.S. constitutional law since the Revolutionary War. Our government represents a compromise between opposing views of where are the most legitimate, efficient, and responsible places for governmental power to be. The country has continually struggled between two political forces in the search for the best model for government. The Federalists advocated the unitary form of central or national government. The Anti-Federalists represented regional interests that advocated stronger local governments. A general theory of government, known as federalism, sometimes called **dual federalism**, recognizes that power can reside at both the central level and at various local levels. Much of American history and the contemporary legal issues affecting business turn on federalism and the separation of powers between and within both state and federal levels of governments.

Constitutional Development during the Revolutionary War

England's pervasive and tyrannical rule over the American colonies led to the Revolutionary War. The English crown was dictatorial and abused the colonists, showing little respect for their opinions. Therefore, the constitutional framers included provisions to restrict any similar misuse of power by separating the power of the central government into three distinct branches. This separation of powers into many subunits of government may not seem the most efficient, but it is a proven deterrent to tyranny.

The original 13 colonies derived their political powers from colonial charters granted by the English crown. These documents eventually developed into separate state constitutions and were ultimately revised to parallel the U.S. Constitution so that the states have similar separations of powers. The colonies had divergent social and economic interests and considered themselves separate, distinct, and sovereign political entities. Although the colonies united during the Revolutionary War to oppose tyranny, they mainly sought to oppose their common enemy and provide for a collective defense, not to unify under a single model of government.

The Articles of Confederation

The colonies' first attempt to unify was an overreaction to the strong English central government. Soon after independence, the states used a confederation form of government that was no more than a loose aggregation of the states, similar to other experiments by the Swiss, Germans, and the Papal states. A confederation is a loose alliance of independent entities that seek to retain separate autonomy and self-determination. Confederating states join together for limited common goals, such as defense. They reject stronger forms of central government. The **Articles of Confederation** created the first American confederation. It provided a benchmark for the strongest form of states' rights in American federalism. Ever since these Articles of Confederation were ratified between 1777 and 1781, the trend has been generally toward increased central government powers and away from strong state powers. The Civil War was a notable example of conflict over states' rights.

The Articles of Confederation gave the new Congress very limited power to conduct foreign affairs, raise armed forces, and levy taxes. It created no branches of government with executive or judicial power. The early Congress had no power to raise money and could only request that the states contribute money for their collective efforts. The states had different currencies that created havoc in interstate commerce and eventually runaway inflation. The central government had great difficulty in maintaining domestic peace and preventing violence. In response, the states attempted to revise the Articles of Confederation; instead, they wrote an entirely new document, the U.S. Constitution.

Development of the U.S. Constitution

The U.S. Constitution is a compromise between the two dominant political groups of that time. The Federalist party initially succeeded in securing a strong national government in international affairs, interstate commerce, and taxation. The Federalist position was exemplified by well-to-do Northeastern merchants who stood to gain the most from unlimited interstate commerce. The Anti-Federalist position represented the states' rights advocates and the populist, agrarian interests of the South. They distrusted both the Federalists and central governments in general. This power struggle resulted in a compromise reserving the police power to the states and providing regional strength through each state's representation in the U.S. Congress.

THE POWERS OF GOVERNMENT

Most governmental powers are provided in the U.S. Constitution. **Enumerated powers** are expressly delegated to the federal government by the states. Implicit powers permit Congress to legislate where it is **necessary and proper** to implement particular enumerated powers. The **reserved powers** of the states include the police power to look after the general health, safety, welfare, and morals of their people.

Not all powers are allocated exclusively to either the federal government or the state governments. Both levels of government share or have **concurrent powers** to make laws in several areas (e.g., taxation). Certain potential powers are **prohibited** to both the state and federal governments. For example, neither level of government may make laws that establish a religion. The supremacy clause denies to the states the power to legislate in areas where the federal government power is exclusive.

Enumerated, Delegated, or Exclusively Federal Powers

The federal government has several **exclusive powers**. The most important to business is the power to regulate interstate commerce. The states are prohibited from making laws that would unduly burden interstate commerce. (The commerce clause is discussed in a later section.) Other exclusive powers give to only the federal government the power to act in matters of foreign affairs. For example, the states have no power to make war, sign treaties, naturalize citizens, or regulate aliens. The federal government has power over the post office, now the quasi-governmental U.S. Postal Service. The power to build post roads has given rise to federal interstate highways.

Reserved and Concurrent Powers

The Tenth Amendment reserves to the states any powers not specifically delegated to the federal government.

The Tenth Amendment

The powers not delegated to the United States by the Constitution, nor prohibited by it to the States, are reserved to the States respectively, or to the people.

Despite this reservation by the Tenth Amendment to the states of all remaining governmental powers, the states share many powers with the federal government. Examples include the power to tax and the powers of eminent domain.

The **police power** permits each state to protect its citizens' "health, safety, welfare, and morals." It enables the states to legislate in the areas of criminal law, tort law, contract law, commercial law, divorce law, regulatory law, and property rights. However, the state police power is not unlimited, so legislation is often invalidated when it imposes an undue burden on interstate commerce or constitutes an uncompensated taking of private property.

Takings

States have the power of **eminent domain**, permitting the **taking** of private property for public purposes, such as condemning homes to build a highway, a city lot to construct a government building, or farmland that will flood and become a lakebed when a dam is built. The power of eminent domain has also been important to create the **rights of way** for utilities and communications companies that are fundamental to Internet operations. Networks of wires are either strung overhead or put in pipes under public streets, but frequently they cross private land. The Fifth Amendment requires the government, or a private utility acting with eminent domain power, to pay "just compensation" for the value of property taken. This clause was included in the Constitution because of England's practice of confiscating colonists' property for use by the English crown. What constitutes a taking and what rights does a property owner have if the government or a utility wants to use the power of eminent domain to take that owner's property? Several recent takings cases illustrate balancing individual property rights with society's various interests.

A partial taking is of particular interest to business. When the taking is complete, the government or utility must pay the reasonable value of the property, essentially a measure of fair market value. However, when the taking deprives the owner of substantial rights, but does not take it all, there is a **partial taking**. This may arise where (1) a landowner is prevented from exploiting the property's greatest economic value, (2) a landowner must let others use the property, or (3) a landowner does not receive just compensation for the taking. Government regulations that limit land use, such as a zoning regulation, generally involve no compensable taking because the property is simply restricted from *some* uses. To do otherwise would severely restrict government's ability to regulate. Nevertheless, the Supreme Court considers some partial takings as compensable. For example, partial compensation was required when a government body took an easement for public beach access[1] and when the use of property in a flood plain was temporarily restricted.[2] A more expansive taking occurred when a regulatory agency sought to prevent coastal beach erosion by denying a building permit to a residential beach lot.[3] The Supreme Court balances the economic impact of a regulation against its anticipated public benefits in determining the extent of compensation for such regulatory takings.

Takings are also at issue in construction and maintenance of infrastructure for public services such as utilities and communications. For much of the twentieth century, state and federal statutes have authorized public utilities to condemn land through eminent domain so long as the land is taken for a public purpose, typically utility services.[4] This power permitted utilities to build and maintain their distribution networks that crisscross the nation: wires for electricity, telephone, and cable TV and pipes for water, natural gas, and sewers. Today, the public's hunger for high-speed Internet access will probably not decrease the need to build physical networks with at least some nonwireless elements, or **landlines**, which are needed for at least part of their networks. Most state statutes provide for structured condemnation proceedings in which the utility seeks to route its wires or pipes through private land or buildings. For example, there were such condemnation disputes when some apartment owners tried to prevent installation of lines as cable TV spread in the 1970s and 1980s. Eminent domain issues will continue as the nation becomes more connected.

Although wireless telephony would seem to alleviate some of the pressures and expenses of acquiring rights of way, it is not clear that wireless services will end the need for physical rights of way over land anytime soon. First, wireless is making only slow penetration into Internet access, and most Internet subscribers still use landlines through modems over traditional phone lines, DSL, or cable systems. Second, cell towers are needed for most wireless service. Many cell towers are sited on private property and are connected and/or powered by using landlines. Finally,

---

1. *First English Evangelical Lutheran Church of Glendale v. Los Angeles County*, 482 U.S. 304 (1987).
2. *Nollan v. California Coastal Commission*, 483 U.S. 825 (1987).
3. *Lucas v. South Carolina Coastal Council*, 505 U.S. 1003 (1992).
4. *Berman v. Parker*, 348 U.S. 26 (1954).

many wire-based utilities share pole space that strings the network wiring through-out each service area. For example, the power company's poles are often used by the phone and cable TV companies under a federal law that requires access but assures compensation. This law seeks to avoid excessive duplication of pole capacity, but it is argued that the law gives pole users a tremendous cost advantage over pole owners. Some other aspects of the regulation of public utilities and the electronic media are discussed in Chapter 14.

JUDICIAL REVIEW

The common law legal heritage in English-speaking nations like the United States has evolved into a hybrid of the common law and civil law legal systems. Both types of law periodically require interpretation, a function historically provided by the courts. Many constitutional provisions are precise enough to so that interpretation is unnecessary. For example, most of the numerical limitations seem clear enough. The minimum age is 35 years for the president, 30 for senators, and 25 for house members. Similarly, the simple majority vote required to pass legislation, the two-thirds needed to override presidential vetoes, and the three-fourths of state legisla-tures needed to amend the Constitution all seem quite precise. However, much of the remainder of the Constitution and many statutes contain vague terms. The founders and some legislatures deliberately use vague terms to permit flexibility as society's needs change. They realized they could not find precise and timeless language that would effectively anticipate the whole range of potential human behaviors. The courts' flexibility and discretion in interpretation helps to encourage compliance with the "spirit" and not just the "letter" of the law.

Judicial Restraint

The Supreme Court's power to interpret the Constitution is important because the formal constitutional amendment process is so cumbersome. Only 27 constitutional amendments are currently effective (Prohibition was repealed). By contrast, the Supreme Court constantly interprets the Constitution, thereby effectively changing it. Nevertheless, the courts' power to make laws is limited in several important ways. First, most courts may adjudicate and interpret only after a real **case or controversy** arises. Advisory opinions are not generally permitted except in a few states. Second, most judges exercise judicial restraint by trying not to make sweeping changes in the law. Judicial decisions are generally made in conformance with established prece-dents. The common law rule of precedent ensures consistency, provides some notice, and restricts judges from constantly imposing their personal economic or social beliefs. **Strict constructionism** is a view contrary to judicial activism in that it pre-sumes the legislature is better suited to solve societal or economic problems because this is precisely the legislature's purpose and because it is more immediately respon-sible to voters.

Although courts have significant lawmaking powers, they are generally power-less to enforce their decisions. The legislature must appropriate funds for enforce-ment by the executive branch. Legal precedents are also subject to later legislation.

In 1944, for example, the Supreme Court held insurance was within interstate commerce, which would have exposed the insurance industry to federal antitrust law.[5] However, Congress quickly passed the McCarran-Ferguson Act to reverse the decision and provide antitrust exemption to the insurance industry.

Supreme Court Review of Legislation

Before 1803, judicial review of legislation was generally unknown. Today, any conflicts between the Constitution and a statute subject the legislation to **judicial review**. The power of judicial review flows naturally from both the common law of precedent and from the supremacy clause. Although no specific constitutional provision empowers the Supreme Court to hold legislation unconstitutional, the Supreme Court conferred this power on itself in the landmark 1803 case, *Marbury v. Madison.*[6]

In the last few days of his administration, President John Adams made several special appointments to federal office before the inauguration of the new president, Thomas Jefferson. After Senate confirmation, President Jefferson directed James Madison, the new secretary of state, to withhold the paperwork needed to legitimize several of Adams's appointments, including Marbury's commission as justice of the peace for the District of Columbia. Marbury sought a **writ of mandamus** in the Supreme Court, an order to force Madison to deliver Marbury's commission. Chief Justice John Marshall declined to grant Marbury's request because no statute gave jurisdiction to the Supreme Court to sit as a trial court in mandamus cases. In this ruling, Marshall effectively made it a judge's duty to interpret statutes in light of constitutional provisions. When a controversy involves the constitutionality of legislation, Marshall's decision empowered the courts to invalidate legislation in conflict with the Constitution.

The advice and consent process was designed to permit open debate of a nominee's ideology and qualifications. The president should be given some free rein to select ideologically compatible individuals for the cabinet. These people must regularly work with the president's team and harmonize with the administration's objectives. However, judges and other independent government officials, like Securities and Exchange Commission or Federal Trade Commission commissioners or the Federal Reserve chairman, are separate from the presidential administration. Their experience and job qualifications are more important than ideological conformity. The nomination and confirmation process has permitted a shift of emphasis from ideological compatibility to qualifications that suit the position. The president and Senate might do well to return to the true spirit of the U.S. Constitution's "advice" provision, which appears to require the president to first seek counsel from the whole Senate. Doing so could help avoid the divisiveness of nominating an ideologically unacceptable candidate.

---

5. *United States v. South-Eastern Underwriters Association*, 322 U.S. 533 (1944).
6. 1 Cranch 137 (1803).

SPECIFIC POWERS OF GOVERNMENT

COMMERCE CLAUSE

The power over commerce is an enumerated power of the federal government. The commerce clause forms the primary basis for economic regulation and is probably the most important constitutional provision with impact on business.

> **The Commerce Clause**
>
> The Congress shall have the Power . . . To regulate Commerce with foreign Nations, and among the several States, and with the Indian Tribes.

Two major aspects of the commerce clause affect business. First, it gives Congress power to regulate interstate commerce. Second, by implication it denies the states power to regulate or impede interstate commerce. It seems to leave the states with somewhat freer control over **intrastate commerce**—that is, the local incidents of commerce. States may validly use their police power to protect the health, safety, welfare, and morals of their citizens. In practice, both federal and state laws may regulate certain aspects of commerce, providing the state law's purposes are proper.

Regulation of Foreign Commerce

Under the Articles of Confederation, the states made inconsistent compacts with foreign nations. The Constitution makes the regulation of trade with foreign nations an exclusively federal power. This provision presumes that decisions to make treaties, conduct foreign relations, and regulate foreign commerce are best made by a single, unified entity representing the will and needs of the whole nation.

The definition of foreign commerce is unclear because foreign commerce with the United States necessarily begins or ends within a state. In practice, the states have been prohibited from regulating certain aspects of foreign commerce. For example, state regulation of imports from or exports to foreign nations is invalid if it restricts trade or requires any special treatment of foreign goods. The states may exercise limited regulation over foreign goods once these goods are in the hands of a retailer and the bulk of a wholesale lot has been broken down into smaller commercial units, for example, when a large shipping container has been broken down into pallets or boxes. State regulation is invalid if it discriminates between domestic and foreign commerce, even if the regulation is arguably based on public welfare concerns. Some nations permit their political subdivisions to affect foreign commerce. For example, the Canadian provinces regulate Canada's securities markets. Provincial regulators can make international agreements with other nations' regulators and have done so on enforcement matters with the U.S. Securities Exchange Commission (SEC).

Federal Regulation of Commerce

The constitutional framers intended the commerce clause to grant Congress sufficient power to govern in all areas of economic activity. In 1824, however, the

Supreme Court, in *Gibbons v. Ogden*,[7] restricted Congress from regulating *intrastate* (matters wholly within only one state) by narrowly interpreting the word *interstate*.

Interstate Commerce

Commerce, undoubtedly, is traffic, but it is something more: it is . . . commercial intercourse between nations, and parts of nations, in all its branches, and is regulated by prescribing rules for carrying on that intercourse.[8]

By the early twentieth century, the Supreme Court restricted Congress's interstate commerce powers to include only those matters involving actual transportation of goods across state lines. This left almost all manufacturing as intrastate and therefore not subject to federal regulation.

Commerce Power and the New Deal

New Deal political economy influenced the Supreme Court's interpretation of the commerce clause. During the Great Depression, public pressure mounted for federal solutions to the economic devastation. The legislative efforts of FDR and Congress pitted them against the Supreme Court's laissez-faire predisposition. After FDR's 1937 power struggle with the Supreme Court, the Court validated nearly all of Congress's remedial legislation regulating commerce, including such major laws as the National Labor Relations Act, the securities laws, and the Fair Labor Standards Act. Since 1937, the commerce clause has become the most significant source of congressional power to regulate business. Today, federal legislation is upheld even when it develops a federal police power to preserve health, safety, and welfare. The **affectation doctrine** invalidates regulation over interstate commerce unless some reasonable link exists between that activity and an aspect of interstate commerce. The determination by Congress that such a link exists is usually sufficient to satisfy the courts, even though the link may be tenuous.

Necessary and Proper Clause

The broad commerce power to regulate business can be further implemented through the necessary and proper clause, a catchall phrase in Article I, Section 8, following the list of delegated powers. It permits regulation even beyond an enumerated power. Legislation covering such additional matters is valid when it makes regulation of an enumerated power more effective. For example, a limit on tort remedies against nuclear power generators was based on the necessary and proper clause as a way to encourage development of the nuclear power industry.

The Necessary and Proper Clause

The Congress shall have Power . . . To make all Laws which shall be necessary and proper for carrying into Execution the foregoing Powers.

---

7. 6 L.Ed. 23 (1824).
8. Ibid.

State Regulation of Commerce

Although the Constitution does not specifically deny the states power to regulate interstate commerce, case law has limited state power. The dual federalism concept permits the states to regulate intrastate activities so long as they impose only minor burdens on interstate commerce under a "balancing test." First, the state regulation must bear a rational relationship to a valid state goal. Second, the effect of the state regulation on interstate commerce must be slight. Third, the extent to which the state regulation discriminates against interstate commerce must be small. Fourth, the necessity for the state regulation must be great. These four factors balance the state's interests in regulating against the need for federal uniformity. If a state law regulating commerce is reasonably related to a strong and necessary state goal and the burdens and discrimination that it places on interstate commerce are small, the law should be valid. A long line of cases on the states' powers to regulate interstate commerce fall into three basic groups: (1) state regulation of interstate transportation, (2) state regulation of production and trade, and (3) state taxation of multistate and multinational businesses.

In the 1925 case of *Buck v. Kuykendall*,[9] a Washington State statute for licensing common carriers was held an invalid burden on interstate commerce. Buck was refused permission to use the Washington State highways to operate an "auto stage line" because the territory was "already being adequately served." The Supreme Court found the state was attempting to unconstitutionally regulate interstate commerce, not simply the safety of its highways. In the 1938 case of *South Carolina State Highway Dept. v. Barnwell Bros.*,[10] the state's restriction on truck width and weight was upheld as a legitimate safety concern, despite the incidental burden that the restrictions placed on interstate commerce. Long trucks presented similar safety concerns to Iowa, which validly restricted double trailers over 60 feet long.[11]

State safety concerns must be actual and not conjectural, a problem addressed by the arbitrary train-length restrictions in the 1945 case of *Southern Pac. Co. v. Arizona*.[12] Arizona attempted to collect penalties from Southern Pacific Railway for violating the 14-car passenger-train maximum limit and the 70-car freight-train limit. This case introduced the "balancing test," and the Supreme Court then used it to invalidate the Arizona statute as arbitrary. *Bibb v. Navajo Freight Lines, Inc.*[13] presented a similar problem in 1959. Illinois attempted to require all trucks to use a particular type of curved mudguard for their wheels. The statute was found unconstitutional because the mudguards, manufactured only by an Illinois company, were expensive and offered little additional protection compared with the equipment already in use by most trucking companies. This ruling illustrates that there must be a compelling local interest before local regulations imposing burdens on interstate commerce are upheld as constitutional.

---

9.   267 U.S. 307 (1925).

10. 303 U.S. 177 (1938).

11. *Kassel v. Consolidated Freightways Corp. of Delaware*, 450 U.S. 662 (1981).

12. 325 U.S. 761 (1945).

13. 359 U.S. 520 (1959).

Most state restrictions on out-of-state products are discriminatory and therefore impose an undue burden on interstate commerce. However, there is an exception for state quarantine restrictions. For example, laws prohibiting transportation of diseased cattle into Iowa and New York were upheld. To protect their fruit trees from disease, Arizona and California can legitimately restrict the import of fruit. However, local efforts to prevent local disposal of imported solid wastes are generally unsuccessful.[14] Although state regulations may ostensibly try to prevent the spread of disease, unwholesome foods, or undesirable materials, their economic effect is to favor in-state producers. There is seldom a justification to burden interstate commerce when a state or local law gives preference to locally produced products, conserves local resources, maintains favorable local prices, or otherwise restricts exports outside the state.

The celebrated **milk import cases** have been particularly troublesome. Although states may use the police power to assure food safety, several milk regulations have been invalidated. States have attempted to control the price, place of production, or distance that milk travels to market on the pretext of maintaining the milk's wholesomeness. The New York State Milk Control Act of 1933 established minimum prices for milk to ensure sanitary conditions. The city of Madison, Wisconsin, restricted milk sales in the city to milk produced within 25 miles of the city.[15] A Mississippi regulation allowed the sale of milk produced out of state only if the state of origin permitted the import of Mississippi's milk. All these state laws were found to be excessive regulation for their limited objective because other means existed to control milk purity.

States may tax interstate commerce if the out-of-state business has some connection, local operations, or nexus with the taxing state. Several types of tax are valid, although each must apply fairly to both in-state and out-of-state businesses: property taxes on real estate or personal property residing within the state on "tax day," income taxes on the portion derived from within the taxing state, and use taxes on an out-of-state mail, phone, Internet, or other direct marketing method. These state taxation methods are so important to the future of e-commerce that this subject is covered in detail in Chapter 14.

CONTRACT CLAUSE

The **contract clause** prohibits the states from impairing private contracts. This limitation restricts the states, but not the federal government, from passing statutes or administrative regulations that modify the duties owed under *existing* contracts. Nineteenth-century Supreme Court decisions interpreted the contract clause so pervasively that states were effectively prohibited from imposing economic regulations.

14. *Fort Gratiot Sanitary Landfill, Inc. v. Michigan Dept. of Natural Resources*, 504 U.S. 353 (1992).
15. *Dean Milk Co. v. Madison*, 340 U.S. 349 (1951).

The Contract Clause

No State shall … pass any … Law impairing the Obligation of Contracts.

The framers included the contract clause in response to the economic chaos that existed under the Articles of Confederation and to prevent the passage of **debtor relief laws** by political pressure. Because more people were debtors than creditors, the framers feared that the debtors might elect legislators who promised to pass laws modifying debt contracts.

Some early interpretations of the contract clause restricted public grants by the states to individuals and institutions (colleges). Modern interpretations of the contract clause permit the states to modify existing contracts only in emergency situations, for example, when necessary to protect the public's health, safety, welfare, or morals.

FULL FAITH AND CREDIT CLAUSE

An important element of federalism is that each state must recognize the laws and legal processes of the other states. Without this recognition, some of the states could become a refuge for those evading their legal obligations elsewhere. To prevent such misuse of the states' borders, the constitutional framers formulated the **full faith and credit clause**.

Full Faith and Credit Clause

Full Faith and Credit shall be given in each State to the public Acts, Records, and judicial Proceedings of every other State.

Full faith and credit is distinguished from stare decisis, the rule of precedent. Precedents are previous cases that establish rules of law applicable to different but similar disputes arising later in that jurisdiction. Full faith and credit does not require states to adopt other states' precedents, only to enforce other states' laws or judgments between particular disputing parties when suit is brought in another state. The full faith and credit clause requires application of the doctrines of **res judicata** and **collateral estoppel**. These doctrines require that when a competent court with jurisdiction over the subject matter renders a final decision, there can be no further litigation, except for appeals. These two doctrines are similar to the criminal law doctrine of **double jeopardy**, which prohibits the prosecution of an individual twice for the same crime. All of these doctrines require a halt to litigation so that a defendant cannot be subjected to repeated suits on the same issues. The courts of other states must recognize and enforce the final decisions of all other states. For example, if a creditor wins a judgment against a debtor in one state and the debtor flees to another state, the creditor may enforce the decree in the second state, even if the second state does not have the same law as the state rendering the decree. Thus, Indiana need not require the payment of alimony in divorce actions between its citizens. However, it must enforce the alimony awards decreed in other states. Otherwise, Indiana could become a haven for alimony defaulters from other states.

Another important effect of the full faith and credit clause is that the courts of each state must apply the law of the state having the closest relationship to the events at issue in a suit. For example, parties may form a contract in one state, but one of the parties might bring suit for breach of the contract in another state. The **forum state** in which the suit is brought must apply the law of that state with the closest connection to the contract. The Supreme Court has approved several definitions of this "closeness." A complex **conflicts of law** analysis may be required to predict the proper choice of law if the forum state's substantive law differs from that of the other states involved. Similar problems exist in tort, domestic relations, and corporation law. For example, the law of the state of incorporation applies to questions of corporate governance. Conflicts of law rules often make it difficult to **forum shop**—that is, look around for a court in a state with a more favorable law. Similar difficulties about international law are discussed in other chapters.

PRIVILEGES AND IMMUNITIES

The **privileges and immunities clause** is another aspect of federalism that prohibits the states from erecting barriers at their borders.

> **Privileges and Immunities Clause**
> The Citizens of each State shall be entitled to all Privileges and Immunities of Citizens in the several States.

No state may discriminate against the citizens of other states by prohibiting travel or denying access to its courts. Corporations do not have all the same rights as natural persons under the privileges and immunities clause. Thus, out-of-state corporations may be charged higher taxes than domestic corporations as long as the taxes are not unfair or confiscatory. Foreign corporations, those chartered in another state, must register when doing business in other states to have the privileges and immunities of domestic corporations chartered in that state. Because state taxes support state educational institutions financially, nonresident students may be required to pay higher college tuition at state universities than do resident students. The commerce, full faith and credit, and privileges and immunities clauses work together to unify the nation while preserving states' rights.

TAXING AND SPENDING POWER

The federal government has the power to tax to raise revenue or even to discourage particular activities. Even if Congress does not have a specific power to directly regulate a particular activity, its taxing and spending power may be used for that purpose. Earlier cases invalidated taxes intended only as indirect regulation rather than for revenue raising. However, the Supreme Court today focuses less on Congress's motives to levy the tax and more on whether the tax is valid as a regulatory measure. For example, taxes have been validated to discourage sales of marijuana, firearms, and gambling. These taxes are, in reality, indirect regulation of these activities.

Congress also has the constitutional power to spend tax receipts on matters both connected to an enumerated power and on matters not directly related to an enumerated power. Funds raised by taxes may be spent on nearly any policy Congress chooses, so long as it does not violate another constitutional provision. Both the taxing and spending powers of the federal government are used to expand its powers to regulate in many areas not originally enumerated in the U.S. Constitution. Today, political constraints are more influential than are constitutional constraints on Congress's taxing and spending habits.

INTELLECTUAL PROPERTY CLAUSE

Many areas of government regulation are derived, but only indirectly, from some broad grant of power. For example, most of the federal regulations of antitrust, the securities and investment markets, labor and employment relationships, consumer protection, and environmental quality are based on the commerce clause. Congress infers its power after experience with problems in these substantive areas and after political pressure is triggered to regulate. There is direct legislative power in the Constitution in only a few areas. The power of taxation is one well-known example of a regulatory power directly enumerated as a federal power. However, e-commerce and cyberspace are also intimately affected by another directly enumerated federal power, the grant to enact and administer intellectual property (IP) laws (e.g., patent, copyright).

> **Intellectual Property Clause of the U.S. Constitution (Article I, Section 8, Clause 8)**
>
> [Congress shall have the power] To promote the Progress of Science and useful Arts, by securing for Limited Times to Authors and Inventors the exclusive Right to their respective Writings and Discoveries.

The IP clause is unusual; few other regulatory areas have such comprehensive enablement. The IP clause not only directly *grants* the specific regulatory power but also states the framers' *purpose* to promote science and useful arts, as well as the *method* Congress should use to achieve this purpose in the grant of exclusive rights for limited times. Congress has had IP laws since 1790. The commerce clause has also been an important source of IP law, providing the constitutional authority for antitrust, trademark,[16] and unfair competition law. More recent **sui generis** IP rights, such as plant patents and chip designs, are based on both the IP clause and the commerce clause.

The IP clause does not answer many nuances of IP law. However, legislation and/or regulators have defined many of these details, and the courts sometimes limit or confirm these details. For example, the Supreme Court has confirmed Congress's

---

16. *The Trademark Cases*, 100 U.S. 82 (1879) (holding that the commerce clause, not the IP clause, is the source of legislative power to enact trademark laws because trademarks are neither writings nor discoveries).

power to establish standards for patentability (novelty, obviousness) and copyrightability (originality). The courts also must balance federalism. In the IP realm, this means there are still state police powers about some IP matters, such as trade secrets, trademarks, and trade dress, as well as the property rights, criminal, tort, and contract law aspects of technology transfer. Many of these issues are addressed throughout this handbook.

CONSTITUTIONAL RIGHTS OF BUSINESSES AND INDIVIDUALS

The adoption of several fundamental rights known as the **Bill of Rights** amended the Constitution shortly after the initial ratification. Those amendments with the greatest impact on business are discussed here. The **First Amendment** contains several rights, most notably freedom of speech, freedom of the press, freedom of assembly, and freedom of religion. The **Fourth Amendment** ensures the right to be secure from searches and seizures except on the issuance of a warrant. The **Fifth Amendment** includes several provisions ensuring fair judicial process, such as protection against self-incrimination, the right to a grand jury indictment, protection against double jeopardy, and the right to due process. The **Sixth Amendment** guarantees a speedy trial, an impartial jury, the right to confront witnesses, subpoena powers, process to obtain witness testimony, and the right to legal counsel. The **Seventh Amendment** preserves the right to a trial by jury in actions at common law. The **Eighth Amendment** prohibits excessive fines. The Ninth, Tenth and Eleventh Amendments limit federal powers and preserve states' rights.

These constitutional rights are not absolute; they have been interpreted and refined over two centuries. Courts balance the need for constitutional protection against other important policies. The Bill of Rights protections specifically apply to natural persons, but they frequently extend to other entities, such as corporations, because they are considered artificial persons. Corporations have the protection of many constitutional rights, particularly during criminal investigations and proceedings. Constitutional rights affect nearly every field of law, as reflected in recurring references and further discussion in other chapters throughout this handbook.

THE FIRST AMENDMENT

The First Amendment has been one of the most important collections of fundamental rights: freedom of speech, press, assembly, and religion. People are specifically protected from action by the federal government under this amendment. There are also protections from a state's action under the absorption doctrine: the Fourteenth Amendment applies the Bill of Rights and other constitutional protections to governmental action at all levels and branches of government.

Freedom of religion was a major reason that many colonists left for the New World. Religious freedom was so important that it was made an integral part of the

First Amendment. The First Amendment's freedom of religion has two parts. First, government may not "establish" any religion. Contemporary establishment issues are raised by school voucher proposals for use at schools sponsored by religious groups. Second, government may not enact laws that interfere with the "free exercise" of religion. Many of the constitutional issues concerning the freedom of religion are beyond the scope of this book. Nevertheless, religious freedom can have a significant impact on business, particularly because the First Amendment requires that employers must provide reasonable accommodation for observance of the Sabbath and varying religious holidays and for other religious customs.

> **The First Amendment**
>
> Congress shall make no law respecting an establishment of religion, or prohibiting the free exercise thereof; or abridging the freedom of speech, or of the press; or the right of the people peaceably to assemble, and to petition the Government for a redress of grievances.

The freedom of speech guaranteed by the First Amendment provides society with open access to the general marketplace of ideas. It protects speakers by affording expressive access to the public and improves the quality and quantity of available ideas. It protects the ability of recipients of this expression to listen, read, and learn. Speech includes written, verbal, and nonverbal methods of expression. For example, the courts uphold union picketing for lawful purposes as nonverbal speech. However, the First Amendment's right of free speech is *not absolute*. Laws may regulate some incidents of speech to preserve safety and public order. For example, in a labor strike, local law may limit the number of pickets and the manner of picketing.

Not all types of speech are protected because society's need for some types of expression does not outweigh the social costs of allowing them. For example, obscenity, defamation, incitement to riot, fraudulent statements, and subversive speeches receive little protection under the First Amendment. **Prior restraint** laws that prohibit certain classes of speech are suspected to violate the First Amendment. Prior restraint arises, for example, if a city denies a permit to assemble, a court prohibits a public meeting even though the potential for violence is quite low, or a magazine is banned because it might have some obscene content. It is impermissible prior restraint when government restricts speech opposing politicians in power. There are three rough classifications of speech for First Amendment analysis: (1) commercial speech, (2) political speech, and (3) unprotected speech.

The First Amendment has a broad impact on various business issues, many of which are introduced in this chapter and discussed in detail. However, some aspects of the First Amendment's impact on particular business problems are discussed in other chapters where specific areas of law are covered. For example, the impact of the First Amendment on defamation and trade libel is discussed more fully in Chapter 3, the First Amendment's impact on privacy is covered in Chapter 13, the interaction between the First Amendment and intellectual property is discussed in Chapters 4 and 7, and commercial free speech in the advertising context is detailed in Chapter 14.

Commercial Speech

Initially, the courts were not sympathetic to the protection of commercial speech. Legislation regulating advertising was approved under the presumption that advertising and other forms of commercial speech are less justifiable than political speech. The underlying reasoning was that commercial speech primarily results only in personal gain for the advertiser and therefore that advertising was not presumed to have the lofty social legitimacy of political speech. However, more recent cases recognize that commercial speech disseminates important information. By making adequate information available to all market participants, commercial speech contributes to the efficient operation of markets.[17]

Despite the increasing recognition of the social value of commercial speech, it may be regulated as to time, place, and manner, but only if society's need for such restrictions outweighs the speaker's interest. The criteria for regulation of commercial speech are listed in Exhibit 2.1. Consider how these criteria apply to restrictions on advertising tobacco, pornography, and alcohol.

During the energy crisis, some states believed that the need to conserve energy clearly outweighed an electric utility's right to advertise. The New York Public Service Commission issued an order that prohibited electric utilities in New York from advertising to promote electricity use. The order permitted only informational advertising to encourage consumption shifts from peak to off-peak times. The U.S. Supreme Court invalidated the order under the First Amendment as a

"highly paternalistic" view that government has complete power to suppress or regulate commercial speech. [P]eople will perceive their own best interests if only they are well enough informed, and . . . the best means to that end is to open the channels of communication, rather than to close them. Even when advertising communicates only an incomplete version of the relevant facts, the First Amendment presumes that some accurate information is better than no information at all. . . . [This] governmental interest could be served as well by a more limited restriction on commercial speech, [so] the excessive restrictions cannot survive.[18]

EXHIBIT 2.1 Criteria to Regulate Commercial Speech

1. The commercial speech must concern lawful activity and not be misleading.
2. The degree of restriction must directly relate to the degree of governmental interest.
3. The restriction must reach no further than necessary to protect the governmental interest, and no other practical method may exist to protect this interest.
4. The time, place, and manner of the speech may be regulated, provided that no change is made in the substance of the speech.

---

17. *Virginia Pharmacy Board v. Virginia Citizens Consumer Council*, 425 U.S. 746 (1976).
18. *Central Hudson Gas & Electric Corp. v. Public Service Commission*, 447 U.S. 557 (1980).

The analysis above from the *Central Hudson* case is important in Chapter 14, where there is a more detailed discussion of the regulation of advertising generally and of the regulation of Internet advertising in particular.

The commercial speech doctrine may also be important for **encryption** software that converts recognizable expression (e.g., text/data file, e-mail message, digital music, video) into a coded, unrecognizable format sometimes called "ciphertext." Using various means (e.g., symmetric encryption, public/private key encryption), an encrypted file is made difficult or nearly impossible to read or use without a decryption "key." Strong encryption is fundamental to reliable e-commerce, the security of electronic payment systems, and the confidentiality of electronic messages (e.g., digital signatures, PGP). However, encryption is also important to maintain military secrecy. Law enforcement agencies have difficulty monitoring criminal and terrorist activities unless encryption is weakened, either with "back door" access for law enforcement or by limiting available encryption technologies to weaker forms.

O N L I N E

For a discussion on cryptology, visit the Center for Democracy and Technology Web site **http://www.cdt.org**

The U.S. State Department once limited exports of strong encryption by classifying them as "munitions" subject to strict export controls. There have been recent changes in export regulations covering encryption software and encryption devices, as well as the electronic dispatch of messages or files protected by strong encryption. Exports have been banned only to certain listed nations (e.g., Cuba, Iran, Iraq, Syria, Sudan, Libya, North Korea). Nevertheless, exporters may be required to obtain an export license granted only after review by the U.S. Commerce Department's Bureau of Export Administration (BXA). By contrast, free speech advocates support the general availability of strong encryption. Contradictory encryption case law is confusing. Is encryption protected free speech under the First Amendment? Are export controls or law enforcement access to encrypted messages impermissible prior restraint on free speech? Is encryption given less protection under the First Amendment because it is "merely" commercial speech?

Political Speech

First Amendment protection also extends to political speech by individuals as well as commercial entities. Corporations may validly disseminate ideas and influence political thought. However, the subject of the political speech should be more general. Political speech may not receive full protection if it identifies specific political parties or candidates, or violate the campaign finance laws.

In *First National Bank of Boston v. Bellotti*,[19] a Massachusetts statute prohibited a corporation from making expenditures or contributions for the purpose of influencing the vote on questions submitted to voters unless the questions materially affected the corporation. The statute also prohibited corporate advocacy on legislation involving taxation. Corporate violators could be fined up to $50,000, and the corporate officer who authorized the expenditures could be fined and imprisoned for up to one year. First National Bank of Boston and others desired to publicize their

19. 435 U.S. 765 (1978).

views that a ballot question on a graduated individual income tax was unconstitutional. The court held:

[The First] Amendment protects the free discussion of governmental affairs. . . . The inherent worth of the speech in terms of its capacity for informing the public does not depend upon the identity of its source, whether corporation, association, union, or individual. . . . The press does not have a monopoly on either the First Amendment or the ability to enlighten. . . . The First Amendment goes beyond protection of the press and the self-expression of individuals to prohibit government from limiting the stock of information from which members of the public may draw.

If a legislature may direct business corporations to "stick to business," it may also limit other corporations—religious, charitable, or civic—to their respective "business" when addressing the public. Such power in government to channel the expression of views is unacceptable under the First Amendment. The First Amendment is plainly offended when a statute suppresses speech and thereby gives one side an advantage in any debate. The proliferation of content on corporate Web sites is another example of political speech that should receive First Amendment protection.

Obscenity

The third classification of communications not protected under the First Amendment is **unprotected speech**. This includes incitement, sedition (advocating violent overthrow of the U.S. government), fraud, defamation, fighting words, words posing a clear and present danger (shouting fire in a crowded place), and obscenity, which is discussed here. Regulation of some of these forms of speech, such as fraud and defamation, are discussed elsewhere in this handbook.

Many forms of written and visual expression are subject to assessment as pornographic or obscene. Indeed, novels, magazines, movies, and interpretive dance have all been tested under local ordinances or state laws that ban obscenity. The states retain police powers to protect the health, safety, welfare, and morals of their citizens from the harmful effects of obscenity. Indeed, there is strong sentiment to protect children from pornography. However, there are two major difficulties. First, it is difficult to distinguish genuinely obscene materials from materials that are not obscene. The First Amendment prohibits censorship, a form of prior restraint, unless the materials are obscene. Local laws might not provide law enforcement with sufficient guidance, and the public's definition of obscenity differs, based on many demographics (e.g., religious belief, gender, age, location). Second, society is generally more protective of children and therefore more willing to limit minors' access to pornography.

The Internet upsets the traditional balance between freer adult access to pornography and the controls that society has fairly effectively exercised over children's access to pornography in its traditional forms—restrictions on selling print pornography to minors, movie ratings, and pay-per-view TV controls. These traditional controls are generally ineffective to block children's access to obscene materials on the Internet. Of course, technological solutions are filling some of this gap. For example, the V-chip on TVs, Internet service provider (ISP) filtering for known pornographic sites, and Internet security software (firewalls, virus protection, block lists for known pornography sites) may all enhance parental control capability. Federal telecommunications regulations are validly used to prohibit broadcast of indecent material when children are most likely to be watching (daytime, prime time).[20] Nevertheless, the Internet has reawakened controversy over the definition of obscenity and the effectiveness of controlling children's access to it.

What *is* obscene? A long line of cases, many in the U.S. Supreme Court, have resulted in a localized test that balances the offensiveness of the suspect expression with its social value. Under the formulation of obscenity announced in *Miller v. California*,[21] the trier of fact in a criminal prosecution may determine whether the expression is obscene using the three factors in Exhibit 2.2.

The definition of the terms in this three-part test is the subject of additional court interpretation. **Prurient interest** requires a "tendency to excite lustful thoughts" and can be expanded to include "a shameful or morbid interest in nudity, sex, or excretion." *Patently offensive* probably defines "hard core" pornography that exhibits ultimate sexual acts, normal or perverted, actual or simulated, including masturbation, excretory functions, and lewd exhibition of the genitals. The suspect expression must also **lack serious literary, artistic, political, or scientific value**. This objective test requires the use of the mythical reasonable person and not the impression of a single juror. Testimony of experts and local community members may be relevant on this point. The local standards of the *Miller* test can be met once a community's contemporary definitions of *patently offensive* and *prurient interest* are understood. For example, Larry Flint's *Hustler* magazine is still banned from Hamilton County, Ohio (Cincinnati). Local TV affiliates sometimes refuse to carry broadcasts believed to be obscene under local standards. However, such local standards seem impossible to apply when the suspect expression is available nearly anywhere from the Internet.

The U.S. Congress responded to mounting political pressure to control Internet pornography with the Communications Decency Act (CDA), passed as part of the

EXHIBIT 2.2 Miller Test of Obscenity

Basic Obscenity Guidelines for the Trier of Fact

1. The average person applying contemporary community standards would find that the work, taken as a whole, appeals to prurient interest.
2. The work depicts or describes, in a patently offensive way, sexual conduct specifically defined under state law,
3. The work, taken as a whole, lacks serious literary, artistic, political, or scientific value.

---

20. *Sable Communications of California v. FCC*, 492 U.S. 115 (1989).
21. 413 U.S. 14 (1973).

Telecommunications Act of 1996. The CDA made it a federal crime to knowingly transport obscene material for sale or distribution through an interactive computer service, with fines up to $100,000 and imprisonment up to five years for the first offense and ten years for subsequent offenses. The CDA covers expressive "matter" including magazines, books, pictures, paper, film, video and audio recordings. The CDA also prohibits on-line communications, involving comments, requests, suggestions, proposals, images, or other communications, that are obscene, lewd, lascivious, filthy, or indecent if intended to annoy, abuse, threaten, or harass another person. It is a separate crime to transmit such material to a minor under 18 years old. The CDA has created major comfort for ISPs, with various defenses against secondary, contributory, or republisher liability for merely carrying the communication containing prohibited obscenities. Key terms in the CDA are not well defined, particularly the term **indecent**. Although the prohibitions against transmitting obscene materials to minors is still valid, recent cases invalidate some CDA provisions.[22]

THE FOURTH AMENDMENT

Of all the constitutional provisions discussed, the Fourth Amendment provides business with the greatest protection from unfair governmental investigations. Typically, the Fourth Amendment protection arises before a criminal defendant is indicted or before a civil administrative case is filed. The Fourth Amendment protects both natural persons and corporations from unreasonable searches and seizures.

> **Fourth Amendment: Unreasonable Searches and Seizures**
>
> The right of the people to be secure in their persons, papers, and effects, against unreasonable searches and seizures, shall not be violated, and no Warrants shall issue, but on probable cause, supported by Oath or affirmation, and particularly describing the place to be searched and the persons or things to be seized.

The Fourth Amendment is a major constitutional source of privacy. The constitutional basis for privacy is developed more fully in Chapter 13.

THE FIFTH AND FOURTEENTH AMENDMENTS

The Fifth and Fourteenth Amendments contain two major provisions to maintain fundamental fairness: the due process and equal protection clauses. The Fifth Amendment applies these protections to actions taken by the federal government.

> **Fifth Amendment: Due Process Clause**
>
> No person shall be . . . deprived of life, liberty, or property, without due process of law.

---

22. *Reno v. ACLU*, 521 U.S. 844 (1997).

The Fourteenth Amendment applies the Fifth Amendment to the states under the **absorption** or **incorporation** doctrine. This doctrine assures that the fundamental protections of most constitutional rights also apply to the actions of state government.

> ### Fourteenth Amendment: Due Process and Equal Protection Clauses
> … nor shall any State deprive any person of life, liberty, or property, without due process of law; nor deny to any person within its jurisdiction the equal protection of the laws.

The Fifth Amendment also includes the well-known right against self-incrimination. This is a fundamental constitutional right to privacy that is discussed more completely in Chapter 13.

Equal Protection of the Laws

The need for equality under the law after the abolition of slavery demanded a definitive constitutional statement. The equal protection clause of the Fourteenth Amendment was originally intended to provide blacks with protection from arbitrary legislative distinctions. Today, that clause applies to all types of arbitrary and unreasonable classifications in legislation and to all ethnic and demographic groups. By its very nature, legislation necessarily selects which persons or entities are subject to the law, based on such classifications as conduct, size of business, or level of income. However, establishing fair classifications of this kind is difficult, requiring careful statutory design. For example, only murderers should receive punishment under criminal statutes prohibiting murder. Similarly, the Uniform Commercial Code imposes special obligations on merchants; it requires a higher level of conduct in commercial transactions from merchants than from nonmerchants. These classifications are fair only when they adequately discriminate.

Legislative classifications with no reasonable purpose are unconstitutional under the equal protection clause. There are three tests of equal protection, and each is progressively stricter in its standards for valid legislation. Under the least restrictive approach, the rational basis test, laws should have general applicability unless there is sufficient reason to discriminate against certain people. This test applies in many situations, but it seldom invalidates legislation. Another test, the strict scrutiny test, applies in situations involving discrimination against protected classes of persons or discrimination in matters of fundamental rights. When strict scrutiny applies, many statutes are held unconstitutional. Quasi-strict scrutiny is an intermediate test that is important in some business contexts.

Equal protection issues arise most often in cases of racial segregation. Equal protection has required reapportionment of state legislatures under the principle of "one person, one vote," as when two nearby congressional districts in a state have grossly unequal numbers of citizens. The courts have ruled military regulations as unconstitutional that afford spouses of servicewomen lesser benefits than the spouses of servicemen. The denial of voting rights in school district elections to nonparents or nonowners of property was found unconstitutional under strict scrutiny.

Rational Basis. The equal protection clause does not disturb the constitutionality of a statute if there is a rational connection between the statute's classification scheme and a permissible governmental purpose. Under this **rational basis** test, the statute is first presumed constitutional. Government may regulate in areas that are normally and legitimately the role of government. For example, Congress may pass laws pursuant to an enumerated power, such as the regulation of interstate commerce. State legislatures may pass criminal laws implementing the police power. Any classifications used in statutes enacted for such purposes must have a reasonable basis and not be arbitrary.

In *Minnesota v. Clover Leaf Creamery Co.*,[23] the Supreme Court found that a Minnesota statute provided adequate equal protection even though it prohibited only plastic disposable packaging for milk. The statute sought to diminish the solid waste problem and save energy by banning nonreturnable plastic milk containers, yet it permitted the use of nonreturnable plastic containers for other products. The rational basis test, which was used here, invalidates only the most outrageously arbitrary classification schemes. This case permits states to implement a regulatory program in steps, eliminating evils only partially at first and deferring complete elimination to future regulations.

Strict Scrutiny. In more recent years, courts have used the **strict scrutiny** test to invalidate legislation that violates certain fundamental rights or discriminates against suspect classes. When the rigorous criteria of the strict scrutiny test are applied, legislation is seldom acceptable if any conceivable alternative could achieve the same legitimate regulatory end. Under strict scrutiny, the suspect legislation must be necessary and the only means to achieve a compelling governmental interest. To survive a strict scrutiny attack, a statute must relate to the governmental interest more closely than is required under the rational basis test, and the governmental purpose must be more important. There must be clear legislative intent to reach the legitimate governmental goal.

Strict scrutiny applies only to fundamental rights and to discrimination against suspect or protected classes. **Fundamental rights** include voting rights, interstate travel, immunity from mandatory sterility, and criminal procedural protections. **Suspect classes** are demographic classifications of people who deserve greater protection because they have been subjected to intentional discrimination. Suspect classes include classifications based on race, national origin, and alien status.

Quasi-Strict Scrutiny. A third classification, **quasi-strict scrutiny**, has arisen in recent years. It falls between the rational basis and the strict scrutiny tests. This standard applies where the rights involved are clearly important but are not quite considered fundamental rights, or where the classifications in the statute are only partially suspect. For example, classifications based on gender or legitimacy must be substantially

---

23. 449 U.S. 456 (1981).

related to an important government objective under this middle-ground test. The quasi-strict scrutiny test validates some classifications while invalidating others. Clearly, every equal protection inquiry is quite fact-specific.

Due Process of Law

The due process clause is intended to prevent unfair and predetermined outcomes at criminal trials like those in colonial times held before English judges. Due process requires that governments observe at least a minimum level of fairness in trial procedures. This fairness doctrine prohibits arbitrary, biased, and unreasonable outcomes in trials and administrative hearings. The due process clause applies to a wide variety of criminal, civil, and administrative hearings. Certain private determinations by nongovernmental entities are also subject to some form of due process. However, due process rights are not identical in all cases. Criminal defendants usually receive more specific and extensive protections than do the parties in civil trials or administrative hearings.

Due process prohibits government from depriving any person of **life, liberty, or property** without due process of law. A person in this context is broadly construed to include both natural persons and artificial persons, such as corporations or unincorporated associations. A **deprivation of life** usually denotes capital punishment and also arises in right to die or euthanasia cases. A **deprivation of liberty** occurs when one is denied the ability to move freely in public areas—that is, while not trespassing on private property. A **deprivation of property** occurs when a person must pay a fine or money damages or when property is taken by government. Be aware that due process actually *permits* government to deprive one of life, liberty, or property, *but only if* due process is followed.

Due process has developed into two separate limits on unreasonable governmental action. **Procedural due process** incorporates the traditional issues regarding the processes of investigation, arrest, detainment, trial, and appeal. **Substantive due process** involves issues concerning the fairness of legislation in the way it defines rights and duties. These due process issues arise whenever government attempts to vindicate rights, whether those attempts are prosecuted by government attorneys, initiated in court or administrative agencies, or conducted by private entities affected with a public character (e.g., private universities). To successfully claim a due process right, some form of **state action** or governmental process must be involved because constitutional rights provide protection only from oppressive governmental actions, not oppressive private acts. There is no constitutional protection from an individual's actions unless the individual is acting under the color of government. For example, a basketball coach suffered no due process violation when the National Collegiate Athletic Association (NCAA) required the university to punish its coach for alleged NCAA rule violations. The NCAA is a private organization, so there was no state action involved, even though the state university implemented the NCAA's order.[24]

---

24. *National Collegiate Athletic Ass'n v. Tarkanian*, 488 U.S. 179 (1988).

Procedural Due Process. Two basic rights in litigation involve due process protections. The first right is intended to assure defendants a fair opportunity to offer a defense and the use of fair trial procedures. In some cases, a notice of suit, a **service of summons**, must be personally delivered to the defendant. **Substituted service** of process is a valid alternative if it is impossible to deliver the notice directly.

The second stage where basic due process rights exist is in litigation and the conduct of trials. The precise fair trial procedures vary according to the rights adjudicated, the type of trial, and the severity of the penalties. The trial procedures should afford the utmost protection to a criminal defendant charged with a capital crime. At the other extreme, a college disciplinary proceeding can provide sufficient due process even without many of the procedural technicalities of a criminal trial. The Fifth, Sixth, and Seventh Amendments also require several fair trial procedures. These procedural rights are detailed in Chapters 3 and 13, where criminal procedure and privacy are discussed. Of particular note is a discussion of the **USA Patriot Act**. This antiterrorist law passed following the September 11, 2001, terrorist attacks. The new law may significantly diminish the rights of suspected terrorists.

Is a full trial by jury necessary to review a university's dismissal of a student for poor scholarship? Informal administrative processes need not include the full spectrum of evidentiary rules to provide minimum due process. In *Board of Curators of the University of Missouri v. Horowitz*,[25] Horowitz was dismissed from the university's medical school for failure to meet academic standards. She had been fully informed of the faculty's dissatisfaction with her progress and the adverse impact on her timely graduation. The ultimate dismissal decision was deliberate and careful. Horowitz sued the university, claiming a lack of due process in the dismissal process. The Supreme Court compared academic dismissal to disciplinary proceedings, reserving the broader due process procedural steps like notice and opportunity to present evidence for only disciplinary proceedings. Justice Rehnquist said that:

The decision to dismiss respondent rested on the academic judgment of school officials that she did not have the necessary clinical ability to perform adequately as a medical doctor and was making insufficient progress toward that goal. Such a judgment is by its nature more subjective and evaluative than the typical factual questions presented in the average disciplinary decision. Like the decision of an individual professor as to the proper grade for a student in his course, the determination whether to dismiss a student for academic reasons requires an expert evaluation of cumulative information and is not readily adapted to the procedural tools of judicial or administrative decision making.

The tort and product liability system has evolved to permit significant awards of damages beyond those needed solely to compensate the plaintiff. In the more egregious product liability, malpractice, and negligence cases, the jury (or sometimes the judge) has ordered a further component of damages, called punitive damages,

---

25. 435 U.S. 78 (1978).

amounts in addition to the compensatory portion of the damage amount. Unlike compensatory damages, which simply reimburse the victim, punitive damages are a form of punishment, justified as a heightened incentive that deters harmful behavior or carelessness. However, many critics argue that recent history in product liability cases shows punitive damages may be unfair and violate both due process and the Eighth Amendment prohibition against excessive fines. Several states have specified limitations on punitive damages, and some recent cases now require controls on juries ordering punitive damages. This topic is discussed in more detail as a form of tort reform in Chapter 3.

Substantive Due Process. The substantive due process doctrine allows a court to declare a statute unconstitutional if the statute fails to provide due process. In the late nineteenth and early twentieth centuries, the **economic due process** doctrine was applied to invalidate early regulatory statutes that required minimum wages or maximum working hours or that allowed union membership. Many such statutes were unconstitutional because they unjustifiably restricted the freedom of business to contract or they deprived business of its property without due process. Today, this economic substantive due process is inapplicable.

In the area of personal liberty and rights, the substantive due process doctrine retains some validity. It requires that legislation meet two tests. The first test is an ends-means test similar to that in equal protection cases. This test requires that legislation be directed toward a legitimate governmental purpose and that the means used be closely connected to that purpose. Second, the test prohibits vague legislation. A statute is unconstitutional if it does not provide ascertainable criteria for the identification of unlawful conduct. For example, a law enforcement officer cannot arrest someone based on the officer's interpretation of what constitutes wrongdoing. Laws permitting this level of discretion are vague. In *Coates v. City of Cincinnati*,[26] the city passed a criminal ordinance prohibiting "three or more persons to assemble . . . on any of the sidewalks . . . and there conduct themselves in a manner *annoying* to persons passing by . . ." (emphasis added). On the basis of this ordinance, the Cincinnati authorities prosecuted Coates for participating in a student demonstration. The ordinance violated due process because it subjected Coates's constitutional right of assembly to an imprecise standard, the term "annoying conduct." Conduct that some people find "annoying" does not annoy others, so people of common intelligence must necessarily guess at the word's meaning. Substantive due process also protects business from prosecution under vague laws.

THE ELEVENTH AMENDMENT

Much in the original U.S. Constitution concerns federalism—the proper balance between power given to the central government versus powers distributed to state

---

26. 402 U.S. 611 (1971).

and local governments. Federalism is also the issue at the heart of several amendments. For example, the Second Amendment authorizes state or local militias. The Ninth Amendment reserves rights to the people even if such rights are not enumerated in the Constitution. The Tenth Amendment reserves powers not delegated to the federal government to the people or to the states. The Twelfth, Fifteenth, Seventeenth, Nineteenth, Twenty-Fourth, and Twenty-Sixth Amendments prohibit states from restricting election matters. The Thirteenth, Fourteenth, and Fifteenth amendments prohibit states from tolerating slavery.

Since the 1980s, the U.S. Supreme Court has shifted firmly to support states' rights. Among the tools used in this shift is the Eleventh Amendment, a relatively inactive provision that has been reawakened with significant impact on e-commerce and a particular impact on IP. The Eleventh Amendment prohibits jurisdiction in the federal courts for many types of suits against the states.

The Eleventh Amendment

The Judicial power of the United States shall not be construed to extend to any suit in law or equity, commenced or prosecuted against one of the United States by Citizens or another State, or by Citizens or Subjects of any Foreign State.

The Eleventh Amendment stands alongside common law precedents as the strongest sources of sovereign immunity for the states. **Sovereign immunity** is a government's immunity from suit, based on the outmoded old English notion that the "king can do no wrong." Since the 1940s, many states, as well as the federal government, have relaxed or partially waived their sovereign immunity, thereby subjecting themselves to civil liability on some matters. For example, most states have opened themselves to civil tort liability for various types of physical injury, such as those resulting from defective conditions on state owned and operated roads.

The **abrogation of state sovereign immunity** may also be accomplished by Congress. However, under recent Supreme Court decisions, this is not easily done, so one of three avenues is open to enforce federally created rights against the states. First, suits may be brought against state officers who violate federal law,[27] such as a state university employee who reproduces copyrighted expression either without permission or outside an exemption such as fair use. These suits are against the officer and not against the state itself. However, the copyright owner can be awarded only prospective relief, such as an injunction against future infringement. There could be no damage suit for past infringement under this theory. Second, states may validly waive their Eleventh Amendment sovereign immunity. Some IP strategists suggest that Congress should amend the IP laws to withhold from states the right to enforce the states' own IP rights in copyrights or patents unless each state specifically waives its sovereign immunity for IP infringement suits brought against the

---

27. See *Ex Parte Young*, 209 U.S. 123 (1908).

state. The third method is for Congress to abrogate the states' Eleventh Amendment sovereign immunity. Under this method, Congress would enact legislation that subjects the states to jurisdiction for infringement in the federal courts. Although Congress tried this several times prior to 1996, a recent series of IP abrogation cases has thrown this third method into question.[28]

---

28. College Savings Bank v. Florida Prepaid Postsecondary Educ. Expense Board., 119 S.Ct. 2219 (1999).

CHAPTER 3
CRIMES AND TORTS

Among the best known areas of traditional law is the punishment or vindication of wrongs. These wrongs may have been committed against society generally or more specifically against individual private parties. They may be committed intentionally or result from unintentional, negligent acts. Two distinct but related branches of law that address these wrongs are covered in this chapter: criminal law and tort law. Imagine that a hacker invades a computer network, intercepts orders for goods, captures credit card account numbers, and then uses them to make fraudulent purchases. Many of these acts would be illegal under criminal law, exposing the hacker to criminal prosecution and penalties (fines, imprisonment). The very same acts could also expose the hacker to civil liability to those directly injured: the credit card issuer, card holders, and the Internet service provider (ISP).

CRIMINAL LAW VS. CIVIL LAW

The purpose of criminal law is to punish wrongdoers and isolate them from society. Criminal law sets standards for duties that all persons and businesses owe to society. Criminal prosecutions are brought by the government, most typically by a local or state prosecutor or district attorney. There are also federal crimes prosecuted by the Justice Department. Prosecutors seek criminal punishment remedies, including fines and imprisonment, and even the death penalty in capital punishment cases, to protect society and deter future wrongdoing. Criminal prosecutors must generally prove the defendant's guilt **beyond a reasonable doubt**, that is, the trier of fact (jury or, if there is no jury, judge) must be thoroughly convinced of criminal guilt.

By contrast, civil law enforces duties owed primarily to individuals or business entities. The civil law of torts imposes duties on persons to act carefully or refrain from intentional aggression. The civil law of contracts enforces duties that are voluntarily assumed by the contracting parties. A civil plaintiff must generally prove the defendant's liability by a **preponderance of the evidence** (more likely than not); this standard of proof is lower than for criminal guilt.

Government units are sometimes the victims of crimes or torts, and governments are sometimes the wrongdoers held responsible in tort suits. Governments can also make, enforce, and be held responsible on contracts, although government contracting and government procurement are specialized fields with rather esoteric rules, not covered in this book. In some tort cases, the judge or jury sometimes assesses punitive damages. Deterrence is a secondary objective of tort law in the most egregious cases.

THE CHALLENGES OF CYBERSPACE FOR LAW ENFORCEMENT

Cyberspace poses many new problems in deterring crime, punishing it, and compensating victims for injuries that wrongdoers commit against society and individuals. Consider these difficulties in the following comparison. First, think of the malicious injury resulting from a burglar's physical intrusion into someone's home or a place of business. Once inside the premises, the wrongdoer might steal property or money, perhaps by cracking open a wall safe. While inside, the burglar might discover valuable secrets by examining confidential files, maybe without leaving fingerprints or a trace of DNA evidence. The burglar might also damage physical property, such as breaking the door and lock while entering, or a burglar might destroy information or records. Now compare this example with the intrusions a computer hacker makes by using networked telecommunications to access others' computers. Hackers can perpetrate similar injuries: After breaking codes to enter a computer or network, the hacker might steal software or data, otherwise wreak havoc with a virus, orchestrate a denial-of-service attack, or crash a hard disk.

The differences between traditional unlawful physical intrusions and cyberspace intrusions are key to the evolution of law to make cyberspace a safer place for individuals and electronic business activity. First, computer intrusions can be committed from far away, sometimes without leaving any of the electronic or physical evidence that is usually recovered from crime scenes by forensic investigators. This distance impedes investigations by hiding evidence, and it complicates jurisdiction over remote defendants, witnesses, and ISPs. Second, many observers believe that computer security measures, such as passwords or encryption, can never be as effective as well-established physical controls. Physical controls include fences, locked doors, security guards, serial numbers, video monitoring, and the difficulty of concealing the mass and distinctiveness of physical assets. Third, hackers sometimes "anonymize" their communications and cover up evidence that could identify them or reveal their whereabouts and accomplices. Some experts believe that many more computer intrusions than physical intrusions go undetected. Fourth, computer attacks, fraudulent schemes, and other harmful communications can too often be carried out on a much broader scale than was possible with traditional technologies. For example, securities fraud, virus attacks, and obscenity or defamatory remarks can be more widely and cheaply disseminated than with traditional means such as face-to-face contacts, the telephone, or postal mail.

FACTORS DISTINGUISHING CRIMINAL LAW FROM CIVIL LAW

This chapter addresses criminal law and tort law, both as they are applied in the traditional physical world and as these bodies of law are adapting to the tough challenges of cyberspace. Some crimes, such as assault and battery, trespass, and false imprisonment, are also unlawful under civil law as intentional torts. For such crimes, the act that may be prosecuted as a criminal offense may also be the complaint in a civil tort suit, and the defendant may be exposed to criminal prosecution as well as civil liability to the individuals, firms, or even governments that are injured.

Criminal Law vs. Tort Law

A wrongful act that results in personal injury may also be a criminal act. Although criminal law was originally derived from common law precedents, it is now based primarily on statutory laws passed by the federal and state legislatures. Similarly, tort law principles emerge primarily from common law precedents, although an increasing number of statutes affect tort law liability. Most crimes and torts are made unlawful by state law.

How can a person be tried twice for the same offense, first under criminal law and then under tort law? Would that not constitute unconstitutional double jeopardy under the Fifth Amendment, as introduced previously in Chapter 2? The answer is generally no. Criminal law punishes wrongdoers, and civil law compensates victims. The law's purposes would be frustrated if prosecutors and injured victims were required to race against each other to the courthouse or if one type of suit preempted the other. Therefore, there is no competition between criminal and civil suits over the same wrongful conduct. In fact, the two paths are often complementary, as when a conviction precedes a civil suit and makes the civil plaintiff's case easier to prove.

Double jeopardy is interpreted so that it is not violated by parallel proceedings. Recall the multiple cases triggered by the O. J. Simpson events. He was successfully sued for the civil tort of wrongful death by the relatives of Nicole Brown Simpson despite his previous acquittal by a jury on criminal charges of murder. Therefore, there is no double jeopardy if a person is sued in a civil tort action and tried for the same criminal act under the same facts. Double jeopardy occurs only when a person is tried twice for the same "crime." The substantive law, trial procedures, and burdens of proof are different for tort cases than for criminal cases. Thus, although a tortious action could be a crime, it need not be. A tort is a wrong for which the injured party can be compensated.

Tort Law vs. Contract Law

Tort law and contract law are both branches of civil (noncriminal) law. If a business or an individual breaches a contractual obligation while also committing a tort, the injured party may bring both a breach of contract case and a tort case. Because both cases are civil actions arising from the same events and involving the same parties,

Exhibit 3.1 Criminal Law vs. Civil Law

Comparative Factor	Criminal Law	Civil Law
Plaintiff/complainant	State or federal prosecutor or district attorney	Injured party: individual, business entity, or government
Objective of law	Protect society, punish wrongdoers, deter wrongdoing	Compensate particular injured parties; only in egregious cases, punishment as deterrence
Nature of wrongful act	Duty owed to society Violation of criminal statute prohibiting certain conduct and intended to protect society	Wrongful act violates private tort duty imposed by law or violates contractual duty voluntarily assumed
Burden of proof	Beyond a reasonable doubt	Preponderance of the evidence
Remedies/penalties	Fines and/or imprisonment; capital punishment in only the most severe cases	Money damages, declaratory judgment, and/or equitable remedies of specific performance or injunction

the two actions can be brought together in one legal proceeding. For example, suppose an on-line consumer purchases a software program over the Internet. After downloading and installing the program, the consumer discovers the program has destroyed important data stored in the consumer's hard drive memory. Contract law requires that the software be fit for its ordinary purpose. In that the software did not meet that standard, the seller breached the contract, as discussed further in Chapters 8 and 10 on contract warranties and licensing. However, the purchaser could also sue the seller or manufacturer of the software in tort because the manufacturer breached its responsibility for being reasonably careful in the design, manufacture, or shipment of its software. Both the manufacturer and the seller could be sued in one suit, alleging a negligent tort against the manufacturer and a breach of contract by the seller. Money damages could be recovered if the plaintiff could prove breach of contract, the commission of a tortious act by the defendant, or both. Punitive damages are generally not available in the breach of contract portion of the suit. Distinctions between criminal and civil law are so important to this chapter that these matters are summarized in Exhibit 3.1.

CLASSIFYING CRIMINAL LAW

Crimes are classified in a number of ways. Most common and street crimes are made illegal under state law, and some crimes are illegal under federal law. The traditional classification scheme for crimes focuses on the severity or seriousness. First,

misdemeanors are less serious crimes traditionally punishable by smaller fines or incarceration in jail or imprisonment for a year or less. Examples include trespass and theft of low-value property. Petty offenses are usually considered misdemeanors and can include building code violations or drunk driving (DUI/DWI). Civil or summary offenses, which are even less serious, can include minor traffic or parking violations for which no criminal record is kept. As with most other crimes, the precise name of the crime, its classification, the precise definition, and the range of applicable penalties vary considerably from state to state.

Second, **felonies** are crimes more serious than misdemeanors, and there are a full range of constitutional protections because the penalties are more serious, such as larger fines and/or longer prison terms. Felonies include homicide, robbery, and arson. The **model penal code**, not one of the uniform laws, further divides felonies into four categories reflecting society's assessment of seriousness, use of deadly weapons or force, the perpetrator's intent, and the suffering inflicted by the criminal act: (1) **capital offenses** possibly punishable by death, (2) **first-degree felonies** punishable by up to life imprisonment, (3) **second-degree felonies** punishable by up to 10 years imprisonment, and (4) **third-degree felonies** punishable by up to five years imprisonment.

CONTEMPORARY CLASSIFICATION OF CRIME

Crimes are also now popularly classified according to other factors, such as the general nature of the damage caused, the means used to commit the crime, or even generalizations about the perpetrators. Although the hundreds of different particular crimes could be classified in many other ways, the following taxonomy is useful to describe crimes. First, **violent crimes** are usually directed against human individuals (such as the familiar urban *street crimes*); they can include homicide (murder, manslaughter), assault and battery, rape, robbery (taking property from another by using force or fear), kidnapping, and "aggravated" forms of various crimes such as assault or robbery, when a deadly weapon is used. Second, **property crimes** cause destruction or deprive owners of their property. They include theft, burglary, extortion, larceny, receiving stolen goods, forgery, fraud, false pretenses, theft of services, infringement, arson, trespass, and vandalism. Third, **public order crimes** generally encompass acts that violate society's mores or threaten order, responsibility, or government, for example, intoxication; use, possession, or sale of controlled substances or items (illegal drugs, weapons, explosives, bioterrorism agents); prostitution; gambling; pornography; hate crimes; stalking or harassment; bribery; treason, sedition, or espionage; incitement to riot; counterfeiting; and various forms of terrorism.

A fourth category includes **white-collar crime**, which is illegal, nonviolent behavior by employees of business firms, and **corporate crime**, illegal behavior intended to benefit business firms. These two categories obviously overlap and often are financial crimes and property crimes that are made to appear part of a legitimate, ongoing business activity. For example, fraud, mail and wire fraud, embezzlement, theft of intellectual property (including trade secrets), industrial espionage, bribery, insider trading, and criminal forms of regulatory offenses such as antitrust law, securities regulations, transportation system regulations, and banking regulations fall in this category. A fifth category, **computer crime**, includes these crimes when the activities at least partially involve computers. Computer crime also includes theft of hardware, software, or computer time, as well as the destruction or deprivation from use of others' computers. **Cyber crime** is a fairly new subclass that describes computer crime committed over telecommunications networks. Cyber crime may cause much broader injuries than other computer crimes. For example, the intentional spread of a computer virus or the launch and orchestration of a denial of service attack against a Web site or ISP affects hundreds, even thousands of others. Other contemporary examples of cyber crime include stalking, pornography, gambling, hacking, electronic terrorism, and theft.

The final broad category of crimes is **organized crime**. Organized crime is often the result of racketeering activities by criminal gangs or syndicates, many of the most infamous of which have been operated by crime families and ethnic clans. Organized crime is operated by a centrally controlled, formal structure and most often the participants satisfy the public's demand for illegal activities such as liquor, drugs, gambling, weapons, prostitution, pornography, and loansharking. Organized crime frequently uses terroristlike tactics of selective violence and intimidation to discipline its members and the public, protect its turf, and insulate its illegal markets. Money laundering is often needed to funnel illegal profits into legitimate investments. Laundering, discussed further later, helps to reinforce the organization's strength and can permit its members to withdraw and use illegal criminal profits. In recent years, organized crime has expanded into financial crime, including credit card and securities fraud.

Clearly, the traditional and more contemporary classifications of crimes are neither exclusive nor exhaustive. Some crimes belong in two or more categories. More detailed discussion of some particular crimes and the applicable law enforcement tools are discussed throughout this chapter. Several other particular crimes involving intellectual property, trade secret theft, securities fraud, insider trading, antitrust violations, tax evasion, environmental pollution, and violations of regulations in food and drug safety, consumer product safety, and health care privacy are discussed in other chapters.

CRIMINAL PROCEDURE

The criminal procedure followed by state and federal law enforcement officials and the criminal courts varies somewhat according to which governmental units have jurisdiction and on the seriousness of the alleged crime. Criminal prosecutions differ from civil cases because the plaintiff is a local prosecutor, staff attorney in the office of the state's attorney general, or a U.S. attorney working for the U.S. Department of Justice (DOJ). Prosecutors are bound to protect the public, which is a different perspective than that followed by a private party vindicating personal rights. Of course, private citizens are often involved in initiating criminal actions when they report suspicious activity to prosecutors, bring charges, or supply key evidence. Criminal procedure begins with investigations and proceeds through arrest, booking, indictment, arraignment, and plea bargaining. If the charges are not dropped or settled in the plea bargain, the matter goes to trial, and criminal procedure governs the trial process, sentencing, and appeal or punishment.

CRIMINAL INVESTIGATIONS

Detection of a criminal act initially prompts an investigation, including the questioning of suspects, possible accomplices, and witnesses. This may lead to an arrest by law enforcement officials. Thereafter, the investigation may continue with interviews of the accused and witnesses and perhaps seizure of hard evidence such as documents, weapons, articles with fingerprints, DNA samples, other identifying evidence, and increasingly computer memories and other records. Criminal charges may be initiated if the district attorney's office believes the defendant can be convicted, given the weight of the evidence and their limited prosecutorial resources. The prosecutor files charges in an affidavit, complaint, accusation, or an information brought against the person or persons implicated in the crime.

Constitutional Protections for the Accused

The U.S. Constitution constrains the tactics used by investigators and requires fairness in trial procedures. The Sixth Amendment requires notice of criminal charges, a speedy and public trial, trial by an impartial jury, representation by legal counsel, confrontation of accusers, cross-examination of witnesses, and the right to call witnesses. Recall the discussion in Chapter 2 of the Fourth, Fifth, and Fourteenth Amendments. The Fourth Amendment prohibits unreasonable searches and seizures, a topic further detailed in Chapter 13. Various testimonial privileges promise secrecy for confidential communications between attorney and client, between spouses, and with some others, also discussed in Chapter 13. Chapter 2 also introduced the due process requirements of the Fifth and Fourteenth Amendments, which provide other general criminal procedure safeguards and set fairness standards for the conduct of all trials.

The Fifth Amendment also requires an indictment and provides the double jeopardy right and the self-incrimination privilege. Since the landmark 1966 case *Miranda v. Arizona*,[1] law enforcement officials must give **Miranda warnings** to all suspects who may be subjected to custodial interrogation. More recent Supreme Court cases have limited this right by creating exceptions to the Miranda rights. For example, there is a limited public safety exception, convictions will not be overturned if there is sufficient evidence for conviction outside the confession, and the suspect must clearly assert the right to counsel during questioning.

Miranda Warning

You have the right to remain silent. Anything you say can and will be used against you in a court of law. You have the right to consult with an attorney and to have one present with you during interrogation. If you cannot afford an attorney, one will be appointed for you.

---

1. 384 U.S. 436 (1966).

The use of evidence acquired through search or seizure for proof of criminal guilt is subject to the Fourth Amendment's protections. They are interpreted to require that law enforcement officials must generally have a search warrant issued by a judge, magistrate, or other public officer before conducting the search. Warrants may be issued only if based on **probable cause**, a legal standard discussed further in Chapter 13. Generally, search warrants are granted only when law enforcement officials can convince the judge that evidence of a crime is likely to reside in the area to be searched and that if the evidence were found it would be relevant to their investigation. The warrant must describe both the evidence sought and the location to be searched. With some exceptions, only the evidence described may be used to prove criminal guilt. Warrants for arrest must also be based on probable cause that the suspect committed the crime described in the warrant.

When these constitutional rights are violated, the evidence obtained is generally inadmissible to prove guilt under the **exclusionary rule**. Further, if investigators acquire leads from illegally acquired evidence, that further evidence is tainted, which means it will be excluded from use at trial as **fruit of the poisonous tree**. For example, assume e-mail records are seized in an illegal search for obscene materials on a suspect's hard drive. If investigators find evidence of illegal gambling on that hard drive, or if the original sender of the e-mail messages is contacted and then provides additional incriminating evidence, then all this additional evidence would be excluded as tainted fruit of the poisonous tree.

In cyberspace, law enforcement needs to access information quickly, given that evidence of wrongdoing is often fleeting and temporary; that is, computer records are easily erased and may exist only for moments as electronic impulses. This impermanence may be counterbalanced by the often large number of intermediate electronic copies made. As discussed in Chapter 13, it is becoming difficult to erase e-mail messages or their file attachments. Many people mistakenly believe there are no copies of their e-mail, clickstream, or on-line activities, but most messages can be intercepted, and they are not easily disavowed. In litigation, the prosecutor can subpoena most print and electronic records from the accused or from others. Many still fail to recognize that their frank, hostile, or incriminating e-mail and other electronic records are preserved on many hard drives, that copies often are saved on their employer's server and at their ISP, and that printouts and electronic copies are made by recipients or are forwarded widely to others. Crime statistics can be found at the FBI's Web site.

FBI Web site
**http://www.fbi.gov/
ucr/ucr.htm**

USA Patriot Act

In the wake of the September 11, 2001, terrorist attacks on the Pentagon and World Trade Center, Congress strengthened federal law enforcement's investigatory powers by passing antiterrorism legislation, the Uniting and Strengthening America Act (USA Patriot Act). This law permits the U.S. Attorney General to detain aliens suspected of terrorist activity, the U.S. State Department to designate **terrorist organizations** to prevent their fund-raising, and the FBI to use **roving wiretaps** on any phone line used by suspected terrorists (e.g., business line, home phone, cell phone, etc.) in a single warrant. Widespread public support quickly developed to lift investigatory obstacles and thereby protect U.S. citizens, property, and free markets from terrorist attacks. Indeed, a major shift in public opinion resulted in huge new majorities favoring the use of facial recognition technologies, TV monitors in public places, and broader government monitoring of various communications. It remains uncertain whether this represents a temporary or permanent shift in public opinion to trade off privacy for security. In most past situations, citizens tolerated increased intrusions only until the threats subsided, but some law enforcement officials argue that the threat of terrorism requires a permanent reduction in privacy.

To ease the difficult task of coordinating antiterrorism activities by various government agencies, as well as the responsibilities of the new director of homeland security, the USA Patriot Act permits greater sharing of investigatory files among various federal agencies. It authorizes secret searches of certain information without notifying the investigation's target. Some aspects of bank secrecy are now relaxed; investigators can obtain payment information such as credit card and bank account numbers of suspected terrorists. The provisions to detect money laundering are discussed later in this chapter. The act also substantially increases funding for U.S. border control. Several of the USA Act's provisions are subject to automatic expiration under a sunset provision.

The USA Patriot Act also enhances law enforcement surveillance powers over on-line activities. For example, the federal government now has authority to subpoena ISPs for e-mail addresses, URLs visited, e-mail recipients, and sender information. Federal law enforcement officials need not have probable cause but need only show that the information sought is relevant to an ongoing investigation. Federal investigators will now routinely have access to information similar to the on-line profiling data collected by the private data industry. Profiling is discussed further in Chapter 13. Many state law enforcement personnel are now seeking similar powers under revised state laws.

PRETRIAL PROCEDURES

A valid arrest initiates pretrial criminal procedure. Arrests are generally made in two ways. First, law enforcement officials may directly observe a suspect in suspicious or criminally related activity, which provides sufficient probable cause to make the arrest. Alternatively, after criminal activity is reported, law enforcement may learn sufficient information to seek an arrest warrant from a judge. Under the Sixth Amendment, warrants are issued only if evidence is presented to show probable cause—a sufficient likelihood that the suspect has committed or is about to commit a crime. Formal arrest includes statements indicating the nature of the activity, and law enforcement usually takes the suspect into custody, a form of temporary detention.

After charges are filed by the arresting officer, there are screening processes to prevent law enforcement officials from abusing the criminal process or bringing false accusations against the innocent. In a **preliminary hearing**, the prosecutor must demonstrate the existence of probable cause that the evidence connecting the defendant to a crime is sufficient to "hold the defendant over" for prosecution.

These proceedings are held before a magistrate, who possesses judicial power to permit a prosecution to proceed. When there is sufficient evidence of wrongdoing, the magistrate issues an **information**, which represents the formal criminal charges. Alternatively, in cases alleging more serious crimes, a grand jury may be used. The **grand jury**, consisting of numerous local citizens, performs a similar function by reviewing the evidence against the accused for probable cause. When grand juries recommend prosecution, they issue an **indictment** showing that there is sufficient evidence against the defendant. Grand juries operate in secrecy to encourage reluctant witnesses to volunteer forthright testimony because the secrecy deters retaliation by the accused.

Following these formal charges, the accused defendant makes an appearance before a judge or other magistrate at an **arraignment**. The defendant may then file a **plea**—that is, the accused's answer to the prosecution's allegations. The most common pleas are not guilty, guilty, or **nolo contendere** (no contest, no admission of guilt but submitting to the court's resolution). A defendant who does not plead not guilty may be immediately sentenced. Indigent defendants may be assigned a free public defender attorney under the constitutional right to counsel. **Bail** may be set to ensure that the defendant will appear at the trial. Bail is often provided by a bail bondsman or, in some cases, may be waived if the judge believes the defendant will not flee, thereby releasing the defendant on his or her own recognizance. The defendant may waive the right to a preliminary hearing or review by the grand jury.

Many accused suspects negotiate the type of crime they plead guilty to, often submitting to the prosecution's preferred sentence. This process is known as **plea bargaining**, and it is memorialized in a **plea bargain agreement**. For example, the prosecutor might initially argue that the defendant's conduct amounted to a serious crime, such as murder. However, during plea bargaining, the defendant may show remorse or agree to provide evidence or testify against other criminals. The plea bargain might obligate the defendant to plead guilty to a lesser offense, such as manslaughter rather than murder, or to fewer from among several charges. This process conserves public resources when the defendant understands that the prosecution could probably win a conviction on some of the charges. By some accounts, plea bargaining is highly successful in resolving criminal cases, probably accounting for nearly 90% of all criminal complaints.

Before trial, both parties may conduct additional investigation, the prosecution to strengthen its case and the defense to prove innocence, find the real perpetrator, gather evidence for cross-examination of opposing witnesses, or show improper evidence gathering by law enforcement. Often each side must provide its information, witness lists, and other sources to the opposition. Hard evidence includes weapons, documents, computer information, and objects with fingerprints or other identifying information. As in civil discovery, the process is intended to elicit the truth.

CONDUCT OF THE CRIMINAL TRIAL

Criminal trials follow a sequence similar to civil trials: (1) a jury is impaneled, (2) both sides make opening remarks, (3) the prosecution presents its case-in-chief by examining and cross-examining witnesses and showing tangible evidence, (4) the defense similarly presents its case-in-chief, (5) both sides make closing remarks, (6) the judge instructs the jury with the applicable law, (7) the jury deliberates, and (8) the jury renders its verdict. Criminal verdicts must usually be unanimous; otherwise, a "hung jury" results, necessitating either another trial or the defendant's release. When defendants are found guilty, they are sentenced, an official judgment as to the punishment, sometimes by the judge but meted out by the jury in many serious crimes.

Juries are impaneled in a process known as **voir dire**. Prospective jurors are questioned to determine whether they have severe biases that would invalidate the accused's due process. For example, the judge should dismiss a prospective juror **for cause** if the prospective juror is related to the parties, has already formed an opinion about guilt from news coverage, or does not believe in the illegality of the particular crime charged or the potential form of punishment (opponent of capital punishment). In addition, sociological and demographic factors about particular prospective jurors might make their participation inappropriate. Each side in criminal trials and in many civil trials has a limited number of **preemptory challenges** to remove such jurors when their attorneys or their trial consultants believe that the prospective juror might not treat the accused or litigating party objectively.

Criminal prosecutors must usually prove two elements of an alleged crime to gain a conviction. First, a criminal act, also known as *actus reus*, as defined by the criminal code, must have been committed by the defendant. Second, the defendant must have had the **criminal intent** to commit the criminal act, which is known as **mens rea**. These elements must be proved beyond a reasonable doubt, a much higher burden of proof than the preponderance of the evidence standard used in civil cases.

SENTENCING

Sentencing is a process in which the judge and/or jury metes out the punishment to the defendant. Many criminal statutes create a range of potential penalties between a minimum and maximum fine and/or imprisonment of those convicted. The defendant may be sentenced immediately if the law requires a mandatory sentence. Sentencing may be postponed in capital crimes or if sentencing guidelines give the judge discretion. In some serious cases, a later hearing is held to consider additional evidence—a **bifurcated trial**. In such a sentencing hearing, the judge or jury may consider the defendant's background and likelihood of **recidivism** (return to crime).

Federal Sentencing Guidelines
Congress established the U.S. Sentencing Commission in the Sentencing Reform Act of 1984. The commission issued the U.S. Sentencing Guidelines to standardize sentencing in the federal courts and respond to evidence that any two defendants convicted of the same crime could receive vastly different punishments. Generally, federal judges must consider a specified range of sentences for particular crimes by considering factors such as the defendant's prior criminal record, the seriousness of the offense just convicted, and any other factors specified in the guidelines.

Many states have also enacted sentencing guidelines to standardize sentencing. For example, a few states have adopted "**three strikes you're out**" laws. These effectively mete out life sentences after three felony convictions. Such sentencing guidelines force judges to sentence repeat offenders with this maximum penalty.

In 1991, the commission promulgated sentencing reforms for federal white-collar and business crimes. Firms with a strictly enforced compliance program or corporate code of conduct may receive leniency.[2] The **U.S. Sentencing Guidelines** promulgate a formula judges must use to calculate a **culpability multiplier** that can supply credits that reduce a defendant firm's criminal sentence. For example, a corporation's criminal sentence could be reduced to as low as 15% of the potential maximum penalty for violations committed by their employees. To qualify, the corporation must have a compliance program that is reasonably designed, implemented, and enforced to be generally effective in preventing and detecting criminal conduct. This "mitigation" of the corporate penalty depends on whether the firm (1) reported the violation voluntarily, (2) instituted an effective compliance program (such as a code of conduct and effective enforcement mechanism) before and after the violation, (3) had no high-level policy-setting official with knowledge of the violation, (4) cooperated fully with the government's investigation, and (5) accepted responsibility and took prompt, reasonable steps to remedy the harm. Other mechanisms include the use of an ombudsman and executive training programs to reinforce the importance of compliance programs. Sentencing reforms like the U.S. Sentencing Guidelines add force to the trend to adopt effective **compliance programs** that enforce corporate codes of conduct.[3]

CRIMINAL APPEALS

Generally, the defendant may appeal a conviction. However, criminal appeals generally address only defects in the criminal process, often constitutional issues from the Bill of Rights. In some states such as California, appeal is automatic in capital punishment cases. The appeals court may permanently dismiss the charges or order a new trial. Absent a trial court error, the double jeopardy provision prohibits another prosecution on the same charges.

SECONDARY LIABILITY

Many criminal prosecutions are complicated by the difficulty of assessing individual responsibility. Consider crimes committed by groups or by a business. Businesses are large organizations that perform complex acts in which many people have a part, which can make the legal determination of criminal intent problematic. It is difficult to assign direct responsibility for the overall effect of such complex behavior. However, there are several legal doctrines that assign criminal liability for major and minor participants in complex or group crimes. For example, parent corporations

---

2. *United States v. Beusch*, 596 F.2d 871 (9th Cir., 1979).
3. In re *Caremark Int'l, Inc.*, 698 A.2d 959 (Del.Ch., 1996).

can sometimes be held liable for crimes committed by subsidiaries under the civil theory of piercing the corporate veil. When the parent so controls the subsidiary's decision making, it would be inequitable to shield the parent from responsibility for the deeds of a related corporation within the larger unified enterprise.[4]

An **accessory** is someone who aids the perpetrator of a crime but is not present at its commission. An **accessory before the fact** provides assistance before the commission of the illegal acts, and an **accessory after the fact** provides assistance after the commission. A **conspiracy** is an agreement among two or more persons who plan the commission of a crime. A criminal **attempt** includes all the activities of the perpetrator(s) to plan and carry out a criminal act, such that, if successful, would result in the criminal act. All these are separate crimes for which additional convictions and penalties can be assessed if adequately proven.

BUSINESS CRIMES

Society increasingly believes it is wrong for business to generate undesirable side effects. Unique temptations and opportunities encourage some business crimes, and criminal acts are often blended with legitimate transactions to avoid detection. Enforcement is frustrated because existing laws do not address all aspects of corporate crime. Many laws target individual conduct or organized crime groups while ignoring the unique attributes of criminality within the business firm. Increasingly, however, new laws specifically address white-collar crime and corporate crime.

Many corporate crimes involve fraud or violations of various regulatory schemes (e.g., labor, environmental, manufacturing) that are not immediately obvious. Unlike the more common street crimes involving violence, property damage, or disturbance of public order, corporate crimes often go undetected because their effects do not surface immediately. The traditional law enforcement emphasis on immediate and personal crimes also tends to shield corporate crime from attention.

Law may not be a sufficiently effective control over much of this aberrant corporate behavior.[5] Some structural and procedural aspects of law reduce its effectiveness as a motivator of corporate responsibility. For example, business crimes tend to affect much larger financial interests than do personal crimes. In addition, judges tend to be more lenient with corporate wrongdoers than with "common" criminals. Why this special leniency? Corporate officers are usually seen as upstanding community members with reputations for responsibility who can usually afford to hire the best defense lawyers. Defendants charged with corporate crime often claim that their actions were motivated not by personal greed or hatred but by the goal of business survival. In communities where the business has many employees and suppliers, these people may be sympathetic to the corporate defendant, and they are the ones who elect the local prosecutor or district attorney.

---

4. See *U.S. v. NYNEX*, 788 F.Supp. 16 (D.D.C. 1992).
5. See Christopher D. Stone, *Where the Law Ends: The Social Control of Corporate Behavior* (New York: Harper Colophon, 1975).

EMBEZZLEMENT

Embezzlement is the wrongful appropriation of property entrusted to an individual. Embezzlement differs from larceny or theft in that the embezzler is initially given rightful possession of the misappropriated property. A thief has no rightful possession of stolen property. Therefore, embezzlement is committed by those who are entrusted with another's property, typically agents, brokers, consultants, accountants, attorneys, or corporate officials. Consider, for example, cashiers, who receive currency from customers as payment for goods or services. A cashier can rightfully possess the cash during working hours, even though it really belongs to the employer. However, handling the money becomes embezzlement when the cashier takes money from the cash register while on the job. By contrast, it is larceny for a cashier to steal cash out of the employer's unguarded safe because the cashier has no rightful custody of that money. The act of embezzlement may also trigger civil tort liability for conversion, as discussed later in the torts section.

MAIL AND WIRE FRAUD

Federal statutes make it a criminal offense to perpetrate fraud by communicating misrepresentations in the mail or by telephone, telegraph, radio, television, or most other electronic telecommunication means. These laws prohibit the use of the mail or wire to conduct an intentional scheme or artifice to defraud in order to obtain money or property. Most businesses communicate to potential clients or customers by mail, over the phone, and increasingly by some electronic means (e.g., electronic data interchange, computer modem, satellite, e-mail, Internet, cell phone, pager). When even an incidental part of perpetrating the fraud includes such communication, the businessperson may be liable for mail and wire fraud. These crimes carry stiff penalties of fines up to $1,000 and imprisonment for up to five years per count. Elaborate fraudulent schemes may constitute numerous separately punishable crimes, and this pattern is also illegal under racketeering laws.

Mail and wire fraud is often combined with prosecution of other regulatory crimes such as copyright infringement over the Internet, hacking as a form of computer fraud and abuse, electronic publication of pornography, and theft of trade secrets by electronic means. For example, the mail and wire fraud statutes were used in the infamous insider trading case involving the *Wall Street Journal*'s "Heard on the Street" columnist. The reporter used the phone to tip his friends about a forthcoming article in which he discussed particular stocks. The friends then traded in the stocks before stock prices were affected by the publication of the stories. The Supreme Court decisively outlawed the participants' insider trading under the misappropriation theory when the case was prosecuted under the mail and wire fraud statutes.[6] Insider trading is illegal as mail or wire fraud if confidential information is misappropriated and securities are traded by mail or coconspirators are tipped by

---

6. *Carpenter v. United States*, 484 U.S. 19 (1987).

phone or wire. These activities are separately illegal under Rule 10b-5 of the Securities Exchange Act of 1934.

Online fraudulent schemes plagued the early days of e-commerce. The mail and wire fraud statutes apply to communications and computer crimes.[7] For example, fraudulent stock fraud, devices promising antiterrorism protection, and various get-rich-quick schemes have been perpetrated via e-mail and Web sites. These activities are a form of wire fraud, even though some links in these communications do not use traditional phone calls or they use wireless devices. There may be a mail and wire fraud violation if nearly any part of the fraudulent transaction uses the mails or wire (wireless, computer networks), including the knowing use of an electronic payment.[8]

COMPUTER CRIME

Today, computers are an integral part of nearly every business. This ubiquity significantly raises the potential for computer crime. Computer crimes include criminal activities at least partially involving computers and increasingly involving cyber crime, which is computer crime committed over telecommunications networks. Computers and networks provide many new opportunities for creative forms of crime. Computer crime includes more than the following list of examples: embezzlement by unauthorized computerized funds transfer; industrial espionage or misappropriation of confidential computer files; theft of hardware, software, or valuable computer-use time; sabotage through tampering with computer files or destroying data, programs, or hardware (e.g., virus infections, denial of service attacks); fraud in making misrepresentations in computer-collected data; destruction or deprivation of computer use by others; and criminal infringement. A new federal agency, the National Infrastructure Protection Center, acts as a clearing house to coordinate the response to cyber crime, hacking, and other unlawful Internet attacks.

ONLINE

National Infrastructure Protection Center
http://www.nipc.gov

Computer crimes are difficult to detect because the more artful hackers carefully cover their tracks to conceal any audit trail. Firms must be vigilant in using effective computer security controls (e.g., encryption, restricting access to computer hardware, firewalls, passwords, ID codes). Until recently, the enforcement of computer crime has simply required the extension of existing law. Today, most states, the federal government, and many other nations are now customizing computer laws to accommodate these unique problems. Some of these laws, such as the Economic Espionage Act, are discussed further in Chapter 5, and the Computer Fraud and Abuse Act is discussed in Chapter 13.

Stalking
Stalking is another traditional crime that has moved to the Internet. **Stalking** is a fairly recently defined crime involving the pursuit of another by tracking them, in a

---

7. *U.S. v. Riggs*, 739 F.Supp. 414 (N.D.Ill. 1990).
8. *U.S. v. Bentz*, 21 F.3d 37 (3d Cir., 1994).

ONLINE

DOJ Cyber stalking
Web site
**http://www.usdoj.
gov/criminal/
cybercrime/
cyberstalking.htm**

stealthy manner, often anonymously. It usually involves repeated acts of harassment perceived as threatening to the victim. The harm is in fear and apprehension about a credible threat of potential physical assault to the victim or the victim's family or damage to the victim's property. The federal government and most states outlaw stalking when it results in harassment, annoyance, or alarm. Stalking may involve tortious activity such as the infliction of emotional distress, as discussed in the torts section later.

Cyber stalking may involve the use of hacker methods to intercept the target's e-mail and Web activity or to pose as a friendly correspondent in chat rooms or other communications. Arguably, cyber stalking is less threatening because of the anonymity and distance between the stalker and the victim. However, experience shows that the potential for fear or electronic theft is realistic. Therefore, several states are amending their stalking laws to include acts of stalking that use telecommunications devices. Children are vulnerable to cyber stalking by predatory adults when trusting children are lured to unprotected places where they may suffer physical, emotional, or financial harm.

Identity Theft

There has long been a crime of impersonation, a form of identity fraud. Today, the Internet makes it easier to acquire an individual's personal information (e.g., name, address, social security number, bank or credit card account numbers) and then misuse that information to convincingly pose as the person, either on or off line. In cyberspace, it is often too easy to evade traditional physical safeguards: examining IDs, observing an impersonator's demeanor, or authenticating signatures. Identity thieves can ruin an individual's reputation, credit history, or insurability or even create a false criminal record. Congress enacted the Identity Theft and Assumption and Deterrence Act in 1998. Most states have identity theft protections for victims, as well as penalties for the thieves.

The Fair Credit Reporting Act (FCRA) is a financial privacy law detailed in Chapter 13. The FCRA is increasingly used to vindicate identity thefts. Victims are suing credit reporting bureaus when they wrongfully provide the victim's credit history to impersonators. In one form of this crime, the identity thief uses credit history information to pose as the victim and thereby obtain credit cards, or utility accounts, borrow money, or obtain fake IDs. Credit bureaus are liable to the victim if they release such information to the wrong person.

In *TRW v. Andrews*,[9] the U.S. Supreme Court limited credit bureau liability by starting the FCRA's two-year statute of limitations when the credit reports were wrongfully supplied rather than later, when the victim discovered her or his identity was stolen by the impersonator. A receptionist in a Los Angeles doctor's office used a patient's personal information to obtain a credit report from TRW (now Experian). Thereafter, the receptionist posed as the patient to obtain a credit card and a utility account. The patient did not discover the damage to her credit rating until a year

---

9. 122 S.Ct. 441 (2001).

later and sued TRW on some of the claims more than two years after the reception-ist obtained the patient's credit history. This important decision puts much more responsibility on the shoulders of the victims of identity theft; they must discover and resolve such problems quickly. Many states help the victims of identity theft with the often daunting task of discovering and correcting errors in their credit histories caused by identity thieves.

Many antiterrorism tools are readily adaptable to reduce identity theft and can also inspire confidence in the safety of e-commerce. For example, identity technologies useful in both areas may include **biometrics** (fingerprinting, retinal scanning, facial recognition, DNA analysis) or **national ID cards** containing digitized records of biometrics, password, photographs, signature specimens, and account numbers. These techniques are controversial among privacy advocates.

Gambling

Gambling has had a long and varied past. Ancient people believed that gambling outcomes were an expression of supernatural powers. This idea survives today because many gamblers believe in luck. Eventually, gambling became a widespread pastime. However, by the nineteenth century, pressures to regulate gambling mounted as it became associated with many negative consequences. For example, gambling restrictions were rationalized after experience with "Old West" saloons, where gambling was linked with alcohol abuse, prostitution, and violence. Many naive gamblers and their families suffered financial ruin. In the twentieth century, gambling became connected with organized crime and with manipulation of sporting events. By the late twentieth century, government regulation relaxed somewhat, as revenues rose from gambling taxes and from state-run lotteries. At least some forms of gambling are illegal in all 50 states and in most foreign nations. However, enforcement of illegal gambling varies considerably. As discussed in Chapter 10, contracts to pay illegal gambling debts are unenforceable.

Gambling is the creation of a risk with no prior existence primarily for the purpose of shifting the risk to expose the parties to gain or loss. These risks are usually based on uncertain events that solely rely on chance (simple card games, dice, roulette), rely entirely on external factors (sports outcomes), or are based on a combination of chance and the gambler's skill (complex card games). Gambling proliferates on the Internet for several reasons. First, local law enforcement officials have great difficulty detecting illegal on-line gambling. Gamblers usually operate from the privacy of their homes, and electronic settlement of gambling debts uses credit cards or peer-to-peer payment systems that are difficult to police. Illegal gambling can involve money laundering, as discussed in a later section. Second, on-line gambling sites operate most successfully from states or foreign nations where on-line gambling is legal. States or nations that generally outlaw gambling or specifically prohibit on-line gambling face very difficult enforcement problems. The jurisdiction problems of the Internet are particularly daunting in cyberspace. Opponents of new restrictions on on-line gambling argue that the costs of enforcement outweigh any benefits, that legalizing gambling would weaken organized crime, and that the negative social context of gambling has changed.

RACKETEER INFLUENCED AND CORRUPT ORGANIZATIONS

A portion of the Organized Crime Control Act of 1970 is known as **RICO**, an acronym for that law's provisions on racketeer influenced and corrupt organizations. RICO has criminal and civil provisions. Civil RICO permits private plaintiffs to sue for civil treble (triple) damages against persons found guilty of racketeering activities. RICO outlaws a pattern of illegal activities that include the **predicate offenses** of securities fraud, murder, arson, extortion, drug dealing, mail and wire fraud, bribery, loan sharking, and other enumerated state and other federal crimes. Many of these crimes can be committed by using telecommunications and computer networks, such as the Internet.

RICO requires a private plaintiff to prove the following essential elements to win triple damages: (1) the defendant committed at least two prohibited acts (2) that constituted a pattern (3) of racketeering activity (4) by which the defendant (5) invested in, maintained an interest in, or participated in (6) an enterprise (7) that affected interstate or foreign commerce. Critics claim RICO has been expanded to cover many activities that were not traditionally considered part of organized crime.

RICO makes it unlawful to invest proceeds derived from racketeering activities, a practice used by organized crime to launder its illegal profits. In one case, the proceeds from the sale of a firm tainted by securities fraud were invested in another firm. In another case, a fraud was perpetrated by general partners who sold their brokerage business. The pattern of racketeering activity outlawed by RICO may be proved, for example, by the artificial inflation of a company's market price. RICO's special powers and penalties promise treble damages and attorney's fees to civil plaintiffs. Criminal conviction can carry fines of up to $25,000 and/or imprisonment for up to 20 years per violation. RICO authorizes judges to order the defendant to forfeit any property acquired with the illegal racketeering profits, which permits prosecutors to request a pretrial freeze or seizure of the defendant's assets. This powerful settlement inducement was allegedly used to bring down the "junk bond king" Michael Milken and his employer, the investment banking firm of Drexel Burnham Lambert.

Nearly half of the states have passed RICO-type statutes. The state laws combined with the expansive federal RICO provision make significant liabilities possible in business litigation. In addition, the RICO criminal procedures provide stiff penalties and permit prosecutors to freeze the defendant's assets during a criminal RICO trial. This tactic has allegedly been used to bully investment banking firms accused of stock manipulation and securities fraud into settling RICO charges.

Dissatisfaction with civil plaintiffs' and federal prosecutors' alleged misuse of RICO has led to reform. For example, the Supreme Court in *H.J. Inc. v. Northwestern Bell Telephone Co.*[10] required better proof of a relationship between the predicate offenses, such as the same or similar purpose, results, participants, victims, or methods of commissions. Prosecutors cannot easily prove the required

---

10. 492 U.S. 229 (1989).

"pattern" from only two isolated events unless they clearly pose a threat of continuity. *Reeves v. Ernst & Young*[11] held that most auditors, investment bankers, and legal counsel are relieved from RICO liability for such crimes as securities fraud committed by their clients. RICO requires that the defendant must actively "participate" in committing the predicate offense to be held liable. The RICO threat on auditors of fraudulent financial statements is eliminated unless they knowingly participate in the management or operations of the client. This point was further reinforced with passage of the Private Securities Litigation Reform Act (PSLRA). Under PSLRA, securities fraud and securities fraud applications of the mail and wire fraud statutes are no longer predicate offenses for civil RICO. However, they still remain part of criminal RICO.

BRIBERY AND THE FOREIGN CORRUPT PRACTICES ACT

Scandals in the 1970s focused public inquiry on the misuse of corporate funds for unethical and illegal purposes. The SEC investigated questionable payments made by domestic firms, including bribery of domestic and foreign officials, illegal campaign contributions, and kickbacks. This prompted Congress to pass the **Foreign Corrupt Practices Act (FCPA)** in 1977. The FCPA was amended twice, first with the Foreign Corrupt Practices Act Amendments of 1988 and again with the International Anti-Bribery and Fair Competition Act of 1998. The FCPA outlaws foreign bribery and establishes accounting standards to prevent bribery. The accounting standards provisions require publicly traded companies to keep books and records that accurately and fairly reflect the transactions of the corporation and to devise and maintain an adequate system of internal accounting controls. These standards are designed to prevent the accumulation and use of bribery funds. Bribery is also a criminal offense under other state and federal laws.

After 20 years' experience with the "high ground" represented by the FCPA, the United States convinced the governments of more than 30 other nations to agree to adopt similar antibribery legislation. This was accomplished with the implementation of a treaty negotiated through the Organization for Economic Cooperation and Development (OECD), the Convention on Combating Bribery of Foreign Officials in International Business Transactions. Congress implemented the convention with passage of the 1998 amendments to the FCPA.

Prohibited Bribery

The FCPA criminalizes foreign bribery intended to "secure improper advantage" when made by all persons, including publicly traded corporations, companies of various legal structures (e.g., **domestic concerns**), various unincorporated organizations, persons within the United States, and persons outside the United States who are working for a U.S. company. The FCPA antibribery provisions outlaw any corrupt

---

11. 507 U.S. 170 (1993).

payments, offers to pay, and offers to give **anything of value** to foreign officials to influence decisions to grant business. **Foreign officials** include government officials, officials of foreign political parties, candidates for foreign public office, and officials of international organizations.

Grease payments (facilitating payments) are not considered bribes under the FCPA. **Grease** payments are made to lower-echelon foreign government agents when they make **routine governmental actions**. In some countries, for example, customs officials routinely expect a "gratuity" to expedite the clearance of incoming goods. An exporter might feel pressured to make a grease payment to get a shipment of perishable goods quickly cleared through foreign customs. In this situation, the payment would not be an illegal bribe so long as it is permissible in the foreign country. Bona fide promotional expenditures and contract performance expenses, including lodging for foreign officials, are not illegal bribes.

Foreign Corruption Practices Act Enforcement

The FCPA gives enforcement powers to both the SEC and the U.S. Justice Department (DOJ). The DOJ conducts criminal investigations, prosecutes criminal bribery, and may seek civil penalties and injunctions. The SEC has civil enforcement powers over publicly traded firms and enforces the accounting standards provisions of the FCPA. Violators of the FCPA bribery provisions are subject to fines of up to $2 million, and individual violators are subject to possible imprisonment for up to five years. The SEC may assess civil penalties of up to $10,000 for individuals, whether or not they are U.S. nationals. An employer may not pay an individual violator's fine.

The 1988 amendments give the U.S. attorney general power to issue guidelines and to assist compliance by providing opinions on the legality of specific proposed conduct by U.S. companies, persons, or their foreign agents in the DOJ's FCPA Opinion Procedure Releases. The new antiterrorism law, the USA Patriot Act, includes foreign bribery as a form of illegal money laundering, discussed later in this chapter.

TERRORISM

Increasingly, the criminal law is directed at **terrorism**, a threatened use of violence reinforced by actual violent, criminal acts, usually for political or religious purposes. Terrorism is often performed by small, zealous groups who intend to coerce and intimidate. They rely on fear from widespread publicity of their illegal acts. Terrorism targets particular victims who are usually linked together by a demographic factor such as their religion, race, ethnicity, or national origin. The impact of terrorism is often much broader, going beyond national borders. Terrorist acts include the development and use of weapons of mass destruction, erratic murders and bombings, hijackings, kidnappings, and creating fear of credible threats of various criminal acts.

Several waves of terrorism in modern times have encouraged public support for new criminal laws and enforcement procedures. For example, infamous waves of terrorism accompanied Nazi expansionism, the Irish Republican Army, the Palestinian crisis, and associated Arab-Israeli conflicts in the Middle East. Except for the Ku Klux Klan's long-standing terrorism against blacks, terrorism was largely unknown in the United States until the Oklahoma City bombing in 1995 and then the attacks on the World Trade Center and Pentagon on September 11, 2001. Increasingly, terrorists use modern tools and technologies that increase the impact of their acts, such as high-powered explosives, hijacking of transportation systems, computers, and telecommunications networks. Terrorists often use these means for spying, malicious destruction or disturbance, and transactions to finance and organize their terrorist networks.

Cyber Terrorism

Cyber terrorism involves activities by **hackers,** people skilled in computer programming. *Hacker* is now generally perceived as a derogatory term. Malicious hackers pride themselves in overcoming the security features of computer networks, and many gain unlawful entry into others' computer systems to steal information or money or do damage. Malicious hacking involves illegal acts that use computer networks for spying, financial fraud, malicious destruction (denial of service, virus attacks, falsifying data), or exerting unauthorized control over dams, power systems, air traffic, transportation systems, utilities, or other systems with broad impact.

Counterterrorism

The United States took steps to combat terrorism and cyber terrorism following several incidents in the 1990s, and particularly after the terrorist attacks of September 11, 2001. First, the United States has negotiated international agreements with other nations and through international organizations such as the United Nations. These agreements require signatory nations to cooperate in antiterrorist activities. For example, many nations are cooperating in apprehending, prosecuting, and terminating terrorist organizations and their networks by using various law enforcement tools. Second, the United States now designates various groups as suspected terrorist organizations, which expands law enforcement monitoring and triggers greater financial scrutiny for money laundering. The FBI's Internet monitoring software program, **Carnivore,** selectively searches for e-mail containing language believed to suggest terrorism and other criminal activity. Third, the United States offers rewards for assistance in apprehending known terrorists. Fourth, antiterrorism preparedness, or **counterterrorism,** has been enhanced by the creation of coordinating agencies such as the U.S. Office of Homeland Security and the State Department's Office of the Coordinator for Counterterrorism. Fifth, the United States and other cooperating nations have increased the effectiveness of their border controls and travel documents (visas). These nations are also monitoring and restricting terrorist fund-raising and improving their information exchange and antiterrorism law enforcement.

ONLINE

U.S. Counterterrorism Web site
http://www. state.gov/s/ct/

MONEY LAUNDERING

Criminal law increasingly focuses enforcement efforts on **money laundering,** a varied set of practices that create an illusion of transactions to disguise the origin and movement of criminal proceeds. The critical element is to mimic legitimate transactions so that criminals can provide plausible explanations for their cash flow and cash reserves. This practice has led to a reliable enforcement method to find the criminal leaders and their accomplices: "Follow the money." Law enforcement often examines a suspect's finances for suspicious expenditures beyond the suspect's reported earnings and financial means.

The term *money laundering* literally means to "clean" or legitimize the appearance of money made "dirty" as the proceeds of crimes. The term may have originated from the 1920s and 1930s gangster era, when legal slot machine gambling proliferated. The cash flow of coins from this gambling and from coin-operated laundries provided plausible and practically untraceable excuses for handling huge amounts of currency and coins from criminal activities. Today, a major argument against gambling is that it facilitates money laundering and organized crime. However, money laundering has probably been done for more than 4,000 years. It was originally used to hide legitimate earnings from taxation or from unfair confiscation by oppressive governments.

Money laundering guidance for financial institutions
**http://www.
moneylaundering.
com**

The tools of money launderers are well known but are still in use because detection is difficult and enforcement is costly. Launderers use transaction methods that minimize records. Cash payments of $10,000 and more must be reported by businesses and banks, creating an audit trail. Using cash rather than checks, wire transfers, or credit cards reduces the record keeping and thereby hides transactions. Conversion of criminal proceeds into gold, diamonds, or other valuable hard assets can also conceal the flow of value. The use of "fronts" is another component of successful money laundering. These apparently respectable businesses are used as a cover for illegal activities.

In recent years, government has tried harder to restrict money laundering, which is an indispensable component of many illegal schemes that society seeks to eliminate: the illegal drug trade, terrorism, organized crime, and smuggling. The purposes of laws against money laundering are to (1) identify criminals and their accomplices for prosecution, (2) reveal the criminals' accessories and coconspirators, who may provide incriminating evidence that brings down criminal organizations, (3) seize the money or freeze accounts holding laundered money, and (4) deter crimes generally because the incentive is reduced if it becomes risky to spend the criminal proceeds. Civil penalties for each money laundering violation can include fines of either twice the amount involved or $1 million, whichever is greater. Several of the key U.S. statutes used to stop money laundering are listed in Exhibit 3.2.

DEFENSES TO CRIMES

Defendants guilty of some crimes may offer an excuse or justification for the criminal act. As in other areas of law, a **defense** either partially or completely relieves the defendant from liability. These defenses are in addition to the basis for acquittal if

Exhibit 3.2 U.S. Laws Against Money Laundering

Federal Statute	Purposes and Methods
Bank Secrecy Act of 1970 (BSA)	Currency transaction report ("paper trail" for transactions over $10,000); civil and criminal penalties
Money Laundering Control Act of 1986	Creates three new federal money laundering crimes: (1) assistance in laundering, (2) engaging in $10,000 transactions involving property from criminal activity, and (3) structuring transactions to avoid BSA disclosures of currency transaction reports
Anti–Drug Abuse Act of 1988	Increased civil and criminal sanctions. Forfeiture of property involved in violating BSA or other anti-laundering statute. Requires record keeping of large cash purchases of monetary instruments (bank drafts)
Crime Control Act of 1990, §2532	Federal banking regulators authorized to negotiate with foreign banking regulators for help in certain criminal investigations
Federal Deposit Insurance Corporation Improvement Act of 1991, §206	Federal banking regulators given discretion to disclose information to foreign banking regulators to enforce anti–money laundering laws
Housing and Community Development Act of 1992, Title XV (Annunzio-Wylie Anti–Money Laundering Act)	Authorizes seizure, closing, and/or revocation of charter of financial institutions guilty of money laundering or BSA offenses; specifies mitigation factors
USA Patriot Act of 2001	Broadens definition of financial institutions regulated under money laundering laws, requires anti–money laundering programs and training, regulates private and correspondent banking; FCPA now defines money laundering as a form of bribery; stiffens civil and criminal penalties for money laundering

the accused's constitutional rights are violated during criminal processing or the defendant creates reasonable doubt about guilt or can disprove the prosecution's allegations.

Some defenses directly undermine the prosecution's proof of *mens rea* or criminal intent. Infancy is a defense for defendants under the legal age of majority, usually 18. Most states have a separate **juvenile court system** for children, although some older minors may be "tried as an adult" in the regular system for particularly serious crimes. **Intoxication** and insanity are also defenses that may show the defendant could not have had the criminal intent needed to be found guilty. Courts are generally more willing to accept intoxication as a defense if it is involuntary—the defendant was forced or tricked into ingesting the intoxicating drugs or alcohol. There are several different tests of criminal insanity: (1) the M'Naghten rule, still used in several states, shows the defendant to be incapable of distinguishing right from wrong, (2) the **irresistible impulse** test is used in a few states, and (3) the Model Penal Code's test, used in most states and federal courts, shows the defendant is lacking substantial capacity to appreciate wrongfulness because of mental disease or defect. **Mistake** of fact may be a defense if the defendant has a genuine mistaken belief in the objective of the act, such as someone who mistakenly takes another person's coat from a checkroom because it looked like the defendant's coat. Ignorance of the law is almost never a defense.

Other defenses examine the circumstances that might justify the criminal act. A victim might grant **consent**, as football players do for assault and battery during practice or games. **Duress** involves a credible threat of serious bodily harm to the defendant, and the defendant commits the crime to avoid the threatened harm. **Self-defense** is similar to duress—the justifiable use of force to repel a physical attack or in defense of one's home or family. The defendant can use only as much force as is needed to repel the attack. Deadly force is justified only when the defendant is threatened with death or serious bodily harm. **Necessity** is another derivation of self-defense. **Entrapment** prevents law enforcement from promoting a crime by staging the circumstances and suggesting that the defendant do the criminal act. There is no entrapment if the defendant was predisposed to the crime. Law enforcement may set up traps so long as they do not push the defendant into the criminal act. The **statute of limitations** prevents prosecution after the statutory period has run out. Finally, some defendants may be granted **immunity**, barring prosecution in exchange for the defendant's cooperation and information leading to successful prosecutions against other criminals.

TORTS

Unlike most of criminal law, which seeks to punish and deter unlawful wrongs committed against all of society, tort law seeks to award compensation to remedy wrongs committed against individuals or identifiable groups. Many intentional torts closely parallel the similar crimes. For example, assault, battery, and trespass entitle the victim to compensation under tort law but are also are criminal acts. The growth in tort law mirrors somewhat the evolution of society. Tort law has become concerned with protecting the individual's reputation, right to privacy, freedom from interference with property rights, and freedom from externally caused mental distress. In recent years, tort liability has expanded to cover interference with personal rights (sexual harassment), interference with economic relations, and injuries from defective products and malpractice.

Exhibit 3.3 Comparison of the Four Types of Torts

Type of Tort	Requirements	Examples
Intentional torts	Intent to commit tortious act Causation Injury	*Battery:* hit another person *Trespass:* unconsented touching of land or personal property of another person
Quasi-intentional tort: defamation	Defamatory (false) statement about the plaintiff Publication by the defendant Damage to plaintiff's reputation	*Libel:* false written statements made in newspaper *Slander:* false spoken statement made on TV
Negligence	Duty to act as reasonable person Breach of duty Proximate and actual causation Injury	Careless driving Unskilled professional malpractice in person or remotely (over the Internet)
Strict liability	Ultrahazardous activity or inherently defective product that is unreasonably dangerous Defect existed while under defendant's control Defendant in business as seller Causation and injury	Use of dynamite that destroys structures on adjoining property Product liability injuries

There are four types of torts: intentional torts, quasi-intentional torts, negligence, and strict liability. Although each type has distinctly different proof requirements, all four require both proof of a causal connection to the tortious act and proof that an injury occurred that the law would compensate. Tort law is much broader and more pervasive than the coverage it is given in this chapter alone. Indeed, tort law is the source of many other forms of liability discussed throughout this book. For example, tort law is the direct foundation for product and service liability, privacy liability, civil securities law liability, and environmental cleanup liability, which are discussed in Chapters 8 and 13. Tort law is closely related to intellectual property infringement (discussed in Chapters 4, 5, 6, and 7) and to agency and employment liability (discussed in Chapter 11). Finally, civil remedies in other regulatory programs closely resemble tort law, such as antitrust and Internet regulation (discussed in Chapters 12 and 14). Clearly, this introductory discussion of tort fundamentals is a necessary prerequisite to most other discussions of civil remedies. Exhibit 3.3 compares the four major types of torts.

BUSINESS AND VICARIOUS LIABILITY

Tort law is a pressing legal concern for business because there may be liability for the actions of employees. Most businesses act through other people: officers, employees, and independent agents. Corporations, partnerships, and many sole proprietorships employ people and other firms to implement their activities. The law holds a business responsible for acts of employees if the business has the right to control the employee.

The Agent and the Independent Contractor

If an agent commits torts while working on behalf of a business, the injured person can sue the business, the agent or employee, or both. This type of risk exposure is **vicarious liability**. In this analysis, the business is a **master** or principal, and its agents or employees are **servants** or agents. Vicarious liability arises when an agent causes injury to a third party—to an individual or to another business—while acting on behalf of the principal.

A business is not held vicariously liable for the act of an agent if the business has no right to control that agent's means or methods of conducting the act. For example, if a person is employed by a business solely to do a particular job without the business having any control over how the job is to be done, only the agent is responsible for his or her acts. The business is not generally liable for the torts of such a person, referred to as an **independent contractor**. The vicarious liability of businesses for the acts of agents or contractors is a major basis for determining ownership of copyrights under the work made for hire doctrine discussed in Chapter 4.

Vicarious Liability and Individual Direct Liability

Although a business is held vicariously liable for an employee's torts, this fact does not alter the **direct liability** of the employee. All persons are directly liable for their own tortious acts. The vicarious liability imposed on a business for the torts of servants is an alternative source for compensation. For example, if ABC Trucking employs Jeff to drive a delivery truck and Jeff's negligent driving causes injury to pedestrians, Jeff is directly liable *and* ABC is vicariously liable to the pedestrians for their injuries. However, such victims are permitted only one recovery. Vicarious liability provides some greater assurance that the victim will be fairly compensated, not overcompensated.

There are several reasons why the vicarious liability of a business is generally more significant than the direct liability of an employee. First, because both the business and the employee may be held liable, the injured party usually sues both of them. The injured person may be unsure whether the employee is solely responsible as an independent contractor or whether the business is also liable because the employee is a servant acting within the scope of employment. By suing both, the injured plaintiff forces the business and the employee to determine through litigation the extent of the control that the business can exercise over the employee. Second, the business usually has greater financial resources than the employee. This basis for suing the business is known as the **deep pocket theory**. Most businesses are well advised to insure these risks. Too often, the employee's wages or assets are insufficient to satisfy large damage awards. Given this disparity in resources, the business, with its deep pockets, is often the injured person's primary target. The deep pocket theory is justified because the master should screen and monitor its servants to assure safe operations.

INTENTIONAL TORTS

An intentional tort is an intentional, wrongful act performed by the person committing the tort, the tortfeasor. The plaintiff must prove that the defendant intended to do the act that caused the injury. Tortious actions that interfere with personal rights can cause physical or mental injury, interference with private property (trespass), or interference in economic relations. Intentional torts require the plaintiff to prove only that the defendant intended to do the act that caused the injury; it is not necessary to prove that the defendant intended to cause the resulting injury. If, however, the plaintiff can prove evil motive or desire to harm, then punitive damages may be appropriate in addition to compensatory damages. **Compensatory damages** are payments to reimburse damages such as medical expenses, lost income, and pain and suffering. The standard is that compensatory damages are awarded only to compensate the injured person for the losses actually suffered. By contrast, punitive damages are additional amounts intended to punish the wrongdoer for the wrongfulness and to deter similar wrongful acts. Punitive damages are discussed in the last section of this chapter.

The clearest cases of intentional torts generally occur when one person causes physical injury to another. For example, a punch in the nose can be a battery if it causes injury. The law requires that people refrain from intentional actions that injure others. It allows recovery of damages for an injury caused by someone's intentional interference with the right not to be injured. Some types of intentional acts interfere with personal rights, and some result from physical or mental injury, interference with property rights, or interference with economic relations.

INTENTIONAL TORTS THAT INTERFERE WITH PERSONAL RIGHTS

Assault
Assault is a crime and intentional tort resulting from an intentional act of putting another person in apprehension of immediate offensive harmful touching. The victim may be afraid but need not be; **apprehension** here means expectation. Words alone do not typically constitute an assault because they are not sufficient to make an ordinarily reasonable person apprehensive of immediate harm. Words coupled with a menacing gesture, however, can constitute an assault. The relevant intent in assault is that of the actor but the apprehension is based on the victim's state of mind, judged by a reasonable person standard. Note that actual physical contact

need not take place for an assault to occur. A person who points a gun or a knife at another person in a threatening manner commits an assault, even though the victim is not actually touched. Given that words alone are insufficient for an assault, it may be difficult to commit assault using e-mail, in chat rooms, or otherwise over the Internet.

Battery

Battery is the intentional offensive touching of another person without justification or consent. Battery also includes the unprivileged touching of another with some instrumentality put in motion by the aggressor. For example, shooting a bullet that hits someone constitutes a battery. Like self-defense and use of force in criminal law, a **reasonable justification** is usually the key to determining whether a battery is wrongful under tort law. A person imminently threatened or battered by another may respond in self-defense with similar force without incurring liability. However, if another person is the victim or the victim's property is threatened, many courts would not excuse a "defensive battery" as self-defense. Minimal, social, or unavoidable touching, as on a crowded bus or at a sporting event, is usually not considered battery because it is expected, justified, and not offensive to a reasonable person. However, "crowd surfing" at a concert might result in unconsented contacts that are more invasive than would be reasonable to expect in most crowded public situations.

False Imprisonment

False imprisonment is the intentional confinement of a nonconsenting individual within a bounded area for an appreciable time. False imprisonment may be charged against a business that attempts to deal with suspected shoplifters or with employees suspected of dishonest behavior. Under common law, a storekeeper could be held liable for detaining a suspected shoplifter if that person was later found to be innocent.

Most states have statutes that limit the false imprisonment liability of storekeepers to unreasonable actions or bad faith detentions. If storekeepers have probable cause or act in good faith in detaining a suspected shoplifter, they are not liable. The privilege is a qualified one; if it is abused, the storekeeper could be held liable for detention without reasonable cause. It is unlikely that false imprisonment could be committed over the Internet. However, where security controls like gates or doors are controlled electronically or with computer networks, there might be liability for false imprisonment.

Intentional Infliction of Emotional Distress

The courts are beginning to recognize that the **intentional infliction of emotional distress** is a separate tort. Liability is usually limited to outrageous acts that cause detectable emotional injury. Although courts frequently hold that there has to be some physical injury to allow recovery for mental distress, some courts allow recovery even in the absence of physical injury.

Invasion of Privacy

The right of privacy provides tort remedies that are intended to protect a person from unwarranted interference with the right to be left alone. The Internet and the reawakening of antiterrorism law enforcement have thrust privacy rights forward as a major public policy issue for the foreseeable future. Privacy has become multi-faceted; that is, privacy is not simply a tort but also subject to constitutional rights, property rights, regulatory requirements, and contractual agreements. Given the increasing importance of balancing individual privacy rights with societal rights, all of Chapter 13 is devoted to the various aspects of privacy.

INTENTIONAL TORTS THAT INTERFERE WITH PROPERTY RIGHTS

Interference with property rights concerns one person's unauthorized use or appro-priation of another's property. The person owning or possessing the property may be injured even if the property is not damaged. Trespass and conversion are torts that interfere with property rights. The right to exclusive possession and use of real property is violated by trespass. Similarly, rights in personal property are also vio-lated by interference or by a conversion that takes or destroys the personal property. Trespass is often a separate crime.

Trespass to Land

A person who enters someone else's real property without consent is committing a trespass. The intentional act of entering the possessor's property causes the injury. Even if the property is not damaged, the possessor is harmed by the unpermitted entry. A person who owns land or is a tenant on real property has the right to have that property remain free from interference. This right protects the owner's exclu-sive possession and use of land, the growing crops attached to it, the minerals under-ground, and/or the buildings and structures built thereon, Of course, if the trespass causes damage to the property, such as pollution, greater compensation is needed. Airplane overflights are not actionable as trespass as long as sufficient minimum alti-tude is maintained under aviation regulations. By contrast, subsurface trespass is wrongful, such as when a mineshaft or oil well drilling crosses property lines under the surface.

Trespass to Chattels

Trespass to chattels is an intentional and wrongful interference with the possession or use of personal property. The rightful owner, possessor, or tenant (lessee) may sue for an injunction. When the trespass is so severe that there is considerable damage, the owner may prefer to sue for conversion. Trespass to chattels is experiencing resurgence as malicious hackers carry out destruction on others' networks or com-puter systems. For example, denial of service and virus attacks may constitute trespass or even conversion if the damages are severe. Is it a trespass to gather data from "free" Web sites if their terms and conditions of service prohibit access except in furtherance of the Web site owner's business? This question was answered in favor of the Web site owner in *eBay v. Bidder's Edge*,[12] disfavoring the operation of shopping bots, a topic discussed in greater detail in Chapter 5.

Conversion

Conversion occurs when one person appropriates personal property that is rightfully in another person's possession. The theft of goods from someone's house represents not only a crime but also the tort of conversion. Thus, the defendant may be held responsible both for the criminal act of larceny and for compensatory damages. Conversion also occurs when a person fails to return borrowed property or property placed in a bailment for a specific purpose. For example, if Joe lends Sue his computer for one month but she keeps it for three months, Sue commits conversion. Sue has wrongfully denied Joe the use and enjoyment of his computer for two months. Generally, a successful conversion suit requires proof of the owner's demand for the return of property, followed by the tortfeasor's intentional refusal to return it.

The victim of conversion may sue for damages measured by the rental value of the converted property. Thus, in the example, Joe could sue for damages based on two months' rental value of a similar computer. If the defendant destroys or permanently deprives the owner of property, the damages would equal the market value of the property. A related tort is misappropriation, which is appropriate for intangibles such as intellectual property rights. For example, the infringement of trade secrets is often vindicated in a civil tort suit for misappropriation, as discussed further in Chapter 5.

INTENTIONAL TORTS THAT INTERFERE WITH ECONOMIC RELATIONS

Both individuals and businesses are protected from unreasonable interference with their economic relations. The intentional torts of disparagement, interference with contract rights, and interference with prospective business relations all pertain to economic relations. The economic interference aspects of privacy rights, such as appropriation, are discussed in Chapter 13. Fraud is another intentional tort covered as a defense to contract liability in Chapter 10.

Disparagement

The tort of **disparagement** protects against the tortfeasor who makes disparaging statements about the business activities of a person or a business. This tort arises if the plaintiff can prove that specific business losses occurred as a result of the statements. For example, if one company's advertising falsely claims that a competitor's products are inferior, that the competitor stocks stolen goods, or that the competitor does not pay its bills, the disparaged business could sue in tort.

---

12. 100 F.Supp.2d 1058 (N.D.Cal. 2000).

Disparagement is sometimes referred to as **trade libel**. Unlike traditional defamation, disparagement protects only an individual's business or trade; it does not protect an individual's personal activities. Further, the plaintiff in a disparagement suit must prove that the disparagement is false. By contrast, the defendant in a defamation suit must prove that the statements were true to have a defense. Trademark law may also be implicated when the disparaging statements are directed at registered trademarks of a firm or at its trademarked products. The problem of using trademark law to block criticism targeting firms is discussed in Chapter 7. Many of the problems that the Internet has thrust into modern defamation law may also apply in disparagement cases.

Interference with Contract Rights or Prospective Business Relations

The tort of **interference with contract relations** involves intentional tampering with the contract of a person or a business. This tort covers existing contracts between an employer and an employee, between a business and a supplier, or between a business and a customer. Intentionally causing the breach of a valid contract constitutes wrongful interference with contractual relations. The tort occurs if the defendant, knowing of a contract between the plaintiff and another party, intentionally induces that other party to breach the contract, and if the breach injures the plaintiff.

The tort of interference with the prospective economic advantage of an individual or a business is similar to the tort of interference with contract relations. Individuals and firms have a legal duty not to tamper with the business relations of others, whether those business relations involve currently enforceable contracts or merely the expectancy of contracts. A famous case involved Pennzoil's fight with Texaco to take over Getty Oil Company. Pennzoil sued Texaco for its wrongful interference with an agreement between Pennzoil and Getty Oil. Texaco claimed that it did not knowingly interfere with their agreement. Texaco's takeover was successful, but Pennzoil initially won the largest punitive damage award in history in the case.[13]

QUASI-INTENTIONAL TORTS: DEFAMATION

Defamation is the publication of an untrue statement about another person that injures the person's reputation or character. **Slander** is oral defamation; **libel** is written defamation. Libel was traditionally considered the more serious offense for two reasons. First, the spoken word is ephemeral; it lasts only as long as the words are spoken. Second, published writings, particularly newspapers and books, are more permanent and influential, so the damage is potentially more widespread. Today, however, technology may draw into question the distinction between libel and slander. For example, radio, TV, and now the Internet are very widely influential. Although radio and TV broadcasts are ephemeral, lasting only the duration of the

---

13. *Texaco, Inc. v. Pennzoil Co.*, 729 S.W.2d 768 (Tex.Ct.Ap. 1987), *cert.denied* 108 S.Ct. 1305 (1988).

statements, they can be recorded and replayed. Many broadcasts are heard or seen by millions of people. Internet communications are increasingly considered published writings, so the rules of libel may be more appropriate. Most of this discussion focuses on defamation, a general tort that includes both.

The reason for the publication requirement is that a person's good name exists only when perceived and evaluated by others. If the audience does not consider the statement derogatory or if no one hears or reads the statement, there is no injury. The interest protected is the subject individual's reputation, so money damages are computed as the victim's lost reputation and lost economic advantages resulting from the extent of publication of the untrue and damaging statements.

DEFENSES TO DEFAMATION

In the United States, the First Amendment is a major component of defamation law. Freedom of speech requires that **truth is a complete defense**. True statements are justified under the U.S. Constitution's protection for the open marketplace of ideas. Certain statements are **defamatory per se**; that is, liability is established automatically and without further proof of the injury to reputation. For example, accusing a person of murder or alleging that a person has a venereal disease could be defamatory per se. Another defense to defamation exists if the person who makes the statement has a qualified or absolute privilege to do so. During litigation, judges, at- torneys, and witnesses have an **absolute privilege**. A **qualified privilege** exists for private matters if the statement is made by someone who has a duty to make statements and if the statement is communicated only to those with an immediate interest in the information. For example, in many states, if a prospective employer asks a former employer about a former employee's character, the former employer's statement is probably privileged. Thus, if the former employer acts in good faith and not in malice, there is usually no defamation, even if the statement is untrue.

There is another defense when the defamation is about public figures. No defamation of a person who is a public figure exists unless the statement is both untrue and made with malice. **Malice** is often difficult to prove. However, if, for example, a reporter writes an untrue story about a public figure, the defamation may be regarded as malicious if the reporter did not take reasonable steps to substantiate the sources. Malice is a particularly important problem for the news media—print, broadcast, or online.

Liability of ISPs
Internet defamation may occur in several contexts. Defamatory statements could be posted to a bulletin board or Web site, they may be uttered in chatrooms, the statements may be included in e-mail messages, the statements may be **Webcast** as streaming audio or video from Web sites, or the statements may be made over Internet telephony (the use of the Internet to carry phone calls). Computer telecommunications networks such as the Internet might eventually be used for new forms of communications still unforeseen today.

Should ISPs whose services transmit defamatory statements be held liable for publishing defamatory statements as **republishers**? The question forces the application of laws developed for older technologies to the Internet. Generally, the courts have not held phone companies liable for spoken defamation because they are common carriers that distribute communications and have no control over the sender's content. Similarly, bookstores are not held liable as republishers of defamation if they have no knowledge of the defamatory contents.[14] This status contrasts with the potential republication liability (1) by publishing companies for statements made in books, (2) by broadcast networks for defamatory broadcasts, and (3) by newspaper publishers for defamation contained in editorials, articles, or ads.

The groundbreaking case of *Cubby v. CompuServe* recognized that ISPs are more like common carriers and should not be liable as republishers when they do not monitor or mediate the communications on their facilities. CompuServe Information Service (CIS) was a component product of CompuServe's ISP service that supplied many special interest bulletin boards, interactive chat rooms, and databases of related information. Derogatory statements about Cubby were initially published by an independent daily newsletter, *Rumorville, USA*. These statements were distributed on one of the CIS services, the *Journalism Forum*, which focuses on the media industry. In shielding CompuServe from republication liability, the court stated:

> *"CompuServe has no more editorial control than does a public library, bookstore or newsstand, and it would be no more feasible for CompuServe to examine every publication it carries for potentially defamatory statements than it would for any other distributor. Technology is rapidly transforming the information industry. A computerized database is the functional equivalent of a more traditional news vendor."*[15]

A key concept in *Cubby v. Compuserve* is whether it would be practical for an ISP to monitor all communications. To the extent an e-mail list, chat room, bulletin board, or Web site is monitored by the ISP or sponsor, there may be republication liability under defamation law or even liability for publishing criminal obscenity.

To deal with this issue, Congress passed the Communications Decency Act (CDA). As noted previously in Chapter 2, ISPs have the benefit of a safe harbor from republisher liability for defamation, obscenity, or infringing materials. However, Congress still sought to encourage ISPs and other technology companies to continue developing methods and software to block and filter offensive or unlawful content. Therefore, §230 of the CDA eliminates ISP liability as a republisher if the ISP makes good-faith action to restrict access or availability of obscene, harassing, or otherwise objectionable content posted by others. The effects of *Cubby* and the CDA are to

---

14. *Smith v. California*, 361 U.S. 147 (1959).
15. 776 F.Supp. 135, 140 (S.D.N.Y. 1991).

make the Internet into an effective new outlet for nonmediated speech. Before the Internet, only the traditional print and broadcast media could effectively reach large segments of the population. The CDA's safe harbor nearly assures that some uncensored outlets will persist.

NEGLIGENCE

Under the law of negligence, all persons and businesses must act responsibly in all their activities. Nearly anyone can be held liable for breach of the duty of care if others are injured as a result. Negligent torts differ from intentional torts because the tortfeasor may be liable for unintentional, careless acts. Negligence is based on fault, not intent. When the carelessness injures others, tort law holds the individual or business liable for the injury.

GENERAL REQUIREMENTS

Four requirements must be proved by a plaintiff in a negligence case. First, the defendant must be shown to owe a duty of care to the plaintiff. Second, it must be proved the defendant breached or did not perform that duty. Third, the plaintiff must link the defendant's breach to the plaintiff's injury as the actual and proximate cause. Fourth, the plaintiff must prove that an injury was suffered and that money damages can be determined as compensation.

Duty of Care

All individuals and businesses must act carefully when others could be affected—that is, when it is foreseeable that a lack of reasonable care could cause injury. Many actions involve a predictable danger of injury. It is not necessary to foresee the precise harm that could occur if the defendant was negligent, only that the failure to exercise reasonable care poses an unreasonable risk of some harm. By contrast, if no risk of harm is foreseen, there is no **duty to use reasonable care**. In such situations, causing an injury to someone would not be negligence. For example, it is reasonable to foresee that driving a car too fast risks harm to other drivers and pedestrians. The duty to use reasonable care requires the driver to guard against such harm. A driver who fails to perform the duty of driving carefully may be committing a negligent tort. Some states apply no-fault laws to motor vehicle accidents, and the injured party need not prove the driver's negligence to be entitled to compensation.

Breach of Duty

The plaintiff must prove that the defendant did not perform the duty of care or is responsible for the nonperformance of that duty. For example, if you have a party in your home or apartment, the law imposes a duty to use reasonable care in maintaining the property and in conducting the party so guests are protected from foreseeable risks. Does a room have loose rugs on which a guest could slip and fall, or loose ceiling tiles that could fall on someone? If the homeowner or apartment tenant does not take precautions with regard to such items of foreseeable danger, the duty of care is not performed; that is, the duty is breached. Thus, nonperformance of the duty of care occurs if a person acts in a careless, reckless, or unreasonable manner. For example, in a case filed against the Los Angeles International Airport,[16] the airport was not liable for the death of a person killed by a bomb left in a public coin-operated locker. The airport was not in a dangerous condition, and the city had taken reasonable steps to guard against terrorism.

The law does not require that a person or a business be an insurer or a guarantor of the absolute safety of others. Negligence is based on a comparison of a person's actions with the standard for the actions expected from the mythical **ordinary, reasonable person**. Sometimes a person or a business acts reasonably yet still causes injury to others. For example, a company that manufactures room heaters uses a process to ensure that they do not overheat and cause fire. If the company has acted reasonably, as compared with the standard expected of manufacturers of similar products, there would be no negligence even if the heater became defective and caused injury to its user. In such a case, the company could not be held liable for negligence, although it might be held liable on some other basis, such as an implied warranty or strict liability.

Proximate Cause

Once the plaintiff has shown that the defendant breached the duty of care, the defendant's act must also be shown to be the proximate cause of the plaintiff's injury. **Proximate cause** is the standard used in negligence cases to establish the reasonability of a causal relationship between the defendant's nonperformance or breach of duty and the plaintiff's injury. Only injuries with a close (proximate) causal connection to the defendant's actions are negligent. These injuries are caused by actions whose consequences are reasonably foreseeable. There is no liability for actions with only a weak or remote link to an injury. For example, it is reasonably foreseeable to expect pedestrian bystanders to be harmed by reckless driving. By contrast, it is probably unforeseeable that the injured pedestrian's best friend would suffer emotional distress from that injury.

Injury

To win a case, plaintiffs must prove they sustained some **injury** that can be compensated for by an award of money damages. Injuries include physical injury, property damage, lost profits, pain and suffering, and many other components that are the consequence of the defendant's negligent act. Expert witnesses are often used to prove and disprove damages. For example, economists testify as to lost profits, orthopedic surgeons as to the diminished capacity of the victim's arms, legs, and hands, and appraisers as to the repair costs of damaged property. The jury considers this testimony in its assessment of a compensatory damage amount.

---

16. *Moncur v. City of Los Angeles Dept. of Air*, 137 Cal. Rptr. 239 (1977).

Negligence Per Se and *Res Ipsa Loquitur*

In two circumstances—negligence per se and *res ipsa loquitur*—the burden of proof on the plaintiff is lessened. **Negligence per se** enables the plaintiff to use the defendant's violation of a criminal statute to prove the defendant was negligent. For example, if a statute imposes criminal penalties if a moving firm does not have certain safety equipment on its trucks, the statute creates a conclusive presumption that the defendant was negligent. Some states allow the presumption to be rebutted by other evidence. This is another important relationship between criminal law and tort law.

Res ipsa loquitur means "the thing speaks for itself." In some situations, circumstantial evidence is used to establish a prima facie case of negligence. Unless the defendant counters this evidence, the doctrine of *res ipsa loquitur* is sufficient to prove negligence. This doctrine is used when the plaintiff cannot know the exact cause of negligence, as in cases involving product liability or negligent building construction. A building will not usually crumble or collapse unless there was some negligence in its design or construction; thus, even though the exact cause of the failure is not known, circumstantial evidence suggests that there was negligence.

DEFENSES TO NEGLIGENCE

There are three basic defenses to negligence claims: contributory negligence, comparative negligence, and assumption of risk.

Contributory Negligence

The defendant may raise **contributory negligence** as a defense when the plaintiff was also somewhat negligent. Even though the defendant may have been negligent, the law prohibits any recovery for the plaintiff. This defense is commonly known as the all-or-nothing rule because the plaintiff wins all if contributory negligence is not proved and nothing if contributory negligence is proved. The harshness of this rule prompted an innovation of comparative fault, the comparative negligence defense.

Comparative Negligence

Most states use comparative negligence rather than contributory negligence as the most common defense in negligence cases. **Comparative negligence** weighs the relative negligence of the plaintiff against the negligence of the defendant. In some states, it does not matter how much negligence is attributable to the plaintiff. Even if the plaintiff can prove that the defendant is only 15% negligent in causing the plaintiff's injuries, the plaintiff (who might be 85% negligent) can still recover damages equal to 15% of the money needed to totally compensate for those injuries.

Consider the following examples. Suppose that a two-car accident occurs in a state using this type of comparative negligence defense. Assume that the plaintiff driving Car 1 is found to be 85% at fault for his own injuries. If $100,000 were needed to totally compensate the plaintiff for his injuries, the plaintiff would be able to recover $15,000 from the defendant driving Car 2, who was 15% at fault. Other states permit the plaintiff to recover damages from the defendant only if the defendant is responsible for at least 50% of the plaintiff's injuries. In these states, the plaintiff in this example above would recover nothing.

Assumption of Risk

The assumption of risk defense is also based on comparative fault. If the plaintiff knew, or should have known, of the risk inherent in a particular situation and voluntarily assumed that risk, the defendant is not responsible for the plaintiff's injuries, even though the defendant was also negligent. A classic example of this defense occurs when a plaintiff is injured while riding in a car with an intoxicated driver. Although the defendant driver is negligent in driving while intoxicated, the plaintiff, who knows the risk of riding with an intoxicated driver, nevertheless voluntarily does so. In such cases, the plaintiff may be denied recovery because of the assumption of that known risk.

Some states using the comparative negligence defense do not use assumption of risk. Under this view, the plaintiff's assumption of risk is a form of negligence that is compared with the defendant's negligence, which effectively merges assumption of risk and comparative negligence into one defense. **Assumption of risk** occurs when a person who knows of a risk nevertheless proceeds in the face of that risk. Contributory or comparative negligence compares the action of the one person with the action of the reasonable person (to determine whether there is any negligence) and of the defendant (to determine the relative negligence of the parties). A person's actions can contribute to causing an injury even if he or she does not know of the risk involved.

STRICT LIABILITY

Strict liability is held against a person who engages in inherently dangerous or **ultrahazardous activity**. There is liability to any injured party, regardless of the actor's intent or fault. Therefore, strict liability is different from intentional torts and negligence because strict liability requires proof of neither intentional wrongdoing nor fault.

GENERAL REQUIREMENTS

The plaintiff's recovery under the strict liability theory is somewhat easier than under the proofs required for either negligence or intentional torts. A strict liability tort occurs if one person does something dangerous and the act injures another person who is within the scope of risk. The determination of whether an activity is ultrahazardous is the most important question in strict liability cases. The precedents can be summarized, although not exhaustively, in the following list: the dusting of crops, the keeping of wild and vicious animals, and the use of explosives and dangerous chemicals. On the other hand, such activities as mining coal, driving automobiles, and keeping gasoline in service station tanks are not ultrahazardous.

Strict liability is also generally applicable to product liability cases. A product is defective if the product is unreasonably dangerous and the danger is not readily apparent to the buyer. Typical strict liability cases involve such products as foods and drinks, playground equipment, consumer appliances, and automobiles. Product liability may also rest on the negligence theory or warranty liability under contract.

DEFENSES TO STRICT LIABILITY

Because proof of negligence is not required in strict liability cases, the defenses of contributory or comparative negligence are not available. However, most states recognize the assumption of risk and misuse defenses. **Misuse** is a form of assumption of risk based on improper product use. For example, a misuse might exist if the injured plaintiff used inside a house an insecticide labeled for only outdoor use. Similarly, if a cigarette package warns users of a specific risk such as lung cancer, the manufacturer is generally not liable for those injuries.

POLICY UNDERLYING STRICT LIABILITY

Society tolerates some ultrahazardous activities that have sufficient social value. Compensation for a victim is more likely in strict liability cases than in negligence cases. Strict liability allows the defendant to spread the costs of the injury among many users, enabling society to receive the benefits of the ultrahazardous activity while sharing the cost of compensating the injured party. For example, society benefits when the mining and road-building industries use explosives. Strict liability balances the danger with society's needs as long as the costs of compensation are shared by society.

TORT REFORM

Because there are so many product liability cases and the ever-increasing jury awards are widely publicized, strong pressures have built to reform tort and product liability laws. Even the U.S. Congress has repeatedly considered imposing national tort reform, preempting this area of traditional states' rights. Existing federal reforms extend to securities litigation, accountants' malpractice liability, civil aviation, and airline disaster litigation. State reforms have passed in many states for strict product liability and other torts such as negligence, warranty, and misrepresentation. The 1980s were a period of dramatic growth in litigation. Tort law expanded as the courts recognized more extensive duties. Juries became more sympathetic to victims of accidents, product failures, and unsafe conditions, applying the deep pocket theory to hold accountable corporate defendants that were perceived to have extensive financial resources. Eventually, insurers claimed they were unable to accurately predict the outcome of tort litigation, and insurance premiums skyrocketed. Some types of insurance became unavailable. Insurers and potential corporate defendants called for tort reform in the media, through various legislatures, and in the courts.

COMPONENTS OF TORT REFORM

Proponents of tort reform claim that reforms create a fair, predictable, and equitable fault system while reducing the costs of litigation. They assert that a tort crisis has increased the cost of goods and services, stifled innovation in new products, delayed the introduction of new drugs, and postponed the sharing of benefits in many research breakthroughs. Tort reforms enacted in some states include changes in the allocation of liability among several defendants, limits on certain types of damages, restriction of double recoveries by plaintiffs, reduction of the contingency fee incentives of plaintiff attorneys, sanctions against frivolous suits, and structured settlements made in periodic damage payments over several years. Astute managers must closely monitor reform legislation and judicial decisions.

Joint and Several Liability

Joint and several liability requires the complete satisfaction (full payment) of a plaintiff's damage award from any or all of the responsible defendants, regardless of the degree of fault of any single defendant. In some cases, a particular defendant may be required to pay more than its share of the damage award. For example, a deep pocket insurer of a local retailer might have to pay the whole judgment if the manufacturer is **judgment-proof**—that is, uninsured or insolvent.

Joint and several liability provides an incentive for plaintiffs to include deep pocket entities as named defendants. Even when they are only slightly at fault, the whole compensatory and punitive amount might fall on a defendant with sufficient financial resources. For example, drivers injured in traffic accidents often sue the state as well as the other driver because the state is responsible for the safety of road conditions. If the other driver is at fault but has insufficient insurance to satisfy the plaintiff's damages, the state's deep pocket may be held liable for the remainder. Most proposals to reform joint and several liability would impose **proportionate liability** among defendants. This system is similar to comparative negligence because it would require the jury (judge, if no jury is used) to assign percentage proportions of fault between defendants and limit their financial exposure to their proportionate amount.

Damage Caps

Tort reform efforts usually attempt to significantly limit or eliminate such **noneconomic damages** as (1) pain and suffering, (2) loss of consortium with a spouse, (3) emotional distress, (4) embarrassment, and (5) punitive damages. For example, some states have imposed specific dollar-amount ceilings for noneconomic damages in all negligence cases. Other states have such ceilings for only specific types of suit, most notably medical malpractice, product liability cases, or cases in which the state is a defendant (hazardous road conditions). Still other states require "clear and convincing evidence" before allowing noneconomic damages to exceed the ceilings.

Punitive Damages

There is a widespread perception that juries are awarding increasingly larger punitive damage awards. **Punitive damages** are an additional component of damages above and beyond compensatory damages. Compensatory damages reimburse the plaintiff for losses actually suffered. Advocates of retaining punitive damages argue they deter the adverse side effects of business activities. Their argument is that without the threat of severe penalties, business managers have little incentive to avoid endangering the public with harmful products, manufacturing processes, or business practices. Additionally, managers are personally too well insulated from lawsuit pressures; that is, they seldom directly bear the wealth effects of their decisions because the firm pays. Finally, they argue that highly visible punitive awards send signals to managers that convince them to act more carefully and consider the impact of their decisions on others.

Opponents of punitive damages argue that they adversely affect companies. Punitives damages can be unpredictable and counterproductive for the economy. For example, a multimillion-dollar punitive award could wipe out a company's profitability for several years, force it to drop useful products, slow its innovation, force the closing of facilities, require layoffs, or even drive the company into bankruptcy.

Several comprehensive empirical studies of damage awards contest the exaggerated claims of some tort reformers. Critics of the tort reform movement charge that stories about punitive damages are distorted to advocate abrupt legislative changes. Researchers find that most large damage awards (1) were made in asbestos cases, (2) have declined since 1986, (3) are made in state courts, (4) predominate in the South, (5) are usually based on the failure to warn consumers of known defects, and (6) have plaintiffs who are victims of catastrophic injuries.[17] Other studies confirm that few of the huge damage awards publicized are ever paid out in full. Although most large punitive awards receive widespread news coverage, they are eventually reduced after settlement or on appeal through the legal device of **remittitur.** Many newsworthy awards are never paid out, and many tort reformers fail to acknowledge these facts.

Recent challenges to punitive damages allege that they violate two fundamental constitutional rights: (1) Punitives allegedly constitute excessive fines prohibited by the Eighth Amendment, and (2) unrestrained jury discretion to assess punitives violates the defendant's Fourteenth Amendment due process rights. In *Browning-Ferris Indus. v. Kelco Disposal*,[18] the Supreme Court rejected the Eighth Amendment argument. A regional BFI executive instructed the local BFI office to cut prices and drive Kelco, a competing waste collector, out of business. The Supreme Court reaffirmed the jury's award to Kelco of $51,146 in compensatory damages and $6 million in punitive damages in Kelco's monopolization suit. The Eighth Amendment was intended to protect convicted defendants from excessive punishment by government, not from civil actions between private parties.

In *Pacific Mutual Life Ins. Co. v. Halsip*,[19] an insurance company was held liable for its agent's misappropriation of health and life insurance premiums. The cover-

---

17. Michael Rustad, *Demystifying Punitive Damages in Product Liability Cases: A Survey of a Quarter Century of Trial Verdicts* (Washington, D.C., Roscoe Pound Foundation, 1991).
18. 492 U.S. 257 (1989).
19. 499 U.S. 1 (1991).

age lapsed when the agent failed to remit premiums deducted from the insured's paychecks. The agent concealed cancellation notices sent out by the insurance companies. A jury verdict held the insurer vicariously liable under *respondeat superior*. Halsip was awarded $1,040,000, of which nearly $840,000 was punitive damages. In upholding the Alabama punitive damage computation procedure, the U.S. Supreme Court held that the common law method for assessing punitive damages is not so inherently unfair as to deny due process and be per se unconstitutional. The Alabama procedure to review punitive damages considered the following factors: (1) the relationship between the punitive damages award, the harm likely to result from the defendant's conduct, and the harm that actually occurred; (2) the degree of responsibility of the defendant's conduct, the duration of that conduct, the defendant's awareness, any concealment, and the existence and frequency of similar past conduct; (3) the profitability of the wrongful conduct and the desirability having the defendant sustain a loss; (4) the "financial position" of the defendant; (5) all the costs of litigation; and (6) mitigation from the imposition of criminal sanctions or other civil awards against the defendant for the same conduct.

Courts after *Halsip* are in conflict. Many are narrowing punitives, some invalidate limits on damage awards, and others continue awarding punitives without any arbitrary dollar limitation. In the much publicized decision of *BMW of North America v. Gore*,[20] a punitive award of $2 million was reversed when weighed against the $4,000 representing compensatory damages for the decreased value of a new BMW automobile. The BMW distributor had repaired a paint scratch that occurred during shipment for a cost of about $600. In 2001, the punitive award of $5 billion was reduced in the infamous case about the *Exxon Valdez* oil tanker spill off the Alaska coast. The appeals court held that the punitives were excessive in relation to the $287 million in compensatory damages. The trial court was ordered to lower the amount of punitives.[21]

Punitives are also available in several state and federal regulatory programs, such as treble damages in antitrust and securities litigation and in employment discrimination cases, as discussed elsewhere in this handbook. In 2001, a federal appeals court held that there is no prerequisite for compensatory damages for the award of punitives in hostile work environment discrimination cases under the federal civil rights law.[22]

---

20. 517 U.S. 559 (1996).
21. In re *Exxon Valdez*, No. 99-35898 (9th Cir., 2001).
22. *Cush-Crawford v. Adchem Corp.*, 271 F.2d 352 (No. 00-7617, 2001).

CHAPTER 4
COPYRIGHTS

Business law in the twentieth century largely addressed tangible assets (e.g., product, plant, equipment, real estate) as the predominant form of property. However, in the twenty-first century, intangible property rights, like the expression protected by copyright law, are becoming the central theme. As noted in the discussion of Constitutional law in Chapter 2, expression is protected under the First Amendment because it is essential to democracy and to commerce. Expression describes the research results that specify inventions, which makes expression both the object and the medium of most creativity. Now consider the human need and passion for entertainment, news, and personal interaction. It is easy to see how expression contains information that lies at the heart of all communications and commerce.

Expression is the most pervasive of all forms of intellectual property (IP). Patents and trade secrets protect ideas but are described in text and drawings. Some creative designs can be protected as design patents, and others function as commercial symbols protectable as trademarks. Even with all these alternative forms of IP, none of them is possible without expression, making copyright as the most pervasive form of IP. This point is particularly important to e-commerce, given that nearly everything on the Internet is expression.

IP is intangible property that suffers greatly when compared with tangible property. Owners must invest often large amounts to invent, create, or acquire IP assets, and IP is much more easily misappropriated than is tangible property. Therefore, it is good that government fosters creativity and innovation by establishing special forms of property rights for IP: copyrights, patents, trade secrets, and trademarks. Technologies such as encryption can also play important roles in preventing misappropriation. Copyrighted expression is particularly vulnerable, and several emerging technologies intensify these risks.

Digital copying and distribution has great potential to weaken traditional business models in the software, music, and video industries. In the 1990s, these industries successfully lobbied for new copyright protection laws. Given the public attention over the modern subject matter of copyright (digital entertainment, Internet communication, creative Web sites), copyright law is ascending to a central role in e-commerce and in cyberspace. This chapter discusses how copyright law protects traditional forms of expression and how expression is adapting to digital forms.

OVERVIEW OF COPYRIGHTS

The law of **copyright** protects original **works of authorship** once they are fixed in a tangible medium. Initial copyright protection arises when an author or creator writes, saves, records, or otherwise forms expression in a physical process. The resulting product is called a **work**. For example, literature, music, or software is written on paper or input into a computer. Music, drama, or dance is also recorded in a medium. For example, images are created, drawn, formed, recorded, or captured as photographs, architectural plans, sculpture, maps, or other visual works. Authors and creators of copyrighted works must often transfer some or all of their rights to others who are more skilled, better connected, or better financed to effectively exploit the work.

Copyright law gives the creator or author several important exclusive rights. These rights are often called a "bundle of rights" because they represent different interests in the work. They include the right to **reproduce** (make copies), **distribute** (sell copies), make **derivative works** (adapt), perform or display (exhibit to the public), make **digital transmissions**, and transfer rights by license or assignment. It is an unlawful infringement when other people use the copyrighted work in these ways but are unauthorized to do so. **Infringement** entitles the owner to legal remedies (compensation). Purchasers of a physical embodiment of the copyrighted work, such as a book, CD, or video, may resell these. This very important right for purchasers is called the **first sale doctrine**. A few infringements are excused under the **fair use** exception. For example, it may be a fair use to use another's work for teaching, scholarship, or research or to parody, criticize, or comment, such as in news reporting. Fair use is one of the most contentious copyright issues today because digital technologies make copying easier.

Copyrights last for a very long time. The **copyright term** has been lengthened for works created after 1978 to more than 70 years in some instances and up to 120 years for some works. The owner's rights under copyright law become stronger when the work is registered and deposited with the Copyright Office of the Library of Congress, although doing so is not always necessary. Similarly, it is no longer mandatory to place a copyright notice on the work, although doing so is still advisable. These matters are detailed throughout this chapter.

THE EVOLVING HERITAGE OF COPYRIGHT

The U.S. Constitution gives Congress the power to make IP laws for copyrights and patents. Before passage of the 1976 Copyright Act, the state common law provided an alternate protection scheme. However, Congress has made the federal law of copyrights exclusive, so the states may no longer provide rights or remedies covering copyrightable subject matter. Much of the ongoing and probable future struggle over copyrights will explore how much the public may use expression protected by copyright. This conflict is really over the **public domain**. A majority of the copyright litigation and regulation concerns how soon, how much, and how others may use expressive works.

Contemporary copyright law had its beginnings in England with Parliament's passage of the **Statute of Anne** in 1710. By the late eighteenth century, the U.S. Constitution had recognized the unique role government plays in providing copyright as an incentive to creativity. Various copyright laws have been passed since that first U.S. statute in 1790. The 1909 and 1976 U.S. copyright laws are the most important. Today, copyright law is again in transition. Most of the world's copyright laws still reflect traditional conceptions of the range of expression, turn-of-the-twentieth-century technologies, and the traditional business models used to exploit copyrighted works. These laws were designed mainly for literary, musical, and artistic expressions and not for functional or coded methods like software or encryption.

Radical changes in technology have pushed traditional copyright concepts to the limit, requiring Congress, regulators, and the courts to improvise as they adapt copyright law to new technologies. Some well-financed interests such as publishing and media conglomerates have been extraordinarily successful in getting legislation passed that favors their interests. Many critics argue these recent law revisions have unduly benefited copyright owners at the expense of consumers, users, and the public domain. They argue that the traditional concepts such as "ideas are not copyrightable, only the expression of ideas is protected under copyright," fair use, and the first sale doctrine are being whittled away. Other nations are also a source of pressure to change copyright law.

The impact of international treaties and domestic laws with an effect on international copyright is significant, as discussed throughout this chapter. A key copyright treaty, the **Berne Convention**, has become the focal point of the different conceptions of expression from various nations and cultures. Other important laws and treaties include the U.S. Tariff Act, the Universal Copyright Convention, the "TRIPS" provisions of the World Trade Organization (WTO), and the regional trade agreements covering the European Union and North America. The United States is often a bellwether in first identifying new copyright issues and has exerted leadership in providing compromise to accommodate the opposing factions of creators and owners versus users and consumers. Nevertheless, some observers charge that the United States fails to protect some rights adequately (e.g., moral rights) and overprotects others (e.g., copyright duration). Some of the more significant international copyright laws and treaties are summarized in Exhibit 4.1.

Exhibit 4.1 Major International Copyright Treaties and Laws

International Agreement, Treaty, or Law	Major Participants and Successes	Major Provisions
Tariff Act §337	U.S.	Authorizes International Trade Commission (ITC) hearings; ITC may issue *exclusion order* directing U.S. Customs Service to block imports of infringing products
Berne Convention	U.S. is among 79 nations; now the leading treaty	Requires national treatment; no formalities for acquisition of copyright rights; strong moral rights
Universal Copyright Convention	Initially favored by U.S. as preferred alternative to Berne	Requires national treatment; substantive provisions: notice, registration
WTO trade-related intellectual property (TRIPS)	Many nations; most successful of all international IP treaties	Requires compliance with Berne, except for moral rights, software, and data compilation protections; permits copyright owner to prohibit rental
EU Treaty of Rome	19 EU "member states"	Various EU directives requiring consistent and harmonized national laws
North America Free Agreement (NAFTA)	Canada, Mexico, and U.S.; some slow progress	Calls for harmonization and effective trade enforcement of national laws

COPYRIGHTABLE SUBJECT MATTER

The Copyright Act defines the types of expression that may be protected.

> **Copyrightable Subject Matter**
> original works of authorship fixed in any tangible medium of expression, now known or later developed, from which they can be perceived, reproduced, or otherwise communicated, either directly or with the aid of a machine or device.[1]

There are several elements to copyrightability. First, the work must be **original**; that is, it is not copied but created independently by the author. This standard is not as rigorous as the novelty standard required under patent law. Further, litigation is not a good forum to assess artistic merit.[2] Nevertheless, the work must have at least

---

1. 17 U.S.C. §102(a) (2000).
2. *Bleistein v. Donaldson Lithographing Co.*, 188 U.S. 239 (1903).

a minimum level of creativity or authorial ingenuity. Second, the expression must be **fixed in a tangible medium of expression**, which requires a stable, permanent, and physical rendering either in a copy or in a phonorecord. The term **phonorecord** is a catchall for recording media; it includes most recordings of sound, video, or software in various media: vinyl, tape, disk.

Copyright does not protect oral renditions or performances unless there is recording or documentation of the original. However, **ephemeral copies** of software or other works loaded into a computer's RAM are potentially infringing copies, even though they disappear when the computer is turned off or moves on to do another activity.[3] Live performances have been problematic but now may be fixed if they are simultaneously broadcast. Third, the work must be perceivable by humans either directly or indirectly. **Direct perception** occurs while a person reads a book or views a photo, painting, or sculpture. **Indirect perception** requires the aid of a machine or device, such as listening to an audio CD or watching a DVD movie played on a machine. Video games in software or on a cartridge are fixed, even though the user's progress through the game can change the images actually viewed from all those possible in the game's memory.

CLASSIFICATION OF WORKS OF AUTHORSHIP

What types of works are copyrightable? The Copyright Act lists eight types of works of authorship permitted copyright protection: (1) literary works, (2) musical works (including accompanying words), (3) dramatic works (including accompanying music), (4) pantomimes and choreography, (5) pictorial, graphic, and sculptural works, (6) motion pictures and other audiovisual (A/V) works, (7) sound recordings, and (8) architectural works. These categories can be complex because some works may not fit neatly in just one category. Categorization can be important because some of the special rights discussed in the next section are not available for all types of works. The classification of copyrightable works is summarized in Exhibit 4.2.

Literary works are the most basic and include expressions in words or numbers. Novels, nonfiction books, databases, and poetry are all literary works. There was significant litigation about the copyrightability of computer software until Congress implemented the recommendations of the National Commission of New Technological Uses of Copyrighted Works (CONTU) with passage of the **Computer Software Copyright Act** in 1980. Software is now classified as literary work when composed of "a set of statements or instructions to be used directly or indirectly in a computer in order to bring about a certain result." It includes source code written by either programmers or another computer. Software also includes object code that runs on computers, as well as operating systems and applications programs.[4]

Musical works include the words and tune as fixed in sheet music, sound recordings, and arrangements but arbitrarily do not include the soundtrack to a motion

---

3. *MAI Systems Corp. v. Peak Computer Inc.*, 991 F.2d 511 (9th Cir., 1993).
4. *Apple Computer Inc. v. Franklin Computer Corp.*, 714 F.2d 1240 (3d Cir., 1983), *cert.denied* 464 U.S. 1033 (1984).

Exhibit 4.2 Types of Copyrightable Works

Works of Authorship	Definition	Examples
Literary	Expressions in words or numbers	Novels, nonfiction books, databases, poetry, software
Musical	Composition: tune, melody, parts, and words but not if in motion picture or other A/V soundtrack	Sheet music, arrangements
Dramatic	Directions guiding portrayal of story in performance using dialogue or acting; includes associated music	Script with accompanying sheet music
Pantomime, choreography	Dance movements and patterns (successive static and kinetic body movements) following rhythmic relationships	Video, film, dance notation
Pictorial, graphic, sculpture	Two- and three-dimensional works of fine, graphic, and applied art; must be physically or conceptually severable from functional aspects	Photographs, maps, paintings, 3D sculptures, pottery, textiles, macramé, jewelry, furniture, computer graphics, still cartoon and characters, prints, art reproductions, maps, globes, charts, technical drawings, diagrams, models, games
Motion picture, audiovisual	Series of related images shown by machine, accompanied by sounds	Disks or tapes shown by projector or TV
Sound recordings	Series of musical, spoken, or other sounds	Phonorecords (tape, disks)
Architectural	Building design, architectural plans, or drawings, including overall form, arrangement, and composition of spaces and design elements	Plans, blueprints, drawings, models, structures built after 1990

picture or other types of A/V work. Sound recordings were not protected until after the passage of the **Sound Recording Act** in 1971. **Sound recordings** capture the performance of a music, literary, or dramatic work by fixing it as a series of musical, spoken, or other sounds regardless of the medium: disks, tapes, or phonorecords. There is an important distinction between the composition and the sound recording: The owner of the composition can prevent performances of the composition, but the sound recording owner cannot. This point is made in Chapter 11 where the compulsory license is discussed. No federal copyright provides protection for sound recordings made before 1972.

The Copyright Office defines **dramatic works** as directions guiding the portrayal of a story in a performance by use of dialogue or acting. **Pantomimes** and **choreographic works** are dance movements and patterns, including both successive static and kinetic body movements that follow rhythmic relationships. They are typically fixed in video or film but can be recorded in notation form. **A/V** and **motion picture** works are series of related images shown by machine (projector, TV) and are accompanied by sounds. The music accompanying A/V works is protectable as part of the A/V work and not separately as a sound recording.

Pictorial, graphic, and sculptural works include two- and three-dimensional works of fine, graphic, or applied art. This classification includes photographs, prints, art reproductions, paintings, maps, three-dimensional sculptures, pottery, jewelry, globes, furniture, textiles, charts, technical drawings, computer graphics, diagrams, models, still cartoons, characters, and other forms. Artistic items that have some physical function have always raised concerns about the public domain. There is continuing concern that copyright protection of a particular artistic design might preempt similar useful objects. When copyright protection is so extensive that it covers the functional aspects of a work, other artists could be prevented from designing artistically different but functionally similar objects. For example, outdoor lighting fixtures were held not copyrightable unless the artistic aspects deserving copyright protection (artistic lampshade) could be separated physically from the functional aspects (fixture and mounting bracket). The **severability rule** requires that functional aspects must remain in the public domain.[5]

Since passage of the **Architectural Works Protection Act** in 1990, copyright protection now extends to architectural plans, drawings, blueprints, and models. The 1990 act protects the design of a building, architectural plans, and drawings, including the overall form, arrangement, and composition of spaces and design elements. Protection does not cover standard features but does cover both habitable (e.g., houses, office buildings) and uninhabitable structures (e.g., bridges, walkways). The severability rule discussed previously applies to buildings already standing before the act's passage; that is, functional aspects are in the public domain. However, for buildings constructed after the act's 1990 passage, copyright protection extends to the whole design.

NONCOPYRIGHTABLE SUBJECT MATTER

Ideas are not copyrightable; only the expression of ideas is protected under copyright. This statement is so often quoted because it underlies much of the controversy about infringement, it defines the public domain, and it also separates fair use from infringement. The Copyright Act specifically excludes the following from copyrightability: ideas, procedures, processes, systems, methods of operation, concepts, principles, and discoveries. This rule makes the public domain richer, enabling other creators to build upon the public domain as new expression reveals new ideas. Creators can maintain control over ideas only if they qualify as patentable or remain concealed as trade secrets.

This rule is the **idea-expression dichotomy**. It was clarified in *Baker v. Selden*, the original case in which copyright protection was denied to a system of bookkeeping, essentially because bookkeeping is a functional process.[6] Often the essential inquiry in distinguishing ideas from expression is whether another person would be prevented

---

5. *Esquire, Inc. v. Ringer*, 591 F.2d 796 (D.C.Cir., 1978).
6. 101 U.S. 99 (1879).

from using the idea unless they also used some form of the expression. As discussed in Chapter 5, sweat of the brow is not protectable under copyright; that is, when facts, data, or their interpretations are produced by hard work (the "sweat"), the result is ideas, not expression. Ideas standing alone are not copyrightable subject matter.

> **Idea versus Expression Dichotomy**
> Ideas are not copyrightable; only the expression of ideas is protected under copyright.

Generally, documents produced by the U.S. government are not copyrightable. This rule increases the public domain, particularly for public affairs. Citizens as a group own government documents because they were produced at taxpayer expense and are intended to benefit the public. Most federal and many state government documents are immediately placed in the public domain. In the United States, no copyright is possible for the reports, opinions, guidance, or other works prepared by government employees performing their government duties. This rule makes it difficult for the U.S. government to protect software produced by government agencies. However, federal agencies may purchase, license, and own software produced by others. Although there is no explicit copyright exclusion for state government works, nevertheless, the laws, regulations, and court decisions contained in many state documents are generally in the public domain. Some nations, such as the United Kingdom, claim proprietary interest in many of their government documents.

THE BUNDLE OF EXCLUSIVE RIGHTS

Copyright law grants several different rights to the author, creator, or owner of the work. These rights essentially define what the copyright owner can do with the copyrighted work and what rights the owner can license or assign to others. These rights are actually a **bundle of exclusive rights**, called **statutory rights**. They include the right to reproduce, make derivative works, distribute, perform or display, license and/or assign, and the newest right of digital transmission. The importance of these rights varies considerably and depends on the type of work and on the business models used in the particular industry involved. The exclusive rights sometimes overlap and can be combined to fully exploit the copyright. Exploitation is often best done by others, such as publishers or studios. The media industry commonly requires authors to assign their interests in their work before they will market the work. Copyright ownership and the licensing or assignment of some or all of the exclusive rights in the bundle are complex matters introduced in Chapter 11 as forms of technology transfer contracting.

REPRODUCTION

The most basic right under copyright is to **reproduce**—that is, to fix the work in a tangible and fairly permanent medium. Copying can also be done without fixation, such as when performed or displayed. The owner typically makes copies by the most efficient production process available: high-speed printing presses for printed materials, high-speed presses for vinyl phonorecords, high-efficiency burning of optical media (CDs), and deliberate, authorized downloads. Unauthorized copying is the most typical form of infringement, whether for personal use or for further distribution or sale. It does not matter that the copier is unaware that the work is protected under copyright. Unauthorized copies are often made by low-efficiency, consumer-oriented copying technologies such as photocopies, tapes, scans, CD burners, and PCs. Of course, there have been cases of large-scale pirating of entertainment products and software in efficient, modern factories. Many such Asian operations have been the focus of international trade negotiations and have held up the grant of "most favored nations" status with the United States as a trading partner.

Unauthorized copying is a persistent and emotion-driven problem. Purchasers of copyrighted works believe they should have the right to make copies and use the work in any way they please. By stark contrast, copyright owners repeatedly use complex technicalities of copyright law to inhibit owners from freely using their works in ways made possible by new technologies. This tension is not easily resolved and has repeatedly resulted in compromise legislation that preserves some aspects of copyright owners' existing business models but permits the emergence of new technologies for copying, performance, and distribution. Nearly perfect digital copying poses a huge threat to the entertainment industry if endless copies are made from legitimately acquired originals and legitimate sales of new copies are prevented that would have otherwise occurred.

The right of purchasers to make tapes from vinyl records, off-the-air broadcasts, or CDs for home use was an unsettled question until the 1992 passage of the **Audio Home Recording Act** (AHRA). Negotiations among the powerful record and electronics industries were triggered by the entertainment industry's fear that digital audio tape (DAT) would lead to widespread illegal copying. The Copyright Office now refers to DAT and other digital recording technologies as **digital audio recording technology** (**DART**). The AHRA requires that **digital audio recording devices** be equipped with copy protection technologies, called **serial copy management systems** (**SCMS**), that prevent making copies from copies. Copies from originals are not prevented by the law. It is ironic that the infringement threat of DAT never really materialized but was reborn in the late 1990s as MP3 and CD burner technologies proliferated.

A compulsory royalty must be paid from the sales proceeds of both digital audio recording devices and blank digital recording media. These proceeds are pooled for distribution to copyright owners and artists by the Register of Copyrights of the Library of Congress. Purchasers may not be sued for infringement if they make noncommercial home copies. There is a similar exception for software purchasers but not for licensees to make backup copies of their software. Some software vendors nevertheless authorize licensees to make limited backup copies.

Are computer-based music-recording devices exempt from restrictions on the use of digital sound recording devices? *RIAA v. Diamond*

ONLINE

Recording Industry of America (RIAA)
http://www.riaa.org

Multimedia weakened enforcement rights of digital music rights owners.[7] It may also have contributed to the migration of consumer listening from a preference for traditional hi-fi quality audio equipment using phonorecords, CDs, and tapes to portable and computer-based listening methods.

DERIVATIVE WORKS

A copyright owner has the exclusive right to base further works on the original by adapting or changing the original work into an abridgment, newer version or translation that caters to another market or is fixed in another medium. Derivative works are more than copying; they arise when editorial changes are made to a preexisting work, annotations or elaborations are added, or detail is removed to condense the original. For example, a book might be abridged, transformed into a screenplay for a motion picture, or rewritten into a stage play. Musical compositions may be arranged differently or interpreted differently by other musicians during a performance. A dramatization might change a literary work.

Derivative works usually add enough original, new expression to be considered an authorial work in and of themselves. The right to make a derivative work belongs to the copyright owner, although this right can be licensed or assigned to others. The digital practice of **morphing** usually results in a derivative work. For example, Web designers who base their Web site on another's Web site by adding, subtracting, or modifying the original could be guilty of infringing on the original owner's exclusive right to make derivative works.

DISTRIBUTION

Many of the exclusive rights of copyright owners would be nearly worthless unless copies or phonorecords could be sold, rented, leased, or otherwise transferred to paying customers. Publication was required under prior law before the author or owner could have rights under federal copyright law. **Distribution** is a form of publication. For example, it would infringe the distribution right if pirated copies of musical recordings were sold by street vendors. The unauthorized posting, downloading, uploading to bulletin boards, and forwarding of e-mail or its attachments are infringements on the distribution right. Ignorance is no excuse for this type of infringement.

First Sale Doctrine

The distribution right is limited by the first sale doctrine. This rule allows the buyer to resell, give, lend, or even destroy the work after the first sale. Without this limitation, copyright owners could prevent a used market from developing in copyrighted products. The record and software industries were successful in lobbying Congress to prohibit commercial rentals of music in 1984 and software in 1990. This first wave of potential widespread piracy triggered industry fears of lost profits. A resale royalty

---

7. 180 F.3d 1072 (9th Cir., 1999).

exists in Europe that requires payment of a royalty from the proceeds of resales after the first sale. Imagine if such a right were to become politically and practically feasible in the United States. Software companies and the entertainment media might be willing to relax their insistence on copy protection or soften their resistance to P2P file-sharing techniques such as Napster if there were a reliable method to collect royalties on sales of used copies.

PERFORMANCE AND DISPLAY

Performance and display are similar in that the copyrighted work is viewed by the public, whether for an admission fee or for free. **Performance** is the more active method used to recite, render, play, dance, or act the work directly or with a device or process such as a projector or public address system. For example, an orchestra performs when the live rendition is broadcast, and another performance occurs if a videotape of the live broadcast is rebroadcast. Among the several limitations on this right is that it applies only to public performances. Individuals may sing in the shower or play their CDs and DVDs in private. Of course, most consumers expect nothing less when entertainment products are purchased.

Public performance occurs in public places, where there are a substantial number of persons outside a normal circle of friends and family. There is no precise guidance on what constitutes a substantial number of outsiders, although it would approach substantiality as the audience becomes larger and the number of outsiders increases. Probably routine meetings of business associates is not substantial. The owner can also control transmission, such as by radio, TV, or Webcast, when this results in a public performance. Other details of music licensing are discussed in Chapter 11.

The right to display was traditionally a right to more passive activity. **Display** of a work entitles the copyright owner to show a copy directly or by mechanical means such as projection of film or slides or on TV. An exception permits the purchaser of a copy of the work to exhibit or project up to one image at a time if the viewers are physically present where the copy is located. The display right does not apply to sound recordings or architectural works.

DIGITAL TRANSMISSION RIGHT

The **Digital Performance Right in Sound Recordings Act** was passed in 1995 to manage rights and uses when digital sound recordings are transmitted. It prohibits unlicensed digital transmissions and creates a compulsory license similar to the mechanical license discussed in Chapter 11. This act requires copyright owners to license digital transmissions of their works when these are made in interactive, on-demand specific requests to order particular types of music or particular titles. For example, XM Satellite Radio is a subscription automobile music service with a hundred different channels, mostly of various music styles or talk programming. Such services may someday have the capacity to broadcast precisely the consumer's particular selection on demand. Other visions of such services could "Webcast" music to a customer's PC on demand. Digital transmissions are a hybrid of distribution and performance. Traditional analog radio broadcasts and existing music subscription services like Muzak seems similar but are not affected.

Consider how digital transmission technologies could change the record companies' current business model. If they can devise effective security technologies to prevent customers from repetitiously replaying these sound recordings, there would be little need to distribute physical copies of music through record stores. Further, record companies could charge fees every time the music is played. The lack of physical copies of new music would give record companies complete control over listening and user fees. If consumers ever accept this "pay-per-use" model, similar revenue models could then spread to computer software and become even more prevalent than pay-per-view video is currently. License fees for digital sound transmissions such as these are negotiated.

Disputes about many forms of licensing are settled through arbitration held by **Copyright Arbitration Royalty Panels (CARP)**. These panels are essentially royalty rate-making tribunals for several licensing schemes, including cable TV, digital audio recording technologies (DAT), digital phonorecord deliveries, and satellite broadcasts. Loopholes in the law were addressed by the Digital Millennium Copyright Act. For example, interactive services that supply consumers with durable copies, rather than simply supplying one-time broadcasts, must negotiate royalties directly with copyright owners or perhaps through performing rights societies discussed in Chapter 11. The bundle of exclusive rights under copyright are summarized in Exhibit 4.3.

ONLINE

Copyright Arbitration
Royalty Panels (CARP)
**http://www.loc.gov/
copyright/carp/**

DIGITAL MILLENNIUM COPYRIGHT ACT (DMCA)

In 1997, the United States signed two international copyright treaties negotiated in the **World Intellectual Property Organization (WIPO)**. The two WIPO treaties obligate all signatory nations to pass legislation implementing provisions of two treaties.[8] One result is the **Digital Millennium Copyright Act (DMCA)**, which creates civil and criminal prohibitions against tampering with copy protection schemes or tampering with the billing data that may accompany a digital copy of the work. The DMCA does not add a new exclusive right to the bundle held by copyright owners. Indeed, the DMCA is not well integrated into existing copyright law because it prohibits *access* to a work rather than *use* of a work. Use is the traditional focus taken by infringement law. As a result, some commentators argue the DMCA may eventually make it unlawful to make a fair use of copyrighted material, as discussed in a later section.[9] At this writing, bills may be introduced in Congress to change this difficulty.

---

8. The two treaties are the WIPO Copyright Treaty and the WIPO Performances and Phonograms Treaty. They were originally adopted by WIPO in 1996, signed by the United States in 1997, and implemented by the DMCA in 1998.
9. See, e.g., Julie E. Cohen, *Lochner* in Cyberspace: The New Economic Orthodoxy of Rights Management, *Michigan Law Review* 97 (1998), 462.

Exhibit 4.3 Comparison of Rights in the Copyright Bundle

Statutory Right	Definition	Examples
Reproduction	Fix the work in a tangible and fairly permanent medium	Make copies using tapes, photocopiers, computer disks
Derivative work	Adapt or change original work for another market or medium, using editorial changes, adding annotations or elaborations, and/or removing detail	Screenplay made from book, new musical arrangement, abridgment or translation of literary work, morphing digital work
Distribution	Initial public transfer of copyright work through sale, rental, lease, or other transfer; limited by first sale doctrine	Retail sale, rental, or lease of copies or phonorecords (not wholesale); copy shelved at public library; downloading
Performance and display	Performance: public viewing or other sensory reception (touch, see, hear) directly or using device or process; public includes substantial number of persons outside a normal circle of friends and family Display: show copy directly or by mechanical means	Recite, render, play, dance, or act the work; live orchestral performance; videotape rebroadcast; projection of film or slides or on TV
Digital transmission	Digital broadcast of sound recordings, on demand	Satellite transmission or Webcast of listener's selections
License or assignment (discussed in Chapter 11)	License: temporary, revocable transfer of right to use work Assignment: permanent and irrevocable transfer of element(s) of bundle	Most agreements for use of software Author's transfer of a work to publisher in exchange for publication, marketing, and royalties

The DMCA applies to a variety of digital works, including sound recordings, A/V works, software, and literary works. Four of the DMCA's major provisions are discussed here: (1) anticircumvention rules, (2) anticircumvention exceptions, (3) copyright management information, and (4) the safe harbor for ISPs. Discussion of the DMCA's civil and criminal penalties and on its impact on fair use follows.

ANTICIRCUMVENTION

Owners of copyrighted works have always relied on standard technologies to inhibit infringement of their rights. Over the years, control over choke points in the creation, production, distribution, or performance of works has been reasonably effective to prevent pervasive misappropriation—at least until the digital age. For example, media and entertainment companies have controlled the capacity of printing presses, vinyl and CD mass production, and broadcast of TV and radio. However, new technologies have opened up substantial leaks in these physical controls. Copyright owners have reacted by plugging them with contract restrictions or by seeking new protective legislation. For example, software has stronger protection when copy-protected, reverse engineering is prohibited, and software is licensed or leased rather than sold. The DMCA attempts to plug a widening hole in the copyright owner's technical or legal protections by making it illegal to evade technologies that impede access or copying. The DMCA anticircumvention rules prohibit unauthorized access to a work protected by **standard technical protection measures** intended to restrict access. Separately, the DMCA has **antitrafficking provisions** that prohibit the manufacture or sale of software or devices that circumvent access controls.

Anticircumvention Exceptions

During Congressional debate on the DMCA, many groups argued that the anticircumvention provisions would adversely affect law enforcement, education, scholarly research, the fair use exception, and the development of encryption (as a form of technical protection measure) and would prevent many traditionally legal methods of reverse engineering. As a result, Congress created several limited exceptions for the six uses listed previously. Exceptions were also created for parents to protect minor children from obscenity or other objectionable material, for accessing or disabling privacy intrusions (e.g., cookies), and for testing the effectiveness of security or encryption technologies.

The DMCA also directed the librarian of Congress to periodically review whether the anticircumvention rules were adversely affecting parties. In 2001, two exemptions were created: (1) decrypting filtering software to evaluate the propriety of Web site databases that block children's access to inappropriate material and (2) circumvention of malfunctioning software or databases if the copyright owner has not fixed the problem quickly. In the rule making, the Copyright Office rejected many exemptions proposed by various groups. Conflict will probably continue between copyright owners and users on these anticircumvention rules.

COPYRIGHT MANAGEMENT INFORMATION

Accompanying the digital content sought by consumers, there is increasingly additional information used for identification, to make records, to meter fees, or to discover infringement. The additional data are called **copyright management information**. Consider how meta-tags in Web pages or in e-mail messages contain routing and subject information. Similarly, copyrighted works may contain the owner's contact information, pricing, links, and licensing terms. This information could be revealed to users as needed, provide record keeping of authorized and unauthorized uses, or be used by electronic agents in automated contract negotiations. The DMCA prohibits intentional tampering with copyright management information that is conveyed with the work.

SAFE HARBOR FOR ISPS

Like the Communications Decency Act, the DMCA provides safe harbors from liability for Internet service providers (ISPs) when they are innocent and acting as mere conduits for their users' infringement. ISPs are not liable for copyright infringement or for contributory infringement as long as they enforce a program to terminate subscribers who repeatedly infringe. Additionally, the ISP may not interfere with standard technical protection measures used by copyright owners. ISPs are not liable for providing a hyperlink to infringing material if they meet several strict requirements, including compliance with the DMCA's **notice and take down** provisions, which require the ISP to remove or block access to infringing materials when the ISP is sufficiently notified by the copyright owner. The DMCA also provides an ISP safe harbor for system caching and ephemeral copies.

MORAL RIGHTS

The author or owner's right to make derivative works may not be enough to prevent negative side effects. In general, Europeans historically feel strongly that only the author has a natural right to prevent desecration of the author's unique, creative works; that is, the author should be able to prevent others from changing the work if the author believes the changes are harmful to the work's artistic integrity. These natural rights are called **moral rights** because they naturally extend from the author's own personality to prevent dishonor or damage to the author's reputation. There are four major components to moral rights: (1) the right of paternity, attribution, or acknowledgment; (2) the right of disclosure; (3) the right of integrity; and (4) the right of withdrawal. Moral rights are most compelling when the author's creative contribution is largely artistic.

The **right of attribution** is essentially a statement that accurately identifies the author as the creator. This right also prevents false claims that someone was the author or creator of a work that she or he did not really create. The **right of disclosure** allows the author control over when, how, and where the work is publicly displayed or performed. Authors can make sure their works are not displayed in galleries, art shows, or public places that they believe might damage their reputation. The **right of integrity** allows authors to prevent physical mutilation, distortion, modifications, or any other changes they believe would injure their reputation. This right can also prevent destruction of the work. Finally, the **right of withdrawal** allows the author alone to change the work and to prevent others from making reproductions. The United States has never adopted this comprehensive, European vision of moral rights. However, aspects of federal and some state laws (e.g., California), as well as federal implementation of the Berne Convention, approximate several aspects of moral rights.

The leading U.S. moral rights case involved an instance when the ABC network cut substantial portions before it rebroadcast the taped shows of a British comedy,

Monty Python's Flying Circus.[10] By shortening the shows, the network violated the express license and created an unauthorized derivative work. This new, shortened work was inaccurately attributed to Monte Python, violating the federal unfair competition law, §43(a) of the Lanham Act. State laws may also provide authors with remedies for moral rights violations. For example, the torts of defamation or privacy might protect some aspects of moral rights. In addition, some states have passed art preservation laws to protect works of fine art, either by prohibiting its destruction or by prohibiting display of altered works. However, these laws may be preempted by the **Visual Artists Rights Act** of 1990 (VARA), which implements U.S. participation in the Berne Convention.

VARA protects only works of visual art that are either in a single copy, such as a famous painting or sculpture, or are part of a limited set of reproductions, such as signed and numbered print editions of 200 or fewer copies. **Visual arts** under VARA include paintings, drawings, prints, sculptures, and photographs. Other visual works are specifically excluded from VARA's moral rights: posters, maps, globes, motion pictures, A/V works, books, periodicals, databases, electronic publications, advertising materials, and works for hire. Neither musical works nor sound recordings are included. The moral rights under VARA include (1) attribution to claim authorship and (2) integrity to prevent intentional distortion, mutilation, or modification that prejudices the author's honor. The author has VARA rights even if the work was sold to another person. Unlike in Europe, VARA permits the author to expressly waive these rights in writing. VARA moral rights last for the life of the artist.

COPYRIGHT PROCEDURES

Copyright protection is much easier to obtain than protection for a patented invention or a trademark. The general requirements under copyright law are only that some unique authorial expression be fixed in a permanent medium of expression. Since the 1976 revision to the U.S. copyright law, it is no longer necessary to register the copyright, deposit a copy with the Library of Congress, publish the work, or attach copyright notice to the work. However, there are still some advantages to using these procedural steps.

ONLINE

Library of Congress
Search Facility
**http://www.loc.gov/
copyright/search**

COPYRIGHT OFFICE

The **Copyright Office** of the **Library of Congress** is the primary U.S. regulatory agency for copyrights. It serves as the point for registration of works and for deposit of works into the Library of Congress, it advises Congress on copyright policy, and it has some rule-making authority. The chief administrative officer is the **register of copyrights,** who is appointed by the librarian of Congress. The Copyright Office

---

10. *Gilliam v. American Broadcasting Cos.,* 538 F.2d 14 (2d Cir., 1976).

provides records of 50 million catalogue entries showing copyright ownership and ownership transfers. These records help potential users discover if a work is in the public domain, and they assist in locating owners so users can seek permission or license to use copyrighted works. These and other copyright records dating back to 1978 are available for on-line electronic search.

Much of the law of copyright, the Copyright Office's various records, copyright regulations, and links to related sites are available online. This section discusses the copyrighting procedures of registration, deposit, and notice, as well as the duration or term of copyright protection.

COPYRIGHT REGISTRATION

The United States stands alone in the world by requiring a registration system for copyrighted works. Registration provides initial validity of copyright ownership, it documents the timing of first creation, and it facilitates a market for copyrighted works. The formalities of registration, deposit, and notice are complicated because of changes in the copyright laws that Congress implemented in 1978 and 1989. Therefore, careful attention is required to determine the creation date for existing works. Registration was important for works created before 1978 because owners could extend their term of copyright protection by filing a renewal with the Copyright Office in the twenty-eighth year, as discussed later. For works created between 1978 and 1989, registration was required if copyright notice was left off a substantial number of copies.

To comply with the Berne Convention, copyright registration was made optional for works created after March 1, 1989. However, even for these newer works, registration is still a useful step because it enables infringement remedies: An infringement suit cannot be brought until after registration if the work was created in the United States or in other nations not part of the Berne Convention. Registration is a prerequisite to seeking statutory damages and attorney's fees, and the owner has few remedies for infringements occurring before registration. The fee for registration is $30 until 2004, when the register of copyrights may make adjustments for inflation.

Most interactions with the U.S. Copyright Office are painless, particularly when compared with interactions with many of the other regulators discussed throughout this book. First, there is no qualification or examination process by the Copyright Office to determine copyrightability, as there is for patents and trademarks by the Patent and Trademark Office (PTO). Fewer interactions with the Copyright Office are adversarial, unlike so many interactions with some agencies (e.g., IRS, Justice Department). Second, copyright registration is relatively easy, inexpensive, and straightforward. The Copyright Office is testing an on-line registration system, the **Copyright Office Registration and Deposit System (CORDS)**, that will permit authors and owners to register and deposit their works via the Internet. The payment of license fees is facilitated by electronic funds transfers using the FedWire system.

ONLINE

Copyright Registration
Forms Online
**http://www.loc.gov/
copyright/forms**

Deposit

Copyright law requires the applicant to **deposit**—that is, to submit—two copies of the best edition of the work. This requirement applies to all types of works. Deposit enhances the archival collection of the Library of Congress. Fines are levied for failure to make the deposit within three months after publication. Clearly, deposit would be impractical, if not impossible, for three-dimensional works, such as the sole copy of a sculpture. Works published outside the United States generally need not be deposited. The Copyright Office has issued regulations that permit the owner to block out the trade secrets contained in the source code listing of software that is deposited.

COPYRIGHT NOTICE

Copyright notice is a familiar public signal that the author or owner claims copyright and that the work is not in the public domain. It consists of the copyright owner's name, one of three permissible forms of the copyright symbol (the "c in a circle" ©, copr., or copyright), and the year the work was first published. Notice should be placed in a reasonably visible location on the work. Copyright Office guidelines help owners make good placement choices. Right now, check the title page to this book. You should find something like this: ©2003 by West Legal Studies in Business. The United States is the only major nation that still actively encourages the use of copyright notices. Although notice in the United States is an imperfect method to determine what lies in the public domain, the process is even more uncertain and potentially costly when notice is not widely used.

Notice serves to inform the public of the copyright. It provides the year copyright protection begins and identifies the original author or owner. Critics argue that notice can be misleading if ownership was transferred after the initial printing of copies that are still in circulation. Copyright notice was a mandatory requirement for copyright protection until the 1988 copyright law revision by which the United States complied with the Berne Convention. Works created before 1989 were subject to forfeiture: They fell into the public domain if the copyright notice regulations were not complied with strictly.

Although Berne implementation has made copyright notice optional, nevertheless, notice still has some legal impact. For example, infringers will probably not be successful in arguing their infringement was innocent if the owner has placed a reasonably conspicuous copyright notice on the work. In such cases, the court should impose on the defendant full liability for statutory or actual damages. No reduction should be made for innocent violation. Suitable posting of copyright notice adequately warns potential infringers that the work is protected.

DURATION OF COPYRIGHT PROTECTION

When compared with patents lasting only 20 years, copyrights seem quite lengthy, having a term of protection lasting for the remainder of the author's life plus another 70 years. Recall that the U.S. Constitution in Article I, §8, cl. 8 restricts copyright protection to "limited times." This phrase represents a balance between the incentive given authors and the social costs of an excessive monopoly that would deprive the public domain. Copyright term is another complex procedural matter because it varies as a result of some key factors defined in several revision laws: the date of creation or publication, status of the renewal term, and whether the work was created in the United States. As introduced in Chapter 11, many, if not most, authors of commercially viable works assign their copyrights to a publisher in exchange for production and distribution of the work. Given this complexity, only generalizations about copyright terms are made here.

Unpublished works could be perpetually protected under state common law until passage of the 1976 Copyright Revision Act, which eliminated common law copyright altogether. Unpublished works created before 1978 were previously protected forever under state common law of copyright. The 1976 act now preempts all state copyright laws, substituting the federal scheme. Common law copyrights are now protected under federal copyright law, so the life-plus-70-years duration is generally applicable to them. For works published before 1964, the author had an initial 28-year term and then a chance for a renewal term of another 28 years. This option permitted the author to renegotiate terms with the publisher. For example, assume a record company acquired a famous and commercially successful blues song from an indigent blues artist for a mere pittance. Copyright law gave the artist a chance to renegotiate more favorable royalties before the second copyright term began by requiring that the artist apply for the extension. The second term was extended from 28 years to 67 years by the 1976 Act. Term renewal was made automatic by the Copyright Renewal Act of 1992. Renewals are eliminated altogether for works created after 1977. Works published before 1923 are now in the public domain. (See Exhibit 4.4.)

The **Sonny Bono Copyright Term Extension Act** was passed in 1998 to extend the terms of some existing copyrights by 20 years. This act results in the general duration of life plus 70 years rule. However, there is a different term for anonymous or pseudonymous works and works for hire created primarily by institutional "authors." They all have a term of 120 years after creation or 95 years after publication, whichever term is shorter. At this writing, there is a Supreme Court challenge pending to the Sonny Bono extension law that could invalidate Congress's lengthening of copyright term. Opponents of the extension law claim the Constitution limits copyright duration to "reasonable" terms and that the term extension is unreasonably long.[11]

COPYRIGHT INFRINGEMENT

Much of copyright law focuses on the unauthorized intrusion into one of the bundle of exclusive rights held by the author or owner. An infringement occurs when the

---

11. See, e.g., *Eldred v. Ashcroft*, U.S. Sup.Ct. No.01-618 (2002).

Exhibit 4.4 Copyright Duration

Date of Work	Date Protection Starts	Duration of Copyright Protection
Published before 1923	When published with copyright notice attached	Now in public domain
Published between 1923 and 1977	When published with copyright notice attached	Up to 95 years for works published between 1923 & 1977 under "two term" systems: • Works first published before 1964—first term 28 years from publication; second term 28 years from renewal; 1976 law increased second term to 67 years; author required to initiate official renewal process if first term ended before 1964 • Works first published after 1963—first term 28 years from publication; second term 67 years from renewal; renewal automatic
Created after 1977	When fixed in tangible medium of expression	Remaining life of author plus 70 years Exception for works for hire (institutional author): • 95 years after publication, or • 120 years after creation, whichever is shorter

infringer makes an unauthorized copy, distributes, performs or displays in public, or makes a derivative of the original work. Infringement analysis requires a complex assessment that often focuses on (1) copying, (2) illicit copying, and (3) whether the copying might be excused because copyright law tolerates some infringements that are fair or necessary for the progress of science and the useful arts. This section focuses on the first two of these factors that must be proved by the owner of the original. The third factor, detailed in a later section, must generally be proved by the alleged infringer.

INFRINGEMENT ANALYSIS

The author or owner's case of infringement first requires proof of a valid copyright (appropriate subject matter, originality, procedural compliance). Registration is a prerequisite to many infringement remedies. Analysis of infringement involves two steps: first consider expert testimony to determine whether copying has occurred, and second consider interpretations by laypeople, usually a jury, about whether the amount taken is qualitatively substantial.[12]

---

12. *Arnstein v. Porter*, 154 F.2d 464 (2d Cir., 1946).

Proof of copying can be difficult. Proving infringement is easy in the case of blatant plagiarism, where the infringer made a substantial, literal, word-for-word copy by "lifting" exact portions from the original work. However, few alleged infringers ever admit to copying, and it is often done secretly, so it must be proved by comparing the two works. This difficulty is made worse because Congress has never successfully defined infringement with precision. Therefore, infringement is an ad hoc determination that varies, depending on the type of work involved: literary, software, musical or visual art. Generally, a comparison is made between the original work that was allegedly infringed and a second work that allegedly infringes on the original work.

Copying

If the second work was independently created, not copied, it cannot infringe the original. Two works could conceivably be protected under copyright, even if they were identical, as long as the second work was created independently. This rule is like the rule in trade secrets but different from the rule under patent law. Independent creation is a complete defense to trade secret misappropriation, but independent creation is no defense to patent infringement. Therefore, the owner of the original copyrighted work must prove that the infringer derived the second work from the first.

In the real world, many copyright infringements are not verbatim takings from the original; that is, many second works are not identical in all respects to the original. Instead, the infringer copies only certain aspects, perhaps paraphrasing prose, changing the meter of poetry or song lyrics, taking only a catchy melody, or modifying some of the instrumental parts or the medium (e.g., oil on canvas to computer graphics, carved stone sculpture to plastic casting).

It is still infringement if the infringement is innocent and the author of the second made no conscious effort to take from the original. Consider the famous example of the 1970s hit song "My Sweet Lord," written and recorded by the late Beatle, George Harrison. The court held he infringed the basic melody of the 1962 hit "He's So Fine," which was written by Ronald Mack and recorded by the Chiffons. Note what the trial judge concluded after inquiring closely into Harrison's inspiration in writing the song:

> *The composer, in seeking musical materials to clothe his thoughts, was working with various possibilities. A particular combination pleased him . . . this combination of sounds would work. Why? Because his subconscious knew it already had worked in a song his conscious mind did not remember. It is clear that My Sweet Lord is the very same song as He's So Fine with different words, and Harrison had access to He's So Fine.*[13]

---

13. *Bright Tunes Music Corp. v. Harrisongs Music, Ltd.*, 420 F.Supp. 177 (S.D.N.Y., 1976) *aff'd sub nom ABKCO Music, Inc. v. Harrisongs Music, Ltd.*, 722 F.2d 988 (2d Cir., 1983).

Typically, the owner of the original may ask the judge or jury to infer copying from circumstantial evidence. If the alleged infringer had **access** to original work and there is **substantial similarity** between the two works, these points may support an inference of copying. The Internet provides considerable and nearly unfettered access to many works, and disproving access to Internet postings may become difficult.

Of course, access should not be conclusive of infringement because copyright does not protect the ideas in the original, only the form of expression. Scientific progress would be difficult unless researchers could have legitimate access to the prior works of previous scholars, but most important, they need access to their ideas. Therefore, the testimony of experts is often helpful to determine whether the similarities result from two independently gifted artists who simply worked from the same public domain reservoir or whether they resulted from copying protected expression. Both unprotected ideas and protected expression are compared, then, to determine whether there was copying and whether the copying was unlawful. Disproving access is a key part of the clean room techniques discussed later.

Access can also be inferred if the two works have **striking similarity**; that is, the similarities are so numerous and so close that it is hard to believe the infringer did not have access to the original and use it. Striking similarity is evident by comparison. For example, try to listen to George Harrison's "My Sweet Lord" after first listening to the Chiffons' "He's So Fine." The court found three musical phrases to be identical in both songs: (1) sol-me-re, (2) sol-la-do-la-do, and (3) sol-la-do-la-re-do.[14] Clearly, listening is the most effective comparison. Many songs have similar melodies or patterns, but infringement analysis is concerned with similarities in the most dominant portions, the creative essence. Once the first step of copying is proved, the judge or jury must then move to the second step: Is the copying illicit?

Illicit Copying

Once expert testimony has helped the judge or jury determine that the original was copied, the testimony of laypersons is used to determine if the copying was an illicit, unlawful appropriation. The substantial similarity standard is again used—this time to determine if the original's expression was taken. The similarities, not the differences, are the critical factor. At this second stage, similarity in the ideas of both works is also irrelevant. Therefore, lay observers who are potentially in the market for that type of work may testify as to whether there is substantial similarity in the expression of the two works. When the case is tried before a jury, they may represent a lay audience and make this determination.

Infringement may take a wide variety of forms, at least as broad as the bundle of rights. First, a common form of infringement occurs when the infringer violates the reproduction right, which generally means the infringer made a verbatim partial or

---

14. These notations are called *tonic sol-fa*. You may recognize these syllables because they represent the different notes of the musical scale (do-re-me).

complete copy. For example, software and sound recordings might be infringed by making analog tapes or digital copies saved on disk. Photographs and books might be copied by photographic means such as photocopiers or even with another photograph. Controversy surrounds the temporary ephemeral copies of audio, video, software, or other digital media made in computer RAM or on other intermediary facilities. Ephemeral copies are necessary to transmit, rebroadcast, load, or use the work.

Second, infringement also frequently occurs when the infringer makes a derivative work that uses only parts of the original while adding original expression. For example, George Harrison's "My Sweet Lord" probably constituted a derivative work of the original "He's So Fine"; it was not a verbatim copy. Third, the distribution right is also infringed when infringing copies or derivative works are distributed to the public. Similarly, infringing copies publicly performed or displayed are another form of infringement.

COMPUTER APPLICATIONS OF INFRINGEMENT ANALYSIS

Infringement analysis for computer programs is a process that has matured through an evolution of cases in the 1980s and 1990s. A three-step software infringement analysis involves (1) abstraction, (2) filtration, and (3) comparison.[15] The first step, **abstraction**, requires a conceptualization of the original work. The program's sequence, structure, and organization are determined, revealing the original program's functions. Second, the various elements dissected in the abstraction phase must be forced through **filtration**, a process of separating unprotected ideas from protected expression. There can be no infringement of elements already in the public domain or for external elements, such as interfaces and communications protocols; mechanical computer specifications permitting compatibility and widely accepted programming practices are removed from consideration. For example, the "video game" cases have established that the interface connecting game cartridges to the game console are functional elements and generally not protected expression. It would be impossible to build compatible software if a competing manufacturer could not determine how the cartridge communicated with the game console. The third step is **comparison**, in which only protected expression of the second work remains and is compared with the original work. It is similar to the illicit copying step discussed previously.

The design of compatible software and hardware has been a daunting task. A copy of the original work must be acquired legally and then reverse-engineered to discover its functions. Only ideas can be duplicated; the expression cannot be used by the maker of the compatible product. However, many vendors do not want unauthorized competitors to produce compatible products. The discussion of network effects in Chapters 9 and 12 are relevant. The owner of the original has an incentive to block compatible products. The resulting competition would undermine the monopoly profits the original's owner enjoys because consumers become locked in

---

15. *Computer Assoc. Int'l, Inc. v. Altai, Inc.*, 982 F.2d 693 (2d Cir., 1992).

and can use only the original owner's "family" of compatible or licensed products. Owners of the original often license or lease their software and hardware so they can prohibit reverse engineering. Nevertheless, reverse engineering may still be permissible as a fair use, as discussed later.

Clean Room Techniques

A special technique—the **clean room** method—is used to reverse-engineer software and hardware. It typically involves two separate teams: The first team analyzes the original work, and the second team designs the competing product. The first team works in a dirty room, where reverse engineering reveals the unprotected ideas and separates them from the protected expression. The dirty room team clearly has access to the original work and must separate unprotected ideas from the protected expression. The designers in the clean room do not see the protected expression but must develop their own from scratch.

For example, a potential competitor seeking to produce compatible game cartridges would first use a dirty room team to decompile the software and discover how the programming conventions are used to make the game work. Expression items such as the graphics and the characters in the original must be separated from the unprotected ideas that show how the game functions and operates. The dirty room team prepares a report that contains only unprotected ideas, public domain expression, and, most important, the functional characteristics of the game. The clean room team uses only the report, not the original work. The clean room team works independently to develop the new game so it is different but still functionally compatible. The clean room technique was legitimized in the watershed case *Sega Enterprises v. Accolade, Inc.*[16]

SECONDARY LIABILITY

In another watershed case, *Sony v. Universal City Studios*,[17] the owners of video content attempted to expand secondary liability theories to hold other parties liable for infringement if they assisted infringers. **Contributory infringement** would hold liable someone who provided technology to or otherwise assisted the infringer. Unlike the patent law, the copyright act has no explicit provisions for **vicarious infringement**, but such liability can be implied when someone is responsible for others who actually do the infringement. For example, a publisher, studio, or broadcaster may be held vicariously liable for the actions of its employees. The *Sony* case held that the maker or seller of a device, the VCR, could not be liable for contributory infringement because the VCR has **substantial noninfringing uses**. VCRs can make legal, imperfect analog copies of public domain works, VCRs can make legal copies when the works' owners authorize copying, and VCRs can "time shift" by copying protected works to enable more convenient viewing.

---

16. 977 F.2d 1510 (9th Cir., 1992).
17. 464 U.S. 417 (1984).

Despite this broad language in *Sony* and similar rulings, copyright owners and the entertainment and software industries continue to press for application of vicarious infringement. The most frequent targets of vicarious infringement are manufacturers, distributors, and resellers of copying technologies (VCRs, CD burners, PCs); the communications intermediaries used to broadcast or download infringing copies (ISPs); and authors or distributors of software that facilitates copying.

Liability of ISPs

Printing presses, broadcasting transmitters, distribution contracts with bookstores or local TV affiliates, and the like were the unique facilities needed for effective large-scale infringement in the traditional world. However, in cyberspace, nearly anyone can become a publisher by distributing works through chat rooms, by e-mail spam, or by providing hyperlinks to infringing materials stored elsewhere or stored directly on their own Web sites. Owners of original works who want to halt infringement must now focus attention on even more entities to remedy infringement.

Internet and on-line service providers are logical targets for secondary liability for various wrongs or offenses: obscenity, defamation, and harassment, as well as infringement. Early cases had conflicting holdings: some held ISPs liable for infringement,[18] and others denied contributory infringement liability if the ISP was unaware of the infringing material.[19] Remember the previous discussion in this chapter about the DMCA's safe harbor for ISPs. The DMCA releases ISPs from secondary liability for merely transmitting infringing materials if the material is stored for only short times. However, if the ISP hosts Web sites for users or otherwise stores allegedly infringing materials for long periods, then more complex notice and take down procedures apply under the DMCA. Generally, the ISP must remove or block access to infringing materials when sufficiently notified by the copyright owner.

INFRINGEMENT REMEDIES

The author or owner's rights under copyright law would be superficial without legal remedies to halt and compensate for the infringement. The Copyright Act provides for equitable remedies (injunctions, seizure, destruction) and legal remedies (statutory damages, actual damages, lost profits, costs and attorney's fees). In addition, criminal penalties deter infringement under the Copyright Act, the DMCA, and the No Electronic Theft Act.

Equitable Remedies

Often the most effective remedy is to simply halt the infringement as soon as possible. The injunction is a classic court order prohibiting the infringer from continuing the infringement. For example, an injunction would stop further infringing

---

18. *Playboy Ent., Inc. v. Freena*, 838 F.Supp. 1552 (M.D.Fl. 1993).
19. *Religious Tech. Ctr. v. Netcom On-Line Comm.Servs., Inc.*, 907 F.Supp. 1361 (N.D.Cal. 1995).

performances of a Broadway play or a movie. An injunction would halt further sales of infringing sound recordings or books. A permanent injunction is possible only after a potentially long trial. However, preliminary injunctions are frequently used to halt the infringement before a full trial can be held if the author or owner of the original work can prove three things. First, the owner must have a strong probability of success at the infringement trial on the merits of the case. Second, the owner must show that it will suffer irreparable harm unless the infringement is enjoined immediately. Third, the court hearing the motion for the preliminary injunction must balance the harms of continued infringement to the author against the harm of shutting down the alleged infringer's business. Typically, hearings for preliminary injunctions are held on short notice, they are not lengthy, and the preliminary injunction is effective only temporarily, until a ruling following the full trial.

After infringement is determined at the full trial, another remedy may be available if there are infringing copies in the supply chain or there is special production equipment suitable just to make them. Infringing copies may be impounded, and production facilities unique to the infringing articles may be destroyed. For example, infringing books, phonorecords, or CDs can be seized from warehouses and retailers. The photographic negatives, presses, plates, or molds used to produce the infringing articles may be destroyed. Destruction is a severe remedy that should be reserved for serious cases.

Legal Remedies

The legal remedies most often given in infringement cases are compensatory, the payment of money damages. Infringers may be held liable either for actual damages, including the infringer's profits, *or* for statutory damages. **Actual damages** are computed as the drop in market value of the author or owner's work that results from the infringement. This determination is difficult, so lost profits are a somewhat more reliable measure. For example, the owner's lost sales might be determined by comparing periodic sales volumes over the period before the infringement with the reduced sales volume after infringement. Of course, economic factors can affect sales, and the infringer may be selling at lower prices, so the lost sales measure is often too speculative to be useful. In addition to lost profits, the owner is entitled to the infringer's profits. In both computations, assumptions must be made about the production costs and the allocation of overhead. Infringer profits and the owner's lost profits can be quite contentious issues at trial.

Because actual damages are difficult to determine, Congress provided for an alternative measure, **statutory damages**. Recall that U.S. law requires registration of the original copyright before statutory damages are available. There can be no statutory damages for even proven infringements that occurred before registration. This legal point is an important inducement for copyright registration. Statutory damages are within the trial court's discretion between $500 and $20,000. If the infringement is willful, the court may assess up to $100,000 in statutory damages.

The trial court may also order the losing party to pay the winner's costs for the infringement trial and the winner's attorney's fees. Traditionally, attorney's fees were paid to winning authors or owners routinely but were difficult for winning defendants to receive when they were absolved of infringement. Does that seem fair? In *Fogerty v. Fantasy, Inc.*,[20] the Supreme Court held this disparity was not fair to defendants because it gave authors and owners an advantage in choosing to go to trial. John Fogerty, a songwriter and member of the band Creedence Clearwater Revival (Southern country-blues) was sued by the owner of a song John Fogerty originally wrote, "Run through the Jungle." John Fogerty recorded a similar song on another label with different words that he titled "The Old Man on the Road." John Fogerty won the infringement suit but was denied attorney's fees by the trial court. The Supreme Court found no compelling reason to favor owners over successful defendants, so it reversed the trial court on the attorney's fee issue.

Criminal Penalties

It is a federal felony to willfully infringe copyright in any type of work for commercial advantage or private financial gain. The federal crime is committed when ten or more copies or phonorecords having a retail value of more than $2,500 are reproduced or distributed within a 180-day period if done without the owner's authorization. Fines of up to $250,000 can be levied for individual repeat offenders or $500,000 for organizations. Imprisonment for individuals for up to five years is alternative. Before passage of the **No Electronic Theft Act** (NETA) in 1997, criminal penalties for copyright infringement applied only to willful infringement for personal financial gain. NETA amendments now include a sliding scale of penalties for aggregate retail values down to $1,000 and also increase possible imprisonment to six years. This means that unauthorized Web posting or e-mail distribution of stolen software, audio, or other works online is illegal under NETA, even if the infringer makes no profit.

Only the Justice Department (DOJ) can prosecute criminal copyright actions. The DOJ has the tougher "beyond a reasonable doubt" burden of proof in criminal copyright infringement cases. Criminal penalties for violation of the DMCA are even more severe, fines up to $500,000 or imprisonment for first-time offenders and fines up to $1,000,000 or imprisonment up to 10 years for repeat offenders. The DMCA's statute of limitations is five years. Not-for-profit organizations are not subject to the DMCA's criminal penalties.

FAIR USE DEFENSE

Many intellectual property theorists argue that copyrights were never intended to be as strong as patents. Patents are strong rights. They protect ideas but last for a much shorter time, generally only 20 years. The secrets behind a patent are disclosed to the public when the patent is granted. By contrast, copyrights last a long time, so the public should not be made to suffer a strong monopoly over the ideas embedded in copyrighted works. As the preceding sections illustrate, infringement analysis is highly uncertain and carries the threat of severe civil and criminal liability. These factors

---

20. *Fogerty v. Fantasy, Inc.*, 114 S.Ct. 1023 (1994).

suggest society is best served by a narrowing of owners' control over copyrighted works. The courts and legislatures have long shown some agreement with these arguments. The English courts originally created an exception to strong copyright protection, called the **abridgment** of the owner's rights. It permits later authors to advance learning by building on existing works.

The abridgment right has evolved into today's most important limitation on an owner's bundle of rights: the fair use exception. Fair use is a defense to copyright infringement that permits reasonable uses of the owner's work without permission. Fair use was developed in English common law cases and then adopted by famous U.S. Justice Story in the 1841 case *Folsom v. Marsh*.[21] Congress codified fair use in §107 of the 1976 Copyright Act so that the threat of infringement litigation does not produce unfair results or weaken the progress of science and the useful arts.

§107 Fair Use Doctrine

Notwithstanding [the author or owner's bundle of rights under §106] the fair use of a copyrighted work, including such use by reproduction in copies or phonorecords or by any other means specified by that section, for purposes such as criticism, news reporting, teaching (including multiple copies for classroom use), scholarship, or research, is not an infringement of copyright.

Fair use is an ambiguous concept. Its uncertainty is further complicated because the case law and statutes do not provide clear guidance and often seem contradictory. Fair use determinations nearly always require ad hoc, case-by-case analysis. Users who forthrightly seek to stay within the lawful bounds of fair use still risk infringement litigation. When they feel uncertain about a particular use, they may decline to use another work because of this risk. Of course, copyright owners prefer narrow fair use, and they may think they benefit when users reluctantly choose not to make a fair use because of their apprehension and the law's ambiguous guidance. The available guidance is too often worthless for most users and probably results in two inferior outcomes: (1) careful users conservatively avoid fair uses they could legally make, and (2) scofflaws ignore the limits of fair use and frequently infringe.

TRANSFORMATIVE USES

One important and developing theory of fair use is that transformative uses are a very important type of fair use. **Transformative uses** are productive uses of the original work that add potentially valuable and creative expression. For example, new works derived from an original may advance the art by adding new information, reinterpreting ideas in light of new conditions, providing more imaginative insights, using different creative or artistic expressions, reaching different conclusions, or targeting different audiences. Transformative uses are more defensible than reproduc-

---

21. 9 F.Cas. 342 (C.C.D.Mass. 1841).

tive uses. Reproductive uses probably seldom qualify as fair uses because they seek only to mimic the original or compete with the original and do not serve new markets or new purposes.

THE FOUR FACTORS OF FAIR USE

Case law and §107 of the Copyright Act set out a list of the types of situations that may constitute a fair use: "criticism, news reporting, teaching, scholarship, or research." This list is not exclusive because the language in §107 precedes the list with the phrase "for purposes such as . . ." This phrasing clearly indicates that the list is not exhaustive but depends on the circumstances. The determination of fair use is an equitable inquiry about the reasonableness of the use. In the 1841 case of *Folsom v. Marsh*, Justice Story first suggested a set of factors that should be used to identify reasonable uses. These criteria have since grown in judicial decisions until this history was codified by Congress in the 1976 Copyright Act.

These factors balance the hardships on the owner against those of the user by applying a form of the rule of reason. Today, all four factors must be used, they are weighed, and some are given greater weight in particular cases. Also, the courts may consider other factors, such as good faith and usages in the trade. They identify new types of reasonable uses, and they are also used to evaluate whether a claimed use is reasonable. The factors are (1) the purpose and character of the use, (2) the nature of the copyrighted work, (3) the amount and substantiality of the portion used, and (4) the effect of the use on the potential market for the work. These complex criteria are discussed next but are probably familiar to most people who have seen them posted in libraries and on photocopiers.

The Four Factors of Fair Use

1. the *purpose and character of the use*, including whether such use is of a commercial nature or is for nonprofit educational use;
2. the *nature of the copyrighted work*;
3. the *amount and substantiality of the portion used* in relation to the copyrighted work as a whole; and
4. the *effect of the use upon the potential market for the work* or the value of the copyrighted work.

Purpose and Character of the Use

The first factor focuses on the alleged infringer's purpose and type of use of the original work. The factors clearly favor some types of uses over others. (See Exhibit 4.5.) For example, nonprofit educational uses are more likely to be considered fair use, and the user's personal commercial purpose is less likely to be fair use. Other uses more likely to be fair include scholarship, protected forms of speech, and uses that transform the original work. Most publishers are *for-profit* businesses, so the profit motive standing alone does not prohibit a fair use. Instead, the commercial character must be less significant than other meritorious factors. Uses less likely to be judged fair under this factor are those in which the commercial aspects predominate.

Exhibit 4.5 Fair Use Factors

Fair Use Factor	Analysis of Use for "Fairness"
1. Purpose and character of the use	More favored uses: • Nonprofit educational uses • Transformative uses Less favored uses: • Commercial uses; user must prove use is reasonable • Verbatim reproductions or no permission fee paid
2. Nature of the copyrighted work	More favored uses: • Original was factual, scientific work Less favored uses: • Original was creative, fictional, artistic work, was unpublished, or if factual was an educational consumable
3. Amount and substantiality of the portion used	More favored uses: • Small amounts of the original's expression used Less favored uses: • Large amounts of the original's expression used • Significant qualitative amount taken, the "creative essence" of original even if just a small amount
4. Effect of use on potential market	More favored uses: • Does not directly compete with original work • Criticism or parody of the original work Less favored uses: • Directly competes with original work

Commercial use weighs most strongly against the user if the uses are simple reproductions of the original that are in competition with the original or if the user could have easily paid for a license.

Nature of the Copyrighted Work

The second factor focuses on the amount of creative expression in the original work. Highly creative and entertaining works with substantial artistic or fictional content are given maximum protection against unauthorized use. Also, unpublished works are given stronger protection. The unauthorized use of an unpublished work probably involves a breach of confidence or maybe even misappropriation. Theft clearly contradicts any "fairness" in the use.[22] Unpublished works are a recurring and legitimate source for news reporting. By contrast, factual or scientific works contain more public domain information, so users may exploit them more readily than they can exploit creative works. However, there are limits. Fair use of factual works should not undermine the only market for authorized copies of the original, such as for educational consumables like preprinted tests, worksheets, or exercises.

---

22. *Harper & Row, Pub. v. Nation Ent.*, 471 U.S. 539 (1985).

Amount and Substantiality of the Portion Used

Many people crave a mechanical rule of thumb that would enable them to comfortably use just under the threshold amount that would surpass fair use. Indeed, some publishers use a proportional **quantitative** maximum—say, no more than 5% of the original. Others use absolute limits, such as no more than 200 words from a book or no more than 25 words from a magazine before permission must be obtained. These methods have only gross validity because sometimes just a small portion constitutes the **qualitative** "creative essence" of the original work. The proper quantitative comparison is between the original work and the amount taken, not how much the portion taken constitutes in the infringer's work. Fair use is less likely as more is taken quantitatively and/or more important parts are taken qualitatively.

The famous case of *Campbell v. Acuff Rose*[23] dramatically illustrates the distinction between quantitative and qualitative substantiality. Roy Orbison's famous ballad "Oh Pretty Woman" was the subject of a parody by the rap group Two Live Crew. The two versions were very different in style, lyrics, most of the melody, and audience. In finding the parody was a fair use, the Supreme Court insisted that the parodist should take only enough of the original work to conjure up the original in the audience's mind.

Effect of Use on the Potential Market

The fourth factor concerns the negative impact that the use might have on the market for the original work. It often carries the most weight. Indeed, this factor is already considered in the first factor, which disfavors commercial uses, and again in the third factor, because taking large amounts effectively becomes a substitute for the original work. This substitution would occur if the use diminished the potential sale of the original, interfered with the original's potential marketability, or substituted for potential demand for the original work.[24] There is an important exception to this rule. When criticism is effective, it weakens demand for the work. Criticism and parody are not really substitutions for the original work, so they are generally permissible as fair uses.

AUDIOVISUAL ENTERTAINMENT

Fair use continues to plague the entertainment and software industries as new technologies enable consumers to make copies of audio, video, games, and software more easily, cheaply, and perfectly. There have been several expansions of fair use theory in influential cases and also in legislation directly involving entertainment. Consider the watershed *Sony* Betamax case previously discussed. The Supreme Court legitimized **time shifting**—that is, taping a broadcast show for later viewing—largely for two reasons: (1) There are substantial noninfringing uses for the VCR, and (2) the permitted taping is only for personal, noncommercial purposes. The

---

23. 510 U.S. 569 (1994).
24. *Hustler Magazine, Inc. v. Moral Majority Inc.*, 796 F.2d 1148 (9th Cir., 1986).

MP3 case interpreted the AHRA so that general-purpose PCs are not digital audio recording devices. This effectively reaffirms that there are substantial noninfringing uses for computers and computer memory. Similar theory underlies the home copying of music authorized by the AHRA because it is for personal use, as well as the making of software backup copies.

Peer-to-peer (P2P) file-sharing technologies like Napster may have finally reached the limits of fair use. Courts are now limiting the growth of entertainment-related fair use and the first sale doctrine. For example, Napster enabled hundreds of thousands of unrelated strangers to make and distribute millions of copies of musical sound recordings. P2P networks are essentially virtual databases of information and copyrighted works that can search, find, download, and save multiple new copies of a single copy of a purchased work. Napster facilitated the unauthorized reproduction and distribution of original works. Was Napster contributing to the wholesale infringement of the musical sound recordings, or should Napster be excused under the fair use doctrine?

Continuing Saga of P2P File Sharing in *Napster's* Aftermath

Many Internet visionaries see P2P file sharing as one of the most important new technologies of the digital age. By contrast, the entertainment and software industry view unregulated P2P as anathema to their existing business models because P2P can be used for widespread infringement. After an injunction shuttered Napster, the top five record companies finally became more serious and began to create two separate joint ventures to distribute music over the Web. However, Judge Marilyn Patel, the trial court judge in *Napster*, is weighing the public interest in the ongoing Napster infringement suit.[25] Judge Patel will permit Napster to defend itself against infringement if it can prove the antitrust defense: copyright misuse. Misuse in this situation is further detailed in Chapter 12.

ONLINE

What services does Napster provide today?
http://www.napster. com

At this writing, users and the entertainment industry are widely reported to be locked in an arms race over P2P file sharing. Users now find several music-swapping services (e.g., Gnutella, Aimster, Morpheus) available that eliminate the central server and database features found unlawful in the *Napster* case. The entertainment industry is introducing music CD copy protection that may prevent the use of MP3 and computer CD-R/W drive technologies. However, early versions are reportedly imperfect and may not play on some CD players, so customer resistance may further depress sales—and anger artists. Similar P2P file sharing may soon proliferate (e.g., Morpheus) now that DeCSS enables decryption of DVD video programming. It should now be clear that the fair use exception does not provide clear guidance for users. However, one thing seems assured: The content industries will try to severely limit fair use, and users will gravitate to each new threatening technology as it becomes available.

---

25. *A&M Records, Inc. v. Napster*, 239 F.3d 1004 (9th Cir., 2001).

OTHER DEFENSES TO INFRINGEMENT

Fair use is the most important defense to infringement. Nevertheless, a few other defenses deserve a brief mention. The alleged infringer may argue **invalidity** of the original work's copyright. For example, the work may not be copyrightable subject matter, or the technical requirements of registration may have been violated. The owner may have waited too long before bringing suit, beyond the statute of limitations period, which is three years after infringement. The owner may be unable to convincingly prove infringement or cannot overcome the user's fair use claims. The first sale doctrine provides a defense to infringement by distribution because the distribution right of the owner of the original ceases when a copy or phonorecord is first sold to a consumer. However, purchasers may not use the first sale defense if they are renting or leasing copies or phonorecords.

CHAPTER 5
TRADE SECRETS AND DATABASE PROTECTION

How does the law fill in the gaps of intellectual property rights? Patents protect ideas but are expensive to prosecute. Patents can be difficult to acquire, they last for only 20 years, and their details are published for the whole world to see. Although copyrights last much longer, they protect only the form of expression and not the underlying ideas or concepts, which are often the primary source of value. Trademarks protect only commercial symbols, goodwill, and brand image. What is the incentive to innovate in developing valuable information or data management when it falls outside these federal protection schemes?

Consider the problem of an Internet business called Everything-Anywhere (EA). Assume EA provides mobile-commerce services to thousands of fiercely loyal clients. EA uses its wireless network to provide travel information, instant discounts at nearby merchants, shopping bot searches, transaction payments, instant messaging, and other services by using clients' various Web-enabled, portable devices such as PDAs, wireless Web phones, and laptops. To fulfill these services, EA has invested considerable sums to build and maintain a huge, perpetually updated database of information. EA integrates private information from multiple sources and continually creates valuable customized reports, which are delivered frequently each day to each client. These services are made possible by EA's use of confidential, proprietary software, both on its servers and installed on each customer's device. Other firms could save a great deal of development expense by copying confidential portions of the software, by marketing their competing services to existing EA customers, and by mimicking the favorable relationships EA has with vendors who sell the goods and services EA filters and selects for its clients. A few technologies in this system are protected by patents, copyrights, and trademarks. However, EA can best exploit its unique business model, valuable data, and proprietary software only if they are protected as trade secrets.

A **trade secret** is secret business information, protected by various laws against misappropriation via improper means or breach of a confidential relationship. The problems facing EA might be solved by using some protective measures to maintain secrecy. For example, the most vulnerable assets are EA's customer list, the architecture of its software, and the database of its clients' preferences. Trade secret law provides a remedy when such things are misappropriated. This chapter discusses the creation and protection of trade secrets, as well as remedies for trade secret misappropriation under various theories of contract, tort, and criminal law. The chapter concludes with a discussion of database protection. References are made throughout to technology transfer and employment concepts detailed in Chapter 11.

NATURE OF TRADE SECRETS

Trade secret law sets standards for business ethics. These standards are often derived from visceral notions of fairness and morality. They constrain competitive practices used among competing firms as well as between firms and their employees. Trade secret law distinguishes information already in the public domain from the product of unique ingenuity developed at the employer's expense. Employees create most trade secrets, and employers and employees often have adverse interests in information uniquely developed for the employer. It can be difficult to distinguish trade secrets from practices recently adopted and widely used throughout the trade or profession. The pace of change increases the importance of trade secret protection, particularly for products that combine various technologies. Today, the predominant innovative activity of business is the creation of proprietary information and business models that are largely protected as trade secrets.

HISTORY OF TRADE SECRET LAW

Trade secret law dates back at least to Roman times, when *actio servi corrupti* was the wrongful corruption of another citizen's slave. Damages were recoverable against outsiders who maliciously enticed the slave to divulge business secrets.[1] Society eventually balanced these property rights with the employee's rights. Even after involuntary servitude ended, during the guild era, there remained long-term employment restrictions for apprentices. The apprentice's livelihood was seen as unduly restricted by a long-term indenture under the master's direction.

Many influential early English trade secret cases involved recipes for medicine. The English courts of equity upheld agreements promising confidentiality for non-patented secrets. Later, the U.S. courts of equity upheld trade secrets, finding that licenses were not unlawful restraints of trade, such as in a secret process for chocolate making[2] or pump design plans secretly copied by a repairman.[3]

---

1. Schiller, Trade Secrets and the Roman Law: The Actio Servi Corrupti, *Columbia Law Review* 30 (1930), 837.
2. *Vickery v. Welch*, 36 Mass. 523 (1837).
3. *Tabor v. Hoffman*, 23 N.E. 12 (1889).

SOURCES OF TRADE SECRET LAW

In a sense, there is no law of trade secrets like there is for other forms of IP. Other forms of IP give more comprehensive protection than does trade secret law. For example, patent and copyright law defines the property interest fairly precisely. They also give the owner exclusive rights for use and possession. By contrast, trade secret law blends various laws that address the challenge of trade secrets' unique vulnerabilities.

Modern trade secret law has its roots in confidentiality duties that are implied from fiduciary principles and are often expressed in employment contracts. Modern trade secret practice is traced to the 1939 publication of *Restatement of Torts* by the American Law Institute (ALI). They are syntheses of the common law in several major subject areas. They are produced by judges, academics, and prominent lawyers to provide uniformity and predictability.

A major problem with the *Restatement*'s vision is that it refused to allow trade secrets to be an innovation incentive. Under this view, trade secrets are not a form of IP but instead are simply a form of commercial morality, which the law remedies for victims of breach of faith.[4] Although the *Restatement* helped make trade secret law uniform, only six states still use it.[5] The ALI eventually dropped the trade secrets provisions from later versions of the *Restatement*, so most states are transitioning to the similar Uniform Trade Secrets Act. In 1995, a new *Restatement* covering trade secrets resurfaced when the ALI first published the *Restatement of Unfair Competition*.

ONLINE

American Law Institute
http://www.ali.org

Today, 44 states have adopted the **Uniform Trade Secrets Act** (UTSA). The UTSA was published in 1979 by the National Conference of Commissioners for Uniform State Laws (NCCUSL). Thirty-four of these states have adopted the 1985 UTSA revision. The UTSA is now the predominant trade secret law in the United States. This uniformity encourages the courts to examine decisions from other UTSA states for interpretation guidance. Coverage of trade secrets in this chapter largely follows the UTSA, but some court interpretations of the *Restatement* are still valid, and the *Restatement* clearly inspired the UTSA. Exhibit 5.1 summarizes the major trade secret laws.

ONLINE

NCCUSL
http://www.nccusl.org

Several states reinforce trade secret law with criminal sanctions. The state laws vary from outlawing theft or possession of stolen computer information to criminal sanctions for unlawful use of secret scientific material. However, the most significant criminal law is federal: the **Economic Espionage Act of 1996** (EEA). Two separate EEA offenses are intended to overcome weaknesses in the civil law of trade secrets and increase the deterrence to trade secret theft. First, the EEA defines the crime of **economic espionage**.[6] Second, the EEA outlaws the **theft of trade secrets**.[7] Both crimes require proof that the defendant (1) stole or, without permission, obtained, destroyed, or conveyed trade secret

---

4. *Restatement of Torts* §757, comment b.

5. The Restatement is the law of trade secrets in North Carolina, New Jersey, New York, Pennsylvania, Texas, and Massachusetts.

6. 18 U.S.C. §1831 (2000).

7. 18 U.S.C. §1832 (2000).

Exhibit 5.1 Sources of Trade Secret Law

Trade Secret Laws	Application
Restatement of Torts	Only 6 states now, main source before UTSA, civil tort-style remedy
Uniform Trade Secrets Act (UTSA)	44 states, civil tort-style remedy
Restatement of Unfair Competition	Minimal current impact
State criminal laws: trespass, theft	Local prosecutor or state attorney, general enforcement, varying standards and penalties
Economic Espionage Act (EEA)	Federal criminal statute, DOJ enforcement, severe penalties
Confidentiality duties derived from agreement	Reinforces civil remedies and criminal penalties
Confidentiality duties derived from employment or agency fiduciary duty	Reinforces civil remedies and criminal penalties

U.S. Justice Department
http://www.usdoj.gov

information and (2) knew the information was proprietary. The economic espionage offense also requires the Justice Department (DOJ) to prove that the defendant intended the action to benefit a foreign government or foreign instrumentality or agent. To convict under the theft of trade secrets offense, the DOJ must also prove that the defendant (3) intended to benefit someone other than the trade secret owner (4) and knew the owner would be injured, and (5) the trade secret was related to a product in commerce.

There are significant penalties for firms under the EEA: maximum fines of $10 million for economic espionage and $5 million for theft of trade secrets. Penalties for individuals include fines up to $500,000 and/or prison terms up to 25 years for economic espionage or 15 years for theft of trade secrets. Substantial forfeiture sanctions may require disgorgement of profits made and forfeiture of any property used during the crime. Congress clearly intended the EEA to apply to crimes involving computer information and theft methods using network communications.

DOES FEDERAL INTELLECTUAL PROPERTY LAW PREEMPT STATE TRADE SECRET LAW?

State trade secret law and the policies underlying the federal IP laws are sometimes in conflict. For example, trade secret law might frustrate the objectives of patent law, such as when trade secrets persist beyond the defined 20-year duration of a patent or trade secret owners must not disclose their invention, as is required for patents. These potential conflicts raise criticisms that perhaps trade secret protections are inappropriate or that trade secrets are a class of lesser inventions. However, consider the impact of Coca-Cola's trade secret formula. The formula has been of potent commercial value for more than a century. Only in recent years have technologies developed (i.e., spectral analysis) that permit reverse engineering to discover the components and proportions of ingredients in the Coke recipe. State trade secret laws may coexist with federal patent law policy.

Could copyright law preempt state trade secret protection? The 1976 copyright revision eliminated the state common law of copyrights. That law also preempts any other state IP laws if they create rights equivalent to any of the exclusive rights under federal copyright—that is, to reproduce, distribute, make derivative works, display, or perform, as discussed in Chapter 4. Therefore, state trade secret protections that mainly protect the subject matter of copyrights are preempted and invalid. Furthermore, trade secret law is preempted even for the elements not protected by copyright if the trade secret law protects the elements protected by copyright law. All this means that it could be difficult to archive trade secrets because any trade secret embodied in expression that is fixed in a tangible medium is preempted because it is covered exclusively by copyright. Most trade secrets are written or stored in electronic form, so they are clearly covered by federal copyright law. How do trade secret laws survive preemption when most trade secrets are stored in forms protected by copyright?

Fortunately, many courts try to preserve trade secret law when the trade secret is contained in a copyrighted work. The key to the continued validity of trade secret laws is that there must be some "extra element" in the trade secret law beyond the requirements of copyright law. This point is usually satisfied where the misappropriation law involves something more, such as the protection against theft of physical copies (documents, disks, files) or a breach of confidentiality. Trade secret laws are not generally preempted by copyright law when they contain additional wrongful acts that are qualitatively different components from the elements of copyright law.[8] Separately, the Copyright Office permits copyright holders of software programs to blank out printed code showing trade secrets when they submit their source code to the Library of Congress.

SUBJECT MATTER OF TRADE SECRETS

Trade secrets include confidential information that has commercial value. Recall that the *Restatement* originally took a conceptual view of trade secrets, recognizing them only as a tort arising from the breach of a confidential relationship. This view effectively denied that trade secrets were property. However, society expects trade secrets will have property-like characteristics, so the UTSA and many courts hold that **"information is property."**[9] Status as property gives the trade secret owner some special rights, and the importance of this distinction is evident.

---

8. *Alcatel USA Inc. v. DGI Technologies, Inc.*, 166 F.3d 772 (5th Cir., 1999).
9. *U.S. v. Carpenter*, 484 U.S. 19 (1987) (material nonpublic information is property in insider trading context) and *Ruckelshaus v. Monsanto Co.*, 467 U.S. 986 (1984) (trade secrets are property interests for government takings purposes).

DEFINITIONS OF TRADE SECRETS

The definitions of trade secrets are very important because they indicate both what subject matter can be protected as trade secrets and the essential steps to create them. Definitions under the *Restatement*, the UTSA, and the EEA are quite similar. Note that over time these laws include specific types of eligible subject matter in progressively greater detail. The *Restatement* definition is worded most generally.

Restatement of Torts Trade Secret Definition

[A]ny formula, pattern, device or compilation of information which is used in one's business, and which gives him an opportunity to obtain an advantage over competitors who do not know or use it. It may be a formula for a chemical compound, a process of manufacturing, treating or preserving materials, a pattern for a machine or other device, or a list of customers. [It may include] a process or device for continuous use in the operation of the business [but not] information as to a single or ephemeral event.[10]

The *Restatement* requires continuous use of the trade secret; the UTSA does not and so permits protection for one-shot deals, such as takeovers, mergers, business plans, or salaries.[11] The UTSA definition includes most of the same elements yet adds some broad forms of eligible information and clarifies the need for reasonable efforts to maintain secrecy.

UTSA Trade Secret Definition

Information, including a formula, pattern, compilation, program device, method, technique or process, that:

(i) derives independent economic value, actual or potential, from not being generally known to, and not being readily ascertainable by proper means by other persons who can obtain economic value from its disclosure or use, and

(ii) is the subject of efforts that are reasonable under the circumstances to maintain its secrecy.[12]

The EEA definition is modeled on the *Restatement* and the UTSA. However, the EEA is more recent legislation, which gave Congress an opportunity to include some more specific examples of eligible subject matter. The EEA clearly recognizes that information is processed, stored, and protected on networked computers.

---

10. *Restatement of Torts*, §757, comment b.
11. New York uses the *Restatement*, so *Lehman v. Dow Jones & Co., Inc.*, 783 F.2d 285 (2d Cir., 1986) held that the attractiveness of a takeover target was not eligible for protection as a trade secret.
12. UTSA §1(4).

EEA Trade Secret Definition

[T]he term "trade secret" means all forms and types of financial, business, scientific, technical, economic, or engineering information, including patterns, plans, compilations, program devices, formulas, designs, prototypes, methods, techniques, processes, procedures, programs, or codes, whether tangible or intangible, and whether or how stored, compiled, or memorialized physically, electronically, graphically, photographically, or in writing if

    (A) the owner thereof has taken reasonable measures to keep such information secret; and

    (B) the information derives independent economic value, actual or potential, from not being general known to, and not being readily ascertainable through proper means by the public.[13]

Case law interprets these lists to include many additional specific types of information. For example, the following are eligible subject matter for trade secret protection: engineering data, customer information, lists or preferences, raw material sources, manufacturing processes, design manuals, operating and pricing policies, price codes, bid information, bookkeeping methods, market studies and research, sales data, marketing plans and strategies, new product information, business plans, optimal use of equipment and machinery, software, flow charts, drawings, blueprints, negative results, and know-how. Even a unique selection, compilation, or combination of information taken from the public domain can be protected, an important feature of database protections discussed later in this chapter.

Note that many items on this supplemental list are competitively valuable confidential business information. Some are **know-how,** the experience and intelligence to make processes work most effectively. Know-how is similar to the specifications in a patent that reveal the best mode to practice the patent—that is, the inventor's knowledge of the optimal method to use the patent in a useful way. **Negative results** show what does not work as desired; they come from experiments or testing. Negative results are valuable because competitors might need to repeat the tests, which gives the trade secret owner an economic advantage. The eligible subject matter for trade secrets is much broader than the subjects for patenting: machines, processes, and compositions of matter.

CUSTOMER INFORMATION

Many trade secret cases are litigated over lists of customers, customers' personal preferences, and other related information. Customer lists are more likely to receive protection if effort and expense is used to compile the list and the list includes associated information that creates a database, such as contact agents and sales histories. Lists known generally throughout the industry or that are readily ascertainable from public sources may not be protected. This means that trade secret protection is more likely when the information is difficult to obtain.[14]

---

13. 18 U.S.C. §1839(3) (2000).
14. *Morlife, Inc. v. Perry*, 56 Cal.App.4th 1514 (Cal.Ct.App. 1997).

An interesting contrast is evident between the law of agency and the emerging interpretation of trade secret law. Agency law provides that customer information retained in a former employee's memory (brain) is exempt from trade secret protection.[15] However, some recent trade secret cases would hold otherwise, such as *Ed Nowogroski Ins. v. Rucker*,[16] in which a former employee recalled, by unaided memory alone, customer lists from a former employer. This was found to be a misappropriation of trade secrets, even though no physical files were copied or stolen.

TRADE SECRETS IN SOFTWARE AND ON THE INTERNET

Trade secrets are increasingly used in software and Internet applications. The major criteria are whether the information, algorithm, links, indexes, methods, or processes would save a competitor time in developing the software or making it more useful. If so, the software information could be a trade secret. Similarly, secret Internet operations, methods, or application programs may qualify as trade secrets. In both cases, the owner must use confidentiality restrictions to retain the secrecy. Users and support personnel can be obligated by agreement to maintain confidentiality and not misappropriate the trade secrets. For example, most software licenses prohibit the licensee from decompiling the program. Decompiling is a form of reverse engineering that could reveal trade secrets to a skilled programmer. Reverse engineering is discussed later in this chapter, and confidentiality agreements are discussed in Chapter 11.

ACQUISITION, CONTROL, AND OWNERSHIP OF TRADE SECRETS

Unlike most other forms of IP, trade secrets do not depend on government agencies to create them. Trade secrets are largely created and maintained by the owner's efforts, based on fundamental factors discussed in this section. Trade secret ownership largely depends on contractual controls and confidentiality agreements. These methods cover users as well as the innovators who contribute to devising and assembling the secret information. Confidentiality must be exercised over all people exposed to the secrets. Other types of control—physical, administrative, and contractual—may be needed, depending on the circumstances.

Trade secret rights are not perfected by making applications or filing registrations with regulators. That is not to say that government enforcement is never involved with trade secrets. Increasingly, the criminal aspects of trade secret misappropriation, such as trespass or theft, are addressed by the FBI, state attorneys general, the DOJ, or other law enforcement agencies. Also, many regulatory agencies use procedures to maintain the secrecy about the regulated entities under their control or about investigatory matters.

---

15. *Restatement of Agency* §396.
16. 971 P.2d 936 (Wa., 1999).

Traditional trade secret law under the *Restatement* envisioned that the subject matter must have **concreteness**. The trade secret should be more specific and certain than a mere idea or theory, and the trade secret must relate to some useful application. Although the UTSA does not require concreteness, many courts impose this requirement implicitly, such as when they define what is eligible subject matter. Some courts would not require that the trade secret have novelty—some unique newness—but other courts impose a **novelty** requirement. It is not so stringent that it amounts to an invention requirement, as is required by patent law. Novelty is closely related to secrecy, discussed in the next section. Interestingly, court decisions requiring concreteness for trade secrets somewhat parallel patent law's specific requirements for an adequate description and novelty. Exhibit 5.2 lists six factors from the *Restatement* that provide guidance for giving trade secret protection.

Conceptually, trade secret status could be perpetual if the owner keeps the information secret. It is difficult to measure the average value of trade secrets or their longevity because so many are successfully kept secret and firms' own records are incomplete. Recall the long-standing success of the Coke formula. As a practical matter, when the existence of highly valuable trade secrets becomes known, competitors probably expend considerable effort to reverse-engineer, misappropriate, or independently develop similar or alternate methods. This section discusses how these *Restatement* factors inspire the de facto trade secret requirements: secrecy, commercial and economic value, and use causing damage.

REASONABLE EFFORTS TO MAINTAIN SECRECY

Secrecy is the critical element in most trade secret cases for two main reasons: First, the owner must undertake reasonable measures to preserve the secrecy; otherwise, the information will not be protected practically or under trade secret law. Second, there is no reason to sue unless the trade secret has been stolen, misappropriated, or disclosed. Absolute privacy is not needed because the cost burden would too often overwhelm the secret's economic value. Instead, an ad hoc, case-by-case analysis of the circumstances is made to determine whether the owner has "taken all proper and

Exhibit 5.2 Trade Secret Factors: *Restatement of Torts*

1. Extent to which the trade secret is known outside the business.
2. Extent to which it is known by employees and others involved in the business.
3. The extent of measures taken to guard the secrecy of the information.
4. The value of the information to [the owner and to] competitors.
5. The amount of effort or money expended in developing the information.
6. The ease or difficulty with which the information could be properly acquired or duplicated by others.[17]

---

17. *Restatement of Torts* §757, comment b.

reasonable steps . . . considering the nature of the information sought to be protected as well as the conduct of the parties."[18] Although trade secret laws do not
directly define secrecy, many cases discuss it, and the trade secret laws define it negatively; that is, they define when secrecy is lacking. For example, the *Restatement*
denies trade secrecy to "matters of public knowledge or of general knowledge in an
industry." Secrecy can be lost even if the general public does not know the secret. A
potential competitor's knowledge is enough.[19]

Relevant factors in secrecy include the general knowledge of security in the
industry and the offensiveness of the misappropriator's conduct. In building a
secrecy program, it may be necessary to examine past trade secret practices in the
industry, conduct periodic IP audits (including the firm's trade secrets and existing
protections), develop scenarios of misappropriation, and design protocols to avoid
loss. The audit team needs expertise in several areas, including IP law, technical
expertise in the invention field, computer security, and business decisions (strategy,
marketing, and/or finance).

These efforts can seem burdensome. However, many management service firms provide consulting to develop new control programs and update existing programs. For
example, big accounting firms, law firms specializing in IP, security consultants, and
computer security firms regularly help perform IP audits and design trade secrets protections. The major methods are discussed later in this chapter. They are useful beyond
trade secrets; much of this regimen is important to develop patents or copyrights.

Will trade secret law still provide remedies if information is inadvertently disclosed outside the "circle of approved employees and third parties"? Secrecy is
always most effective when the information is retained by a controlled inner circle.
However, there are several recurring situations in which information is released and
the courts must determine whether trade secrecy continues as a practical matter.
First, information may be determined through **reverse engineering** of products
embodying the trade secret that are acquired legally. Second, published information
that is **readily ascertainable** from trade journals, reference books, or other published
materials is not secret. Third, trade secrets may be revealed to government entities.

Trade Secrets Revealed to Government

Another regular form of trade secret disclosure is the information contained in
patents. Patent law requires the PTO to keep confidential trade secrets divulged
in patent applications during examination. If worldwide patent protection is
sought, patent applications are published after 18 months, revealing these secrets.
Once patents are granted by the PTO, publication of the patent reveals the invention's trade secrets. These trade secrets then enter the public domain. Of course,
patent law gives the inventor a limited monopoly to prevent others from directly
using the secrets, but their revelation often encourages innovation to work around
and even surpass the patent's claims. The patent applicant may withdraw the

---

18. *USM Corp. v. Marson Fastner Corp.*, 393 N.E.2d 895 (Mass. 1979).
19. UTSA §1 comment.

application at any time before the patent application is rejected or published or the patent is issued. This usually preserves trade secrets contained therein.[20]

Some trade secrets are revealed to government, such as disclosures to regulatory agencies or during litigation. Most agencies have rules requiring that trade secrecy be respected whenever possible. However, agencies sometimes release trade secrets for the public good or during enforcement litigation with the secret's owner. The Freedom of Information Act (FOIA) requires federal agencies to release information whenever a reasonable request is made by any person.[21] FOIA permits most agencies to exercise discretion[22] to withhold disclosing trade secrets in satisfying FOIA requests. Further, an agency can override its promise to maintain secrecy of information submitted by its owner. Nevertheless, a regulator's disclosure of a trade secret may constitute a taking, entitling the owner to compensation under the Fifth Amendment, because "information is property."[23] Similar trade secrecy problems arise with state open records laws; many are patterned after the federal FOIA.

Trade secret information could be revealed during litigation over IP, trade secrets, product liability, or environmental or other issues. Information presented at most trials is placed in the "public record," permitting examination by anyone. However, all is not lost in litigation because many judges place protective orders on information revealed during pretrial discovery. **Protective orders** are court orders to preserve secrecy. Further, testimony likely to reveal trade secret details may be taken **in camera**—that is, privately before the judge and not in open court. Finally, judges often **seal records** from the trial that would reveal trade secrets. Judges also order the opposing parties and witnesses not to disclose trade secret details without court approval.

WHAT ARE REASONABLE SECURITY PRECAUTIONS?

Firms with substantial or key trade secret assets must develop security protection programs and keep them updated. These programs are even useful to competitors to disprove charges of misappropriation because they provide a complete catalogue of the firm's trade secrets that helps prove rightful development and use. Many components to these programs should be familiar to law enforcement, management accountants, auditors, security professionals, and national security experts because the design of similar systems are so important to these professionals.[24] The firm should first establish sound policies on trade secrecy. From these policies, security measures should be generated that address activities of and interactions among three separate areas: (1) information-centered controls, (2) employee-centered controls, and (3) outsider-centered controls. Of course, there are other ways to classify controls, and many security measures could be usefully applied in two or more classifications.

---

20. 35 U.S.C. §122 (2000).
21. 5 U.S.C. §552 (2000).
22. *Chrysler v. Brown*, 441 U.S. 281 (1979).
23. *Ruckelshaus v. Monsanto Co.*, 467 U.S. 986 (1984).
24. M. Epstein and S. Levi, Protecting Trade Secret Information: Plan for Proactive Strategy, *Business Law* (May 1988).

Deliberate evaluation of trade secret protection is necessarily a **risk-benefit analysis**. The cost of each security control measure must be balanced against the financial risk of losing the secret to competitors. Then this analysis is adjusted by the probability that particular combinations of controls can prevent or impede misappropriation, resulting in the net benefits likely to be derived.

Information-Centered Controls

The initial focus should be made on the information itself: Identify sensitive information; list all employees and outsiders who have access; create a "need to know basis" for future access; place warning labels and then log sensitive documents, files, and facilities; use lock-out techniques such as vaults, restricted areas, and computer and network passwords; encrypt or otherwise code data; erase, shred, or destroy stale information; control photocopying; segregate data that has value when integrated; and install alarms, video surveillance, and monitoring devices. With so much proprietary information now created by computer, distributed throughout the firm's locations, and stored for retrieval on networks, the importance of computer security is seldom overstated. Network security techniques such as changing passwords, firewalls, hacker prevention, and Internet policies are becoming very important. Logs should be kept showing when network information was accessed, downloaded, printed, or saved and by whom (IP address).

Reconsider the Coke formula example. The formula is reputedly separated into two major components: one is locked up at one facility, accessible by only one scientist; the other is locked up at a different location and known only to another scientist. The two scientists never meet; their contact is largely prevented. Batches of the two formula components are assembled separately and later combined at a third site. Such information-centered controls significantly reduce misappropriation risk.

Employee-Centered Controls

Few firms can create or use trade secrets without divulging some portion of them to the employees who invent or implement firm activities. Employee-centered controls are directed at delegating strong confidentiality duties and controlling the misuse of trade secrets. The most basic controls are created in employment agreements in which the employee is bound to confidentiality in various nondisclosure agreements (NDA); a noncompete clause; the nonsolicitation of clients, customers, and co-workers; required sign-in after hours, identification cards while on site, and special access codes to enter sensitive areas; and various work rules generally prohibiting misappropriation and specifically prohibiting personal misuse of employer trade secrets and other assets. Many employers clearly inform their employees that phone records are retained, e-mail using the firm's computers or networks belong to the employer, and workplace surveillance must be expected. Employers generally require employees to assign their IP ownership rights to the employer and agree to assist in obtaining patents or copyrights. Exit interviews and posttermination reminders may encourage compliance. They can also provide a convenient opportunity for the return of the employer's documents, computers, and files. Many of these employment contracting terms are detailed in Chapter 11. Additionally, Chapter 11 discusses the developing inevitable disclosure doctrine, under which a court may impose restrictions that prevent former employees from using trade secrets for a competitor.[25]

Employee-centered controls run some risks. Constant reminders seem advisable so employees are encouraged not to relax their vigilance. However, overextensive security controls may harm morale. They can show a lack of trust, raise employee turnover, and ultimately discourage beneficial risk taking. When controls are well balanced and periodically reviewed during IP audits, employees may better appreciate how their ingenuity contributes to the firm's value.

Outsider-Centered Controls

It is almost inevitable that outsiders will be exposed to at least some trade secrets. Visitors are given plant tours. Employees of service and maintenance firms are often summoned in emergencies. Specifications and new product plans are shared with suppliers who design parts and provide expertise. Consultants are exposed to strategies, product specifications, and production processes to help the firm. Customers are diverted from competitors when shown details of promising, innovative products. As with employee exposure to trade secrets, it is best to reveal only on a need-to-know basis, solicit NDAs, and reveal incomplete information wherever practical. Firms should carefully review product catalogues and specifications, Web site postings, and press releases to prevent disclosure of important trade secret data. Although licensing trade secrets can be tricky, study the techniques discussed in Chapter 11. For example, most software contains trade secrets, most purchasers of software license its use, and licensors generally impose confidentiality through prohibitions on decompiling or other reverse engineering.

Individuals often submit ideas to firms perceived as capable of effectively developing them into profitable businesses. Idea submissions require delicate progressive revelation and NDAs to create confidentiality and prevent the recipient from appropriating the idea. These techniques are also detailed in Chapter 11. Some of this effort may seem to be unnecessary, excessive secrecy that will only create mistrust and is hardly conducive to good relations. The professional duties of many consultants, accountants, and lawyers prohibit disclosure of client confidences, even without NDAs. Maybe this is so, but it is usually advisable to log and specify confidentiality for all valuable trade secrets shared with outsiders to facilitate their consultation with the owner. Many nations around the Pacific Rim develop long-term, trusted relationships with suppliers and customers to improve confidentiality expectations resulting from loyalty and trust. Such cultural norms may substitute for some costly controls.

---

25. See *PepsiCo, Inc. v. Redmond*, 54 F.3d 1262 (7th Cir., 1995) and *EarthWeb, Inc. v. Schlack*, 71 F.Supp.2d 299 (S.D.N.Y. 1999).

COMMERCIAL VALUE

The *Restatement* implicitly requires the trade secret to have commercial value, derived from the requirement that the secret must give an advantage over competitors. The UTSA and EEA more clearly require trade secrets to give the owner some commercial advantage; these laws require that the owner "derives independent economic value, actual or potential, from [the information] not being generally known." For example, the trade secret could give the owner a cost advantage in raw materials, production, or distribution. Alternatively, the trade secret might make the product superior in quality, features, or performance.

USE CAUSING DAMAGE

The final requirement is that trade secret protection will be available when the owner is damaged by the use of the trade secret. This use arises when a competitor can avoid costs or increase quality or productivity by using the trade secret. Damage from use also arises when the misappropriation occurs because the owner will suffer potential loss from a competitor's future use of the trade secret or from public disclosure.

TRADE SECRET OWNERSHIP

Ownership generally falls to the inventor, discoverer, or developer of the trade secret. Employers may rightfully capture secrets developed at the firm's expense and by its employees by using employment contract provisions such as work for hire, hired to invent, NDAs, noncompetes, and work rules establishing ownership. Ownership is so closely related to secrecy that ownership is lost when the information enters the public domain. Nevertheless, the owner has remedies under trade secret law against employees or outsiders who misappropriate the trade secret or cause it to be publicly disclosed. Misappropriation is discussed next, remedies are discussed later in the chapter, and employment contracting is discussed in Chapter 11.

MISAPPROPRIATION

Although secrecy is the fundamental concept in creating trade secrets, the fundamental concept in trade secret infringement is misappropriation. Misappropriation is the conduct triggering liability and legal action. Suits for wrongful misappropriation are the primary means to protect trade secrets. Misappropriation is both a tort and a violation of contractual confidentiality; many trade secret owners make claims under both theories. A general definition of **misappropriation** covers a range of unethical activities including knowing, wrongful conduct resulting in theft, and wrongful disclosure of secret information using either improper means or in violation of a confidential relationship. The UTSA definition of misappropriation is somewhat complex.

Misappropriation under UTSA

(i) acquisition of a trade secret of another by a person who knows or has reason to know that the trade secret was acquired by improper means; or

(ii) disclosure or use of a trade secret of another without express or implied consent by a person who

(A) used improper means to acquire knowledge of the trade secret; or

(B) at the time of disclosure or use, knew or had reason to know that his knowledge of the trade secret was

(I) derived from or through a person who has utilized improper means to acquire it;

(II) acquired under circumstances giving rise to a duty to maintain its secrecy or limit its use; or

(III) derived from or through a person who owed a duty to the person seeking relief to maintain its secrecy or limit its use; or

(C) before a material change of his or her position, knew or had reason to know that it was a trade secret and that knowledge of it had been acquired by accident or mistake.[26]

Although the *Restatement* definition is substantially similar, there is one major difference. Before an alleged misappropriation violates the *Restatement*, a disclosure or use of the information must be proved. By contrast, the UTSA provides a tougher standard. The UTSA is violated by mere wrongful acquisition—activities that can occur even before a wrongful use or disclosure might occur. The UTSA definition can be clarified by reclassifying the misappropriation factors into four major forms of misappropriation: (1) improper means, (2) receipt, (3) disclosure, and (4) use. As illustrated in the section on reasonable security precautions, any form of misappropriation could be performed by employees, trusted third parties (e.g., consultants, suppliers, customers), or third-party strangers.

MISAPPROPRIATION: ACQUISITION BY IMPROPER MEANS

Acquisition of trade secrets by using improper means includes actions such as "theft, bribery, misrepresentation, breach or inducement of a breach of duty to maintain secrecy, or espionage through electronic or other means."[27] These are probably the most severe forms of trade secret misappropriation because they involve actions often unlawful under criminal law. For example, employees and entrusted third parties often have access to trade secrets needed to perform their jobs. This type of "information is property"; it belongs to the employer and not to the employee or the entrusted third party. It is misappropriation if one of these parties acquires the information by stealing, bribing others, or using espionage. Similar activities committed by competitors or complete strangers, such as while on a plant tour or by enticing an employee or entrusted third party, are also wrongful.

---

26. UTSA §1(2).
27. UTSA §1(1).

This form of misappropriation specifically targets unlawful capture of electronic information or unpermitted access into computers, networks, or telecommunication systems. It includes both trespass to land and trespass to chattels. Trespass is an ancient legal concept that is experiencing a revival as hackers probe computers attached to networks and the Internet. All these situations involve intrusion into the zone of expected privacy, a topic developed more fully in Chapter 13. Many physical and computer security controls are regularly used to prevent this problem.

MISAPPROPRIATION BY DISCLOSURE

Trade secret law seeks to prevent disclosure of trade secrets, mostly by employees or entrusted third parties. However, it also prohibits disclosure by strangers who receive the information unlawfully. For example, it is unlawful to disclose trade secrets acquired *directly* from a discloser who used improper means or to *indirectly* acquire information known to come through a chain of tipping. It is also unlawful to disclose trade secrets for a person who knows the information was originally acquired through improper means or in breach of a confidence. Note that disclosure is a separate wrong that is derived from another wrong: acquisition by improper means. Why should there be two separate wrongs in what might often be a single act? Trade secret law reinforces commercial morality by assuring that several forms of the wrong are made illegal and that wrongdoers cannot easily escape liability.

MISAPPROPRIATION BY RECEIPT

Trade secret law also prohibits the receipt of protected information. Misappropriation often involves a "tipping chain" that transmits stolen information from an insider or thief through others to a competitor. Passive and accidental receipt of trade secrets is not generally unlawful. Instead, it is wrongful for a recipient to encourage another person, insider or outsider, to communicate the information, when the recipient knows the secret was misappropriated by improper means or a breach of confidentiality. For example, when a competitor receives trade secrets from a former employee of the owner, this constitutes misappropriation by receipt. The recipient could also be another employee of the owner, an entrusted third party, or some other stranger.

MISAPPROPRIATION BY USE

The most direct damage occurs to the owner when the trade secret is used, usually by a competitor, to gain an economic advantage. The owner loses the advantage, and the value of the trade secret is at least partially lost. For example, like with unlawful disclosure, it is unlawful to use trade secrets acquired *directly* from a discloser who used improper means or *indirectly*, if the user knows the information came through a chain of tipping. It is also unlawful to use trade secrets if the user knows the information was originally acquired through improper means or in breach of a confidence. Use is the final but most damaging activity along the chain of misappropriation, as depicted in Exhibit 5.3.

Exhibit 5.3 Chain of Unlawful Forms of Misappropriation

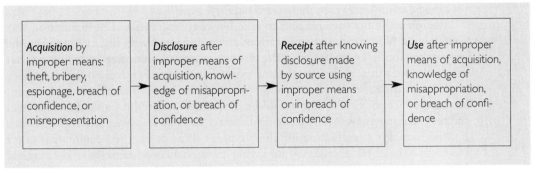

DEFENSES TO MISAPPROPRIATION

Someone accused of misappropriation may counter the trade secret owner's allegations with evidence disproving the owner's claims or even with an excuse—a defense. Several defenses partially or fully relieve the alleged misappropriator from liability: (1) independent development, (2) proper means of discovery, (3) innocent receipt, (4) reverse engineering, (5) public domain, and (6) various standard equitable and procedural defenses.

INDEPENDENT DEVELOPMENT

Unlike the protection under a patent, a trade secret may be rightfully developed and used by multiple inventors or discoverers. By contrast, it is patent infringement for a second inventor to practice the innovation contained in an existing patent, even if the second inventor was unaware of the patentee's invention. Not so with trade secrets—independent development, either before or after the owner's development, is a complete defense to misappropriation. Of course, the independent development must not have been informed or inspired by confidential information received from the owner. For example, assume one firm has developed an algorithm to evaluate the sale price of derivative securities. After a second firm became known for using a similar technique that it developed previously, the first firm sues for misappropriation. The second firm may use the algorithm because it was developed independently by that second firm but not if it hired away the inventor.

INNOCENT RECEIPT

There is no duty to refrain from using information received accidentally and innocently. The recipient can defend against a misappropriation suit when no confidentiality breach was known to the recipient or no improper means was used. For example, consider the innocence of a recipient of information overheard in public. If the recipient made no effort to extract the information and there is no indication that the speaker breached a confidence, then there is no liability.

Recipients' innocence reduces to whether they had notice the information was confidential. Notice can take many forms but is answered with this analysis: Did the recipient actually know or, given the circumstances, should they have known that the disclosure was confidential or came from a confidential source? Sometimes notice comes after the recipient has in good faith paid value for the secret or the recipient so changed its position that it would be inequitable to hold it liable. For example, the recipient may have licensed the trade secret from an imposter and then invested heavily in making products using the secret. In these cases, the *Restatement* urges courts to balance the equities by not giving an injunction or damages to the original trade secret owner. In these late-notice situations, the UTSA would require the innocent recipient to pay a reasonable royalty to the original owner.

REVERSE ENGINEERING

Throughout this chapter, reverse engineering is discussed as a legitimate method to discover trade secrets and a complete defense to a misappropriation suit. **Reverse engineering** is the analysis of a product to discover its components and structure. The *Restatement* generally defines it as "inspection or analysis of the commercial product embodying the secret." The UTSA defines it as "starting with the known product and working backward to find the method by which it was developed."

Reverse engineering can often reveal trade secrets in the structure or design of products. The process involves retracing the steps in design and then re-creating the formula or process used in production. For example, when GM embarked on a program to improve the crashworthiness of its sedans, it bought ten Volvos and painstakingly disassembled them to discover how Volvo makes such safe cars. By contrast, trade secrets in the production or administrative process generally cannot be revealed when products are disassembled by experts in the fields of design or manufacturing so they are naturally safer from reverse engineering.

There are limits to reverse engineering. First, software licenses routinely prohibit disassembly—reverse engineering by decompiling object code to become source code. Analysis of source code by experienced programmers would usually reveal trade secrets. Second, the products studied must be acquired legally, according to the UTSA: "The acquisition of the known product must, of course, be by a fair and honest means, such as purchase of the item on the open market for reverse engineering to be lawful." For example, it would not be legitimate to reverse-engineer stolen preproduction products or bribe suppliers to provide components containing the trade secrets.

INFORMATION ALREADY IN THE PUBLIC DOMAIN

Information in the public domain cannot be a trade secret and therefore cannot be misappropriated. Unique combinations, including selection and arrangement of public domain information, could be a trade secret. The public domain defense is directly tied to secrecy. Remember the discussion earlier that information provided to governments or which is readily ascertainable from trade journals, reference books, or other published materials is not secret. But what about secret information wrongfully published? The Internet is a very effective and convenient way to quickly destroy trade secrecy for vindictive or altruistic reasons. Given the breadth of the First Amendment's freedoms of speech and press and absent a confidentiality duty or theft, preventing such postings may be difficult, at least beforehand. Some cases hold that Internet postings destroy secrecy and place the information into the public domain.[28] However, if the owner acts quickly to contain the damage by taking down postings, some courts may be willing to analyze the extent of the publication without mechanically ruling that trade secrets are always destroyed by Internet posting.[29]

OTHER DEFENSES TO MISAPPROPRIATION

Other defenses to misappropriation deserve passing mention. The **statute of limitations** for tort suits is usually applicable. Trade secret owners waiting too long to bring suit may be barred. Equitable defenses are also generally available because the injunction remedy can be so effective. For example, laches is equity's flexible version of a statute of limitations. The **unclean hands** defense could bar an owner who used improper means in acquiring the trade secret. **Laches** would bar an owner's misappropriation suit if there were unexplained delays in bringing suit. If the owner proves its trade secret was misappropriated and no defense applies, the owner is entitled to remedies.

REMEDIES

Trade secret owners suffering misappropriation have two major civil remedies: (1) an injunction against further disclosure or use of the trade secret and (2) money damages resulting from loss of the competitive advantage from the secret information. Separately, the owner may initiate a criminal complaint for state crimes (e.g., theft, trespassing, burglary) or federal crimes, such as the EEA or privacy crimes discussed in Chapter 13, including the Computer Fraud and Abuse Act or the Electronic Communications Privacy Act. Of course, political pressures may influence criminal prosecutors. Their investigatory resources are limited, and they must allocate their constrained resources among a wide variety of crimes and current criminal investigations.

INJUNCTIONS

Injunctions are the most basic and immediately effective remedies. A court order can prohibit the misappropriator from actual or threatened use of the secret. An

---

28. *Religious Technology Center v. Netcom On-Line Communications Services, Inc.*, 923 F.Supp. 1519 (N.D.Cal. 1995).
29. *DVD Copy Control Association, Inc. v. McLaughlin*, 2000 WL 48512 (Cal.Sup. 2000).

injunction is also useful to prohibit further disclosures of the secret to others. These may be the most effective remedies when the information is still secret and has not been disclosed widely into the public domain because they effectively prevent economic damages. The injunction may target an entrusted outsider, a competing firm, or a former employee, such as in the inevitable disclosure situation, from disclosing or using the information.

An injunction should be limited to the time the information remains secret. Once the trade secret goes into the public domain, the misappropriator should be able to use the information just as anyone else could. However, a few courts delay this use to prevent any head start in getting products to market made possible by the misappropriation. A temporary restraining order (TRO) or **preliminary injunction** can be appropriate where disclosure is imminent. For example, if the misappropriator is ready to deliver to a client a report containing the secrets, then a preliminary injunction would delay the disclosure until after a trial is held on the secrecy and misappropriation issues.

MONEY DAMAGES

If an injunction to prevent disclosure or use of a trade secret is not possible, then money damages are the next most effective remedy. Damages may result from the owner's loss of sales or market share to competitors' sales that include the infringing trade secret, lower prices for the owner's sales due to competitors' sales, and the misappropriator's profits from products sold using the trade secret. Under the UTSA:

Damages can include both the actual loss caused by misappropriation and the unjust enrichment caused by misappropriation that is not taken into account in computing actual loss.

The owner must prove the compensatory damage amount. The misappropriator has the burden of proving that none of its profits are attributable to the trade secret. If damages are too difficult to prove, a reasonable royalty may be ordered. The UTSA permits punitive damages up to double the amount of the compensatory damages for willful, wanton, and malicious misappropriation. Additionally, attorneys' fees are sometimes ordered in cases of blatant, oppressive, and bad faith conduct. Attorneys' fees could be ordered against the trade secret's owner for a bad faith claim of misappropriation or bad faith opposition to terminate an injunction after the trade secret has gone into the public domain. In extraordinary cases, where the misappropriator has produced products that include the trade secret technology, called embodiments, these products could be seized and destroyed.

PROTECTION OF DATABASES

The information age runs on data, facts, collections of artistic expression, and the like. Consider the business models for such profitable firms as Lexis-Nexis, Westlaw, Moody's, eBay, DoubleClick, Rand-McNally, and proprietary libraries. The one common thread is their need for a reasonable cash flow to fund investment in acquiring data, both digital and analog. Without some legal protection for their databases, only public libraries and universities would be apt to make systematic accumulations of data available for research, learning, and commerce. Databases are as old as manual record-keeping systems, as ubiquitous as telephone books and CD-ROMs, and as new and innovative as Napster was in creating peer-to-peer (P2P) network applications.

Databases are collections of works, data, or other materials arranged in a systematic or methodical way for retrieval or access by manual or electronic means. Data are raw facts that most often become meaningful only when collected and arranged in some logical fashion so that meaning can be given. Then users can access the information and aggregate particular aspects of it in different ways that reveal meaningful relationships. Many useful databases are constantly updated with new information, purged periodically of useless or stale information, and constantly managed to maintain usefulness, data security, confidentiality, and value.

The types of information contained in databases often are such diverse subject matter as literary works, artistic works, texts, sounds, images, numbers, facts, production figures, shipping information, transactions, financial data, geographic information, and personal data. Today, databases are most useful when compiled electronically. Databases are usually stored on computers and electronic media so they can be retrieved according to defined aspects of the data. The function of databases is often to create reports that are communicated to remote locations via telecommunications, such as the public Internet or in closed, proprietary intranets.

Database technology has advanced significantly from ledger paper and spreadsheets. Today a database may stand alone on a PC or mainframe computer or be part of a distributed processing system. Either is well suited to database construction and operation. For example, modern databases may be composed of several separate repositories that are formally linked together by telecommunications. Many firms link their geographically dispersed databases into an enterprise-wide intranet. Increasingly, informal links are arising under the P2P techniques of survey, indexing, and access.

Some databases contain so much information and are so huge that they are comprised of terabytes of information. They are often called **data warehouses**. The dramatic drop in costs for electronic storage and retrieval makes such mass data techniques practical. Large-scale and distributed databases raise both database protection and privacy concerns. (The latter is discussed in Chapter 13.) Relational databases run quickly and efficiently, revealing associations among data and permitting talented people to find new relationships, a practice called **data mining**. New associations are discovered, new sequences are uncovered, and new data classifications or clusters are constructed. All this enables better forecasts, a clear competitive advantage that can also be sold to others.[30]

---

30. Jane Kaufman Winn, and James R. Wrathall, Who Owns the Customer? The Emerging Law of Commercial Transactions in Electronic Consumer Data, *Business Lawyer 56* Bus Law 235 (2000), 235.

The Europeans have gone much further than the United States in protecting databases. As discussed later, the EU Directive on the Legal Protection of Databases[31] rewards people or firms who gather data and invest in its organization into a potentially useful database. The EU Directive requires each separate EU nation to enact national laws that create **sui generis** forms of IP. These modern databases are thus new forms of IP, not previously recognized under traditional copyright, patent, trade secret, or trademark law. However, this "sweat of the brow" theory is not part of current U.S. law. In the United States, databases receive incomplete protection under one or a combination of several theories of law: tort, trade secret, copyright, and contract. This section discusses these incomplete protections that U.S. law offers for databases.

TORT THEORIES

Tort theories of database protection have existed for decades but offer rather limited protection. Several tort theories are available to database owners to protect their databases from unauthorized access, use, or resale by an infringing outsider: misappropriation, trespass, conversion, and trade secrets. Database infringement may include aspects of one or more of these theories, as well as some other legal theories such as breach of contract, database license violations, and breach of employment or confidentiality agreement.

Hot News

The landmark case resolved a 1918 misappropriation dispute in *International News Service v. Associated Press*.[32] International News Service (INS) transmitted news stories about World War I as reports on its wire service. INS originally acquired these stories off the Associated Press (AP) newswire. INS members used these reports as the basis of newspaper stories in direct competition with AP member newspapers that wrote similar stories based on the same timely **"hot news."** The U.S. Supreme Court held that it is wrongful to unfairly misappropriate factual material acquired by another to compete with the data's owner. This decision spawned a form of database protection called the hot news theory, so named because the time value of the information was the property of the original owner.

Later legislation and cases have severely limited this doctrine. Recall from the trade secret preemption discussed before that state law is invalid if it covers copyright subject matter and creates rights similar to those under federal copyright. Hot news is expression covered under copyright, and copying is one of the copyright bundle of rights. However, state misappropriation laws may still protect hot news because they involve "extra element(s)" protected beyond the copying. For example, state misappropriation law generally addresses other elements, such as the time-sensitive nature of the facts, the investment by the owner ("sweat"), the infringer's

31. OJ 1996 L77/20.
32. *International News Service v. Associated Press*, 248 U.S. 215 (1918).

free riding, the infringer's direct competition with the database originator in using the information, breach of confidence, or passing off. Hot news data may be protected against misappropriation if one or more of these (or other) noncopyright elements are protected by the state law.

Problems with hot news protections were addressed in a series of more recent sports information cases involving real-time play-by-play and score information delivered via wireless or the Internet to various devices, including pagers, PDAs, and PCs. Consider *National Basketball Association* (NBA) *v. Motorola, Inc.,*[33] Motorola marketed a pager promising to deliver real-time NBA scores but failed to license this content from the NBA. This information was acquired through Sports Team Analysis and Tracking Systems, Inc. (STATS), which gathered the data from various broadcast sources. STATS then transmitted the data to Motorola via satellite, and Motorola distributed the information to pagers and through the Internet. About the same time, the NBA was attempting to launch its own "Gamestats" service. The New York trial court protected the NBA data and decided in favor of the NBA. It held that STATS and Motorola made no contributions to the data and that they deprived the NBA of its property. However, this trial court decision was reversed on appeal. The Second Circuit found no "extra elements" in this case because the copyrighted broadcasts and noncopyrightable scores should not be separated to permit state claims. This case narrows the hot news protection for databases substantially.

Trespass to Chattels

Trespass to chattels or **cyber trespass** may be a more promising tort theory to protect databases, as well as any data on individual computers or spread among Internet Web sites. Trespass is an intentional invasion of another person's property interest, the owner's exclusive right to possession. In the electronic database context, trespass could be accomplished locally or remotely by (1) physical acts on site that intrude into another's computer storage and (2) remote access, probably via Internet or network connections, wired or wireless, by which the trespasser gains access to a computer's memory, storage, or data transmission. Trespass causes harm by reducing the condition, quality, or value of personal property even if there is no physical damage.

Trespass seems to be a robust theory whenever there has been unauthorized access to another's computer, any unauthorized storage onto or destruction of data residing on another's computer, and any unauthorized reading or accessing of data taken from another's computer. Trespass could be a major threat to several computer and networking transaction methods, such as cookies, copying data from a local hard drive during an interactive session to make capacity available for the session, or any other probing of another computer for information. Courts could excuse the trespass and thereby permit remote access if (1) permission is granted in a user agreement, (2) the public gains a widespread understanding and accepts that many Internet methods require access to user data, or (3) users realize their RAM and permanent storage

---

33. 105 F.3d 841 (2d Cir., 1997).

must be invaded by outside programs or probes to accomplish the user's on-line experience. However, there is evidence that few users understand either the fact of outsider probes or the privacy and security significance of such probes. It may take some time before there is widespread user acceptance.

Data Aggregation

Data aggregation requires probing another's Web site for information. **Data aggregators** are a cottage industry that locates data from widely varying sources such as the Internet to produce reports useful to users. In many of these situations, the firms initially posting the raw data would prefer to shield the data from the "prying eyes" of these new Internet firms. The originators hope to capture for themselves the value of reselling the information, prevent competition, force the aggregators to license the data, or generally prevent the diversion of user attention away from the originator's site. In a simple sense, search engines and Web crawlers are a form of data aggregator because they compare the user search terms with meta-tag and content or text files to produce reports that rank order the information by relevance. The owner of the probed Web site may claim the probe was an intrusive trespass in an attempt to prevent the aggregator's activity.

Many content aggregators use even more sophisticated methods. For example, on-line bill-paying services probe the bank accounts of bank customers to process automated bill paying. This practice has become known as **screen scraping** because the banking customer grants permission and password access to the aggregator to access the customer's account information, which is "scraped" or taken off the bank's site to facilitate the automated bill payment. Some banks hope to capture fee income from such services when they finally implement their own electronic bill presentment and payment services. The factual data about a bank customer's account are not protected by copyright. Indeed, the data are arguably the customer's property, not the bank's property. A few banks have sued, using trespass and IP theories, to prevent probes by such aggregators. For example, a few banks include copyrighted screen designs or trademarks so that when aggregators probe bank Web site information with the customer's consent the screen scraping inadvertently infringes the bank's IP rights. If banks are successful with trespass or infringement theories, bill payment services could be forced to license the data or go out of business.[34]

Content aggregator—bill payment service
http://www.paytrust. com

Shopping Bots

Intelligent agent software improves the accuracy and usefulness of information obtained from Internet sites. **Shopping bots** can search for particular models or classes of goods and then return comparative reports showing on-line sellers that satisfy the customer's price and other specifications. Shopping bots may run each search de novo or create databases from which other customers' comparison shopping

---

34. See discussion of bots, intelligent agents, and similar automated data collection services in Ballon, Ian, *E-Commerce and Internet Law*, Glasser LegalWorks (2000) at Chapter 13.

requests are provided. For example, Bidder's Edge would satisfy customer requests for on-line auction data by searching well-known auction sites such as eBay. However, eBay attempted to block Bidder's Edge and finally sued, claiming the bot trespassed on eBay's Web site. A preliminary injunction against Bidder's Edge illustrates that trespass may be a viable theory to shield publicly available data from wholesale extraction by using its terms and conditions for Web site access to stop information scavengers like the shopping bots.[35]

COPYRIGHT PROTECTION OF DATABASES

As discussed in Chapter 4, copyright law protects the form of expression but not the underlying ideas in the expression. This limitation makes copyright law only a weak protection for databases. Copyright may protect a database as a compilation when it includes a unique selection and arrangement of facts. A **compilation** is the product of selecting, coordinating, arranging, or organizing existing material, irrespective of whether these underlying facts were ever protected under copyright. For example, compilations have included personal organizers, standardized tests, a country music show, greeting cards, a collection of logarithms, and a seed suppliers' directory.

It is copyright infringement if another person copies the selection and arrangement of a protected compilation. Others may independently make similar selections and arrangements. A second compiler may use the first compilation to check for errors or omissions. The copyright law recognizes that there can be sufficient originality or creativity for copyright protection in the selection and arrangement of facts into a database. Creativity is the element of making nonobvious choices from among numerous choices.[36] Courts no longer extend copyright protection to compilations of facts without regard to the necessary creative elements of selection and arrangement.[37]

TECHNICAL AND CONTRACT PROTECTIONS

In U.S. database protection experience, two common methods are probably the most useful: technical security measures and contract restrictions against infringement. Technical methods include a variety of electronic, security, programming, and physical safeguards that lock up the data. For example, encryption of the data on a CD-ROM would impede infringement. Similarly, it would be very time-consuming to acquire all the data served from a Web site if the site's search engine responds to queries with only piecemeal answers. Database protection is available to the extent the database owner can use technical security measures to restrict access, meter use, and generally impede comprehensive extraction of large portions of its data.

---

35. *eBay, Inc. v. Bidder's Edge, Inc.*, 100 F.Supp.2d 1058 (N.D.Cal. 2000).
36. *Matthew Bender & Co. v. Hyperlaw, Inc.*, 168 F.3d 674 (2d Cir., 1990).
37. *Feist Publications, Inc. v. Rural Telephone Service Co., Inc.*, 499 U.S. 340 (1991).

However, technical progress eventually overcomes many of these security controls. Therefore, technical security measures are best reinforced with contractual restrictions.

Contractual terms of use and restrictions on decompiling, reverse engineering, and reselling data are all important means to prevent database infringement. Owners of databases often treat their information as IP and choose to license the content rather than sell it or assign it outright. Licensing is completely appropriate for databases containing IP, such as a collection of copyrighted works, video, music, or images. However, licensing factual databases requires the owner to exert physical and contractual controls that make the database into a trade secret. Contract terms may limit the licensee's use, resale, and manipulation of the database. Assent to these terms of use is likely to be part of a negotiated transaction between businesses. However, on-line access to databases is increasingly accomplished when agreement is made by clicking an "I accept" button in a dialog box, known as "click-wrap" agreements. Tort and contract theories of database protection merge because the tort theory of misappropriation becomes useful when employees and licensees are bound by contract to preserve secrecy and make only allowable uses under the license.

The Uniform Computer Information Transactions Act (UCITA) is a new law for the licensing of computer information. When adopted, UCITA would make licensing databases much easier and more certain. UCITA would give the database owner very strong control over database licenses and uses. UCITA is controversial because it deviates from the consumer expectations developed over many years in sales contracts for goods. UCITA and its controversies are detailed in Chapters 8, 9, and 10.

SUI GENERIS DATABASE PROTECTION

In recent years, particularly following the 1991 *Feist* decision, pressures from the database management industry, from media giants, and from foreign nations have resulted in international treaty negotiations for new forms of database protection. These new forms are called **sui generis database protections** because they are unique, one of a kind, and new to the type of IP interests involved. In 1996, the EU urged the WIPO to add two forms of database protection to the international trade agenda: (1) copyright protections and (2) sui generis database protections. Since that time, the EU adopted (March 1996) the **EU Directive on the Legal Protection of Databases**,[38] which has been implemented with national legislation by about half the EU member nations. Since that time, the U.S. Congress has introduced several controversial database protection bills. As of this writing, the prospects for sui generis database protections in the United States are improving.

---

38. OJ 1996 L77/20.

EU Database Protection Directive

The EU database directive calls for two independent types of protection for databases. First, the EU directive calls for copyright protection that closely parallels U.S. law: protection for the selection or arrangement of the database contents produced by the author's own intellectual creativity. Much like in the United States, the contents (facts and ideas) may not be protected by national copyright laws. In most respects, the EU's copyright protection of databases must provide all the characteristics of other copyright rights, as discussed further in Chapter 4.

ONLINE

EU Database Directive
**http://europa.eu.int/
eur-lex/**

The second form of EU database protection is a sui generis right. The maker of a database who has made a substantial investment in either obtaining, verifying, or presenting the database's contents has a right to prevent others from infringing. Infringement is wrongful and unpermitted extraction or reutilization of the whole or a substantial part of the database's contents. EU database rights can be economically exploited through licensing, transfer, assignment, or other grant. National laws passed under EU directives generally apply only to EU citizens. For EU databases, the law is applicable from the nation of residency of the database owner. For corporations, this means the nation of its incorporation if it has its central administration or principal place of business within the EU or where it has a registered office and genuine ongoing operations. The actual data entry or other investment may be made in another nation. For example, considerable keyboarding is done in India for firms from around the world. An English firm could outsource the actual database construction to India yet be protected under the UK's database protection legislation.

EU database rights nominally last 15 years from the date of completion. However, the 15-year period is restarted in two major ways that may extend the duration to more than 30 years in some instances or indefinitely in typical practice. First, a 15-year extension is granted if the database owner makes the database available to the public "in any manner" before the first 15-year term expires. Second, the 15-year term restarts from the time the owner makes a substantial change to the database contents, whether additions, deletions, corrections, or other alterations. Of course, database management is a common practice because maintaining the database keeps it a valuable asset. Protections for many EU databases will last indefinitely.

Both copyright and sui generis database protection rights have exceptions similar to fair use that permit unconsented or unlicensed use. It is permissible to extract or reutilize insubstantial portions, but not repeatedly or systematically. Database contents may be used for noncommercial teaching or scientific research if the source is attributed. EU nations may also add exceptions for public security or administrative and judicial procedures. The EU directive leaves it up to the EU nations to design remedies. Copyright infringement actions are envisioned for the copyright database right. The sui generis right presumes the owner may sue to prevent infringement or use a breach of contract action for users exceeding the rights they actually acquired. (See Exhibit 5.4.)

Exhibit 5.4 Database Protection Laws

Type of Database Law	Strengths	Weaknesses
Tort: misappropriation	Protects data even if technical security measures or contractual restrictions are not used	Protects only "hot news" or other elements not part of copyright law protections
Tort: trade secrets	Most common in U.S.; requires technical security measures or contractual restrictions	Rights are lost when information is disclosed into the public domain
Tort: trespass to chattels	Protects information stored in owner's personal property, such as computer or network storage	Trespass theory could be expanded so far that interactivity would be severely impeded in network settings
Copyright	Strong prohibition against copying; rewards creativity in selection and arrangement	*Feist* limits protection to compilations made with creativity in selection and arrangement; underlying ideas and fact are not copyrightable
Contract	Common protection in the U.S.; enforceable to prevent misuse, disclosure, copying, or reverse engineering	Requires privity; not applicable unless user assents to restrictions; form and conscious understanding of assent required remains unclear
Sui Generis	Stronger protection than under nearly any other theory; validates the "sweat of the brow" theory	Constitutionality suspect; could impede research and narrow the public domain; offers excessive rewards for some uncreative work

CHAPTER 6
PATENTS

Innovation is essential to the increasingly competitive business environment. Innovation is pervasive. For societal progress, these must be innovation in new materials, new products, and more effective and more efficient production processes. In all markets—in the traditional bricks-and-mortar economy, in the "new" e-commerce sector, and in the convergence of these two industrial sectors—innovation is important. Firms in both the goods and service sectors must also enhance their business methods by refining existing processes or creating brand-new methods.

However, business innovation is becoming more difficult, particularly for individual entrepreneurs and small to medium-sized firms. One important reason is that business methods are now clearly patentable. Consider the highly publicized examples of Amazon.com's "one-click" e-commerce ordering system[1] or Priceline.com's "reverse auction" process.[2] Literally thousands of business method patents have been issued since the 1998 watershed case of *State Street Bank vs. Signature Financial Group*.[3] Now business method patents exist in such diverse areas as accounting and bookkeeping, payment systems, electronic commerce transaction processing, pricing and marketing techniques, inventory control, manufacturing, financial instruments, and transactions systems for telecommunications. Business method patenting has been hotly controversial.

---

1. *Amazon.com, Inc. v. Barnesandnoble.com, Inc.*, 73 F.Supp.2d 1228 (W.D.Wash., 1999). U.S. Pat. No. 5,960,411, Method and System for Placing a Purchase Order via a Communications Network.
2. U.S. Pat. No.5,794,207, Method and Apparatus for Effectuating Buyer-Driven Commerce.
3. 149 F.3d 1368; *cert.denied* 525 U.S. 1093 (1999).

This chapter discusses patents—a strong form of IP. Patents are the primary protection for inventions. Patents cover much more than business methods; they are a fundamental source of value for nearly all technology firms. In the future, few firms will be able to rely solely on their IP attorneys to adequately understand the strategies needed to manage IP assets and infringement risks. This chapter first previews the field of patents. Next, the patentability of inventions is discussed, followed by a description of the patenting process. Throughout this chapter, patenting strategies are explored, including the avoidance of infringement litigation and, when necessary, the realization of remedies. This chapter concludes with a discussion of some special forms of patent-related IP: plant patents, design patents, and semiconductor chip designs.

OVERVIEW OF PATENT LAW

Patent law protects **invention**(s). Invention is both a process and the thing(s) resulting from the invention process. The invention process involves the production or contrivance of something previously unknown—that is, discovery achieved through study, experimentation, or imagination. The invention thing is a physical object or device or finding that contributes to the creation of a new procedure or practice. A **patent** is a limited monopoly granted by government to the first creator of a useful, novel, and nonobvious invention. Patents are granted on machines, articles of manufacture, compositions of matter, and processes.

Many patentable inventions are difficult to distinguish from trade secrets. The overlap between trade secrets and patents is discussed in Chapter 5. A simple distinction is that trade secrets are information that was not generally known. Patents go further by implementing such unknown information into an **embodiment**—that is, a thing or process that becomes functional by using the basic information in some beneficial way. For example, a trade secret might result from a discovery made by experimentation that shows properties of a new type of metal alloy. A patent might put that raw information into practice in several ways. First, a patent might cover a new process used to produce the new alloy (e.g., smelting, casting, forging, coating). Second, a separate patent might cover a new product made from the alloy that benefits from the alloy's unique characteristics (e.g., strength, lightness, corrosion resistance, flexibility).

What types of things should society recognize as patentable? This old but recurring question has again become important in recent years, as several scientific advances have raised cultural, philosophical, theological, and practical concerns. For example, should life forms or clones be patentable? Should the human genome be patentable? Should patents be granted to hospitals on new medical therapies derived from raw material such as the tissue samples of their patients? Other types of new inventions threaten to weaken the public domain by taking basic laws of nature, formulae, or algorithms away from the public during the patent's near 20-year-long term. For example, the courts worried about protecting the public domain for nearly 22 years before the patentability of software was clarified. Similar reasons kept the patentability of business methods in doubt for more than a century before their patentability was clearly established in 1998.

Patentability is a complex **qualification** procedure—an adversarial process that tests the invention under the stringent standards of patentability. Inventors typically must carefully and confidentially document their diligence in the invention process. A registered patent lawyer or registered patent agent is usually hired to assist in preparing the patent application, which contains highly technical patent claims describing the invention, with drawings and specifications. After the application is filed with the Patent and Trademark Office (PTO), a long and iterative process follows, called **patent prosecution**. It can take 12 to 24 months, or even longer for complex new technologies. During prosecution, an expert PTO **examiner** reviews the application. The inventor must typically negotiate with the PTO to narrow the scope claimed for the patent, which gives the patent applicant a narrower monopoly. If the invention is novel and nonobvious, the PTO issues the patent. The patent application generally remains confidential during prosecution but is eventually published when the patent is issued. However, if the inventor also applies for patents in nearly any foreign nation, the patent application will be published 18 months after filing.

The theory of IP was first introduced as a Constitutional matter in Chapter 2 and then revisited in Chapter 4. Thomas Jefferson was an active inventor and the father of the U.S. patent system. He believed that stringent patentability standards are desirable because government should not suffer the "embarrassment" of a patent monopoly without something substantial and useful given to the public in return. His sentiment here implies the limitations on patents that underlie the **contract theory** of IP. This theory holds that patents are a bargain between society and the inventor. Society provides the inventor with a monopoly to exploit the invention. In return, the inventor's rights are limited: (1) The invention must be "qualified" through stringent patentability standards before the patent is issued, (2) the patent is limited to a fixed term (today 20 years) after the patent application is filed, and (3) when the patent is issued, the inventor must publicly disclose the invention's secrets. All parties should benefit because the patent is an incentive to innovate, disclosure adds new knowledge, useful new information becomes available, and the invention eventually becomes part of the public domain.

Qualification of patentability is *the* major problem in patent law. The inventor must prove the invention is novel, nonobvious and useful. Experts examine the technology claimed in the patent application to determine novelty and nonobviousness. This entails an iterative **examination process** involving several parties: (1) the inventor, who is usually represented by a registered patent lawyer or patent agent, and (2) examiners working for the PTO. The PTO is a federal agency and a branch of the U.S. Department of Commerce. The examination process is designed to assure that the invention is not already in the public domain (part of the prior art) and was not too easily foreseen by persons skilled in the art (nonobvious). Patent litigation sometimes occurs during this patent prosecution process but may occur later if there is infringement.

The inventor may try to personally exploit the invention. However, others may be more effective in using the invention in their existing products or processes or in incorporating the invention as part of existing or new products. Sometimes established firms are better at marketing the new product through existing and successful supply chains. These matters are part of patent strategy, an area that is becoming vitally important to business decisions because managers need an understanding of IP.

The Constitution's framers included details about the purpose and governmental powers over IP in Article I, §8, clause 8. Several patent laws or revisions have been passed by Congress, the first in 1790 and others in 1793, 1836, 1890, and 1909. The 1952 act is still in effect, but amendments were passed in 1982, 1984, 1988, and 1999.

INTERNATIONAL PATENT PROTECTION

International treaties have had a significant influence on U.S. patent law. Usually, the presidential administration authorizes the United States to participate in negotiations in an international organization. Sometimes these negotiations result in multi-lateral agreements among several major industrialized nations, and some treaties also include developing countries. Thereafter, the U.S. Senate considers the treaty; many are officially ratified. International treaties require each signatory nation to pass legislation that implements the treaty. This pattern has been followed in numerous instances by the U.S. Congress and by the European Union (EU).

There are several important IP treaties with impact on patents. First, the **Paris Convention** requires "national treatment"—foreign patents are given all the same rights and status as domestic patents. However, the impact of the Paris Convention is limited because it does not require common patentability or patenting standards among the nearly 80 signatory nations. Second, the **Patent Cooperation Treaty** creates procedural advantages for patent applications made in the nearly 100 signatory nations. Third, the **European Patent Convention** applies to the 19 "member states" of the EU. This treaty simplifies and harmonizes patent application filing requirements and requires EU nations to enact uniform domestic patent legislation. Fourth, the **Patent Law Treaty** was an attempt by the World Intellectual Property Organization (WIPO), a division of the United Nations, to harmonize substantive patent law in member nations. However, its impact has been limited because the United States refused to change certain policies.

Fifth, the World Trade Organization (WTO) concluded various **Trade Related Intellectual Property (TRIPS)** agreements that are probably the most successful of all international IP treaties. TRIPS requires phased compliance deadlines, creates dispute resolution mechanisms in the WTO, has effective national IP enforcement and remedies, and requires criminal sanctions and judicial review of IP matters. The United States has changed several aspects of its patent law to comply with TRIPS, including changing to the 20-year patent term, broadening the subject matter of patents and requiring publication of patent applications before issuance, after 18 months.

Finally, the North American Free Trade Agreement (NAFTA) requires eventual harmonization and effective enforcement of national IP laws in Canada, Mexico, and the United States. The most significant patent treaties are summarized in Exhibit 6.1.

Exhibit 6.1 International Patent Policy

International Intellectual Property Agreement or Treaty	Unilateral, Bilateral, or Multilateral	Major Participants	Major Provisions and Impact
Paris Convention	Multilateral	80 signatories	Requires national treatment, but success limited; requires no common standards
Patent Cooperation Treaty	Multilateral	100 signatories	Procedural advantages for patent applications within signatory nations
European Patent Convention	Multilateral, regional	EU's 19 member states	Simplified and harmonized patent application filing requirements; requires signatories to enact uniform domestic patent legislation on certain substantive points
Patent Law Treaty	Multilateral	Several nations but not U.S.	WIPO (UN) attempted harmonization of substantive patent law in member nations; momentum stalled after U.S. refused to change certain policies
World Trade Organization (WTO): TRIPS	Multilateral	Many nations participating	Phased compliance deadlines; WTO dispute resolution mechanisms, effective national enforcement and remedies, criminal sanctions, judicial review; must comply with Paris Convention, 20-year patent terms, broadened subject matter, limited compulsory licensing; probably most successful international IP treaty.
North American Free Trade Agreement (NAFTA)	Multilateral, regional	Canada, Mexico, and U.S.	Calls for harmonization and effective enforcement of national law

PATENTABILITY

Probably the most important and contentious issues in patent law are whether a particular invention should be patentable and the scope of the patent. **Patentability** is determined by the complex analysis of whether the invention has: (1) patentable subject matter (statutory subject matter), (2) novelty, (3) nonobviousness, and (4) utility. Section 101 of the patent law defines the proper subjects for patenting.

Patentability under §101

Whoever invents or discovers any new and useful process, machine, manufacture or composition of matter, or any new and useful improvement thereof, may obtain a patent therefore, subject to the conditions and requirements of this title.

Initially, the inventor has control over how the invention is classified and defined as it is tested for patentability. The patent application must accurately and fully describe the invention's architecture and function in detailed patent claims and specifications—the heart of the patent application. The four key patentability issues are now explored.

PATENTABLE SUBJECT MATTER

Utility patents are possible on only four types of subject matter: (1) machine, (2) manufacture, (3) composition of matter, and (4) processes. (See Exhibit 6.2.) Special forms of patents and patentlike protections (sui generis) exist for plants, designs, and semiconductors, discussed at the end of this chapter. The four utility patent categories overlap somewhat but are largely identical to the original definition from the 1793 act. Some complex inventions can be classified in more than one category.

The four classes are not well defined in the Patent Act, so the courts have largely used definitions from the dictionary. A **machine** is a mechanism, device, apparatus, or instrument with parts that are organized to cooperate when set in motion to produce predictable results. An article of **manufacture** is produced from raw or processed materials and/or from component parts. Manufacturing with labor or machinery gives new forms and characteristics to these components. This is the catchall category, and it includes goods and "anything under the sun" human made and not clearly within the other categories. A **composition of matter** is any combination of two or more substances. Compositions of matter include composite articles derived from chemical union or mechanical mixture, such as life forms, gases, liquids, powders, and solids.[4]

A **process** is defined in the Patent Act in terms of itself: "process is a process, art or method, and includes a new use of a known process, machine, manufacture, composition of matter, or material." Cases refine this as "a mode of treatment of certain materials to produce a given result . . . an act or series of acts, performed upon the subject matter to be transformed and reduced to a different state or thing."[5] New uses of known materials are also processes. For example, assume a pharmaceutical firm develops an arthritis drug that was only partially successful. If another firm testing the drug accidentally discovers that it can grow hair, this would be a patentable process separate from the original patent on it as a composition of matter.

Finally, **improvements** on existing machines, manufactures, compositions of matter, or processes are also patentable. Patent law encourages additional research into new uses and into enhancements to the functioning of existing products. Interesting strategic issues, such as blocking patents, arise when the new use or the improvement is made on an item already protected under an existing patent. These strategies are discussed throughout this chapter.

---

4. *Diamond v. Chakrabarty,* 447 U.S. 303 (1980).
5. *Cochrane v. Denver,* 94 U.S. 780 (1877).

Exhibit 6.2 Patentable Subject Matter: Utility Patents

Subject Matter	Definition	Examples
Machine	Mechanism with parts organized to cooperate in motion to produce predictable results	Engine, appliance, computer, vehicle
Manufacture	Articles produced by labor or machinery in which new form and characteristics are given to raw or processed materials and/or components	Catchall category, includes most goods as well as machines and compositions of matter
Composition of matter	Combinations of two or more substances; composite articles derived from chemical union or mechanical mixture, including gasses, liquids, powders, and solids	Molecules, chemical compounds, life forms
Process	"Process means process," art or method and includes a new use of a known process, machine, manufacture, composition of matter, or material; also treatment of materials, act, or series of acts that transform a subject matter	Chemical production, business methods, software, new uses of known materials

NONPATENTABLE SUBJECT MATTER

The policies of patent law are much more thorough in protecting the public domain than is copyright law. This is evident in the rigorous qualification process for the patentability of new inventions and in the **nonpatentable subject matter** defined by statute and cases. Exceptions to patentable subject matter are called **nonstatutory subject matter**. First, patent protection is not available for **naturally occurring** things such as life forms. For example, many herbalist remedies come from plant extracts or other living things. Perhaps a cure for cancer might be found in the bark of a yew tree. Although such research is very important, there can be no patent protection for this type of discovery. However, a patent might be appropriate if the naturally occurring substance is changed in a newly invented process or its modified form is new and human-made.

A second major area of nonpatentable subject matter is **abstract ideas, laws of nature**, and **mathematical formulae**. Like naturally occurring things, ideas and natural laws are not invented; they already exist. Their discovery is laudable, but it is not invention. The public domain must be protected so that others can use ideas and formulae (algorithms), which are the fundamental building blocks of science and engineering. For example, Albert Einstein's theory of relativity is generally considered a colossal contribution to theoretical physics. However, Einstein's $E = mc^2$ is a law of nature, which other scientists must be able to use. Similarly, Isaac Newton could not have patented the law of gravity. Of course, the laws of nature, algorithms, and abstract ideas are part of the functioning of nearly all inventions. Practical applications and implementations of ideas and algorithms, are patentable, just not the underlying laws themselves.

These two nonstatutory subject matters lie at the heart of the controversy over the patentability of biotechnology inventions, software, and business methods. All three new areas are now clearly patentable. However, a long period of resistance preceded the patentability of each because many people were concerned that such matters were merely discovered, not invented. Also, many people strongly believe there is a duty to protect the public domain. Biotechnology inventions trigger strong theological opinions. Each of these new technologies has followed a similar three-phase trajectory. First, the courts refused patentability by designating them as non-statutory subject matter. Second, there was an intermediate, maturing phase when some courts were more careful with their reasoning and contradictory case law resulted; some cases permitted partial patentability. Third, there was final acceptance and recognition of patentability.

BIOTECHNOLOGY

The patentability of biotechnology is a very broad subject. Congress has clearly provided for sui generis protection of new, bioengineered plant species in two laws: the Plant Patent Act of 1930 protecting asexually reproduced plants and the Plant Variety Protection Act of 1970 protecting new plant varieties bred with sexual reproduction techniques. Utility patents are also now possible for new plant species.[6] Plant patent protections are discussed in a later section.

Nearly two-thirds of all prescription and over-the-counter drugs have at least some naturally occurring components. Patents on such drugs cannot cover the natural components but may cover the unique mixture, any novel processes to produce them, or a human-made, purified version of the naturally occurring component. Monopoly profits for critical drugs raise fairness questions and controversy in developing nations (AIDS treatment) and in national crises (Cipro, the anthrax antibiotic).

Medicines are a very important part of biotechnology patenting. The pharmaceutical industry continues to successfully argue that strong patentability is needed to maintain private-sector funding of research into lifesaving or life-enhancing drugs. The Food and Drug Administration (FDA) has authority over the regulation of drugs. The distribution or sale of new drugs is prohibited until after clinical trials prove their **efficacy**—their effectiveness in treating the conditions as intended. FDA qualification of new prescription and over-the-counter drugs often discovers that the drugs have side effects. These drug trials may continue for several years before the FDA releases the drugs for public use, and extended trials can cut short the patentee's 20 years of monopoly protection. Shortened patent terms for drugs, medical devices, and some other inventions makes it more difficult to recoup research expenses from the monopoly profits before generics (work-alike or identical formulations) undercut their monopoly profits. Congress relieved some of this "unfairness" in the **American Inventor's Protection Act (AIPA)**. The AIPA authorizes the PTO to extend patent terms if delays in patent prosecution or FDA trials continue for more than three years.

6. *J.E.M. AG Supply v. Pioneer Hi-Bred Int'l.*, 121 S.Ct. 2566 (2001).

The protection of genetic engineering, cloning, or other more modern biotechnology methods for reproduction of both plants and animals was an uncertain and controversial issue until 1980. Many cases denied utility patents to bioengineered life forms for two reasons. First, naturally occurring life forms are unpatentable subject matter. Second, many forms of bioengineering evoke strong theological emotions and religious issues. Should some corporation be permitted to patent life forms, animals, or humans? Consider the storm of controversy surrounding the acquisition of stem cells ("harvesting" from human embryos) and their use in disease research. The watershed 1980 case of *Diamond v. Chakrabarty*[7] shattered much of the resistance to modern biotechnology patents. During the patent prosecution, a PTO examiner rejected Chakrabarty's claims for an oil-eating strain of bacteria that could be used to clean up oil spills. The U.S. Supreme Court permitted patentability, stating that "Chakrabarty's microorganism plainly qualifies as patentable subject matter." Citing congressional intent in the 1952 Patent Act, the court reiterated that patentable subject matter includes "anything under the sun that is made by man." The PTO had argued that broad new types of subject matter should not be permitted patentability until Congress accepts them after considering the competing economic, social, and scientific considerations. However, this argument contradicts the very core of patent law: Patents are issued only for novel and unforeseen inventions.

The Supreme Court also dismissed the PTO's lament that patentability of life forms might trigger a "gruesome parade of horribles" such as "frankenfoods," genetically engineered plants or animals with unknown side effects; resistant forms of fungi, bacteria, or viruses that could devastate whole species; monsters made up of genetic components from different species of plants and animals; and further destruction of biological diversity if genetically engineered species harm natural species. These complex questions are well beyond the purposes of patent law. Any additional incentive offered by patentability is minor, given the well-financed biotechnology industry and the rather considerable health research system.

COMPUTER SOFTWARE

Computer programs met with similar strong resistance to patentability. In early cases, courts fretted that patenting software might result in removing the mathematical formulae contained in the program's code from the public domain; that is, algorithms that cause the software to function could become unavailable to others if the software was patented. These courts prohibited software protection by permitting patentability only if the program was embedded in a machine. In the 1980s, the courts applied the Freeman-Walter-Abele test denying patentability if the software merely solved equations.[8] This test required that physical changes occur in work performed by physical processes before patentability would be permitted. However, after a watershed case in the 1990s,[9] the PTO issued new

---

7. *Diamond v. Chakrabarty*, 447 U.S. 303 (1980).
8. A trilogy of companion cases comprise this test: *In re Freeman*, 573 F.2d 1237 (C.C.P.A., 1978); *In re Walter*, 618 F.2d 758 (C.C.P.A., 1980); *In re Abele*, 684 F.2d 902 (C.C.P.A., 1982).
9. See *In re Alappat*, 33 F.3d 1526 (Fed.Cir., 1994).

guidelines for software patentability that now permit patents over software embedded in a machine or on a chip as well as software that can be loaded from disk on a general-use programmable computer. Software patentability does not hinge "on whether there is a mathematical algorithm at work, but on whether the algorithm-containing invention, as a whole, produces a tangible, useful, result."[10]

METHODS OF DOING BUSINESS

Another new area of patentability involves methods of doing business, as introduced at the beginning of this chapter. **Business method patents** are now available for a wide range of business processes. For more than a century, business methods were not generally considered patentable. The **business method exception** was widely believed to make business methods unpatentable, and many business methods are implemented in computer software, a type of invention that was also generally considered unpatentable before 1994. Furthermore, process patents were long disfavored. This point was illustrated in one business method patent case that held a standardized fire-fighting system as merely unpatentable "mental steps."[11]

Cases at the turn of the twentieth century denied protection of bookkeeping systems under both copyright and patent law as "methods of transacting common business."[12] In another case, a 1934 forerunner to computerized trading systems like the NASDAQ was held unpatentable.[13] Also the now well-known drive-in theater was unpatentable.[14] The business method exception became such a significant barrier that few inventors ever attempted to patent their business methods.[15] However, things are different today. *State Street Bank v. Signature Financial Group* opened the floodgates to thousands of business method patent applications after 1998.[16]

Following the business method patent revolution ignited by the *State Street* decision, the PTO has issued thousands of business method patents. The quality of these business method patents raises concerns for several key reasons. First, in the early years, most PTO examiners were not trained in business. Expertise in the underlying art has always been a key requirement for the quality of a "qualification" patenting system. Second, PTO examiners initially searched mainly through existing patents to see if the business method was already protected by patent or in the public domain. However, so few business method patents were issued before *State Street* that the PTO was unlikely to find any useful prior art—they were looking in the wrong place. Furthermore, most academic business journals and the business press are not organized or indexed to reveal precisely when business methods were first used or invented or by whom. Therefore, PTO examinations were not informed by

---

10. *ATT Corp. v. Excel Communications, Inc.,* 172 F.3d 1352, 1361 (Fed.Cir.), *cert. denied* 120 S.Ct. 368 (1999).

11. *In re Patton,* 127 F.2d 324, 327-38 (C.C.P.A., 1942).

12. *Hotel Security Checking Co. v. Lorraine Co.,* 160 F. 467 (2d Cir., 1908).

13. *In re Wait,* 73 F.2d 982 (C.C.P.A. 1934).

14. *Loew's Drive-In Theatres v. Park-In Theatres,* 174 F.2d 547 (1st Cir., 1949).

15. One notable exception was the Merrill Lynch Cash Management System that hastened the combination of investment and commercial banking; *Paine, Webber, Jackson & Curtis v. Merrill Lynch,* 564 F.Supp. 1358 (D.Del. 1983); U.S. Patent No. 4,346,442 ("Securities brokerage-cash management system" issued Aug. 24, 1982).

16. 149 F.3d. 1368, *cert. denied* 525 U.S. 1093 (1999).

any comprehensive or accurate understanding of business processes. Third, business methods are not clearly defined under patent law. Members of the patent bar are trying to characterize business methods as something else—software or other types of processes—to avoid business method patent difficulties. Fourth, the cost of patent practice may make business method patents a luxury for only large, high-tech firms that can afford the expense of patenting and infringement risk management. Fifth, the quality of business method patent has been highly suspect. There is reasonable evidence that many of the dot.com firms that suffered bankruptcy in 2000 were largely based on business method patents that could not sustain profitability. Further, observers allege that many of these business method patents would satisfy neither the novelty nor nonobviousness requirements.

At least two factors may now begin to reduce the problems with business method patents, Internet patents, and e-commerce patents. First, Congress included a **prior user or first inventor's defense** with the passage of the AIPA in 1999. Many business methods are developed and used in confidence as trade secrets. If another party receives a patent on that business method, the AIPA permits the first inventor to continue using the business method without risk of infringement liability. A workable definition of business method patents is critical because this first inventor's defense applies only to business methods and not to any other subject matters. Many in the patent community are apprehensive that the first inventor user defense concept might spread to other processes, machines, manufactures, or compositions of matter. Some case law already suggests that there is a prior user defense for other patentable subject matters.[17]

The second reason there is hope for entrepreneurs and small and medium-sized businesses despite these problems is the widespread belief that the many bad business method patents issued in the early years will make infringement litigation inevitable. The courts will likely test the validity of these business method patents at great social cost over the next several years. Many of the early business method patents issued will be invalidated because they were obvious, not novel, or both. As business method patent case law and settlements expand the body of knowledge over business methods, fewer bad business method patents will be written and issued by the PTO in the future.

NOVELTY

Patent law is intended to protect the public domain. No patent monopoly should remove knowledge that is freely available to all from the storehouse of human knowledge. The novelty requirement is designed to prevent patents being granted on known ideas or on inventions already in use. The potentially very lucrative patent monopoly should not be given for inventions already in the public domain.

Section 102 of the Patent Act defines novelty in a complex set of "statutory bars." These bars are significant legal barriers to patentability. They define instances when the invention is not patentable, hence they "bar" or disqualify patentability for an invention that was previously publicly known, used, published, made, or sold.

---

17. *Dunlop Holdings Ltd. v. Ram Golf Corp.*, 524 F.2d 33 (7th Cir., 1975); *cert.denied* 424 U.S. 958.

35 U.S.C. §102 Conditions for Patentability: Novelty

A person shall be entitled to a patent unless—

(a) the invention was known or used by others in this country, or patented or described in a printed publication in this or a foreign country, before the invention thereof by the applicant for patent, or

(b) the invention was patented or described in a printed publication in this or a foreign country or in public use or on sale in this country, more than one year prior to the date of the application for patent in the United States,

(c) he has abandoned the invention, or

* * *

(g)(2) before such person's invention thereof, the invention was made in this country by another inventor who had not abandoned, suppressed, or concealed it. In determining priority of invention under this subsection, there shall be considered not only the respective dates of conception and reduction to practice of the invention, but also the reasonable diligence of one who was first to conceive and last to reduce to practice, from a time prior to conception by the other.

The public domain in patents is part of the prior art. **Prior art** represents the accumulation of specialized knowledge that describes the status of technology, and it informs all inventors. The prior art is important in determining novelty and later in determining nonobviousness. It is also important to analyze the prior art aspects of novelty and nonobviousness from the perspective of **persons of ordinary skill** in the art. They are hypothetical professional specialists in the technologies involved. They can be expected to know the prior art and to have struggled with making improvements.

Publicly Available Knowledge

Section 102(a) focuses on the extent of publicly available knowledge about the invention before the inventor conceives of the invention. It prohibits inventors from patenting knowledge in the previously existing public domain. The scope of this knowledge is defined in §102(a) as whether the invention was publicly known or used in the United States, whether it was patented anywhere in the world, or whether it was disclosed in a printed publication anywhere in the world. No patent may be issued on an invention that is sufficiently described in a single reference or single source found in the prior art. This means that an invention is unpatentable if *other persons* have known or used the invention in the United States. Section 102(a) also bars patentability if the invention was described in a publication or previously patented by *someone else* anywhere in the world. Was the prior art description or patent sufficient to describe the new invention? If so, the prior art reference is said to **anticipate** the later invention. The sufficiency of the description is judged by hypothetical persons of ordinary skill in the art. For example, experienced accountants, finance professionals, or database designers would understand the prior art describing a new record-keeping invention.

Section 102(a) is the most important definition of the prior art. It helps preserve the public domain by prohibiting patenting of information already described in various ways. For example, an invention is unpatentable by anyone in the United States if a foreign scientist presented findings at an academic conference, published the findings in an international research journal, obtained a U.S. or EU patent, demonstrated a prototype at a U.S. trade show or shipped an embodiment into the United States. Sales, uses, or demonstrations of the invention can reveal the invention's secrets or be reverse-engineered to expose the new technologies.

The limitation to printed publications in §102(a) is an anachronism. Prior art is expanding to include electronic information retrieval systems. Scientific journals and patent offices around the world are posting prior art on the Internet and using other modern database techniques to make prior art available electronically.

What is the date of invention or knowledge of prior art? Why are these dates important? **Conception** is the "aha moment" when the inventor conjures up how the invention's components will interact to produce its function. It usually concludes a design phase when a mental or written plan is finally composed that envisions how the invention will work. Conception is complete when it would be possible for a hypothetical person of ordinary skill in the art to use the plans to produce a working model, prototype, or embodiment. After the inventor conceives (largely a mental step), there must be the physical construction of an embodiment, a step known as the reduction to practice. Invention occurs at conception if there is sufficient detail in drawings and plans describing the invention. Reduction to practice is also relevant because it is an important way for prior art to become known or used by others. Both events may become important if multiple inventors claim the invention in competing applications as discussed later.

Inventors, including the firms that employ inventors, must be careful to document the invention process so they can prove the date of conception. The date that an embodiment is made public is important because that is an important way for it to become part of the prior art. Secret uses of a similar invention are not usually sufficient to become part of the prior art. Either the date of conception, the date of reduction to practice, or both may become issues at trial about the patent's validity. Therefore, record keeping, as discussed further in a later section, is an important regimen under the patent law.

One-Year Grace Period

The United States is one of the few nations to give the inventor some development time to perfect the invention before the patent application must be filed. Under §102(b) the inventor may delay filing the application for up to a full year after conception and reduction to practice, during which time the inventor may publicly disclose, sell, publish descriptions in scholarly journals, and otherwise reveal the invention to the public, to venture capitalists, or to other firms that are better able to finance or develop the invention. The one-year rule applies to actions of anyone but overlaps with §102(a), which already covers public use, publication, or patenting by others. Patentability is "barred" by §102(b) if the invention was patented or described in a printed publication by anyone, anywhere in the world, more than a year before application.

Section 102(b) also denies patentability if the invention was on sale or in use in the United States more than a year before the inventor's application. Section 102(b) most clearly affects the inventor because it gives a **grace period** after invention to find financing or test the market's reaction to the invention. It adds another important disqualifier to those found in §102(a) by creating the **on-sale bar.** No patent will be issued for an invention "on sale" more than one year prior to filing the patent application. "On sale" means actual completed sales, held "for sale," demonstrated at trade shows, or described in literature available to potential buyers. There are exceptions for **experimental uses** or experimental sales purposes. Experimental uses or sales do not trigger the §102(b) statutory bar so long as the public cannot discover the invention's secrets. For example, the buyer of a prototype must be using the invention for testing and must be restricted to secrecy in a nondisclosure agreement like those discussed in Chapter 11.

The one-year rule is very important for academic scientists and entrepreneurs and in marketing strategy. The "publish or perish" regimen requires that academics publish their work quickly. Furthermore, many academics have deep convictions that their work should be shared freely with their colleagues and become part of the public domain. Their scholarly reputations are their most important assets. Academics are only mildly interested in patent protection, particularly given the patenting costs and considerable uncertainty over their inventions' value when exploited in the market. Entrepreneurs and marketers often must "sell" their invention to venture capitalists or corporate management and then arouse the interest of potential buyers before they can afford the costly patenting process. They may feel the need to disclose new products to the market quickly to preempt competitors' sales and build their firm's brand image. Although a year may seem like a long time for some simpler technologies, those inventions containing complex technologies require considerable additional work to perfect them. It can be difficult for entrepreneurs and small businesses to fund the $10,000 to $50,000 patenting costs. On balance, §102(b) gives inventors some breathing room but requires that they act diligently to apply for a patent.

First to Invent

Section 102(g) grants patentability to the inventor who first invented. The United States is also the only significant nation to award patents to the **first to invent.** Nearly all other industrialized nations award patents to the inventor who is **first to file.** The difference may seem technical, but it has enormous consequences. The first-to-invent standard rewards the original inventor with the patent irrespective of the inventor's financial or technological resources. First to invent denies the patent to later inventors who are shrewd or better financed and use these advantages to file earlier than the original inventor. By contrast, first to file rewards the quickest to start the patenting process and probably works to the advantage of better financial firms that are most experienced in filing patent applications.

The side effects of these two systems are considerable. In the United States, the first-to-invent rule and the one-year grace period encourage entrepreneurs and small inventors, even if they do not have large R&D and IP budgets. By contrast, first-to-file systems reward large, well-financed high-technology firms. These firms can much better afford the considerable expense of developing the invention quickly. Firms with big IP budgets can command IP resources and rush to make patent applications. But a balance must be drawn between two public policies: Fairness dictates rewarding the original inventor, but society is best served by diligent, methodical, and pragmatic inventors who move steadily to refine the invention in a practical way.

Many other nations are pressuring the United States to abandon the first-to-invent system in favor of first to file. Many IP observers expect the United States could give up first to invent in negotiations on some future international IP treaty in return for other concessions. The most persuasive reason to adopt first to file is that the first-to-invent standard is vague and inefficient. Litigation is arguably required more often in the United States to settle inventorship disputes under the first-to-invent standard. By contrast, first to file seems more decisive, and fewer conflicts should arise over which among competing inventors is entitled to the patent. The U.S. defenders of the first-to-invent standard argue that the certainty of first to file unfairly penalizes entrepreneurs and small to medium-sized businesses that can never be as savvy or financially prepared for the considerable IP and patenting expenses to which large technology firms are already accustomed.

The first inventor who conceives of the invention and then diligently reduces it to practice is the first to invent and should be entitled to the patent. Among competing inventors, the patent is awarded to the one with priority. However, there can be difficult questions of priority when one inventor conceives first buts moves slowly to reduce the invention to practice. During this interval, another inventor might conceive of the same invention and move more quickly to reduce it to practice before the first inventor. Although this scenario may seem far-fetched, it actually occurs quite often. For example, in many of the biotechnology and software fields, several scientists or inventors may be working independently to solve similar problems. It is quite possible that two inventors might conceive of the same invention nearly simultaneously. Actual physical reduction to practice is not always required. A **constructive reduction to practice** is possible if the patent application is so detailed that it clearly informs the hypothetical person of ordinary skill how to build a working prototype or use the process.

Inventors must be conscientious in reducing their inventions to practice and in filing their patent applications. This duty of **diligence** is required by at least two provisions of the Patent Act. First, §102(c) bars patentability if the inventor has abandoned the invention, expressly or by implication. For example, an inventor can expressly dedicate the invention to the public, thereby waiving all rights to a patent. Alternatively, the inventor could simply wait too long after reduction to practice before filing the patent application, which can imply an **abandonment**. Second, §102(g), introduced previously, denies priority to an inventor who abandons, suppresses, or conceals the invention, which can occur if there are unexcused delays in reducing to practice. **Concealment** is precisely the strategy used to protect trade secrets. The original inventor who chooses trade secrecy protection rather than a patent filing could lose rights in the trade secret if a later inventor is diligent and files before the first inventor. These strategies are discussed in this and other chapters. Finally, **suppression** is the deliberate act of hiding the invention. An inventor who suppresses an invention may lose priority to a second, diligent inventor.

Searching the Prior Art

It should be clear by now that "knowing" and understanding all the prior art for the technologies underlying an invention is a difficult but important task. This task is made worse when the invention is complex or includes several different types of technologies. Patent law assumes that inventors know the prior art. However, prior art is highly dispersed, it is often expressed in foreign languages, and it lurks in the files of foreign patent offices, in obscure scientific journals, or in B2B and industrial advertising. An inventor working with his or her patent attorney or agent should usually search the prior art to assure the invention is novel. Prior art is becoming much more accessible today than was possible just a decade ago. The U.S. PTO has posted published patents dating back to 1790 online at http://www.uspto.gov. Many of the more recent patents include complete drawings and specifications.

Many publishers of law and technical materials archive, index, and sell access to huge databases of published patents and scientific literature. These were traditionally available only in print publications but are now contained on CD-ROM or through on-line pay-per-use databases such as Lexis and Westlaw. IBM provided much needed stimulus for the on-line versions of patent databases and the vastly superior capabilities of electronic database search. In 2000, IBM's on-line patent database was sold to Delphion Corporation, which operates it as a subscription-fee service. It has some unique search capabilities and offers some of them free at its Web site.

ONLINE

Delphion's patent search engine
**http://www.
delphion. com**

In the next few years, expect that new, more complete, and better indexed databases or prior art will become available. More foreign patents may be translated into English, and more inexpensive search services may be performed by third parties (technical professionals). Better search engines will use plain language queries and a more complete electronic thesaurus of equivalent technical terms, and these databases will be distributed on high-capacity media (DVD).

Many scientific disciplines are supplementing their printed journals with on-line publications. Some are even abandoning print publications altogether because the publication process simply takes too long. For example, in high-energy physics, the most important research papers are largely available online soon after drafting. This practice enhances distribution to all in the community of relevant scientists who might be interested, and it enables electronic search. Search of printed journals is long, arduous, and limited by the indexing and classification scheme used by authors and editors.

Consider a hypothetical example of patent search problems, which are not that different from Internet search difficulties. Imagine that a finance professor was the first person to invent a new valuation method that used a modified version of the discounted cash flow technique. The new invention was described in an article published in a finance journal six months before the inventor filed a patent application. Before the publication, a financial engineer working at an investment banking firm separately invents a similar evaluation technique but is unaware of the finance professor's prior work. In searching the prior art, the financial engineer fails to use the academic term "discounted cash flow" but instead uses the industry term "present value" in searching for prior art. In a paper-based search system, only patent lawyers or agents who are intimately familiar with both the academic *and* industry perspectives would understand that "discounted cash flow" and "present value" are sufficiently equivalent to represent similar methods of using the "time value of money" for a new valuation method.

As electronic search engines become more sophisticated, they should become capable of translating such technical terms at the conceptual level, much as an expert in the field could. Search engines show great promise for the quality and efficiency of prior art searches, which should improve dramatically over the next few years. This progress will probably parallel similar improvements in Internet search engines and shopping bot technologies that are used by Web surfers. Prior art and the hypothetical persons of ordinary skill in the art are also critically important to the second fundamental patentability standard: nonobviousness.

Additional patent search databases
http://www.lexis.com
http://www.westlaw. com

NONOBVIOUSNESS

The third major criteria for patentability, the **nonobviousness** requirement, is stated in §103(a) of the Patent Act. Nonobviousness was added by the 1952 revision that replaced, but closely parallels, a former requirement for **inventiveness**. Today, a patent should not be granted on a novel invention if the advancement is small and represents merely minor improvements over the prior art. Minor improvements make the invention obvious to the hypothetical person of ordinary skill in the art.

> **35 U.S.C. §103 Conditions for patentability; nonobvious subject matter.**
>
> (a) A patent may not be obtained though the invention is not identically disclosed or described as set forth in §102 of this title, if the differences between the subject matter sought to be patented and the prior art are such that the subject matter as a whole would have been obvious at the time the invention was made to a person having ordinary skill in the art to which said subject matter pertains.

The *Graham v. John Deere* Test

The Supreme Court first requires a three-step analysis of nonobviousness, which was expressed in *Graham v. John Deere Co.*[18] First, a court reviewing a patent for obviousness must determine the scope and content of the prior art. This requires a meticulous search and analysis of the prior art that was available at the time the invention was made. Prior art is found in published patents, scientific journals, textbooks, and the like. There is often so much prior art in a particular technology that it must be selected carefully, or this step could quickly become overwhelming. For example, imagine the difficulties of determining obviousness of a novel e-commerce electronic payment method. Is the prior art limited just to the necessary steps for electronic funds transfers, or should the processing of payments by checks and drafts also be explored? Perhaps the search should grow even larger to include all computerized

---

18. 381 U.S. 1 (1966).

network communication technologies from the telecommunications field, encryption techniques from computer science, and the network effects of currencies from the literature of economics.

Second, there must be a determination of the level of skill held by the hypothetical person of ordinary skill in the pertinent art. This step is necessary because the reviewing court must take only the perspective of experts before evaluating obviousness. The nonobvious test is made only from the perspective of possible inventors, who are assumed to be from among those skilled in the art. These people are the most likely to have the skill and inclination to conceive of such an invention. Obviousness can be judged only after the prior art and persons of ordinary skill in those arts are accurately identified.

The third step is to compare the prior art with the invention to evaluate whether the invention has made any significant advances. If the differences are slight, the invention is obvious and not patentable. However, if the advance is substantial, the invention is nonobvious and may be patentable. Judges make this comparison from the perspective of one skilled in the art and knowledgeable of the prior art. However, experience has shown that nonobviousness tests are difficult to apply because lay judges are seldom skilled in the art. Too often they may try to second-guess the hypothetical person of ordinary skill or substitute their own judgments using hindsight or common knowledge.

That is precisely what happened in *Panduit Corp. v. Dennison Mfg.*[19] The trial court used improper perspectives in holding a patent on the "cable tie" was obvious. Panduit invented the cable tie, a one-piece plastic fastener that holds together a bundle of wires. The cable tie is a strap that wraps around the bundle, and the pointed end is inserted into a looped opening on the other end that locks the strap together. There are teeth all along the cable tie that engage with the one-way locking device in the looped opening. Panduit spent several million dollars on R&D over a nine-year period to develop the locking mechanism so it would be easy to insert but difficult to remove. This effort was needed to make the cable tie convenient but effective in tightly holding the bundle of wires. Dennison's R&D effort had failed, but eventually Dennison became the second largest supplier of cable ties by copying Panduit's patented design. When Panduit sued for infringement, Dennison claimed the locking device was obvious. The trial court erred by improperly using hindsight, ignoring the perspective of persons of ordinary skill, and dissecting the claims in Panduit's patent.

Both obviousness and nonobviousness must be measured at the time the invention was conceived, not later, when a judge has the benefit of hindsight. But obviousness is determined by actuality, while nonobviousness is determined hypothetically, without inventive insight. Hindsight is a later perception that benefits from seeing the significance of events that were much more difficult to see previously. Judges using hindsight later on during suit over validity and/or infringement are

---

19. 774 F.2d 1022 (Fed.Cir., 1985), *on remand* 810 F.2d 1561 (Fed.Cir., 1987).

suggestions. However, many inventions are made in large R&D laboratories where several human contributors collaborate. It is possible to have co-inventors if each makes a substantial contribution to the conception of the patent's novel aspects. If two or more persons conceive of the essential germ of the novel idea, then they are equal joint inventors. Some joint inventors may contribute different aspects, but all must be contributors to the novel aspects. All **joint inventors** must sign and participate in the application process.

Provisional Patent Applications

Since 1995, it has been much easier to establish the date of invention and obtain priority in international patent filings by using an abbreviated **provisional application**. As discussed next, regular patent applications must provide a highly accurate and detailed description of the invention. The provisional application can omit most of this. It allows the inventor to file an abbreviated description without taking the time and care necessary to meticulously draft clear and complete patent claims. Provisional applications have advantages: (1) First-to-file standards and shorter grace periods in foreign nations are satisfied by a provisional application, and (2) the inventor may have up to an additional year to test the invention's market appeal before investing in a full patent application. The inventor has one year after filing the provisional application before the full application must be filed.

The PTO's Electronic Filing System (EFS)

As part of the PTO's modernization initiatives, it has established the **Electronic Business Center (EBC)**, a group of related transaction-processing systems. The EBC processes upgrade interaction with the PTO from the historical use of paper-based, in-person, mail, and telephone interactions to electronic transaction processing. These are similar to the e-government initiatives being implemented throughout other federal agencies and in many states and some municipalities. The EBC includes electronic search for issued patents and trademarks, including full graphic images, the electronic payment of fees and account maintenance, electronic PTO job applications, and PTO subcontractor qualification. The EBC also includes the **Electronic Filing System (EFS)** for electronic filing of patent applications and **Patent Application Information Retrieval (PAIR)**, a faster and less costly method to check the status of a patent application.

Generally, the EBC systems require an initial registration of each individual or corporate user so all communications can be authenticated before transmission of highly confidential information. Registration and the use of bar codes simplifies interaction between the PTO and large, high-technology firms that have numerous applications filed at any one time. Public Key encryption Infrastructure (PKI) helps assure confidentiality. Special software is used for "clients" (inventors or assignees) to interact with the PTO's EBC. All these systems hold promise to improve service, reduce service times, and reduce the costs of the ever burgeoning patent information system.

unfairly using the very insight of the inventor to conclude that the invention was obvious. Second, the court substituted its judgment for that of persons of ordinary skill. Third, the *Panduit* court erred by dissecting Panduit's claims into the component parts of the cable tie invention. Nearly every invention combines at least some existing technologies. Nonobviousness must be judged by considering the invention as a whole: A unique combination of existing factors constitutes inventiveness.

Secondary Considerations (Objective Factors)

Nonobviousness is the most important patentability criteria. The *Graham* three-part analysis is the conceptually accurate method, but it is too often difficult to apply. Prior art determinations are lengthy and complicated, judges have difficulty accurately mimicking the perspective of persons of ordinary skill that change with every technology, and the temptation is strong to use hindsight, general principles, and common experience. For these reasons, the Supreme Court has acknowledged that sometimes **secondary considerations** may be appropriate. These are additional factors that tend to show that the invention was not obvious at the time it was invented. The Federal Circuit now considers these factors to be very important and much easier to apply than the *Graham* test, so they are now called **objective factors**: (1) long-felt, but unmet need, (2) commercial success, and (3) use or copying by others.

First, **long-felt, but unmet need** occurs when an industry has unsuccessfully tried to solve a problem that the invention finally does resolve. The failure of others' efforts, when combined with the inventor's success, is often convincing evidence that the invention was not obvious; otherwise, others would have invented it. Second, if the **commercial success** of the invention is strong, it can be inferred that it was not obvious; otherwise, other inventors would surely have developed a similar invention sooner. The invention's success must come from its inventive, nonobvious features and not from some other cause, such as promotional expenditures, the seller's market dominance, or other product features not part of the invention. Third, **use of copying by others** can be persuasive. The authorized licensing or outright infringement by competitors is an additional market test of the invention's nonobviousness. Licensing implies competitors accept that the patent is valid; infringing copies imply that competitors were unable to develop adequate substitutes, so the invention must have been nonobvious. For example, in the *Panduit* case, Dennison was not successful in designing a workable cable tie other than by using the method Panduit used to solve these problems in its patent. Both Panduit and Dennison had tremendous commercial success in producing the patented version of the cable tie.

Amazon.com v. Barnesandnoble.com, Inc. is a recent high-profile case illustrating nonobviousness in the business method patent, Internet e-commerce area. What was particularly remarkable about this case is that it received considerable press coverage and provoked many people to publicly participate in the debate over what constitutes nonobviousness. Such technical discussions seldom occur outside the close-knit members of the patent bar or among experts in the technologies involved. Indeed, this case became the cause célèbre on the public policy issues of business method patentability.

UTILITY

Recall that §101 permits patents to be granted to "whoever invents or discovers any new and *useful* process, machine, manufacture or composition of matter." This creates a requirement that the invention have **utility**, beneficial use for the invention or for products produced by a patented process. This threshold of practical value is low because the invention need not work any better than technologies in the prior art. Indeed, many inventions are refined long after they are patented. Some older cases denied utility if the invention was frivolous, injured public well-being, or was immoral. However, later cases prefer to leave the public policy aspects of the invention's function to other laws, such as regulation of gambling devices or sexual devices. A few cases prohibit patentability of inventions for not being useful if the primary function is illegal or unsafe. For example, patented drugs must prove their efficacy both under FDA drug trials and under the utility standard of patentability.

THE PATENTING PROCESS

Obtaining a patent on an invention is a much more complicated and expensive process than is obtaining a copyright or perfecting a trade secret. Patenting requires qualification, an adversarial process proving the invention is patentable subject matter and that it is novel, nonobvious, and useful. Patenting is seldom successful without careful record keeping during the invention process, the preparation of the patent application advised by a patent attorney or patent agent, and many months of interaction between the inventor and the PTO's patent examiner. Frequently, the inventor is an employee, so employment responsibilities are involved, such as patent assignment and assistance duties often contained in the employment contract. Patenting is so costly ($10,000 to $50,000 in out-of-pocket expenses plus various opportunity costs) that patentability and commercialization sometimes involve third-party experts and venture capitalists. This section discusses the regulatory requirements for patent prosecution.

THE PATENT AND TRADEMARK OFFICE (PTO)

The U.S. PTO is a division of the Department of Commerce. This makes the PTO different from the Copyright Office, which is an agency of Congress and independent of the president. The PTO is a dependent regulatory agency under direct control of the president through the Cabinet. The PTO is the agency Congress created to qualify patents and trademarks, to promulgate interpretive regulations on patent and trademark issues, and to organize the fields of patentable technologies. The PTO's regulations set procedures for various patent-related activities. For example, the procedures that PTO examiners must follow in examining patent applications are assembled into the **Manual of Patent Examination Procedure** (**MPEP**). Like most other federal administrative agencies, the PTO must follow the Administrative Procedure Act (APA) in its rule making, hearings, investigations, and responses to requests by the public under the Freedom of Information Act (FOIA) for information held in the PTO's files. The PTO's work burden is

ONLINE

PTO's MPEP
http://www.uspto.gov/
web/offices/pac/dapp/
mpepmain.html

enormous. With the number of patent applications approaching a quarter million e— year, it is impressive that the PTO manages the workload fairly well. Of course, with other information businesses, the PTO's computerization efforts have improve— productivity.

THE PATENT APPLICATION

Despite the U.S. first-to-invent standard, it is still sensible to file a patent application as soon as the invention is reduced to practice. This is particularly important for firms engaged in active international trade that expect their patented products to be competitive in international markets. The first-to-file standards in other nations create risks if filing in foreign nations is delayed. Similarly, many other nations do not have the one-year grace period. Therefore, publication, sales, or use of the invention before filing in many other nations risks patent rights.

An important step before filing is to assure that the inventor keeps detailed records in lab notebooks that are periodically signed and witnessed. Lab notebooks should be bound with no blank or missing pages to represent an accurate chronological journal that logs the invention process in accurate sequence. An initial patentability search of the prior art can be advisable so the benefits of patenting costs are better known and thereby provide an initial assessment of novelty that can encourage continuing with the expense of a patent application.

There are several major parts to a patent application. The inventor must describe the invention in a specification including at least one claim that provides sufficient detail that a person of ordinary skill in the art would be enabled to practice (reproduce or use) the invention. The specification should describe the invention and the manner and process of making and using it. Drawings are required when needed to illustrate the invention's architecture and aid in understanding it. The inventor must make an oath declaring original inventorship. The appropriate filing fee must also be included. After the patent is granted there are periodic **maintenance fees** owed by the patent owner.

Inventorship

As discussed in Chapters 4 and 11, inventorship under patent law is a different matter than authorship under copyright law. Although an employer can claim authorship for a work made for hire by one or more employees, this is generally not possible for inventorship. Generally, a patent application is made by the actual human inventor. The inventor must sign the application and declare that he or she is the first inventor. Of course, employers often contract with their employees for an assignment of patent rights and further require confidentiality and assistance in prosecuting the patent application.

A sole inventorship occurs when only one person conceives of the essential elements that are the "germ" of the invention's novel aspects. There is but a sole inventor even if others assist in the effort, pose problems to solve, or make minor

ONLI—
Trilateral Web site
http://www.trilateral.
org

ONLINE
European Patent Office
http://www.european-
patent-office.org
Japanese Patent Office
http://www.jpo.go.jp

DISCLOSURE

The major premise of patent law is that a limited monopoly on the invention is given in exchange for the inventor's **disclosure** of the invention's secrets. Disclosure occurs in a **specification** that has two parts. First, claims describe the invention, the "what description" that precisely defines the scope of the patent owner's rights. Second, specifications are the "how description" details of construction and use that must enable a person of ordinary skill in the art to practice (make or use) the invention in the best mode known by the inventor. PTO regulations require a ten-part format, including the inventions title, various cross-references, a summary, a brief as well as a detailed description of the drawings, claims, an abstract, the oath, and the drawings. Although there are no rigid requirements for the format of claims, successful patent claim drafters tend to use esoteric and somewhat standard terminology to describe the particular physical functions of an invention. The language of claims often seems convoluted to the layperson.

Enablement and Best Mode

Adequate description can be a difficult problem. There are natural incentives that create tension between inventors and everyone else (PTO, competitors). Inventors want their claims written broadly to maximize the value of their patent monopoly. Inventors are often reluctant to be as clear and complete as PTO examiners might demand. Ambiguous claims are more difficult to copy or design around, and this also makes the patent potentially stronger than the law permits. Two tests of adequacy are applied to the disclosures: (1) They must provide **enablement** (to a person of ordinary skill in the art), and (2) they must reveal the **best mode** for practicing (using, making) the invention.

The specification need not be a step-by-step production task list or cookbook approach. However, if a person of ordinary skill would be required to perform extensive experimentation before they could construct a working embodiment, then the disclosure is not enabling; that is, it is insufficient and must be revised by the inventor. The best mode requirement is intended to prevent inventors from concealing known examples of the best ways they have discovered to practice the invention. For example, consider the difference between a good cookbook and a bad one. The author of a good cookbook knows the common mistakes that cooks of ordinary skill might make, such as taking steps out of order, inaccurate measurement, improper mixing, inaccurate heating, and insufficient interlude between procedures. The good cookbook warns of these trouble spots and thereby strives to communicate the best mode for cooking the recipe (practicing the invention). By contrast, a bad cookbook fails to warn of possible problems, raising the probability of failure and requiring even cooks of ordinary skill to be persistent and experiment until they get it right.

It takes considerable experience in the technology involved before most people can develop an adequate understanding in the reading, interpretation, and writing of good claims. Technical professionals, patent lawyers, and patent agents usually develop expertise in only a few narrow but related technologies because the technical details are just too numerous in the most valuable arts. Nevertheless, it is useful to see how claims and supporting specifications are written so that the enablement and best mode standards are better understood.

Secrecy

Traditionally, patent applications have remained secret during prosecution. Only the inventor, the patent attorney or agent, various employees, the PTO examiner, and a few PTO staff are typically exposed to a patent application until after the patent finally issues. All these parties already are obligated to maintain secrecy until the patent is issued, or they should be. After issuance, the patent is published for anyone to see. Secrecy of patent application contents serves very useful purposes for the inventor. If the patent is rejected, the inventor can try to maintain it as a trade secret. Often during prosecution, the PTO examiner demands that claims be reduced in scope, which diminishes their value. Applicants may become dissatisfied if a narrow patent results. They can still withdraw their application and try to use the invention as a trade secret. Secrecy encourages frank and open prosecution activities between the PTO examiner and the inventor.

The advantages of secrecy largely benefit the inventor. Society also has an interest in patent applications before patents are issued. For example, the public could often contribute to the examination process. Persons of ordinary skill might supply prior art that might narrow the patent's scope or invalidate it. Publication of patent applications reduces the surprise element that surfaces when "submarine" patents undercut industry practices. Most other industrialized nations now require the publication of patent applications at some fixed time after filing irrespective of whether the patent is yet issued.

The United States finally gave up the absolute secrecy rule for patent applications when the examination process takes more than 18 months. If the application is also filed in foreign patent offices, the AIPA requires publication. The AIPA implemented the WTO and TRIPS treaties by standardizing the secrecy of patent applications to 18 months. Small U.S. inventors won an important exception: Secrecy may continue beyond 18 months if the inventor does not also file in foreign nations. This rule pressures the PTO to speed up the average examination process closer to 18 months. PTO examination can take several years for new and complex technologies like software, business methods, and biotechnology. Applicants uncertain about their application's prospects can still withdraw them before 18 months to avoid publication. This strategy can be used to preserve trade secrecy. Secrecy orders are possible for technologies with national security or defense reasons (secret weapons system), so these are also exempt from publication. Patent applications are now available from the PTO Web site and from other sources.

ONLINE

USPTO Patent
Application Searches
**http://www.uspto.gov/
patft/**

PATENT INFRINGEMENT

Patents are strong IP rights because, unlike copyrights, the patent protects both the idea and the expression (embodiments). The patent owner, often an assignee from the original inventor, has several exclusive rights that are protected by the threat of infringement litigation. These are the rights to exclude others from (1) making embodiments of the patented invention, (2) using the patented invention, and (3) selling (making the first sale) the patented invention. If the patent covers a process, ownership includes the right to exclude others from (1) using the process and (2) selling goods produced by the process. These are the most basic rights from the bundle held by the patent owner. Additional rights permit the patent owner to exclude others from importing into the United States infringing goods or goods produced using infringing processes made outside the United States and provide export restrictions on components of patented combinations and making an application to sell patented drugs.

LITERAL INFRINGEMENT

Infringement analysis is a three-step process: (1) a literal infringement inquiry, (2) a doctrine of equivalents inquiry, and (3) and a reconsideration of the inventor's history of negotiating the claims during patent prosecution. First, the court will look to whether there was **literal infringement**. This is similar to literal infringement under copyright because there is a comparison made between the patent claims and the alleged infringing embodiment. If every element claimed in the patent is also present in the allegedly infringing thing, then there is literal infringement. An exact duplicate infringes under the rule of **exactness**. If one of the claimed elements is missing, there can be no literal infringement under the rule of **omission**. However, there may still be infringement under the doctrine of equivalents discussed next. The rule of **addition** applies when all the claimed elements are reproduced in the infringing embodiment but additional elements are added. Infringement by addition is still a literal infringement even if it is an improvement.

For example, imagine a patent on a machine used to cut grass to an even height between three and six inches; it is called a "lawn mower." The original patent claims describe a nonpower, manual mechanism with the following elements: (1) a long handle, (2) metal frame and housing, (3) cutting blades, (4) the riding wheels drive the blade, and (5) the riding wheels adjust to maintain a variable but uniform cutting height. It would be literal infringement by exactness if a competitor produced a closely resembling machine with all five of these elements. It would be literal infringement by addition if another competitor produced a power mower with the only difference being a gasoline motor to drive the blades. However, it would not be literal infringement by subtraction if an electric motor powered a wheelless power mower that used a propeller-like blade to force airflow downward to hold the mower's cutting blades at a uniform height. Nevertheless, the wheelless mower might still be infringing under the doctrine of equivalents unless the PTO examiner rejected the cutting height claim during the original prosecution under the doctrine of file wrapper estoppel.

DOCTRINE OF EQUIVALENTS

The second step in patent infringement analysis frequently determines whether the allegedly infringing thing is highly similar to the patented invention. The doctrine of equivalents is one aspect of patent law that is stingy with the public domain. The **doctrine of equivalents** defines infringement more broadly by including competing products that closely resemble the patented invention's design, even when they are not literally infringing. For example, the wheelless mower had many of the same elements as the original mower; it added an engine for power, omitted the wheels, and substituted a propeller-like blade to maintain the uniform cutting height. Should patent law recognize the wheelless mower as an infringement?

Since 1853, the Supreme Court has recognized infringement when similar elements are substituted in an effort to avoid infringement.[20] There can still be infringement under the doctrine of equivalents if obvious changes are made by using known substitutes and the resulting product "performs substantially the same function, in the same way, to achieve the same result."[21] This is an ad hoc determination that must compare the prior art, from the perspective of a person of ordinary skill in the art, as to each substituted element(s). It is essentially a nonobviousness test; it is applied to the element substituted for the missing element(s). It is not judged from the perspective of when first invented, as was nonobviousness. Instead, it is judged from a later perspective: at the time of alleged infringement. Would the designers of lawn and garden implements easily think to use blowing air rather than wheels to maintain the mower's cutting height? The doctrine of equivalents is justified as a method to prevent "fraud on the patent" and unscrupulous copiers. Clearly, the doctrine of equivalents tends to expand patent rights but at the cost of making IP infringement determinations much more uncertain and costly. However, there is an important limitation that may reduce some of this ambiguity: file wrapper estoppel.

File Wrapper Estoppel

What if the substitute element had been the subject of contention during the inventor's prosecution history with the PTO examiner? Should the inventor be allowed to resurrect a claim rejected by the PTO examiner during prosecution? For example, suppose that the PTO examiner rejected the inventor's claim to use a gasoline motor to power the cutting blade but instead allowed the claim for a manual, wheel-driven, push-powered blade finally described by the original patent as issued. Given that the inventor was required to give up the gasoline motor during prosecution, should the inventor be allowed to use the doctrine of equivalents to prevent infringement if a competitor later sells a power mower? The doctrine of **file wrapper estoppel** prevents the original inventor from bringing back a claim as an equivalent in infringement litigation that was surrendered during to a PTO examiner during prosecution.

Prosecution is a process in which the PTO examiner carefully studies the invention claims and looks through prior art cited by the inventor and for other prior art the examiner finds independently by using other sources, databases, and cross-referencing indexes. The PTO examiner might find that some aspect of the invention's

---

20. *Winans v. Denmead*, 56 U.S. 330 (1853).
21. *Graver Tank & Mfg. v. Linde Air Products Co.*, 339 U.S. 605 (1950).

unfairly using the very insight of the inventor to conclude that the invention was obvious. Second, the court substituted its judgment for that of persons of ordinary skill. Third, the *Panduit* court erred by dissecting Panduit's claims into the component parts of the cable tie invention. Nearly every invention combines at least some existing technologies. Nonobviousness must be judged by considering the invention as a whole: A unique combination of existing factors constitutes inventiveness.

Secondary Considerations (Objective Factors)

Nonobviousness is the most important patentability criteria. The *Graham* three-part analysis is the conceptually accurate method, but it is too often difficult to apply. Prior art determinations are lengthy and complicated, judges have difficulty accurately mimicking the perspective of persons of ordinary skill that change with every technology, and the temptation is strong to use hindsight, general principles, and common experience. For these reasons, the Supreme Court has acknowledged that sometimes **secondary considerations** may be appropriate. These are additional factors that tend to show that the invention was not obvious at the time it was invented. The Federal Circuit now considers these factors to be very important and much easier to apply than the *Graham* test, so they are now called **objective factors**: (1) long-felt, but unmet need, (2) commercial success, and (3) use or copying by others.

First, **long-felt, but unmet need** occurs when an industry has unsuccessfully tried to solve a problem that the invention finally does resolve. The failure of others' efforts, when combined with the inventor's success, is often convincing evidence that the invention was not obvious; otherwise, others would have invented it. Second, if the **commercial success** of the invention is strong, it can be inferred that it was not obvious; otherwise, other inventors would surely have developed a similar invention sooner. The invention's success must come from its inventive, nonobvious features and not from some other cause, such as promotional expenditures, the seller's market dominance, or other product features not part of the invention. Third, **use of copying by others** can be persuasive. The authorized licensing or outright infringement by competitors is an additional market test of the invention's nonobviousness. Licensing implies competitors accept that the patent is valid; infringing copies imply that competitors were unable to develop adequate substitutes, so the invention must have been nonobvious. For example, in the *Panduit* case, Dennison was not successful in designing a workable cable tie other than by using the method Panduit used to solve these problems in its patent. Both Panduit and Dennison had tremendous commercial success in producing the patented version of the cable tie.

Amazon.com v. Barnesandnoble.com, Inc. is a recent high-profile case illustrating nonobviousness in the business method patent, Internet e-commerce area. What was particularly remarkable about this case is that it received considerable press coverage and provoked many people to publicly participate in the debate over what constitutes nonobviousness. Such technical discussions seldom occur outside the close-knit members of the patent bar or among experts in the technologies involved. Indeed, this case became the cause célèbre on the public policy issues of business method patentability.

UTILITY

Recall that §101 permits patents to be granted to "whoever invents or discovers any new and *useful* process, machine, manufacture or composition of matter." This creates a requirement that the invention have **utility**, beneficial use for the invention or for products produced by a patented process. This threshold of practical value is low because the invention need not work any better than technologies in the prior art. Indeed, many inventions are refined long after they are patented. Some older cases denied utility if the invention was frivolous, injured public well-being, or was immoral. However, later cases prefer to leave the public policy aspects of the invention's function to other laws, such as regulation of gambling devices or sexual devices. A few cases prohibit patentability of inventions for not being useful if the primary function is illegal or unsafe. For example, patented drugs must prove their efficacy both under FDA drug trials and under the utility standard of patentability.

THE PATENTING PROCESS

Obtaining a patent on an invention is a much more complicated and expensive process than is obtaining a copyright or perfecting a trade secret. Patenting requires qualification, an adversarial process proving the invention is patentable subject matter and that it is novel, nonobvious, and useful. Patenting is seldom successful without careful record keeping during the invention process, the preparation of the patent application advised by a patent attorney or patent agent, and many months of interaction between the inventor and the PTO's patent examiner. Frequently, the inventor is an employee, so employment responsibilities are involved, such as patent assignment and assistance duties often contained in the employment contract. Patenting is so costly ($10,000 to $50,000 in out-of-pocket expenses plus various opportunity costs) that patentability and commercialization sometimes involve third-party experts and venture capitalists. This section discusses the regulatory requirements for patent prosecution.

THE PATENT AND TRADEMARK OFFICE (PTO)

The U.S. PTO is a division of the Department of Commerce. This makes the PTO different from the Copyright Office, which is an agency of Congress and independent of the president. The PTO is a dependent regulatory agency under direct control of the president through the Cabinet. The PTO is the agency Congress created to qualify patents and trademarks, to promulgate interpretive regulations on patent and trademark issues, and to organize the fields of patentable technologies. The PTO's regulations set procedures for various patent-related activities. For example, the procedures that PTO examiners must follow in examining patent applications are assembled into the **Manual of Patent Examination Procedure (MPEP)**. Like most other federal administrative agencies, the PTO must follow the Administrative Procedure Act (APA) in its rule making, hearings, investigations, and responses to requests by the public under the Freedom of Information Act (FOIA) for information held in the PTO's files. The PTO's work burden is

ONLINE

PTO's MPEP
**http://www.uspto.gov/
web/offices/pac/dapp/
mpepmain.html**

enormous. With the number of patent applications approaching a quarter million each year, it is impressive that the PTO manages the workload fairly well. Of course, as with other information businesses, the PTO's computerization efforts have improved productivity.

THE PATENT APPLICATION

Despite the U.S. first-to-invent standard, it is still sensible to file a patent application as soon as the invention is reduced to practice. This is particularly important for firms engaged in active international trade that expect their patented products to be competitive in international markets. The first-to-file standards in other nations create risks if filing in foreign nations is delayed. Similarly, many other nations do not have the one-year grace period. Therefore, publication, sales, or use of the invention before filing in many other nations risks patent rights.

ONLINE
Trilateral Web site
**http://www.trilateral.
org**

ONLINE
European Patent Office
**http://www.european-
patent-office.org**
Japanese Patent Office
http://www.jpo.go.jp

An important step before filing is to assure that the inventor keeps detailed records in lab notebooks that are periodically signed and witnessed. Lab notebooks should be bound with no blank or missing pages to represent an accurate chronological journal that logs the invention process in accurate sequence. An initial patentability search of the prior art can be advisable so the benefits of patenting costs are better known and thereby provide an initial assessment of novelty that can encourage continuing with the expense of a patent application.

There are several major parts to a patent application. The inventor must describe the invention in a specification including at least one claim that provides sufficient detail that a person of ordinary skill in the art would be enabled to practice (reproduce or use) the invention. The specification should describe the invention and the manner and process of making and using it. Drawings are required when needed to illustrate the invention's architecture and aid in understanding it. The inventor must make an oath declaring original inventorship. The appropriate filing fee must also be included. After the patent is granted there are periodic **maintenance fees** owed by the patent owner.

Inventorship

As discussed in Chapters 4 and 11, inventorship under patent law is a different matter than authorship under copyright law. Although an employer can claim authorship for a work made for hire by one or more employees, this is generally not possible for inventorship. Generally, a patent application is made by the actual human inventor. The inventor must sign the application and declare that he or she is the first inventor. Of course, employers often contract with their employees for an assignment of patent rights and further require confidentiality and assistance in prosecuting the patent application.

A sole inventorship occurs when only one person conceives of the essential elements that are the "germ" of the invention's novel aspects. There is but a sole inventor even if others assist in the effort, pose problems to solve, or make minor suggestions. However, many inventions are made in large R&D laboratories where several human contributors collaborate. It is possible to have co-inventors if each makes a substantial contribution to the conception of the patent's novel aspects. If two or more persons conceive of the essential germ of the novel idea, then they are equal joint inventors. Some joint inventors may contribute different aspects, but all must be contributors to the novel aspects. All **joint inventors** must sign and participate in the application process.

Provisional Patent Applications

Since 1995, it has been much easier to establish the date of invention and obtain priority in international patent filings by using an abbreviated **provisional application**. As discussed next, regular patent applications must provide a highly accurate and detailed description of the invention. The provisional application can omit most of this. It allows the inventor to file an abbreviated description without taking the time and care necessary to meticulously draft clear and complete patent claims. Provisional applications have advantages: (1) First-to-file standards and shorter grace periods in foreign nations are satisfied by a provisional application, and (2) the inventor may have up to an additional year to test the invention's market appeal before investing in a full patent application. The inventor has one year after filing the provisional application before the full application must be filed.

The PTO's Electronic Filing System (EFS)

As part of the PTO's modernization initiatives, it has established the **Electronic Business Center (EBC)**, a group of related transaction-processing systems. The EBC processes upgrade interaction with the PTO from the historical use of paper-based, in-person, mail, and telephone interactions to electronic transaction processing. These are similar to the e-government initiatives being implemented throughout other federal agencies and in many states and some municipalities. The EBC includes electronic search for issued patents and trademarks, including full graphic images, the electronic payment of fees and account maintenance, electronic PTO job applications, and PTO subcontractor qualification. The EBC also includes the **Electronic Filing System (EFS)** for electronic filing of patent applications and **Patent Application Information Retrieval (PAIR)**, a faster and less costly method to check the status of a patent application.

Generally, the EBC systems require an initial registration of each individual or corporate user so all communications can be authenticated before transmission of highly confidential information. Registration and the use of bar codes simplifies interaction between the PTO and large, high-technology firms that have numerous applications filed at any one time. Public Key encryption Infrastructure (PKI) helps assure confidentiality. Special software is used for "clients" (inventors or assignees) to interact with the PTO's EBC. All these systems hold promise to improve service, reduce service times, and reduce the costs of the ever burgeoning patent information system.

DISCLOSURE

The major premise of patent law is that a limited monopoly on the invention is given in exchange for the inventor's **disclosure** of the invention's secrets. Disclosure occurs in a **specification** that has two parts. First, claims describe the invention, the "what description" that precisely defines the scope of the patent owner's rights. Second, specifications are the "how description" details of construction and use that must enable a person of ordinary skill in the art to practice (make or use) the invention in the best mode known by the inventor. PTO regulations require a ten-part format, including the inventions title, various cross-references, a summary, a brief as well as a detailed description of the drawings, claims, an abstract, the oath, and the drawings. Although there are no rigid requirements for the format of claims, successful patent claim drafters tend to use esoteric and somewhat standard terminology to describe the particular physical functions of an invention. The language of claims often seems convoluted to the layperson.

Enablement and Best Mode

Adequate description can be a difficult problem. There are natural incentives that create tension between inventors and everyone else (PTO, competitors). Inventors want their claims written broadly to maximize the value of their patent monopoly. Inventors are often reluctant to be as clear and complete as PTO examiners might demand. Ambiguous claims are more difficult to copy or design around, and this also makes the patent potentially stronger than the law permits. Two tests of adequacy are applied to the disclosures: (1) They must provide **enablement** (to a person of ordinary skill in the art), and (2) they must reveal the **best mode** for practicing (using, making) the invention.

The specification need not be a step-by-step production task list or cookbook approach. However, if a person of ordinary skill would be required to perform extensive experimentation before they could construct a working embodiment, then the disclosure is not enabling; that is, it is insufficient and must be revised by the inventor. The best mode requirement is intended to prevent inventors from concealing known examples of the best ways they have discovered to practice the invention. For example, consider the difference between a good cookbook and a bad one. The author of a good cookbook knows the common mistakes that cooks of ordinary skill might make, such as taking steps out of order, inaccurate measurement, improper mixing, inaccurate heating, and insufficient interlude between procedures. The good cookbook warns of these trouble spots and thereby strives to communicate the best mode for cooking the recipe (practicing the invention). By contrast, a bad cookbook fails to warn of possible problems, raising the probability of failure and requiring even cooks of ordinary skill to be persistent and experiment until they get it right.

It takes considerable experience in the technology involved before most people can develop an adequate understanding in the reading, interpretation, and writing of good claims. Technical professionals, patent lawyers, and patent agents usually develop expertise in only a few narrow but related technologies because the technical details are just too numerous in the most valuable arts. Nevertheless, it is useful to see how claims and supporting specifications are written so that the enablement and best mode standards are better understood.

Secrecy

Traditionally, patent applications have remained secret during prosecution. Only the inventor, the patent attorney or agent, various employees, the PTO examiner, and a few PTO staff are typically exposed to a patent application until after the patent finally issues. All these parties already are obligated to maintain secrecy until the patent is issued, or they should be. After issuance, the patent is published for anyone to see. Secrecy of patent application contents serves very useful purposes for the inventor. If the patent is rejected, the inventor can try to maintain it as a trade secret. Often during prosecution, the PTO examiner demands that claims be reduced in scope, which diminishes their value. Applicants may become dissatisfied if a narrow patent results. They can still withdraw their application and try to use the invention as a trade secret. Secrecy encourages frank and open prosecution activities between the PTO examiner and the inventor.

The advantages of secrecy largely benefit the inventor. Society also has an interest in patent applications before patents are issued. For example, the public could often contribute to the examination process. Persons of ordinary skill might supply prior art that might narrow the patent's scope or invalidate it. Publication of patent applications reduces the surprise element that surfaces when "submarine" patents undercut industry practices. Most other industrialized nations now require the publication of patent applications at some fixed time after filing irrespective of whether the patent is yet issued.

The United States finally gave up the absolute secrecy rule for patent applications when the examination process takes more than 18 months. If the application is also filed in foreign patent offices, the AIPA requires publication. The AIPA implemented the WTO and TRIPS treaties by standardizing the secrecy of patent applications to 18 months. Small U.S. inventors won an important exception: Secrecy may continue beyond 18 months if the inventor does not also file in foreign nations. This rule pressures the PTO to speed up the average examination process closer to 18 months. PTO examination can take several years for new and complex technologies like software, business methods, and biotechnology. Applicants uncertain about their application's prospects can still withdraw them before 18 months to avoid publication. This strategy can be used to preserve trade secrecy. Secrecy orders are possible for technologies with national security or defense reasons (secret weapons system), so these are also exempt from publication. Patent applications are now available from the PTO Web site and from other sources.

ONLINE

USPTO Patent
Application Searches
**http://www.uspto.gov/
patft/**

PATENT INFRINGEMENT

Patents are strong IP rights because, unlike copyrights, the patent protects both the idea and the expression (embodiments). The patent owner, often an assignee from the original inventor, has several exclusive rights that are protected by the threat of infringement litigation. These are the rights to exclude others from (1) making embodiments of the patented invention, (2) using the patented invention, and (3) selling (making the first sale) the patented invention. If the patent covers a process, ownership includes the right to exclude others from (1) using the process and (2) selling goods produced by the process. These are the most basic rights from the bundle held by the patent owner. Additional rights permit the patent owner to exclude others from importing into the United States infringing goods or goods produced using infringing processes made outside the United States and provide export restrictions on components of patented combinations and making an application to sell patented drugs.

LITERAL INFRINGEMENT

Infringement analysis is a three-step process: (1) a literal infringement inquiry, (2) a doctrine of equivalents inquiry, and (3) and a reconsideration of the inventor's history of negotiating the claims during patent prosecution. First, the court will look to whether there was **literal infringement**. This is similar to literal infringement under copyright because there is a comparison made between the patent claims and the alleged infringing embodiment. If every element claimed in the patent is also present in the allegedly infringing thing, then there is literal infringement. An exact duplicate infringes under the rule of **exactness**. If one of the claimed elements is missing, there can be no literal infringement under the rule of **omission**. However, there may still be infringement under the doctrine of equivalents discussed next. The rule of **addition** applies when all the claimed elements are reproduced in the infringing embodiment but additional elements are added. Infringement by addition is still a literal infringement even if it is an improvement.

For example, imagine a patent on a machine used to cut grass to an even height between three and six inches; it is called a "lawn mower." The original patent claims describe a nonpower, manual mechanism with the following elements: (1) a long handle, (2) metal frame and housing, (3) cutting blades, (4) the riding wheels drive the blade, and (5) the riding wheels adjust to maintain a variable but uniform cutting height. It would be literal infringement by exactness if a competitor produced a closely resembling machine with all five of these elements. It would be literal infringement by addition if another competitor produced a power mower with the only difference being a gasoline motor to drive the blades. However, it would not be literal infringement by subtraction if an electric motor powered a wheelless power mower that used a propeller-like blade to force airflow downward to hold the mower's cutting blades at a uniform height. Nevertheless, the wheelless mower might still be infringing under the doctrine of equivalents unless the PTO examiner rejected the cutting height claim during the original prosecution under the doctrine of file wrapper estoppel.

DOCTRINE OF EQUIVALENTS

The second step in patent infringement analysis frequently determines whether the allegedly infringing thing is highly similar to the patented invention. The doctrine of equivalents is one aspect of patent law that is stingy with the public domain. The **doctrine of equivalents** defines infringement more broadly by including competing products that closely resemble the patented invention's design, even when they are not literally infringing. For example, the wheelless mower had many of the same elements as the original mower; it added an engine for power, omitted the wheels, and substituted a propeller-like blade to maintain the uniform cutting height. Should patent law recognize the wheelless mower as an infringement?

Since 1853, the Supreme Court has recognized infringement when similar elements are substituted in an effort to avoid infringement.[20] There can still be infringement under the doctrine of equivalents if obvious changes are made by using known substitutes and the resulting product "performs substantially the same function, in the same way, to achieve the same result."[21] This is an ad hoc determination that must compare the prior art, from the perspective of a person of ordinary skill in the art, as to each substituted element(s). It is essentially a nonobviousness test; it is applied to the element substituted for the missing element(s). It is not judged from the perspective of when first invented, as was nonobviousness. Instead, it is judged from a later perspective: at the time of alleged infringement. Would the designers of lawn and garden implements easily think to use blowing air rather than wheels to maintain the mower's cutting height? The doctrine of equivalents is justified as a method to prevent "fraud on the patent" and unscrupulous copiers. Clearly, the doctrine of equivalents tends to expand patent rights but at the cost of making IP infringement determinations much more uncertain and costly. However, there is an important limitation that may reduce some of this ambiguity: file wrapper estoppel.

File Wrapper Estoppel

What if the substitute element had been the subject of contention during the inventor's prosecution history with the PTO examiner? Should the inventor be allowed to resurrect a claim rejected by the PTO examiner during prosecution? For example, suppose that the PTO examiner rejected the inventor's claim to use a gasoline motor to power the cutting blade but instead allowed the claim for a manual, wheel-driven, push-powered blade finally described by the original patent as issued. Given that the inventor was required to give up the gasoline motor during prosecution, should the inventor be allowed to use the doctrine of equivalents to prevent infringement if a competitor later sells a power mower? The doctrine of **file wrapper estoppel** prevents the original inventor from bringing back a claim as an equivalent in infringement litigation that was surrendered during to a PTO examiner during prosecution.

Prosecution is a process in which the PTO examiner carefully studies the invention claims and looks through prior art cited by the inventor and for other prior art the examiner finds independently by using other sources, databases, and cross-referencing indexes. The PTO examiner might find that some aspect of the invention's

---

20. *Winans v. Denmead*, 56 U.S. 330 (1853).
21. *Graver Tank & Mfg. v. Linde Air Products Co.*, 339 U.S. 605 (1950).

claims is already in the prior art. Some claims are written so broadly that they could include things already in the prior art. It is common for the PTO examiner to require the inventor to revise the application by making **amendments**. Only when the examiner is satisfied with these revisions is the patent, as rewritten, **allowed** when the PTO examiner recommends the patent be granted. Patent prosecution takes a long time because newer technologies are complex, the PTO has a substantial workload, and patent prosecution is iterative, requiring amendments to the application. If the PTO examiner finds there are no novel or nonobvious claims, the application can be totally denied in a **final rejection**.

Festo Clarifies Doctrine of Equivalents

The doctrine of equivalents creates sometimes costly uncertainty because there is ambiguity in determining equivalents that arise later in time. The doctrine of equivalents raises three very serious risks and thereby imposes costs on society and competitors while conferring benefits on patent owners. First, competitors using elements that are possible equivalents may be sued for infringement. Second, many competitors are deterred from using equivalents because of uncertainty that these might be infringing. This leads them to forego innovation that might have been beneficial to society. Third, competitors probably pay unnecessary license fees to inventors to avoid these two risks causing society to suffer dead-weight welfare loss as innovation is prevented or unnecessary payments are made to patent holders.

Some of these problems are clarified by the 2002 case of *Festo*.[22] Festo alleged that SMC infringed patents for "magnetically coupled rodless cylinders" used in robotics by substituting an equivalent element. The Supreme Court's interpretation of *Festo* now creates a rebuttable presumption that equivalents are not available for an amended claim element. Had the Supreme Court upheld the Federal Circuit's "complete bar" rule, this would have threatened all patent owners who make narrowing amendments to their applications during patent prosecution. Narrowing claims is a very common practice during prosecution. Such a sweeping change would have undermined the value of 1.2 million patents currently in force—an outcome so disruptive the Supreme Court would not likely permit without some clear guidance from Congress.

DEFENSES TO INFRINGEMENT

Those accused of infringement have only a few recognized excuses. The most important defense is **invalidity**. Those alleged to have infringed commonly attempt to show that the patent is invalid, nonstatutory subject matter, not novel, obvious, or not useful. Indeed, much patent litigation involves both claims of infringement and of invalidity. There is a presumption of validity for patents issued by the PTO, making issued patents very strong rights. The burden of proof is on the infringer or other

---

22. *Festo v. Shoketsu Kinzoku Kogyo Kabushiki Co.*, 2002 U.S.LEXIS 3818 (May 28, 2002).

person challenging validity to prove the invention was not patentable. For example, the incentives to do more thorough prior art searches are much greater during infringement litigation. Challengers often expend considerable resources to **scour the prior art** or enlist other competitors to help "bust the patent" by finding prior art that makes the patent seem obvious or not novel. The inventor's conduct is also closely examined for fraud or other inequitable conduct that might help invalidate the patent. Some upstart companies actively solicit prior art to help invalidate bad patents.

IP is highly regulated because it is clearly a form of monopoly and remains an exception to the general public policy disfavoring monopolies. Indeed, many IP professionals carefully avoid using the term *monopoly* because most people feel that monopolies are exploitive. Owners of all forms of IP, but particularly patents, may be tempted to extend their patent monopoly to other things that are not protected by IP laws. This is called a **misuse** of the patent. Misuse is a defense to patent infringement and may also be a separate, illegal act under antitrust laws. Antitrust law and patent misuse are discussed in detail in Chapter 12.

Two additional infringement defenses deserve brief mention. Infringement suits are not well limited by statutes of limitations. The six-year limitation on damages or injunctive relief restarts as to each new wrongful act of infringement: producing, selling, offering for sale, or using an infringing embodiment or process. Although suit on some very old acts of infringement may be barred, the continuing nature of infringement usually assures that the patent holder will still have a remedy. Nevertheless, the equitable concept of **laches** may be used to bar an infringement suit if it is delayed too long. Recall the **first sale doctrine** in copyright law that permits buyers of a copyrighted work to resell. This doctrine also applies to embodiments containing patented parts or produced using a patented process.

REMEDIES

The right to exclude others from making, using, or selling a patented invention would be hollow without fairly reliable remedies to enforce these rights. Patent remedies closely parallel those for copyrights discussed in detail in Chapter 4: (1) equitable relief by injunctions and (2) legal remedies in the form of lost profits, reasonable royalties, a form of punitive damages, interest on damages, and attorneys' fees. Typically, the patent owner must first prove infringement as discussed in the previous section. Then, a remedies phase is conducted in the infringement litigation that often raises additional complex issues. Both equitable and legal relief are appropriate in many instances. (See Exhibit 6.3.)

EQUITABLE REMEDIES

Court orders to cease the infringement are important because they can be more immediate. First, the patent owner may seek a **preliminary injunction** at an abbreviated hearing. The four equitable elements must be proved: (1) likelihood of success

Exhibit 6.3 Remedies for Patent Infringement

Remedy	Definition of Remedy	Impact of Remedy
Preliminary injunction	Temporary court order prohibiting infringement until full trial; must prove: (1) likelihood of success, (2) irreparable harm, (3) balancing of hardships, and (4) public interest	Prevents alleged infringer from continuing acts of alleged infringement until full trial; dissolved after full trial
Permanent injunction	Court order following full trial on merits of case; prohibits further infringement; must prove infringement	Prevents infringer from making, using, or selling infringing products or process; dissolved after patent expires
Lost profits	Projection of profits patent holder would have made if infringer's competition had not diverted sales; may include price erosion—lower profitability on patent holder's sales	Requires reasonable prediction of additional sales patent holder would have made without the infringement; not available if reasonable royalty is awarded
Reasonable royalty	Projection of royalties patent holder might have made if infringer had negotiated license; may base on rates from recent licenses on similar technologies or patent holder's standard royalty rate	May require hypothetical "negotiation" of license fees; not available if lost profits are awarded
Treble damages	Assessed in addition to other damages if infringement is willful	Strong deterrent to infringement
Attorneys' fees	Assessed in addition to other damages if infringement is willful	Most fully compensates patent holder for expense of defending patent

at a full trial held later on the merits of the infringement case, (2) the patent owner will suffer irreparable harm unless the infringer's conduct is stopped immediately, (3) the hardships on the patent owner and the alleged infringer are balanced, and (4) the public interest is considered. At one time, preliminary injunctions were difficult to obtain, but this has changed in recent years. A full trial on the infringement questions must be held before a **permanent injunction** is issued. An injunction is dissolved after the patent expires.

LEGAL REMEDIES

A court evaluating infringement may choose from several measures of monetary damages: (1) lost profits, (2) reasonable royalty, (3) treble damages, and (4) attorneys' fees. Remember the difficulties of determining these measures of compensatory damages for copyright infringement, as discussed in Chapter 4. Lost profits arise when the court can reasonably predict that the patent owner would have made additional sales if competition from the infringer's products had not diverted sales.

Another component of these damages is **price erosion,** which involves another fore-cast of damages in which the higher prices the patent owner "might have received" are projected if the infringing products had not competed. As was discussed in greater detail in Chapter 4, all these profitability measures require estimates of costs and overhead, which can be quite contentious, arbitrary, and speculative. Two alternative measures of royalties are possible: (1) a **reasonable royalty** based on rates used in recent agreements concerning similar technologies and (2) an **established royalty** computed at a rate the patent owner is already charging other licensees. Patent owners may recover either lost profits or royalties but not both. However, treble damages and attorneys' fees may be assessed in addition to compensatory damages if the infringement is willful.

INTERNATIONAL REMEDIES

Since the 1980s, trade relations with other nations have changed significantly by international treaties and by U.S. law. Several laws now improve the U.S. patent owner's remedies for infringement from activities in foreign nations. For example, §337 of the Tariff Act authorizes the U.S. Customs Service to block importation of infringing goods. The special 301 powers of the Omnibus Trade and Competitiveness Act authorize the U.S. Trade Representative (USTR) to monitor foreign nations suspected of repeated infringement. Under §301 of that Act, the USTR can negotiate stronger IP protections in other nations and impose trade sanctions on nations that are the source of repeated infringement. Finally, the **Process Patent Amendments of 1988** make it an infringement to import goods produced using patented processes if the patent owner has not authorized use of the process. The law is complex and includes due diligence so that resellers are not excessively burdened. International patent remedies are summarized in Exhibit 6.4.

Exhibit 6.4 Patent Infringement Remedies under International Trade Law

Trade Law	Impact on Patent Infringement Remedies
§337, Tariff Act	Authorizes International Trade Commission (ITC) hearings and findings; may issue exclusion order directing U.S. Customs Service to block imports of infringing products
Special 301, Omnibus Trade and Competitiveness Act	Authorizes the U.S. Trade Representative (USTR) annual review of foreign nations' acts, policies & practices affecting U.S. IP; various watch lists signal dissatisfaction; closely monitor or trigger investigation and possible trade sanctions; successfully raising IP protection in several nations
§301	Authorizes USTR to investigate and negotiate trade agreements to enforce IP rights
§271(g), Process Patent Amendments	Creates new infringement remedy against importer of goods produced using patented processes if unauthorized; due diligence procedures for importers and resellers

SUI GENERIS PROTECTIONS

Several additional types of IP protections have been added to the law in the United States and other nations to protect unique forms of property. For example, a new form of IP is currently proposed for the U.S. to protect databases. These new forms of IP are often called **sui generis** (pronounced "sue-eye generous"), meaning unique, special, or original. Sui generis subject matter does not usually fit neatly into the subject matter acceptable in the existing fields of copyright, trademark, patent, or trade secret. Also, political pressures may prevent the inclusion of sui generis subject matter because the protection might be too great. For example, databases are not well protected under copyright law because they represent public domain ideas and often have little creativity. Similarly, databases do not fit well in patent law because the information they contain is often in the public domain. Furthermore, expanding copyright or patent law to protect databases might not be politically acceptable because the very long term of copyright protection or the strong protection of patent law could stifle research.

Three sui generis forms of IP are discussed here: (1) design patents, (2) plant patents, and (3) semiconductor chip (mask works). Additional sui generis forms are not detailed here but may arise from time to time in other nations, such as in Europe with the European database protection, the German **petty patent,** and the Japanese **utility model.** These rights protect industrial designs that are not well protected in the United States.

DESIGN PATENTS

Congress authorized design patents for ornamental objects to encourage the elimination of unsightly industrial mechanical devices. They created a separate type of patentable subject matter for ornamental design that is fixed in an article of manufacture under §171 of the Patent Law.

> **Design Patents under §171**
> Whoever invents any new, original, and ornamental design for an article of manufacture may obtain a patent therefore, subject to the conditions and requirements of this title.

Design patents differ somewhat from utility patents. First, design patents are intended to encourage the decorative arts by protecting ornamental designs on useful articles. Second, the term of protection is 14 years from issuance rather than the 20 years from filing used for utility patents. They do not protect the useful aspects of inventions. Third, the ornamentation must generally be visible during normal use. By contrast, an invention, including a utility patent, may well hide the patented aspect as a component. For example, the novel decoration on a sports shoe achieves its purpose when seen. However, the utility of a patented fuel injection pump is typically hidden inside the engine of a vehicle when it is working as intended. Fourth, infringement analysis requires a perspective more like copyright or trademark—a comparison of similarities in the overall appearance between the patented article and the alleged infringing article. Further, the test is for similarities as perceived by an ordinary observer. Finally, the application procedure to acquire a design patent is much simpler to complete than is a utility patent application. The primary focus is on whether the drawings accurately capture the design rather than on verbal descriptions of functions, as are needed for a utility invention.

There is an important limitation on design patents: Only ornamental designs are protected, so the patented design cannot serve primarily a functional purpose. Patented ornamental designs may have functional aspects but the design cannot be dictated by the functional needs. Designers are often advised that to better assure design patentability of the ornamental design, it should be made severable from its functional aspects. This controversy is similar to the severability discussion about trademarks that follows in Chapter 7.

Conjure up an image of the bicycle rack that is simply a multiple s-shaped metal tube fixed into the ground, usually set in concrete. This item would seem to be the perfect example of the merger of "form into function." However, there is no practical way to separate the ornamental curves from the functional bike slots, so the bike rack is probably not a patentable design. By contrast, the ornamental design of soles on athletic shoes was held patentable despite the function of the sole in the shoe.[23]

Design and utility patents share several aspects. First, the PTO is the regulator that qualifies both types of patents. Second, both must be qualified under similar novelty and nonobviousness standards. However, the relevant scope of prior art for design patents is broader, including anything with similar appearance regardless of its function. Third, similar processes are followed. **Double patenting** is generally prohibited; a single item cannot receive both a utility and design patent. This is not to say that a particular article of manufacture might not have various patents on some of its components. For example, the typical computer is protected under several patents. However, the component protected as a utility patent must be separate from the portions of the article covered by the design patent.

Modern design patent problems include the visual aspects of computers, software, Web sites, and e-commerce screens. Many observers argue that design patents are an imperfect protection scheme for industrial designs. Designers should explore whether trademark, trade dress, or copyright protection might be an alternative to design patent protection in some instances.

PLANT PATENTS

The United States has two sui generis laws to protect plants. They are different systems administered by two different regulatory agencies. These two sui generis schemes predated the third basis for plant protection, utility patents, which became available under the landmark *Chakrabarty* ruling as clarified in 2001.[24]

---

23. *Avia Group Int'l v. L.A. Gear California, Inc.*, 853 F.2d 1557 (Fed.Cir., 1988).
24. *J.E.M. AG Supply v. Pioneer Hi-Bred Int'l.*, 121 S.Ct. 2566 (2001).

The first scheme is administered by the U.S. PTO. Under the **Plant Patent Act** of 1930, plant patents are an extension of utility patent procedures. They provide patent protection to distinct, new, asexually reproduced plant varieties. **Asexual reproduction** includes horticultural techniques such as the rooting of cuttings, layering, budding, and grafting. Reproduction of plants from seeds and reproduction of bacteria are not covered. The patentability standards of novelty and nonobviousness are generally applicable. The term of protection is 20 years after filing, just like utility patents. Successful plant patent applications concentrate more on the adequacy and quality of color drawings than do utility patents. The drawings must reveal all the new variety's distinctive characteristics.

The second form of sui generis plant protection was created by the 1970 **Plant Variety Protection Act**. This law protects sexually reproduced plant varieties. This technique involves cross-pollination that creates a hybrid in the next generation. Patentability standards are much reduced; there is no nonobviousness requirement. The act is administered by an agency of the Department of Agriculture's Agricultural Marketing Service. The Plant Variety Protection Office examines applications and issues plant variety protection certificates. Fungi and bacteria are excluded but may receive utility patent protection. Protection lasts for 18 years.

ONLINE

PTO's Plant Patent information
http://www.uspto.gov/web/offices/pac/plant/

SEMICONDUCTOR CHIP PROTECTIONS

The Semiconductor Chip Protection Act was passed in 1984 to provide sui generis protection for **mask works**, the microscopic electronic circuit schematic diagram containing thousands of transistors as found in integrated circuits. Their development requires considerable time and investment, but they are easy to copy and pirate. Copyright and patent law standards and processes were unsuitable for the short useful lives of semiconductor chips. Chips are useful articles inseparable from their graphical design. While seemingly appropriate for patent protection, they are more like expression covered by copyright. Congress created a sui generis protection administered by the Copyright Office to protect the investment in chip design, essentially a form of programming. The term *mask* is used because chip making is essentially a photographic technique. The mask is a diagram of each layer of the chip's wiring. The mask stops the light used to etch the tiny circuit pathways into a silicon wafer that separate the conducting pathways from the insulating parts.

The act has standards that are very similar to copyright law. For example, the mask work must be fixed in a chip product, it must represent original design that was created independently, the underlying ideas are not protected, a first sale doctrine applies, and a form of fair use permits copying for teaching, analysis, or evaluation. Further, there is no rigorous qualification as is required for patents. The mask work designer, usually a chip manufacturing firm, must register the work with the U.S. Copyright Office. Mask work protection provides a limited bundle of rights to reproduce, sell and license or assign. Protection lasts for ten years after registration or it is first exploited commercially.

CHAPTER 7
TRADEMARKS

Commercial symbols are powerful tools that build and enhance brand image. Firms spend a lot on their brand images: (1) advertising to stay in the public's consciousness and (2) developing easily recognized logos and other unique identifiers that conjure up favorable memories to trigger repeat transactions. Indeed, much of a firm's goodwill directly results from the brand image sustained by the firm's name, commercial symbols, and reputation. Commercial symbols use imagery and mental pictures to communicate a firm's reputation and thereby distinguish the product's source and qualities from competitors or substitutes. Their vivid verbal descriptions and visual images are enhanced with artistic, literary, or musical expression. Commercial symbols make easy, direct, and influential connections with memories that can reliably direct purchasing decisions.

Trademarks are the most valuable form of modern commercial symbols. Trademarks are a subset of commercial symbols that receive legal protection under the federal laws (e.g., Lanham Act), state common law, and state statutes. Think of a **trademark** as a commercial symbol, word, name, or other device that identifies and distinguishes the products of a particular firm. Trademark law entitles the owner of the trademark, or **mark**, to prevent others, both competitors and those in other industries, from using the trademark to market their products. The principles of trademark infringement illustrate that there are a few exceptions: similar marks for very different products owned by different firms (e.g., Yahoo! chocolate drink vs. Yahoo! Internet portal, Lexis on-line research portal vs. Lexus automobiles). Trademarks are used to help customers find, identify, and distinguish the products of individual firms. Trademarks are the central organizing principle for franchises, detailed in Chapter 11.

This chapter covers trademarks, related intellectual property (IP) rights including trade dress and trademark-related unfair competition, and the trademark implications of the Internet. Trademark law is a complex and challenging area because the standards of analysis and much of the case law are based on artistic and cognitive judgments about human perception and commercial behavior. Increasingly, social science research is needed to prove the impact of trademarks on consumer perceptions and activities. Indeed, market research based on consumer behavior is becoming an important tool in trademark litigation and in administrative determinations by the U.S. Patent and Trademark Office (PTO).

NATURE OF TRADEMARK AS AN INTELLECTUAL PROPERTY RIGHT

Trademarks differ conceptually from other forms of IP such as patents, trade secrets, or copyrights. The constitutional and economic rationales for most other forms of IP are based on two premises: (1) The limited IP monopoly is a powerful incentive to creativity that ultimately benefits society, and (2) IP is really a contract between government and innovators in that a limited monopoly is given in exchange for disclosure of details describing the innovative design. By contrast, trademark policy rewards investment in goodwill only as a byproduct of preventing consumer deception. Indeed, trademark law provides little reward to the visual artist who uses creative imagination and aesthetic skills to design the commercial symbol. Many well-known trademarks were the product of only nominal compensation given to an employee who won a contest to rename the firm; for example, the Standard Oil Co. of New Jersey changed from Humble Oil to Exxon, and Andersen Consulting became Accenture.

GOALS OF TRADEMARK LAW

Trademark law balances four broad goals: (1) the promotion of business ethics, (2) the refinement of distributional efficiency, (3) the development and maintenance of goodwill, and (4) the preservation of competition by expanding the public domain. These broad goals are implemented by three main trademark concepts that pervade this chapter: inherent distinctiveness, likelihood of consumer confusion, and functionality.

First, trademarks promote business ethics. They discourage competitors' promotional activities that weaken the link between a commercial symbol and the firm it represents. Trademark policy evolved from the common law of unfair competition. Competitors may not deceive or confuse consumers about the origin or nature of their products by pretending their products are related to a more reputable firm. Trademarks enable a firm to accurately and exclusively identify itself as the source of particular products. Trademark owners have the right to prevent others from free-riding on the trademark owner's promotional expenses. For example, enforceable trademarks help prevent competitors from palming off their inferior products, such as a competitor that pretends its products were really produced by the trademark owner. These laws may also prevent a counterfeiter from knocking off products protected by a trademark with look-alike imitations. Trademark owners use the infringement remedy to assert these rights.

Second, trademarks enhance distributional efficiency. Buyers and sellers often expend considerable resources to do their business together. Sellers have large advertising, sales, and promotional expense. Many smart buyers spend considerable time and sometimes even money to research product performance before making purchases. Effective use of trademarks helps reduce these search costs that connect buyers and sellers. Buyers can more quickly, easily, and cheaply find sellers using well-known trademarks. Commercial symbols more directly associate the seller's products with that seller's reputation. For example, the McDonald's golden arches can be spotted by motorists even when they are driving quickly along a busy Interstate highway. Motorists' search costs to find a fast food restaurant are lower when the golden arches are so reliably and safely located.

Third, trademark law encourages investment in brand image. The incentive to invest in goodwill would diminish without some assurance that firms would capture the benefits of their investments in making their products uniform in quality. Trademark law helps to prevent unfair competition when a competitor passes off its products as produced by another seller. Consumers clearly benefit from investments in quality. Markets function better when the seller's reputation becomes a primary method to communicate accurate marketing information. For example, if all automakers could use the three-pointed star logo on their cars, Mercedes-Benz could have less incentive to produce high-quality cars. Note that the investment in uniform product quality encouraged by trademark law is often different from the investment in innovation encouraged by patent and copyright law. Investments in quality under trademark incentives need not result in new technologies to the same extent that IP investment encourages R&D efforts to develop new technology.

Finally, there are limitations on trademarks to encourage active competition. Some words, descriptions, or symbols are necessary for all competitors to adequately and accurately describe their products. Therefore, no one may acquire a trademark monopoly over the clearest descriptive terms or images for a particular product. Such a trademark would give its owner an unfair advantage over competitors who could not adequately describe their competing products. As a result, trademark law prohibits the registration of generic trademarks, thereby leaving the major descriptive terms for that type of product in the public domain for use by all competitors. For example, if Sony held a trademark to the term TV, other TV makers would be at a significant disadvantage. Finally, protection should not extend to functional aspects of trademarks, elements that affect the purpose, action, or performance of the product. Trademark protection of such functional or useful characteristics would conflict with the balance drawn under patent law by denying competitors the use of key operating elements.

SOURCES OF TRADEMARK LAW

Unlike federal patent and copyright law, the congressional power to enact federal trademark law is not generally based on the IP clause of the U.S. Constitution.[1] Recall that the IP clause, found in Article I, §8, authorizes IP legislation only "To promote the Progress of Science and useful Arts, by securing for limited times to Authors and Inventors the exclusive Right to their respective Writings and Discoveries." The main purpose of trademark law is not directly related to this grant. Instead, trademark law is derived from the state law of unfair competition. Therefore, Congress's legislative power for trademark law is based on the commerce clause to regulate interstate commerce.

The regulation of unfair competition began in state common law and spread to both state and federal statutes on trademarks; it also includes palming off and dilution statutes. Early cases applied equitable principles to prohibit unfair competitive activities that hinder competition through the use of deceptive, improper, or unfair methods of competition. These laws hold that consumers are harmed when one seller pretends its goods are made by a competitor. This is **free riding** on the other firm's reputation, and it harms both consumers and the competitor. Today, trademarks are protected under state common law and state statutes of unfair competition. In addition, many states permit trademark registration.

State trademark law has been significantly supplemented by federal trademark laws enacted in 1870, 1881, and 1905. The **Lanham Act** of 1947 is the primary federal trademark law in force today. It was revised in 1988 and again in 1996. There is stronger protection under the Lanham Act for trademarks used in interstate commerce. Federal trademarks are registered with the PTO. Applications for trademark registration are subject to **qualification**; that is, applicants should conduct a search to assure their proposed trademark is not already used by another. The applicant's trademark counsel gives an opinion of the uniqueness of the proposed trademark, and then PTO examiners also search to confirm the trademark's uniqueness.

Many protections of state and federal trademark law apply even to unregistered marks. However, registration facilitates stronger rights and remedies. Registration is important to strengthen international rights for exclusive use of the trademark in foreign nations. Trademark-related legislation is summarized in Exhibit 7.1. Some aspects of the commercial symbols covered by trademark law may also be protected by copyright or as design patents.

INTERNATIONAL TRADEMARK LAW

International trademark rights are becoming increasingly important as some nations try to recapture their cultural and national symbols or prevent counterfeit branded goods from flooding their markets. Foreign nations' trademark laws differ; protec-

---

1. *Trademark cases*, 100 U.S. 82 (1879).

Exhibit 7.1 Applicability of Trademark Laws

Trademark Law	Basic Provisions	Applicable in Which Jurisdictions
State unfair competition statutes and common law	Prohibits: unfair competition, palming or passing off, dilution	Limited to activities affecting interests in that state
State trademark statutes	Trademark registration, qualification, infringement, remedies	Limited to activities affecting interests in the state of enactment
Lanham Act of 1943	Trademark registration, qualification, infringement, remedies; enables PTO regulation	U.S. interstate commerce and foreign activities with substantial . impact within the U.S.
Federal Trademark Dilution Act of 1996	Extends state antidilution remedies to famous marks throughout the U.S.	U.S. interstate commerce and foreign activities with substantial impact within the U.S.
Anti-Cybersquatting Protection Act of 1999 (ACPA)	Prohibits domain name pirating or ransom	U.S. interstate commerce and foreign activities with . substantial impact within the U.S.
Trademark System of the European Union	Trademark Law Harmonization Directive of 1988 requires EU nations to pass uniform legislation on trademark subject matter and grounds to refuse registration and defines trademark rights; Community Trademark System of 1993 permits central registration	All 13 EU member nations
Paris Convention	Requires national treatment to foreigners from signatory nations, protection for marks well known in signatory nation	In all signatory nations that implement the treaty's provision with national legislation (U.S.)
Madrid Agreement and Madrid Protocol of 1996	Permits central filing after registration in home nation	In all signatory nations that implement the treaty's provision with national legislation (U.S.-Protocol)
Trademark Law Treaty	Restructures and simplifies trademark registration procedures in signatory nations	In all signatory nations that implement the treaty's provision with national legislation (U.S.)
ICANN Uniform Domain Name Resolution Process	ADR process to settle rightful trademark preemption of domain name registration	All nations bound by WIPO treaties

tion is often given to the firm that first registered the mark, not the firm that used the trademark first, as in the United States. Firms entering international commerce must assess the desired strength for their trademarks in foreign markets, both in nations where they intend to sell products and in nations where competitive products might be produced.

International organizations are important in international trademark matters. For example, affiliated trading groups such as NAFTA and the EU are trying to harmonize trademark protections. Master international trade treaties negotiated through GATT and the WIPO are working toward uniformity. Three multilateral treaties have direct impact on trademarks. The **Paris Convention** gives reciprocity for each separate nation's treatment of trademarks but grants few substantive rights, lacks a centralized registration or filing system, and lacks effective enforcement mechanisms. The **Madrid Agreement** and the **Madrid Protocol** have yet to have major influence but hold some promise for harmonization. The **Trademark Law Treaty** was a 1994 product of the WIPO, and the U.S. Congress passed legislation in 1998 to conform U.S. procedures to this treaty.

TRADEMARK SUBJECT MATTER

Trademarks, also known as marks, may consist of words, names, symbols, devices, or any combination of these elements. Cases have expanded this list to include other elements, including slogans, numbers, colors, smells, sounds, and the overall design of a product's package or the vendor's premises. For example, many of the images used on Web sites are potential subject matter of trademark or trade dress. There is a trend to include new types of elements if they help to distinguish the vendor's products from competitors. It is often necessary to examine what particular products are sold under the mark in question in the analysis of both the subject matter of marks and their distinctiveness.

WORDS, TITLES, NUMERALS, ABBREVIATIONS, AND SLOGANS

Single words and short groups of words are among the most common forms of marks. Single words, titles, abbreviations, and nicknames are all eligible to become marks if they are distinctive. For example, the abbreviation BMW for Bavarian Motor Works is eligible because consumers readily recognize that the abbreviation relates to the firm as a manufacturer of automobiles. Pepsi is eligible as a nickname for Pepsi-Cola.

Titles of literary or other entertainment works generally cannot become registered marks because they describe the contents of those publications. However, titles that are arbitrary, suggestive, or have secondary meaning can be registered. Titles to literary or other entertainment works might also be registered for use on companion goods such as clothing or toys.[2] The use of names is problematic because the Lanham Act conditionally excludes marks that are "primarily merely a surname." **Conditional exclusion** means that names might be trademarked if they are mixed with other words or have acquired secondary meaning (discussed later).

Letters, numerals, and other typeface characters and symbols may be combined to create marks if they are distinctive and not mainly descriptive of the product. It is common practice to use alphanumeric characters that distinguish models of automobiles

---

2. *Lucasfilm, Ltd. v. High Frontier*, 622 F.Supp. 931 (D.D.C. 1985).

or electronics as produced by particular manufacturers. However, they cannot be trademarked if these letters and numerals are used to clearly identify product specifications from among several with differing characteristics. For example, if model numbers are intentionally chosen to refer to a progression of increasing size specifications or performance characteristics in the product, they are descriptive and not protectable. Protection can be lost if competitors in the industry use similar numerals to designate competing products (e.g., Intel's 386 CPU chips).

Slogans and groups of words are also eligible. Slogans could lose their distinctiveness if they are too long to be easily remembered, are buried in text, or mostly convey promotional information. Nevertheless, long slogans may still be copyrightable as advertising copy. A trademarked slogan can validly contain components that are separate marks; the mark "Coke" is part of the slogan "Coke is it," and "Allstate" is used in "You're in good hands with Allstate." To become registered marks, all words, phrases, abbreviations, and slogans must be distinctive.

SENSORY ELEMENTS: DISTINCTIVE SHAPE, COLOR, ODOR, OR SOUND

Trademarks need not be expressed only in text or graphic images. A common and distinctive element in corporate logos is shape. There are also **design marks** that use some nontext elements, such as oval borders, unique fonts, and geometric designs to serve as backgrounds to word marks. These elements contribute to the distinctiveness of many trademarks. Shape may not be merely ornamental. Shapes must create a commercial impression separate from the word mark. Consider the traditional Coke bottle. It uses a vertically ribbed, hourglass shape as its design mark. Even the location of a label might be recognized by consumers as the distinctive element for the producing firm, and therefore it acquired secondary meaning, as discussed later. For example, the red fabric tab on the right rear pocket of Levi's jeans is a trademark separate from the LEVI mark stitched to the tab.[3] However, the Levi's tab did not transfer into a different market, for shirts, where the Levi's tab on the front pocket was not protected as a separate mark.[4]

Other sensory elements can also be used as trademarks or as components of trademarks, including distinctive color, odor, or sound. Color patterns or shapes have long qualified as components of design marks. In recent years, color standing alone, even without being part of a fixed pattern, may also be protectable.[5] For example, color was distinctive when applied to replacement fabric covers for ironing presses in commercial laundries.[6] Critics charge that permitting color trademarks, apart from a graphic symbol or design, could eventually deplete the limited number of available colors in the palette. The protection of color marks may depend on consumer ability to differentiate between subtle shades and hues, a difficult task.

---

3. *Levi Strauss & Co. v. Blue Bell, Inc.*, 632 F.2d 817 (9th Cir., 1980).
4. *Levi Strauss & Co. v. Blue Bell, Inc.*, 778 F.2d 1357 (9th Cir., 1985).
5. *In re Owens-Corning Fibreglas*, 774 F.2d 966 (Fed.Cir., 1985) (pink for fiberglass insulation was distinctive, not functional).
6. *Qualitex Co. v. Jacobson Products Co., Inc.*, 514 U.S. 159 (1995).

Smells can be registered if they are distinctive and not the product's major feature. For example, scented embroidery yarn was held registrable.[7] However, the scents of particular perfumes are not likely to be trademarkable because their smell actually describes the product's main characteristic. Although smell may not seem to be relevant as a trademark in e-commerce, someday computers may have an electronic odor transducer that could transmit an aroma sample. Finally, sounds may now be trademarked. Other motorcycle manufacturers cannot meticulously copy the distinctive rumble of a Harley-Davidson motorcycle in their attempts to duplicate the "hog" experience. Use of distinctive sounds on the Internet may further extend the protectability of sounds as marks. Electronic transducers of aroma are becoming possible so if PCs become equipped with them, trademarked smells might become associated with Web sites.

CHARACTERS AND CELEBRITIES

The personae of characters and celebrities can be powerful marketing tools. Consider the power of cartoon characters to capture repeat business for related products such as theme park admissions, movie attendance, and video sales and for sales of toys, clothing, music, and food (Disney, Warner Bros.). Similarly, the endorsement of famous artists, musicians, or sports figures enhances advertising and brand image (Britney Spears, Michael Jordan). Characters may appear in works that are literary or entertainment or on the Internet. Trademark protection may extend to a character's name, nickname, or outward appearance, but not to their traits or talents.

Certain elements of a celebrity's persona may be trademarked, including their look, dress, actions, and sound. The line separating trademark or unfair competition aspects of celebrity rights from their privacy rights is fuzzy. Digital technologies to morph or simulate a character or celebrity in video or on-line performances will probably raise both trademark and privacy risks if celebrity images are used without license. The privacy aspects of celebrities are discussed further in Chapter 13, and the licensing aspects are discussed in Chapter 11. Clearly, many video games and Web sites use characters extensively as part of entertainment and to distinguish themselves from other Web sites.

TRADE DRESS

Trademark law can also protect the combination of visual design elements used in the overall appearance of a product, its labels and packaging, the business's premises, or a Web site's distinctive look and feel. These visual design features are known as **trade dress**. They cover the way the product or service is "dressed up" and creates a total image. To serve as a protectable mark, the trade dress must be distinctive and indicate that the mark owner is the source of the products. For example, trade dress is a major element of many consumer product franchise businesses.

---

7. *In re Clarke*, 17 USPQ2d 1238 (TTAB, 1990).

Consider how McDonald's restaurants have a uniform look: rectangular red brick building, yellow accents, golden arches (a separate mark) where permitted by local zoning ordinances, uniform service counter, and similar dining room design.

Trade dress is a very broad and vague term because it includes an arrangement of many elements: size, shape, three-dimensional design, ornamentation, color scheme, sounds, and smells. Trade dress for restaurants or taverns includes the emotional, sensory, and aesthetic elements of mood, environment, air, and atmosphere—all part of the "ambience." Trade dress is not merely decoration but must make a commercial impression. It seems likely that trade dress will become even more important as a feature of unique Web site design.

Several factors are used in determining whether trade dress is inherently distinctive.[8] First, distinctiveness is more likely if the shapes and designs are uncommon. Second, the trade dress should be unusual in the market for that type of product. Third, simple refinements on traditional ornamentation used in that product's market are less likely to be distinctive. Trade dress cannot be functional when taken as a whole; that is, the whole look and feel should not be essential to the product's use or have a direct impact on the cost of production or the product's quality. Trade dress analysis considers all the trade dress components taken together as a whole.[9] The individual components may have functions if the whole of the trade dress is not functional. For example, the quarry floor tiles used in the Taco Cabana Mexican restaurants are functional: They seal the floor and provide a finished, decorative surface. However, the tile is only a component of the whole restaurant's ambience, a trade dress that is not functional and not necessary to operate a Mexican restaurant successfully. The analysis of functionality should inquire whether there are commercially feasible alternatives for a competitor's trade dress, whether the trade dress is the simplest and least costly means to manufacture, and whether the trade dress aspects (e.g., color) are inherent and therefore necessary for other competitors.[10] Functionality of Web site features may become problematic for the protection of Web site designs. For example, common color bars, clickable button locations, and locations for particular functionality (e.g., search box, terms and conditions, privacy policies) may eventually limit a Web site's ability to protect these elements as they become standard.

EXCLUDED AS INELIGIBLE SUBJECT MATTER

The Lanham Act prohibits registration of several types of marks. These marks can also be canceled or denied protection under the common law. First, **generic words** that are the common description of the product cannot be trademarked. This implements the fourth goal of trademark law: to maintain competition and safeguard the public domain. (Generic terms are discussed later.) Second, scandalous or immoral marks are disqualified. These are marks that are shocking to a sense of propriety and

---

8. *Lisa Frank, Inc. v. Impact International, Inc.*, 799 F.Supp. 980 (D.Ariz., 1992).
9. *Fuddruckers, Inc. v. Doc's B.R.Others, Inc.*, 826 F.2d 837 (9th Cir., 1987).
10. *Sega Enterprises Ltd. v. Accolade, Inc.*, 977 F.2d 1510 (9th Cir., 1992).

offensive to moral feelings, inspire condemnation by a large portion of the population, or refer inappropriately to religious matters. Unlike copyright, the First Amendment does not give the right to register immoral or scandalous marks, even if they are not obscene. Only a few cases interpret this provision. The following marks were disqualified as immoral or scandalous: "Madonna" as a brand name for wine,[11] a defecating dog as a satirical design mark for clothing,[12] and "Booby Trap" for feminine underwear (brassieres).[13]

Another class of ineligible subject matter includes fraudulent or deceptive marks. **Deceptive marks** falsely connect the product with persons, institutions, beliefs, or national symbols or cause them contempt or disrepute. They are deceptive if consumers are likely to be influenced by the connection. For example, it would be deceptive if a firm unconnected with the family of a famous army general used the general's name as a mark for rifles. A **deceptively misdescriptive** mark makes a false inference about an influential matter such as an inaccurate geographic origin. Much of the litigation over trademarks on the Internet concern deception in the use or descriptive power of marks (meta-tags).

Additional ineligible subjects include government insignia, flags, coats of arms, names, portraits, or signatures of any living person without their permission or of a deceased U.S. president during the life of the widow(er) without permission. Marks that are primarily geographic are ineligible unless they acquire secondary meaning. Such marks can include the names of states, cities, regions, geographic features, or their nicknames ("Big Apple"). If the products are not associated with the geographic place, then the mark is either deceptive or misdescriptive. Names are discussed later.

TYPES OF TRADEMARKS

Trademark law traditionally focused on marks that identified a single source or producer of goods. Eventually marks also became useful to identify services, uniform product characteristics from various producers and members of industry-wide organizations. In the narrowest sense of the term, *trademark* refers to a mark that distinguishes the source or origin (e.g., producing firm) of goods. As discussed further in Chapter 8, **goods** are tangible personal property (not real estate, employment or services). The Uniform Commercial Code (UCC) defines goods as "all that are movable at the time" of contracting." The Lanham Act's definition for *trademark* addresses only goods:

Trademark

any word, name, symbol, or device or any combination thereof . . . used by the producer or reseller . . . to identify and distinguish [its] goods, from those manufactured or sold by others and to indicate the source of the goods.[14]

---

11. *In re McGinley*, 660 F.2d 481 (CCPA, 1981).
12. *Greyhound Corp. v. Both Worlds, Inc.*, 6 U.S.P.Q. 863 (TTAB, 1988).
13. *In re Runsdorf*, 171 U.S.P.Q. 443 (PO TTAB, 1971).
14. 15 U.S.C. §1127; Lanham Act §45.

A trademark is generally registered in relation to a particular type of product or a line of related products. Legal questions about a mark are generally considered as they relate to use with particular types of products. For example, trademarks on particular goods include Pepsi® for various versions of soda pop, IBM ThinkPad® for a broad line of laptop PCs, Toyota Tundra® for pickup trucks with various body and drivetrain configurations, and Sony Diskman® for a line of somewhat different portable CD players. Trademarks registered with the PTO may be displayed with the "R in a circle" symbol right after the registered trademark: ®. Trademarks claimed under state common law or trademark statute may be displayed with the small capital letters "TM" right after the trademark: ™. Domain names function like marks but are not yet recognized under the Lanham Act as a separate category of mark. Mark owners must use notices, or they may not be able to sue for damages. Marks and domain names are discussed later.

SERVICE MARKS

Eventually, trademark law began to recognize that services have become a significant part of commerce and that marks should also protect services. The same questions of source identity, consumer confusion, and investment in quality control are important to markets for services, particularly in dispersed business systems like franchises. Indeed, the information age signals a shift from a predominance of goods transactions in the early twentieth century to a predominance of services in the twenty-first century.

What are services? Provisionally, consider **services** to be contracts in which the predominant value is derived from a customized application of human labor, expertise, and/or information. Service businesses perform human activity, manual labor, or professional practice. The sale of goods is at most a minor, incidental part of a service contract, such as the oil in an oil change, meat in a fast-food hamburger, or the shampoo used in hair styling. The Lanham Act does not define services, but the courts have defined the term expansively. For example, as consulting practices flourish, firms purchase customized "solutions" to operate their business systems.

A key factor in hastening the shift to service products is the characterization of information, software, and computer information as services and not as goods or real estate. Therefore, as the ingenuity of humans increases, services will probably be broadly defined and include activities beyond those in most common use today: lodging, restaurant, consulting, advertising, professional practices, entertainment, financial, software, information, transportation, and Web portals, as well as repairs and maintenance. Marks associated with services are registered under the Lanham Act "in the same manner and with the same effect as are trademarks" for goods.

> **Service Marks**
> any word, name, symbol, or device or any combination thereof [used to] identify and distinguish the services of one person . . . from the services of others and to indicate the source of the services, even if that source is unknown.[15]

---

15. 15 U.S.C. §1053.

A service mark is registered in relation to a particular type of product or a line of related services. For example, service marks used on particular services include McDonalds^{SM} for restaurant services, Mr. Goodwrench^{SM} for automotive maintenance and repairs, and eBay^{SM} for auction and intermediary sales services. Note that many services include an incidental sale of goods: foodstuffs for restaurant services and parts for maintenance and repair services. Some of these goods may be trademarked separately, such as the Delco® or Delphi® parts used in GM's Mr. Goodwrench service or Boar's Head® cold cuts in a deli franchise like Schlotsky's.

Service marks are commonly used with franchise businesses, such as laundry, insurance, restaurants, fast lubes, and product service centers. In the future, product sales and performances may be directly made by computer. Automated performances most closely resemble services unless goods are the predominant output produced by the automated performance. Even if the human labor component declines in these automated performances, they are likely to be classified as services for service mark purposes. A service mark may be displayed with the small capital letters "SM" beside the service mark: ^{SM}. Notice is a prerequisite to using the damage remedy.

Service Marks Must Be More Than Ancillary

Whether service marks can be registered is also limited by the principle that the public domain must be protected. Service marks must be more than merely ancillary; the service must be sufficiently separate from the sale of goods, and each service must be separately significant. This requirement is intended to prevent mark owners from registering excessive service marks to accompany their trademarked goods, which could result in "a whole raft of service mark registrations covering each and every 'service' that every other competitor also provides as an adjunct to the sale of goods."[16] This **more than ancillary rule** helps discourage trademark owners from creating an excessive number of service marks to cover services that other competitors must also necessarily provide. The problem is that competitors could be blocked from adequately promoting "generic" ancillary services if they are covered by ancillary service marks. For example, most full-service gasoline service stations perform oil changes and chassis lubrications, services provided by many other service stations. Service marks like "OilChanger" or "LubeJobber" are probably ancillary, so they should not be registered to only one oil company.

CERTIFICATION AND COLLECTIVE MARKS

Marks are important to indicate the sole source of products but are also useful to indicate more than just a *single* source. For example, franchises operate under systemwide service marks and trademarks. Franchises, detailed further in Chapter 11, are actually groups of independent businesses operating under a single set of quality control and operational guidance imposed by the franchisor, the mark owner.

Two more distinctive types of marks impose systemwide quality control, require uniform product origin, and/or impose operational guidance on independent entities:

---

16. See J. Thomas McCarthy, *Trademarks and Unfair Competition*, 2d ed. §19.30 (San Francisco: Lawyers Cooperative Publishing Co./Bancroft-Whitney, 1984).

collective marks and certification marks. These marks should function in the same manner and with the same effect as trademarks. They are generally owned by independent parties and not by the "industrial or commercial" firm producing the products. Instead, they may be owned by "nations, states, municipalities and the like" if the noncommercial owner exercises "legitimate control over the use of the marks." These marks should not be registered if the noncommercial owner misrepresents that it is the actual producer. For example, regional government units in agricultural regions do not produce the foodstuffs under these marks. Instead, independent growers in that region produce the products under the auspices of the regional authority, such as California Raisin Growers.

Certification Marks

Certification marks certify that the products of all producers using the mark have the characteristics of the group operating under that certification mark. Mark owners cannot discriminate against or deny use of the mark as long as the producers meet the objective certification standards. Otherwise, the mark could be used to exclude disruptive competitors. Note in the **certification mark** definition that the mark's owner must be independent of the producers who produce their products. Otherwise, there could be conflicts of interest and increase the potential that the mark owner would not be objective in overseeing the matters certified. For example, if the state government of Florida owned the "OJ" certification mark, no state agency can either produce orange juice under the mark or use "OJ" as a service mark in promoting the Florida citrus industry.

Certification Mark

any word, name symbol, device or combination thereof [used by producers other than the certification mark owner] to certify regional or other origin, material, mode of manufacture, quality, accuracy or other characteristics … or that the work or labor on the goods or services was performed by members of a union or other organization.

As with service marks, the certification mark owner must exercise some quality control to assure that its standards are met. Consider how Underwriters Laboratories monitors the use of its "UL" certification mark. Use of the mark by product sellers assures a level of safety in operations of mechanical and electrical goods. UL tests samples from participating product manufacturers and then uses a listing contract to require the covered manufacturers to promise that all other goods using the "UL" mark will also meet the safety criteria. This is about all that UL could practically do to assure compliance. It is impractical for a certification mark owner like UL to test every product or impose absolute control over producers' use of the certification mark. Instead, the certification mark owner must impose a compliance program of reasonable steps under the circumstances to prevent the public from being misled.[17]

ONLINE

Underwriters
Laboratories
http://www.ul.com

---

17. *Midwest Plastic Fabricators, Inc. v. Underwriters Laboratories, Inc.*, 906 F.2d 1568 (Fed.Cir., 1990).

Several certification programs are becoming important in e-commerce, such as assurance services for encryption security, privacy, and electronic payment security.

ONLINE
Privacy, e-commerce
certification
**http://www. bbbonline
.org**
http://www.truste.org

For example, the Better Business Bureau provides privacy assurance through its BBBonline program. TRUSTe provides similar certification. New standards and other certification authorities are likely to emerge as e-commerce grows. Service and certification and marks on the Internet will become more important as safe shopping, privacy protection certification, and secure payment mechanisms require standardization to attract customer loyalty and trust.

Collective Marks

Collective marks are similar to certification marks, but collective marks are used by members of an organization to identify their members. They overlap with certification marks if the organization imposes quality control or other standards on its members. For example, the mark "Realtor" refers to members of the National Association of Realtors. They are real estate professionals who pass professional testing and are bound to professional rules of conduct. Membership is the key distinction between certification and collective marks, particularly when the organization requires its members to adhere to codes of conduct or they certify professional conduct or members' moral character.

> **Collective Mark**
>
> Trademark or service mark . . . used by members of a cooperative, an association or other collective group or organization . . . to indicate membership.

SPECTRUM OF DISTINCTIVENESS

Thus far, we have examined several ways to classify trademarks: first, according to the type of subject matter or thing afforded protection, such as words, shapes, and sensory phenomena; second, the source of law affording the protection, either state, federal, or international; and third, the type of commercial activity associated with the mark, either products, services, or groups of producers. This section discusses a fourth and perhaps the most important categorization of marks: the perceived relationship between the mark and its owner. Trademark law provides the strongest protection for identifying marks, the most important function of marks. Identifying marks clearly trigger human memory to associate the mark directly with only one producing firm. A second function of marks is to convey some aspect or attribute of the product. All marks communicate one or both of these two aspects: (1) identification of the producing source and (2) description(s) of the product's attributes. Trademark law makes determinations about distinctiveness and then dictates whether a mark should be registered to one firm or left in the public domain for use by all competing producers.

Firms usually have many choices in selecting the best mark for its products. At one extreme, marks can be chosen that *do not* automatically cause consumers to think about the type of product; that is, the mark does not suggest or describe the characteristics, properties, or features common to all competing products in that category. These marks are the strongest and most distinctive because they uniquely refer to the mark's owner, not to the product category. They are distinctive marks because they are not needed by other competitors to describe their versions of the same product. Marks serve the policies of trademark law best when they promote competition. Trademark law preserves commercial symbols best describing the product for the public domain. No one firm may own the best words, phrases, or symbols that identify the product category.

On the other extreme are marks that do describe each generic category of products. They are the weakest marks because they do not connect directly with a particular producer of the goods. Nevertheless, firms have a natural incentive to use brand names that conjure up images of the product or suggest images of its best features. Suggestive marks may cause consumers to experience multiple hints about the product's suitability or desirability. Some product names strongly imply the product's characteristics as well as identifying the particular producing firm. Trademark law and policy seek to limit this. Only a limited number of best descriptors are available for each product. The best descriptors are generic, so they should remain in the public domain for all producers to describe their products.

The categorization system for marks is known as the **spectrum of distinctiveness**. There are several categories positioned between the two extremes: from arbitrary and fanciful, through suggestive and descriptive, and then finally to generic. The spectrum of distinctiveness discussed in this section is summarized in Exhibit 7.2.

ARBITRARY AND FANCIFUL MARKS

Arbitrary and fanciful marks are inherently distinctive, strong marks that can be protected immediately. The PTO should register arbitrary and fanciful marks without difficulty, and courts should recognize their distinctiveness. The adoption of an arbitrary or fanciful mark easily permits the mark owner to use the mark. **Arbitrary and fanciful** marks in no way describe the whole category of competing products. They are the strongest marks because they identify only a particular producer, or sole source, for the product.

Some arbitrary and fanciful marks have components that are well-recognized words or symbols. For example, Blue Diamond uses a familiar color and shape but this mark has no relationship to the product: nuts (food). Similarly, Carnival[18] is arbitrary and fanciful for a cruise ship line, as is "Just do it"[19] for sportswear and related equipment. Some arbitrary marks are coined or made-up words that did not exist before registration. They have no relationship to the product category: Rolex for watches,[20] Kodak for photographic supplies and services,[21] and Exxon for petroleum products and services.

---

18. *Blumfield Development Corp. v. Carnival Cruise Lines, Inc.*, 669 F.Supp. 1297 (E.D.Pa. 1987).
19. *Nike, Inc. v. Just Did It Enterprises*, 799 F.Supp. 894 (N.D.Ill. 1992).
20. *Rolex Watch U.S.A., Inc v. Caner*, 645 F.Supp. 484 (S.D.Fla. 1986).
21. *Eastman Kodak Co. v. Weil*, 243 N.Y.S. 319 (N.Y.Sup. 1930).

Exhibit 7.2 Spectrum of Distinctiveness

Descriptiveness Category	Definition	Trademark Protection	Examples of Marks and Associated Products
Arbitrary or fanciful	Inherently distinctive, no connection between mark and product category	Strong protection, immediate protection possible	Blue Diamond (nuts), Exxon (petroleum), Kodak (photographic), Rolex (watches), Carnival (cruises), "Just do it!" (sport equipment), Penguin (books), Arrow (shirts), Beefeater (gin)
Suggestive	Mark indirectly suggests feature(s) of goods, but a connection is required using human imagination	Strong protection, immediate protection possible	Coppertone (suntan lotion), Accenture (consultant), Sportstick (lip balm), Gung-Ho (action figure)
Descriptive	Mark describes major feature(s) of the type of product	Weak protection, secondary meaning is required	Beer Nuts (salted snack), Bufferin (buffered aspirin pain reliever), Chap Stick (lip balm), Fashion Knit (sweaters), Beef and Brew (restaurant), Healthy Choice (diet foods), Super-Soaker (high-powered water gun)
Generic	One of the few terms necessary to adequately describe the type of product	No protection, remains in public domain for use by all competitors	TV, phone, blouse, shoe, watch, computer, tape, and almost any term designating a product category; terms adjudged generic: shuttle (airline), 386 (CPU), Swiss Army (multiblade pocketknife); distinctive genericide: terms before escalator, cellophane, aspirin, thermos

SUGGESTIVE MARKS

Suggestive marks have at most a vague relationship to the category of goods. **Suggestive marks** are not precisely descriptive; they require some imagination, thought, or perception by consumers to connect the mark to the goods. They indirectly suggest some relevant characteristic, feature, interesting quality, or concept about the goods. For example, an insecticide function is suggested with the Roach

Motel brand of insect traps, skin coloration change is suggested by Coppertone sun-tan lotion, expertise with an *accent* on a fu*ture* orientation is suggested by the Accenture brand of consulting services, and macho abandon is suggested by the Gung-ho mark for an action figure toy.[22] Suggestive marks are inherently distinctive and deserve immediate protection.

DESCRIPTIVE MARKS

Descriptive marks immediately conjure up some important characteristic about the product. They do so without the need for much imagination. Such marks are weak because they tend to more clearly describe products from all the producers in that category. Because of the scarcity of adequate descriptive terms, trademark policy imposes a conditional exclusion on descriptive marks. Descriptive marks must remain in the public domain and cannot be registered or protected unless they acquire secondary meaning, as discussed in the next section.

Descriptive terms are often adjectives, adverbs, or descriptive nouns because they address aspects of the product, such as the product's nature, quality, characteristics, ingredients, components, or intended use. Marks that are primarily a surname (last or family name) are conditionally excluded from registration. Marks that are primarily geographic are conditionally excluded. Examples of descriptive marks include Beer Nuts (salted snack), Bufferin (buffered aspirin pain reliever), Chap Stick (lip balm), Fashion Knit (sweaters), Beef and Brew (restaurant), Healthy Choice (prepared foods), and Super-Soaker (high-powered water gun toy). Descriptive marks neither are protectable under state unfair competition law nor can they be federally registered until they have acquired secondary meaning.

Secondary Meaning

There is a major exception to the trademark policy that prohibits descriptive terms in marks. Trademark protection can be allowed but only after a descriptive term has acquired secondary meaning. In this context, the mark's **primary meaning** is in its description of the goods. The mark's **secondary meaning** develops only after time passes. Public exposure during this time creates an association between the mark and the mark owner as *the* single producing source. Secondary meaning exists only when consumers immediately link the mark with the mark owner and not with the class of products from all producers. For example, assume the Internet service provider JetWire.com, a suggestive mark, begins using "BroadBand" as the brand name of its Internet access service. BroadBand is probably descriptive because most high-speed Internet access service firms would find the term a useful description for their services. However, secondary meaning develops after the public associates the BroadBand mark with only the JetWire.com firm. Descriptive terms like BroadBand cannot be registered until secondary meaning develops in the public's eyes. When will that happen?

Proving secondary meaning is generally an empirical process that considers the mark's economic impact by examining past events and current conditions. For

---

22. *Hasbro, Inc. v. Lanard Toys, Inc.*, 858 F.2d 70 (2d Cir., 1988).

example, data from validly conducted consumer surveys are direct and fairly persuasive evidence of consumer perception. There is an immediate link of the mark to the particular producer as the only source producing the product under the mark. Consumer survey data can prove the perception of relevant buyers, past purchasers, and prospective consumers for the type of product in question. Circumstantial evidence is also useful to infer secondary meaning. For example, courts may consider long and continuous use of the mark, the amount and nature of advertising using the mark, and the sales volume of products under the mark. These factors help to show the effectiveness of developing a secondary meaning.

Descriptive terms are not immediately permitted registration by the PTO on the **principal register**. This is the more favorable federal registration list because (1) it gives strong notice of the mark's ownership throughout the United States, (2) infringement suits and remedies are enhanced, (3) international registration and protections are enhanced, and (4) a mark becomes incontestable after registration for five years on the principal register.

A secondary list of marks is also maintained by the PTO: the **supplemental register**. It is used when marks do not qualify for the principal register. Generally, the supplemental register is available for descriptive terms but not for generic terms. Supplemental registration permits use of trademark notice symbols ®, as well as reciprocal registration between the United States and some other nations, and it enhances some infringement remedies. However, supplemental registration does not provide all the benefits of the principal register. After a descriptive mark is in exclusive and continuous use for five years and is listed on the supplemental register without legal challenge, it may be moved to the more advantageous principal register.

Until *Two Pesos, Inc. v. Taco Cabana, Inc.*, trade dress could be protected only after it had acquired secondary meaning.[23] *Taco Cabana* permits adoption and PTO registration of trade dress even before secondary meaning is established. Unfortunately, a 2000 case obscures this issue again. In *Wal-Mart Stores, Inc. v. Samara Brothers, Inc.*,[24] the Supreme Court openly worried that registering product design before it develops secondary meaning would give existing mark owners too much power to lock up product designs. The justices are concerned that juries may be too easily convinced to make the vague determination that a particular product design is inherently distinctive. Such unpredictable results could discourage new or upstart firms from costly litigation over product designs that another firm already has registered. The issue may now turn on whether trade dress is a form of product design or whether it is simply a form of product packaging. If trade dress is a form of product design, then secondary meaning would be required for protection.

Taco Cabana's trade dress
http://www.
tacocabana.com

However, if trade dress is merely packaging, then *Taco Cabana* would permit trade dress to be protected immediately after PTO registration. This quandary may encourage firms engaged in e-commerce to characterize Web site trade dress as product packaging to avoid the more onerous requirement of secondary meaning for product designs.

23. 505 U.S. 763 (1992).
24. 529 U.S. 205 (2000).

GENERIC MARKS

Trademark law's primary goal is to promote fair competition, without deception. To further this goal, the common law and the Lanham Act deny protection for marks that are **generic**. They are the most common names and descriptions of the class of products in question. No producer should be given a monopoly over the genus name or class descriptors for all competing products. By definition, generic terms cannot identify the producer as source because all competitors' products are identified by the generic term. The legal question in cases interpreting generic terms is whether the term serves as one of the more common names for products in the minds of most relevant consumers.

The particular generic term in question need not be the only name for the product. Consider how the electronic transmission and reception of full-motion video for entertainment purposes is known by various generic terms: television, TV, the tube, or video. Many generic terms are nouns or adjectives because they designate a product category, such as phone, blouse, shoe, watch, computer, or tape. Some terms are adjudged generic, such as shuttle (airline), 386 (CPU; thereafter Intel adopted Pentium rather than 586), and Swiss Army (multiblade pocketknife).

Genericide

Some mark owners are so successful with their advertising and promotional activities that the consuming public eventually associates the mark with the whole product category. Marks that were once suggestive or distinctive may eventually become the primary term describing the class of products. This outcome is **genericide** because the owner loses protection for the mark. The test of genericide is whether the mark's primary significance to the consuming public is to identify the mark owner as the sole producing source or the mark has come to describe the class of products from all sources. As with many other factual questions in trademark law, the proofs used in a genericide case include data from consumer surveys, advertising, use by competitors, and authoritative sources such as dictionaries and expert lexicographers.

Note that many contemporary mark owners actively seek to avoid genericide of their more valuable marks. For example, the Xerox Corp. frequently advertises that there are no "Xerox copies," and instead there are xerographic copies made on photocopy machines. Similarly, RollerBlade has taken a subtler approach by including the following wording right after its mark, RollerBlade: "brand of in-line skates." In each instance, the mark owner discourages the public from using its mark as the generic descriptor for the product category. Famous genericide examples include aspirin, escalator, thermos, and cellophane. All these marks were distinctive, but after they became widely known as the generic description of the product class, the marks were no longer capable of identifying the mark owner as the sole producing source.

CLASSIFYING MARKS ON THE SPECTRUM OF DISTINCTIVENESS

It can be difficult to differentiate suggestive marks from descriptive marks[25] or even to distinguish arbitrary or fanciful marks from suggestive marks. The spectrum of

---

25. *Franklin Knitting Mills, Inc. v. Fashionit Sweater Mills, Inc.*, 297 F. 247 (S.D.N.Y. 1923).

distinctiveness is a continuous range of classifications; it is not abruptly defined or clearly expressed. Determinations of distinctiveness have very important consequences because an owner may be denied the use of a mark if it is not inherently distinctive: arbitrary, fanciful, or suggestive. In judging how to classify a mark, we must look to actual usage and use one or more of several factors, including (1) recognized meanings from the dictionary or thesaurus, (2) judge or jury determination of what constitutes the reasonable cognitive judgment of average or ordinary customers, (3) empirical evidence of consumer attitudes and perceptions, or (4) a factual history of coining terms or local business traditions. Many distinctiveness determinations are based on subjective judgments by PTO examiners, judges, and juries.

It is also challenging to distinguish suggestive marks from descriptive marks. There are two tests to differentiate them. One test examines the degree of imagination needed to connect the mark with the product. If less imagination is needed, then the mark is weaker and more descriptive; if more imagination is needed, then the mark may be suggestive. A second test looks to whether the mark is a term or descriptor needed by competitors to describe their similar products. If so, the mark is more likely to be descriptive, and the mark owner will have difficulty acquiring exclusive rights. Examples of classifying marks along the spectrum of distinctiveness is summarized in Exhibit 7.3.

FUNCTIONALITY

The trademark policy goal of promoting competition by preserving the public domain is again addressed by the functionality limitation. **Functionality** is a product's feature that affects its purpose, action, or performance or the facility or economy of its processing, handling, or use.[26] Functional aspects of product design cannot be protected by trademark; otherwise, competitors could not compete effectively. For example, trade dress often involves physical aspects of product packaging or the architecture of business premises. Trademark protection extends only to the distinctive visual elements of the design and not to the functional aspects. In the *Taco Cabana* restaurant case, the purpose of the garage doors should be considered functional and not protected as trade dress. They serve an important climate-control function, permitting the enlargement of the dining room onto the adjoining patio areas in good weather while protecting the inside dining space during inclement weather. By contrast, the vertically ribbed hourglass shape of the Coca-Cola bottle is mostly ornamental and unnecessary to strengthen the container.

When is a trademark feature functional? The courts have developed several tests, but unfortunately they do not provide consistent answers. The courts reject the colloquial or de facto definition that the feature simply performs some function. Instead, the courts inquire into whether (1) there are equally appealing alternative ways to accomplish the function, (2) whether the feature was once patented, or

---

26. *Restatement of the Law, Torts, 1st.*

Exhibit 7.3 Classifying Marks along Spectrum of Distinctiveness

Mark	Product	Classification	Rationale for Classification
Suave	Shampoo	Suggestive	Suave and results of haircare are desirable characteristics for humans
Accuride	Tires	Suggestive	Accuracy is desirable trait of tire performance
Wearever	Cookware	Suggestive	Durability is desirable
Verbatim	Floppy disks	Suggestive	Exacting recall is desirable
Tylenol	Pain reliever	Arbitrary	Coined, new word name
Amtrak	Transportation	Suggestive	Coined, suggests America and tracked transportation
Hard Rock Café	Restaurant	Arbitrary/fanciful	No relationship to service
Tea Rose Flour	Food	Arbitrary/fanciful	No relationship to type of food

(3) whether the mark owner touts the feature as functional in advertising.[27] If these facts are true, the feature will probably not be protected because it is functional. A trademark feature could also be considered functional if it lowers production costs, as was the case with a bicycle rim design used by Schwinn. Some cases even hold that consumer demand may be enhanced with aesthetically pleasing designs. Under this reasoning, an artistic element of a mark or trade dress might not be protected because its function is to increase demand.

Of course, certain aspects of functional designs may be protected under patent law if they satisfy the patentability standards of novelty, nonobviousness, and utility. Recall from Chapter 6 that design patents have similar limitations on functionality. Functional designs enter the public domain more quickly, at the expiration of the limited patent term. Another reason to prohibit functional aspects of trademarks is that the potential duration of a trademark is perpetual. The functionality rule helps preserve the public domain and defers to the rigors and limitations of patent law for functional elements.

ACQUISITION, REGISTRATION, AND MAINTENANCE OF TRADEMARKS

Trademark rights are created or acquired in two major, sometimes overlapping ways: (1) use and (2) registration. The commercial reputation necessary for trademarks cannot be created until the owner makes **actual use** of the mark. Use makes consumers aware so they can rely on the mark to identify the owner as producer. Therefore, to obtain such rights, trademark law traditionally requires the mark owner to be the first to adopt and use the mark. The mark must be affixed to the

---

27. *In re Morton-Norwich*, 671 F.2D 1332 (CCPA, 1982).

product. For goods, this means placing the mark directly on the goods, containers, packaging, displays, documentation, or labels. For services, the mark should be displayed along with sales or advertising.

No registration is necessary under state common law. However, stronger rights are available under state or federal trademark registration. To qualify for federal trademark protection and registration, the applicant must be the first to use the mark in interstate commerce or the first to acquire secondary meaning for descriptive marks. Recall the discussion of interstate commerce in Chapter 2. The Supreme Court interprets interstate commerce broadly to include many *intra*state activities that affect *inter*state or foreign commerce.[28] The technology transfer and franchising aspects of trademark licensing are discussed in Chapter 11.

FEDERAL REGISTRATION UNDER THE LANHAM ACT

The Lanham Act provides stronger trademark protection than the automatic protections under the state common law of unfair competition. There are several federal registration alternatives under the Lanham Act and its amendments. Registration and other trademark regulatory matters are handled by the Patent and Trademark Office (PTO). The PTO is currently a separate office within the U.S. Department of Commerce, although there have been proposals to privatize the agency.

ONLINE

USPTO's Trademark
Web site
**http://www.uspto.gov/
main/trademarks.htm**

There are two main types of registration on the principal register: §1(a) for marks already in use and §1(b) for intent-to-use applications. Marks may be registered if they are already in use in interstate commerce. The application must identify the owner and the products covered, state the date of the mark's first use, and include a drawing of the mark and specimens of how it is actually used. The applicant must claim that no other rightful user is known. **Disclaimers** can be made, indicating descriptive or generic elements of the mark such as common shapes (circle, oval) and descriptive words (pizza). Disclaimers excluded the matters listed from protection. The PTO may require disclaimers for particular mark elements. Registration on the supplemental register is also available for "would-be marks," typically descriptive terms, geographic names, or surnames. Supplemental registration, discussed previously, is appropriate for marks that are in the process of acquiring secondary meaning. The PTO now encourages electronic filing using the eTEAS: *Trademark Electronic Application System.*

ONLINE

USPTO's eTEAS on-line
registration
**http://www.uspto.gov/
teas/index.html**

Intent-to-Use Application

The 1988 Trademark Revision Act reversed an old prohibition against trademark registration: the **token use doctrine.** Trademark policy did not develop to encourage the needless proliferation of unused commercial symbols or to reward artists and marketing innovators by granting property rights in unused designs. Instead, the

---

28. *In re Silenus Wines*, 557 F.2d 806 (CCPA, 1977).

trademark goal of preventing consumer confusion is the most important policy. Therefore, mark owners could not lock up a particular mark by making sham transactions—that is, mere token use—to simulate the mark's use in interstate commerce. No trademark protection was permitted for inactive marks: "Ownership of a trademark accrues when goods bearing the mark are placed on the market."[29] Some mark owners actively "warehoused" appealing marks with only vague plans for their future use. These practices frustrate trademark policies of maximizing the public domain because their registration was based on deception. Competitors were denied the use of good but inactive marks.

The token use doctrine was abolished in 1988 when the intent-to-use application process began. When an applicant has a bona fide intention to use the mark in interstate commerce in the future, the applicant may lock in its priority; the application date establishes the date of first use. This "start date" is an important focus when other users try to use the same or a confusingly similar mark. An intent-to-use application is valid for only six months, during which the applicant must begin actual use. A six-month extension is usually granted, and up to three additional six-month extensions may be granted with proof of good cause (e.g., unforeseen production delays). Once the mark is in actual use, a statement should be filed to move the mark to the principal register.

Trademark Searches

Some research is sensible before investing too much in a trademark. A search of trademark databases is useful to uncover similar marks. Searches can be done by many trademark-savvy individuals, but serious and high-stakes searches are best left to professional trademark search firms and trademark law practitioners. Searches are best made before doing certain things: prosecuting an application, advertising to build brand image, or ramping up production if the mark is permanently affixed. As discussed later, searches should include Internet domain name registrations.

Although trademark searches are optional, they are a good risk-averse strategy because trademark searches often uncover others' claims and other uses of the mark. A search is particularly important for suggestive and descriptive marks because another owner may be a direct competitor selling similar products. Trademark applications must confirm that the applicant in good faith knows of no confusingly similar marks already in use. Searches help to confirm this good faith belief. Trademark infringement suits are costly, as are the wasted costs of advertising or production that used another's mark.

Searches can be made on one or more public domain or proprietary databases, including the *Official Gazette* (the PTO's paper-bound publication), the PTO Web site, CD-ROM databases such as CASSIS, on-line databases (Lexis, Westlaw, Dialog), and print publications from public libraries. A cursory, surface search looks for existing marks with nearly identical spelling or pronunciation or close visual similarity. A deeper, analytical search examines synonyms, homonyms, alternative and phonetic spellings, and similar

ONLINE

Trademark search firm, Thompson & Thompson
http://www.t-tlaw.com

---

29. *Blue Bell, Inc. v. Farah Mfg. Co.*, 508 F.2d 1260 (5th Cir., 1975).

overall shapes or visual components. For example, an analytical search for marks similar to "e-commerce" or "cyberlaw" should examine all marks beginning with the lower case *e* or including the prefix *cyber* or the suffix *law*. A deep search covers even more: directories (yellow pages, B2B or trade catalogues), business service firms, and participants in the supply chain. Software using pattern recognition to search digital images is becoming available and should make searches more complete and efficient. In complex searches, professional search assistance may be best to benefit from experienced judgment. Searches range upward from $100.

Prosecution and Examination

After filing, there is an interactive process of **trademark prosecution** between the applicant and the PTO that can take many months. The PTO examines the application to assure compliance with registration procedures and trademark requirements (e.g., proper subject matter, distinctiveness), and a PTO examiner conducts a search to determine the likelihood of confusion. The PTO examiner will issue an office action letter refusing the registration if generic or descriptive terms are used or there is a confusing similarity with an existing mark. The applicant usually responds by negotiating over elements of the proposed mark and with reinterpretation of similar existing marks. If the applicant fails to overcome the examiner's objections, a **final refusal** is issued; failure to respond within six months results in **abandonment** of the application. A mark is approved when the examiner is satisfied with the applicant's responses and the mark is published in the *Official Gazette*. A **registration certificate** is issued for marks in actual use, or a **notice of allowance** is issued for an intent-to-use application.

RENEWAL AND TERMINATION

Marks are renewable every ten years if they are in continuous use. The first renewal must occur in the fifth year and requires filing an affidavit declaring continuous use. After publication in the *Official Gazette*, another person may challenge the registration in an **opposition** proceeding. This permits outsiders to question the mark's confusing similarity to existing marks or claim that the mark contains descriptive elements or generic terms. If a confusingly similar mark is already in use, the PTO may grant concurrent but restricted use. During the first five years of registration, the mark is vulnerable to **cancellation** for the same reasons used in the opposition process. After the first five years, marks become **incontestable**; they cannot be cancelled, even if they are not inherently distinctive or they lack secondary meaning. However, after five years, marks remain vulnerable to cancellation if they become generic, are abandoned, were obtained by fraud, or are ineligible subject matter. The abandonment of a mark is inferred if there is a substantial period of nonuse, if the owner intends to not resume use, or if the owner fails to control use of the mark (unpoliced licensees).

LIMITATIONS ON THE SCOPE OF USE

Historically, there were two major limitations on a mark's scope of use: (1) geographic or territorial and (2) product field of use. Modern statutes diminish the importance of these limitations. Under the common law, a mark's owner held exclusive rights only in the geographic territory where the mark was actually used. Another person could use the same or a confusingly similar mark in a remote geographic territory, if the first mark owner had no presence in that other region and the second user acted in good faith. The remote territory must not be influenced by advertising or reputation of the first mark. **Good faith** means the second user had no notice or knowledge of the first user's use. For example, imagine that a restaurant chain began operating in the 1940s in New Jersey under the mark "Acme Diner." In the 1960s, a California restaurant chain started operating under the "Acme Diner" mark, but the owner had no knowledge or notice of the New Jersey chain or its use of the mark. The California chain would have a defense to infringement in a suit brought by the New Jersey chain's owner.

Traditional trademark law permitted exclusive rights only in relation to specific products with which the mark was used. For example, assume a blues club, the Bent Note, sold no goods under its mark. Anyone else could use the "Bent Note" mark to sell products other than nightclub services. Today, state and federal antidilution statutes provide some protection to mark owners from noncompeting uses of their marks. Dilution laws are discussed further in the next section.

TRADEMARK INFRINGEMENT

The trademark industry continues to refine its methods of describing and distinguishing marks. Despite this progress, marks will probably continue to be defined by very vague criteria. Further, the incentive remains strong to use descriptive terms or to ride free on the brand image of successful competitors. Such acts can be concealed because the law uses so many imprecise standards such as "spectrum of distinctiveness" and "likelihood of consumer confusion." Trademark law permits a mark owner to defend its rights by proving infringement and then seeking remedies. **Infringement** occurs when an outsider uses the same or a similar mark and thus weakens the value of the owner's mark. This section discusses the difficult task of determining when a mark is violated or encroached upon by another mark.

LIKELIHOOD OF CONFUSION STANDARD

The primary test for trademark infringement and unfair competition is the **likelihood of confusion** standard: Would the use of the same or a similar mark by an offending user cause confusion to an appreciable number of consumers about the source of products? This question focuses on whether average, reasonable consumers would be misled into believing the alleged infringer's products were produced by the mark owner or were confused about who produced the products. This concept is fundamental because trademark law primarily remedies consumer misunderstanding about the source of supply for products. The likelihood of confusion standard is also used by the PTO in examining trademark applications. How is the likelihood of confusion determined?

Several key factors are used in determining the likelihood of confusion. Although no one factor alone is decisive, the courts consider a preponderance of factors by weighing and combining them. Unfortunately, the courts do not agree on a single set of factors, but the following summarizes the factors most frequently used. First, the *strength of the mark* is relevant. It measures whether the mark is inherently distinctive—typically more so if the mark is arbitrary or fanciful, but less so if it is descriptive. A mark is also strengthened if the public already associates the mark with its owner, much like the analysis of secondary meaning. Second, a comparison is made to find *similarities between the two marks*. Confusion is more likely if the two marks are closely related in their visual appearances, their phonetic sound (perhaps using a linguistic analysis), and their meanings. Third, the *relationship between the two products* is compared. Products that directly compete or are in related markets would be more likely to confuse people than would products in totally unrelated markets. It is also important to consider how the two products are distributed in the supply chain.

Fourth, empirical *evidence of actual confusion* is very persuasive. This evidence may be drawn from witness testimony. However, consumer behavior data are even more valid if based on scientifically designed and administered surveys or on focus group interrogation. Fifth, *buyer sophistication* is relevant because as purchasers become more discriminating or knowledgeable, they should be more careful about origin. Also, more costly products cause most consumers to do more careful research. Sixth, the *defendant's intent* may show a motive to use a similar mark to ride free on the mark owner's reputation. However, some types of evidence could weigh against an inference of infringement intent. For example, intent might be disproved if the alleged infringer performed an exhaustive search, commissioned a trademark analysis before using the mark, or did considerable advertising. Finally, the courts may examine the *potential for expansion* by either user. If either producer's product lines might move to become in more direct competition, future consumer confusion could result. The likelihood of confusion factors are summarized in Exhibit 7.4.

The likelihood of confusion standard essentially identifies when the goods of the infringer are being passed off as those of the mark owner. An infringer who intends this result is guilty of palming off. State unfair competition law provides remedies for wrongs similar to infringement: misrepresentation and false advertising. **Reverse passing off** occurs when the infringer removes the marks from products made by the mark owner and then sells them as its own. It is a reverse of normal passing off because the infringer pretends the goods of another were produced by the infringer. **Trademark disparagement,** a form of trade libel, protects a mark owner from injurious falsehoods, false statements about another's products. Trademark service firms can help monitor other mark users for potential infringement. Monitoring services scan various media, print and broadcast as well as Internet sites, to find offending uses of an owner's mark. Search bots are also in widening use to find infringers on the Internet.

ONLINE

Infringement monitoring services
**http://www.
cyveillance.com**

DILUTION

Several state and federal laws protect a somewhat different interest than infringement by confusion. **Dilution** is a mark owner's interest in maintaining brand image,

Exhibit 7.4 Likelihood of Confusion Factors

Factors Determining Likelihood of Confusion	How Likelihood of Confusion Factors are Evaluated
Strength of the mark	Distinctiveness; secondary meaning
Similarities between marks	Visual appearance, sound, meaning
Relationship between products	Competing products, related vs. separate markets, supply chain considerations
Evidence of actual confusion	Scientifically valid empirical studies, consumer surveys, focus groups
Buyer sophistication	Confusion less likely where buyers research before purchasing
Intent of alleged infringer	Free riding on mark owner's reputation suggests attempt to cause confusion
Potential for expansion	Suggests potential for future confusion if two mark owners eventually become direct competitors

the commercial magnetism of its brands. Dilution may occur when another party uses the owner's mark on products and this use diminishes the mark's value. The dilution may occur through **tarnishment** of the mark or by **blurring** the distinctiveness of the mark from the diluting mark. The wrongdoer need not be selling products directly competitive to the mark owner's products. Dilution damage may be greatest when the wrongdoer has a reputation for poor quality or for offensive products (e.g., pornography). The difficulties of linking, framing, and the use of metatags all implicate infringement, particularly dilution and tarnishment. These matters are detailed in Chapter 11.

Damages from trademark dilution are greatest when the mark is famous and has built up considerable goodwill. The **Federal Trademark Dilution Act of 1996** (FTDA) provides a federal remedy for famous trademarks, whether or not registered. Some famous marks include the McDonald's golden arches,[30] Toys "R" Us,[31] and the uniforms of the Dallas Cowboys cheerleaders.[32] FTDA guidelines help to identify **famous trademarks** as listed in Exhibit 7.5.

DEFENSES TO INFRINGEMENT

Someone charged with infringement or another wrong under trademark or unfair competition law often argues that the mark owner has a weak case. Alleged infringers often argue the mark in question is invalid, was improperly registered,

---

30. *McDonalds Corp. v. Arche Technologies*, 17 U.S.P.Q.2d (BNA) 1557 (N.D. 1990).
31. *Toys "R" Us v. Akkaoui*, 1996 WL 772709 (N.D.Cal. 1996).
32. *Dallas Cowboys Cheerleaders, Inc. v. Pussycat Cinema, Ltd.*, 604 F.2d 200 (2d Cir., 1979).

Exhibit 7.5 FTDA Guidelines for Famous Trademarks

- Mark's degree of inherent or acquired distinctiveness
- Duration and extent of mark's use with product
- Duration and extent of advertising and publicity with mark
- Geographical extent of trading area in which mark is used
- Channels of trade for products sold under the mark
- Degree of recognition of the mark by the alleged infringer as well as in the relevant market and supply chain
- Nature and extent of usage by third parties of the same or similar marks
- Registration on the PTO's principal register

includes a generic term, or is descriptive but without secondary meaning, that there is no likelihood of confusion, that the mark is functional, or that the owner abandoned the mark. Sometimes the alleged infringer tries to justify its own actions with a **defense to infringement**. Some defenses are invalid after the five-year incontestability period under the Lanham Act.

There is a **fair use** defense to trademark infringement that is similar to copyright fair use. Descriptive and suggestive words used in a mark must remain available for use by others to describe their own goods. For example, surnames and geographic descriptions may be used by others from that region or who have that surname. When a mark is not used in its trademark sense (to identify the origin of products), then the other party's use should be allowed as a fair use. For example, the Web site of a Playboy model accurately described her as a "Playmate of the Month" and "Playmate of the Year" in the site's meta-tags and these titles were prominently displayed on her Web site. This display was a fair use because she was accurately describing herself as well as her past activities and accomplishments.[33] The First Amendment permits news reporting and parody even when trademarks are viewed or described. Some infringement examples are summarized in Exhibit 7.6.

REMEDIES

Owners of marks have several Lanham Act remedies against others whose infringement or dilution causes damage. The most direct and powerful relief is often an equitable remedy, such as an injunction, because it halts the infringement and prevents further damage. Monetary remedies include compensation for two types of loss: damages to the mark and the infringer's profits. The mark owner must have given notice of use (™) or notice of registration (®) or prove the infringer knew the mark was in use. In exceptional cases, such as where the infringement is deliberate, attorneys' fees and costs may be awarded. There are enhanced civil and even criminal penalties for

---

33. *Playboy Enterprises Inc. v. Welles*, 7 F.Supp.2d 1098 (S.D.Cal. 1998).

Exhibit 7.6 Examples of Infringing and Noninfringing Marks

Primary Mark: Product	Secondary Mark: Product	Likelihood of Confusion?
Toys "R" Us: retail toy sales	Guns Are Us: retail gun sales	None; toys is national, guns only local[34]
Post-It: adhesive note pads	Post-it.com	Infringement and intentional consumer confusion likely[35]
Miracle Whip: food	Yogowhip: food	None; *whip* not the most important element of mark
Little Caesar: pizza	Pizza Caesar: pizza	None; toga-clad character sufficiently different from chariot-riding character
McDonald's: various fast foods	McPretzel: soft pretzel	Yes; existing family of marks includes similar uses

using counterfeit marks. Remedies under state law generally parallel the Lanham Act. Unlike federal remedies, some states may permit punitive damages. Attorneys' fees are seldom permitted under state law, but this may be changing. The seizure of imported counterfeit goods by U.S. Customs is discussed later.

Injunctions that order the infringement stopped may be cast in several ways. A **preliminary injunction** can be issued quickly if the mark owner is likely to succeed in the later infringement trial, and fairness favors the mark owner for such an immediate and drastic action. **Permanent injunctions** are the most common remedy under the Lanham Act. After an injunction is ordered, the infringer may also be ordered to **recall** the infringing products—that is, pay to have all products in the supply chain returned. In some cases, the injunction may also order the products destroyed if the infringing aspects cannot be separated (e.g., logos not easily removed). In the Internet context, an injunction might be directed to force the infringer to take down and cease further use of the infringing material.

Under the **Trademark Counterfeiting Act** and the **Anticounterfeiting Consumer Protection Act**, even tougher remedies are authorized: seizure, impoundment, treble damages, criminal penalties, and racketeering remedies under Racketeering Influenced and Corrupt Organization (RICO), discussed in Chapter 3. **Counterfeiting** is the use of a spurious mark, identical to or indistinguishable from a registered mark. Counterfeit goods are fake copies made with the intent to defraud consumers into believing they were produced by the mark owner. For example, fake designer jeans, complete with distinctive labels and unique stitching, are a recurring problem. Destruction of fake jeans may be unnecessary if the counterfeit labels are removed.

Injunctions are the preferred remedy because they are immediate and because monetary damages are often difficult to prove. To get monetary relief, there must be actual consumer confusion, a somewhat more rigorous standard than the infringement

---

34. *Toys "R" Us Inc. v. Feinberg*, 26 F.Supp.2d 639 (S.D.N.Y. 1998).
35. *Minnesota Mining & Mfg. v. Taylor*, 21 F.Supp.2d 1003 (D.Minn. 1998).

standard: likelihood (potential) of confusion. Consumer surveys and testimony are relevant. Confusion is presumed for intentional infringement. **Actual damages** include lost sales and injury to reputation and goodwill. For example, lost sales might be based on the mark owner's reasonable marketing estimates projected from past sales. However, damages are difficult to prove, partly because economics and accounting do not yet provide reliable measures of goodwill and because there are no reliable valuation methods for reputational losses.

By contrast, it may be easier to disgorge the infringer's **undeserved profits** if reliable financial data are available. The mark owner must first prove the infringer's gross sales. Next, the infringer has the burden of proving production costs or profits not due to infringement (e.g., noninfringing components). In some cases, the trial court judge may find the damages computed are substantially lower than the overall damage apparently suffered by the mark owner. In such cases, the trial court may order **treble damages**—up to three times the actual damages as computed. These are not punitive damages.

INTERNATIONAL TRADEMARK

As with most forms of IP, a registration in one nation, as well as satisfaction of a particular nation's laws, does not assure protection in other nations. Unfortunately, there are difficulties in assuring IP rights in international commerce. International trademark law has similar challenges. The Internet offers global opportunities for visual communications associated with commercial symbols. As cross-border sales of trademarked information products expands, the potential for international trademark disputes may also expand. Soon the global reach of trademarks will be much greater than the gray market and counterfeit goods problems discussed here.

Gray goods are imported products sold outside the normal supply chain. For example, the price of Mercedes-Benz cars is significantly higher in the United States than in Germany. This huge price discrepancy gives U.S. car dealers an incentive to purchase cheaper new and slightly used Mercedes cars from foreign distributors, dealers, Mercedes employees, and customers for import into the United States. The manufacturer, Daimler-Chrysler, conditions the use of the Mercedes mark, the familiar circled three-point star, on compliance with strict importation rules it imposes on its U.S. subsidiary and local franchised dealers. This system is fairly effective in preventing importation and sale of Mercedes cars outside the official supply chain. A portion of the gross profits from U.S. sales of Mercedes cars made through the official supply chain is used to fund advertising and warranty repair costs. Cars imported through other nations or directly from Germany do not carry their share of these legitimate marketing expenses, and these unlicensed importers ride free on expenses paid in the regular supply chain. Of course, if there was a cheaper, alternate supply channel, Mercedes would be unable to keep prices so much higher in the United States. Also recognize that some goods first sold abroad are illegal or unsuitable for sale in some other nation. Cars sold in the United States must meet stringent safety and emissions standards that are not used in other nations. As a result, many imported gray market products must be heavily modified. Television sets use incompatible broadcast standards, NTSC in the United States and Canada versus PAL in Europe, making such gray goods nearly useless.

Sales of counterfeit goods in the United States are likely to be trademark infringement. By contrast, sales of gray market goods in the United States are not trademark infringement. If the foreign manufacturer is related to the U.S. importer that has registered the mark, there is no right under the U.S. Tariff Act to request the U.S. Customs Service to block imports of gray market goods. However, if the U.S. importer and foreign manufacturer are independent, importation of the gray market goods can be blocked.[36] The Lanham Act §42 has been used to block goods rightfully produced under the mark overseas if they have different characteristics than do the goods sold in U.S. markets (e.g., differences in soap fragrance or sudsing).[37] However, these laws cannot stop importation of personal purchases by domestic tourists traveling abroad.

TRADEMARKS AND THE INTERNET

The Internet magnifies many things: communication, depth and breadth of discovery, and the visibility of commercial symbols. The full implication of the Internet on trademarks is uncertain but already emerging in several key areas. First, Web sites permit broad communication of commentary and criticism that can adversely affect mark owner reputation through tarnishment. Second, the practices of linking, framing, and meta-tag usage raise the potential for passing off and other false association problems discussed in Chapter 11. Third, this section discusses the connection between trademarks and domain names and how the relationship triggers problems such as cyber squatting.

DOMAIN NAMES AND TRADEMARKS

In the Internet's early years, the assignment of domain names was done largely by Network Solutions Incorporated (NSI), operating under a subcontract from the National Science Foundation (NSF). Domain names were granted on a first-come, first-served basis, and few processes were established to settle ownership or trademark conflict disputes. However, today it is becoming evident that TLDs serve a trademark function much like other components of marks (color, smell, trade dress). Domain names are becoming an integral part of the trademark system because they often satisfy trademark standards.

Some Internet traditionalists are troubled by this development. They insist that URLs are merely technical addresses and were never intended to be marks. However, URLs function like telephone mnemonics (e.g., 1-800-FLOWERS) because they are often accurately guessed. Case law and legislation in the 1990s now recognize that domain names serve trademark functions of source identification, indicate quality,

---

36. *KMart Corp. v. Cartier, Inc.*, 486 U.S. 281 (1988).
37. *Lever Bros. Co. v. U.S.*, 877 F.2d 101 (D.C.Cir., 1989).

and are repositories of goodwill. URLs are susceptible to trademark problems such as consumer confusion and functionality. Nevertheless, there are some important differences between URLs and domain names. Domain names are acquired through registration with a domain name registry, a process separate from trademark acquisition through use or PTO registration.

REGISTRATION OF DOMAIN NAMES

The monopoly NSI held over administering the Internet domain name system expired in June 1999. Since that transitional period, several other domain name registrars have emerged (http://www.register.com) who are accredited by the Internet Corporation for Assigned Names and Numbers (ICANN) (http://www.icann.org). Someone seeking to operate a Web site must first obtain an IP address from an Internet service provider (ISP) (find ISPs at http://www.thelist.com). Next, provide the IP address to an accredited registrar, and, if the domain name chosen is not already registered, it can be registered for a fee. The Internet makes it easy to search for an available domain name or to actually register and pay the registration fee. Domain name registration does not assure all the Lanham Act protections offered to trademarks. It is still necessary to register the inherently distinctive mark with the PTO, a step most established firms have already done for their most valuable marks. Domain names can be transferred, an important step in the process of completing a corporate acquisition or merger.

CYBER SQUATTING

Before 1999, many firms still remained unconvinced that the Internet was important in their business models. Indeed, many mark owners could not see why they should register their marks as domain names. Still, there are significant risks that outsiders may register domain names identical to owners' marks. Some outsiders have registered variations of others' marks or combined others' domain names with alternate TLDs (e.g., .org rather than .com). Also outsiders sometimes register common misspellings of others' marks as well as their nicknames (bigblue.com for ibm.com). Recall that the domain names are registered on a first-come, first-served basis. There are no qualification standards, such as those to avoid confusing similarity that are required for trademark prosecution and PTO examination. Instead, domain name registrars simply accept applications unless the precise domain name sought is already registered to another owner. These circumstances contributed to **cyber squatting**, the practice of acquiring domain names for ransom and resale to the original owners of similar marks.

Consider the landmark example of Panavision International, which owned two famous marks, Panavision and Panaflex.[38] These marks were used in connection with the firm's photographic imaging business. In 1995, Dennis Toeppen registered

---

38. *Panavision Int'l v. Dennis Toeppen*, 945 F.Supp. 1296 (C.D.Cal. 1996), *af'd.* 140 F.3d 1316 (9th Cir., 1998).

panavision.com and later registered panaflex.com before Panavision International fully appreciated the importance of Internet commerce or the risk that others could use these marks as domain names. On simple Web sites using these domain names, Toeppen displayed only an aerial view of the town Pana, Illinois, and on another site he posted only "hello." Toeppen never did any real business using the domain names. Panavision demanded Toeppen cease using these domain names, and Toeppen demanded a $13,000 ransom. When Panavision sued to enjoin this use, the court held Toeppen had diluted Panavision's marks. Dennis Toeppen registered other famous marks and attempted other acts of what is now called cyber squatting.

Anti-Cybersquatting Consumer Protection Act

Congress passed the **Anticybersquatting Consumer Protection Act (ACPA)** in 1999 to remedy this practice. ACPA makes it unlawful to traffic in or use domain names that are identical or confusingly similar to distinctive marks protected under state trademark law or the federal Lanham Act. APCA creates a civil action authorizing the mark owner to sue if the cyber squatter has bad faith intent to profit from the cyber squatting. Remedies include cancellation of the cyber squatter's registration, transfer to the mark owner, actual money damages, and profits or statutory damages up to $100,000. The suits are *in rem*, which means that for jurisdiction purposes, it is irrelevant whether legal process has effectively notified a cyber squatter. Some cybersquatters provided false contact information, cannot be located with due diligence, or cannot be effectively reached using personal jurisdiction.

ACPA does not address all uses or dilution of a mark by someone other than the mark owner. For example, recall the discussion of First Amendment freedom of speech and the press in Chapter 2. Trademark law and dispute resolution of domain names should not prevent legitimate news reporting, parody, criticism or even gripes directed against a mark owner. For example, the legality of the dot.sucks sites or simply adding *–sucks* after a mark to create a domain name is a hotly debated question. Mark owners legitimately seek to protect their marks. However, the use of trademark law to stifle criticism probably violates the First Amendment. On the other extreme are uses of domain names by fans and admirers of the mark owner (fan clubs).

ACPA remedies are triggered when the cyber squatter is guilty of **bad faith** in registering the mark owner's trademark as a domain name. ACPA lists nine factors that courts may consider in determining the cyber squatter's bad faith, as listed in Exhibit 7.7.

ICANN's Uniform Domain Name Dispute Resolution Policy

Before 1999, NSI operated a domain name dispute resolution policy, but it was criticized and there was litigation. A white paper by the National Telecommunications and Information Agency (http://www.ntia.doc.gov) of the Department of Commerce recommended that the World Intellectual Property Organization convene a study to recommend a new dispute resolution procedure. This resulted in the ICANN Uniform Domain Name Dispute Resolution Policy (UDRP), a form of international arbitration that has been in effect since December 1999. In the first year,

Exhibit 7.7 ACPA Factors in Determining "Bad Faith" Cyber Squatting

1. Trademark ownership rights by mark owner
2. Closeness between domain name and cyber squatter's name
3. Cyber squatter's use of the domain name in commerce for access to a Web site
4. Cyber squatter's intent to divert Web traffic from the mark owner
5. Cyber squatter's offer to ransom the domain name to the mark owner
6. Whether cyber squatter gave misleading information in domain name registration
7. Cyber squatter's repeated, similar cyber squatting on other owners' marks
8. Whether mark is distinctive and famous

these were various ICANN approved "providers" (arbitrators) using the UDRP to settle more than 2,000 disputes. ICANN claims that nearly 75% of domain name disputes filed under UDRP processes have resulted in cancellation of the cyber squatter's domain name registration.

Most of the UDRP standards for cyber squatting are similar to the ACPA standards. However, the UDRP differs from litigation in the United States under ACPA in five major ways. First, the UDRP is arbitration, so it has many cost, timing, and confidentiality differences with litigation. Second, the UDRP ostensibly applies to international domain name disputes. Third, the UDRP hearings are ex parte, and all proceedings are based on documents filed; there are no parties present, no witnesses are examined, and legal counsel is not present. Fourth, UDRP awards are not binding on the courts and, *unlike* most other forms of arbitration, they can be appealed. Fifth, the UDRP may be used before or after litigation. UDRP decisions are listed on the ICANN Web site (http://www.icann.org/udrp).

CHAPTER 8
INTRODUCTION TO CONTRACTS AND THEIR FORMATION

In just a few years, the formation of contracts online has evolved from an esoteric process designed by lawyers and data processing experts into something most college students and businesspeople do regularly. Nearly every time computer users click "OK" or "I agree" to install software online or use databases, a contract is formed. How can we integrate our understanding of traditional written contracts resulting from face-to-face negotiations into this emerging world of electronic contracting? This is a pressing question confronting most businesses today as their bricks-and-mortar storefronts converge with their growing on-line presence. Contract law must adapt to new and future forms of communication and automated negotiation.

This chapter discusses the law applicable to contracts and the early-stage aspects of most forms of traditional and e-commerce transactions: their formation and enforceability. The laissez-faire principle is alive and well in the U.S. law of contracts. Therefore, with very few exceptions, contract law does not set the terms of any contract; instead, most terms are negotiated. Contract law sets the ground rules for formation, interpretation, and performance of commercial relations. The following discussion focuses on contracting for most types of business involved in the sale of goods, services, intellectual property licensing, and real estate.

SOURCES OF COMMERCIAL LAW

The many sources of commercial law complicate planning for the wide variety of potential transactions and potential parties from different states or nations. Traditionally, such difficulties concerned only large firms engaged in interstate or international commerce and their expert consultants advising on collateral matters such as transportation, financing, law, or import-export regulations. However, the Internet now permits individuals and small businesses to directly participate in many aspects of global commerce, and many people unaccustomed to these matters need a broader understanding of commercial law. The onset of e-commerce also suggests the need for greater uniformity and harmonization in commercial laws between states and nations.

The starting point for analysis of commercial contracting is with the common law of contracts. The common law comes from case law precedents and was the original basis for U.S. contract law. Today, the common law of contracts applies to sales of interests in land; to employment, services, and consulting contracts; and to many transactions in intellectual property rights. The common law has been collected and rephrased by legal scholars into a compilation, the ***Restatement of the Law Second, Contracts***. Although the *Restatement* is not the definitive law, many courts nevertheless have made it authoritative by citing it as if it were legislation to resolve disputes. In the United States, contract law is a combination of common law precedents, the *Restatement,* and statutory contract law.

The most important statutory law of contracts is found in uniform laws passed by the states. The **Uniform Commercial Code (UCC)** is a product of the National Conference of Commissioners on Uniform State Laws (NCCUSL). The UCC is based on the common law and on the law merchant. The UCC governs the sale of goods and some other types of contracts. The UCC now applies throughout the United States and is summarized in Exhibit 8.1. It is divided into several parts called articles that govern most aspects of commercial transactions: sales of goods, various payment mechanisms and their intermediaries, investment securities, title documents and collateralization.

ONLINE

NCCUSL's Web site
http://www.nccusl.org

Certainty in international transactions is complicated because different nations have varying approaches to contracting that reflect their cultural, political, and historical differences, their different legal systems, and their differing views on the role of government intervention in commerce. The common law system, based on the rule of precedent, is applicable in the United States, Canada, and most other nations of the former British Empire. The civil law system, based on comprehensive codes or statutes, generally applies in nations with a continental European heritage. There are further differences with Islamic law, socialist law, and the law in some developing nations. Despite some uniformity, each system's unique differences can have an impact on contract duties, formation, performance, and expectations. Civil law nations fill in contract gaps with statutory terms common to all contracts. This policy is adopted by the UCC. Indeed, the most successful commercial law is suppletory, as found in most industrialized nations. **Suppletory law** furnishes common terms to agreements the parties have left incomplete in some way(s). Economists believe it is efficient for commercial laws to allow freedom of contract yet provide standard-form, gap-filling terms if these automatic terms are similar to the ones that would have been negotiated by parties dealing at arm's length.

ONLINE

Find the complete UCC
on the Internet
**http://www.law.
cornell.edu/ucc/ucc.
table.html**

Exhibit 8.1 Articles of the Uniform Commercial Code (UCC)

No.	Title of Article	Coverage
Article 1	General provisions	Concepts and definitions common to all UCC Articles
Article 2	Sales	Formation, enforcement, performance, and remedies for sales of goods
Article 2a	Leases	Formation, enforcement, performance, and remedies for leases of goods
[UCITA, formerly Article 2b]	[Uniform Computer Information Transactions Act, only in Va. & Md.]	[Formation, enforcement, performance, and remedies for licensing software, data, and computer-delivered information]
Article 3	Commercial paper	Issue, negotiation, and transfer of payment by checks, notes, drafts, and certificates of deposit
Article 4	Bank deposits and collections	Defines relations among banks and their depositors; governs payment and collection process
Article 5	Letters of credit	Defines rights and duties of parties financing or paying in international trade by using letters of credit
Article 6	Bulk transfers	Notice requirement to protect creditors from merchant debtor disposing of all inventory to abscond with proceeds
Article 7	Warehouse receipts, bills of lading, documents of title	Negotiation and transfer process for documentary titles covering goods in transit or in storage
Article 8	Investment securities	Negotiation and transfer of investment securities (e.g., corporate stocks, bonds)
Article 9	Secured transactions	Creation and enforcement of liens on goods; priorities among creditors established

Trade between developing countries and industrialized nations reflects an imbalance in bargaining power and in the development of their legal systems. The United Nations Vienna Convention on Contracts for the International Sale of Goods (CISG) governs international sales of goods unless the parties choose by contract to apply some other law.

O N L I N E

CISG
**http://www.uncitral.
org/en-index.htm**

Dealings between firms in developing and developed nations raise ethical concerns because contracts are negotiated with foreign government officials. Officials in some nations have been known to expect special favors before granting business to foreigners. Concern over such practices led the United States to enact the Foreign Corrupt Practices Act (FCPA), discussed in Chapter 3, to prohibit bribery by U.S. firms or corrupt payments to gain business. The CISG reflects concerns over these problems.

Privately adopted rules for commercial practice, the original basis for the law merchant, still have significance in both domestic and international trade. The International Trade Commission (ITC) promulgates commercial rules, called INCOTERMS, which parties may choose to implement in their contracts. Affiliated trading groups like North American Free Trade Association (NAFTA) and the European Union (EU) also regulate some aspects of international trade. In the e-commerce area, the EU has become proactive in promulgating new laws that cover several aspects of e-commerce. Many of these new laws, called EU directives, are discussed throughout this handbook.

Specific e-commerce laws are also passing in many U.S. states. Two of these new laws are discussed in depth later in this handbook. The Uniform Electronic Transactions Act (UETA) legitimizes the use of electronic documents, electronic signatures, and electronic agents. UETA has become law in nearly 30 states and is likely to pass soon in the other states. It could eventually become applicable to most types of contracts and other legal documents. The Uniform Computer Information Transactions Act (UCITA) was formerly intended to become UCC Article 2B but now stands outside the UCC. UCITA would apply to the formation, enforcement, performance, and remedies in contracts for the licensing of software, data, and computer-delivered information. However, it has passed in only two states, Virginia and Maryland, and its prospects for further passage are uncertain. If UCITA is not held to apply to a particular licensing transaction, the common law and the UCC would probably apply.

TYPES OF COMMERCIAL CONTRACTS

Contracts are classified in several ways. **Express contracts** arise from the parties' outward expressions of mutual assent, such as their oral or written statements, gestures, or on-line communications. **Implied in fact contracts** are inferred from the parties' actions. For example, a written employment agreement is an express contract. By contrast, a taxi passenger's contract is often implied in fact. **Bilateral contracts** require two promises, one from each party. In a **unilateral contract**, one of the parties does not expect a return promise but instead asks the other party to actually perform. For example, an offer of reward seeks a unilateral contract: The offeror makes an express promise to pay the reward if some other party does an act—provides the information sought. The performing party does not accept the reward contract by *promising* to provide the needed information but instead accepts the reward offer by *performance* in actually providing the information. Both bilateral and unilateral contracts are possible under common law, the UCC, and UCITA. Most contracts are bilateral in nature.

A **valid contract** is completely enforceable by either party if it meets all of the necessary legal requirements. A **void contract** is invalid and unenforceable because the contract has an illegal objective or one party is adjudged to have been insane or incompetent during negotiations. A **voidable contract** allows one or both of the parties to rescind or cancel if there is a problem with incapacity, fraud, misrepresentation, duress, undue influence, or mistake. When all the duties have been fully performed by both parties, this contract is an **executed contract**. An **executory contract** has at least some duties by either or both parties that are not yet fully performed. An **unenforceable contract** is one for which a written document was required by the statute of frauds, but none was signed. These contract problems are discussed further in Chapter 10.

ANALYSIS OF E-COMMERCE USING TRADITIONAL CONTRACTING MODELS

It is useful to analyze emerging e-commerce methods by reference to traditional commercial practice. Electronic contracting is based on existing contract rules and commercial practices. Although some new cyber laws and commercial practices will probably develop to supplement current practice, existing law remains the backbone for e-commerce. Traditional contracting is based on a sequence of conventional activities and resulting conditions that create legally binding mutual obligations between the parties. Contracting between parties has four major components: (1) exchange of information, (2) reaching an agreement with mutual assent, (3) consideration, and (4) performance and payment. Enforceable contracts in both the traditional and on-line environments must have all these elements present.

INFORMATION EXCHANGE MODEL

Under the informational model, prospective buyers and sellers become interested in contracting as they identify each other, begin communicating their interest in contracting, and advertise and describe their products and services. Outside cyberspace, the parties often request and provide information by using various advertising media, trade shows, sales representatives, catalogues, brochures, specifications, and price lists. When third parties are needed to complete the transaction, the parties hire them (e.g., brokers, lenders, carriers). Before the contract is finalized, counterparties often make inquiries regarding terms, revise their product specifications, and modify proposed terms.

Although similar methods are now used in cyberspace, electronic contracting will eventually benefit from the faster speed of communications and the greater access to on-line resources. For example, there will be real-time updates of price and of product availability, and all parties will be able to access larger computer databases of product information. The advantages of cyberspace will permit efficiencies heretofore unavailable in most markets, making it possible to collect and distribute private data about counterparties (e.g., interests, preferences, tastes, creditworthiness, performance quality, reliability). Unless constrained by privacy laws, Web site operators will collect private information about customer demographics and preferences to target their marketing or assemble into dossiers for sale or barter to other firms. Commercial parties will participate in B2B exchanges, where buyers can post specifications, sellers will help design customized products, specific terms will be negotiated, and final agreements concluded. Internet information exchange also permits the use of business models based on Web site exposure, measured as "hits" or "eyeballs," and thereby receive compensation for directing visitors to other sites (hyperlinked referrals) or for banner advertisements. All this customer exposure helps build a brand image that enhances the value of trademarks and goodwill and permits heightened use of customer relationship management techniques.

MUTUAL ASSENT MODEL

A wide variety of contract negotiation and conclusion techniques are used both inside and outside cyberspace. Even though the common law traditions were modified by the UCC to conform to modern commercial practice, the basic framework of common law mutual assent dictates the legal expectations for contracts formed in and out of cyberspace. Contracts are formed when an offer is communicated. An offer confers a power of contracting on the offeree, thereby creating a contract when the power is exercised in an acceptance. Contract negotiations via the Internet will mirror these and other common law behaviors, including revocations, rejections, modifications, and repudiations. Contemporary commercial practices prevailing under the UCC will also be adopted in e-commerce. For example, parties will use electronic versions of purchase orders, confirmations, and invoices—each with different terms. This creates a **battle of the forms** problem. Standard terms will be included to improve the predictability and reliability of contracting, particularly in contracts between consumers and merchants. Standard form contracts between merchants will develop from trading partner agreements for electronic data interchange (EDI).

It seems unlikely that written contracts will be abandoned. Documentary evidence of the parties' agreement and contract terms will still be required and is nearly always advisable. The requirement of the statute of frauds for a signed memorandum and the dependability and completeness of writings under the parol evidence rule should play as significant a role in e-commerce as it plays under traditional practice. Indeed, UETA legitimizes the use of computer communications as electronic records that are legally equivalent to written documents. UETA sanctions the use of digital signatures to satisfy the need for authorized signatures on written contracts. The authentication evidencing that the parties actually signed a record may be performed by cybernotaries. Similar assurance may be provided by various encryption techniques. As in the traditional world, contracts may be implied from the parties' on-line conduct. Parties will be bound to only those agreements negotiated and concluded by agents with proper authority, although UETA legitimizes the use of electronic agents. UETA and the redundant federal e-sign law are discussed in Chapter 10.

CONSIDERATION MODEL

The consideration requirement has always posed conceptual challenges for students of contracting. Traditional contracts are enforceable only when each party's promised performance is supported by consideration, a legally binding obligation arising from the parties' mutual assent. The consideration requirement is used to test the seriousness of the bargained-for exchange. A party's promise is unenforceable unless made in exchange for a legally sufficient counterpromise by the other party; that is, each party must make a new and irrevocable commitment to the other. The significance of the consideration requirement has diminished. For example, consideration is not required in some sales of goods under the UCC, or it may be presumed. In B2B contracts, careful contract drafting by experienced lawyers nearly eliminates consideration risks.

However, e-commerce business models purporting to give users "free access" are again raising consideration questions. The mere accessing of a site may obligate users to the Web site's license restrictions and require them to provide private information or accept privacy-tracking "cookies" that the Web site or its affiliates may access later. It is still useful to analyze e-commerce by using the consideration model because it can resolve legal rights when the profit-making expectations of Web site operators must accommodate the Internet culture's expectations for "free-surfing."

PERFORMANCE MODEL

The performance of contracts via computer communications poses some of the greatest challenges for e-commerce. Currently, only intangible personal property can be transmitted electronically via communications networks like the Internet. Today, it is physically possible to download documents, data, artistic expression or literary works, music, consulting reports, professional advice, software, images, audio or video files, orders, notices, and documentary transfers. For the foreseeable future, the performance of contract duties involving the delivery of tangible property will not be made via the Internet. Physical delivery of tangibles must be made personally or through agents such as a delivery service.

Money, document, and title transfers are contract obligations that can be made electronically. The electronic transfer of payments (e-payments) and electronic recording, custody, transmittal, presentment, and endorsement of formal contracts such as commercial documents (e.g., documents of title, warehouse receipts) can be made via the Internet. Wire transfer of funds began soon after the first telegraph cables were laid in the 1800s. Today, electronic funds transfers (EFT) are a majority of all funds transferred.

The law and commercial practice developed under these four traditional contract components are useful in analyzing e-commerce because they are the paradigm for the evolution of commerce into cyberspace. Although a few cyber laws may radically change this traditional practice, many if not most traditional contracting elements will probably survive the evolution to e-commerce. It is now useful to analyze the needs for new cyber laws by reference to the emerging types of on-line contracts already in use.

TYPES OF ON-LINE CONTRACTS

Several types of e-commerce commercial contracting are in current use. Further innovation in communications, computers, and business methods are likely to encourage additional advances. An accepted method of classifying e-commerce is through traditional supply chain concepts, which generates three distinct on-line markets, each with its separate architecture and differing legal requirements. First, the B2B market involves procurement transactions among suppliers of raw materials or component parts to assemblers, as well as from wholesale suppliers to retailers. There have been extensive e-commerce developments in the B2B markets, including the widespread development of EDI. The ABA's Electronic Messaging Services Task Force defines EDI as "the transmission, in standard syntax, of unambiguous information between computers of two or more independent organizations."

In practice, EDI refers to a system of interconnected computers, using dedicated and secure telephone lines and/or satellite connections to link merchant buyers, sellers, their banks, carriers, warehouses, customs officials, and trade brokers. EDI systems envision repeated transactions between regular suppliers and customers that use electronic ordering, confirmation, invoicing, record keeping, payment or financing, and transmittal or negotiation of trade documents. The terms of EDI contracts are generally stated in an umbrella contract, which the ABA refers to as a trading partner agreement. This contract permits the sale of varying quantities and types of goods at various delivery dates and at changing prices. However, most other terms are held constant. EDI systems may permit some human intervention. Some EDI systems may automatically make daily merchandise restocking orders, much like Wal-Mart's pioneering EDI system. At this writing, there are in development several hundred B2B exchanges (on-line electronic marketplaces) that envision using the Internet rather than dedicated, secure communications. Many of these markets would permit participation by many competing buyers and sellers.

The second major type of e-commerce market is consumer retail or business to consumer (B2C). Such markets sell goods generally through Web site shopping transactions, such as Amazon.com, or dispense computer services and information through fee-based subscription services, such as America Online (AOL). Web site B2C shopping usually involves customers browsing on-line catalogues, specifications, and price lists before communicating a purchase order directly online, through other electronic means (e.g., fax, phone), or via the mail. Consumer payments may be effected online or via other means (e.g., phone credit card, check). Deliveries of tangible goods are usually made off line by delivery service, although customers can sometimes pick up the goods physically at a distribution center. The B2C subscription services include on-line service providers (OSPs), also known as Internet service providers (ISPs), which charge subscribers a periodic fee for access, a pay-per-view fee charged by the amount of time used, or at various rates depending on the different costs of the particular content accessed. The standard subscription agreement often has aspects of a license. Most ISPs have abandoned charging fees in favor of business models deriving revenue from banner ads or the collection and resale of private data. LexisNexis and Westlaw are fee-based subscription computer information and research services that charge variable pay-per-view rates; they are commonly used in legal and financial research.

The third type of e-commerce market is consumer to consumer (C2C). They most resemble electronic want ads, flea markets, or auctions but use Internet facilities such as electronic bulletin boards, chat sites, or e-mail communications. At this writing, eBay is the best known example of this e-commerce model. The contractual terms of trade range quite broadly. Some are open, permitting the parties to negotiate and arrange for payment and delivery, such as those often found on an electronic bulletin board. Other systems impose rules of trade that are set by system software and security features, such as those found in many of the more successful on-line auction sites.

TRANSACTIONS' SUBJECT MATTER DETERMINES WHAT LAW APPLIES

The essential threshold inquiry in analyzing transactions is the classification of the transaction's subject matter; that is, the main consideration exchanged must be identified. Transactions primarily for the purchase of land, professional service engagements, or regular employment are generally governed by the common law of contracts as supplemented by various regulatory regimes. The UCC Article 2 governs contracts for the sale of goods. **Goods** are tangible personal property (not real estate), which the UCC defines in §2-105(1) as "all that are movable at the time of contracting." While the UCC is based in the common law, it also conforms to commercial practice. Therefore, UCC provisions often supplement and occasionally change the common law rules. International sales of goods are covered by the CISG, although many international B2B supply arrangements may choose to apply other laws or private commercial rules. Auctions of goods are covered by the UCC, supplemented by each auction's own rules. Auctions of services were so infrequent historically that the applicable law is uncertain. However, the service auctions beginning to appear in cyberspace will probably follow the common law but be modified somewhat by practices used in goods auctions and with each auction's own unique rules.

E-commerce transactions often involve the licensing (temporary right to use) or assignment (outright sale) of intellectual property (IP) or other data and information. The common law governs licensing and assignments but is supplemented by federal IP law. However, a new licensing law, the Uniform Computer Information

Transactions Act (UCITA), may apply to IP licensing. UCITA is discussed through-out later chapters and is applicable in those states that have adopted it, thus far only Virginia and Maryland. Additionally, UCITA may also apply to contracts where local law permits the contract to invoke the licensing law from another state that has adopted UCITA. UCITA exempts transactions in electronic information in several industries with stable contracting environments: TV, movies, recorded music, and print publishing. The mere use of e-mail or other electronic communications to reach an agreement for land, goods, or services does not make UCITA applicable. At this writing, there is an effort to apply the UCC Article 2 to transactions in software, perhaps preempting the application of UCITA.

Despite the apparent complexity of e-commerce transactions, the discussion in this book usually begins with the common law rules and then considers when other laws may be applicable. Exhibit 8.2 summarizes the application of major laws that affect the formation, interpretation, performance, and terms of e-commerce transactions.

Most commercial contracts have multiple subject matters. For example, most buyers believe that the predominant subject matter in the contract are the goods, the land, or the services purchased. By contrast, the seller is much more concerned with the buyer's payment. The UCC has several other articles (3, 4, 5, 7, and 9) govern-ing performance of the payment, credit, and transfer or custody obligations. In addi-tion, many transactions have subject matter mixed between goods, services, and information. One classic example is the warranty accompanying a sale of goods; another example is a restaurant's sale of food (goods) accompanied by the service of preparing and serving the food. In such transactions, the UCC applies if goods pre-dominate in the transaction, such as the sale of a new car sold with a warranty for service and repair. The common law applies if land or services predominate and the goods sale is only incidental, such as a restaurant's service of food. Despite this lat-ter general rule, the UCC's warranties discussed in Chapter 10 cover restaurant food services.

UCITA is intended to cover transactions to create, modify, transfer, or license computer information or information rights (e.g., software, data) when in electronic form either obtained from or through a computer or if licensed for computer pro-cessing (UCITA §103(a)). UCITA applies only to the information aspects of a trans-action, leaving other appropriate laws to apply to the noninformation subject matter. For example, the UCC applies to the goods aspects of a transaction unless computer information is the "primary subject matter" and the goods aspects are merely an incidental portion. The UCC applies when computer information is embedded in goods, such as the diagnostics in a car engine's control computer. Contracting par-ties may either "opt in" to the application of UCITA or "opt out" of UCITA, as long as the safeguards of UCITA §103(e) are satisfied.

UETA enables business and government to agree to use electronic forms of records, signatures, acknowledgments, and notarization. UCITA permits the use of either electronic or paper documents, calling them **records,** to effect the communi-cations for contracting or to satisfy any need for written contract documents. Both UCITA §102(54) and UETA §2(13) define **record** as "information that is inscribed

Exhibit 8.2 Application of Various Laws to E-Commerce Contracts

Subject Matter of Contract	Law Applicable to Contract Formation, Interpretation, and Performances	Other Laws Potentially Relevant to E-Commerce Transactions
Interest in land	Common Law	Agency; real estate conveyancing; mortgages; environmental regulations; UCC Articles 3, 4, 5, 7, and/or 9, E-SIGN or UETA if enacted
Professional Services	Common Law, UCITA where enacted for independent contractors in information service contracts	Agency; professional ethical regulations; UCC Articles 3, 4, 5, 7, and/or 9, E-SIGN or UETA if enacted
Employment	Common Law	Agency; labor law; regulation of equal employment and compensation; UCC Articles 3, 4, 5, 7, and/or 9, E-SIGN or UETA if enacted
Goods [software]	UCC Article 2	Agency; UCC Articles 3, 4, 5, 7, and/or 9, E-SIGN or UETA if enacted
Leases of goods	UCC Article 2A	Agency; UCC Articles 3, 4, 5, 7, and/or 9, E-SIGN or UETA if enacted
Information, software, IP data: contracts to license, create, modify, or transfer	Common Law or UCITA where enacted [Va. & Md.]	Agency; federal or international IP laws
Securities	UCC Article 8	Agency; state corporation laws; federal securities regulations; UCC Articles 3, 4, 5, 7, and/or 9
Performances: payments, credit, and Goods Transfer or Custody	UCC Articles 3, 4, 5, 7, and/or 9	Agency, E-SIGN or UETA if enacted

on a tangible medium or that is stored in an electronic or other medium and is retrievable in perceivable form." UETA defines **electronic record** as a "record created, generated, sent, communicated, received, or stored by electronic means." UETA is more procedural than substantive, a perspective dramatized by this caricature: "The medium shall not be the message." UETA requires no standard or particular form of electronic transaction. Instead, UETA validates the use of electronic means where traditional paper documents and signatures were previously required. It permits but does not require electronic contracting; that is, parties must agree to use electronic records and electronic signatures rather than their written counterparts. When parties agree to transact electronically, their records, signatures, and contracts must be enforced if made in electronic form. Therefore, electronic records and electronic signatures will satisfy the requirements of other laws that require signatures and writings. UETA must be applied to facilitate electronic transactions, and it must be construed to be consistent with reasonable commercial practice and to promote uniformity among the states. It applies only prospectively—that is, to transactions using electronic records or electronic signatures that are created, generated, sent, communicated, received, or stored after the adopting legislation becomes effective. For states that do not adopt UETA, these matters are governed by the federal **E-SIGN** law officially known as the Electronic Signatures in Global and National Commerce Act. UETA and the federal E-SIGN law are discussed in Chapter 10.

CONCLUDING AN AGREEMENT

The formation of a contract is generally known as mutual assent. In international parlance, these are the activities that **conclude an agreement**. Before a bilateral contract arises, the parties must agree to the contract's terms, a step known as **mutual assent**. In traditional and "big ticket" contracting, the parties begin preliminary negotiations by communicating expectations about what they consider to be favorable terms. For example, an advertisement, salesperson's pitch, or Web site information may start the negotiations. By contrast, contracts with smaller "stakes" have smaller profit margins and generally lesser consequences for both buyer and seller, which usually make it uneconomical for most sellers and many buyers to engage in extensive negotiating formalities that impose high transactions costs. Indeed, **form contracting** is a twentieth-century efficiency innovation that has nearly eliminated the transaction costs of negotiating, particularly in B2C transactions. In most retail contracts, large sellers set "take-it-or-leave-it" terms, sometimes called **boilerplate**. Consumers have little power to change these standardized terms. In a few instances, some sellers find a competitive advantage in varying a few contract terms, particularly the price on big-ticket items. Still, consumers seldom negotiate much, and many prefer the low stress and simplicity of not haggling at all.

Populist pressures for consumer protection legislation illustrate the major exception to laissez faire. Consumer protection laws usually are not passed until after long experience with entire industries that uniformly adopt nearly identical terms that favor sellers. It appears that e-commerce B2C transactions could follow this model. Despite the potential for lower transaction costs with the use of electronic negotiations, most B2C on-line transactions are largely "take-it-or-leave-it," based on arcane boilerplate terms that largely benefit the seller. Buyers often ignore this "legalese," choosing to quickly click through and thereby accept them, often ignorant of the rights they surrender and the duties they accept. The discussion of UETA and UCITA in Chapters 8 through 11 examines a few such consumer protection provisions in both laws.

The stated terms of a contract must usually identify the parties, adequately describe the subject matter, state the price (i.e., the cash, property, or services), indicate the quantity of the product or services, fix the time for each party's performance, and include any other key terms (e.g., credit, warranties). The parties' early communications may be merely informational or can be cast in the form of offers and counteroffers. A fine line distinguishes mere informational communications from the five operative contracting communications: offer, acceptance, revocation, rejection, and counteroffer. This distinction is based on the objective theory of contracts.

OBJECTIVE THEORY OF CONTRACTS

All expressions of the contracting parties are judged objectively by a reasonable person's interpretation. The objective theory of contracts applies to all communications between parties to distinguish mere (1) preliminary negotiations and (2) inquiries regarding terms from more serious communications such as (3) offers, (4) counteroffers, (5) acceptances, (6) revocations, and (7) rejections. The first two of these are informational communications that do not create, exercise, or terminate the power of contracting. By contrast, the latter five do affect the power of contracting. An offeror's statement is a legal offer if a reasonable person would conclude that the offeror clearly intended to confer a power of acceptance on the offeree and that the offeree need only accept to create a contract. The offeror's hidden intent or secret hesitation is irrelevant. For example, a casual person might make a proposal, but only in jest. Such a proposal might be an offer irrespective of the emotional person's intent if a reasonable person believes it was intended as an offer. Many behavioral observers of cyberspace communications believe that e-mail messages are all too often flippant or emotionally inspired. Therefore, care must be taken in making electronic communications or interpreting them as operative contracting communications. Offers and acceptances are particularly critical because society believes that frivolous statements should not lead to binding contract obligations.

THE OFFER

An **offer** is a proposal to contract that contains all of the necessary contract terms. The proposal must be intended by the offeror to confer a power of acceptance on the offeree. An offer becomes effective only after it is communicated—that is, when received by the offeree. The offer is usually oral or written, but occasionally it can be communicated by gestures, such as the way bids are made at some auctions. Written offers may be made in electronic communications, such as by telephone, fax, e-mail, Web site response or submission, chat room communication, or bulletin board posting. As additional electronic communications become commonplace, they will probably satisfy the requirement for effective communication among contracting parties.

Problems may occur in interpreting whether business communications are really offers. Generally, advertisements for goods or services are merely intended as invitations to deal; they are seldom actual offers. The objective reasonable person would presume that advertisements, solicitation letters, catalogues, and price lists are intended merely to arouse the interest of a potential buyer who would negotiate after receiving such information. If advertisements were routinely considered offers, then a contract could be too easily created. For example, not many sellers would be prepared with sufficient inventory if too many of these "offerees" responded to a particular advertisement. Because it is reasonable to assume that advertisers do not want this out-of-stock problem, their advertisements are not offers, only preliminary negotiations. This is not to say that an advertisement could not be worded to clearly indicate an offer. An advertiser could invite immediate acceptance. For example, language such as "while they last" in an advertisement could create an offer. Offer and acceptance are illustrated in Exhibit 8.3.

TERMINATION OF OFFERS

As long as an offer remains open, the offeree is free to create a contract by accepting the offer. However, the offeree's ability to exercise the contracting power can be terminated. Offers are terminated by the passage of time (lapse), revocation, rejection, acceptance, the death of either party, or the destruction of the contract's subject matter.

Lapse of Time

Offers do not confer a permanent power of acceptance. Offers are terminated by the passage of a reasonable time, a period that varies, depending on the circumstances. Offers terminate quickly in volatile markets (e.g., stock, currency, or commodities

Exhibit 8.3 Offer and Acceptance

After preliminary negotiations, A's offer passes a power of acceptance to B, who exercises that power and a contract results when B dispatches an acceptance to A. For example, if A offers to purchase B's house and B mails an acceptance to A, an enforceable contract exists.

exchanges) and when parties leave a face-to-face encounter. By contrast, in more stable markets, such as real estate, an offer can have a longer life, perhaps days, weeks, or even months. These rules should apply to e-commerce negotiations. For example, assent to on-line investments in the financial markets is usually instantaneous or subject to pub-licized rules permitting market-induced delays in executing trades. An offer may expire in virtual negotiations if the parties cease communicating for even a few minutes. An offeror who wants the offer to terminate at a specific time may limit its duration by specifying that the offer lapses under its own terms after the time passes. For example, prospective home buyers often specify that their offers lapse in a few hours or days. This tactic creates an imminence to induce a reluctant seller to accept a particular price.

Revocations

Usually, the offeror may withdraw an offer by the act of **revocation** at any time before acceptance. A revocation is effective when expressed directly by the offeror to the offeree. A revocation may be implied, such as when the offeree receives reli-able knowledge that the offered property was sold to another person. Revocation is illustrated in Exhibit 8.4.

In some instances, an offeror can make a binding promise *not to revoke* an offer. **Irrevocable offers** are useful, for example, when the offeree must spend time and money to survey or research the subject matter before agreeing. If the offer is held open, the offeree has more time to study it without fear of losing the deal. There are two ways to make an offer irrevocable: option contracts and firm offers. An **option contract** is formed when the offeree pays a price (consideration) for irrevocability. The option becomes a separate contractual commitment in which the offeror gives up the right to revoke in return for the consideration. Options are valid in sales of goods, but they are used extensively to tie up real estate while buyers consider other alternatives. Options to purchase securities, called puts and calls, are common forms of speculative investment.

Options to purchase *goods* under the UCC can be made without any considera-tion paid by the buyer. A **firm offer** can be made by a merchant in a signed writing,

Exhibit 8.4 Revocation

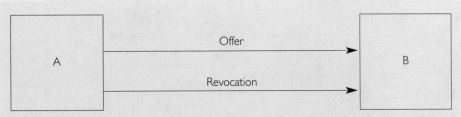

A's offer is terminated by A's revocation of the offer, and if made before B responds, no contract results. For example, if A offers to purchase B's house but has a change of heart before B responds, A may withdraw the offer by revocation and no contract results.

which creates an irrevocable offer even without payment of consideration. A firm offer is irrevocable for a reasonable time, as stated in the offer, but no longer than three months. An offeror who revokes a firm offer or sells optioned property to another person breaches the option contract and would be liable for damages. For example, assume that in a signed writing a merchant makes an offer to sell a buyer 500 widgets at $30 each. If the merchant promises to keep the offer open for two weeks but then withdraws it the next day, the buyer may enforce the contract. In some civil law nations, offers must stay open for a minimum period, such as three days. The CISG makes firm offers enforceable even if they are not made in writing.

Rejection

An offeree may refuse an offer by communicating a **rejection**, which terminates the offeree's power of acceptance. However, care is necessary because not every response by an offeree constitutes an unequivocal rejection. For example, it is not a rejection for an offeree to merely request additional information or to ask the offeror to consider changing the terms. This is an **inquiry regarding terms**, which is compared with rejection in Exhibit 8.5.

Counteroffer

By contrast, an offeree might appear to accept an offer but also attach additional or different conditions to the apparent acceptance. This type of response is often called a **conditional acceptance**. When an offeree revises the offered terms in this or any other way, it is still considered a counteroffer. Both conditional acceptances and counteroffers reject and terminate the offer because they lack exact agreement with the offered terms. When negotiating with counteroffers, the parties exchange several offers, none of which is accepted. If the offered terms and the accepted terms deviate, no contract results because the parties have failed to agree; that is, the offer and the offeree's response are not a mirror image of each other, so there is no meeting of their minds. Instead, each response to the previous offer is a counteroffer. Eventually, a contract may result when the last counteroffer is *un*conditionally

Exhibit 8.5 Rejection

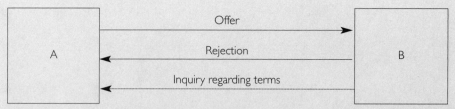

A's offer is terminated by B's rejection of the offer so no contract results. For example, if A offers to purchase B's house and B immediately rejects the offer, no contract results. However, a mere inquiry regarding terms does not terminate the offer.

accepted by the last offeree. Counteroffers are often the negotiating method used in residential real estate sales. *Counter* is a slang term for making a counteroffer.

Both the UCC and UCITA treat conditional acceptances as counteroffers, and contracts are enforceable only when any new conditions are accepted. No contract arises until the original offeror accepts the different terms that the offeree imposes in the conditional acceptance or counteroffer. If the parties use standard forms that include a conditional acceptance, they must wait for acceptance of the conditional terms before performing. Otherwise, a contract exists, but the conditional or additional terms are not accepted. Counteroffer is illustrated in Exhibit 8.6.

ACCEPTANCE

For a contract to be formed, the offeree must accept the offer (recall the illustration in Exhibit 8.3). A contract comes into existence when the offeree accepts all the terms, exactly as proposed. This results in an express agreement, a clear **meeting of the minds**. In one form of negotiating, informal communications between the parties take place before either actually makes an offer. Later, a formal offer, containing all of the terms already acceptable to both parties, is made by one party and formally accepted by the other. Businesses often use this form in more complex contracting, such as with a supplier or commercial customer. Another form of contracting involves negotiating by changing the offered terms, with each party making a counteroffer to the prior offer. In a third variation, the offeree neither inquires nor objects but accepts on the offered terms. Much of the on-line e-commerce in B2C markets uses this third form, a "take-it-or-leave-it" approach using standard terms and form contracts. UCITA has some special rules for **form contracts**.

> Form contracts under UCITA §102(60): "records containing terms prepared for repeated use in transactions [when used if] there was no negotiated change of terms by individuals except to set the price, quantity, method of payment, selection among standard options, or time or method of delivery."

Exhibit 8.6 Counteroffer

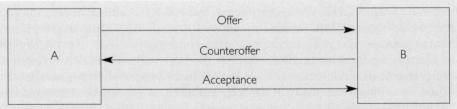

A's offer is terminated by B's counteroffer or conditional acceptance, but B extends a new offer to A. The contract results when A dispatches an acceptance in response to B's counteroffer. For example, if A offers to purchase B's house but B counteroffers at a higher price, then no contract exists unless A accepts B's counteroffer.

An acceptance need not be communicated to be effective. An acceptance can be implied from the offeree's conduct. For example, a Web user who continues accessing a free Web site, after learning of particular terms in the access license, could be bound to those terms. Consider the many Web sites that restrict access to users who agree to the Web site's use license. Many Web sites collect information about users' Web surfing and access history (clickstream) for advertising, target marketing, and resale. Use of the Web site under these conditions could obligate users not to defeat the Web site's collection of private data if the user has impliedly accepted the license's privacy policy.

TIMING AND EFFECT OF CONTRACTING COMMUNICATIONS

For a contracting communication to confer, exercise, or terminate the power of acceptance, the sending party must intend the communication to affect the power of contracting. Most communications between parties are effective only when actually received. Generally, offers, revocations, rejections, and counteroffers are effective when and if received. However, one major exception, the **mailbox rule**, makes certain acceptances effective when dispatched. A dispatch occurs when the offeree has done everything that can be done to send off the acceptance. For example, a contract immediately comes into existence the moment a diligent offeree drops a properly addressed, stamped letter of acceptance into a U.S. Postal Service mailbox. Acceptances are also effective upon dispatch if any other reasonable method is used that has been invited by the offeror. The acceptance is effective even if a rejection or revocation arrives before the acceptance ultimately arrives or is lost.

The relevance of the mailbox rule has diminished. First, if the offeree uses an unreasonable means of communication, the acceptance is not effective until receipt. Second, the offer may specify that no contract becomes binding until the acceptance is actually received. Third, UCC §2-206 is more lenient. An acceptance is effective if it is communicated by any reasonable method under the circumstances in common use, and if it is as fast as or faster than the means used by the offeror. For example, a faxed acceptance would be effective to create a contract based on a mailed letter of offer. Fourth, acceptances communicated by instantaneous communications, such as telephone or telex, are effective upon receipt. However, e-mail is not always instantaneous, so analysis under some special rules of UCITA and UETA may be necessary. Fifth, UCITA §203(4)(a) makes electronic acceptance or performance effective on receipt. Sixth, under international law, the CISG makes acceptances effective upon receipt, and a similar rule applies under the civil law of many nations.

There is a rebuttable presumption that the U.S. mail reliably delivers mail. A return receipt or electronic acknowledgment helps prove delivery. These factors should also apply to private mail services, as should a signature tracing saved to a delivery driver's electronic tablet. As nearly instantaneous electronic messaging becomes more widespread in contract negotiation, all electronic messages are likely to be considered delivered and effective when they arrive in retrievable format on the recipient's system. UCITA encourages the use of electronic acknowledgments; essentially, these are automatic, semiautomatic, or manual electronic replies indicating a message was received by the intended recipient. However, under UCITA §215(b), "Receipt . . . by itself does not establish that the content sent corresponds to the content received." As regular users of e-mail will recognize, replies and forwards often include the text of the prior message(s), but it can be difficult to determine if the earlier text remains unaltered.

UETA does not attempt to change substantive commercial laws; it seeks only to validate use of electronic communications. In UETA §15, electronic records are considered sent when (1) properly addressed to a system designated by the recipient, (2) in a form capable of processing by the recipient's system, and (3) the information enters a system outside the sender's (or sender's agent's) system. Receipt under UETA occurs when the record reaches the recipient's designated system and is capable of processing by that system. Therefore, under UETA, sending and receipt are nearly simultaneous for many contracting partners, almost eliminating the risk of competing revocation and acceptance timing. UETA does not require that the individual recipient must receive personal notice for the receipt to be valid.

CONTRACT FORMATION UNDER THE UCC

The UCC generally requires the same elements of a valid contract as the common law: mutual assent, consideration, no defenses to formation, and legality. The UCC adopts most common law offer and acceptance doctrines but simplifies the formation of sales contracts as is done in commercial practice. UCC §2-206 permits both bilateral and unilateral contracts. The UCC rejects the rigid common law acceptance rules by permitting acceptance in any commercially reasonable manner. An acceptance of an order (offer) is possible with either a prompt promise to ship or with an actual, prompt shipment of goods that conform to the order's specifications. The shipment of nonconforming goods is the simultaneous acceptance of the order, and it also breaches the contract unless the seller indicates the shipment is made as an accommodation.

Auctions

The century-old auction device is changing; many successful auctions today are conducted online. In the traditional "open outcry" form of auction, the owner of goods or land hires an auctioneer to advertise the public sale event to attract bidders. At the appointed time, interested purchasers physically attend the event or communicate bids remotely by telephone or other electronic means. Bidding generally starts low, although some sellers set a minimum bid. Bidders then make successively higher competing bids until only one winning bidder remains—the one who made the last and highest offer. Under free market economic theory, the auction mechanism is the primary method of transaction exchange.

Auction sales present a problem of identifying which party is the offeror and which is the offeree. Under the common law of auction sales, the identities of the offeror and offeree are defined by the apparent intent of the parties. Sellers at many auctions want to retain the right to withdraw goods from the auction block if they decide the bids are too low. To accomplish this, the bids must be designated offers.

This means the auctioneer's final act of knocking down the goods to the highest bidder would work as an acceptance. Most auctions concern goods, so UCC rules often apply. Under UCC §2-328, an auction of this kind is called an **auction with reserve** because the seller is considered to reserve the right to withdraw goods from the auction block before final sale.

Of course, the offeror-offeree designations can be switched in an auction, so that each bid is an acceptance of the auctioneer's offer in placing the goods on the block. A fiction is created to accomplish sales under this system. Each next higher bid is considered to replace the previous bid and cancel the contract created by the previous bid. The final acceptance occurs when the bidding stops, and the enforceable contract is formed when the goods are finally knocked down to the last and highest bidder. An auction of this kind is called an **auction without reserve** because the auctioneer does not reserve the right to withdraw the goods after bidding starts. Most auctions choose to operate with reserve unless the auction notice explicitly indicates otherwise. Auctions without reserve may be necessary when sellers are desperate because auctions without reserve tend to draw bargain hunters.

On-Line Auctions

In practice, few markets still use the traditional auction method. Indeed, there are many auction variations. For example, there are **sealed bids** in which the identity of competing bidders and/or their bids is kept confidential. The time open for receiving bids can be extended for hours, days, or even weeks. Electronic facilities can match orders for sale and purchase much like stocks trade on the New York Stock Exchange's computer, the NYSE DOT. Electronic auctions hold promise for C2C, B2C and B2B markets.

eBay's transaction security
measures description
http://www.ebay.com

On-line auctions in the future will probably enforce terms of auction trade that increase their reliability. Auctions failing to provide such assurance are unlikely to succeed in the long run. Auctions involving B2B commerce are also developing, and some may radically change the supply chain because of **disintermediation**— the elimination of middlemen, wholesalers, and resellers who add no real value for buyers.

E-B2B Exchanges

The Internet has spawned interest in the auctioning of goods and services. Auctions for services were historically limited to charity events. However, B2B and B2C auctions of professional services are emerging. For example, outside independent attorneys can bid on corporate work. The rules for these markets are uncertain, but they may resemble competitive, sealed-bid procurement, processed at Internet communication speed with potential transactions visible to many more parties. Corporate clients will probably post detailed descriptions of packages of related work to the electronic market, essentially a secure bulletin board, and make a request for quotes (RFQ). Law firms could register to gain access to the electronic market, view the RFQs online, forecast the work effort needed, formulate a bid, and finally communicate it via e-mail to the potential client. The client might then select the best price from among firms considered reasonably competent and then award a binding contract, either via return e-mail, phone, mail, or other means. The involvement of corporate counsel in posting RFQs and law firms in bidding probably assures that reasonable auction rules will be adopted and carefully constructed. As the on-line auctions become reliable, other professionals' services (e.g., accountants, consultants), and financing for corporate or consumer loans are moving online.

By early in 2000, nearly 1,000 B2B exchanges had been announced, largely to be implemented on the Internet. The Federal Trade Commission (FTC) calls them **B2B electronic marketplaces**. The FTC provisionally defines them as "software systems that enable buyers and sellers of similar goods to carry out procurement activities using common, industrywide computer systems." At the time of this writing, only a few are functioning. Nevertheless, they hold promise for substantial efficiencies in procurement and probably involve four major areas of law: membership rights, commercial law, IP, and antitrust. In the first area of legal concern, B2B exchanges will probably enforce membership rules, impose terms and conditions for use, and allocate risks among participants by using warranties, indemnification, and dispute resolution methods.

The second major area involves the processing of transactions and the terms of sale. Most goods sales must conform to UCC Article 2. Electronic means of mutual assent will be used, so many of the UETA and UCITA mechanics of contract formation and performance are implicated. Four major transaction methods are envisioned. First, participants may solicit and identify each other online and then move off line to negotiate and conclude a binding contract by using the RFQ format. Second, there are direct auctions in which many parties can bid on specified goods during a finite open time period. *Prices rise* as more bids are made, and the goods are typically sold to the highest bidder.

Another major method is the **reverse auction**, essentially an electronic posting of a buyer's needs. Bidding typically *drives prices down* during a fixed time period, and the lowest bidder wins the contract. Of course, these price movement dynamics may differ if bids are sealed or the bidders' identities are kept confidential. A fourth possible method may emulate the financial markets, which are sometimes called **dual auctions** because they involve the posting of bid and ask prices. Prices for standardized goods, such as in the markets for currencies, commodities, or securities, are bid up to prices asked by sellers or down to prices bid by buyers.

The third major area of legal concern is the unique intellectual property that will emerge. Two types are likely: (1) transaction information and (2) transaction processing methods. First, data are largely protected under trade secret law, and participants may be unwilling to permit other exchange participants or outsiders to benefit from such confidential information. Contractual confidentiality restrictions and various computer security methods are likely. Second, some transaction processing methods will be novel and nonobvious enough to be protected under a business method patent. For example, an Internet-based reverse auction method, as described in Priceline.com's patent, may become the common method for purchaser-initiated B2B systems.

The fourth area of B2B legal concern involves any potentially collusive activity among competitors. There are always antitrust concerns about price fixing, particularly in vertical procurement markets, if they largely involve a single industry. These potential anticompetitive aspects of B2B exchanges are discussed further in Chapter

12. There are precedents to aid in developing these markets: travel reservation systems, agricultural auctions, and the securities and commodities markets.

E-CONTRACTING DEPARTURES FROM TRADITIONAL PRACTICE

Emerging e-commerce methods depart from traditional contracting practices. Two related practices that are coming into widespread use are likely to shape much of the future for B2C and C2C commercial practice online. First, shrink-wrap and click-wrap may operate both as a manifestation of assent and as conclusive proof of the agreement's terms. Second, in B2B commercial practice, many parties already engage in EDI, an electronic form of ordering based on agreed and standardized terms of trade.

Shrink-Wrap Agreements

The software industry has long sought to impose standardized license terms on mass market purchasers by enclosing a printed copy of the license that is viewable from within a clear plastic wrap that is sealed around the software package. This **shrink-wrap agreement** resembles a unilateral contract in which purchasers' assent to the terms is inferred when they open and use the software product. A shrink-wrap typically provides that the act of opening the package constitutes an acceptance of the license on the stated terms. These terms are not negotiated but are imposed on individual licensees, and they generally favor the seller. By contrast, license terms negotiated as part of a **site license** to large purchasers, such as corporations or universities, may differ significantly from shrink-wrap licenses. When shrink-wrap agreements are enforceable, they automatically obligate the licensee to the stated terms. Shrink-wraps are probably enforceable if drafted carefully and clearly, displayed conspicuously to permit review, and do not deviate substantially from industry norms. However, some courts refuse to enforce shrink-wraps or find that particular terms are unconscionable (unfair). Some have been invalidated as a postnegotiation attempt to unilaterally impose additional but unfavorable terms on the buyer.[1]

Shrink-wraps are becoming ubiquitous; arguably, they are so common they constitute a usage of trade that sets a precedent for interpreting similar licenses. Another basis for enforcement is that shrink-wraps simply modify any preexisting contract terms. For example, many software purchases are clustered into periodic shipments: First, the terms for some trial copies are negotiated; then, later shipments include shrink-wraps with modified terms. Some courts refuse to enforce these shrink-wrap terms if unconscionable. In one watershed case a shrink-wrap was enforced as a license limitation on using data contained in a CD-ROM telephone directory.[2]

Shrink-wraps often limit the customer's rights of use as well as the customer's rights against the seller. For example, many licenses limit warranties or the damages recoverable if the software or information is defective, they deny the right to sue by requiring arbitration, and they often apply laws favorable to the vendor. Customers

1. *Step-Saver Data Systems, Inc. v. Wyse Technology*, 939 F.2d 91 (3d Cir., 1991).
2. *ProCD, Inc. v. Zeidenberg*, 86 F.3d 1447 (7th Cir., 1997).

unwilling to assent to the shrink-wrap terms are usually permitted to return the package under a term that gives a choice: to **accept or return**—that is, accept all the standard license terms or return the goods to the seller. Some cases refuse to enforce such take-it-or-leave-it contracts, calling them **adhesion contracts** if customers are unlikely to read or understand terms that are unconscionable or violate public policy. Nevertheless, a few state statutes have attempted to validate shrink-wrap licenses, and UCITA would validate them, as discussed in the following sections. License terms are discussed further in Chapter 11.

Click-Wrap Agreements

Shrink-wraps have evolved into the **click-wrap agreement** encountered while operating a computer. Use of the software or access to a Web site is often prevented unless the user clicks affirmatively "I Agree" during software installation or before accessing Web site content. Packaged software using a click-wrap license can record the assent on the user's computer, although it is more reliable to transmit the assent back to the seller during on-line registration through the user's modem or Internet connection. Web sites requiring click-wrap assent may cause an immediate transmission of the agreement back to the Web site operator. The click-wrap is similar to the shrink-wrap because both impose standardized licensing terms to which users agree by conduct. Click-wraps are likely to be enforceable under the same standards applicable to shrink-wraps. However, both may be vulnerable to invalidation as unconscionable or an adhesion contract. The ruling in the case *Specht v. Netscape*[3] refused to enforce a click-wrap unless the user had scrolled down through all the terms, indicating the opportunity to read them all. They differ mainly in that assent is demonstrated by clicking through rather than by opening the transparent plastic wrapper. Also, click-wraps are more likely than shrink-wraps to govern all future transactions.

ONLINE

FTC's click-wrap enforceability advisory
http://www.ftc.gov/bcp /conline/pubs/buspubs /dotcom/

Contract Formation under UCITA

The Uniform Computer Information Transactions Act (UCITA) was originally proposed to be part of the UCC, as Article 2B, and to validate shrink-wrap mutual assent. Since then, UCITA's scope grew initially but is now limited to traditional and electronic transactions in software, multimedia, data, and on-line information. As of this writing, UCITA has been enacted only in Virginia and Maryland. Iowa law prohibits vendors from imposing UCITA on Iowa consumers. Controversy surrounds UCITA, and many observers believe it will not be as successful as the UCC. Despite this controversy, UCITA settles on electronic contracting rules that may eventually become some of the norms for other forms of on-line contracting. UCITA parallels UETA in legitimizing the parties' use of electronic records, electronic signatures, authentication, and electronic agents. UCITA's broad terms are discussed throughout the electronic commerce chapters. This section discusses the impact that UCITA may have on the formation and conclusion of a contract.

---

3. 150 F.Supp.2d 585 (D.N.Y. 2001).

UCITA's contract formation rules parallel existing sales law because many UCITA rules were derived from the *Restatement of Contracts* and from UCC Article 2. The new law speaks in terms of "manifesting assent," so much of the focus in UCITA mutual assent is on what a reasonable person would infer from the contracting parties' conduct. UCITA §202 permits contract formation in any manner, including traditional offer and acceptance, and by the parties' conduct. Contracts formed using electronic agents are also authorized. UCITA §203 provides that offers can be accepted in any reasonable manner including by shipment or promise to ship a copy of the subject computer information. UCITA §203(4)(a) rejects the mailbox rule when electronic communications are used: Acceptances are effective upon receipt of an electronic message or upon the receipt of an electronic performance.

UCITA §211 establishes an important rule in facilitating mutual assent in Internet types of transactions. UCITA makes it unfavorable for information vendors to prevent customers from exercising the opportunity to review, print, or store the license terms before performance. Of course, customers may choose not to read the terms, so a contract under UCITA is enforceable so long as customers had an opportunity to review. UCITA creates special rules for **mass market transactions**. Generally, these are licenses sold at retail to consumers containing standardized terms, UCITA §102(43). There are special remedies for consumers of mass market licenses.

UCITA adoptions and controversy
http://www. ucitaonline.com

Electronic Data Interchange

In the 1990s, commercial customers began to use electronic methods for customizing B2B contracts, orders, and documents for recurrent purchase transactions with regular customers from their long-standing suppliers. **Electronic data interchange (EDI)** transactions usually anticipate a course of dealing with continuing orders, invoices, payments, and shipments based on standard terms in an umbrella contract, the **trading partner agreement**. The International Chamber of Commerce (ICC) first developed EDI practices with Uniform Rules of Conduct for Interchange of Trade Data by Teletransmission (UNCID).

EDI is a flexible contracting method permitting various models. For example, in an EDI model perfected by Wal-Mart, a large purchaser may provide incentives so that its many suppliers will implement EDI with particular computer and communications hardware and EDI software based on standard trade terms and conditions. In another model, the start-up costs and complexity of all this EDI "infrastructure" is best provided by a third-party EDI firm that specializes in electronic transaction processing. EDI trading partners often expect their counterparty to implement adequate EDI systems and then regularly keep accurate records and log all transactions and transmissions. The amount of human intervention varies in different implementations of EDI systems.

The Electronic Messaging Services Task Force of the American Bar Association (ABA) developed the **Model EDI Trading Partner Agreement**[4] that provides some

---

4. *The Commercial Use of Electronic Data Interchange: A Report and Model Trading Partner Agreement*, 45 Bus.Law 1645 (1990).

standard or benchmark EDI terms that balance the burdens and risks among EDI parties. Terms of the Model EDI Trading Partner Agreement may be adjusted to suit the special needs of particular parties. The ABA model agreement envisions that the parties will use a secure, closed, and dedicated communications system to reduce both errors and unauthorized interference by hackers. Confirmation messages are encouraged to provide "functional acknowledgment" that each counterparty's electronic message was received. EDI messages are typically made effective upon receipt, eliminating the mailbox rule. The parties may agree to use communication methods that clearly indicate the formation of their contract.

ONLINE

Accredited Standards Committee's EDI standards
http://www.x12.org

TERMS OF THE AGREEMENT

Parties often use a written agreement, even if contract law does not require one, because long experience shows that it is prudent to "get it in writing." For example, circumstances can change after the agreement is concluded and before all performances are rendered. These changed circumstances often make it less advantageous for one party to perform the duties as they originally agreed. Of course, the primary purpose of enforceable contracts is to permit parties to allocate the risk of changed circumstances and thereby gain certainty so they can plan for the future. For example, a seller might agree to supply a commodity at a particular price, but the price rises by the time shipment is made. Alternatively, a retailer might agree to buy popular goods from a manufacturer but be unhappy about receiving the shipment several weeks later when an item's popularity has declined.

Written contracts make it difficult for the party disadvantaged by economic or other circumstances to deny terms plainly stated or to add terms not originally stated in the written contract. Experienced business parties prepare written contracts that anticipate many changes in circumstances. Typically, the more sophisticated party, both in business decision-making and legal drafting abilities, takes the initiative to author the written agreement. The author, called the **scrivener**, often takes advantage of the situation by including terms more favorable to the author's side. However, when both parties are relatively sophisticated, the contract is drafted in successive versions that eventually reach some middle ground that reflects the parties' relative bargaining power and the market conditions for the underlying goods or services. Despite the certainty provided by written contracts, it is often necessary for contract law to assist in interpreting the parties' contract by determining what terms should be in a vaguely worded contract, filling in gaps the parties overlooked, defining contract duties by interpreting contract language, and implementing later modifications. This section discusses interpretation of terms.

MIRROR-IMAGE RULE

The common law **mirror-image rule**, applicable to land sales, services, or employment, requires that the acceptance mirror the offered terms. This rule requires that the accepted terms agree in every detail to the offered terms with no variations. The

UCC, applicable to sales of goods, is more liberal, permitting some deviations between the offered and accepted terms. Commercial organizations often fail to adhere strictly to the common law mirror-image rule. Goods sales often involve a "battle of the forms" in which buyers and sellers, with the aid of their attorneys, construct invoices, order forms, and confirmation notices containing terms very favorable to themselves. Inevitably, there are differences between terms found in the offer and acceptance forms. Minor differences usually go unnoticed unless a dispute arises. UCC §2-207 provides a complex solution to this problem.

Additional Terms in Acceptance or Confirmation (UCC §2-207)

1. A definite and seasonable expression of acceptance or a written confirmation which is sent within a reasonable time operates as an acceptance even though it states terms additional to or different from those offered or agreed upon, unless acceptance is expressly made conditional on assent to the additional or different terms.

2. The additional terms are to be construed as proposals for addition to the contract. Between merchants such terms become part of the contract unless:
   (a) the offer expressly limits acceptance to the terms of the offer;
   (b) they materially alter it; or
   (c) notification of objection to them has already been given or is given within a reasonable time after notice of them is received.

3. Conduct by both parties which recognizes the existence of a contract is sufficient to establish a contract for sale although the writings of the parties do not otherwise establish a contract. In such case the terms of the particular contract consist of those terms on which the writings of the parties agree, together with any supplementary terms incorporated under any other provisions of this Act.

UCC §2-207 applies to forming a contract when there are only minor deviations between the parties' written documents in sales of goods. Unlike under the common law mirror image rule, slight differences between the offer and the acceptance do not always cause mutual assent to fail. A contract is formed if there are no material differences on key terms in the parties' communications. However, either party may reimpose the mirror-image rule. Counteroffers are possible only if highly material terms are in dispute between the writings. **Highly material terms** include essential terms like the parties' identity, the price, and significant differences in the quantity or subject matter. For example, differences in the size, color, or grade of apples would be highly material, and a return communication that contains these differences would be a counteroffer.

If the additions, deletions, or changes in the acceptance or confirmation form are not highly material, perhaps they are just material, and this does not prevent mutual assent. In this case, the parties still have an enforceable agreement. If different terms appear in the second communication, they are considered mere proposals to modify, but the contract still exists on the terms as originally offered. Such proposals to modify may be accepted or rejected by the offeror. **Material terms** are those that would cause surprise to either party, such as changes in standard warranty protection or customary credit terms.

When both of the parties are merchants, immaterial differences in the second communication may actually become part of the contract without further negotiation, providing the offeror does not object to the offeree's immaterial new terms. If the parties conduct themselves as if they have a contract despite different terms in their forms, their conduct implies that they acknowledge a contract exists and that it is enforceable. In that case, the contract's terms are those on which the writings agree, together with other terms automatically supplied by the UCC. For example, if the buyer pays for the goods or the seller delivers them, then a contract exists even if the parties' forms do not agree. The CISG rejects UCC §2-207 and follows the mirror-image rule.

The UCITA approach to the battle of the forms is found in §204. It retains much of the UCC §2-207 regimen. A contract is not created if the acceptance materially alters the offered terms, unless the material term is accepted or the parties conduct themselves as if a contract exists. If the additional terms are not material, a contract exists on the offered terms. If the additional terms are immaterial, they are not part of the contract except between merchants, where they can become part of the contract unless the other party objects. In UCITA licensing contracts, the scope, geographical region, field of use, and duration of a license are likely to be material terms in most situations.

OPEN TERMS

Most reasonable and careful parties express all or nearly all the terms they foresee as essential when they make an offer or otherwise negotiate. However, such foresight is not always necessary: The parties may presume that reasonable or customary terms are in use even if some terms are not expressed. UCC §2-204 provides for terms of a contract to be left as **open terms** for future determination or to be inferred later from the circumstances. In such situations, the contract will be enforced as long as a "reasonably certain basis" exists "for giving an appropriate remedy."

The UCC provides **gap-filling terms** to supplement vague sales contracts. For example, the price of goods may be determined later if the parties leave the price term open, if they say nothing about price, or if they intend to use the market price prevailing at the time of delivery. UCC §2-304 infers a reasonable price determined at the time for delivery. An open delivery term is interpreted as requiring delivery at the seller's place of business and at a reasonable time after contracting. A payment term left open obligates the buyer to pay when the goods are received. Even the quantity term can be left vague until determined by the sellers' actual **outputs** or the buyers' actual **requirements**. Terms can also be supplied by trade custom, as discussed in the next section. The CISG does not clearly encourage the use of open terms, except in setting the price according to some outside force, such as by market prices, a market index, formula, or third party. The CISG imposes no good faith duty on the parties, but the UCC and UCITA both do impose a **duty of good faith** on all parties.

UCITA permits open terms and provides several default rules, essentially gap-filling terms, to supply terms when the parties fail to be specific. Not all terms must be conspicuous, negotiated, or expressly assented or agreed to, unless UCITA expressly requires such formality. Under UCITA §305, "An agreement that is otherwise sufficiently definite to be a contract is not invalid because it leaves particulars of

performance to be specified by one of the parties." Any such particulars of performance may be specified by a party but only in good faith and only in a commercially
reasonable manner. There may be several excuses for breach if the other party fails to
specify a term "seasonably" (within the time agreed or within a reasonable time) and
this failure materially affects the other party. For example, if the purchaser of data
delays in setting specifications for the data needed, the supplier is excused for any
resulting delay in its performance and may perform, suspend performance, or treat
the failure to specify as a breach of contract. UCITA §306 requires that performances
under open terms be "reasonable in light of the commercial circumstances existing at
the time of agreement." UCITA special licensing terms are discussed in Chapter 11.

INTERPRETATION

Disagreements over the meaning of contract terms are all too frequent and are
resolved under the objective rule of contracts. Terms are interpreted by how an
objective, reasonable person would understand the words used in the particular context. Common words are given their general meaning unless the particular line of
business applies a unique usage to the words in question. For example, consider the
word *gross*. In common parlance, gross means overall, total, flagrant, disgusting, or
bizarre. However, among wholesalers and retailers, gross is a measure of unit quantity, precisely 12 dozen, or 144.

    Three levels of trade custom or commercial precedent are useful in interpreting
contracts. The first level applies precedents set in a whole industry, and the two other
levels progressively provide guidance developed from narrower experiences among
fewer parties. The broadest source of industry precedent comes from **usages of trade,**
which are methods or expectations in the commercial dealings common to a whole
trade or business, derived from its customs and practices. It may take some time
before the Internet community establishes solid usages that most participants regularly observe. A narrower source of trade customs comes from a recognized course
of dealing. These are practices derived from previous dealings directly between the
contracting parties.

    The narrowest of the three is a **course of performance,** which looks to a single con-
tract between the parties in which there were several or repeat performances, such as
installment payments or deliveries. For example, a buyer who fails to object to consis-
tently late deliveries establishes a precedent that causes the seller to reasonably expect
that tardy future deliveries are acceptable. Once this course of performance is set, the
buyer would be unable to claim breach of contract for another late delivery before first
notifying the seller that future late deliveries would not be tolerated. Both the UCC and
UCITA permit these trade usages to help interpret vague contracts or to define terms.
The UCC's provision is similar to UCITA §302, which provides that when there are
inconsistencies, the parties' agreement and conduct are given precedence over trade
usages. For example, the express terms of a contract override all inconsistent trade
usages; course of performance prevails over course of dealing and usage of trade, and
course of dealing prevails over usage of trade. Trade usages are proven as facts.

MODIFICATIONS

Laissez faire dictates that contract law should not inhibit the parties from modifying an existing agreement. Circumstances change, and parties are often willing to accommodate each other to preserve their ongoing relationship. However, experience has shown that a powerful party may pressure the weaker party into a modification more favorable to the stronger party. As a result, the common law requires that any contract modification be regarded as another contract that should be properly formed and supported by consideration. This rule usually means that both parties' obligations must be changed by the modification. The UCC and UCITA were drafted to ease these requirements. Modifications of goods sales and computer information licenses are enforceable even without consideration and even if only one party's obligation changes.

Many contracts anticipate such changing circumstances and require that particular processes be followed for modifications. Generally, oral contracts may be modified orally. However, many written contracts require that modifications are enforceable only if made in writing and sometimes only if approved by particular parties. Under UCITA §303, an authenticated record may validly require that later modifications be effected only by use of another authenticated record. In a B2C transaction, using the merchant's standard form, the consumer must separately manifest assent to the clause requiring an authenticated record for a modification. Online subscription contracts have frequent periodic changes in terms. Generally, the subscriber must be given an opportunity to "terminate the contract as to future performance if the change alters a material term and the party in good faith determines that the modification is unacceptable." UCITA requires that whenever opposing parties are asked to accept a modification, they must be given an opportunity to review the proposed modification before it becomes binding.

Consideration

As introduced earlier as the consideration model of e-commerce, the law does not enforce all agreements. For two reasons, mutual promises must go beyond a certain minimum threshold to create a contract: First, many promises are made idly or lightly, with no intention of creating binding obligations. For example, promises to make a gift, do a favor for another, or participate in a social arrangement are considered less serious than are business promises. Second, only sufficiently important cases should burden the judicial system. Although it might be socially desirable to rely on all promises, there must be some limit on the enforceability of promises, a limit corresponding to the seriousness and motivation of the promisor and the reasonableness of the promisee's expectations. These reasons justify the **consideration** requirement. Consideration distinguishes serious, enforceable promises from less serious and unenforceable promises. The rule of consideration requires that the parties mutually give value or make obligations. This is the principal measure of the importance of promises, but its significance is declining. The mutual promises necessary for adequate consideration are illustrated in Exhibit 8.7.

Exhibit 8.7 Consideration

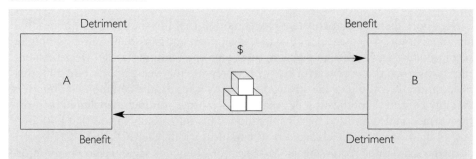

Consideration exists for a contract when the two parties exchange new promises. A promises to pay money to B because B promises to deliver goods to A, and B promises to deliver goods to A because A promises to pay money to B. A's promise to pay B for the goods that B delivers is a benefit to B and a detriment to A. B's promise to deliver goods to A is a benefit to A and a detriment to B.

TESTS FOR THE PRESENCE OF CONSIDERATION

There are several tests of consideration. They vary conceptually and are stated in terms of value, benefits, detriments, mutuality of obligation, and the exchange of promises. A common misconception about consideration is that value must pass physically between the parties. Another misconception is that there must be a real detriment to the promisor and a real benefit to the promisee. Although the consideration requirement is usually satisfied if property or labor is exchanged, it can be satisfied with less, simply by the parties' new promises. Only **legal detriments** or **legal benefits** need be present in the new promises, such as when the parties make promises that obligate themselves in the future. A promise to do something new, something the promisor was not previously obligated to do, is sufficient consideration to support a counterpromise. A promise is quite different from an actual transfer of property or services pledged in a promise. All that is necessary is that the promise creates a legally binding obligation. Promises alone have sufficient legal value to show seriousness. Actual performance satisfies the consideration requirement but is not necessary.

A **forbearance** is *promising not to do* something or to actually refrain from doing it. A forbearance can also constitute sufficient consideration. In the settlement of a dispute over an automobile accident, for example, the party at fault usually promises to pay money in exchange for the victim's promise to refrain from suing for damages. This explains why contracts to release a negligent driver are enforceable to prevent suit after the victim accepts an insurance company settlement. The proper test of consideration is whether the parties make mutually binding new promises. Enforceable promises may be either promises to do something new or promises to refrain from doing something previously permissible. To satisfy the consideration test, the promises made by both parties must change their legal obligations.

MUTUALITY OF OBLIGATION

The exchange element of consideration is an important concept. Parties that exchange promises are more likely to intend to be legally bound because each party's promise is made "on the condition" that the other party is making an acceptable return promise. With few exceptions, the mutual or bilateral nature of the promises clearly indicates their seriousness and the parties' intent to be bound. Each party makes a promise "in consideration" of the other party's promise, so the promises are mutually given in exchange. Each party is induced or motivated to promise something new because the other party has made a new promise in return. Stated another way, each party's promise must be supported by the consideration found in the other party's counterpromise.

The classic formulation of consideration holds that there must be a legal detriment to the promisee or a legal benefit to the promisor when the promises of the parties are analyzed (illustrated in Exhibits 8.8 and 8.9). These tests are efficient because each demonstrates that two new promises are made. Either of these tests also shows that each party gives and receives legal value. Another formulation holds

Exhibit 8.8 Detriments to the Promisee

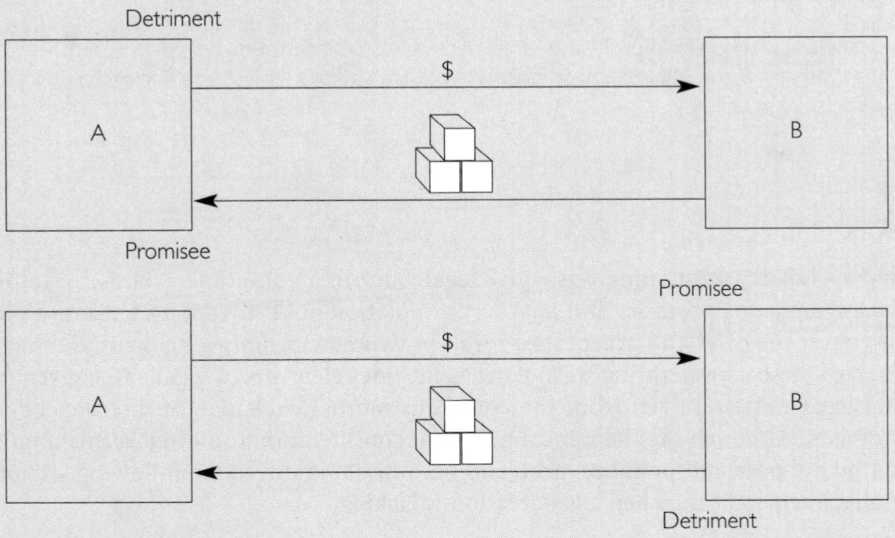

Consideration exists for the whole contract because, from A's perspective, there is a "detriment to the promisee." A's detriment is the promise to pay money to B, made in exchange for B's promise to deliver goods to A. *(top)*

Consideration exists for the whole contract because, from B's perspective, there is a "detriment to the promisee." B's detriment is the promise to deliver goods to A, made in exchange for A's promise to pay money to B. *(bottom)*

Exhibit 8.9 Benefits to the Promisor

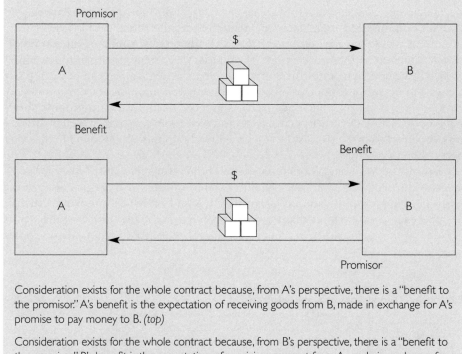

Consideration exists for the whole contract because, from A's perspective, there is a "benefit to the promisor." A's benefit is the expectation of receiving goods from B, made in exchange for A's promise to pay money to B. *(top)*

Consideration exists for the whole contract because, from B's perspective, there is a "benefit to the promisor." B's benefit is the expectation of receiving payment from A, made in exchange for B's promise to deliver goods to A. *(bottom)*

that each party must consciously give legal value in an outgoing promise in return for the incoming promise. Still another formulation holds that consideration exists whenever the offer and acceptance result in two new promises made in exchange. Each of these consideration formulations includes elements of legal value given for and legal value received from the conscious mutual exchange of interdependent promises. Although the theoretical nature of consideration too often seems obtuse, it need not pose interpretation problems because situations in the following sections more clearly indicate when consideration is lacking.

UNENFORCEABLE PROMISES: CONSIDERATION IS LACKING

In several common situations, consideration is found to be lacking, which makes the agreement unenforceable. If either party's promise is subject to that party's wish, will, or desire, then the promise is **illusory**. For example, an unlimited right to cancel the contract gives the promisor a way to back out at any time. A promise that is never binding is an illusion, so a contract supported by such a promise lacks consideration. However, if the cancellation right is limited, such as with 30 days' notice, then the promise is not illusory and provides good consideration.

When one party is already legally bound to perform an obligation and later simply repromises it, that second promise is a mere stale repetition. Nothing new is given in the newly repeated old promise when it is in exchange for the promisee's return new promise. When there is a **preexisting legal duty**, the promisor is already legally obligated to do or refrain from doing some activity and then attempts to use the repromise as consideration for a new contract. However, there is no new consideration, and the second contract based on a restated promise is unenforceable. Consider a jockey who is already under contract to ride a horse in the Kentucky Derby. If that jockey pressures the horse's owner for higher pay as the odds of winning become more favorable, the owner may feel pressure to promise to pay more. However, this owner's promise is not supported by any new consideration. The jockey has a preexisting legal duty to ride in that race under the terms of the original contract.

There is sufficient consideration in an **accord and satisfaction** when a debtor agrees to settle a disputed or **unliquidated debt**. For example, a client may not have agreed to a consultant's fee before the services are rendered. When the bill arrives, the client may dispute the amount or particular itemized entries. When the consultant and client settle their dispute over the bill, the disputed claim becomes liquidated. Each has given up rights by settling, and the settlement amounts to an accord and satisfaction that is supported by consideration. By contrast, agreements to settle undisputed or liquidated debts by which the debtor promises to pay less are usually not supported by consideration because the debt amount is the debtor's preexisting legal duty. However, if the debtor promises to pay the amount sooner or in a different medium, then the creditor receives something different than was originally promised, and consideration is again present to validate the contract.

PROMISES ENFORCEABLE WITHOUT CONSIDERATION

Enforceable obligations do not always require consideration. In a few unusual cases, a single, one-way, or gratuitous promise, though unsupported by consideration, becomes enforceable to preserve fairness and equity. The doctrines of **promissory estoppel** and **charitable subscriptions** permit enforcement by balancing the unfairness when the promisee suffers damage by relying on a promisor's promise (see Exhibit 8.10).

The doctrine of charitable subscriptions is similar to promissory estoppel. It applies when a charity relies on a donor's promise to contribute. Typically, the promisor pledges to donate something, and the charity relies on that pledge to its detriment by changing its position. For example, if a church member's promise to make a big contribution induces the church to remodel its building, the one-way charitable subscription becomes enforceable as soon as the church contracts with a builder, even though the charity has not given consideration.

Exhibit 8.10 Elements of Promissory Estoppel

1. Under the circumstances, should the promisor reasonably expect that the promisee will rely on the promise and then act in some definite and substantial way? This is a detrimental reliance.
2. Has the promisee in fact relied on the promise to his or her own detriment?
3. In balancing the equities of enforcing or not enforcing the promise, would substantial unfairness be avoided if the promise is enforced?

The consideration requirement is waived in several other limited situations. For example, a debt barred by either the statute of limitations or the debtor's discharge in bankruptcy may be revived if the debtor reaffirms the original promise to pay the debt or makes partial payment without new consideration. The repayment of debts barred by bankruptcy must be approved by the bankruptcy court judge. **Composition** agreements entered into by several creditors and a debtor are enforceable without new consideration because the parties have a mutual interreliance similar to actual consideration. Although common law modifications require consideration, UCITA and the UCC permit contract modifications without consideration, and the UCC requires no consideration for written merchants' firm offers and for modifications of existing sales contracts. Consideration is generally unnecessary under UCITA for waivers or releases, which are one party's surrender of rights under a contract.

UCC §2-302 permits the court hearing a contract dispute to modify an adhesion contract—that is, a contract with unfair provisions—under the **unconscionability** doctrine. The parties may present evidence of the purpose and commercial setting of any clause brought into question. A consumer contract may be designated unconscionable if it is one-sided and oppressive, causes unfair surprise, and unfairly allocates risks because one side clearly has superior bargaining power. Courts have applied unconscionability as a form of consumer protection beyond the UCC context to achieve fairness. Unconscionability seldom applies to commercial parties. It is generally reserved for the uniquely vulnerable position of consumers. Commercial parties are presumed to be more experienced and better informed, to have better access to legal counsel, to possess stronger bargaining power, and to negotiate contracts more carefully than most consumers.

Internet transactions may reawaken the quiet area of contract consideration. The law increasingly recognizes that visitations by Web users to Web sites, downloads, and Web site interactivity often involve a license between the Web site and user. Licenses are contracts that must be supported by consideration. Many Web users have accepted license terms at some Web sites, essentially manifesting their assent by clicking "I agree." As the Web site license theory takes hold, users may be limited in the defensive acts taken to preserve their privacy. For example, many Web sites are expressly accessible only on the condition the user truthfully and completely supplies private information and accepts cookies to track the user's clickstream. User access to the Web site would constitute consideration from the Web site in exchange for the user's private information. If the user were to provide incorrect or incomplete data in a Web site registration license application or thwart use of cookies, this act could constitute a failure of consideration or even a breach of the license agreement. Of course, Web site operators who insist on enforcing this contract consideration theory to compel the surrender of private data from privacy-sensitive and savvy users may forfeit advantageous visits from a considerable part of the market. The pressures for privacy laws as a form of consumer protection are discussed further in Chapter 13.

CHAPTER 9
PERFORMANCES AND PAYMENTS

Commerce was at great risk before the law became a reliable incentive to perform contracts as promised. At one time, there were many perils and much intrigue in commercial transactions. Deliveries made over long distances could be lost at sea, damaged by weather, or stolen by pirates. Even as commercial law developed more fully, some parties too often failed to fulfill their obligations: Checks bounced, some goods were defective, and the quantities delivered were late or short. Parties generally trust repeated transactions with reliable counterparties or face-to-face exchanges where the consideration can be inspected before completing the transaction. The development and enforcement of safe commercial law and practices have very substantially reduced transaction risks. Today, commercial law provides highly reliable recourse when contract performance is inadequate or fails completely. This consistency may be among the most important factors supporting trade and prosperity.

Unprotected commerce over the Internet has caused a reversion to the commercial risks of the past. Anonymous interactions and transactions with unknown and untrusted counterparties are again raising many of the same risks that existed before commercial law improved dependability. Goods, data, and software from unknown vendors are too frequently defective or misdescribed. Electronic payments are at risk of interception by hackers or cancellation. Counterparties are often in remote jurisdictions where legal process is expensive, often greater than the value of the transaction at stake. The progress of e-commerce will be inhibited unless commercial law can adapt to reduce these risks. Adaptations of commercial law and practice that made early commerce safe may be the solution to transaction safety in e-commerce.

The primary objective of contracting is to make and receive a performance: the actual transfer of valuable goods, services, information, and payment. In this chapter, the performance of contracts is reviewed, including how contract terms and other standards may condition or assess the accomplishments of each party. This chapter also reviews the participation of outside third parties who may assist in processing or assuring performance. In some instances, a third party is entitled to receive a performance. Payment systems are discussed because, except for barter transactions, payments are the most common form of performance. Parties that satisfactorily fulfill their obligations are entitled to discharge, which recognizes that adequate performance releases them from their duty to perform. Throughout this discussion, it is important to remember that the contract's primary subject matter determines what law applies: common law, Uniform Commercial Code (UCC), Uniform Computer Information Transactions Act (UCITA) and/or Uniform Electronic Transactions Act (UETA).

PERFORMANCES

Most parties hope to discharge their contractual duties quickly and effectively. Contract law measures their performance by examining several basic performance questions: *When* should performance have been made and were these duties performed in a timely manner, *what* was performed, *who* performed it and to whom was the performance made, and *where* was performance made? Adequate and **full performance** by both parties fulfills their duties, and the contract is effectively discharged. These questions are examined in this chapter. With the convergence of e-commerce and the traditional economy, this chapter focuses on traditional physical performances and also integrates an understanding of how traditional performance rules extend into e-commerce through electronic payments, the processing of electronic documents, and electronic deliveries.

CONDITIONS

Conditions address the timing of performance. Certain events or **conditions** are often necessary before a party's rights become enforceable. The parties can expressly agree that some event is the triggering condition, often by using phrases such as "provided that," "contingent on," or "on the condition that." Conditions may also be implied with express conditions or with the circumstances. Some contracts contain **conditions precedent**, uncertain future events that must happen *before* a duty is owed. For example, in a software development contract, the contract terms might not require the purchaser to pay until the software is proved to satisfactorily perform according to prescribed standards. In e-commerce, an on-line seller might require the buyer's payment as a condition precedent before the seller will deliver. A Web site development contract might condition the client's payment duty on the client's personal satisfaction with the Web site's appearance and functionality. **Concurrent conditions** arise when each party's performance is conditioned on the other party's nearly simultaneous tender of counterperformance. For example, in most face-to-face retail store sales, the buyer's payment is concurrently conditioned on the seller's delivery. Similarly, the seller's delivery is concurrently conditioned on the buyer's payment. Occasionally, there is a **condition subsequent**. This is an event that occurs *after* a duty is being performed that relieves one party of any further duty to perform. For example, a customer's failure to pay the monthly bill for Internet service might be interpreted to relieve the ISP from a duty to provide future service.

TITLE AND RISK OF LOSS

Before the UCC, under the common law, the concept of **title** or ownership of property was very important for many reasons. Title gave the owner a right to insure the property, and title gave the owner legal remedies against the seller or a wrongdoer. An owner is liable for taxes. An owner risks financial loss if the property is damaged or destroyed. The UCC has changed some of this by separating the incidents of ownership that title implied from two other concerns: insurable interest and risk of loss. Today, title to goods affects mainly ownership, creditors' rights, and taxation. As discussed further in Chapter 11, ownership of information and intellectual property is distinguished from the more limited licensee rights that most purchasers obtain when acquiring these intangibles.

Title

Title does not pass from the seller to the buyer until *after* the goods are identified to the contract. Goods are **identified** when particular goods are designated as being for the buyer, which can occur in several ways. The contract may explicitly designate particular goods by, for example, listing serial numbers. Identification also occurs when particular goods are shipped or the seller otherwise labels them as intended for the buyer. Generally, the contract of sale dictates when title passes. However, if the timing of title transfer is not mentioned, then title passes when the seller completes delivery. Delivery can happen: (1) when they are delivered to the carrier in a contract requiring the seller to "ship," (2) when they are delivered to the buyer in a contract requiring the seller to "deliver," (3) at the time of contracting if delivery is not mentioned or will occur without moving the goods, such as when the goods are held in an independent warehouse, or (4) when negotiable documents of title are delivered. If the buyer rejects the goods, title immediately reverts to the seller. Most title transfers in international trade are determined by separate, formal documents of title.

Documents of Title

Many domestic and international commercial transactions use formal written documents that accompany the goods in transit for various purposes. For example, commercial documents make or guarantee payment, prove the contents of shipment to various officials (customs, public safety, law enforcement, carrier, bankers, buyer), and prove or actually transfer ownership. These are formal documents, and they are intangible interests in personal property. They are traditionally written on paper; many are still printed on official-looking certificates.

Since the 1960s, many commercial documents have been replaced by **uncertificated** rights, which are generally mere book entries or electronic records held by another party, for example, insurance policies, ATM transactions, savings accounts, and corporate securities (stocks or bonds). This change has been made possible by innovations in technology, such as computerized electronic communication, encryption, and biometrics. Also, UETA now permits many such formal documents to be officially archived as electronic records on computers as well as transferred and negotiated by electronic endorsement. Security measures to minimize errors and irregularities in this electronic world must eventually become as reliable—perhaps even more reliable—than the security measures traditionally used with paper documents.

Traditionally, an intimate understanding of these commercial documents was largely of interest to logisticians, carriers, warehouses, auditors, lawyers, financial service firms (securities, insurance, banking), government officials, and, of course, delivery drivers, loading dock foremen, and mail room clerks. Today, with the migration of commercial practice to e-commerce, such details are becoming important to entrepreneurs, information technologists, marketing and finance people, and professionals in nearly all other business functions because their design of new systems for the converging economy *must* use them effectively.

Many important commercial documents transfer legal rights when negotiated by endorsement. This exchange of commercial documents works to reduce risk, particularly in transactions conducted at a distance. These risks include wrongful payment or delivery, malicious tampering, fraud, and theft. Payment by check is the most familiar form of transferable or **negotiable instruments**. **Commercial paper**, a subset of negotiable instruments, is governed by UCC Article 3. It includes familiar forms of payment obligations, including checks, notes, drafts, certificates of deposit, and bankers' acceptances.

The usefulness of negotiating documents by endorsement is best seen with the classical example of buyers' and sellers' "transaction anxiety." Sellers are often unwilling to transfer title or physical custody of goods to an unknown or uncreditworthy buyer without some kind of assurance. Similarly, buyers are often unwilling to make payment to unknown or untrustworthy sellers, without some assurance. These expectations can be fulfilled when the system uses **trusted and reliable third-party intermediaries**, including the seller's and buyer's banks, the carrier or other freight forwarder, or the warehouse. These trusted intermediaries perform nearly concurrent conditions in transferring the payment to the seller and transferring title to the buyer. In other words, after inspections and government clearances are verified, intermediaries condition their endorsement of payment on the endorsement of the title transfer, and vice versa.

UCC Article 7 governs the use of **documents of title**, which include bills of lading, dock receipts, dock warrants, and warehouse receipts. Documents of title are written instruments entitling the holder to possess, receive, or dispose of specified goods usually then held by a bailee, carrier, or warehouse. Bailees are temporary custodians of goods who usually act for the true owner's benefit. Carriers and warehouses are common bailees. A **bill of lading** is a document of title used by carriers and freight forwarders. A bill of lading can also serve as the contract of carriage Exhibit 9.1). A **warehouse receipt** is a title document issued by a warehouse and it can also serve as the storage contract (Exhibit 9.2).

Documents of title may be nonnegotiable. However, when they are negotiable and physically accompany the flow of documents handled by trusted intermediaries, certainty rises significantly. An endorsement is required to transfer rights from the transferor to the transferee of a negotiable document of title. There is a special status for bona fide purchasers of negotiable documents of title, similar to the holder in due course status for commercial paper discussed later. During shipment, carriers must take reasonable care of the goods in their possession. Carriers must deliver them to the recipient, called a **consignee**, which is designated in the document of title. Similarly, warehouse operators must take reasonable care of goods in their possession, deliver them to the designated consignee, and accurately prepare the warehouse receipt. Risks that the goods may be lost, damaged, or stolen in transit are discussed later.

Electronic Commercial Documents

Negotiable documents can be processed electronically. Currently, this is largely done within secure Electronic Data Interchange (EDI) systems operating among regular trading partners who previously agreed to use electronic commercial documents. However, as UETA is proven reliable, electronic commercial documents will migrate from EDI into more general practice. Theoretically, documents need not physically accompany the goods in transit. Indeed, printed documents cannot physically accompany electronic deliveries of information or software. Instead, various electronic methods may cause electronic documents to arrive right before or soon after the goods arrive. They could directly accompany electronic delivery of information or software. For example, documents showing endorsements can be transferred by fax machine, scanned for attachment to e-mail messages, downloaded from a secure Web site, or sent via EDI.

An original document is first prepared, perhaps by word processor in ASCII characters or by a Web page development tool using the HTML Web markup language. Perhaps a more suitable and emerging new language is **XML**, extensible markup language. XML is broader than HTML, it permits the use of graphics for diagrams, and designers can construct forms for easy and accurate data storage and retrieval. Alternatively, the document can be printed for faxing, or an electronic version can be transmitted via computerized facsimile, sent as an e-mail attachment, or uploaded or downloaded through a secure Web site. As the electronic document is transmitted electronically, all necessary intermediaries can apply their endorsements. Endorsements can be written signatures made either on the original or on a copy printed from the electronic version or made by using some other acceptable electronic signature technology (e.g., encryption). Further endorsement and transfer can be made physically or by another electronic conversion that uses the same or a different technique, such as fax, e-mail, scanning, Web access, or

Exhibit 9.1 Bill of Lading

BILL OF LADING

Shipper	
Consignee: (Complete name and address)	Forwarding agent
	Point and country of origin / Place of receipt
Notify party	Domestic routing instructions
Pier	Place of delivery
Ocean vessel / Port of landing	
Point of discharge	

CARRIER'S RECEIPT		PARTICULARS FURNISHED BY SHIPPER		
Marks and numbers	Number of packages	Description of goods	Gross weight	Measurement

- Received in apparent good order and condition except as otherwise noted hereon the goods, containers, or other packages for transportation from the place of receipt or port of loading subject to exceptions, limitations, and conditions and to be delivered to the consignee or assigns.

(TERMS OF THIS BILL LADING CONTINUED ON REVERSE.)

TOTAL FREIGHTS $ _____

DATE _____   BY _____
                                                              (Agent)

Exhibit 9.2 Warehouse Receipt
WAREHOUSE RECEIPT—NOT NEGOTIABLE

Receipt and lot number _____ Vault no. ____ ____ ____ ____ ____

____ ____ ____ ____ ____

Date of issue _____ 20 _____

Received for the account of and deliverable to _____
of (address) _____
the goods enumerated on attached schedule and stored in Company warehouse, located at
_____. These goods are
accepted upon the following conditions.

That the value of all goods stored is not over $ _____ per pound
unless a higher value is noted on the schedule, for which an additional monthly storage charge of
$ _____ on each $ _____ will be made.

Ownership. The Customer, Shipper, Depositor, or Agent represents and warrants that he is lawfully possessed of goods to be stored and/or has the authority to store or ship said goods. (If the goods are mortgaged, notify the Company of the name and address of the mortgagee.)

Payment of Charges. Storage bills are payable monthly in advance for each month's storage or fraction thereof. The Depositor will pay reasonable attorney's fee incurred by the Company in collecting delinquent accounts.

Liability of Company. The Company shall be liable for any loss or injury to the goods caused by its failure to exercise such care as a reasonably careful person would exercise under like circumstances. The Company will not be liable for loss or damage to fragile articles not packed, or articles packed or unpacked by other than employees of this Company.

Change of Address. Notice of change of address must be given the Company in writing, and acknowledged in writing by the Company.

Transfer or Withdrawal of Goods. The warehouse receipt is not negotiable and shall be produced and all charges must be paid before delivery to the Depositor, or transfer of goods to another person; however, a written direction to the Company to transfer the goods to another person or deliver the goods may be accepted by the Company at its option without requiring tender of the warehouse receipt.

Access to Storage, Partial Withdrawal. A signed order from the person whose name the receipt is issued is required to enable others to remove or have access to goods. A charge is made for stacking and unstacking, and for access to stored goods.

Building-Fire-Watchmen. The Company does not represent or warrant that its building cannot be destroyed by fire. The Company shall not be required to maintain a watchman or sprinkler system and its failure to do so shall not constitute negligence.

Claims or Errors. All claims for non delivery of any article or articles and for any damage, breakage, etc., must be made in writing within ninety (90) days from delivery of goods stored or they are waived. Failure to return the warehouse receipt for correction within _____ ( ) days after receipt thereof by the depositor will be conclusive that it is correct and delivery will be made only in accordance therewith.

Warehouseman's Lien. The Company reserves the right to sell the goods stored, in accordance with the provisions of the Uniform Commercial Code (Business and Commerce Code if stored in Texas), for all lawful charges in areas.

Termination of Storage. The Company reserves the right to terminate the storage of the goods at any time by giving to the Depositor thirty (30) days' written notice of its intention to do so, and, unless the Depositor removes such goods within that period, the Company is hereby empowered to have the same removed at the cost and expense of the Depositor, or the Company may sell them at auction in accordance with state law.

THIS DOCUMENT CONTAINS THE WHOLE CONTRACT BETWEEN THE PARTIES AND THERE ARE NO OTHER TERMS, WARRANTIES, REPRESENTATIONS, OR AGREEMENTS OF EITHER DEPOSITOR OR COMPANY NOT HEREIN CONTAINED.

Storage per month or fraction thereof $ _____	Wrapping and preparing for storage $ _____
Warehouse labor $ _____	Charges advanced $ _____
Cartage $ _____	$ _____	$ _____
Packing at residence $ _____	$ _____	$ _____
	By _____

some future developed electronic or digital communication method. As UETA and the federal E-SIGN law are expanded to cover more types of commercial documents, endorsements may alternatively be made with electronic signatures on electronic records.

As of this writing, neither UETA nor the federal E-SIGN law applies to checks, notes, drafts, or letters of credit. The banking industry has reliable systems and may want to await the proven security of newer systems. However, experience with EDI and the electronic negotiation of real estate promissory notes should eventually demonstrate a workable model for electronic negotiable instruments of all types. As the banking system becomes able to reliably process electronic checks, simple changes in the UETA and E-SIGN exceptions for electronic transferable documents may expand their use. Chapter 8 introduced UETA's approach to electronic commercial documents.

Under UETA §16 and the federal E-SIGN law, electronic **transferable records** can be used as negotiable documents if the parties expressly agree to use them. However, for now, UETA permits the use of electronic transferable records for only real estate promissory notes and documents of title. The mortgage industry appears ready to reduce the paperwork expenses of negotiable documents. The federal E-SIGN law is even more restrictive, in that it permits electronic transferable records for only real estate promissory notes. By permitting electronic promissory notes for real estate loans, UETA and E-SIGN facilitate cost savings for the secondary mortgage industry. All the federal E-SIGN exceptions will be reviewed by 2003, and some exceptions may then be removed by Congress or by federal regulators. The states might also expand coverage to other types of commercial paper.

Like their paper counterparts, transferable records must be created, transferred, and stored under secure conditions that permit only one party at a time to control or possess them. Absent forgery in the paper world, when a negotiable instrument is transferred, it is no longer held by the transferor, only by the transferee. Significant technological difficulties must be overcome before many computer systems could be sufficiently reliable and secure to assure such exclusive control over transferable records. For example, after an electronic transfer, the sending system must be prevented from having any control over the record, and the recipient must have exclusive control. Some possible combination of security methods is needed, including encryption, physical access controls, and/or third parties that record every transfer. Endorsement could be approved or made by humans who review each transaction by computer. Alternatively, the electronic agent provisions of UETA and E-SIGN are intended to permit cost savings with computerized transaction processing and endorsement via electronic agents.

Like many citizens, some courts are suspicious of the validity of electronic documents. Electronic commercial documents must have enough security to build confidence that the system is not prone to alteration, forgery, or other fraud. Based on recent case rulings, key commercial concepts, such as title, require reliable evidence, and the Internet may have a long way to go before it builds confidence that it is accurate.

Warranty of Title

The UCC implies in every contract for sale that the seller has the right to sell the goods, there are no outstanding liens on the goods, and the seller can pass good title to the buyer. This is known as the **warranty of title**. It differs from express warranties and implied warranties of fitness or merchantability, which address product quality, not ownership. For example, the warranty of title would make the seller liable if the true owner of stolen goods were to reclaim them from the buyer after the sale. The warranty of title can be specifically disclaimed. It does not arise if the circumstances suggest the goods are of questionable origin, such as in a sheriff's sale. However, a general statement disclaiming "all warranties" does not eliminate the warranty of title. UCITA's noninterference and noninfringement warranty would serve a function similar to the warranty of title.

Risk of Loss

Risk of loss is still important because goods can be damaged, lost, or stolen during shipment. Loss may result from an intentional act, negligence, or a natural catastrophe. Importantly, before risk of loss passes to the buyer, the seller is liable for breach of contract if a loss occurs. By contrast, after risk of loss passes to the buyer, the purchase price must be paid even if the goods are damaged or lost. Therefore, the parties have conflicting incentives for the timing when they shift the risk of loss. One sensible risk management technique is for both parties to insure the goods during transit. The buyer has the right to insure, called an **insurable interest**, as soon as the goods are identified, and the seller retains an insurable interest for as long as the seller has either title or a security interest (lien) in the goods.

Passage of risk of loss is made according to numerous technical rules. First, the parties may specify in their contract when risk passes. Second, if they do not include such a term and no carrier is used to transport the goods, then risk passes when a nonmerchant seller tenders delivery to the buyer or a merchant seller makes actual delivery to the buyer. Third, when a carrier is used, risk generally passes at either the point of the shipment's origin or at the point of arrival at the destination according to the **mercantile terms** used: FOB, FAS, CIF, C&F, or Ex-Ship. Mercantile terms are established by the UCC and are called **INCOTERMS** by the International Chamber of Commerce. See Exhibit 9.3 for common mercantile terms.

ONLINE

International Chamber of Commerce
http://www.iccwbo.org

Consider the example of goods shipped from a Pittsburgh manufacturer to a Detroit wholesaler. In an "FOB Pittsburgh" contract, risk and title pass when the seller tenders the goods to the carrier in Pittsburgh. In an "FOB Detroit" contract, risk and title pass when the carrier makes actual delivery of the goods to the buyer in Detroit. The risk remains on the seller in a **sale on approval** until the buyer confirms the purchase after testing or other trial period. Risk remains with the buyer in a **sale or return** until the goods are returned to the seller. If the goods are rightfully rejected or there is a rightful revocation of acceptance by the buyer, risk reverts to the seller. These latter two remedies are discussed later in this chapter.

Exhibit 9.3 Mercantile Terms

Mercantile Abbreviation	Mercantile Term	Mercantile Term Meaning
FOB	Free on board	Requires payment of freight charges: (1) by buyer if FOB (named place of seller's shipment), (2) by seller if FOB (named place of buyer's destination), (3) by seller if FOB (named carrier vessel, car, or vehicle). Title and risk of loss pass from seller to buyer at the named place.
FAS	Free alongside	Requires seller to deliver goods alongside vessel designated by buyer. Title and risk of loss pass from seller to buyer alongside the vessel.
CIF (CF)	Cost, insurance, freight	Seller's price includes cost of goods, loading, transit, insurance, and freight charges for transport to the named destination. Seller must contract for the transportation. Title and risk of loss pass from seller to buyer when the goods are delivered to the carrier.
C&F	Cost and freight	Seller's price includes cost of goods, loading, and freight charges for transport to the named destination. Seller must contract for the transportation. Title and risk of loss pass from seller to buyer when the goods are delivered to the carrier.
Ex-Ship	Ex-Ship	Requires unloading of goods from ship at named port; title and risk of loss pass from seller to buyer when unloaded.

THIRD-PARTY RIGHTS

One might think that only the contracting parties may seek enforcement of their contracts. However, in four distinct situations, outsiders have legally enforceable rights or responsibilities in the contracts of other persons or firms. The first two situations involve contracts that specifically identify and intend an outside third party to receive contractual benefits. Such third parties are either creditor beneficiaries or donee beneficiaries. The third and fourth situations arise when a contracting party transfers to an outsider either contractual rights or contractual duties under an existing contract. In such situations, the outsider may enforce the contract or could be required to perform a contractual duty.

Third-Party Beneficiaries

An outsider intentionally identified as a beneficiary to receive the performance is an **obligee** in the original contract and is known as a **third-party beneficiary**, illustrated in Exhibit 9.4. The party who must make the performance is the **obligor**. A third-party beneficiary may enforce the contract against the original obligor. If the person who is promised a performance intends that the contract should confer a gift on the third party, then the third party has no right to sue this promisee. For example, assume someone purchases flowers from a florist, intending them to be a gift for the purchaser's spouse. The spouse, known as a **donee third-party beneficiary**, could enforce the contract against the florist as obligor, but obviously not against the spouse who purchased the flowers. The spouse conferring the gift simply used the florist's services to make the gift. The donee of a gift cannot generally sue the donor for the performance.

Contrast the restrictions on donee third-party beneficiaries with the greater rights of third parties who were previously owed a duty by the promisee. If the promisee uses the obligor to discharge a *duty already owed* to the third-party beneficiary, this is a **creditor third-party beneficiary** situation. Creditor beneficiaries may enforce the obligation against *either* of the contracting parties. The promisee was already previously liable to the third party because that duty preexisted, independent of the third-party beneficiary contract. For example, a home sale contract might identify the

Exhibit 9.4 Third-Party Beneficiary

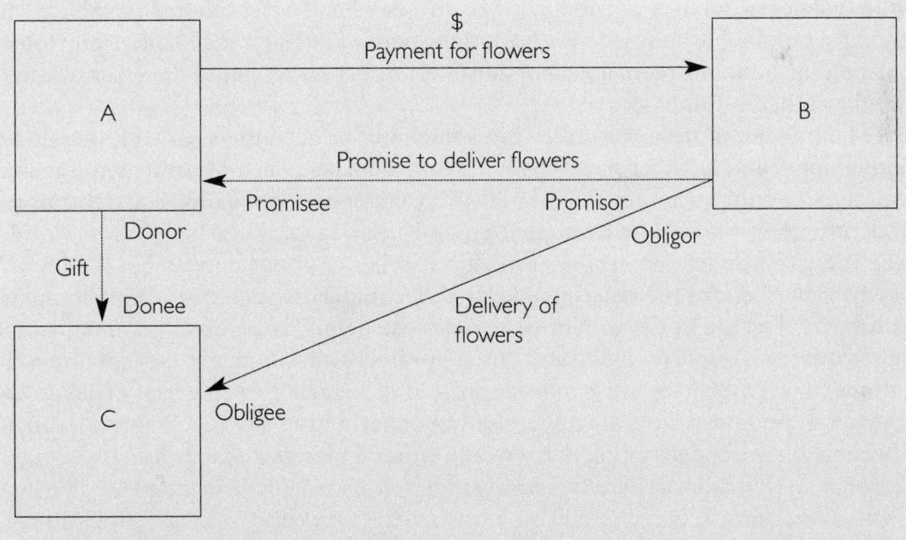

A buys flowers from B to be delivered to C, and the contract between A and B identifies C as the recipient of B's performance. Thus, C is a donee third-party beneficiary of the contract between A and B. C may require B , but not A, to perform the contract.

seller's lender as a creditor third-party beneficiary. If the buyer assumes the seller's mortgage and promises to repay the original mortgage loan, the lender can generally sue either the seller or the buyer. The seller is liable as the original borrower, and the buyer voluntarily assumed the duty to pay. Unless the bank releases the seller from making the payments in a **novation** contract, the bank may sue either the seller or the buyer for loan default, because the seller originally borrowed the money and the buyer promised to perform to the lender on the original loan.

Some outsiders are mere **incidental beneficiaries**. Incidental beneficiaries receive benefit only by coincidence from the side effects produced by others' contracts. These side effects are called **externalities**, or benefits enjoyed by outsiders who are not contracting parties. Incidental beneficiaries have no rights to enforce the contract because they are neither identified in the contract nor intended to benefit from it. For example, contracts for the construction of a new factory often generate significant economic benefits for the surrounding community. However, community members cannot enforce the construction contracts because they are merely unintended and incidental beneficiaries.

Assignment and Delegation

Contract rights and/or duties are sometimes transferred to an outsider in a separate contract. Such **transfer contracts** are often made after the original contract. The law distinguishes between the **assignment of rights** to enforce the original contract, (Exhibit 9.5) and the **delegation of duties** to perform under the original contract (Exhibit 9.6). Consider the sale of a business. The seller assigns rights to enforce contract duties owed to the business *from* others (e.g., accounts receivable) and usually delegates duties previously owed *to* outsiders (e.g., accounts payable). The purchaser of the business receives both rights and duties so it may collect previously outstanding accounts receivable and must perform contract duties the seller formerly owed to other customers.

The transfer of rights or duties can sometimes be accomplished without getting permission from the other party to the original contract. Such unconsented transfers are effective only when they do not materially change the obligations or rights of the nonconsenting party. For example, a wholesaler may assign past-due accounts receivable to a collection agency or factor. A seller of goods may assign the buyer's payment by check to the seller's bank for collection. These debtors cannot complain as long as they are notified. Notice permits the debtor to redirect payment to the new payee, the assignee. Rights and duties are freely transferable if they involve obligations to pay money or are standard repair and construction contracts. The test for transferability focuses on the nonconsenting contracting party. A transfer is unenforceable if the nonconsenting party would suffer a **material change** in duty or right. Personal service contracts are typical examples of unassignable or nondelegable contracts. Nevertheless, it is possible for the original contractor to grant permission for the assignment or delegation, consenting to substitute the new party as assignee or delegate. The original contract can validly limit delegation. Assignment is a commonplace technique, particularly in the endorsement and transfer by negotiation of payments and other commercial documents, as discussed next.

Exhibit 9.5 Assignment of Rights

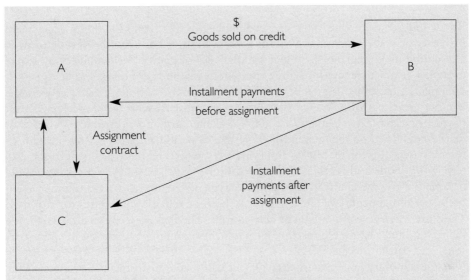

A's account receivable is factored to C, an assignment of rights. C is the factor that obtains the right to receive the installment payments that B originally promised to A. B's consent is necessary only for the assignment of personal services, not this payment duty.

Exhibit 9.6 Delegation of Duties

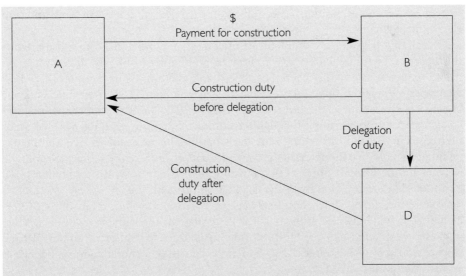

B's obligation to perform construction services is delegated to D. In this delegation of a duty, D is the delegate that becomes obligated to perform the construction services to A. A's consent is necessary to delegate personal services and also to release B's original duty to perform.

PAYMENT SYSTEMS

By the Industrial Revolution, commerce had evolved beyond the limits of payment by barter or cash. Fundamental to the growth in trade has been the development of alternatives to concurrent payment and delivery of goods. Performances by barter or money (e.g., currency) for large transactions in goods, services, and land are seldom made simultaneously by both sides. Key to this evolutionary advance were the banking practices of medieval European **mercantilists**, who developed important payment mechanisms. Generally, today's documentary and electronic payment systems are modeled on the mercantilists' system of permitting the transfer of **rights to receive payment** given by buyers and borrowers, who used these payment documents to pay for goods and services. The mercantilists' customs and practices eventually became the law merchant. Documentary payments facilitated trade, and they eventually permitted negotiable instruments to become reliable substitutes for currency. These are very successful payment mechanisms. The Federal Reserve processes more than 50 billion negotiable instrument payments annually, mostly the familiar personal and corporate checks.

Contemporary law encourages payment with paper instruments and increasingly with electronic alternatives. This transactional infrastructure was made possible as lawmakers recognized that uniformity among the states and between nations is needed to facilitate commerce. The payments section of this chapter discusses the traditional paper-based payment schemes governed by UCC Article 3, "Commercial Paper," and Article 4, "Bank Deposits." Also, electronic payment schemes are discussed, including Article 4A covering electronic funds transfers, Federal Reserve System rules on debit, point of sale, and credit card transactions, and innovations in electronic payments.

Recall that negotiable documents of title, discussed previously, are processed by third parties, including carriers, warehouses, and banks. Similarly, negotiable payments are processed by the seller, the seller's bank, the buyer's bank, and other intermediaries. When the buyer pays using commercial paper, the seller accepts the buyer's check or note as the buyer's performance. Typically, the seller then negotiates the paper, transferring it through the banking system by endorsement for eventual payment by the buyer or the buyer's bank. This concept of **negotiability** is essential to making commercial paper an adequate substitute for money. Negotiable instruments are formal contracts that must meet strict requirements for contents and location. They are transferred by the negotiation process. The law gives a special status to intermediaries, which stand between the payor and payee, to encourage intermediaries to willingly accept the paper in exchange for the value it represents. Most of these intermediaries become **bona fide purchasers for value** or **holders in due course,** who are given greater rights than are assignees of a simple, informal contract as just discussed.

DEFINITIONS

UCC Article 3 covers two types of commercial paper: notes and drafts. A **note** (promissory note, installment note, collateral note, mortgage note) is a *two-party* instrument in which the **maker** promises to pay the **payee** a specified amount in the future. A bank's **certificate of deposit** (CD) is a type of note in which the bank acknowledges the receipt (deposit) of customer funds and promises to repay them at a future time with interest. A **draft** is a *three-party* instrument in which a **drawer** issues a draft that orders a **drawee**, usually the drawer's bank, to pay money to the third-party payee. **Checks** are the most common form of draft. When a drawer writes the check, it directs their drawee bank to pay the specified amount of money to the payee or to someone else to whom the payee endorsed the check. Other forms of draft are widely used in commerce. For example, the **time draft** is payable on a specified date in the future, possibly days, months, or even years away. A **sight draft** is payable on sight—that is, immediately when presented and after a demand is made for payment. A **trade acceptance** is a commercial draft used to pay for goods (also known as a **sales draft**). It can be drawn by the seller of goods on the buyer's bank and sent for the buyer's approval.

NEGOTIABILITY

Negotiable instruments must meet strict rules of form to facilitate accurate and efficient verification of the terms and validity. This regularity encourages participants in the banking system to willingly take the paper by assignment in exchange for value, usually by paying money for the paper or crediting a customer's bank account. Can you imagine the commercial difficulty if sellers and their banks would not accept documentary payments?

Commercial paper must meet the negotiability requirements of UCC §3-104 by being strictly (1) in writing and (2) signed by the maker or drawer, (3) containing unconditional promise or order to pay, (4) indicating a fixed amount of money (sum certain), (6) being payable on demand or at a definite time and (7) payable to order or to bearer, and (8) containing no other undertaking. These requirements create certainty, reducing the risk of forgeries or fraud by imposters. The migration to electronic payments over many years has been slow but steady to permit management of these risks and thereby retain stability in the banking and financial systems.

The writing requirement permits the use of handwritten, typed, preprinted, or mixed inscriptions in a tangible form. Although the use of paper is traditional, it is unnecessary. Computer and telecommunication transfers are covered by UCC Article 4A on electronic funds transfers. The **signature** may be handwritten in cursive or printing; supplied by stamp, computer, or check-cutting device; or provided by some other mechanized form or symbol intended to authenticate a writing. UETA does not yet require use of electronic signatures on notes or drafts. However, if favorable experience accumulates, the states or the Federal Reserve may expand UETA's coverage to electronic payments. Importantly, forgeries do not obligate the maker or drawer who is wrongly named on a forged instrument.

Notes and drafts must include an **unconditional promise or order to pay**, thereby setting the terms of payment. A **promise** makes a commitment to pay. By contrast, a simple IOU is not a promise to pay because it is merely an acknowledgment of a debt. Alternatively, an **order** directs some agent to make the payment. Typically, an order directs the customer's bank or lender to make the payment. The payment cannot be made conditional on some event or on another agreement; otherwise, no one would freely accept such paper in commerce. For example, a promissory note would be nonnegotiable if it was written by a buyer who included an express condition that the payment promise was not binding until the payee (e.g., seller) delivered specified goods. Similarly, paper is nonnegotiable if made expressly subject to or governed by some other writing or contract like a warranty. Why? Banks and other intermediaries would have no easy way to confirm whether the goods were delivered, and they could not easily verify the contents of some other writing. Banks would probably be reluctant to accept such conditional paper if extra work was needed to verify other documents.

Many people write notations on their checks. It is permissible for commercial paper to merely mention another obligation or writing without destroying negotiability. For example, check writers often use a memo line in the lower left-hand corner to reference a particular payment, invoice number, transaction, or the underlying contract. It is also permissible to state that a note is secured with a lien on specified collateral. A payment can be limited to be taken from a particular fund, such as when a customer's check is drawn against only one of several accounts held in a particular bank.

Instruments are negotiable only if the extent of the obligation can be easily ascertained by looking *only* at the paper. Importantly, a **fixed sum of money** (sum certain) must be stated. Nevertheless, some adjustments are permissible. For example, interest may be stated at a specified rate. A formula can state the applicable interest if it is clearly stated on the paper or can be determined by an index that is generally available as a published rate (e.g., "three points over prime rate"). Variable-rate paper is now negotiable under the 1990 revision to UCC Article 3. Paper remains negotiable even if the fixed amount can be adjusted by a stated discount for early payment or a premium charged for late payments. There can also be adjustments for additional costs of collection, such as attorney's fees. Payment must be promised or ordered only **in money**—that is, domestic or foreign currency sanctioned by a government. Payment promised in foreign currency can also be paid in domestic currency; the exchange rate is determined at the spot market rate quoted by banks as prevailing on the date of payment. However, payment cannot be promised or ordered in goods, services, or other intangible, nonmoney credits. A check to pay in gold leaf, cigarettes, bus tokens, frequent flyer miles, or some Internet currency is nonnegotiable even if such "currency" becomes acceptable as a medium of exchange in some communities. This is the most important requirement restraining the use of traditional payment mechanisms in electronic form by using nonmoney credits, as discussed later.

Negotiable paper must make it clear *when* payment is promised or authorized. There is a "time value of money." Intermediaries are willing to handle commercial paper only if their obligations and rights can be determined easily. A **demand instrument** is payable "on demand," when presented, or "at sight" if no time is stated, like most personal checks. Many notes and time drafts are often made payable at a definite future time on a specified date. Sellers and lenders take these instruments as a form of credit, effectively giving the buyer some time to settle up. The **definite time** that payment will be made must be readily ascertainable when the instrument is originally made. Negotiable time instruments include those made payable a fixed period after a stated date (30 days after June 1, 2002), on or before a particular date (payable October 30, 2003), on stated alternate dates, or payable on some other readily ascertainable date. However, paper is nonnegotiable if made payable only after some uncertain event. For example, a note made payable "after I sell my house" is nonnegotiable because when or whether the house might be sold is uncertain. Notes remain negotiable even if they contain an **acceleration clause**, giving the holder a right to demand early payment for some stated reason. For example, it is common in real estate purchases for the buyer to borrow much of the purchase price. The real estate loan is evidenced by a note that may include an acceleration clause requiring full and early repayment if the owner sells the house before the loan is completely repaid. Borrowers are also often given the right to prepay their loan early without destroying their note's negotiability. A note remains negotiable even if the holder is given the right to extend payment to some later date as stated on the note. However, it is nonnegotiable if the maker alone can extend payment.

Commercial paper must contain the **magic words of negotiability**, "payable to order or bearer," which signals intermediaries that they should willingly take the paper because it will flow freely to others and ultimately the maker or drawee will honor the payment. **Bearer paper** is negotiable by anyone who rightfully possesses it. For example, "pay to bearer," "pay to Joan Doe or bearer," and "pay to cash" all contain sufficient magic words of negotiability. **Order paper** is somewhat more restrictive than bearer paper because only a stated person can rightfully demand payment. Order paper requires negotiation; usually an endorsement must be supplied by the person named in the order or by someone else who is the rightful transferee. For example, order paper is negotiable if there are magic words such as "pay to the order of Joan Doe" or "payable to the assigns of John Doe." However, paper is nonnegotiable if it says only "pay to Joan Doe" because this does not encourage intermediaries to handle the paper. The person must be clearly identified, by name, account number, or office. Some preprinted forms use both order and bearer language such as "pay to the order of ___*named person*___ or bearer," and a specific name will be written into the blank when issued. Paper with both order and bearer language is treated as bearer paper. By a special UCC exception, checks commonly indicate "pay to the order of ___*named person*___" but remain negotiable even if the maker crosses out the wording "~~to the order~~" or if the preprinted form says simply "pay to _____."

A negotiable instrument may be antedated, postdated, or undated without affecting its validity. Written words are given preference over contradictory numeric writing, so the written amount on a personal check must be honored even if the numerals do not match. Handwritten terms are given preference over typed or preprinted terms, and typewritten terms are given preference over preprinted terms. An incomplete instrument may be completed by some authorized person. Consider a blank check that the maker authorizes someone else to fill in with the correct purchase price. It is enforceable. However, a blank check completed for a higher amount contains a **material alteration**. The negotiability of instruments must be readily determinable by looking only at the instrument itself for the elements discussed here. These elements must all appear on the face of the paper, with the few

Exhibit 9.7 Negotiability Determined on Face of Draft

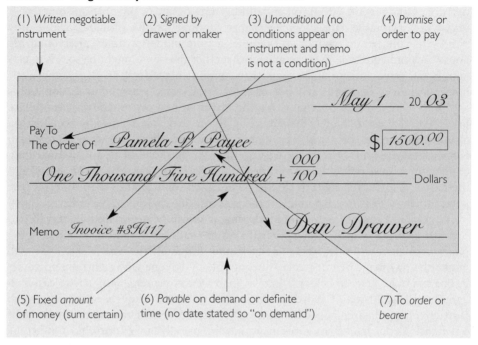

exceptions noted. Exhibit 9.7 illustrates the formal negotiable instrument requirements appearing directly on a check.

NEGOTIATION AND TRANSFER

The transfer of commercial paper is much like an assignment of contract rights covering the right to receive the stated payment. However, in commercial practice, intermediaries generally want better rights than would exist for an assignee under a simple contract. An assignee of a simple contract receives only the rights held by the assignor, nothing more. However, to encourage their participation, commercial paper law adds a special status for intermediaries that transfer the paper. To achieve this special status, it is not enough that the instrument be in the formal negotiable form just discussed. The instrument must be transferred and assigned by due negotiation. Intermediaries thus have a special status, called a holder in due course, generally assuring that payment will be free from many defenses the original maker might assert against a normal contract assignee. Obviously, some clarification and context for the concept of the holder in due course is now needed.

When a maker or drawer initially drafts the instrument and makes the first delivery to another person, this is known as **issue**. Most paper is subsequently delivered many times in later **transfers** from **transferors** to **transferees**. Consider an individual who issues a personal check. First, the check may be issued by the drawer to a merchant in exchange—that is, as payment—for goods or services. The merchant is a transferee who further transfers the check to the merchant's own bank in exchange for crediting the merchant's account by the check amount. The check is likely to be negotiated further—that is, transferred through other correspondent banks— and is ultimately presented for payment to the drawee, which is the buyer's bank. **Negotiation** is a special type of transfer to a **holder** who rightfully possesses (has actual physical control) and has good title (ownership) to the instrument. Anyone in rightful possession of bearer paper has good title. Clearly, it is less risky to make paper to order, to endorse with restrictions, and to safeguard negotiable instruments as if they were cash. Order paper is negotiated when the previous holder physically transfers it after making an endorsement. Endorsement shows the transferor knowingly grants the transferee rights in the paper. If paper is made payable to multiple transferees in the conjunctive (e.g., "to Jack *and* Julia") then both must indorse. If the paper is made payable in the disjunctive (e.g., "to Jack *or* Julia") then either of their endorsements alone will suffice.

Endorsements

An **endorsement** is the signature of a payee, usually made on the back of the instrument. An endorsement is not invalid if it corrects a misspelling or changes the name to that of the holder. If the payee's name is misspelled, it is preferable to endorse by spelling the name both ways. An endorsement can broaden or limit further negotiation. In a **blank endorsement**, the payee simply supplies her or his signature converting the paper from order to bearer paper. In a **special endorsement** the payee supplies a signature but restricts further negotiation to a person named in the special endorsement. This implies that it retains order paper status because it is made to the order of only the newly named person. For example, compare the endorsements on the back of two checks made payable to John Doe in Exhibits 9.8 and 9.9. John's blank endorsement in Exhibit 9.8 makes the order paper into bearer paper. However, in Exhibit 9.9 John alternatively made a special endorsement over to "pay to Joan Roe." This endorsement serves as a security measure because it preserves the check's character as order paper that can be lawfully negotiated by only one person, Joan Roe. Bearer paper can be given a special endorsement, which converts it into order paper.

A **restrictive endorsement** that adds some condition generally does not destroy negotiability. Some restrictive endorsements are ignored. For example, assume the payee John Doe adds the restriction to "pay only if the maker performs the contract." This is a restrictive endorsement, but the added words would not be given any effect. By contrast, further negotiation can be somewhat restricted, such as transfer only through the banking system. "Pay any bank" and "for deposit only" are common and enforceable restrictive endorsements that do not destroy negotiability. For example, anyone giving cash for a stolen check with the restrictive endorsement "for deposit only" may be required to pay a second time to the check's rightful owner.

All endorsers are presumed to make **unqualified endorsements;** that is, they imply that they promise to pay on any instrument they endorse if it is not paid

Exhibit 9.8 Blank Endorsement

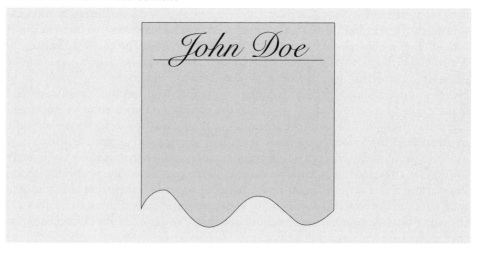

Exhibit 9.9 Special Endorsement

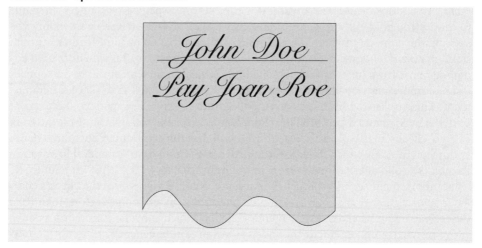

when due. Therefore, all intermediaries usually must deal with a bounced check if the drawee bank dishonors the check for insufficient funds or other reasons. Any endorser may limit this risk by making a **qualified endorsement** by endorsing and writing "without recourse" on the back. Of course, qualified endorsements reduce the willingness of further intermediaries to accept or give value for the paper.

Forged endorsements on bearer paper are irrelevant because the forged endorsement is unnecessary to negotiate. Recall that the bearer need only tender delivery, not supply an endorsement. However, forgeries might be unlawfully used to negotiate order paper. A forgery is ineffective to pass title. Therefore, understanding the **chain of title** on the paper becomes important if forgery is suspected. This often requires identifying each transferor and each successive transferee, noting dates where possible. Although a forged drawer or maker's signature will not obligate the true drawer or maker, it does not affect the holder's status with respect to others in the chain of title. Therefore, the ultimate dishonor gives holders the right to collect from their immediate transferors. This complex concept is discussed next.

Holders in Due Course

Intermediaries in the banking system are encouraged to participate in transferring payment rights so long as they need not worry that they have much risk if the commercial paper is dishonored. Holders can obtain an even more special status as a **holder in due course (HDC)** if they take a transfer of an instrument (1) for **value,** (2) in **good faith,** and (3) **without notice** of any defenses or another's claim to the paper. The HDC's special status is much better than that of a contract assignee or even another holder. Ordinary assignees take commercial paper or other contract rights subject to *any* defense the maker or drawer could assert in the original and underlying contract. The HDC takes commercial paper free of such **personal defenses,** which encourages intermediaries to participate in handling commercial paper. For example, assume a retailer purchases goods from a wholesaler and pays with a nonnegotiable promissory note. Because it is nonnegotiable, the wholesaler then assigns (factors) the note to a finance company, which immediately pays the wholesaler a discounted amount in cash. What effect on negotiability is there if the wholesaler fails to deliver the goods as promised or if the goods actually delivered breach the warranty? The finance company is an assignee of a simple contract right to receive the buyer's payment. The finance company could not force the buyer to pay because the seller has breached the contract.

Commercial practice has developed the HDC as a special status to encourage intermediaries such as banks and finance companies to willingly handle notes and drafts. The HDC takes commercial paper free of personal defenses to the underlying contract; that is, the HDC will not be denied payment even if the maker or drawer has the personal defense of breach of contract against the seller who was the original payee.

The HDC must give value for the instrument; otherwise, there would be no out-of-pocket losses to protect. Generally, value is given if the HDC pays money for the transfer of the paper. However, the value given will also be sufficient when the HDC acquires the paper as collateral, takes the paper as payment for a separate, previous debt (antecedent claim), gives another negotiable instrument in exchange (e.g., pays for a note with a check), or makes an irrevocable obligation to a third party (e.g., issues a letter of credit). Banks usually give value when they pay out cash in return for a check or when a customer's account is given unrestricted credit for the amount of a deposited check. HDC status is given only to a holder who takes the paper in **good faith**—that is, honesty in fact—a subjective standard that inquires whether the person actually knew of any wrongdoing.

The UCC imposes an objective standard of sincerity by prohibiting HDC status to a holder with any *notice* (actually knew) of several specified problems: The paper is overdue, is unpaid after demand, or was accelerated; the paper was obviously altered or forged; the paper was dishonored; or anyone has defenses or claims to payment on the underlying transaction. Checks are presumed overdue 90 days after the issue date, so intermediaries after that date are not HDCs. Nevertheless, the drawee bank may still pay such a check if sufficient funds are available.

Later transferees from an HDC inherit the HDC's special status under the **shelter rule**. Unless a transferee from an HDC was a party to the fraud, the transferee also shares the HDC's special rights to ignore personal defenses in the underlying transaction. For example, assume the buyer of goods issued a note to a seller who, in turn, negotiated the note to an HDC. If the HDC made a gift of the note to his spouse, the spouse would have HDC protections, even though the spouse gave no value to the HDC in return.

The HDC takes free of personal defenses; that is, the HDC can demand payment even if the original maker or drawer can assert a defense against the original payee. Personal defenses include the usual contract law defenses, such as breach of contract, fraud in the inducement (intentional misrepresentation), misrepresentation, mistake, failure of consideration, failure of a condition precedent, and impossibility. However, the HDC will take a negotiable instrument subject to real defenses. This means that in such cases the special HDC status is inapplicable and the HDC may be prevented from receiving payment. The following are **real defenses**: incapacity (incompetence, infancy), fraud in the execution (tricked into signing the wrong instrument, such as a note rather than an autograph as pretended), instrument discharged in bankruptcy, forgery, material alteration, and illegality.

The Federal Trade Commission (FTC) has promulgated a rule that supersedes the HDC rule when the note's maker is a consumer purchasing goods or services. Consumers who purchase on credit can still assert personal defenses like breach of contract for the sale of the goods. The FTC rule constrains the transfer of consumer financing notes, which puts pressure on sellers of goods. If sellers breach the underlying sale contract, they risk holding all consumer financing contracts as their own receivables rather than easily factoring them for immediate cash to third-party finance companies.

LIABILITIES OF THE PARTIES

Holders, HDCs, and other intermediaries in the commercial banking system willingly participate because their rights and liabilities are predictable when a negotiable instrument is dishonored. UCC Article 3 provides for both contract liability and warranty liability. On these bases, most transferees are assured of recourse against either an immediate or remote transferor when a check bounces or a note is not paid. Many of these parties are not natural persons—for example, corporations—so their negotiable instruments are signed by their authorized agents. Only an authorized agent can obligate an entity to liability on an instrument. The agent is not personally liable on the instrument if the principal is identified and the agent clearly signs in a representative capacity.

Different forms of liability are implied by contract for nearly everyone signing a negotiable instrument. There is nearly absolute and unconditional **primary liability** for makers, drawers, and drawees after an instrument is accepted. Endorsers generally have only **secondary liability**; their liability is typically conditioned on certain events or rights. A maker is primarily liable to pay a note according to its terms. The drawer on a check or draft also has primary liability, but it does not arise unless the drawee dishonors the draft. A drawee is not primarily liable until acceptance of the draft by the drawee, which usually occurs after the drawee, usually a bank, verifies the drawer's signature and concludes that a sufficient balance is available to make the payment. However, if a check presented is not dishonored by midnight on the next business day, then it is accepted. Acceptance makes the drawee into an **acceptor**.

An endorser becomes secondarily liable after payment is refused. This happens after the holder made **presentment** of the instrument demanding payment from the drawee or maker; there was **dishonor** by inaction or refusing payment, and a **notice of dishonor** was given to the endorser, either orally, in writing, or electronically. A **protest** is a notarized certificate of dishonor sometimes used in international banking. As stated earlier, an endorser can avoid liability by endorsing "without recourse." If presentment of a check is not made within 30 days from the date of endorsement, the endorser no longer has endorser liability.

Endorsers are also liable to all subsequent transferees under five **implied warranties**: (1) the transferor had *good title* to the instrument, (2) *all signatures are authentic*, (3) the instrument has *no material alterations*, (4) there are *no claims or defenses* against the transferor, and (5) the endorser has *no knowledge of insolvency* by the maker, drawer, or acceptor. If one of the warranties is breached, an endorser may be liable to any subsequent transferee who gave value for the instrument. A subsequent transferee is someone later in the chain of title. Warranty liability is a further inducement, in addition to the protections provided by primary and secondary liability, to encourage holders to participate in handling paper. Both warranty and endorser liability can be disclaimed.

BANK RELATIONS WITH CUSTOMERS

UCC Article 4 governs bank relationships with its customers. The drawee bank is a debtor holding its customer funds, and the bank's customers are creditors, depositors, and drawers. A bank's basic obligation runs only to its customers, not to third-party holders who present checks for payment. The bank must **honor** drafts or other items by making payment upon presentment. Wrongful dishonor makes the bank liable to the bank's customer for compensatory damages that may arise if, for example, the drawer is arrested for bouncing the check. But, of course, banks need not pay an item if there are insufficient funds available on deposit.

Forgeries
The bank may charge the customer's account with properly paid items. However, in certain situations, the bank may not charge a customer's account or, if the bank

makes a mistaken payment, the account must be recredited for items with the following problems: (1) forged signatures of the drawer or an endorser, (2) altered items, (3) payments made before the date stated on the draft, or (4) payments made in violation of a valid stop-payment order.

Bank customers must use reasonable care by promptly examining each periodic bank statement for forgeries or bookkeeping errors. A customer who delays may lose the right to contest forgeries or material alterations. Banks can recover from anyone forging a necessary endorsement. The bank, not the customer, is liable for payment on an item with a forged drawer's signature. However, if the bank dishonors a check with a forged signature of a drawer or endorser or because the item has a material alteration (e.g., zeros added to raise dollar value), the first transferee who took the check from the forger bears the loss.

INTERNATIONAL SALES TRANSACTIONS

Domestic and international commercial law evolved from international practice and the law merchant. International sales transactions are generally far less certain than domestic transactions. The physical distance between parties grows, language and cultural barriers arise, currency fluctuations too quickly eliminate profitability, and the cross-border enforceability of contracts is uncertain in many legal systems. Indeed, some systems are outright hostile to foreigners. Commerce could be significantly reduced if the legal machinery was generally believed to be unreliable. To raise expectations, much of international law is designed to improve the reliability of commercial performances.

International Documentary Sales

The bill of lading is often transferred between the seller's bank and the buyer's bank. This practice permits payment to be conditioned on title transfer using negotiable document of title. Similarly, the simultaneously delivery and title transfer is conditioned on payment by draft or letter of credit. There are four major methods by which the international buyer makes payment. First, many buyers and sellers have long-standing and trusted relations, so the seller has well-founded confidence that a particular buyer, who has made reliable payment of prior bills, will again be "good for this payment." In such situations, sellers may ship based on the buyer's **open account** and expect timely payment in the near future or as agreed. Second, some sellers insist on **prepayment** from an unfamiliar buyer or from a buyer with uncertain credit risks. Of course, the risk shifts to buyers who prepay: The seller might default by not making delivery. Third, payment can be made by draft (e.g., bill of exchange, check, sight draft) payable out of the buyer's bank account or credit line. A seller authorized in the contract of sale may actually prepare the draft and send it to the buyer's bank for payment, along with the bill of lading. Such a sight draft is due immediately upon arrival at the buyer's bank. A time draft is not payable until some future date; essentially, the seller provides credit. The fourth method uses a letter of credit.

Letters of Credit

The buyer's method of payment in much of international commerce is a **letter of credit (L/C)**, a bank's documentary assurance to the seller that the buyer will pay. The L/C is based on the buyer's bank's creditworthiness and on its international reputation. To facilitate processing through the international banking system, L/Cs are often made negotiable. The L/C often accompanies the transaction documents. They can also be made nonnegotiable. **Standby L/Cs** are used for nonpayment purposes, such as performance bonds, guarantees, or other collateral.

In the United States, L/Cs are governed by UCC Article 5. However, most international L/C transactions specifically incorporate the **Uniform Customs and Practices for Documentary Credits (UCP)** issued by the International Chamber of Commerce (ICC). The newest revision of the UCP is **UCP 500**. The UCP governs when the L/C specifies the UPC. When there is any conflict between the UCP and the UCC, the UCC governs only if there is no UCP provision. Exhibit 9.10 shows a sample L/C form.

The typical international sales transaction using the L/C as payment involves four parties: (1) The buyer is the **account party**, who applies to (2) its bank, the **issuing bank**, to establish a line of credit and issue the L/C in favor of (3) the seller, the **L/C beneficiary**, and documents are forwarded and payments transmitted through (4) the seller's bank, known as either a **confirming bank** or **advising bank**. The whole process involves two other primary documents: the underlying contract for sale of goods and the bill of lading. Many international sales transactions also include one or more of the following supplementary documents and relationships: contract(s) of carriage with one or more common carriers, storage contracts with dock and warehouse facilities, customs clearances, inspection documents, the buyer's application for credit, insurance polic(ies), export licenses, certificates of origin, packing slips, and the relationship of trust built up between the two banks. The 1994 UCP revision creates greater flexibility for L/C parties to use new and electronic documents in international sales transactions. Carefully review the order and flow of documents in the typical L/C process as depicted in Exhibit 9.11.

The seller often prepares the primary documents after negotiating the sales contract with the buyer. All matters called for in the sale contract must be included exactly as they are stated in *all* the other documents. This is a strict form of the mirror image or perfect tender rule from contract law. It prohibits the issuing bank from paying on the L/C if there are *any* **discrepancies**—that is, major or even minor differences among the documents in the terms stated. For example, discrepancies include any variance among the documents in the goods description (e.g., size, quantity, quality, color, specifications), misspellings, missing documents like an inspection certificate, late delivery, different named shipping vessel or carrier, expired L/C, and most other errors.

This **strict compliance rule** is so exacting because time and cost pressures make banks generally unsuitable and unable to investigate or resolve discrepancies. Banks must examine L/C documents quickly, or they are presumed to accept them and then become obligated to pay on the L/C. UCC Article 5 gives domestic banks just three

Exhibit 9.10 Letter of Credit

Date: April 6, 1992

Call 828-8327 concerning inquiries on Documents submitted under this letter of Credit.

CREDIT NUMBER

| **DOCUMENTARY CREDIT—IRREVOCABLE** | Of Issuing Bank   0/00/000   Our No.   0000000 |
| FOR ACCOUNT OF | CORRESPONDENT |

| BENEFICIARY | AMOUNT |

FOR ACCOUNT OF

Taiwan Steel Products Co., Ltd.
Taipei
Taiwan

CORRESPONDENT

First Bank
Taipei
Taiwan

BENEFICIARY

John Doe Exporters, Inc.
Chicago, Illinois
U.S.A.

AMOUNT

Six Thousand and
00/100 U.S. Dollars   U.S. $6,000.00

EXPIRY
June 15, 2003

IN ALL COMMUNICATIONS WITH US, PLEASE MENTION OUR REFERENCE NUMBER

Gentlemen:

We have received from the above named bank a **cable** dated **April 5, 2003** requesting us to inform you that they have opened in your favor their irrevocable Credit particulars of which are as follows:

Available by your drafts at   **sight ON US.**

Accompanied by the following documents (full sets required unless otherwise specified):

> Signed commercial invoice in triplicate, describing the merchandise as mentioned below, stating that goods shipped conform with purchase order No. 0/00/0 dated March 5, 2003.

> Packing list in triplicate.

> Insurance policy or certificate in duplicate covering all risks including war risks.

> Full set of clean on board ocean bills of lading issued to shippers' order and blank endorsed, marked "Freight Prepaid" and notify International Forwarders, Keelung.

> Evidencing shipment from U.S. Port to Keelung, Taiwan not later than May 25, 2003 of the following merchandise: 200 sets of cookware at the price of $30.00 per one set CIF Keelung, Taiwan.

> Partial shipments permitted.

> Transshipments prohibited.

> Drawings under this letter of credit must be presented for negotiation not later than ten days after the date of issuance of the bills of lading.

[ ] This credit is not confirmed by us and therefore carries no engagement on our part, but is simply for your guidance in preparing and presenting drafts and documents.

[X] This credit is confirmed by us and we undertake that all drafts drawn and presented in accordance with the terms of the credit will be honored by us.

The above mentioned correspondent engages with you that all drafts under and in compliance with the terms of the Credit will be duly honored on delivery of documents as specified.

If the Credit has been opened by cable, this advice is subject to correction upon receipt of the mail confirmation.

Drafts must be marked "Drawn under **First Bank, Taipei, Taiwan, Letter of Credit No. 0/00/0** " and presented at our office on or before the above indicated expiry date.

The credit is subject to the Uniform Customs and Practice for Documentary Credits [1974 revision the International Chamber of Commerce Publication No. 290]

Should the terms of the above mentioned Credit be unsatisfactory to you, please communicate with your customers and request that they have the issuing bank send us amended instructions. Original credit must be returned with documents for negotiations.

J. Smith
FOR CASHIER

G. Black
FOR CASHIER

Exhibit 9.11 Letter of Credit Process

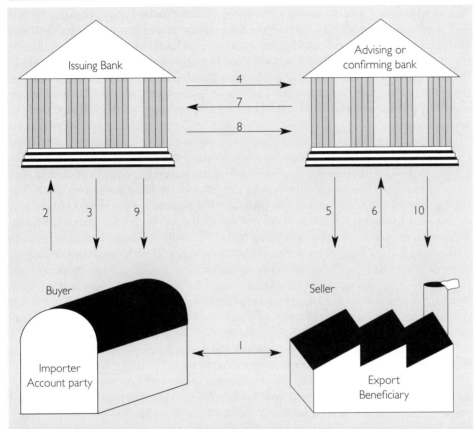

Typical Order of Events:

1. Contract for the international sale of goods.
2. Buyer (account party) applies to the issuing bank for an L/C designating the seller as beneficiary.
3. Issuing bank makes commitment to buyer to issue L/C specifying buyer's terms of full performance.
4. L/C is forwarded from issuing bank to the seller's advising or confirming bank.
5. Advising or confirming bank forwards buyer's L/C to seller for seller's preparation of documents in conformance with L/C.
6. Seller forwards completed documents (e.g., bill of lading, inspection certificates, export license, customs clearance) to advising or confirming bank.
7. Advising or confirming bank carefully checks for discrepancies, advises seller to make any necessary revisions, and forwards documents to issuing bank.
8. Issuing bank carefully checks for discrepancies and either (a) honors L/C by paying seller or confirming bank; or (b) bank dishonors L/C if there are discrepancies or bank revokes a revocable L/C.
9. Issuing bank forwards bill of lading and any other documents to buyer as necessary to claim goods from carrier.
10. Advising bank pays seller, credits seller's account, or pays transferee if beneficiary negotiated L/C.

banking days to do their document examination. The UCP requires banks to use a "reasonable time," which cannot be more than seven banking days. The general rule is that banks need not "look behind the documents" to determine negotiability and performance of an international sales transaction. Therefore, the parties must draft the documents very carefully and provide for others to verify matters, such as inspecting the shipment to assure exact compliance with the sales contract description. The 1994 UCP revision directs banks to ignore any L/C conditions not contained in the documents. The UCP has no fraud exception, so this subject is left to national law.

The bank issuing the L/C has a duty to "pay against the documents" by first checking for discrepancies, endorsing documents as necessary to process the transaction, and then either notifying the seller of discrepancies causing dishonor of payment or honoring the payment by paying the seller or crediting the seller's bank. The UCP presumes L/Cs are irrevocable, although the buyer's bank can make them revocable, but this substantially reduces their usefulness. The L/C is often **confirmed**, obligating the seller's bank (confirming bank) to credit the seller's account as soon as the issuing bank honors payment. If the L/C is **unconfirmed**, the seller's bank provides only advising functions as a correspondent of the issuing bank by processing paperwork but does not credit the seller's account. In most cases, the seller's bank assists in preparing the documents and reviewing them for discrepancies. It forwards the documents to the issuing bank and may need to redraft any noncomplying documents returned by the issuing bank if there is still time remaining.

A standby L/C is not used for payment but instead as a performance guarantee or collateral. Payment is due if the account party breaches some duty. For example, Manufacturers Bank was required to pay on a standby L/C that guaranteed the performance of AT&T's contract to install a telephone system in Iran. AT&T stopped performance after the Shah was ousted and the Islamic regime did not pay its AT&T bills. Despite Iran's breach of the installation contract, the bank was still required to pay the standby L/C because AT&T's performance bond was not conditioned on Iran's payments.[1]

Electronic Letters of Credit

Letters of credit need not be transferred physically by mail or trusted courier. For many years, international practice has recognized and employed electronic L/Cs that are transmitted among participating banks through secure electronic communication networks such as SWIFT, the Society for Worldwide Interbank Financial Telecommunications. Article 11(a)i of UCP 500 specifically authorizes the use of "authenticated teletransmissions." They are regarded as "the operative Credit instrument," and no physical mail confirmation is necessary. UCC Article 5's recognition of electronic L/Cs is somewhat less definite; UCC §5-104 requires the use of a "record" authenticated by signature or other authentication method acceptable under standard practice by financial institutions or a method otherwise specifically

---

1. *American Bell International v. Islamic Republic of Iran*, 474 F.Supp. 420 (S.D.N.Y. 1979).

permitted in the L/C. Electronic L/Cs are clearly envisioned by the UCC §5-102(14) definition of the term **record**, which permits "information inscribed on a tangible medium, or that is stored in an electronic or other medium and is retrievable in perceivable form." The comments to UCC Article 5 authorize current use of electronic L/Cs if the transmission and its data are durable and can be printed as a paper document for controlling and recording payments and assignments.

UCP "authentication" predates UETA, so no traditional signature or symbol-based method is required. Nevertheless, the UCP makes the advising bank responsible to assure that the L/C is authentic. This technology-neutral approach permits authentication by numerous methods, including encryption, password, return acknowledgment, verification by telephone, or a traditional signature or symbol. Authentication under the UCC is also flexible and technology-neutral, encouraging the evolution of practices by the banking industry. Authentication is necessary only for the identity of the L/C issuer, confirmer, or adviser. If there are incomplete or garbled teletransmissions, the electronic L/C is not effective. In such cases, the advising bank should request that the issuing bank resend clear and complete information, which the issuing bank should promptly provide.

Alternatives to Traditional Documentary Sales

International commercial contracting retains some ancient contracting methods while it also evolves with technology. Alternatives to the traditional documentary sales process previously described are widely used today. **Countertrade** is a complex reciprocal barterlike exchange in which international brokers match buyers and sellers who trade goods and services without transferring cash. Many developing countries and former Soviet bloc nations have negative trade balances, their currencies do not convert well into hard currency, they have large debt burdens, or their government restricts currency outflows. These problems restrict the very foreign trade so badly needed to invigorate their economies. There are several types of countertrade. **Barter** is the direct exchange of different types of goods or services between the two parties. In a **swap**, two sellers of the same goods exchange delivery obligations to reduce transportation costs. The most common form of countertrade is **counterpurchase**: A seller from an industrial nation exchanges goods or services for other goods from the buyer, often through an intermediary such as the government or a firm in the developing nation. In a **buyback**, industrial machinery acquired from the seller is paid for with goods eventually produced with those machines.

Countertrade raises many legal, electronic commerce, ethical, trade policy, and economic policy questions. Legal questions include product safety compliance, complex contracting, and the antitrust laws. Electronic commerce questions involve computerized matching and communications among counter trading parties. Ethical issues include foreign bribery and allegations that rich industrial nations take unfair advantage of developing nations. Trade policy issues include trade restrictions and the dumping laws. Economic problems include circumventing foreign currency translation and the rather significant inefficiency of countertrade. Consider the role that the Internet could play in barter and the more fine-tuned adjustments that could be made among all the parties.

ELECTRONIC PAYMENT SYSTEMS

Money, the primary subject of payment obligations, has a long history, an understanding of which informs the design of reliable electronic payment systems. Dating from hundreds of years B.C., the successful forms of money traditionally have two major functions: (1) **storehouse of value** and (2) **medium of exchange**. Money was once considered a storehouse of value because gold or silver coins had intrinsic value from their precious metal content. Today, few circulating coins are struck from precious metal, and few paper currencies are backed by government promises to redeem them for gold or silver. Therefore, today money serves as a storehouse of value only while the public has confidence in it. Public confidence is also essential to money's function as a medium of exchange. Money must be widely available so that most people can use it. Money must also be widely acceptable: most people must be willing to take it in payment for services, intangibles, goods, or land.

The experience with various competing currencies in early U.S. history was negative. During colonial and post-Revolutionary times, paper notes were issued by governments (England, colonies, states, U.S. federal), by private banks, and even by other private parties. Some were backed by agricultural products, such as tobacco, meaning the currency could be redeemed (exchanged) for something of tangible value. However, the proliferation of these currencies caused inflation; many were not universally accepted for payment. The Constitution framers reacted to a proliferation of currencies before the Revolution and during the time of the Articles of Confederation. They envisioned a single predominant currency, so Congress was granted the power to coin and regulate money, and that power was prohibited to the states. The states have since had the power to charter (license) banks. Currency was issued by both federally chartered banks and by state-chartered banks until the taxes levied on nonfederal notes diminished their use. Public confidence in money is enhanced when control is concentrated in a trusted government entity like the Federal Reserve.

Background: Contemporary Use of Electronic Payment Systems

Electronic payments are hardly new. The first international wire transfer of funds occurred soon after the transatlantic telegraph cable was laid in the 1880s, linking the United States with the United Kingdom. The lives of few people today remain untouched by electronic payments. The most frequent experiences are cash withdrawals from bank accounts or credit card accounts via automated teller machines (ATMs). Most credit card charges use electronic account verification and transaction processing. Indeed, the physical handling of credit card carbon impressions is nearly an extinct practice, although it resurfaces occasionally when electronic networks become temporarily inoperative. Most retail merchants offer point-of-sale (POS) transaction processing for debit and ATM cards via electronic networks similar to credit card networks.

Electronic payments systems are less visible, but no less important, in other areas. Consider the growing use of electronic payment systems in transportation: toll tag use at turnpikes, bridges, and tunnels and gasoline purchases charged with electronic token-readers at the pump. Even people who do not use "plastic" are affected by electronic processing of payments at the wholesale level. Nearly all interbank transactions between the buyer's bank and the seller's bank are processed electronically, including the total fund transfers clearing all paper checks, direct deposits, and clearance of credit card or debit transactions by ATM or POS. Electronic payment systems should be viewed broadly to include preconditions to payment such as metering, bill calculating, and invoicing.

The electronic metering and recording of customer transactions facilitates billing of regular and long-distance telephone use, wireless airtime, pay-per-view deliveries, and on-line subscription services (ISP, Lexis-Nexis, Westlaw). **Electronic bill payment and presentment (EBPP)** to customers or to their automated payment services may also trigger electronic payments. Many transactions use analog or digital electronic means to transmit billing and payment information, such as use of the telephone (voice), fax (documents), or e-mail (electronic records) to communicate credit card account numbers and expiration dates to authorize payments, to identify the payor, or to transfer bank draft payment using **automated clearing house (ACH)** facilities. Electronic bill presentment is the first step to performance of payment obligations. It may occur through e-mail, Web banking, or some third-party electronic bill payment service.

The following section discusses the existing legal framework for electronic payment mechanisms, as well as the technical and legal challenges to successful development of alternative electronic payment mechanisms. First is an introduction to the retail electronic transfer of payments involving both credit and debit transactions under federal law. Next, wholesale electronic funds transfer under Federal Reserve regulations, the federal Electronic Funds Transfer Act, and UCC Article 4A are examined. Finally, emerging electronic payment systems are reviewed in light of the key enduring legal and practical characteristics of successful payment systems. These principles are projected onto proposed systems to predict the obstacles and opportunities for reliable electronic payment innovations.

Retail Electronic Funds Transfer: Credit Cards

When consumers directly use electronic funds transfer (EFT), these are retail transactions that can occur in two modes. First, credit card transfers are debt transactions, essentially advances made from a line of credit established between the consumer and the credit card issuer. Credit EFT transactions are based on push technology because a series of payment orders directs banks to make payments through the system to the ultimate payee. Second, debit transfers are deducted directly from assets held by a financial institution or from an existing deposit account with a bank. Like traditional paper-based checks and drafts, debit EFT are based on pull technology because they order or request payment through the system from the payor bank.

Credit cards were first developed in the 1950s. They proliferated in the 1960s as many banks issued cards indiscriminately and without careful screening for the creditworthiness of prospective cardholders. After many issuing banks sustained significant losses, Congress passed the Consumer Credit Protection Act in 1970, as part of the Truth in Lending Act. The Federal Reserve is authorized to implement the act and has done so with the strong consumer disclosure protections of Regulation Z.

Credit card transactions are also regulated by three major types of contracts: (1) There are contracts between merchants and their banks to process credit cards accepted as payment, (2) there are contracts between consumers and their banks that issue credit cards, and (3) all participants are bound by the transaction clearing rules of the sponsoring credit card association (e.g., Visa, MasterCard, Discover, American Express). They are closed systems in several respects. The parties' rights and duties are defined by system rules regulating acceptance of payments, processing of transactions, and the honor or dishonor of the ultimate transfer of funds. Also the transmission of transaction information is often sent via secure networks. However, consumers become vulnerable as they transmit credit card account information via the Internet. Security concerns will require the use of encryption or other protective means. For example, the SSL (secure socket layer) communications technology is in wide use, essentially an encryption of account information during transmission.

The revenue that supports the credit card system is derived from various fees. First, a percentage of gross credit card sales, the "discount," is charged-back against the merchant who accepts credit cards. Effectively, this is a percentage-of-gross-sales fee (1%–5%) the merchant must pay on the amount received in payment for the consumers' use of credit. Second, consumers pay interest on unpaid balances, typically between 10% and 24%. Third, some cardholders pay an initiation fee or recurring annual fees.

Credit card issuers profit from these fees, which allows them to give consumers another big incentive to use credit cards: the rather considerable advantage of **float**. Those consumers who can time their credit card transactions and payments optimally actually borrow the amount of the purchase, interest free, for up to 50 or 60 days if they have no outstanding unpaid balances. Float has been a double-edge sword for many years, affecting both the credit and debit sectors of the banking industry. The float causes many banks to lose profitable opportunities, yet some banks find ways to take financial advantage of float. Float is the result of slow and inefficient transmittal of instruments and documents, as well as less than fully automated record keeping. Today, the elimination of float is a primary incentive driving advances in electronic payment systems.

Regulation Z imposes considerable consumer protection obligations on card issuers. In turn, card association rules shift many of these risks to merchants. Cards may be sent to consumers only upon consumer requests or as a renewal. A cardholder becomes liable for charges only after the issued card is accepted, either by signature, by use, or by authorizing another person's use. Increasingly, acceptance is accomplished when consumers call to activate new cards they receive. Periodic statements of account and notices of the card issuer's error resolution process must be sent to cardholders. Cardholders must attempt to settle disputes that arise over a transaction (e.g., warranty breach) directly with the merchant. Regulation Z gives the consumer a bargaining advantage in this: Payments to the merchant can be suspended until the dispute is resolved. Regulation Z limits this right to contest only those charges over $50, and only those made within the cardholder's state or within 100 miles of the cardholder's home. Some credit card issuers currently waive these restrictions. Without this extension of consumer protection, consumers charging purchases in distant transactions via the Internet, phone, or mail order would not have this dispute-bargaining advantage.

Cardholder liability is limited to $50 for any unauthorized charges made before the issuer is notified that the card was lost or stolen. Merchants who do not inspect the card they accept may not contest the cardholder's claim that a particular charge is unauthorized. Card association rules shift most of this risk to merchants, who must verify the identity of the cardholder. The most common verification methods include a comparison of signatures, although other methods are available, such as a comparison of the cardholder's photograph on the card or other ID, verification using a PIN (personal identifying number), or perhaps some biometric method (fingerprint, retinal scan). Merchants accepting cards via mail, telephone, or the Internet seem particularly vulnerable to credit card fraud. Increasingly, credit card issuers insure these risks in an effort to make Internet credit card use more secure and safe for consumers. Clearly, the relatively high credit card interest rates payable on unpaid balances also defray the expenses of credit card fraud and subsidize losses on delinquent accounts of uncreditworthy cardholders. These consumer protections are unequaled for any other payment method, electronic or otherwise. For this reason, Regulation Z probably accounts for the overwhelming dominance of credit card payments in retail transactions consummated by phone, by mail, or over the Internet. In other words, in the Internet space, "credit card is king."

Retail Electronic Funds Transfer: Debit Cards

The other predominant mode for consumer electronic funds transfer is the debit EFT transaction. Since the 1970s, financial institutions have offered electronic access to retail customer deposit accounts or other assets through customer use of debit cards at ATMs or POS devices. Debit EFT also includes computer or telephone transfers, regular direct deposits such as paychecks or social security benefits, and direct withdrawals such as periodic bill payments, and, more recently, Internet bill payment services. Congress passed the Electronic Funds Transfer Act (EFTA) in 1978, authorizing the Federal Reserve to implement the act, which it has done with Regulation E. Regulation E requires financial institutions to issue an **access device** when EFT debit services are used. Various security methods serve as components of an access device. Redundant controls are usually best. Consider the security involved in using a debit card to withdraw cash from an ATM. The actual card must be used, a secret PIN must be entered, photographs are taken, and the amount of the withdrawal is often limited so an account cannot be quickly depleted. Now consider the authentication process for bill payment by using a home computer. This process might include a written preauthorization for such transactions, an on-screen notice detailing each transaction, identification using a PIN, and a paper receipt for reconciliation of records. The EFTA and Regulation E cover only the bank-to-consumer portion of these transactions. The wholesale, interbank transfer of consumer transactions is discussed in the next section.

Regulation E is less consumer-protective than Regulation Z because it places greater responsibility on consumers. For example, consumers who completely fail to notify the bank of a lost or stolen debit card could conceivably suffer unlimited losses. The $50 limit applies only if notice is given within 2 days after the consumer learns of the loss. The limit rises to $500 if notice is given after 2 days but by 60 days. Increasingly, debit cards are branded as credit cards to broaden their acceptance beyond ATMs and POS devices to include certain merchants. Some credit card companies are not enforcing the higher loss limits for these cards. Such lenient policies could change as consumers become reliant on them. Debit cards may not be issued or activated unless requested by the consumer, and some employers now refuse to offer paper paychecks, pressuring employees to authorize direct deposits. Debit fees currently favor merchants, the so-called PIN authentication.

Regulation E has no provision similar to the right under Regulation Z to withhold payments during the consumer's dispute with the merchant for breach of contract. Debit transactions offer more disciplined spending management to financially responsible consumers because consumers have difficulty spending more than is available as deposited assets. Nevertheless, users of credit EFT methods have stronger regulatory protections under Federal Reserve Regulation Z than do users of debit EFT methods under Regulation E.

Regulation E gives consumers a right to stop payment similar to the right under commercial paper law. For example, a preauthorized EFT may be prevented, before it is actually executed, such as the regular payment of a utility bill. Regulation Z requires that banks investigate and document errors, and consumers must be given documentation of all EFT transactions actually completed. Disclosures of consumer rights under the EFTA are also required. In June 2000, the Federal Reserve proposed revisions to Regulation E to expand disclosures required for ATM fees and to allow recurring EFT from a consumer account when authorized in a signed writing or "similarly authenticated." If the proposal is promulgated, it could permit use of some electronic or biometric means of authenticating regular EFT transactions.

Wholesale Funds Transfers

Before the 1989 introduction of UCC Article 4A, the only guidance for wire transfer of commercial payments among business parties was industry practice. Since then, the widespread adoption of UCC Article 4A has codified many of these practices to achieve a balance of the risks. A typical wholesale business-to-business payment occurs when a commercial customer pays its suppliers. This wholesale transfer of funds totals several trillion dollars each business day. These EFTs are typically made in large amounts, at high speed, and at low cost, using reliable electronic technologies. UCC Article 4A is technology-neutral; it governs wholesale funds transfers whether transmitted by electronic means or by traditional means such as U.S. mail.

Much of the money transferred to or from banks by consumers or other customers is eventually transferred between banks. Federal Reserve Regulation J applies essentially similar rules to the EFT between financial institutions routed through Fedwire, using their regional Federal Reserve branches as conduits. Although the consumer-initiated credit or debit EFTs previously discussed are excluded from UCC Article 4A, this law was prescient because its objectives and methods anticipated the problems with electronic payments arising in contemporary e-commerce. A more detailed example of a wholesale EFT transaction helps identify the parties and provides a better understanding of their major functions and the steps typically involved.

Wholesale EFT Transaction Illustration

Assume that East Corp. owes $45,350 for a truckload of widgets it purchased from InterWidgCo. East Corp. typically pays its bills from an account with All-National Bank. InterWidgCo. has an account with First State Bank. An EFT commences when an authorized person in East Corp.'s accounts payable office uses a computer to issue a *payment order* directing All-National Bank to transmit a second payment order to First State Bank. The All-National Bank payment order specifies that $45,350 currently held in East Corp.'s account will be transferred to First State Bank and the amount should immediately credited to InterWidgCo.'s account. When First State Bank accepts the second payment order, it notifies InterWidgCo. that the $45,350 has become available. Settlement of these payment orders usually occurs later, when accounting entries are made netting all the transactions between the two banks, perhaps by the close of that business day.

In this example and under UCC Article 4A, both East Corp. and All-National Bank are **senders** of payment orders. Each order, in turn, is triggered by its predecessor. East Corp. is the **originator**. First State Bank is the receiving bank, and InterWidgCo. is the **beneficiary** of the payment orders. If these two banks have not had regular, frequent transfer activity between them, one or more **intermediary banks** may be needed to act as conduits to process these payment orders.

Today, most EFT payment orders are transmitted electronically through communications systems called value-added networks (VAN). Significant VANs include the regional automated clearing houses (ACH), the New York Clearinghouse Interbank Payments System (CHIPS), and, in international commerce, the Society for Worldwide Interbank Financial Telecommunications (SWIFT). Payment orders can also be transmitted by EDI, fax, e-mail, phone, and even on paper. When an EFT transaction is processed through intermediary banks, several VANs may be involved. VANs are closed and secure information-processing systems transmitting EFTs only among members or as intermediaries for other banks or other parties.

UCC Article 4A requires that **security procedures** be established to authenticate transactions, verify the parties' identities, and detect errors. These concerns are similar to the problems addressed by electronic signatures, discussed in Chapter 10. UCC Article 4A encourages banks to develop, regularly use, and impose security procedures on customers, so long as they are **commercially reasonable**. Security procedures can be expected to evolve and improve over time. Examples include the use of algorithms or other codes, identifying words or numbers, encryption, callback procedures, or similar security devices.

The overriding incentive of EFT is to reduce the cost of individual verification of payment orders, making EFT more efficient. When commercially reasonable security procedures are in place but an unauthorized payment order is processed, the loss allocation rules of Article 4A and the parties' contract usually shift this risk to the customer. UCC Article 4A helps settle disputes concerning potentially costly errors, such as mistaken beneficiaries or amounts, improper notices, fraudulent payment orders, and even bank failures. EFTs are typically large dollar amounts, and their transaction costs are low. UCC Article 4A helps the transmitting and receiving banks to carefully design EFT procedures for themselves and their commercial customers with a view to minimizing the risk of costly errors and the opportunity for fraud.

Future Prospects for Electronic Payment Systems

Many experimental consumer electronic payment systems have been announced. The accompanying promotional fanfare has attracted dot.com venture capital and investor attention. However, most of these systems have eventually failed, and none has yet achieved widespread success. Nevertheless, electronic payment systems may experience the greatest near- to medium-term growth in peer-to-peer (P2P) payments systems like PayPal, smart card use, electronic customer loyalty point systems, escrow services, electronic bill presentment, and electronic access and manipulation of account records at banks and vendors. All these systems rely on computerized, electronic telecommunications to do one or more of the following: authorize or order payments, verify customer identity and availability of account status, documentation, and record keeping.

ONLINE

PayPal P2P system
http://www.paypal.com

Some day, secure electronic packets of value may actually transfer electronic currency without the assistance of trusted third-party intermediaries (e.g., banks). However, third parties will remain involved with all forms of payment until electronic payment innovations are much more reliable and resistant to tampering, legal, and commonplace. E-commerce will probably rely on credit cards for at least part of most consumer transactions in the near to medium term. An estimated 95% of Internet commerce payments in 2000 involved credit cards, and many electronic payment innovations depend on credit cards.[2]

As with most other cyberlaw concerns, returning to the basic principles underlying our existing law and financial institutions may be necessary. With a clearer understanding of the function of these institutions, we can then project how such legal protections should be configured in e-commerce and determine whether existing law can adapt. If not, society can consider new legislation that is technology-neutral, will accommodate existing payment methods, and then will foster the development of new payment methods.

The barriers to widespread use of electronic payment innovations are considerable. Uncertainties about the safety and security of payment innovations may slow acceptance by the public and businesses. The Federal Reserve is reluctant to surrender its control over the money supply, and banks are not eager to relinquish their control over payments. However, the economic incentives to reduce the transaction costs of payment performances are substantial. Compare the estimated cost (in 2000) of an in-person bank transaction with a human teller at $1.07, an ATM trans-

---

2. See e.g., Julia Angwin, "E-Money: And How Will You Be Paying for That?" *Wall Street Journal*, October 23, 2000, p. R37.

action at 27¢, and a smart card transaction (discussed later) less than 1¢.[3] The combined costs of billing consumers and their payments by check are estimated at 85¢ per transaction. As discussed in Chapter 6, there are significant incentives to innovate in electronic payment systems, now that business methods are clearly patentable. Indeed, as of 2000, the U.S. Patent and Trademark Office (PTO) had issued nearly 100 patents covering electronic payment systems. As payment laws are modernized in the future to facilitate innovation, many more patent applications for electronic payment systems can be expected.

Adapting Payment Law and Business Practices to E-Commerce

The law of electronic payments is developing slowly. Before the Internet's full potential can be unleashed, the constraints of law and business practice must be accommodated. A central constraint is that compliance is required with banking and payment laws.[4] First, state laws require banks be licensed. Banks have a near oligopoly control over the deposit and payment order business. Electronic payment products have been proposed by nonbanks. Nonbanks that accept customer deposits or link their payment products to a bank account may violate state banking laws. Nonbanks may engage in the business of transmitting money (e.g., Western Union, GE Credit, money orders), including the movement, distribution, and clearing of payments. However, such nonbanks must also be licensed under most states' money transmitter laws. Second, Regulation E may apply to electronic payments, such as the stored value systems discussed later, which would trigger the Regulation E consumer protections previously discussed. Third, the Stamp Payments Act of 1862 makes it a criminal felony to circulate coins, tokens, or obligations under $1 if they are intended to circulate as money. Unless repealed, this old law could severely constrain the development of micropayments, point systems, and the electronic coin purses. Fourth, the deposit insurance system is designed to protect depositors from bank failures. Some firms can be expected to try to remain outside the extensive regulations of the FDIC. However, customers of some other firms may still seek the safety of deposit insurance.

Innovation in the design of electronic payment schemes must also account for business practices and economic incentives. The lessons learned from the major characteristics of money and from the evolving payment schemes should be addressed. As innovations in electronic payments are analyzed, consider the following factors:

- Confidence in money is gained when its value is linked or it can be converted into something of value, such as an acceptable denomination of a respected currency ($, £, ¥, €) or another liquid asset with reliable value (gold).
- Electronic payment forms should be as convenient as cash—that is, readily transferable, capable of convenient exchange in scalable denominations, and easily stored and transmitted to or received from various locations.

---

3. Thomas P. Vartanian, "The Future of Electronic Payments: Roadblocks and Emerging Practices," testimony before the Subcommittee on Domestic and International Monetary Policy of the Committee on Banking and Financial Services, U.S. House of Representatives (September 19, 2000) citing Kevin P. Sheehan, *Electronic Cash*, Banking Rev. (FDIC) 1.
4. Ibid.

- There must be security and accuracy in transactions.
- There must be reliable means to authenticate electronic money as genuine, not counterfeit or forged.
- Anonymity for the purchaser is a contentious issue. Some users may seek an audit trail of all prior transactions, including the identity of payors, payees, and intermediaries. This capability is now possible with checks, wire transfers, POS, or credit card transactions. Law enforcement prefers traceable payments for evidence of criminal activity, such as the money laundering discussed in Chapter 3. Paper currency has serial numbers and can be marked, and contemporary coins have too low a value to be practical for large transactions. By contrast, many other users prefer to maintain transaction anonymity. Some privacy advocates suspect that comprehensive transaction records weaken personal freedoms and can become a tool for a repressive government.
- Few payment schemes are practical without the participation of trusted and reliable third-party intermediaries. Third parties, like banks, provide useful services such as experience, transmission of orders, account information or documents, useful relations with correspondents; they provide security and safekeeping; and they can connect the payment scheme to reliable sources of value.
- New forms of money created outside the traditional framework of regulatory oversight may weaken control over the economy. Alternative forms of money and payment schemes processed outside the banking system threaten the power of the Federal Reserve and other financial regulators to control the money supply, maintain the solvency of financial institutions, and maintain the integrity of deposit insurance (FDIC), suggesting a role for government in electronic payment success.

The involvement of third parties seems indispensable to the success of electronic payment innovations. These third parties would usually include banks, financial institutions, credit card issuers, and VANs. The emerging electronic payment innovators might also find additional third parties useful, including lenders, Federal Reserve, FDIC, clearing houses, and escrow agents. Aside from the network effect problems of scale economies, the success of electronic payment innovations must find the right mix of third party involvement and hit the market at the right time. Consider the potential range of involvement of such third parties: (1) investment, ownership, and operation of the electronic payment system; (2) research, development, standards setting, and system design; (3) issuance of electronic value to consumers and financial liability for the electronic value; (4) resale agent for other issuers of electronic value; (5) recruitment of participating merchants; (6) recruitment of consumers; (7) operation of computer data and storage; (8) operation of telecommunications network infrastructure; and (9) escrow services.

Electronically Stored Value and Smart Cards

Persistent efforts to use electronic memory devices to store value for ultimate use in payments probably will continue. Value stored on computers could be used in Internet transactions. Value stored on plastic cards or other portable storage devices could be used to shop in person through computer communications terminals physically held at a merchant's premises or mounted as a PC peripheral. Stored value is really an electronic wallet, purse, or piggy bank. Most such systems envision that value is added into storage by a third party who accepts traditional payment by cash, check, or credit and/or debit card transfer and converts this to the storable electronic value. When purchases are made, precise deductions of the appropriate value are made from the storage device. Optional features of the transaction include remote authentication and authorization, documentation, transmittal of notices, accumulation of private consumer behavior information, creation of permanent records, and even maintenance of anonymity. The stored value experiments thus far attempted are distinguished by the precise combination of these factors, as well as identity of the third party, the computer and communications infrastructure used, and other architectural aspects.

In the United States, most smart card experiments have failed (e.g., 1996 Atlanta Olympics, 1998 Manhattan Upper West Side). Stored-value cards offer consumers less protection than do credit or even debit cards under Federal Reserve Regulations Z and E (limitation on theft losses, unauthorized use). The Mondex and CyberCoin projects are repeatedly mentioned. However, American consumers seem satisfied with existing payment technologies. By contrast, smart cards are becoming popular in Europe, Japan, and U.S. college campuses, where the finality of cashlike transactions is appreciated and there are no realistic expectations to benefit from the float.

Federal Reserve Proposal for Electronic Check Presentment

In 2000, the Federal Reserve proposed a system to reduce the costs of physically moving checks between banks and Federal Reserve branches and around the country. This system involves automated clearinghouse debits or **electronic check presentment (ECP)**. Under this proposal, the bank that "cashes" the payee's check would retain the paper check rather than return it for payment as done currently under UCC Articles 3 and 4. Instead, the depository bank would make and transmit an image of the check to collect from the drawee bank. If the drawer who issued the check ever requested a copy, the depository bank would electronically produce and mail an **image replacement document (IRD)** to the drawer. Federal Reserve regulations would make this IRD an equivalent of the original check for all legal and evidentiary purposes. Although a few rights and duties must be revised under Federal Reserve regulations and the UCC, the ECP proposal described here appears to be a substantial efficiency innovation for the back office handling of traditional paper checks and may be a step toward broader acceptance of electronic checks.

Micropayments

Considerable Internet content is not particularly valuable and will probably not be sold for high prices, which is not to say that healthy markets cannot develop in low-priced content such as clips of sound, music, or video, images, data, information, and analysis. Rather, the availability of such content is restrained until efficient and effective payment schemes are devised. As of this writing, most "low-value content" is available only under one of four general business models: (1) free, supposedly as part of building elusive "brand image," (2) ostensibly free sites that generate revenue from banner advertisements, referrals, or secondary use and resale of users' private information profiles, or (3) subscription services and (4) metered pay-per-view services. Until content providers can be paid fairly for their low-value content, the willingness to supply more content will be restrained. Web site practices may not respect visitor privacy. Some content providers remain unwilling or unable to have their content effectively bundled with other subscription services. An obvious solution to this problem is the development of effective **micropayment** technologies—small, electronic payments made automatically and at low transaction costs.

Most existing payment schemes pose transaction costs that may consume too large a percentage of low-value transactions. Consider the difficulties with credit card use. The transaction fees force many merchants to require minimum purchases of $10 to $20 per charge. Some credit card issuers charge merchants up to 5% of the total sale in fees for processing the payment. These economics make it difficult to profitably use credit cards for sales of low-value content. It is generally uneconomical to make micropayments to access Web content on a pay-per-view basis. Potentially lucrative new business models would be possible if Web users could make small electronic payments, perhaps as low as a few pennies, to receive low-value Web site content. For example, reliable micropayment capabilities might replace some of the free access to Internet sites under current usage. Micropayments could stimulate accessibility to more creative and useful Web page information, video and audio content, images, and networked data if Web site operators had greater incentive from more direct profits. Of course, many in the Internet community are unreceptive to this pay-per-view model because Web content has long been freely available. However, their fears may be an overraction. There is a compelling analogy: Video content proliferated as television viewing migrated from free advertiser- supported broadcast transmission to subscription cable television, premium channels, video rentals, and pay-per-view.

The lack of universal micropayment capabilities relegates Web commerce to either (1) larger transactions for goods, software, or subscription services or (2) speculative and uncertain business models. Although this dilemma probably constrains very few B2B transactions, it forces business-to-consumer and consumer-to-consumer transactions into a few controversial business models, such as (1) banner advertising and referrals, (2) the collection and resale of private user data, and (3) customer relationship, brand image building. The introduction of reliable and efficient micropayment technologies arguably would release a flood of content, reducing reliance on models that are contingent on revenues from advertising or private data profiling. At this writing, the most promising models permitting micropayments are subscription services, e-malls, and e-wallets. Although some form of digital coin might be more effective, failures of the Millicent, flooz.com, and CyberCoin experiments because of insufficient critical mass probably reflected a user population that was not ready to pay for content they still believed should remain free.

Electronic Payment Epilogue

As of this writing, at least four broad types of experimental electronic payment systems were underway. First, digital cash requires the involvement of an intermediary (InternetCash Corp., DigiCash Inc., EZPass). The intermediary takes in money from registered consumers who establish a credit balance with initial payment by cash, check, or credit card. Payments are then dispensed for Internet purchases made from registered vendors. Second are digital wallets, which also require consumers and vendors to register with an intermediary (Yahoo!, AOL's Quick Checkout, Microsoft's Passport). The intermediary's software holds the consumer's credit card numbers and shipping address, facilitating quicker on-line transaction processing. In a variation of this type of system, the vendor assigns a different credit card number for each new transaction so that the vendor never learns the consumer's actual credit card number, which enhances security. Third, systems that more closely resemble frequent flyer points, bonus coupons, or green stamps are typically issued by point-granting intermediaries (Beenz.com, E-Centives, MyPoints.com). Both consumers and vendors must register and points are earned for providing personal information or viewing ads. Fourth, escrow agents are trusted third parties who hold the consumer's payment for the vendor's benefit until the consumer notifies the escrow agent that the goods actually arrived and conform to the vendor's description. Escrow payments must be released to the vendor when the escrow terms are satisfied. Escrow has long been used to protect both parties in various types of transactions, notably sales of real estate.

Despite all the publicity surrounding electronic payment experiments, the most successful systems are largely extensions of existing systems, illustrating two important points. First, consumers' and commercial parties' acceptance of new payment systems will depend on the proven security and reliability of those systems. Second, payment system performance depends on trusted third parties—commercial banks and other financial intermediaries—which will probably control the handling of most payment processes. E-commerce must rely on credit cards, checks and drafts, and EFT until there is widespread acceptance of reliable electronic currency. Indeed, Federal Reserve Chairman Alan Greenspan has predicted, "Electronic money is likely to spread only gradually and play a much smaller role in our economy than private currency did historically."

CHAPTER 10
WRITINGS AND RECORDS, DEFENSES, REMEDIES, AND CREDITORS' RIGHTS

Individuals and businesses make on-line agreements daily, from complex loan applications and brokerage account applications to simple Web site access agreements. These contracts are made and performed as discussed in the previous two chapters. Should signed writings be necessary to enforce these contracts? How is an electronic contract proved if there is no traditional written contract? Can either party get out of their duty by pleading some defense or coercion to enter the contract? What good are legal rights without some reasonable remedy? These matters were critically important in the traditional economy and are of equal importance to e-commerce. This chapter addresses various remaining commercial law and regulation issues. First, the requirement for written contracts and its evolution into electronic records are explored. Next, defenses to contract formation are examined, followed by a discussion of the authority of agents to make and perform contracts, including both human and electronic agents. Then the failure to complete obligations and remedies for such breach of contract are covered. The chapter concludes with a discussion of special remedies for creditors when the debtor fails to make timely payments or otherwise defaults on a financial obligation.

WRITINGS AND SIGNATURES, RECORDS AND AUTHENTICATION

Contrary to a popular misconception, most oral contracts are fully enforceable and legally binding. Generally, contracts need *not* be in writing. Indeed, retail purchases are contracts, and there are usually no written contracts used, other than the ubiquitous receipt. Of course, if a dispute over any contract's interpretation arises, proving the precise terms may be difficult without consulting a reliable written document. There are several purposes for signed writings. It may be difficult to **authenticate** who really accepts an offer if the acceptance is done remotely and without witnesses. A signed writing helps prevent **forgery**. Signing a contract also serves a cautionary purpose: The ceremonial execution of a written contract more clearly demonstrates each party's approval of the particular terms memorialized in the writing, and it reminds them of the seriousness of their new duties.

To reduce the possibility of inaccurate fact findings in court, the law does require that some contracts be evidenced by a writing that includes all essential terms. For contracts that fall into one of several special classes, the **statute of frauds** requires a written contract *signed by the party to be charged*. The party to be charged is the one who denies the existence of a contract and who may be sued for breach. Written contracts need be signed only by the party against whom the plaintiff seeks enforcement. As discussed in Chapter 8, writings or records are often used to communicate the offer and the acceptance. Even when no writing is required by the statute of frauds, most parties consider writings and records to be very important to contract enforceability.

MEMORANDUM

To be effective in satisfying the statutes of frauds, a written contract must appear in a certain form, known as a **memorandum.** A memorandum may be an informal document or even a collection of several documents if they refer to the same transaction. A memorandum may be pieced together from separate documents, receipts, telegrams, mailgrams, letters, order forms, confirmations, addressed envelopes, and the like.

There is now no good reason to exclude electronic documents or records from satisfying the writing requirements. In the same way the courts have validated telegraph, telephone, and Telex communications, various communications tools (e.g., fax, e-mail, Web-interactive communications) are likely to be adequate substitutes for writings.

SIGNATURES

The signature required for a memorandum may be satisfied by any tangible sign that is used to authenticate a writing. Of course, a cursive signature of the party is the traditional method. However, parties may also use a stamp, corporate seal, initials, the signatory's name as printed or typed, or even a fingerprint or the letter X. The key factor is that the party making the sign must intend that it be used for authentication at the time the sign is affixed to the writing or record. **Authentication** under UCITA means either (1) to sign or (2) with the intent to sign a record, otherwise to execute or adopt an electronic symbol, sound, message, or process referring to, attached to, included in, or logically associated or linked with, that record.

Electronic forms of authentication are becoming satisfactory as signatures. A few courts have held that audiotape or videotape recordings of the parties executing the agreement could be sufficient authentication. Facsimile signature devices, which are essentially signature machines, can make valid signatures if there is reliable proof that the machine was operated by someone with authority. Authority to negotiate and authenticate contracts is discussed at the end of this chapter. Electronic signature pads record signatures needed for credit card payments at many retailers and are used increasingly in commercial transaction documents, such as by UPS. These machines record, archive, and transmit a digital copy of the actual cursive signature as proof of the transaction or delivery.

Digital signatures are encrypted data bits used to authenticate electronic records. They are attached to a communication to attest to one or more of the following: a particular person created the record, access to view or modify the record is limited to designated persons or recipients, and/or verification of the source of the communication. In the future, other digital signature technologies may develop, including biological certification (e.g., biometrics such as retinal scan, fingerprint, voiceprint) and third-party certification authorities, effectively **cyber notaries** that perform a function for electronic commerce similar to that performed by notaries public on paper documents. Electronic signature enforceability is addressed further as part of the discussion of UETA later.

STATUTE OF FRAUDS CATEGORIES

Written contracts in the form of a memorandum are necessary in several major business-related activities, including (1) sales of land, (2) guarantees to pay the debts of others, (3) contracts incapable of performance within one year of their making, and (4) sales of goods worth $500 or more under the UCC. UCITA adds another category in computer information contracts: A record must be authenticated (the cyberspace equivalent of a signed writing) if the agreement requires the payment of a contract fee of $5,000 or more. Many other signed writing requirements are found in variations of the statute of frauds spread over various commercial laws. For example, the UCC requires signatures and endorsements for negotiable instruments (checks, notes), documents of title, warehouse receipts, bills of lading, and sales of investment securities.

Sales of Land

A contract that calls for the transfer of any **interest in land** must be evidenced by a memorandum to be enforceable. This requirement applies to contracts that transfer a variety of real estate interests, including full ownership (called a fee simple), an easement, covenant, mortgage, condominium ownership, mineral rights, growing vegetation, and leases lasting more than one year in most states (three years in a few states, such as Pennsylvania).

The **part performance** exception to the statute of frauds permits enforcement of an oral land sale contract if the buyer has (1) paid part or all of the purchase price and (2) either taken possession of the property with the seller's knowledge or made valuable improvements on the land. Enforcement of an oral land sale is justified because it would be unfair to let the seller use the technicalities of the statute of frauds to back out of an oral deal later turned unattractive after the buyer takes possession.

In such instances, most courts grant a specific performance, ordering the seller to formally deed the property over to the buyer. It is expected that the passage of UETA will encourage expanded use of electronic records in place of the many current paper-based documents for real-estate transactions (e.g., contracts of sale, inspection certificates, deeds), land use processes (e.g., zoning applications, subdivision plats), and real estate financing (e.g., loan applications, mortgages, recording).

Guarantee Contracts

If an outside third party promises a creditor that the outsider will pay the original debtor's debt, the promise must be in writing. These promises are known as collateral contracts of **guarantee**. Although the original debtor's contract of debt need not be in writing, the guarantor's promise to pay if the debtor defaults *must* be evidenced by a memorandum. A true collateral contract of guarantee is enforceable only after the debtor defaults. For example, assume that C, a creditor, is willing to extend credit to D, the debtor, only if G, the outside guarantor, provides additional assurance that the debt will be repaid. G's promise to pay D's debt if D defaults is a collateral contract of guarantee that must be evidenced by a memorandum.

An exception to this requirement exists when the guarantor's **main purpose** or **leading object** is merely to protect the guarantor's own interests. An oral guarantee is enforceable in this situation because fraud is less likely. For example, a corporation in financial difficulty may be unable to borrow money unless its president agrees to guarantee the loan. Because the president's main purpose in guaranteeing the loan is to protect the company and his position as president, the guarantee need not be in writing. Guarantee contracts should also be distinguished from other forms of collateral and security arrangements that need no writing to be enforceable. Because loan cosigners or comakers are both primarily liable on the debt, their promises are not collateral guarantees and need not be evidenced by a memorandum.

Contracts Incapable of Performance within One Year

Long-term and complex contracts are more susceptible to problems of proof as time passes. If a breach of contract suit is brought long after contracting, witnesses may forget the facts or the circumstances may have changed. Therefore, a contract that is incapable of being performed within one year after the contract was made must be evidenced by a memorandum. The statute of frauds does not require writings for all long-term contracts. In many instances, the parties choose to take longer than a year to perform contracts that were capable of full performance within a year. The fact that a contract *might* take longer than a year to perform is not the important factor. No writing is required if the contract could reasonably be completed within one year.

Generally, only those contracts that require more than one year from the date the contract was made and the last day on which a performance is required must be memorialized with a memorandum. The one-year time begins to run when the contract is made and ends with the last required performance. Contracts that require several years for full performance must be evidenced by a memorandum. For example, a two-year employment contract or a professional engagement requiring performance at a time more than a year after the contract is made must be in writing under this provision.

UCC's Sales of Goods over $500

The common law statute of frauds has been amended by the UCC for contracts involving the sale of goods for $500 or more. The UCC statute of frauds is less restrictive than the common law. The memorandum required by the UCC need not state all the terms of the contract, but it will be enforced only up to the quantity stated in the writing. The UCC has "gap fillers," automatic terms that are implied in a goods sale contract if there are missing terms. For example, testimony may supply terms of price, delivery, quality, or industry customs. There are four major exceptions to the UCC statute of frauds in which oral contracts are enforceable.

First, if both parties to an oral contract are merchants and one party sends a written confirmation of an oral agreement to the other party, then no writing is necessary if the recipient fails to object within 10 days. This is the **receiver bound** exception. It provides an incentive for merchants to carefully read and quickly respond to their mail. A second UCC exception exists for **specially manufactured goods**, defined as goods unsuitable for sale in the seller's ordinary course of business. Consider an oral telephone order for $1,000 of unique manufactured goods. Even without a writing, the oral contract becomes enforceable as soon as the seller makes a substantial beginning in procuring or making the goods. Goods requiring special printing, embossing, unusual colors, trademarks, or emblems are typical examples of specially manufactured goods.

A third UCC exception permits enforcement of an oral contract if the party seeking to deny the contract nevertheless confirms the agreement by making a judicial **admission**. The admission may appear in testimony, in pleadings, or otherwise in a court proceeding. The statute of frauds will not aid a party to renege on a contract actually entered into orally. The fourth UCC exception permits enforcement of oral contracts if there has been either a **part payment** for goods by the buyer or an acceptance of a **partial delivery** by the seller. Contracts are enforced under this part performance doctrine only for the quantity paid for or accepted.

Statute of Frauds for Licenses under UCITA

UCITA's statute of frauds is based on the UCC. Most important, and consistent with UETA, the focus turns away from a primary reliance on cursive signatures written on paper documents by pen. UETA and UCITA now permit the use of physical or electronic records. A record is sufficient even if it omits or incorrectly states a term. No contract is enforceable beyond the number of copies or subject matter as shown in the record. Terminology under UCITA changes; instead of a signed writing, UCITA requires an **authenticated record**. Recall that a **record** includes both information inscribed on a tangible medium (writing) or stored in a retrievable format (electronic record), and authentication is either a signature or the execution of an electronic symbol linked with that record. UCITA validates current digital signature technologies and many other technologies that may develop in the future.

The main UCITA rule is that contracts requiring payment of a contract fee (price) of $5,000 or more must be supported by an authenticated record showing that a contract was formed. The party against whom enforcement is sought must authenticate the record, and the record must reasonably identify the subject matter. However, a party can agree that any future UCITA license between the parties need not be stated in authenticated records if the party against which enforcement is sought agrees to this in the first authenticated record.

UCITA's exceptions to the statute of frauds expand on exceptions found in both the common law and in the UCC. First, no authenticated record is needed if the license terms call for an agreed duration of one year or less. Also, no authenticated record is needed if the license may be terminated at will by the party against whom the contract is asserted. Second, there is a part performance exception: No authenticated record is needed when a tendered performance is accepted or the information licensed is accessed by the licensee. For example, no writing is required when the buyer takes and accepts the goods or downloads the information. Third, there is no authenticated record requirement when a party admits in court, by pleading or by testimony or otherwise under oath, that a contract was made. An admission is not enforceable beyond the number of copies admitted or the subject matter admitted. Fourth, there is a merchant's receiver bound exception. No authenticated record is required between merchants if, within a reasonable time, a record confirming the contract and sufficient against the sender is received and the party receiving it has reason to know its contents. Like the UCC, this exception is inapplicable if a notice of objection to the contents of a merchant's confirming record is given by way of a record within 10 days after the confirming record is received. UCITA's statute of frauds would govern only licenses of information.

UNIFORM ELECTRONIC TRANSACTIONS ACT

The Uniform Electronic Transactions Act (UETA) may be the most significant cyber law for electronic commerce. UETA validates electronic contracts, electronic signatures, and the use of electronic agents for electronic contracting. UETA's passage by all the states seems likely, following passage in Congress of the Electronic Signatures in Global and National Commerce Act (federal E-SIGN) in June 2000. This federal law effectively encourages states to adopt the more favorable provisions of UETA.

Impact of UETA

A working understanding of UETA is important to businesses that create, process, and accept paper-based contracts but seek to convert to electronic forms of these documents. Many states' regulatory agencies will implement UETA in government documents. Most state agencies must promote consistency and interoperability between their agencies and with other states and the federal government.

Electronic forms of various traditionally paper-based negotiable instruments are now valid, including notes, bills of lading, warehouse receipts and other documents of title. However, UETA does not yet apply to several key classes of documents, such as wills, codicils (revisions of a will), and testamentary trusts, or to the most common negotiable documents, such as checks, drafts, letters of credit, and investment securities. Nevertheless, the experience of UETA should influence how all negotiable instruments eventually migrate to electronic form. UETA does not alter many states' consumer protections, such as requirements for written or mailed notices. UETA should be distinguished from UCITA; the latter applies only to transactions in computer information. UETA applies to transactions in several but not all underlying subject matters, including land, services, and goods, with the exceptions noted previously. UETA does not apply to computer information transactions covered by UCITA; however, these two laws have many similar provisions.

ONLINE

On-line Information about UETA
**http://www.
uetaonline.com**

Overview of UETA's Provisions

UETA establishes several new terms of commercial practice and thereby expands traditional contracting concepts to work in the digital age. As in UCITA, a UETA record is information inscribed in a tangible medium or stored and retrievable in perceivable form. An **electronic record** is a record that is created, generated, sent, communicated, or received by electronic means. Information means data, text, images, sounds, codes, computer programs, software, databases, and the like. An **electronic signature** is an electronic sound, symbol, or process attached to or logically associated with a record, used with the intent to sign the record. It is the equivalent of an authentication under UCITA. UETA permits the use of electronic agents to effect automated transactions, as discussed later in this chapter.

Electronic Records and Electronic Signatures

The centerpiece of UETA is found in §7, which validates the use of electronic records and signatures. Electronic records satisfy legal requirements for writings so that the enforceability of a record or signature cannot be denied simply because it is in electronic form. Electronic records must still satisfy any other formal requirements, such as notices, disclosures, and completeness of terms. For example, if the parties' e-mail messages show an agreement on the sale of widgets, these electronic records would still need a quantity term to create a valid contract for the sale of goods under the UCC. Electronic records and signatures simply satisfy requirements under existing law, such as the statute of frauds, when they require documents to be signed writings.

Legal requirements to provide information in a memorandum are satisfied with an electronic record if it is capable of retention (printing and storing) by the recipient when received. UETA makes electronic records the equivalent of writings but does not alter other substantive requirements of contract law. Many other laws have specific requirements for the posting, display, communication, and transmittal of records; usually a physical, printed form is required. Although UETA validates electronic records, it does not override these existing legal requirements under other laws mandating particular methods of posting, sending, or formatting records. For example, eviction notices generally must be posted where the tenant is most likely to see it, right on the front door of the dwelling. Even if the landlord and tenant agree to electronic transactions, UETA cannot override property law requirements for physical posting of paper eviction notices.

Electronic transactions pose different security problems than traditional practices that use printed documents or voice telephone conversations. Electronic information is vulnerable to corruption by electronic interference or intentional forgery by hackers. UETA authorizes the use and innovation of security procedures (e.g., encryption) to verify the identity of the sender. UETA makes an electronic record or electronic signature attributable to a particular sender if it was the act of that person, which can be shown in any manner from the context and surrounding circumstances, such as an effective security procedure.

UETA's recognition of electronic signatures differs somewhat from existing digital signature law and practice; the latter focuses on security and encryption. By contrast, UETA simply permits the substitution of an electronic sound, symbol, or process when the law requires a physical signature if it is attached to or logically associated with a record and used with the intent to sign the record. Electronic signatures may take many forms, including a PIN number, password, server identification, biometrics, click-wrap using the "I Agree" button or some form of encryption.

Changes and Errors in Electronic Transmissions

Electronic transmissions can be prone to errors caused by individual users, and sometimes they are prone to changes caused by electronic computers or during communication. UETA encourages the use of security procedures to detect and correct changes or errors. In §10, UETA provides that if one party fails to use a security procedure that both parties had previously agreed to use, the conforming party may avoid the change or error if the security procedure would have discovered it and permitted its correction. Additionally, UETA strongly encourages simple error-checking mechanisms in business-to-consumer transactions, such as confirmation screens that help detect errors. These and other types of changes or errors are resolved under the doctrine of mistake discussed later.

Retention of Electronic Records

Many laws require certain documents to be saved as evidence for future use. UETA §12 permits the retention or presentation of electronic records to satisfy these retention requirements if the information accurately reflects the original and remains accessible for future reference. Accessibility of electronic records becomes problematic over time. Obsolete computer systems may become incompatible or accessible only by data-recovery experts. Floppy disks are not stable over time, and conversion between systems is time-consuming and expensive. Nevertheless, electronic records must remain accessible if they are to satisfy legal requirements for retention. For example, if a law requires retention of a check, that requirement is satisfied by electronic retention of all information on the front and back of the check. Unless there is a requirement to the contrary, written documents can be discarded once transferred to electronic form. However, care should be taken until electronic archives are proven reliable.

Sending and Receipt of Electronic Records

The law often requires inquiry into the time or place that a document is sent or received. For example, recall that a contract is created under the mailbox rule when the acceptance is dispatched. Similarly, the UCC requires that some notices must be delivered to a party's place of business. UETA §15 does not address proof of time of receipt. In the situation of multiple e-mail addresses, the recipient can designate the particular e-mail address to be used. When the precise location is an issue—for example, in a conflict of laws or tax issue—the location is that of the sender or recipient, not the location of the information system. General broadcast messages that are sent to systems rather than individuals are not considered a sending. The key element is whether the sender or recipient has control.

Transferable Records

UETA facilitates electronic negotiable instruments but only in the limited areas of the electronic equivalent of paper promissory notes and paper documents of title, and then only if the issuer agrees that the electronic record should also be an **electronic transferable record**. UETA does not apply to checks, drafts, investment securities, or letters of credit. Rules parallel to UETA may be developed in the future, but the banking system is not yet ready for these documents to "go electronic" under UETA.

UETA creates the concept of "control" over an electronic record, which should be the equivalent of the concept of "possession" as traditionally used in a paper context. Systems must be in place to ensure that the record is transferred in such a manner that there is only one "holder" of the record. The transferable record must remain unique, identifiable, and unalterable. UETA's provisions are summarized in Exhibit 10.1.

Additional Laws Covering Electronic Signatures

The original impetus for UETA in 1996 was the international effort by UNCITRAL, which drafted the Model Law on Electronic Commerce. UETA was intended to displace the proliferating number of electronic and digital signature laws passed by the states in recent years. UETA is technology-neutral and intended to avoid state laws that favor particular technologies. For example, a few state statutes, such as Utah's, validated electronic signatures only if dual-key encryption was combined with third-party certification of the encryption keys. Such technology-specific laws could lock in particular technologies and dampen the incentive to innovate.

Now UETA has spawned imitation. A federal electronic signature law was passed in June 2000, formally known as the **Electronic Signatures in Global and National Commerce Act** (E-SIGN). The E-SIGN law preempts—that is, it overrides—all state electronic signature laws, with an important exception. UETA's electronic contracts and signatures provisions, §§1–16, will apply in states where UETA is enacted without substantial change from the official version discussed previously. Although Pennsylvania's UETA is nearly identical to the official version, California's initial passage of UETA contained more than 50 amendments. E-SIGN may preempt California's UETA if the courts interpret it as not being uniform. Therefore, the applicability of UETA or E-SIGN law may depend on the outcome of future court challenges.

There are some key differences between UETA and E-SIGN. UETA covers more types of transactions than does E-SIGN. For example, as discussed before, UETA covers attribution, defines when records are sent or received, covers mistakes or

Exhibit 10.1 Summary of UETA Provisions

Section	Subject	Summary of Provisions
§1	Short title	Cite as Uniform Electronic Transactions Act (UETA)
§2	Definitions	Definitions for 16 key UETA terms
§3	Scope	Applicable to electronic records and electronic signatures in contracts, notes, documents of title, and certain government documents; not applicable to wills, codicils, testamentary trusts, checks, UCITA transactions, and others prescribed by law
§4	Prospective application	Applies to validate electronic transactions only after the effective date chosen in the adopting state statute
§5	Use of electronic records and electronic signatures; variation by agreement	Use of electronic means is not required; applicable only if parties agree to conduct transactions by electronic means, determined by context and circumstances; any party may refuse to conduct future transactions electronically, and this right cannot be waived; other UETA provisions may be varied by agreement
§6	Construction and application	Construed and applied to facilitate electronic transactions, be consistent with reasonable commercial practice, and facilitate uniformity
§7	Legal recognition of electronic records, signatures, and contracts	Records, signatures, and contracts may not be denied enforceability solely due to their electronic form; electronic records and electronic signatures satisfy legal requirements for signatures and writings
§8	Provision of information in writing; presentation of records	Legal requirement to provide information in writing is satisfied with electronic record if capable of retention (printing and storing) by recipient when received. Validity of electronic records under UETA does not override legal requirements of other laws requiring paper document posting, sending, or formatting
§9	Attribution and effect of electronic record and signature	An electronic record and electronic signature are attributed to a particular sender if they were the act of that person; shown in any manner from the context and surrounding circumstances, such as an effective security procedure (e.g., encryption)
§10	Effect of change or error	Use of security procedures encouraged to verify changes and correct errors; penalizes party using electronic agent in automated transaction with an individual unless an opportunity is provided to verify communication and check errors
§11	Notarization and acknowledgment	Notarization requirements satisfied by electronic signatures made by the authorized person if all required information is attached or logically associated with the electronic signature or electronic record
§12	Retention of electronic records; originals	Electronic record satisfies laws requiring document retention if the information accurately reflects the original and remains accessible for future reference; check retention requirements satisfied by electronic retention of all information from front and back of check; written documents may be discarded after transfer to electronic form; laws passed later may specifically require retention of nonelectronic records
§13	Admissibility in evidence	Evidence of a record or signature cannot be excluded from a legal proceeding solely because it is in electronic form
§14	Automated transaction	Machines acting as electronic agents can form contracts; the lack of human intent does not negate the transaction, inferred from computer programming and use; contract may be formed between electronic agent and individual, e.g., click-through; no legal relationship created with unidentified site access if user is not identified; validates user's click-through license agreement, constitutes a sufficient signature

Exhibit 10.1 Summary of UETA Provisions (continued)

Section	Subject	Summary of Provisions
§15	Time and place of sending and receipt	Parties may agree as to effective timing of electronic messages; otherwise, electronic record is sent when properly addressed or directed to an information processing system designated by the recipient, in a form capable of processing, and it enters a system outside the sender's; receipt occurs when the record reaches the recipient's designated system in a form capable of processing, not when recipient becomes aware of it; return receipt of acknowledgment verifies the record's receipt but not its contents
§16	Transferable records	Framework for negotiation of electronic promissory notes and documents of title but not for other commercial paper (checks, drafts), letters of credit, or investment securities; issuer must agree to use electronic transferable records; "control" over an electronic record depends on the reliability of the system to identify the person as rightful transferee; copies must be identifiable as not the authoritative original; systems must assure there is only a single authoritative copy and only one "holder" of the record; the transferable record must remain unique, identifiable, and unalterable

errors, requires the admission of electronic records in legal proceedings, permits the use of transferable records in transactions beyond real property, and better defines the use of electronic agents in automated transactions. E-SIGN does not cover these subjects precisely. By contrast, E-SIGN provides more consumer protection by requiring notices and protection from unannounced electronic communication system changes. Where UETA merely requires the retention of electronic records for later reference, E-SIGN requires more: that records be accessible to all who are entitled under law. E-SIGN specifically excludes the use of several documents in electronic form—in family law matters (divorce or custody settlements, antenuptial agreements) and for various cancellation notices (utility shutoffs, insurance benefits)—and it prohibits giving notice only by electronic means concerning a primary residence (eviction, mortgage default, repossession, foreclosure). E-SIGN requires assessment of its exceptions and the effectiveness of electronic consumer notices. On balance, the states have an incentive to avoid federal preemption by E-SIGN, so most are likely to pass UETA in its original form. Nearly 30 states have passed UETA as of this writing.

PAROL EVIDENCE

Before a contract is finalized, the parties frequently negotiate or dicker about its terms. The negotiation process often involves proposals and counterproposals of alternative terms that replace previously offered but withdrawn terms. As the negotiators change their proposed terms, they grant advantages to the other party and may take on new performance burdens. The final agreement is usually a compromise in which both parties give up some of their original demands and find agreement in a middle ground. This process of give-and-take through negotiation has led to the parol evidence rule.

The **parol evidence rule** prohibits either party from proving any different terms than those stated in the written document. If the parties litigate over breach of contract, the parol evidence rule prevents the jury from considering any oral or written evidence that would alter or vary the terms in the written contract. Neither party may seek the jury's sympathy by introducing evidence of a contract term that might have been proposed during preliminary negotiations but was later omitted when the parties reached a complete and final agreement. It also prevents fraud because false evidence of terms allegedly adopted is excluded.

The statute of frauds is further distinguished from the parol evidence rule because the latter is "triggered" when the court finds the writing is an **integration**. This means that the parol evidence rule excludes evidence of terms not in the writing when the court finds that the writing was intended by the parties to be so complete that it should not be supplemented. The parties can make this outcome even more certain by including a **merger clause** that clearly states that the writing is intended as an integration. As a practical matter, the rule requires the party that did not prepare the writing to read it carefully before signing. This extra care assures that all of the finally agreed-upon terms actually appear in the written contract. The parol evidence rule does not exclude evidence needed to clarify ambiguities or to show fraud, duress, mistake, illegality, incapacity, or later modifications.

UCITA §301 adapts the traditional parol evidence rule to protect the integrity of records felt to provide the exclusive source of terms, called **confirmatory records**. UCITA permits the explanation or supplement of confirmatory records by using evidence of usage of trade, course of dealing, or course of performance, even if the confirmatory record is not deemed ambiguous or does not amount to an integration. However, under some circumstances, the court may find that the proposed additional terms would not have been omitted from the confirmatory record, so the evidence will be excluded. It is also useful to consider UETA's transferable record rules as an alternate form for safeguarding the terms in a record. Transferable records must be secured by technical means, such as by system architecture or encryption, to prevent alterations.

CONTRACT DEFENSES

Canceling an agreement is difficult. The law generally favors stability and thereby satisfaction of the reasonable expectations of the parties. However, in some cases public policy finds that the circumstances of the parties' mutual assent favor releasing one party from a bad bargain because of actual or potential coercion during negotiations. A contract defense may exist if the parties' mutual assent is not genuine, such as when either party is coerced. An agreement can be canceled if the misunderstanding or coercion is so great that enforcement would be unfair. Such situations typically arise in dealing with incompetents, when one party misrepresents material facts to the other, when certain mistakes are made, or when there is coercion. Neither UETA nor UCITA displaces contract defenses. Indeed, UCITA §114 specifically embraces the contract defenses discussed next with this provision: "principles of law and equity, including the law merchant and the common law of this State relative to capacity to contract, principal and agent, estoppel, fraud, misrepresentation, duress, coercion, mistake, and other validating or invalidating cause, supplement [UCITA]."

CAPACITY

Not all persons are legally capable of entering into contracts. Some persons lack the mature judgment, experience, cognitive development, or ability needed to understand the effects of their promises. Minors as well as drunken, drugged, and insane persons lack contractual capacity, so they are protected from the harsh dealings of another party. However, the mental and negotiating capabilities of incapacitated persons are not usually evaluated in every case. Rather than invalidating outright all the contracts of incompetents, the law gives each incompetent the right to avoid unfair contracts at their choice. An incompetent may usually withdraw or **disaffirm** a contract. This protection lasts until the minor reaches the age of majority, usually 18, or the drunken, drugged, or mentally impaired person becomes lucid. Adults cannot disaffirm contracts made with incompetents.

In most states, both deserving and shrewd minors are protected by the right to disaffirm a contract. For example, a minor can disaffirm a reasonable contract even if the adult party is damaged by the disaffirmance. Adults can protect themselves by assuring they deal only with adults or by insisting an adult parent or guardian join in, cosign, or guarantee the contract. Much of the contemporary regulation of Internet activity involves interaction with minors, with particular emphasis on regulating the collection and use of private information and regulating minors' access to "adult content." Regulation of on-line activity with children is covered in greater depth in Chapter 13.

Although identifying minors is a well-understood problem in face-to-face transactions, it is more problematic when transactions are remotely concluded via phone, fax, or mail. Electronic commerce transactions pose even more difficulty because many use automated transaction processing or electronic agents that are not sufficiently sophisticated to reliably identify the customer's incapacity. Two major methods appear in current use: (1) customer affirmation that they are adults, usually to access adult material, and (2) requiring the use of credit cards to access Web site material, based on the assumption that few customers under age 18 legitimately possess credit cards.

Voidability of an Incompetent's Contracts
Before majority, minors may disaffirm their contracts at any time but must generally return the contractual benefits still in the minor's possession. It is usually irrelevant that some of these benefits are missing or depreciated. Many states now limit this

absolute right of disaffirmance if the minors misrepresented their age. In such situations, the minor may disaffirm but is held liable for the adult's losses. After a minor attains majority or after a mental incompetent becomes lucid, there is a short window of opportunity for disaffirmance, which must be done within a reasonable time. During this grace period, the incompetent is enabled to assess the fairness of contracts made during minority and decide to either disaffirm or ratify them. Once a minor reaches majority and accepts the contract by **ratification**, the right to disaffirm is lost.

The contracts of minors and other incompetents are not automatically considered void. Instead, they are voidable contracts, and only the minor's intentional act of disaffirmance releases the minor from liability. A voidable contract may be ratified only after the incapacity is removed. A minor cannot make a legally binding contract during minority, and it follows that it is impossible to ratify a contract during minority. Ratification can occur only after the minor reaches majority or after an impaired person becomes lucid. The law may **imply ratification** if the incompetent either has not disaffirmed within the reasonable time or acts in a manner inconsistent with disaffirmance. For example, if after reaching 18, the person continues to use property bought during minority, the courts will imply a ratification from that conduct.

Necessaries

In some instances, an incompetent's right to disaffirm is further limited by making them responsible to pay for **necessaries,** the necessities of life: food, clothing, and shelter. Necessaries may also include contracts for services and property that aid in sustaining life, such as tools of the trade, employment placement services, vocational education, and medical services or supplies. This determination is subjective. Of course, the possibility of an unfair bargain still exists, for example, overpriced or defective necessaries. Balancing these considerations, the law implies quasi-contractual duties on the incompetent to pay the reasonable value of the necessary items, which may be less than the price originally agreed to. Items are not necessary if the incompetent's parent or guardian could have provided them.

MISREPRESENTATION AND FRAUD

It is unjust for either party to provide incorrect information to the other about the contract's subject matter. From an economic perspective, the allocation of resources is not optimal if contracting parties have inaccurate or incomplete information. The law prohibits a wrongful party from enforcing a contract based on such misrepresentation. The innocent victim may rescind a contract tainted by misrepresentation if it involves material facts on which the victim has justifiably relied and has suffered damages. The UCC imposes good faith requirements of "honesty in fact in the conduct or transaction concerned," and UCITA further requires the "observance of reasonable commercial standards of fair dealing" in every contract or duty.

The initial focus in a misrepresentation case is on the misstatements themselves and also on the person making the misstatements. Not all statements are facts that can be misrepresented. **Facts** are matters susceptible to exact knowledge and verification, such as past events or current conditions. Usually, predictions of future events are not facts but merely opinions, so they cannot be misrepresented as facts. However, if the opinion is made by a recognized expert or appraiser, then their statements of opinion or prediction could actionable as misrepresentation if they are untrue. For example, a salesperson's use of generalized statements concerning the value or quality of goods is known as **puffing**. Most reasonable buyers understand that puffing statements are usually too vague to be misrepresented as facts. However, if the person making representations of facts knows, or should know, that their statements are false, then this behavior is more serious and the act of misrepresentation becomes fraudulent. **Fraud** is not only a reason to cancel a contract but also the basis for monetary damages based on the tort of **deceit**. Fraud is a criminal act and a regulatory violation under state and federal law.

The next focus in a misrepresentation case is on the victim. In negotiating a contract, the victim's **reliance** on the other party's representations must be reasonable. Sometimes the victim should not believe a particular representation. If the victim has superior experience with the contract subject matter, then the victim should make an independent investigation. If there is no actual reliance by the victim, then there is no causal link between the misrepresentation and the victim's alleged damage. A lack of reliance releases the misrepresenter from liability, because contract law aids only victims damaged as a direct result of another's wrongdoing. However, if the victim of fraud honestly and reasonably believed the misrepresenter's statements, the contract may be canceled. For example, if a landowner promises that no toxins were ever dumped on the land, the buyer may rescind if later there is proof the landowner knowingly contaminated the land.

MISTAKE

In most instances, the law refuses to aid those who blunder in contract negotiations by making mistakes of judgment either in assessing the contract's value or in estimating their own capability to perform. However, some mistakes concern such key terms as the identity, existence, or character of the contract's subject matter. When both parties are mistaken about the subject matter, a **bilateral** or **mutual mistake** occurs, permitting either party to rescind or cancel. If only one party is mistaken, then there is a **unilateral mistake**. The contract is voidable for a unilateral mistake only if the nonmistaken party knows of or should have known of the victim's mistake and takes advantage of the victim.

UETA and UCITA both recognize recurrent areas for error with provisions to prevent mistakes in computer transactions. A mistake may occur in the execution by completing or authenticating the wrong document or misentering keyboard information. A mistake may be the result of computer interface frustration, such as madly clicking through. UETA §10 was introduced previously; it addresses this problem when automated transactions are made with an individual. The party using an electronic agent must give the individual an opportunity to prevent or correct the error. For example, consider an individual who strikes the numeric key "1" to order a single copy of a book from an on-line bookseller but the "1" key sticks or delays in displaying the "1," or the "1" is mistakenly rekeyed causing "111" to be sent. In such a situation, the electronic agent facility of the on-line bookseller must send a confirmation screen that permits the individual to review the quantity ordered. This confirmation might be as simple as a box saying, "You ordered 111 books; click yes if this is correct." UETA §10 provides that without using some such security procedure, the individual may avoid the mistaken contract for the quantity of 111 books. Electronic agents are discussed further at the end of this chapter.

Restitution is usually required to unwind a mistaken transaction. If UETA gives one party a right to rescind a mistaken transaction, any consideration already received must be either returned or destroyed or instructions from the other party followed. However, a party may be prohibited from rescinding if the consideration was already received and used. For example, it may be impossible not to have used information after it is revealed, because the information *is* the consideration. Once information is received and understood, it may be impossible to avoid using it or receiving its value, and this situation limits the right to avoid the error or change.

UCITA §206 empowers the courts to grant appropriate relief if the use of electronic agents results in an automated contract involving fraud, electronic mistake, or the like. UCITA §214 gives consumers a defense to avoid contracts resulting from electronic errors. An **electronic error** occurs in an electronic message if the information processing system provides no reasonable method to detect and correct or avoid errors. In an automated transaction, a consumer is not bound by an electronic message that the consumer did not intend and that was caused by an electronic error, if the consumer promptly notifies the other party, returns the computer information or destroys all copies, and has not already used the benefits of the information or redistributed it to a third party.

DURESS

The terms of most contracts are dictated by market forces or by one party's business needs. Laissez-faire freedom of contract prevents the law from changing the terms of freely negotiated contracts. However, if one party unduly pressures the other party, the resulting contract may be voidable. The threat or actual use of force is an obvious type of coercion that might make a person to agree to unfavorable terms. This constitutes **duress,** and the victim may rescind the contract. The threat of criminal prosecution is duress, but the threat of civil suit is not duress unless the claim is unfounded and malicious. The threat of force may seem nearly impossible in electronic transactions because of the anonymity and separation of the parties. However, hackers have done considerable damage from their remote locations. Some parties identify themselves, or their locations may become known by various means. Some contracting partners can access the other party's assets, perhaps even taking control over another party's computer, information system, or critical Web site. Therefore, duress may become a problem even in the seemingly isolated Internet environment.

Economic duress arises if one party threatens to breach an existing contract unless the victim agrees to another, usually unfavorable, contract. However, economic duress is not a justifiable basis for cancellation if the economic circumstances are imposed by the market or if the victim makes mistakes of judgment. Tying is another form of economic duress discussed further in Chapter 12 on antitrust law. Unfair commercial contracts may be modified under the UCC concept of **unconscionability**, discussed in Chapter 8.

In a more subtle form of coercion, **undue influence** is exerted by someone owing a fiduciary or close relationship to the victim. Victims of undue influence may rescind a contract if a position of trust was used to divert property from its normal course. For example, a young boy's grandmother became his guardian after his parents died, leaving him as the heir to their corporate stock. However, the grandmother induced the boy to sign over the stock to her. Her undue influence deprived him of the stock, so after he became an adult he disaffirmed the stock transfer to his grandmother and the corporation was required to replace his shares.

ILLEGALITY

The common law doctrine of **illegality** holds that the law should not aid lawbreakers; therefore, the courts usually do not assist either party to an illegal contract. Illegality arises if the principal contract objective calls for the commission of a criminal or tortious act. Illegal contracts are void and unenforceable. However, the illegality doctrine is not so straightforward if the contract calls for acts that may not appear illegal but an illegal performance is likely. When the most likely method of performing the contract's legal objective is through illegal means, the contract itself may be illegal. By contrast, an otherwise legal contract is not made illegal simply because one party may do an illegal act during performance. Courts must determine the legality of the subject matter and assess how the principal duties are likely to be performed.

Because the courts refuse to enforce the duties of either party to an illegal contract, it is often said that the parties will be left as the court finds them. For example, if one party has already paid for an future illegal act, the other party will not be required to perform that act or ordered to repay for the unperformed illegal act. Despite the apparent unfairness, illegal contracts cannot be rescinded or enforced when both parties are *in pari delicto*, that is, they both know of the illegality.

Types of Illegality
There are four common areas in which illegality seems to exist but the rule prohibiting enforcement is relaxed: (1) licensing, (2) gambling, (3) public policy, and (4) restraints of trade. Restraints of trade may arise from covenants not to compete (discussed in Chapter 11) and may constitute antitrust offenses (Chapter 12).

Licensing Statutes. Many states and municipalities require certain professionals and most businesses to obtain licenses before doing the licensed activity. A court may refuse enforcement of certain contracts made with unlicensed persons, but first the type of license must be determined. Some licensing statutes, such as municipal business licenses, have only a **revenue-raising** objective. These laws do not usually require a test of the licensee's expertise or qualifications, so contracts made by unlicensed persons or businesses are generally enforceable, even if they have neglected to obtain the required license. However, penalties may apply.

On the other hand, all states and most nations require the licensing of many professionals. The primary objective of professional licensing is to protect the public from unscrupulous and unskilled practitioners. **Regulatory licensing statutes** require satisfaction of certain minimum qualifications before professional practice. For example, lawyers, doctors, engineers, teachers, real estate brokers, and barbers must be licensed before practicing by demonstrating their good character and professional skills. An unlicensed professional's contracts to provide regulated services are illegal and unenforceable. Therefore, a customer or client is usually permitted to rescind such a contract for professional services and regain any funds they paid because they are the type of person protected from unskilled and unscrupulous practitioners by the statute.

Gambling. In all states, the unrestricted free exercise of gambling is illegal. Legal gambling generally occurs in licensed casinos, at licensed pari-mutuel racetracks, at licensed off-track betting parlors, at sales locations for state lotteries, or at limited charitable functions (e.g., bingo games). Contracts to pay illegal gambling debts are unenforceable. The proliferation of Internet gambling sites has challenged law enforcement because gambling sites are often located outside the state or in international havens, generally beyond the practical reach of local law enforcement. Problems of illegal Internet gambling were discussed in Chapter 3.

One of the most perplexing problems with gambling is determining what activities are really illegal gambling. **Gambling** occurs when the parties enter a gaming transaction that creates a risk from an uncertain event. That risk had no prior existence and is created primarily to shift that risk and expose the parties to gain or loss. For example, neither party has a risk of losing the bet before they start the game. However, as a result of playing, they both risk loss. If two parties bet on the price level that a particular stock will reach on a particular day, they create an unenforceable gambling contract. A similar economic event seems to occur if one party sells a stock and another party buys it. However, there is a fundamental difference between betting and a legitimate securities transaction. Stock ownership carries the risk of uncertain price movements, a previously existing risk. By contrast, betting on stock prices creates a brand-new risk that is not associated with stock ownership but is created only in the gambling contract.

Insurance contracts are also susceptible to characterization as gambling. An insurance contract is legal and not gambling if the beneficiary or loss payee (the person selected to receive the policy proceeds) has a close connection with the insured person or property. The beneficiary's risk existed before the insurance was purchased. This close connection or nexus is called an **insurable interest**. An insurance policy is not illegal gambling when there is an insurable interest. An insurable interest in a person's life exists if there is a close family relationship (e.g., spouse, child, parent) or the insured is a key employee of a business. "Janitor life insurance" raised controversy in 2002 because it raised income at some companies but stretches the meaning of "key employees." An insurable interest in property exists if the beneficiary owns, leases, or holds a lien on the property (collateral) or arises for the buyer after the seller identifies specific goods as destined for shipment to a particular buyer under the UCC. If the purchaser of insurance has no insurable interest, the insurance contract is illegal gambling. In the case of a loss, no benefits are paid, but the premiums are returned to the insured party.

Public Policy. As a matter of public policy, the courts usually do not enforce agreements that violate society's ethical and moral norms as found in statutes and court decisions. Public policy prohibits contracts that seek to bribe or unduly influence public officials, fiduciaries, agents, or law enforcement officials in the performance of their duties. Such contracts are illegal and unenforceable. For example, public policy prohibits certain terms in the contracts of parking lot operators, pawn shops, or checkrooms. These parties are bailees because they hold custody of other people's property. Bailees often try to enforce **exculpatory clauses** in an attempt to escape liability if the owner's property is damaged or lost while the bailee has custody. However, such clauses are generally unenforceable if the bailee tries to avoid liability for willful misconduct. Exculpatory clauses are valid only to relieve the bailee of liability for negligence and only if the terms are effectively communicated to the property owner.

AUTHORITY TO NEGOTIATE AND CONCLUDE CONTRACTS

Few contemporary businesses can expect to manage significant growth without hiring employees to do production, administration, procurement, and sales activities. Although the Internet may seem to permit sole entrepreneurs to go it alone, eventually in the expansion of most successful start-ups, they must use other people or firms as agents to perform the increasing workload. This section discusses the parts of agency law needed for others to negotiate, conclude, and perform contracts. The discussion includes the agent's duties, the agent's authority, and the principal's duties resulting from contracts made by agents or from automated transactions that use electronic agents. Agency law is largely taken from case law precedents and summarized in the *Restatement of the Law Second, Agency*, produced by the American Law Institute.

ONLINE

American Law Institute
http://www.ali.org

NATURE OF PRINCIPAL AND AGENT RELATIONS

An agency is initially a two-party relationship between the **principal**, who hires or otherwise consents to accept the services of a second party, the **agent**. An agency is a fiduciary relationship in which the principal consents to have the agent only act for the principal. All corporations are artificial persons under the law that can act only through agents. All corporate contracts, including purchasing, hiring, and selling, are performed by corporate agents. Corporate agents may be persons—usually managers and employees or other firms such as independent contractors. The law of agency becomes important when the principal's legal relationships with outside third parties are affected by the agent's actions. These acts regularly include negotiation, conclusion or performance of contracts, receipt of information, processing of payments, and various forms of decision making. Agencies are most often created formally in a written or oral contract for employment or retainer. However, agencies may also arise by implication from the circumstances, even if there is no formal employment relationship.

Agents are fiduciaries that generally owe duties to perform carefully and with loyalty to the principal. Agents must avoid conflicts of interest; they cannot simultaneously represent the counterparty in a contract. Agents may not favor their own personal interests over their principal's interests. It is unethical and unlawful for an agent to take a profit in a transaction made for the principal without the principal's fully informed consent. An agent must also keep the principal's trade secrets confidential. Agents must obey all the principal's reasonable and lawful orders in connection with the subject of the agency. Agents must use reasonable skill and care by giving the principal's business reasonable diligence and attention. These and other topics related to the rights and duties owed by agents and their principals are detailed further in Chapter 11. The agency relationship is depicted in Exhibit 10.2.

AGENT'S AUTHORITY

The most important point about agency in the contracting context is that the agent's contracting activities bind the principal only if the agent is authorized. This point is significant both for contracting by traditional means and in most electronic com-

Exhibit 10.2 Authority of Agents

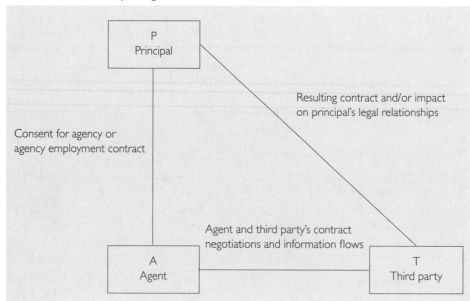

merce activities. Principals may assent to a contract by using their authorized agents. An authorized agent's actions bind the principal in the contract to the third party. Much of this chapter has been devoted to the creation of binding contracts via traditional offer and acceptance or with substitute technological methods. Principals may use agents to negotiate and conclude agreements, and when they do, the resulting agreements are binding, but only if the agents are authorized.

Authorizing agents in a clear manner is critically important to commerce and to understanding the principal's contractual duties. Of the four major methods to authorize agents, the first two forms are actual authority: (1) express authority and (2) implied authority. The second two forms are **circumstantial authority**: (3) apparent (ostensible) authority and after-the-fact authorization by (4) ratification. The clearest and most effective method for authorizing an agent is by **express authority**. As illustrated in the section on written contracts, express authority is best given in a written contract. Express authority can also be granted orally but must be in writing in a few instances. The **equal dignities rule** requires a written authorization if the agent negotiates a contract for the principal that the statute of frauds requires must be in writing: land sale, guarantee, performance for more than one year, sales of goods worth more than $500, and computer information or securities worth more than $5,000.

The principal has the power to control the amount, scope, and timing of the agent's authority. However, if an agent has been granted at least some express authority, the law may permit these powers to expand as an **implied authority** when needed to implement the express grant. For example, assume that a Web-based retailer has authorized its purchasing agent to negotiate and conclude contracts with suppliers at prevailing market prices for up to 5,000 units in any month. One supplier with excess inventory offers a steep discount, but only if the Web retailer's agent will commit to purchase 7,000 units. In some instances, courts may imply the agent has authority to purchase the additional 2,000, even though this quantity exceeds the agent's express authority, because the discount is so favorable. Of course, given sufficient time and an immediately accessible principal, the agent should request express authority. Implied authority is intended to permit the agent to push the limits in an urgent or emergency situation. Implied authority also supplements an express grant of authority when it is vague or silent on a particular point.

An agent's authority may also be expanded when the principal's acts suggest to third parties that the agent is authorized. The principal gives the agent apparent or ostensible authority when the principal's words or actions hold out or intimate that the purported agent has some authority. Even volunteers, who are not authorized agents, may be given apparent authority in some instances. For example, imagine that the trademarked logo of a retail company appears on a manufacturing company's Web site. Additionally, text on the manufacturer's site strongly suggests that the retailer can negotiate prices in sales made directly to the consumer from the manufacturer. In this example, even if the retailer has no actual authority, the manufacturer has held consumers to believe that the retailer is an authorized agent and can make binding contracts.

Authority is best when clearly expressed before the agent negotiates a contract. However, a fourth type of authorization is conferred *afterwards* by ratification.

Ratification may arise either when agents exceed their actual authority or when non-agents volunteer to represent the principal. The contract becomes binding on both the principal and the third party when the principal learns of the unauthorized agent's act and retroactively approves the entire transaction. Ratification may also be implied if the principal remains silent while retaining the benefits of an unauthorized contract with the third party. For example, an unauthorized friend might buy insurance for you. You are not liable to pay the premiums, but if you do, the payment is a ratification of your friend's unauthorized act.

CONTRACT LIABILITY OF PRINCIPAL AND AGENT

Under the **conduit theory**, the contract made by an authorized agent binds only the principal and the third party. Agents usually take on only a representative role and seldom expect to have personal liability if the principal breaches the contract. For example, a corporate purchasing agent would not expect to be held liable if the corporation failed to pay a supplier for goods the agent ordered. The purchasing agent is a mere conduit through whom the principal and third party negotiate. When two corporations are contracting, they each use agents as conduits for their negotiations. However, if the agent is unauthorized, the conduit theory does not apply, and the agent can be held liable for the unauthorized commitment. For example, many corporate employees are not authorized to assent to a click-wrap software license or to bind their employer to a Web site agreement. Some employees may be unaware that the employer may not be responsible on these agreements and that the employee may have personal liability on these electronic commerce agreements.

An agent is also personally liable when pretending to represent a nonexistent principal. An agent may be legally responsible in two additional instances, even if the principal authorizes the negotiations. First, an agent can voluntarily assume the liability of a principal when the agent cosigns or comakes the contract. Second, an agent may be personally liable if the principal's existence or identity is withheld from the third party. Agents are generally not liable when the third party knows that a principal exists; that is, the agent is known to be only a representative, and the principal's identity is also known to the third party. However, some agents withhold the principal's identity to preserve the principal's confidentiality. For example, a principal's negotiating experience may be so well known that third parties might hope to seek better terms when dealing with that principal. To avoid this, the principal might use an agent to negotiate contracts and hide the principal's identity. In such situations, the agent may be specifically instructed to conceal the principal's existence and/or identity and thereby preserve the principal's confidentiality. This is not illegal; it is an undisclosed principal situation.

When the third party knows the agent represents someone else but does not know who the principal is, the principal is **partially disclosed**. Few third parties are willing to accept uncertain responsibility from some unknown principal, so they insist the agent assume responsibility on the contract. When the third party does not even know that there is a principal, the authorized agent appears to actually be the principal in the contract. This is an **undisclosed principal** situation. The third party may elect to hold either the agent or the principal liable on the contract, but not both. This **election** cannot be made until the third party learns the principal's identity and verifies authority. Undisclosed principals are sometimes used in land sales to conceal the identity of a purchaser such as a big company or a wealthy individual.

ELECTRONIC AGENTS UNDER UCITA AND UETA

UCITA and UETA both accept the law of agency. They further envision the use of automated, mechanical, or computerized communications as substitutes for human agents to negotiate or conclude contracts. UCITA §107(d) authorizes electronic agents to authenticate, perform, or manifest assent to create a contract. UCITA §102(27) defines an **electronic agent** as a computer program (or electronic or other automated means) used by a person to initiate an action (take a step in an electronic transaction) or to respond to electronic messages or performances on the person's behalf without review or action by an individual. The UETA definition is similar. The principal is bound by the operations of the electronic agent, even if no individual is aware or reviews the electronic agent's actions. The acts of an electronic agent may be attributable to that person or company.

Electronic agents may conclude **automated transactions,** contracts formed without human intervention by one or both parties. Automated transactions may also be formed with interaction between a human and an electronic agent. Electronic agents may manifest assent to a record or term after an opportunity for review. The assent may occur after the electronic agent has an opportunity to authenticate the record or term. Alternatively, assent may occur after the electronic agent starts to perform by delivering the licensed information or by making a payment due. For an electronic agent to have sufficient opportunity to review a record or term, it must be in a form that a reasonably configured electronic agent could be technically capable of using. Eventually, electronic agents may develop artificial intelligence, enabling totally autonomous negotiations.

DISCHARGE OF OBLIGATIONS, BREACH OF CONTRACT, AND REMEDIES

The vast majority of contracts are performed satisfactorily; goods are delivered and accepted, services are adequately rendered, land ownership is transferred and possession taken, and payments are accurately made and credited. Small disputes may arise concerning the quantity, quality, form, or timeliness of both parties' performance, but most are quickly settled amicably. Of course, there are two major incentives to avoid contract disputes. First, most parties genuinely seek repeat business and need to build and maintain their good reputations by performing satisfactorily. Breach of contract is generally believed to harm commercial reputations. Second, the threat of legal process looms over contract performances. The law provides aggrieved parties with a remedy.

Early experience with e-commerce shows that performance and payments pose a challenge to the effectiveness of traditional economic and legal incentives. These traditional methods of resolving contractual disputes are under stress in the e-commerce world. For example, many on-line retailers in the B2C world have failed to provide adequate customer support, failed to accurately deliver customer orders in a timely manner, or failed to process payments fairly. As a result, some e-commerce businesses have collapsed. Many e-commerce firms are developing new policies and procedures, including the use of trusted third parties to oversee or assist in performance. Two key observations should be made. First, initial designs of e-commerce transaction processing, particularly by dot.com entrepreneurs inexperienced in traditional commerce, may not satisfy customers. This undermines confidence in e-commerce generally and may delay its growth. Second, political and economic pressures will mount to prevent recurrence of e-commerce service failures. If the public comes to believe that remedial efforts are failing, additional consumer protection regulations seem likely.

In this section, the traditional methods of determining satisfactory performance are explored, including the discharge of contractual duties, measures of adequate performance, breach of contract, and legally enforceable remedies. Measures of performance and remedies are standardized under contract law. Nevertheless, laissez-faire allows the parties considerable flexibility to customize such terms to best suit their needs. This section also discusses the difficulties in fashioning new laws that balance the need to encourage e-commerce growth and the need to adequately protect both sides in e-commerce transactions. The primary focus is on the common law as modified for goods sales by the UCC and for licenses under UCITA where it is the law. Many of UCITA's provisions define licensing, and they are detailed in Chapter 11.

DISCHARGE BY PERFORMANCE

Each party's performance is judged by the degree of perfection that a reasonable person can objectively expect to receive. To adequately discharge their contract duties, both parties must perform exactly as promised; otherwise, they will have committed a **material breach.** This is the **perfect tender rule:** The buyer must pay fully and on time, and the seller must deliver on time exactly the quality and quantity. If either party materially breaches its obligation, the innocent party may postpone counter-performance and sue for a remedy. In many instances, contract law relaxes this strict rule. Strict and exact performance of many complex contracts is not always realistic. In some situations, the law or the parties may permit something less than perfect and full performance.

Consider two compelling examples that support relaxing the perfect tender rule when the seller produces a product customized for the buyer's particular needs. The first is a classic example, a building construction contract. The contractor, acting in good faith, is permitted by law to deviate slightly from the plans and specifications if the deviations are only minor and unintentional and they scarcely cause the buyer any real harm. For example, the building materials called for in the contract may become unavailable, permitting the contractor to make substitutions. The law requires that the contractor should still be paid. The second example is similar: the design and production of complex software or Web sites. Technology and consumer tastes change quickly during performance. Sometimes the customer may call for changes after construction starts; perhaps the vendor takes advantage of new tools or technological capabilities. When the performance made is not exactly as stated in the contract, it may be best to adjust the purchase price to reflect the slightly lesser but still reasonably acceptable quality because it still amounts to a **substantial performance.**

The distinction between the perfect tender rule and the substantial performance doctrine is illustrated by the difference between mass production and individually customized production. The industrial revolution made possible much higher efficiency and more consistent quality. Innovations included routine tasks and repetitive production with standardized and interchangeable parts. Mass production permits more consistent quality, which justifies the perfect tender rule for standardized goods. By contrast, the difficulties of achieving perfection in specially manufactured products is complicated by uncertainties in production, fitting custom parts and materials availability, justifying a relaxation of perfection.

How these two rules of performance quality will adapt to the "mass customization" plans of some e-commerce companies is uncertain. **Mass customization** promises the quality control and efficiency advantages of mass production with the made-to-order customization that customers increasingly demand. Mass customization promises to reduce inventory costs and shorten production delays. The closest contemporary example of this manufacturing-to-order concept is the on-line ordering and configuration of personal computers. It may take some time before mass customization of hardware or software products can achieve its promise of satisfying consumer choice, cost savings and consistent reliability. Until manufacturers can adequately test the performance of all combinations of options, the unknown interactions among them can conceal reliability problems.

The lateness of deliveries, payments, or performance of services is also judged. If the delay in performance is too serious, it may constitute a material breach. If there is a material breach, the innocent party is relieved from performance and may sue for a remedy. Slight delays must be tolerated, though, perhaps with small price adjustments made. However, at the time of contracting either party may insist the contract include a provision making **time of the essence.** This provision requires perfect tender and timely performance. For example, a real estate sale contract might require the buyer to search diligently for financing and require that time is of the essence so that if the financing cannot be found the seller can quickly find another buyer or the buyer find another property.

Anticipatory Breach

Either party may notify the other party of an inability or unwillingness to perform in the future. This is an **anticipatory breach** under the common law and an **anticipatory repudiation** under the UCC or UCITA. Such a preannounced breach gives the innocent party a choice if breach is threatened before the time set for performance:

either await performance or immediately sue. In either case, the aggrieved party may suspend its performance after receiving this anticipatory notice. Anticipatory repudiation permits the innocent party to sue for damages, cancel the contract, or ignore the repudiation and await performance. The breaching party may withdraw the repudiation if the aggrieved party has not yet acted on it, such as by contracting with someone else or by bringing suit. At any time, either party may demand **adequate assurances of performance** from the other party. For example, if a seller is uncertain about the buyer's solvency or if a buyer is disturbed about recent erratic deliveries, either party could lose trust. If the other party fails to give assurances after a request, the innocent party may pursue remedies for breach even though the time for performance has not yet arrived.

IMPOSSIBILITY OF PERFORMANCE

The doctrines of delegation and **impossibility of performance** are interrelated. Sometimes an obligor becomes ill and cannot perform services or cannot deliver goods that were destroyed or unobtainable if a supplier halted production. A strike or a boxcar shortage might also prevent performance. In such situations, the contract becomes *subjectively impossible* to perform. That is, the obligor (the subject) cannot personally perform as promised, but perhaps an outsider could be substituted to perform as a delegate.

Consider the differences between a contract for the services of a famous portrait painter and those of a house painter. If the artist becomes ill, there is simply no direct substitute for the quality of the expected performance. Because no one else can paint like the artist, performance is either justifiably delayed or excused altogether by impossibility. By contrast, if the house painter suffers a strike, there is no objective legal impossibility of performance because house painting is not generally considered so unique. Why? Because another house painter could be appointed to paint the building. In such cases, the obligor *must* delegate the duty or risk breaching the contract. The doctrine of impossibility excuses performance only when unique services are justifiably excused or unique subject matter is destroyed before performance. Other variations of this defense are the **frustration of purpose** and **commercial impracticality** doctrines. Some courts release an obligor if, after the contract has been made, events occur that render the other party's performance worthless or too costly.

Force Majeure Clauses

The parties may agree to define the particular events or conditions that trigger impossibility of performance. **Force majeure** clauses are often used when one or both parties could be exposed to uncertain and debilitating events. Force majeure clauses are enforceable as privately bargained-for impossibilities. They are customized to the parties' particular needs or their industries. For example, oil and gas supply contracts typically contain force majeure clauses that excuse performance if oilfield difficulties are experienced. Force majeure clauses are generally enforceable if, through no fault of either party, performance becomes impossible because of listed events. Typical subjects of force majeure are labor troubles (strikes), war, transportation failures, acts of God, and any other event the parties mutually agree to include in the clause.

DAMAGES

Contract law is intended to satisfy the parties' reasonable expectations of performance. In most cases, money damages are an efficient and satisfactory remedy. **Compensatory damages** are the most typical damage awards because they represent the losses actually suffered in obtaining a replacement, realizing the promisee's original expectations, or obtaining a substitute performance. For example, the party breaching a contract must usually pay any of the innocent party's out-of-pocket expenses. Of course, the nonbreaching party has a **duty to mitigate damages** by avoiding and minimizing their damages when possible. Punitive damages are rarely awarded in breach of contract cases unless the promisor is also guilty of tortious and willful misconduct.

Damages for breach can sometimes be made more certain if the parties agree to a **liquidated damage** provision in which the parties specify the amount of damages if one party breaches. Liquidated damage clauses are enforceable only if they are legitimate estimates of uncertain future damages. An attempt to use liquidated damages to penalize and discourage breach is generally unenforceable. For example, if a wholesaler presold a quantity of goods to be acquired from a manufacturer, it would be unreasonable to charge the manufacturer liquidated damages that were considerably more than the wholesaler might expect to profit on the transaction. A large liquidated damage provision in such a supply contract would be unenforceable as a penalty because the wholesaler's potential loss is limited to the difference between wholesale and resale price, plus expenses or diminished goodwill and reputation. However, if the wholesaler had not presold the goods and the market for the goods was uncertain, a liquidated damage provision approximating the wholesaler's markup could be a reasonable amount.

SPECIFIC PERFORMANCE

Although damages are the most typical remedy, a specific performance of the contract may be ordered in cases involving unique property such as land, collectibles, or goods previously designated for purchase. **Specific performance** is a court order requiring the parties to perform exactly as originally promised. When money damages are inadequate to satisfy the promisee's expectations, the extraordinary remedy of specific performance may be ordered. No specific performance will be ordered for personal services. Both the UCC and UCITA provide for specific performance in appropriate circumstances.

ARBITRATION CLAUSES

Arbitration is a traditional dispute-settlement mechanism in international commerce. It is used increasingly in domestic commercial disputes for the reasons discussed in

Chapter 1—namely, efficiency, privacy, and avoidance of litigation difficulties. However, an arbitration clause may not always result from balanced bargaining. Indeed, critics charge that the stronger party usually *imposes* arbitration on the weaker party, who may have little choice but to accept.[1]

UCC REMEDIES

The UCC remedies are intended to put the innocent party in the same position as if the breach had not occurred. An innocent but aggrieved party may seek a court order, the recovery of money damages, or other rights designed to give the innocent party benefits equivalent to what full performance would have given. The UCC imposes a general duty of good faith on all parties. The remedies for breach of contract track the steps in each party's performance so that the impact of a breach can be corrected precisely and quickly. Both parties must stand ready to perform until the other party fails to **tender** performance as required; that is, they must indicate a willingness and an immediate ability to perform ("here, take the money!").

The UCC generally permits either buyer or seller to recover **consequential damages,** those additional damages that flow naturally from the breach, including lost income or profits. However, the UCC requires any aggrieved party to mitigate damages by trying to minimize them whenever practical. Either party can cancel the contract if the other party is in breach of contact. The UCC imposes a four-year **statute of limitations** period, which requires suit for breach of contract within four years after the contract was performed. However, much of the focus of the UCC is providing reasonable self-help mechanisms to avoid confrontation or litigation. The UCC releases parties from performing if an unforeseen event makes the obligor's performance highly impractical. For example, if a seller's cost of goods increases by 10 times or more, then the contract might be discharged for commercial impracticality.

Seller's Obligations and Buyer's Remedies

In addition to rights under the extensive UCC express and implied warranties of quality, the buyer has several more remedies. The most fundamental buyer remedy is the right to receive **conforming goods** that exactly meet the contract description. The seller must tender delivery at a reasonable time and place, give the buyer notice, and hold the goods for a reasonable time to give the buyer the opportunity to take delivery. The buyer has the right of **inspection** before accepting goods to assure they conform to the description, unless the delivery is COD or a "shipment against documents" (e.g., document of title, draft, letter of credit). However, the inspection right imposes a duty on the buyer that may limit warranty protection. For example, to the extent the buyer fails to discover a defect while making a reasonable inspection, the buyer's warranty is excluded, and there is no remedy.

If the seller delivers **nonconforming goods** that do not meet the contract specifications, then the buyer has three choices: (1) accept the nonconforming goods,

---

1. *Hill v. Gateway 2000, Inc.,* 105 F.3d 1147 (7th Cir.) *cert. denied* 522 U.S. 808 (1997).

(2) reject nonconforming goods and sue for damages, or (3) accept whatever commercial units (e.g., case, crate, pallet) that are reasonable under the circumstances and sue for damages. An **acceptance** of goods occurs when the buyer indicates willingness to keep them, fails to reject within a reasonable time, or treats the goods as belonging to the buyer (e.g., uses or resells them). Even after an acceptance, the buyer has a limited right of **revocation of acceptance**; the buyer may withdraw or cancel the acceptance if there are defects that were difficult to discover in a normal inspection (latent defects) or the buyer reasonably believed the seller would cure but the seller never did. After the buyer rejects or revokes acceptance, the buyer must reship the goods back to the seller or hold them for the seller to pick up.

The buyer's rights after rejecting nonconforming goods are limited by the seller's right to cure. **Cure** is the seller's right to correct the breach by notifying the buyer that substitute conforming goods will be provided. Then the buyer must receive the conforming goods before the time originally set for performance. If the seller fails to deliver conforming goods by the time set for performance, the buyer may **cover** (purchase substitute goods from another seller). Alternatively, the buyer may sue for specific performance to force the seller to give up unique goods or for **replevin** of goods already identified in the contract. The buyer has the right to collect compensatory damages when the seller fails to perform. Damages are computed as the difference between the contract price and the higher market price on the day of the breach. An alternate measure is the increased price paid for cover, including incidental and consequential damages.

Consider how these remedies would affect a retailer who was promised a shipment of desktop personal computers on Thursday just before the retailer's well-advertised Saturday sales event. If the wrong goods arrive (laptop computers) on Tuesday, the supplier still has until Thursday to cure this by delivering conforming goods—desktop PCs. However, if nothing shows up by Thursday, the buyer may cover by purchasing desktop PCs from another supplier on Friday. The buyer is not required to cover, so if no goods arrive for the Saturday sales event, the buyer can still sue the supplier for consequential damages, probably lost profits from the desktop PCs that would have been sold on Saturday.

Buyer's Obligations and Seller's Remedies

The seller's most basic right is to receive payment of the contract price on or before the time set for performance of the payment obligation. The seller has four basic monetary remedies if the buyer refuses to accept delivery of conforming goods: (1) collect damages equal to the difference between the contract price and a lower market price prevailing at the time of breach, (2) collect damages on the difference between the contract price and a lower resale price to some other buyer, (3) recover lost profits if the buyer's breach causes the sale of fewer units by the seller, or (4) sue for the total sale price if the goods are unsuitable for sale to anyone else (highly customized).

When the buyer's solvency is in question, the seller has some additional remedies: (1) stop the shipment of goods already in transit with a common carrier, (2) refrain from delivering goods the seller still holds, or (3) demand return of goods anytime during the 20 days following delivery if the buyer is insolvent. However, the seller must deliver as promised if an insolvent buyer tenders cash. The CISG closely mirrors the UCC remedies for both buyer and seller.

REMEDIES UNDER UCITA

In those states where UCITA is effective, the remedies parallel the UCC's remedies in many ways. UCITA's laissez-faire perspective permits the parties considerable freedom to design their own remedies by contract. This makes the UCITA remedies controversial because licensing is unique and many of the balances the UCC draws between vendor and buyer rights in goods sales may not work well for the licensing of software or information. Indeed, many observers predict that transactions governed by UCITA will show systematic bias favoring sellers in consumer transactions and bias favoring large corporate buyers in B2B transactions. Generally, UCITA includes a cancellation right after notice to either party if the other party breaches. The parties may agree to a liquidated damage provision. UCITA has a complex statute of limitations of ostensibly four years. However, the statute of limitations may be changed in nonconsumer contracts, but not to less than one year. Limited forms of money damages are a primary focus of UCITA remedies, but they are much more regulated than under the common law or the UCC. As in other areas of the law, the parties must mitigate damages whenever it is reasonable to do so.

Limitations on Electronic Self-Help

UCITA has a controversial contractual remedy that some software producers and information providers apparently are hoping to use widely: **electronic self-help**. The licensor can disable some software with several possible technologies. One clear example of electronic self-help termination occurs when the licensor shuts off the licensee's access to programs or databases at the licensor's server. This electronic self-help remedy may be legitimate if the licensee has missed payments and is nearly insolvent. The licensor should not be required to continue supplying when the licensee is in breach of contract.

It is typical for software or data to reside on the licensee's system. However, even when the licensee physically controls the information, it can still be remotely shut off by electronic means. Examples of these electronic self-help methods include

- Periodic electronic reauthorization
- A time-activated shut-off device (electronic time bomb)
- Periodic entry of changing authorization codes
- Web-based probes from the vendor that disable the system, or the system may require periodic retrieval of reauthorization from the licensor over the Web, by telephone, or by mail

Self-help has long been acceptable in leasing and in secured lending (discussed later). Repossession of automobiles is a prime example. However, there is strong public opinion that electronic self-help is an intrusive violation of privacy. Public policy tolerates self-help only if it does not cause great surprise, does not breach the peace or damage third parties, and does not permit economic abuse of a vulnerable customer. For example, if electronic self-help were used to shut down key accounting software or disable an essential data system, there could be potentially huge consequential damages for the licensee. Therefore, electronic self-help may be deemed to be *illegitimate* if the licensee is not really in breach, the licensor pressures the licensee to pay more or buy other products, or there are risks to public safety, potential harms to third parties, or the risk of personal injuries, property damage, or information destruction. Without these safeguards, electronic self-help could actually serve to hold the licensee's business for ransom.

UCITA prohibits electronic self-help in mass market licenses. In other licenses, the licensee must specifically consent to the self-help provision, but this could be a "take-it-or-leave-it" proposition. The licensor must give the licensee 15 days notice before invoking electronic self-help. UCITA remedies are derived from licensing practices; other details are discussed in Chapter 11.

ONLINE

Controversy over UCITA's Self-Help Provisions
http://www. ucitaonline.com

CREDITORS' RIGHTS AND DEBTOR PROTECTIONS

A critical underpinning to the commercial law system is the protection given parties when contracts are breached. Much of commerce depends on seller-financed transactions or on transactions financed by third-party financial institutions. Long experience with abuses by both debtors and creditors shows a need for legal and contractual safeguards that balance their interests. When a debtor's insolvency leads to default on a loan, two major sources of law are implicated: (1) state commercial law including secured transactions and (2) federal bankruptcy law. Insolvency protections include the orderly and fair administration of the insolvent debtor's remaining assets, which can minimize creditor losses if the debtor tries to disappear with the assets or if the debtor favors some creditors over others. It also addresses the creditor's harsh treatment of the debtor. This section examines the planning and practice of "definancing," first, as provided by contract and state law on creditors' rights and then under federal bankruptcy law. Federal bankruptcy law is divided into components generally called chapters, which are frequently referred to in this discussion: Chapters 7, 11, and 13.

ONLINE

Insolvency information and data
http://www. bankruptcydata.com

SECURED FINANCING

The creditor's willingness to extend credit depends on the probability of default and on how adequately the debtor can assure repayment. The debtor's promissory note provides the basic legal right to debt repayment. **Insolvency**—the unwillingness or inability to make debt payments—too often makes it impractical for creditors to collect. This reality has led to the development of other repayment assurances. For example, a creditor should investigate the debtor's creditworthiness before making the loan. Credit insurance, surety, and guarantee contracts are sometimes used, making third parties accountable if there is a default. Frequently, creditors insist that the debtor grant a lien in collateral—that is, **pledge** property actually held by the creditor or grant a right to foreclose on property the debtor uses.

A **lien** permits the creditor to take steps to repossess and foreclose on the collateral if the debtor defaults. **Foreclosure** is a regulated process of selling the collateral to produce **proceeds**, usually money paid by the buyer at the foreclosure sale. Foreclosure proceeds are used largely to pay down the outstanding debt. Common examples of **security interests** include mortgages on land, new car liens, and a corporate bondholder's lien on factory machines.

UCC Article 9 provides the legal machinery for securing loans by creating lien rights in personal property but not in real estate. A major revision of Article 9 became effective in July 2001 and is being adopted by most states, effective when designated in the state's adoption statutes. During the transition from old Article 9 to Revised Article 9, it is still useful to understand both versions, even if all 50 states adopt the revision. Although Revised Article 9 continues the use of paper documents, it now recognizes electronic records; it permits the use of traditional signatures while also recognizing electronic authentication. These advances should enhance efficiency and accuracy in credit transactions, such as electronic loan applications, electronic communications between debtors and creditors, and electronic creation of liens using public filing and retrieval. Revised Article 9 also makes new distinctions between consumer debtors and commercial borrowers.

The only party who can grant a lien and create a security interest is the owner or rightful possessor of property. Often, the **secured party** (lender) will not make a loan unless the owner grants a lien. A security interest gives the secured party special rights to keep or sell the collateral if the debtor defaults. **Default** is not defined in Article 9, which gives the parties freedom of contract to define default in the loan documentation. Default is most often triggered by missed periodic loan payments. Default can also be triggered by other financial conditions or behaviors that lenders find typical of an imminent breach.

Commonly, the borrowed money is used to purchase the collateral. This creates a **purchase money security interest (PMSI)**. Many UCC Article 9 rules depend on the type of property: intangibles, accounts, inventory, consumer goods, farm products, or equipment. Revised Article 9 adds several new classes of property important to the information economy, including software, payment intangibles, investment property, health care insurance receivables, and commercial tort claims.

Security interests must generally be created in two basic steps. The first step is attachment, the grant of a security interest. The second step is **perfection**, determination of the secured party's priority. Priorities are important if a debtor grants several liens in the same collateral to different secured parties. Article 9 priority rules settle these conflicting claims when the proceeds of a foreclosure sale are insufficient.

Attachment

The creditor is responsible for making the security interest become effective. Attachment using a **security agreement** is the most common method. The security agreement is a written document or electronic record, signed or authenticated by the debtor, describing the collateral and granting the lien. Attachment makes the lien effective between the debtor and the creditor. Attachment is accomplished when three things occur. First, the borrower must sign a security agreement or authenticate such an electronic record. Alternatively, the creditor could take possession of the collateral to make attachment possible. Second, the secured party must give **value**, a form of consideration. Usually a lender advances the loan principal to be used for the purchase of either the collateral or some other property. Third, the borrower must have some **rights** in the collateral, although full ownership is not necessary. After the security interest attaches, the secured party should be careful to assure that no other secured party acquires superior rights in the collateral. Assurance of this priority is the second major step: the perfection process.

Perfection by Public Filing

Debtors are usually free to grant numerous security interests in the same collateral to several lenders or secured parties. This practice may be appropriate if the asset is so valuable that it could cover several loans or be useful in a later round of financing. For example, homeowners commonly borrow money by taking out a second mortgage on their home. However, disputes inevitably arise among several secured parties who all have security interests in the same collateral. For example, if the collateral is worth less than the total of all outstanding debts, some lien holder(s) may not be fully paid. To be assured of their precedence, secured parties must take the additional step of perfection. This puts other potential lenders on notice that the secured party has priority. Perfection usually occurs when the secured party files a **financing statement**, known as Form UCC 1. This document or electronic record is separate from the security agreement. A financing statement describes the collateral and the security interest and must be filed at the local government office (county courthouse) or state government office (secretary of state) as required by law.

The public filing of liens on both real estate and personal property serves a very important function: It facilitates efficient financing. The availability of these public databases permits potential lenders to make a loan conditional on a reliable foreclosure value of particular collateral. The lender can search for other security interests on the property that the borrower is offering as collateral. Lenders can avoid making loans if liens are already outstanding on the property. Public policy disfavors secret liens because they pose excessive risk to later lenders and thereby restrict the availability of credit. The current local and state filing system for secured transactions is archaic and fragmented, frustrating efficiency. A comprehensive, national, searchable electronic database of secured transaction filings could greatly enhance the protection of lenders and eventually lower the cost of credit.

The revision of Article 9 should help advance the filing system from today's numerous local and state paper-based databases into a national electronic system. Electronic databases may be inherently more efficient, rigorous, and potentially exhaustive in retrieving relevant data. Today, a few private vendors are integrating access to many states' electronic filing systems. Further, there are national secured transaction filings for a few types of collateral—IP and mobile equipment like railroad cars and commercial aircraft. However, a single, federally operated, secured

transaction database for most types of property would be difficult to achieve politically. The efficiency and fairness of secured financing may not reach its potential
until search costs and accuracy are improved. Revised Article 9 holds great promise
but may not eliminate secured transaction costs so long as the information trail is
easily broken by debtors moving the collateral to other states, changing their individual or business names, or becoming acquired by other companies.

Perfection: Alternatives to Filing

UCC Article 9 allows alternative methods of perfecting a secured transaction. First,
the secured party may perfect by taking possession of the collateral. If other potential lenders act carefully, another lender's possession is a clear signal that a security
interest exists. Second, most vehicles have title certificates that are needed to transfer ownership. Notice of a security interest is typically written directly on a vehicle's
certificate of title, and this clearly notifies buyers or lenders considering a transaction that a lien exists. Third, perfection of a PMSI is automatic for consumer goods,
instruments, and health care insurance receivables. Fourth, floating liens are particularly useful for rolling inventories through the use of **after-acquired property
clauses**. For example, inventory collateral can be generally or vaguely described, so
that liens on goods sold to consumers from the inventory are released upon sale.
However, the secured party's lien can then be automatically extended, via the after-
acquired property clause, to any replacement goods that replenish the inventory.
Fifth, the lien on property the debtor sells can extend to the proceeds received in that
sale; that is, the security interest covers the money received by the seller or any goods
the seller receives in trade for the secured property that was sold.

Financing Transactions in IP and Telecommunications Intangibles

Intangibles such as IP pose conceptual and practical financial problems. Of course,
all assets, tangible or intangible, are most reliably valued *ex post*, using the hindsight
of completed transactions and cash flows. Tangible assets seem much easier than
intangibles to value with reliability and precision *ex ante*, particularly if there are liquid markets that can value similar assets. Traditional accounting principles do not
adequately standardize the valuation techniques for IP and many other intangibles.
Most IP assets are valued at acquisition cost. It is inherently misleading to simply
capitalize research and development (R&D) expenses. R&D is frequently irrelevant
to the IP asset's potential for cash flow. Research is inherently risky, and the commercialization of innovation is uncertain. IP is often a mere component of other
products or services, raising additional uncertainty. Even modern techniques of
financial forecasting (e.g., discounted cash flow, options pricing) are more speculative when applied to intangible assets.

Goodwill is a convincing example of the difficulties in valuing IP. Goodwill cannot be recorded as an asset unless it is acquired in a transaction involving tangible
assets. Goodwill may be valued for financial accounting purposes only to the extent
the purchase price for an acquired company or a business unit exceeds the fair market value (FMV) of its tangible assets. This surplus is simply presumed to be goodwill

if the tangible assets purchased are available in a liquid market at FMV. Goodwill is often represented by trademark(s) so the trademark's value may be inferred from the value of goodwill.

Secured transaction law also poses risk in the financing of intangibles. Given the higher inherent risk that intangibles will be profitable, creditors need even more effective techniques to reduce the risk of debtor default. The legal process for securing loans on IP and other intangibles is fragmented and uncertain. The acquisition of effective liens on trademarks, patents, *unregistered* copyrights, and FCC broadcast licenses is governed by UCC Article 9. These assets are classified as **general intangibles** under both the old and the revised versions of UCC Article 9. Case law legitimizes the traditional UCC attachment process using a security agreement and the UCC perfection process through filing in the applicable state or local office. Although the IP laws generally require federal filings for outright assignment (a complete sale of the IP asset), cases hold that the federal IP laws allow UCC filings for secured transactions because they are not outright assignments. The trademark and patent laws have no secured transaction provisions. Therefore, the only method to create enforceable liens in trademarks, patents, *unregistered* copyrights, and broadcast licenses is by using state UCC law and processes. Although domain names are closely related to trademarks, how liens on domain names will be resolved is uncertain. It is also unclear whether domain names are assets available to satisfy creditors' claims. UCC security interests can also be extended to cover the proceeds of IP, which essentially are the royalties and other fee income from licensing the IP.

All this stands in stark contrast to the process required for *registered* copyrights. The *only* method to create enforceable liens in registered copyrights is to follow the federal secured transaction filing process at the federal Copyright Office. Copyright law opens the Copyright Office's filing system only to registered copyrights. Therefore, *unregistered* copyrights generally cannot use the Copyright Office services, so they must rely on the UCC secured transaction process. Federal law will likely trump state law in the growing area of telecom licenses. The FCC appears to have the legal right to recapture licenses to use portions of the airwave spectrum that had been auctioned to a wireless firm that went bankrupt. A license to use a portion of the airwave spectrum is a very valuable intangible asset, essential to wireless service providers. Although this federal right of recapture is not really a contractual form of lien, it nevertheless works to preempt other creditors' claims on the license.

Priorities

Disputes are inevitable among secured parties competing for the proceeds of a foreclosure sale. Generally, the secured party that perfected first will have its debt completely satisfied out of the foreclosure sale proceeds before other creditors with lower priority receive anything. If the dispute is among unperfected parties, the party whose security interest attached first will win. UCC Article 9 provides for many complex additional priority rules based on a number of factors: the types of secured parties, the types of collateral, whether the loan created a PMSI, whether the debtor is in bankruptcy, and whether the collateral was purchased by a good faith purchaser for value.

Default

After priority problems are resolved, the secured party may choose between remedies: selling the collateral in a public or private sale or simply keeping the collateral to satisfy part or all of the debt. If the sale brings more money than is needed to pay off the secured party's debt, the surplus first pays the expenses of the repossession and sale. Next it repays all other secured debts, and then any remainder is returned to the debtor. The debtor is responsible for any deficiency if sale proceeds are insufficient to pay all debts.

BANKRUPTCY

The Constitution empowers Congress to pass uniform bankruptcy laws. The Bankruptcy Act of 1898, which governs bankruptcy in the United States, has been revised several times. Substantial amendments were made in the Bankruptcy Reform Acts of 1978, 1984, 1986, and 1994. Another revision effort that is likely to favor creditors began in 2000 but remained unresolved by 2002. After a bankruptcy filing, the debtor may lose control and ownership of many assets. These assets are liquidated (sold), and the proceeds are eventually distributed to creditors. Usually, most of the unpaid portion of the bankrupt's debts are **discharged**—that is, eliminated altogether—resulting in the debtor receiving a "clean slate." Thus, bankruptcy law provides the overextended debtor with a fresh start and assures fair and equal treatment of all creditors within each of several creditor classes. There are several different forms of bankruptcy that may be used by individuals, businesses, and certain government units.

American Bankruptcy Institute
http://www.abiworld. org

Straight Bankruptcy

The best known form of bankruptcy is Chapter 7 of the bankruptcy code. Known as **straight bankruptcy**, it provides for a complete liquidation of the debtor's assets and partial satisfaction of most debts. The bankruptcy courts oversee the process of (1) collecting and selling the debtor's assets, (2) verifying creditor claims, (3) distributing the proceeds, and (4) granting the debtor a discharge of most remaining debts. Insolvent individuals, partnerships, and corporations may be liquidated in straight bankruptcy. A debtor may choose to file a **voluntary petition** with the bankruptcy court, or creditors may "throw" a debtor into bankruptcy by filing an **involuntary petition.** The fact of **insolvency** is determined on either the cash flow basis or the balance sheet basis. A debtor unable to pay debts as they come due is insolvent on the cash flow basis. A debtor with liabilities in excess of assets is insolvent on the balance sheet basis. Either debtor may take advantage of bankruptcy laws. From the time that the bankruptcy petition is filed until the final disposition of the case by the bankruptcy court, a stay or suspension order is in effect. The **bankruptcy stay** prevents creditors from collecting debts or foreclosing on collateral.

To qualify for a discharge from debts, the debtor must perform several duties and cooperate in good faith during bankruptcy proceedings. The debtor must file documents with the bankruptcy court, including (1) a list of creditors, (2) a schedule or list of assets and liabilities, and (3) other financial statements. The debtor must give up all nonexempt property to the bankruptcy trustee, who becomes the legal owner until liquidation. Most tangible and intangible property, such as goods, real estate, intellectual property rights, and accounts receivable are surrendered.

The bankruptcy trustee is elected by majority vote of creditors to manage the proceeding by carefully collecting and disposing of the property and thereby accumulating a fund used to pay off creditor claims. The trustee determines whether each creditor's claim is genuine and may challenge any fraudulent claims against the debtor. The trustee must collect property and debts owed to the debtor and may choose to reject executory contracts, excusing the bankrupt debtor from performing in the future. The trustee must keep adequate accounting records and file a detailed accounting with the bankruptcy court. Professionals such as accountants, appraisers, attorneys, and auctioneers are hired as necessary to assist the trustee. The trustee uses the proceeds from liquidating the bankrupt's property, called the bankrupt's estate, to pay these and other costs of bankruptcy before proceeds are distributed to creditors.

There are three basic types of creditors in bankruptcy proceedings. First, **secured creditors** have security interests, such as mortgages or liens on specific property. Security interests give these creditors a preference on the sale proceeds after the secured items are sold in liquidation, but only up to their contractual security or up to the liquidation value of the collateral, whichever is less. To the dollar extent that the collateral sale is insufficient to satisfy a secured creditor's claim, the secured creditor becomes equivalent to an unsecured creditor. Second, **unsecured** or **general creditors** have no security interests. They must take their shares of the distribution proceeds equally as a group on a pro rata basis after secured creditors are paid from the proceeds of their collateral. For example, trade creditors that supply inventory or equipment without retaining a lien are unsecured. Credit card issuers are unsecured on most of their customer accounts. Third, **priority creditors** generally have priority over unsecured creditors. Each class of priority creditors may have its claims totally paid before the next class receives payment. Priority creditors include bankruptcy administration expenses, certain wages and benefits of the bankrupt's employees, taxes, certain consumer claims, and alimony and child support. If there are insufficient funds to pay all the claims of a particular class of priority creditors, they share the remainder of the fund pro rata and all lower priority creditors receive nothing.

After liquidation, a discharge in bankruptcy is usually ordered, giving the bankrupt a clean slate for preexisting debts. However, a discharge can be denied if the bankrupt conceals assets, makes fraudulent transfers, destroys books or records, disobeys a bankruptcy court order, fails to explain the loss of assets, or makes fraudulent statements in the bankruptcy proceeding. If no discharge is granted, the bankrupt will lose its assets in the liquidation yet still owe the unpaid portion of all debts. Some debts, such as alimony, child support, federal taxes, and federally insured student loans, cannot be discharged in bankruptcy, so they are still owed after discharge of other debts.

ONLINE

Bankruptcy forms online
**http://www.uscourts.
gov/bankform/**

Alternatives to Liquidation

All debtors in financial difficulty need not be completely liquidated. A debtor with only moderate financial difficulties may be able to work out suitable arrangements with creditors under alternative procedures. Under a Chapter 13 **debt adjustment,** an individual person with regular income from salary, wages, or commissions as an employee may have debts adjusted but not discharged. Usually a very strict subsistence budget is imposed on the debtor until solvency is reached via various work-out techniques. The debtor's employer or the debtor pays a certain sum periodically (usually monthly) to the bankruptcy trustee. The trustee apportions that sum among the creditors according to the adjustment plan. **Composition** arrangements with creditors may allow the debtor to pay lower principal and/or interest rates. **Extension** terms permit the debtor to make smaller payments and extend the maturity date and/or the number of debt payments. If the debtor complies with the plan, there is a discharge, even if some creditors receive less than the original amount of their debts plus interest and penalties.

For corporations, Chapter 11 provides a **reorganization** process somewhat similar to the Chapter 13 arrangement just discussed. Chapter 11 permits businesses with going-concern value to continue operating during financial difficulties. The purpose is to minimize the negative impact of business failures on the economy, creditors, customers, suppliers, employees, and the community. In a Chapter 11 proceeding, a debtor corporation is reorganized pursuant to a voluntary or involuntary petition. Texaco may be the largest firm to have successfully emerged from Chapter 11. At this writing, Enron continues to operate under the "protection from creditors" provided by Chapter 11.

The reorganization process is usually more complex and time-consuming than a Chapter 13 proceeding. Each class or group of similar creditors and shareholders forms a separate committee to propose, negotiate, modify, and approve a master **reorganization plan**. The plan may include elements of composition, extension, and/or reduction, which means that the debtor corporation's shareholders, bondholders, and creditors are likely to receive less than their full claims. For example, some creditors may be converted into shareholders, preferred shareholders may be converted into common shareholders, and common shareholders, as residual claimants, may lose most of their stock.

If the bankruptcy court finds that a particular plan is fair and equitable to all the classes of creditors, then the whole plan may be approved, even if some committees have not approved it. The final court approval of the plan discharges the corporation from its former debts and equity interests and substitutes the new claims as defined in the plan. In some Chapter 11 proceedings, referred to as "prepacks," the various claimants negotiate the plan before filing the bankruptcy petition. This practice permits the plan to be worked out amicably and reduces the bankruptcy court's involvement to approval of a plan that the parties already feel is fair. A prepack can be more efficient and avoids goodwill losses because the proceeding occurs quickly and without much fanfare. A corporate reorganization can be converted into a Chapter 7 liquidation proceeding when it is in the best interest of all involved.

Insolvency and the Dot.coms

By the year 2000, much to the disappointment of "new economy" supporters, dot.com start-up companies finally became subject to traditional financial expectations. The mere promise of revolutionary new e-commerce business models could not overcome the need for conventional cash flow and enduring wealth creation. Many over-valued stock prices fell to levels more consistent with customary models of revenue production. Without solid cash flows, many new ventures could not long maintain their high cash "burn rates" (underfunded expenditures). Firms in the infor-mation economy pose commercial and financial challenges because many rely heavily on intangible and intellectual property assets that are difficult to evaluate and can be risky collateral. Investors and venture capitalists can be expected to withdraw or dis-continue financing when dot.coms appear headed for financial trouble.

Unlike firms in the bricks-and-mortar economy, many dot.com start-ups have few tangible assets to secure loans. Many also are equity financed, making it less appropriate to seek the debt relief of bankruptcy. Bankruptcy administration expenses may quickly overwhelm a troubled dot.com's tangible assets. Financial dif-ficulties in e-commerce are widespread; they destabilize intellectual property asset values and therefore are harmful to creditors and investors. At least three insolvency problems can plague financially troubled dot.coms. The first and most fundamental is that the primary intellectual assets of most dot.coms are their employees. Many dot.com employees hold stock options. However, employees can too easily lose their incentive to remain employed when the company's financial troubles depress their options' value.

Licensing of IP both *to* a dot.com and *from* a dot.com raises two more impor-tant areas of insolvency issues. If the IP is "licensed-in" to a financially troubled company from a financially healthy outside third party, the license may not survive in the licensee's bankruptcy to be available as an asset of the bankruptcy estate. Recall the discussion of contract assignments earlier in this chapter. Contracts are not assignable without the permission of the obligor if the contract's subject matter is unique. The IP licensed-in to a financially troubled dot.com from a licensor may not be freely assignable by the trustee to raise cash. Royalty payments fundamen-tally depend on the licensee's unique products, so the licensor's permission to assign is probably needed. Such licensors may often be better off abandoning the bankrupt, in which case new licenses can be negotiated with other licensees without interfer-ence from the trustee.

A third problem area arises when the IP is "licensed-out" from a financially trou-bled company. Generally, bankruptcy law permits the trustee to use reasonable busi-ness judgment to either accept or reject any of the bankrupt's executory contracts in order to maximize the bankrupt's estate. The outside licensee can be left in limbo until such a choice is made. Under bankruptcy law, ongoing IP licenses are consid-ered **executory contracts** because both parties continue to owe some future duty to perform. For example, the licensee must make future royalty payments, and the licensor must continue to grant permission to use the licensed technology. Until 1988, bankruptcy law permitted the trustee to reject ongoing licenses, thereby can-celing the bankrupt debtor's permission, and the licensee was often left in limbo until the rejection decision was made. However, the Intellectual Property Bankruptcy Act now requires the trustee to respect ongoing licenses by giving the licensee an option to terminate or continue the license.

Intangible information is a primary asset for many financially troubled dot.coms. As discussed in Chapter 13 of this book, private data can be valuable both to the individuals profiled in the information and as a marketing tool in commerce. ToySmart, an Internet toy retailer, collected considerable private information about children who visited the ToySmart site. ToySmart's announced privacy policies prohibited resale of this information without each individual's permission. However, when ToySmart filed for Chapter 9 bankruptcy protection in June 2000, it proposed to sell the database of children to raise cash and help it survive as a going concern. The FTC intervened to block the data sale. Nevertheless, the value of private data might still be realized in this or similar situations if, rather than selling the data outright, the financially troubled dot.com were acquired by another company and survived as a subsidiary. Such a survival technique would probably leave the dot.com free to use its intangible assets as originally permitted by its privacy policy. Restrictions on a dot.com's ownership are not generally part of privacy policies.

CHAPTER 11
TECHNOLOGY TRANSFER: EMPLOYMENT, SERVICE, AND DISTRIBUTION CONTRACTS

How does a firm protect its intellectual assets? This problem is becoming more acute as job tenure practices change. Increasingly, employees change jobs several times during their careers, broadening their skills and experience. Lifetime employment with a single firm is becoming rare. Imagine a typical modern scenario: Employees work on projects developing new products and services. They become attractive to competitors and to other firms for two main reasons: (1) These employees know secrets about the particular products or processes of their current employer, and (2) employees have valuable general experience in developing products, giving them strong potential on related projects. Successful employees are often lured away to other firms with offers of higher salaries, stock options, and challenging new assignments. The departure of one influential employee can stimulate other employees to change employers. The exodus of their cumulative knowledge effectively transfers significant intangible assets about technologies to the new firm.

Can the original firm protect its knowledge base with contractual and other legal restrictions? If they can, how do employees retain the flexibility to advance their careers? The law balances these parties' rights. Employees need to maintain freedom of job mobility, they have the right to seek rewarding work, and they need financial rewards. Society is best served when workers are most productive by working up to their greatest potential in their chosen fields of expertise.

Increasingly, the value of firms depends less on the fair market value or cash flow potential of tangible assets (real estate, product, plant, and equipment) and more on ideas, as created and implemented by employees. In the knowledge economy, value is derived increasingly from information and expertise supplied by employees. Firms have legitimate interests in protecting any intellectual property (IP) resulting from investment in R&D or from employee training. IP is valuable whether held as registered patents, copyrights, and trademarks or held as proprietary information and trade secrets secured in filing systems and known only by key employees. These two realities, job-hopping and the ascendance of intangible assets, raise risks for both employers and employees. The law creates technology transfer mechanisms that balance these often conflicting interests.

EXHAUSTIBILITY OF TANGIBLE VERSUS INTANGIBLE PROPERTY

The risk of losing proprietary information from employee movement is one example of the main problem in technology transfer: the exploitation of intangible property. Information and other intangible property are seemingly inexhaustible, making them uniquely different from tangible property. Tangibles are totally **exhaustible**; when tangibles are transferred or wrongfully misappropriated, the rightful owner loses *all* value in the property, and the ownership advantages are completely exhausted. For example, when an automobile is sold or stolen, the owner is suddenly aware of the obvious fact that the property is gone. The owner cannot economically exploit the tangible asset because no one would buy it without tangible proof that it exists.

By contrast, intangible property is only partially exhaustible. The original persists even when copied. Intangible property can be possessed simultaneously by many people. Often, the value of intangibles to the original owner is not immediately or completely eliminated when only a few copies are sold, licensed, or even stolen. For example, when patented processes, computer software, sound and video recordings, or information are licensed, sold, or misappropriated, only a "copy" is taken. The owner still has the "original," which can be exploited financially when the original owner sells additional licenses to others. Indeed, the original owner could make a nearly infinite number of copies, which makes the intangible seem to be inexhaustible. However, eventually the market would become saturated, eliminating all paying customers. Therefore, intangibles are only **partially inexhaustible**, or partially exhaustible. If too many licenses are sold or too many illegal copies are made, eventually the marketability becomes exhausted. For example, if numerous illegal copies of a rock group's latest album are pirated, eventually royalties from legitimate sales diminish. This is the result predicted by the artists and record companies in the case that shut down Napster.[1] The same holds true for illegal copies of books, software programs, games, data, videotapes, or nearly any digital media. Similarly, if a competitor's spy obtains a company's newly developed secret production process, the innovation loses much of its value to the original inventor.

Most people understand the partial exhaustibility of intangibles. For example, most people understand that use of unauthorized copies often goes undetected. As long as the original remains intact, the owner of intellectual property may never even

---

1. *A&M Records, Inc. v. Napster*, 239 F.3d 1004 (9th Cir., 2001).

know about the unauthorized copies. Some people believe that no harm is done if the owner is unaware of the misappropriation. However, the owner receives decreasing profits when there is uncontrolled and unauthorized distribution of intangible IP. Society gives incentives to inventors and creators by establishing IP rights and enforcing the technology transfer contracts needed to exploit IP. Licensing permits the owner to control distribution. Without a method to identify what IP legitimately belongs to a particular owner, people could ignore the license and misappropriate the IP. The federal laws concerning patents, copyrights, and trademarks and the state common law protecting trade secrets, trademarks, and technology transfer contracts are essential to an owner's exclusive claim to IP.

This chapter discusses the methods used to exploit intangibles and distribute them through the supply chain. IP laws prohibit most unauthorized uses, as discussed in Chapters 4 through 7. IP law endows the owner, inventor, or creator with a bundle of rights to exploit their IP largely through technology transfer. Employment contracts are examined first in this chapter. They specify the employer's and employee's rights in IP, inventions, and job experiences, often through assignments of innovations. Next, licensing is discussed because it is the primary method to distribute technology. Leases and franchising are then discussed at the end of this chapter.

LAWS APPLICABLE TO TECHNOLOGY TRANSFER AND DISTRIBUTION

Technology transfer creates business relationships that are formed by contract. These relationships manage and structure the financing, allocate property rights, arrange production, establish control, provide funds, anticipate expansion, and/or create uniform controls for a business that is often composed of numerous related yet independent parts. Managers negotiating employment or distribution contracts hire employees and independent contractors. These relationships create the design of the supply chain. Under American law, laissez-faire freedom of contract is given great weight. The parties may design their contract terms to achieve nearly any desired result unless public policy is offended. Most subjects of bargaining are open to negotiation, resulting in a mix of terms that reflect the parties' needs and relative bargaining power. Of course, the stronger party can often extract concessions at the other party's expense.

Agency law supplements these employment and distribution contracts by clarifying the various parties' duties, automatically providing for allocation of certain business risks, and implying fiduciary duties of care and loyalty. Regulation addresses some problems in employment and distribution contracts, although no single and coherently integrated body of law has developed. During the twentieth century, the laws of contracts and agency have been supplemented by various employment regulations. Employment law is a general umbrella term for various state and federal regulatory programs such as the antidiscrimination laws administered by the Equal Employment Opportunity Commission (EEOC), workplace safety rules from the Occupational Safety and Health Administration (OSHA), workers' compensation, regulation of wages and working conditions, collection of employment taxes, and laws concerning lie detector use, drug testing, immigration, garnishment, plant closing duties, and termination of employment. Labor law governs unionization and collective bargaining between employers and employees. The antitrust laws discussed in Chapter 12 constrain supply chain relations with distributors, franchisees, and in licensing IP.

EMPLOYMENT CONTRACTS

An employer generally has the incentive to specify contract terms that enhance the employer's flexibility, business opportunities, and profitability. Employers usually desire to minimize expenses, protect assets, and retain flexibility to deploy their employees as needed. On the other hand, employees desire stability in their compensation and work environment, job security, fair treatment, and generally increasing compensation and benefits. Some employees seek stable work tasks, but many others expect ever-changing challenges in their work assignments that permit them to grow professionally. Employees also want freedom to resign at will, go work elsewhere, or even start their own businesses, using all their accumulated skills and experience. Sometimes these goals come into conflict, presenting a zero-sum struggle, much of which is resolved during negotiation of the employment contract. Sometimes public policy intervenes to equitably balance the parties' reasonable expectations or protect outsiders affected by the employment relationship.

The parties to employment and distribution contracts understandably use their contract to control performances. For example, manufacturers and wholesale distributors often require retail outlets to carry large inventories, hire knowledgeable sales staffs, use only trained repair technicians, and diligently promote their product lines. Employers may impose work rules to assure product quality and employee loyalty while maintaining a congenial workplace. The flow of benefits and funds between the parties is also an essential contract term. Both sides must be concerned with termination provisions as changes occur in the parties' needs or performance quality. This section discusses several contract terms that can protect these interests. Many are applicable to both employment and distribution contracts.

EMPLOYER'S RIGHT TO AN EMPLOYEE'S INNOVATIONS

There is a shift in innovation today; less is developed by independent individuals and more by institutions. The complexity and technical sophistication of most processes and new products require considerable expenditures for research. Many important discoveries could not be developed except with the use of extensive scientific equipment in expensive laboratory settings. Today, teams of researchers employed in corporate R&D departments, government labs, or research universities predominate. The institutional sponsorship of R&D raises critical questions of ownership and the permissible use of these innovations.

An employer may lay claim to ownership of innovations developed by employees, based on agency law, the employment contract, and/or IP law. Most fundamentally, the fiduciary duty generally prohibits an agent from competing with the principal. If an employee develops and sells something that is close to the employer's line of business, the employee's acts could violate the duty of loyalty. An employer's claim to ownership becomes stronger when it is based on contract. An employee may be specifically hired to do research, create expression, or develop a particular technology. The employment contract may shift ownership and control of copyrights, patent rights, or trade secrets to the employer, often in an assignment.

An employer may not own the innovations produced by an employee if the employee's duties do not specifically include conducting research or fostering innovations. If the employee can prove that personal investment of time, money, and effort was made to develop an invention, innovation, or trade secret, then the employee may own it. This claim is even stronger if the innovation was developed entirely on the employee's own time. Employee ownership gives the employee exclusive rights to use it personally or license it to others. Contrast this innovation with an invention that was developed on the employer's time and using the employer's resources and facilities. Most savvy employers specifically include **assignment** provisions in employment contracts that transfer ownership of such innovations to the employer. Assignments were introduced in Chapter 9.

Even without an assignment, the employer may still have a limited shop right to use the invention. Under the **shop right doctrine**, the employer has a *nonexclusive right to use* the innovation without paying royalties to the employee. This right persists after the employment terminates and can also apply to an inventor who is an independent contractor. During the negotiation of an employment contract, some employers clearly inform each new hire that they are **hired to invent** particular innovations or in specific technologies. This statement generally vests ownership in the employer.

An invention may be developed by a single individual or by several members of a design team. Patent applications must by made or authorized only by the inventor(s) unless excused, such as when an inventor cannot be found or refuses to participate. The **inventor** is the person who conceives of the essential "kernel" of features or elements that makes the invention novel—an advance over known prior art. Two or more persons may be co-inventors if each collaborates to contribute, even if their work is done separately or at different times.

Employee's Assignment of Innovations

To avoid uncertainties, employers often insist that a term appear in the employment contract requiring the employee to assign to the employer all patents, inventions, innovations, or trade secrets. Because patents are typically issued to individual inventor(s), employers need employees' cooperation to own them. Patent-assignment clauses usually say that: (1) inventions developed during employment are transferred to the employer, (2) the employee will assist in securing the patent but usually at the employer's expense, and (3) any patent issued is assigned to the employer.

Before R&D starts, it is difficult to know which employees will be successful innovators. To confidently capture control over all new technologies, many employers simply require all employees to assign their rights, usually when first hired, even if few employees actually invent anything useful. Some very valuable employees may have the bargaining power to refuse assigning all their patent rights. Many progressive research universities split patent royalties with the faculty researchers responsible for the development. These policies are argued not only to be more equitable but also to enhance faculty motivation by retaining and attracting high-quality researchers. Employment, salary, and bonuses are valid consideration for an employee's assignment of patent rights.

The courts may choose not to enforce an unreasonably broad assignment clause. For example, an assignment would probably not be enforceable for an invention made entirely off the employer's premises, financed wholly with the employee's funds, and developed on the employee's time. A few states have statutes that reinforce the employee's ownership of personal developments. However, this can be a gray area, particularly for inventors actually employed to do R&D and who are exposed to component technologies developed for the employer that could arguably contribute to the employee's invention. Clear guidance is particularly problematic for inventions made during an employee's off-work time but in the same general area of expertise used in employment.

Work Made for Hire

Copyrighted works generally belong to the author or coauthors of the work. Joint authors create a work when they intend that their contributions be merged into inseparable or interdependent parts of a single whole work. For example, joint authors include the composer and lyricist of a song or the coauthors of a textbook. Authors are generally the human individuals who actually create the work. However, a corporate or business firm may be the author holding all the bundle of rights in copyright if it hires employee(s) or independent contractors to create part or all of a work under a **work made for hire,** including (1) works created by employees **within the scope of their employment** or (2) specially commissioned works created by independent contractors. **Specially commissioned works** can be used only as part of a (1) collective work, (2) motion picture or other audiovisual work, (3) translation, (4) compilation, (5) supplementary work, (6) instructional text, (7) test, (8) answer key, or (9) atlas. Additionally, the written contract must be signed by both parties and must be executed before the work starts to expressly designate it as a "work made for hire." The employee–independent contractor distinction was created in the 1976 revision to the copyright law. Works created by employees or commissioned before 1976 generally belong to the employer. The Supreme Court reinforced the individual author's rights in interpreting control over a commissioned statue in *Community for Creative Nonviolence v. Reid.*[2]

Consider how these ownership problems can complicate contracts for writing software or for Web site creation and maintenance. For example, a computer programming company might develop software or Web pages under a supply contract

---

2. 490 U.S. 730 (1989).

for a client. The customer is generally best served if they get an assignment of all copyrights developed during the course of the contract's performance. However, if the contract does not include an assignment of the program's copyright or fails to include wording that the agreement is a "work for hire," the programmer will own the program. Software and Web pages may not qualify under one of the nine categories of works made for hire. Under the federal copyright law, the programming company would own the source code and could sell a second copy to the client's competitor. Such copyright ownership issues can extend to written text, computer programming, sound recordings, Web site pages, browser applets or plug-ins, and film or television video sequences. These issues are discussed in the final section in this chapter.

Master-Servant and Scope of Employment

The two forms of work made for hire use the two major criteria for vicarious tort liability under *respondeat superior* introduced in Chapter 3: the master-servant relationship and activities within the scope of employment. Courts evaluate several factors in distinguishing servants from independent contractors. First, the parties' intent may provide some insight, although this form of relationship may be chosen to achieve tax benefits. Second, the level of supervision commonly required for the type of work is important. Where employers usually supervise closely the type of work in question, the master's right to control the servant is implicated. However, if the employee is generally left to work independently with only cursory monitoring, the employee is more likely an independent contractor. Third, an independent contractor usually has a higher level of skill than a servant. Servants typically possess more generic skills possessed by many people. An independent contractor usually has extensive experience, training, and education, particularly if it leads to a recognized profession or occupation. The supervision factor is also related to the skills factor. An employer's supervision is more likely when the employee's skills are lower and the employer's skills are higher.

A fourth factor concerns the employee's service arrangements. Servants generally work exclusively, regularly, and continuously for the same employer. By contrast, independent contractors tend to work for numerous employers on specific tasks and only when needed. An independent contractor may reject an employer's instructions and may refuse engagements for various reasons. Fifth, the manner of payment is often indicative: Servants are paid a recurring salary based on pay periods. Independent contractors are usually paid by the job. Sixth, if the employer owns the facilities and tools required for the work, the employee is probably a servant. Independent contractors typically have many of their own tools and often work at their own premises. Finally, the local customs for the type of work involved may also be relevant.

These criteria are helpful to decide close cases. For example, consider the two primary methods for hiring an attorney. When an attorney in private practice is retained by a client, the parties probably enter a contract for services that may contain a clause preserving the attorney's independence. Second, the attorney probably supervises his or her own work. Third, in most situations, the attorney is hired specifically to render professional expertise. Therefore, the client's direct and close supervision would be improper. Fourth, many attorneys in private practice work for several different clients on an irregular basis. Fifth, the attorney is paid for the particular job. Sixth, the attorney typically works at the courthouse, the attorney's law office, and at various other locations. These factors strongly suggest that the attorney in private practice is an independent contractor. However, an attorney working for a corporation is viewed quite differently. A corporate staff attorney is typically subject to the employer's supervision, works exclusively at the employer's site on a regular and continuous basis, and is paid a salary. These examples emphasize that it is difficult to reliably designate an employee except by using a preponderance of these factors. In some states, it is difficult to regularly retain personnel and designate them as independent contractors if that would reduce their rights.

The second element, **scope of employment,** is also ambiguous and unpredictable in close cases. There is an enormous amount of case law interpreting the phrase "scope of employment." Two main inquiries have developed. First, was the servant pursuing the master's business objectives? Second, was the servant's act foreseeable by the master? Both of these tests are ambiguous and could lead to conflicting results. Acts that are most clearly outside the scope of employment are done solely for the servant's benefit. The *Restatement of the Law Second, Agency* in §228 attempts to clarify this confusion:

> **Section 228 of the *Restatement of the Law, Second, Agency***
>
> (1) Conduct of a servant is within the scope of employment if, but only if:
>   (a) it is of the kind he is employed to perform;
>   (b) it occurs substantially within the authorized time and space limits;
>   (c) it is actuated, at least in part, by a purpose to serve the master; and
>   (d) if force is intentionally used by the servant against another, the use of force is not unexpected by the master.

ONLINE

American Law Institute's
Restatement of the Law
http://www.ali.org

The general law of agency provides the method used to analyze work made for hire issues under federal copyright law. This ignores any special exceptions under a particular state's law. This analysis should not give sole reliance to the control issue— that is, whether the employer had the right to control or took actual control over the author's activities.

RESTRICTIONS ON COMPETITION

An employer risks several potential losses when an employee disassociates from the firm. First, it may be difficult to replace the employees whose services are unique or who know the business thoroughly. New employees must be trained for complex tasks and must become familiar with the employer's business. This problem has led to the use of fixed-term employment contracts that require notice before termination.

A second problem is the information an employee learns or develops while on the job. The employer could suffer irreparable harm if an employee quit and immediately joined a competitor or started a competing firm and used confidential information.

For example, sales personnel are given lists of existing customers and develop lists of new customers. They learn about new products before their release and may learn innovative sales tactics. Top management, designers, engineers, and production personnel learn trade secrets about new products and secret production processes before they are disclosed outside the firm. This information and other competitive strategies and marketing plans could be immensely useful to a competitor.

The employer confronts a dilemma: Can employees be effective without learning such information, or will the employer's success be compromised if employees quit and take or disclose valuable confidential information? To analyze this question, an understanding is needed of how freedom of employment contracting is affected by the balancing of interests between employers and their employees.

Covenants Not to Compete

An employee's rights after termination may be limited by a **covenant not to compete**; a contract term prohibiting the employee from competing with the employer after termination of their employment. These provisions are also known as **restrictive covenants, noncompetition clauses,** or simply **noncompetes** for short. They restrict an employee's freedom to work, usually irrespective of whether the employee is fired or quits. Noncompetes supplement the general fiduciary duty of loyalty (discussed later), which requires confidentiality and prohibits competition during employment. Today, most savvy employers require new hires to sign noncompetes as one of many hiring documents. However, many smaller firms or employers without knowledge or experience with competition by former employees may seek to impose noncompetes in midstream on existing employees. These employees may argue that their employer gives them no new consideration in return for the noncompete restriction. Such a lack of new consideration could bar enforcement of the noncompete if the employee is already working under a fixed-term employment contract. However, many employees work under an employment-at-will contract, so the employer's consideration for imposing a noncompete in midstream could simply be the promise of continued employment, making the noncompete enforceable. Employment-at-will is discussed later in this chapter.

Reasonable Restriction

Some employers attempt to make excessive restrictions on their former employees' activities. The law generally disfavors such overrestrictive covenants because they restrain trade. Noncompetes may deprive former employees of a livelihood or restrict their use of professional talents and skills used at a former job. Indeed, as a matter of public policy in California, noncompetes are generally unreasonable and invalid. In other states, a noncompete must be reasonable to be enforceable. Some courts and a few state statutes limit the use of noncompetes to executive, managerial, or professional employees, those who are more likely to have access to valuable confidences. For example, noncompetes are most likely to be enforceable on agents who deal with clients, like brokers of real estate, securities, and commodities. A few states outright refuse enforcement to unreasonable noncompetes, leaving the employer totally unprotected. Employers seeking reliable protection from restrictive covenants generally must draft them narrowly, precisely limiting their effect as to time, space, and field of use. Some states use the **blue pencil test,** which permits the judge to limit the unreasonable aspects of a noncompete to more reasonable dimensions.

The restriction may be only as broad as necessary to prevent misappropriation of the former employer's trade secrets and confidences or unique relationships with customers (goodwill). For example, assume an employee is required to sign a restrictive covenant when first hired. The covenant will be considered unreasonable and unenforceable if it restricts competitive employment for an excessive period of time, say 10 years. Six months to two years is usually considered the useful life of the former employee's confidential knowledge. Thereafter, confidential information becomes obsolete, or competitors obtain it by other means. Clearly, the reasonable time varies by industry, permitting the employer and employee to present evidence on labor markets in their industry, as well as the useful life of confidential information. For example, a two-year restriction might be reasonable in traditional manufacturing industry but an "eternity" (unreasonably long) in the Web site design industry. In the sale of a business or professional practice, the time restriction may be much longer, even permanent. No reasonable person would purchase a business at a price including a premium for goodwill unless the seller is restricted by a noncompete for a long time. In such situations, the seller is usually prohibited from competing against the purchaser because competition would dilute the value of the purchased business.

Restrictions are also unenforceable if they extend to geographic regions where the former employer is not doing business. Geographic restrictions may be larger if the employer is engaged in interstate or international commerce. Restrictions are generally unenforceable outside the field of use made during the former employment. For example, it would probably be unreasonable to restrict a computer programmer from working for a bank unless their former duties included writing financial software. Employers are at increasing risk when they impose, rather than negotiate, unreasonable or vaguely defined restrictions without evidence that the former employee was exposed to real and valuable trade secrets. Increasingly, the terms of contracts with suppliers and customers are considered proprietary. Along with unique business methods potentially patentable as methods of doing business, the trade secrets protected by noncompetes and confidentiality agreements may include such business transaction information.

Ancillary to an Agreement

The restrictive covenant must be **ancillary;** that is, it must be necessary to protect interests transferred in a contract. A noncompete is ancillary when it is necessary to protect trade secrets divulged during an employment contract or to protect goodwill purchased in a business. Restrictive covenants unconnected with employment, franchise, or the sale of a business are generally unenforceable. It is never legitimate to use noncompetes to simply prevent competition. Although stating a separate consideration paid for the noncompete may not be necessary, it can be useful to do so. For example, a noncompete could be written to protect the sale of business, stating a lower value for the business's tangible assets and a premium separately stated for the intangible goodwill. In such a situation, it is easier to conclude that a separate consideration was paid for the restrictive covenant to protect the goodwill. In many states, an employer's agreement to hire is sufficient consideration for a noncompete if the employment probably involves sharing trade secrets or confidences with the employee.

Inevitable Disclosure Doctrine

Some observers argue that noncompetes are draconian—that is, more stringent and severe than needed, like killing a fly with a hammer. Former employers have legitimate interests in restricting only the *use* of confidential information; they have no legitimate interest in preventing former employees from vigorously competing against the former employer. However, noncompetes do both these things and sometimes provide the former employer with a wider margin of protection than is deserved. It would be much fairer to former employees to use more precise methods to limit the *misuse* of particular confidential information, such as the confidentiality duties that are discussed in the next section. However, employers may be justified in arguing that they are at greatest risk when former employees move into very similar jobs at direct competitors. It may be impossible for these former employees not to divulge confidences. Indeed, many observers argue that firms routinely hire employees away from their competitors more to gain confidences than to gain employees generally experienced in the field. If this is true, then it may be that disclosure of the former employer's confidences is inevitable when employees change jobs.

For some years now, a few courts have enjoined former employees from working for a direct competitor in a job with nearly identical duties under the **inevitable disclosure doctrine**. It applies to employees not bound by a noncompete but who have such intimate knowledge of the former employer's trade secrets that the employee could not possibly work for a competitor without using or disclosing the confidences. For the inevitable disclosure doctrine to apply, the trade secrets allegedly involved must be precisely and validly defined and highly valuable to both employers.[3] What should be the remedy? Courts use an **inevitability injunction** that prevents the employee from taking the new job immediately. It might extend for only short periods (e.g., six months) as was ordered in the watershed case of *Pepsico, Inc. v. Richmond.*[4]

FIDUCIARY DUTY OF LOYALTY

The most fundamental duty that agents or employees owe to their principals and employers is the **fiduciary duty of loyalty**. It is a duty of trust and confidence requiring the agent to act with the utmost good faith in relation to the principal's business affairs. The agent must also render service with reasonable care and skill, which requires the agent to perform the contract duties promised and give due attention to the principal's business. Additionally, the agent must communicate information about the principal's business, account for money and property received for the principal, and act with obedience to the principal's reasonable directives.

---

3. *EarthWeb, Inc. v. Schlack*, 71 F.Supp.2d 299 (S.D.N.Y. 1999).
4. 54 F.3d 1262 (7th Cir. 1995).

The agent must conduct the principal's affairs with the highest integrity. The principal's business and financial interests must be put first and all other interests subordinated. While authorized, the agent must act solely for the principal's benefit in all business matters concerning the subject matter of the agency. This duty prohibits the agent from acting in the interests of others or in the agent's own personal interests if it conflicts with the principal's interests. Some aspects of the fiduciary duty may continue even after the agency is terminated. The fiduciary duty is necessarily stated imprecisely in the abstract but becomes more specific in certain recurring situations: (1) potential conflicts of interest, (2) the agent's comminglement of the principal's property, (3) the agent's competition with the principal, and (4) the maintenance or misappropriation of the principal's confidential information.

Conflicts of Interest

From biblical times, there has been a fundamental principle that no one can serve two masters. Any action that would favor one principal necessarily causes harm to the other. This zero-sum assessment assumes that benefits flowing to one principal must necessarily come at the expense of the other. It is best illustrated where the two principals are contracting together or are competing for the same limited stakes. An agent who represents both principals is a dual or double agent. An agent representing both sides in the same transaction is incapable of satisfying fiduciary duties to both principals simultaneously. Gains by one side are translated into losses by the other.

For example, a real estate agent representing both the seller and the buyer is incapable of fully satisfying the seller's need for a high price and the buyer's need for a low price. The dual agent provides professional judgments to each and learns confidential knowledge about the seller's willingness to reduce the price and pressures to sell quickly and about the buyer's ability to pay more than initially offered. In all probability, one of the principals will receive more information or better advice than the other. Even if the agent scrupulously attempts to "split the difference" by negotiating "fair terms," both principals receive a lesser caliber of service than if each had an independent and loyal agent. Today, several states specifically permit buyer's agents who owe their loyalty only to the buyer. Fidelity and trust given to one principal is incompatible with the trust owed the other.

Agents violate the fiduciary duty of loyalty by receiving secret gifts, gratuities, commissions, kickbacks, or bribes from the other party in a transaction. Such payments are believed to influence the agent's judgment, and this harms the principal. Both the agent and the third party are liable for the principal's losses when the two collude to breach the agent's fiduciary duty. For example, a corporate purchasing agent might be treated to extensive entertainment or provided gifts by a supplier to influence the agent's decision to make corporate purchases. Receipt or solicitation of such inducements amounts to kickbacks, even bribes made as compensation that violates the agent's fiduciary duty.

Despite this prohibition against an agent's adverse interests, in some instances an agent may lawfully represent two parties to a transaction. An agent must generally disclose to the principal all matters that have an impact on the agency, including the existence of another principal. There is no fiduciary violation where both principals are fully informed that the other principal exists and then give consent to the dual agency. An agent may also act as a finder to bring together two potential contracting partners without informing either of the dual agency if neither principal expects advice or help with negotiations. A **nonexclusive agent** may represent numerous principals and the agent's own interests even if the multiple representation competes with any one principal. Consent for such competition must appear in the employment contract or be inferred from the parties' past dealings or other circumstances. For example, theatrical agents typically represent many different performers. The agent's reputation for representing numerous performers is probably sufficient to communicate any potential adverse interests. High-quality theatrical agents must have flexibility to decide whether a particular performer is suitable for a particular role. These agents can then provide a reliable clearinghouse to fulfill the varying needs of third parties for different characters or styles of music.

Self-Dealing

Another form of conflict occurs when the agent's own financial interests directly conflict with the principal's interests. Any personal interest the agent has in a transaction that is adverse to the principal's interests breaches the fiduciary duty. For example, without the principal's fully informed consent, an agent cannot secretly purchase the principal's property. Even if the price was allegedly "fair" or was determined by an appraiser or closed at the market price, this practice is self-dealing. Similarly, the agent may not advance the interests of close friends or relatives if doing so conflicts with the principal's interests.

During the agency, an agent may not compete with the principal in matters that fall within the scope of the agent's employment without the principal's fully informed consent. An exclusive agency prohibits the agent from competing with the principal on either the principal's time or even on the agent's own time. For example, most corporate employees are required to apply themselves full-time and only for the corporation's business interests. This rule probably does not prohibit the agent's moonlighting on the agent's own time in a line of business distinct from the principal's business.

Duty to Account

Agents often hold property and funds belonging to the principal. Any such property received by the agent during the course of operating the principal's business must be safeguarded for the principal's benefit. Any payments the agent receives must be forwarded directly to the principal unless the agent is permitted to retain amounts as reimbursement for expenses, compensation, or commissions. For example, it is customary for waiters to retain tips given by restaurant patrons.

The duty to account has two additional aspects: the duty to keep accurate records and the duty not to commingle the agent's property with the principal's property. Accurate records are essential if the agent executes numerous transactions for the principal and the principal's profits come into question. When the principal requests to see these records, the agent must produce them. Additionally, the agent must not commingle the principal's property with the agent's property. This generally requires an agent to open a separate bank account before depositing the principal's funds. For example, the agent may not use the principal's funds as a short-term loan or for the agent's personal investment purposes, even if the funds are eventually returned. The agent must keep accurate records. Any doubts about the true ownership of commingled funds are resolved in favor of the principal.

Confidentiality Duty

Another aspect of loyalty is the agent's duty to maintain confidentiality. Principals commonly expose their agents to numerous confidential matters to facilitate the effective operation of the business. Confidences are facts that are not known widely or that could harm the principal if they became widely known, including the principal's trade secrets, formulas, manufacturing processes, business plans, financial condition, customer lists, sales tactics, and new product information. Such information is often communicated to agents but is intended solely for the principal's benefit. The agent is prohibited from using such information for personal purposes and may not communicate it to a competitor. Information is the principal's property, and the agent is prohibited from misusing it, irrespective of whether the information was originally produced by the agent, the principal, or another agent.

After termination, an agent may always use any generalized knowledge and skills acquired during the agency. The employer has no right to demand confidentiality for matters that are generally known or for information the employee has a privilege to use personally. A distinction is drawn between "generalized knowledge" of a profession or trade, which a former employee may use or reveal, and "confidences," which may not be used or revealed because they belong to the employer.

A general framework for distinguishing generalized professional information from proprietary information requires analysis of several factors. First, consider the employer's restriction on the employee's ability to compete and the reasonableness of any restriction. Second, the employee's participation in developing the confidential information may be relevant. Third, the employee's knowledge of the employer's claim of exclusive rights to the information is important. Fourth is the extent of the employer's investment in developing the information and how the disclosure would affect future incentives to invest. Under the various testimonial privileges, such as the attorney-client privilege, a client may require confidentiality for communications made to receive legal advice. The privilege may also require confidentiality by secretaries, accountants, and other technical experts.

Nondisclosure Agreements

Of increasing importance are **confidentiality agreements**, also widely known as **nondisclosure agreements (NDA)**. They are often signed between suppliers, customers, and all their employees involved in a transaction. For example, consider the scenario where one party is presenting a proposal or other innovative ideas to attract the other party into a business relationship. During preliminary negotiations, the parties evaluate the proposed contract by making presentations and submitting data, specifications, or strategic plans. The NDA requires confidentiality and thereby prohibits disclosure of any secrets revealed in such presentations.

Increasingly, contracting parties insist on confidentiality for secret information for assessing contract feasibility or during contract performance. An NDA can be required before permitting outsiders' access to confidential information. The NDA may limit the purposes for the communication, itemize the particular information covered, indicate how it is transferred, and require its use only for the contract in question. Each document can be identified separately by number, such as customer lists, drawings, reports, specifications, and confidential exhibits. Anyone agreeing to receive confidential information should attempt to limit his or her duty to maintain secrecy to a particular time frame. Information that will be revealed when a patent is granted can be made confidential for a few years. However, trade secret information should be kept confidential indefinitely or until the secrets become known publicly.

Such NDAs may create a level of trust that can encourage other revelations of proprietary information. For example, information can be discovered during plant tours or disclosed in separate discussions explaining the itemized documents. Therefore, it is often prudent to extend the coverage of the NDA to all confidential information exchanged or discovered during the parties' relationship. However, the NDA should not cover information that is already known by someone else in the firm or information that is already in the public domain.

The NDA should prohibit copying the information, transferring it to outsiders, or divulging it to consultants. All documents should be returned when demanded by the disclosing firm. All individuals exposed to confidential information covered by the NDA should also sign. Often both parties sign the NDA, particularly if both parties disclose and both parties are to receive information. Recipients of confidential information should attempt to limit their duty to maintain secrecy to a particular time frame. NDAs are an essential safety net for employers if an employee's noncompete might ever become unenforceable.

TERMINATION OF EMPLOYMENT

The employer's and the employee's interests may conflict when the employee is terminated. The injury suffered by the parties can depend on the circumstances. The employee must find new work if laid off by the employer. By contrast, the employer must find a replacement employee if the employee quits. The employer's IP and trade secrets can be protected by noncompetes and NDAs, as discussed previously. However, there is a continuing fiduciary duty owed by the employee after termination. This section discusses how the law further constrains the employee's activities after the employee's departure from the employer.

Preparatory Steps

A former employee's conduct just before leaving the firm is often closely examined after termination for evidence of conflicts of interest. A former employee may legitimately take preparatory steps to start or join a new business before quitting the former employer. For example, contracts with suppliers and leases may be negotiated, a new corporation may be formed, and customers not then serviced or sought by the former employer may be solicited. However, these acts can appear sinister, or even conflicts of interest. The former employer's documents should not be taken. Many firms today try to avoid such thefts by escorting a terminated employee from the building. Additionally, customers or coworkers should not be solicited. An employer may validly prohibit the hiring of coworkers with a separate contractual covenant. Solicitation of employees serving under fixed-term contracts exposes the departing employee who solicited them to liability for tortious interference with contractual relations.

SETTLING WORK RULE DISPUTES

The increasing complexity of employment, service, and distribution contracts raises the likelihood of disputes among the parties. Increasingly, employers impose work rules, often embodied in employee manuals that supplement the employment contract. These terms may include additional employee duties. Many employment contracts **incorporate by reference** employee manuals that thereby become express terms of the employment contract with binding legal effect on the legal obligations of both the employer and employees. The same effect may be given to other company documents that carry various titles: company handbook, management handbook, corporate code of conduct, and corporate policy manuals. For example, such handbooks may be introduced as evidence to clarify an ambiguous employment contract. Publicity of the code projects a public image of ethical and socially responsible behavior. Codes of conduct may be required by law or by a self-regulatory body. Some become part of a consent decree made with a government agency that was investigating the company. For example, the U.S. Department of Defense has insisted that several defense contractors institute codes of conduct to prevent defense-procurement fraud or overcharging the government.

Corporate codes of conduct often prohibit employees from engaging in a wide range of illegal or unethical activities, including bribery, sexual harassment, destruction of documents, insider trading, environmental violations, software piracy, misappropriation, fraud, and copyright infringement. Additional policies address the employee's duties during government investigations, antitrust compliance, international boycotts, and relations with suppliers and customers.

Arbitration

Arbitration was initially introduced in Chapter 1. Increasingly, employment and distribution contracts require the parties to arbitrate disputes, a form of alternative dispute resolution (ADR), rather than litigate. Many U.S. workers are covered by agreements to settle employment disputes through arbitration. For example, labor union contracts require arbitration of workplace disputes between union members and the employer. **Arbitration** is a binding ADR method by which the parties' dispute is submitted to a nonjudicial third party who renders a legally enforceable decision. The arbitrator's decision is an award of damages or other relief (reinstatement, restored seniority). The recent Supreme Court case *Adams v. Circuit City*,[5] reaffirmed that the Federal Arbitration Act (FAA) applies to employment disputes and that employers can require the settlement of employment disputes with arbitration.

---

5. 532 U.S. 105 (2001).

The Supreme Court remanded the case back to the Ninth Circuit Court of Appeals to reconsider whether the Circuit City arbitration clause was valid. The Ninth Circuit held that even though the FAA validates employment arbitration, if the employer drafts the arbitration clause to be too favorable to the employer, it can be invalidated under state contract law.[6] Therefore, litigation, rather than arbitration, for workplace disputes can occur in three ways; first, when arbitration clauses are not used; second, when arbitration clauses like the one used in the Circuit City case are held invalid; and third, when Congress specifically exempts employment disputes from the Federal Arbitration Act, such as it has done for transportation workers.

LICENSING

License is a very broad yet vague term because it refers both to governmental privileges and private contracts. The **governmental privilege** aspect is familiar to anyone who licenses vehicles or businesses and to those who become qualified to drive a vehicle or practice their profession. Usually a governmental entity seeks to raise revenue and/or control the persons conducting the licensed activity. For example, businesses must obtain a municipal business license to conduct their activities. Professionals such as doctors, lawyers, engineers, and more than 100 other trades and callings must have government licenses to assure professional character and competence and protect society. Although governmental licenses are important in technology transfer, the following discussion concerns private licenses.

A **private license** is a special privilege that is defined and conferred by contract on some firm or person, called the **licensee** by the owner of property or producer of a service, the **licensor**. A license usually confers lesser rights than would be transferred in an outright sale or assignment. The licensor usually retains rights in the property. Many licenses permit the licensor to revoke the license if the licensee breaches limitations on use as stated in the license. Licenses are often standardized form contracts with nonnegotiable terms to reduce transaction costs. However, under the laissez-faire, freedom-of-contract principle, licenses may be individually negotiated, so they can have an almost infinite variety of forms. Like all contracts, licenses are created with valid mutual assent and must be supported by consideration. Some licenses must be in writing and are subject to limitations, such as defenses to formation. As discussed in Chapter 8, the mutual assent that concludes many contemporary licensing contracts in the consumer mass market is accomplished with click-wrap or shrink-wrap. Licenses are a common part of contracts for employment, distribution, franchising, and software purchases and are becoming increasingly important in Internet use and information sales.

Licensing is a common method to distribute property directly to consumers. Licensing is also essential in organizing franchise businesses because independent outsiders distribute the franchise system's products. Limited property rights are created, narrowing the licensee's use of intangible property. Usually, licensing is only a

---

6. *Circuit City v. Adams*, 279 F.3d 889 (9th Cir., 2002).

limited sale of intangible property, unlike transactions in tangible property such as the temporary lease or permanent outright transfer of land or goods. Tangible property has material substance that can be possessed physically and exclusively. Leasing is the primary method to create and transfer limited property rights in tangible real estate (e.g., office, building) or personal property (e.g., vehicles, computers, telecommunications equipment). By contrast, intangible property rights are not directly related to physical property but are recognized as rights between persons. This point is sometimes confusing because intangible IP can be represented in physical objects, such as a copyrighted book, a patented process using machines, software on disk, a patented component in a product, or the trademarked logo on a sign or product packaging. Licensing most often involves a transfer of the right to use intangible property: ideas, information, discoveries, knowledge, expressions, designs, writings, words, program steps, symbols, logos, trade names, slogans, endorsements, or software. Some transactions are a hybrid of leasing and IP licensing. For example, the tickets to watch a movie or sporting event, attend a concert, or view a theatrical performance are usually called licenses despite the incidental real estate interest in occupying a seat for a short time.

The licensor's primary incentive is to exploit its IP to maximize revenue. The licensor, in **licensing out** the IP, usually tries to impose restrictive license terms and retain maximum rights so they can be relicensed to others. The licensee has somewhat rival interests when **licensing in** IP rights, attempting to minimize license restrictions and lower the compensation paid while maximizing its opportunities for exploitation.

Licenses almost always grant lesser rights than transfer in a sale or assignment. An **assignment** is generally an outright transfer that forever conveys all or a substantial part of the seller's rights to the buyer. When the seller assigns IP, the seller cannot generally assign that same IP to anyone else. Therefore, assignment is inappropriate if the seller's business model depends on multiple resales of the same IP. An assignment of IP is most appropriate if the buyer purchases a customized IP product that will not be sold to another customer.

GENERAL LICENSING TERMS

Many standardized licenses are similar to other types of form contracts: Consistency in terms and conditions reduces transactions costs. Lower licensing costs can be passed on to consumers, and eventually more content should become available to the public. Consider how appropriate it is to use standard, mass-market licensing for Internet content. Much Web content is of such low value—worth just pennies per page—that individually negotiating each license for user access would be prohibitively expensive. In high-volume, consumer transactions, many licensors carefully craft a single, uniform contract. This "take-it-or-leave-it" approach uses a single statement of terms and conditions. For example, the conditions for Web site use become a license to access the Web site's material. Sometimes an incentive emerges to modify these set terms, such as when the market resists by demanding a better deal. A contemporary example is that many Web sites are increasing privacy protections under pressure from consumers and the threat of regulation.

In the future, automated electronic agents could negotiate some terms, particularly where the trade-offs between factors are susceptible to deterministic substitution. For example, a user's browser could initially specify the user's privacy expectations. Next, the Web site could either change its privacy policy to conform to the user's demand or it could counterpropose somewhat less privacy protection in exchange for giving the user free access to normally pay-per-view data. If the user's electronic agent were programmed to accept this counteroffer, the transaction costs of negotiating a low-value license could be accomplished automatically. Automated bargaining by electronic agents raises some interesting new complications.

Many of the licenses that cover high-value content or become the major foundation for ongoing business relationships are custom tailored to the specific situation with deliberate and thoughtful human oversight. Few terms in such contracts are standard because the stakes are high enough for the parties to commit human resource investments to customize their relationship, balancing the relative risks and rewards in the package of terms. An important feature of licensing is evident in the adage that "there are many ways to slice the [IP] salami." This means that laissez-faire freedom of contract is alive and well in the law of licensing. Parties negotiating licenses can make conscious trade-offs by varying any or all contractual terms and thereby define the rights created and conveyed in the license.

Many license terms are actually limitations on the licensee's right to use or exploit the IP. The following terms are typically used to limit the license granted: field of use, duration, territory, noncompetition, transferability, termination, and liability for consequential damages. Other typical terms define the form of compensation, make warranties, may require confidentiality, and provide for dispute settlement. Some of the principal licensing terms are discussed in the following text. Licenses restrain trade to some extent, so they are scrutinized under antitrust law as discussed in Chapter 12. The Federal Trade Commission and the Justice Department have issued antitrust guidelines for IP licensing.

Scope of Grant

The heart of any license is the **grant,** the clause(s) that describes the IP involved, creates the right, and then transfers it to the licensee. The grant defines the content. For example, data sets are described, official titles are used for registered copyrighted work(s) or a description of the invention(s), and patent number(s) and/or registered trademarks are separately listed. Commonly, the rights are **nonexclusive,** which permits the licensor to use the IP as well as license it to others. In an **exclusive** license, only the licensee may use the IP, thereby prohibiting use by either the licensor and/or other licensees. **Sublicensing** is the licensee's right to further license the IP to others. It is often prohibited. However, when sublicensing is permitted, the licensor may require the licensee to use particular licensing terms or a specified form for all sublicenses. The licensor may specify particular rights retained, thus expressly permitting the licensor to use certain aspects of the IP rights.

A problem concerning the technological scope of grants in both assignments and licenses reemerged in the mid-1990s. When a license is first negotiated, the terms usually address uses and technologies known at that time, raising the question of whether old grants should be interpreted to include each new technology as new markets are built. Consider how negotiations for an author's rights to a novel written in the 1950s could not have foreseen the development of consumer electronics or digital technologies. The publisher may have had standard form contract language that effectively captured the rights to adapt the novel into known technologies such as a script for a Broadway play, a Hollywood movie, or a TV drama. However, few publishers would have thought to include grant language to capture unknown fields of use such as videotape sales or rentals. These technologies did not exist in the 1950s when the contracts were drafted. Similarly, few publishers in the early 1990s were farsighted enough to capture an author's rights to many current electronic formats such as DVDs or Web downloads of streaming video. This gap creates uncertainty about whether a license or assignment will cover uses involving future technologies. The law implies that many book authors retain electronic distribution rights to their books unless the grant specifically included all technologies presently known or developed in the future.

A recent controversy illustrates the problem of publishing in new technologies not specifically described in the original grant. Freelance writers are independent contractors who supply stories to newspapers, magazines, and the trade press. The publisher evaluates each story, and the parties enter into a new contract each time a story is published. The grant is often made according to the publisher's standard form contract that traditionally granted rights for publication only on paper and not in electronic formats. As publishers have moved their content onto the Internet, they have electronically republished stories originally granted only for print uses.

One recent Supreme Court case caps a developing line of similar lower court cases to illustrate part of this problem. In *Tasini v. New York Times Co.*,[7] the U.S. Supreme Court held that grants in one medium do not extend to grant uses in other media. Tasini was a freelancer who wrote stories for various media outlets. This practice permits the newspapers to have smaller in-house staffs while encouraging a thriving group of writers who cherish their status as independent contractors. Tasini's assignment to the *Times* granted print rights but did not mention electronic rights. Tasini sued for infringement when the *Times* posted his article to its electronic archive of stories. Many large media companies like the *New York Times*, *Wall Street Journal*, *Washington Post*, *Business Week*, and *Time* have found value in archiving all their previously published articles to provide access free or to fee-paying customers via the Internet. Some authors have demanded additional royalties or sought to block use of their articles in electronic databases of published articles.

Tasini's victory for freelance writers may come at a price—a loss for the public. Many publishers refuse to negotiate new royalty agreements for electronic rights, choosing instead to remove these writers' content from their electronic databases. This creates a "gap in history." Cases like *Tasini* have led publishers to change their standard form contracts for both licensing and assignments. Many publishers now specifically acquire rights to future but currently unknown technologies, as illustrated in the following sample language. Of course, famous authors and talented

---

7. 533 U.S. 483 (2001).

inventors have stronger bargaining power. These authors may be able to insist on retaining rights to some future technologies or negotiate more favorable royalties for themselves.

Grant for Use in Future Technologies

The author grants all rights to the Work, including reproductions, whether in media now existing or hereafter developed, including, but not limited to, print, electronic communication or storage by magnetic or optical means, including all video, movie, audio rights and the public performance or display of the Work or any derivative works using electronic means now existing or which may come into existence.

IP Audit

Licensors must assure they have solid rights to the IP they license out. An **intellectual property audit** is advisable to marshal all of the firm's IP assets and determine the enforceability of rights. Audits help the firm precisely monitor assets and avoid licensing out IP when the licensor does not have full rights. Licensees frequently insist that licensors must make a warranty of title, possibly called warranty of non-infringement, assuring that they have the right to license and that the licensee's allowable use under the license will be rightful. Audits may also be advisable for licensees and during mergers and infringement litigation, and they are a prerequisite to cross-licensing.

Duration and Termination

An important business issue is the duration, length of time, or term of the license, the starting date and the ending date outside of which the licensee has no rights. Licensees naturally seek longer terms to permit full development of the licensed IP, particularly if it is successful. By contrast, some licensors may prefer retaining control, perhaps to substitute potentially more successful licensees or to renegotiate more favorable terms when it becomes clear the IP is becoming successful. The duration may be defined by precise calendar dates or could be indefinite, such as when terminated by specified events: "for as long as the licensee sells the licensed product."

Sometimes the licensor may have the right to terminate the license earlier if certain conditions are not met. For example, grounds for termination may include the licensee's failure to make required payments, failure to reach milestones (production quantities, quality), or the licensee's breach of key license terms. After termination, a licensor may find it desirable to obligate the licensee to a continuing confidentiality duty and to complete unfinished performances after termination.

The **first sale doctrine** prohibits the licensor from exercising control after the product embodying the IP is sold the first time. Buyers of patented goods or copyrighted expression are not bound by the licensor's restrictions. For example, a patent holder cannot prevent the consumer from reselling an automobile containing patented technologies. Similarly, the copyright holder cannot prevent a consumer from reselling a music CD, video, or used textbook. By contrast, licensors hope to restrict further use or transfer of digital copies of licensed software or information, precisely the issue holding back Web music.

Territorial Limitations to a Geographical Region

Many licenses limit the particular geographic regions in which the licensee may do business using the IP. For example, in the entertainment industry and in franchise businesses, the licensee is commonly granted marketing rights solely within a specified metropolitan area, in a particular state or states, within the continental United States, or in particular nations. This practice permits the licensor to license out to different firms in other regions that have local expertise or a successful track record. Sometimes differences in cultural aspects or language, as well as local regulatory restrictions, make it necessary to license differently in various locations, particularly in international transactions.

The Internet makes enforcing traditional geographic limitations more difficult. Markets are becoming global, advertising extends beyond borders, and the Internet's architecture works against restricting marketing activities to particular regions. Nevertheless, licensees can be prohibited from directing their selling efforts to particular regions, states, or nations.

Another method of limiting marketing rights is to restrict the field of use by prohibiting the licensee from selling in particular supply chains, outside particular industries, or to particular customers or markets (wholesale, retail). Such supply chain restrictions have antitrust implications, discussed in Chapter 12.

Compensation

Payment is usually the most important licensing term. Compensation structure can vary widely. The license typically requires payment of some consideration for the privilege granted in the license. Consideration may come from a number of sources: money, the cancellation of past debts the licensor owed to the licensee, the settlement of a infringement claims between the parties, or cross-licensing of the licensee's other IP back to the licensor. The licensee frequently pays a monetary licensing fee or royalty. Licensees typically must keep accurate records so that royalties can be precisely paid, the licensee's success determined, and audits facilitated.

Royalty traditionally refers to consideration paid for mineral interests under lease or for the licensed use of a registered patent, copyright, or trademark. Royalties are computed at a percentage rate that is applied to a **royalty base**, which depends on the volume of the licensee's unit production, dollar sales activity during the license duration, or other quantity measure of production or sales. Royalties for Internet content can be metered in other ways, such as Web site "hits," the number of viewers or downloads, and time of viewing (eyeballs). **Residuals** are royalties paid in the entertainment industry. **Running royalties** are set annual fees and generally not variable by units or dollar volume. A **license fee** generally refers to an initial or fixed payment made to purchase the license right or to acquire a franchise that includes license rights. Such fees are generally fixed and are not paid periodically or in variable payments. Compensation schemes under many licenses combine fixed fees with variable fees.

How much should the licensor charge? The licensee can be successful only when the fees are reasonable, considering the contribution made by the licensed IP to the value of the whole product. For example, the royalties charged for a patented automobile component could not exceed the cost of a reasonable substitute component. Similarly, the consumer cost of basic cable TV service would probably not support fees for premium movie channels. Therefore, pricing a royalty requires analysis of economic factors such as the existence of substitute components, price elasticity for substitute components, the added utility that the IP contributes to the product, and the competitive environment for the finished products. Adjustments are often needed to better balance the burdens of production expenses, taxes, shipping, returns, and discounts. Finally, licensors are often obligated to indemnify licensees if the IP licensed infringes a third party's IP rights.

PATENT LICENSING

Patent license grants a privilege to practice the patent—that is, permits the licensee to engage in conduct that the patent owner could otherwise attack as patent infringement, such as manufacturing the patented product or using the patented process. Licenses are made for existing patented technologies and can be made for technologies covered by patent applications even before they are issued. The U.S. patent law requires that licenses be in writing. Licensees are often in the best position to observe the performance of a patented invention and make design improvements. However, the licensor's consent may be necessary to experiment with or modify the patented process or goods and then to regularly practice the improvement developed by this R&D. The licensor of the original technology cannot practice the improvement without a license from the licensee who developed the improvement. These patents block each other unless the parties enter into cross-licensing.

Cross-Licensing

This problem underscores the importance of having a portfolio of patents and the benefits of cross-licensing. Under **cross-licensing**, each party owns IP and exchanges licenses in one or more of their technologies with an opposing party. Cross-licensing is an efficient process. Often no money changes hands, and only licensing rights are exchanged. Cross-licensing can be used whenever mutually beneficial, such as in settlement of IP disputes between the parties. The promise of cross-licensing has led to strategic behavior by many technology firms: They build up IP portfolios, particularly patents, so they can use the threat of patent infringement litigation to negotiate settlements based on cross-licensing. Therefore, some licensing does not produce much royalty revenue but instead provides a shield against the threat of infringement damage liability. Royalties cannot be collected after a patent expires.

TRADE SECRET LICENSING

A common misconception is that trade secrets are used only by the firms that develop them. The very nature of secrecy makes it difficult to conceal such information if it were to become widely known. However, many trade secrets cannot be effectively exploited by their discoverer, and perhaps full exploitation can be accomplished only by sale or license to others. Two key secrecy conundrums create challenges in the licensing of trade secrets. First, the buyer must be convinced of the value in a technology, but, if it is revealed, the information might no longer be secret.

Second, the licensee must agree to maintain confidentiality. Trade secrets are often described in documents, but they may also be discovered by reverse engineering, such as in dissecting a product or decompiling software, as discussed in Chapter 5.

The owner of a trade secret faces a potentially daunting dilemma in licensing the technology. Potential licensees are often unwilling to license a technology without knowing many of the key secret factors that make it valuable. However, the owner could lose its value when the secret is divulged. To engage serious interest by a potential licensee, one or both of the following conditions must exist: (1) The secret product has a well-known reputation for value and quality, or (2) the licensor must divulge enough to stimulate the recipient's serious interest. When the trade secret is too new to have developed a reputation, the licensors must hope to persuade the recipient that the idea has value. To do so, the recipient must enter a confidential relationship to allow a review of the secrets by using the strategies discussed next.

Submission of Unsolicited Ideas

Many inventors are unable, by themselves, to effectively exploit their innovations. Some are simply not interested in undertaking all the trouble and risk of starting up a new business. They often seek the interest of a successful firm already in the field or in a related trade. Established firms have acknowledged goodwill and may be better able to develop and market the innovation. It's a big strategic challenge for an inventor to find the right firm and then provoke interest without running the risk that the firm will simply use the idea without paying. Unless patented, ideas are "as free as the air,"[8] so the law does not generally protect an innovator who blurts out an innovative idea without first making a contract for compensation. Sometimes the law provides protection under an express or implied contract for compensation or if the innovator had a confidential relationship with the recipient firm. However, without such confidentiality, the recipient is generally free to use the idea after disclosure.

What types of ideas might be submitted? Submissions can concern trade secrets, possibly patentable inventions, business strategies, marketing plans, new products, new designs, business methods, and other forms of inspiration. Some ideas are **know-how**, the expertise to make innovations work or work better. Copyright law largely protects only the form of expression and not the underlying ideas. Therefore, it is not easy to protect an abstract concept or story line for a movie, television show, or theatrical work; a slogan and skit underlying an advertising campaign; or the abstract concepts underlying a sculpture, artwork, or Web site. A submitter would nearly always have a stronger position if the idea could first be patented. However, patenting is often prohibitively expensive for independent inventors. Submission to another firm may seem attractive if the recipient has special expertise that is needed to analyze the idea's profitability, if the idea may not be patentable, or if it could be better protected as a trade secret.

The submitter may be entitled to compensation from a recipient under any one of four theories from state law. Many states recognize rights in novel, original, and

---

8. *Desny v. Wilder*, 299 P.2d 257 (1965).

concrete ideas once they are well developed and nearly ready for implementation. Industry customs are also relevant to show the practice in compensating for idea submissions. First, there is a property rights theory in ideas presented orally, in writing, or in a mock-up. To be protected as property, such ideas cannot be already in common use or well known. The recipient may be liable for misappropriation by having access to the idea and then producing a product substantially similar to the one submitted without the inventor's permission. Second, recipients are bound to express contracts to compensate the submitter, but there must be contractual consideration. Waivers that release the recipient from liability must clearly state their terms, and some states require them to be reasonable.

The last two theories are implied contracts. The third theory examines the parties' conduct. A contract may be implied-in-fact by considering four factors: (1) whether the recipient solicited the idea, (2) whether the recipient could prevent disclosure, (3) whether the disclosure was confidential, and (4) the nature of the parties' interactions. The submitter's case is strengthened when the idea submission was intentionally solicited by the recipient; the recipient could have prevented the disclosure and knew the submitter expected compensation. By contrast, an implied contract is less likely if the submission was received involuntarily and there was no expectation of confidentiality. The fourth theory is quasi-contract, a form of equitable relief that is implied-in-law. A remedy could be required if the disclosure was confidential, the recipient would be unjustly enriched by using the disclosed idea, and the parties intended to agree on compensation later. Remedies under these four theories could include actual value or the reasonable value of the recipient's benefits. Alternatively, the industry's going rate for reasonable royalties might be used as a benchmark.

Recipients also have risks when unsolicited ideas are submitted. Many large firms are inundated with submissions of unsolicited ideas. Some firms may already have similar R&D efforts underway somewhere in their various divisions or at some other location. No recipient should ever agree to pay for ideas that it already knows, are in the scientific literature, or are in the public domain. However, screening submitted ideas for utility and profitability can be costly. Submitters can sue, claiming misappropriation. Many large technology firms use routine procedures to handle and review submissions. For example, submissions can be handled by separate offices within the firm or even by an independent third party. These procedures create a **Chinese wall** to isolate the actual recipient from the firm's operating divisions that might use the idea.

Many firms require the submitter to sign a **waiver** before the recipient will evaluate the idea. Waivers are essentially contracts that release the recipient from liability for misappropriating the idea or breaching confidentiality. They frequently allow copies to be made and can permit disclosure onward to others. Unless the submitter has a patent, many of these waivers could allow the recipient to keep or use the idea. Filing for a patent before submission may protect the submitter. However, if a patent is unaffordable or impossible, the submitter must devise a strategy to entice the recipient into confidentiality. One method is to gradually reveal just enough information to convince the recipient of the idea's value, and then the recipient may agree to maintain confidentiality while further details of the idea are evaluated.

Database Licensing

Until databases are given **sui generis** status as a separate and unique type of statutory IP right, their protection must rely primarily on trade secret law. Therefore, databases are most effectively licensed when kept secret or when technical features deter misappropriation or enhance the database's utility. For example, data stored on a Web site could be effectively licensed if users consent to confidentiality and they have difficulty copying substantial portions of the data. Data that must be constantly revised or updated has an inherent licensing advantage if the original owner has preferred access to the updated data stream, such as a stock exchange has to daily trading information. In sum, the best current methods to protect databases include limited licensee access, a valuable brand image, a unique user interface, and contractual confidentiality.

COPYRIGHT LICENSING

Licensing of copyrighted IP is probably the most common form of licensing. Most Web content is protected by copyright, although Web licensing may also involve trademarks, trade secrets, patents, and endorsements. Copyright licensing is somewhat more complex than licensing of these other forms of IP because copyright is a bundle of rights with separate licensable interests in reproduction, derivative works, and distribution, as well as performance and display. Distinctions are made between exclusive and nonexclusive licenses. Over the years, the licensing of copyrighted works has become less complicated, as the owners of works recognize new business models and forms for the use of their works. The most influential factors are standardized license contracts, reasonable fees, recognition of profit potential in customized content, technological solutions that permit selective unbundling of content, and a greater willingness to explore new marketing channels.

Consider the example of **custom anthologies** created by college faculty for their students' readings. For many years, professors collected articles from newspapers and trade magazines, problems and exercises, scholarly research, and book chapters to produce an optimal readings package. In many subjects, this practice is necessary because textbooks lag behind the understanding of emerging and fast-changing fields. However, many such anthologies were made without the permission of the publishers or authors. Before the 1980s, the permissions process was cumbersome, and many publishers resisted any attempt to parcel out portions of their works in independent compilations, occasionally preferring to assemble their own custom anthologies. However, after the famous Kinko's case,[9] most publishers, copy shops, and university printing services now work together more effectively to provide timely and efficient permissions clearance. Today, most such anthologists respect the copyrights of the owners by securing permissions more easily, and they pay royalties to the publishers. Still, many professors complain that the high costs of permissions are passed on to students, which forces much higher prices, and many professors have deleted important materials as too costly. Nevertheless, the Internet holds great promise for efficient permissions licensing by connecting licensors with licensees.

---

9. *Basic Books, Inc. v. Kinkos Graphics Corp.*, 758 F.Supp. 1522 (S.D.N.Y. 1991).

Licensing Music

There are many practical differences in copyright licensing depending on the type of expression involved: literary; musical; dramatic; choreographic; pictorial, graphic, and sculpture; audiovisual; sound recordings; and architectural works. Digital fixation and storage and Internet transfer add further complexity. In the United States, practices have developed to facilitate the licensing of copyrighted expression, such as the compulsory licensing of music and broadcasts and the private management of the permissions process by performing rights organizations. Chapter 4 illustrates several separate copyrightable interests in music. Foremost are the typically inseparable interests in the **composition** for which the tune or melody is written by the composer-songwriter and the words are written by the lyricist. Most often, the composer and lyricist assign these interests to a music publisher, either a corporate affiliate of a recording company or an independent firm. Sheet music and "fake books" are often published. However, today the larger market involves a separate copyright interest in a **sound recording**, made by a particular group of musicians who join to record their rendition of the composition. There may be several individuals or firms with rights in the copyright of the sound recording, including the author of the **arrangement** (adaptation or modification to different voices, instruments, rhythms, verses, etc.), the musicians, vocalists and singers, and recording technicians who modify (morph) many aspects of the sound. In most instances, the rights of these parties are assigned to the record company in exchange for marketing, regular employee compensation, and/or royalties. Some of these persons may be employed under a work made for hire contract, obviating the assignment. The classic treatise explaining licensing music is *Kohn on Music Licensing*.

ONLINE

Kohn on Music Licensing
**http://www.
kohnmusic.com**

The Europeans have a strong tradition in according **moral rights**—the artist or author's right to accurate attribution and to maintaining the integrity of the original work. Moral rights are generally weaker in the United States than in Europe. Consider the issue of compulsory licensing and cover. In the United States, very few IP rights are subject to **compulsory licensing**, by which the government mandates permission to use an owner's IP for a fee set under government oversight, not by market forces. Under a compulsory license, the owner may neither refuse to license nor negotiate license fees. Compulsory licensing was initiated in the 1909 Copyright Act to balance rights in the automated playing of player pianos.

The 1976 Copyright Act continues compulsory licensing for five types of content: (1) nondramatic phonograph records, called the **mechanical right;** (2) cable television retransmission of broadcast TV; (3) jukebox playing of phonograph records; (4) noncommercial, public broadcasting of certain copyrighted works; and (5) satellite retransmissions to the public. Compulsory licenses are administered by the Copyright Royalty Tribunal, but there has been significant litigation. The Recording Industry Association of America (RIAA), a trade association, is closely involved in music licensing and infringement enforcement.

ONLINE

Recording Industry
Association of America
http://www.riaa.org

The **mechanical license** for phonograph records is among the most significant compulsory licenses. The mechanical license arises after a musical composition is recorded by one band or group of musicians and it is distributed to the public.

Thereafter, another musical group may apply for and receive a mechanical license to make an independent recording of that composition, even if it will be recorded in a different style. That is, once a composition is **covered**, others may record and distribute to the public or publicly perform their version. It is also significant for Internet music because the Digital Millennium Copyright Act (DMCA) applies the mechanical license to **digital phonorecord deliveries**, essentially streaming or downloading music via the Internet. There are limitations on the mechanical license: It does not require licensing for dramatic musical works (operas, soundtracks), and the original song cannot be distorted; that is, the basic melody cannot be changed without infringing the composition owner's right to adapt the original into a derivative work.

Performing Rights Associations

Public performance licenses are needed when a sound recording from a phonorecord is broadcast via radio, TV, or the Internet. Licensing is also needed for a public performance of a musical composition, played by some other group of musicians. For example, a license is needed when a "cover band" plays others' compositions or the rendition is styled like the sound recording of a particular musical group. How could composers, musicians, and record companies monitor all the radio airplay or live band performances and negotiate reasonable royalties? The administration of such permissions, licensing, and collection and distribution of royalties could be prohibitively cumbersome without form contracting. To simplify this process, **performing rights associations** provide clearinghouse services by supplying **blanket licenses**, which are standardized licenses at standardized rates. They substantially increase the economies of scale by reducing transaction costs and probably increase the replay and cover of compositions and sound recordings. As discussed in Chapter 12, these societies are generally pro-competitive but are regulated under antitrust law to prevent price-fixing or bias favoring established composers or musicians.[10]

Performing rights licensing organizations
http://www.ascap.com
http://www.bmi.com
http://www.sesac.com

Performing rights associations include the American Society of Composers, Arrangers, and Performers (ASCAP), Broadcast Music Incorporated (BMI), and the Society of European Stage Authors and Composers (SESAC). Licensees may license through these organizations or can approach copyright owners, mostly the record companies, to negotiate licenses directly.

The mechanics of licensing music from its owner usually comes after the selection of the best music to use in the licensee's particular application. This is itself an art and a challenging process because of the many styles and tastes involved in optimally selecting compositions and particular recordings or excerpting the most useful passages. As discussed later, the personnel involved in designing a complex collection of IP must understand IP law and how it is licensed. It is also possible to draw music from the public domain or from music libraries. Public domain music must still be arranged and performed by musicians the user hires. Sound recordings from music libraries may be the easiest method to acquire rightful use, but care must

---

10. *Broadcast Music Inc. v. CBS*, 441 U.S. 1, 32 (1979) (J. Stevens dissent).

be taken to acquire *all* the rights the user may conceivably need as the product's success expands. Finally, the licensing of digital copies of software, information, music, images, and video is unsettled at this time. Chapter 4 discusses the peer-to-peer (P2P) exchange of copyrighted works through Internet music-trading facilities such as Napster, Morpheus, Gnutella, and MP3 that poses potentially irreconcilable conflicts between copyright holders and emerging consumer expectations. It is possible that the technical and legal issues will crystallize to enable Web delivery of such works, perhaps on a subscription or pay-per-view basis.

SOFTWARE LICENSING

Software licensing primarily involves creating and transferring copyrighted IP because software is expression written in symbolic language that defines process steps to control computer hardware. However, software licensing can sometimes be a hybrid of various forms of IP. Software can include methods and processes that are protectable as trade secrets, and some software programs may be sufficiently novel and nonobvious to be patentable. In addition, many successful software programs have brand images protected by trademarks that are used in various places to complement and reinforce the other IP protections. Increasingly, software licensing is accomplished through the shrink-wrap or click-wrap techniques discussed in Chapter 8.

Software licenses are perhaps unique largely because of the reproduction right under copyright that gives exclusive rights to the copyright owner to make and distribute copies. To use software effectively, it is necessary to make several types of software copies and then to use the copies in various ways. To be useful, software licenses must permit users to do at least some copying. Nearly all purchasers of software licenses receive a copy of the original program, whether distributed on disk, on CD, as written lines of code, or as a file when downloaded. Loading the software on a system's hard drive makes another copy, and most users seek the right to make backup copies to restore their systems after hardware failures. Each time the software loads up for use, substantial parts of the software must be copied into temporary storage (RAM). Some software licenses permit installation on a single user's desktop and another copy on their laptop computer, so long as both are not in use simultaneously. **Site licenses** give firms and other large institutions the right to make multiple copies for employees, members, or students. Therefore, at least some attention must focus on the extent of copying permitted under a software license. Many information licenses must accommodate intermediate, ephemeral or temporary copies as necessary to use information contained in a database.

To adequately protect the trade secrets contained in many software programs, licenses typically forbid reverse engineering. The user may not **decompile** or otherwise convert the machine-readable **object code** back into **source code**—the form in which programmers write software. Trade secrets could be discerned if the software was analyzed to determine how its components work. The prohibition against decompiling can create problems, particularly if the licensor is unwilling, unable, or unreasonable about providing later services for the software. Repairs to fix bugs or modifications to evolve the software's functionality usually require making changes to source code. Many software programs anticipate this need and build in some user flexibility. However, the prohibition against reverse engineering could severely inconvenience the licensee, particularly if the licensor went bankrupt. In special situations, a **source code escrow** may be an appropriate compromise. It employs the services of an independent third party to protect the trade secret confidentiality but gives the licensee a right to decompile and repair or customize when needed.

The furor during 1999 over the Y2K problem helps underscore the central role that software plays in successfully running government, business, safety-related aspects of the transportation system, flood control, and electric power generation and distribution. The importance of software licensors' quality warranties was highlighted. Considerable societal cost to update software systems had been delayed until the Y2K crisis. There is good news in all the Y2K difficulties in that millions of dollars were expended to upgrade software that will probably have lasting positive impact. Nevertheless, experience and litigation over these expenditures emphasize the importance of carefully analyzing software warranties and then developing strategies for substitutes that replace mission-critical software systems.

Multimedia Works

Multimedia works are combinations of various types of content, largely protected under copyright, that can include text, audio, graphics, and video expression. Multimedia products are generally embodied in software that is designed to be used in education and entertainment and will run largely on computers or networks. Multimedia products may also include other types of IP, such as trade secrets, patents, trademarks, and data.

A multimedia project poses three broad challenges in technology transfer. First, its development must be commissioned. Content experts, programmers, pedagogical experts, and media experts are generally all needed to create a high-quality product. Second, the developer must create or acquire rights to many small bits of content that are to be orchestrated into the multimedia collage or montage. Third, the product must be distributed, usually under license, using either fixed storage (CD-ROM) or network delivery (Web-streaming) via a potentially profitable business model. Multimedia products are very complex and require significant IP management of permissions. They have many of the same cyber law problems as any other e-commerce project, including general IP, copyright in particular, payments, e-contracting, privacy, and constitutional protection of First Amendment expression.

COMPUTER INFORMATION LICENSING UNDER UCITA

At the heart of UCITA is the different treatment given licensing of computer information (software, data) than the traditional commercial practice for sales or leases in goods, land, and services. UCITA's drafters made many aspects of licensing consistent with the familiar practices of UCC. UCITA attempts to strike a balance that preserves innovation incentives without inhibiting the growth of simple and efficient network distribution. Many of UCITA's contract law provisions were introduced in previous chapters. Formation and consideration rules were introduced in Chapter 8;

recall that UCITA embraces the transaction costs savings in the developing law of shrink-wrap and click-wrap assent. Chapter 9 introduced UCITA's title warranties. Chapter 10 details UCITA's integration with UETA, as well as discussing how UCITA establishes a visionary framework for the evolution of contractual writings and remedies applicable to electronic contracting and performances. In this section, some of UCITA's unique licensing aspects are introduced.

Mass Market Licenses

Like most other uniform laws, UCITA creates a legal framework around recognized and common commercial practices. Current licensing practice generally falls into two broad categories: (1) large, wholesale, B2B transactions and (2) retail transactions that are both B2B and B2C. The large transactions require considerable customization. The law has generally presumed large transactions are negotiated at arm's length and that both parties are reasonably sophisticated and represented by legal counsel competent in licensing. These underlying assumptions and these contracts are explored later in this chapter.

Under UCITA, **mass market** licenses are small-dollar, routine transactions that include all consumer contracts. In addition, they include B2B transactions in which marketing efforts are directed to the general public, under substantially similar terms consistent with retail transactions, and are not for customized products, site licenses, or access contracts. For example, both consumers and employees use Web-browsing software and various plug-ins to display particular types of documents (pdf) or play audio and video clips. UCITA covers licensing in both markets because they are mass market transactions based on similar terms and they are neither customized products nor site licensed in the corporate market.

UCITA imposes special rules for mass market licenses, largely to recognize the needs for consumer protection while promoting economies of scale to achieve efficiency in standard form licenses. Consumer protections for mass market licenses include a requirement for mutual assent before or during initial access to the information, an opportunity to review and retain copies of the license terms, and restrictions on unconscionable terms. If the licensee's assent comes after payment, then there is a right to return the product, and certain consequential damages are recoverable. UCITA's efficiency provisions expressly condone the use of shrink-wrap and click-wrap as a legitimate manifestation of mutual assent to create licensing contracts.

Access Contracts

UCITA may bring some clarity to subscription service contracts with Internet access providers (ISPs). UCITA covers **access contracts**—contracts "to obtain by electronic means access to, or information from, an information processing system of another person."[11] This category includes ISP contracts with providers such as AOL, AT&T, and CompuServe, as well as remote data processing such as Reuters, Lexis-Nexis, and Westlaw; e-mail systems such as Hotmail; and automatic database updating. UCITA

---

11. UCITA §102(a)(1).

§611 sets default rules for ISP service quality, including (1) keeping the system available in a manner consistent with contract terms and industry practice but permitting occasional access failures, (2) permitting periodic change to content unless specific content availability is guaranteed, and (3) clearly indicating use restrictions for the information accessed. In the future, UCITA could conceivably apply to wireless telematics (OnStar) and telecommunications (wireless Web services) and to permitting license termination without notice if the licensee is in breach of contract.

Other Licensing Terms in UCITA

UCITA provides default rules for most of the standard licensing terms discussed here. In most instances, laissez faire gives the licensor the freedom to negotiate a contract that specifies these terms, although some licensees may be able to negotiate more favorable provisions. Care must be taken when the license is prepared by one party because surprise and disappointment to the other party are likely. First, if the number of permitted users is not expressly limited, although it often is, UCITA limits it to a reasonable number of users in light of the information involved and the commercial circumstances. For example, if UCITA applied to recorded music, sharing one licensed sound recording with all students attending a particular university would be unreasonable. Second, there is no automatic right to receive error corrections, updates, improvements, or new versions of software or information. Third, UCITA favors licensors in matters involving ownership, transfer restrictions, and inspection rights.

UCITA report
**http://www.wsba.org/
businesslaw/lcc/
report/2000/ucita.htm**

Finally, UCITA licenses are not perpetual; they last for a term that is reasonable in light of the information involved and the commercial circumstances. Great care must be taken that the licensor's right to terminate does not permit the extortion of huge fees under threat of termination when the licensee has become highly dependent on the information. For example, a threat to terminate enterprise software just before the licensee's annual inventory needed for preparation of financial statements and its tax returns could amount to economic duress. UCITA provides no automatic protection from such extortion. To avoid such pressure, licensees must carefully examine license terms and negotiate fairer termination provisions.

TRADEMARK LICENSING

The licensing of trademarks is usually a B2B matter between two parties: (1) the licensor, who either manufactures a trademarked product or who owns a business service system, and (2) licensees, who independently do business selling the licensor's products or services. Trademark licensing benefits both the licensor and licensee because sales are enhanced with a strong brand image of the product or service. This image is created from the licensor's reputation for product quality, as enhanced by advertising and by the product's visibility at the licensee's retail level.

Consistency and coherence in the supply chain are key to maintaining the enforceability of trademark-licensing contracts. Early cases held that a licensor abandoned and lost rights in its trademark when it failed to control licensees' use of the trademark.[12] Today, the Lanham Act requires that the trademark owner must exercise control over the quality and nature of the products sold under the trademark. As discussed in Chapter 7, the basis of trademark rights is to assure that consumers are protected. Trademark is not premised on a pure private property rights theory that commercial symbols constitute a separate type of property. Instead, the validity of trademark licensing is tested by the fundamental principle that commercial symbols function as a method to prevent consumer confusion. In modern business practice, trademark licensing is the fundamental organizing principle for a highly successful business method: the franchise.

FRANCHISES

Franchise, like *license*, is a somewhat imprecise term because it refers generally to the grant of a privilege. Franchise describes both governmental grants and private-contract relations. The early governmental grants of franchises were to public utilities (e.g., electric, gas, water, telephone). They were essentially legal monopolies to provide the service within a fixed geographic area. By contrast, the **private franchises** discussed here grant a privilege to conduct the business defined in the franchise agreement. Franchises are a form of business organization because they permit an owner to profit from the business's growth while retaining some control and limited liability.

Since the 1950s, franchises have grown tremendously and contribute significantly to retail sales of manufactured products and consumer services. Common franchise businesses include automobile dealerships, fast food and other types of restaurants, soft drink bottlers, and gas stations. There are also numerous service franchises such as hotels, motels, photocopying, vehicle rentals, tax preparation, cleaning or laundry, law, hair salons, and real estate brokerages.

What Is a Franchise?

There is no single definition of franchise. A **franchise** is generally recognized to be a contract that grants a license to conduct business under a registered trademark in which all participants share a community of interest in selling goods or services under specified conditions. A franchise system is a business-distribution organization composed of numerous independent retail units, the **franchisees**, which pay franchise fees and royalties to the **franchisor**, which supplies products, formulas, a trademark, and/or methods of operation. An FTC trade regulation rule defines a franchise as any continuing commercial relationship in which franchisees distribute goods or services identified by a trademark, service mark, trade name, or other commercial symbol. The franchisee is required or advised to meet the franchisor's quality standards, the franchisor secures a retail outlet or location for the franchisee, and the franchisee is obligated to make a payment or commits to make future payments to the franchisor or an affiliate.

---

12. *Everett O. Fisk & Co. v. Fisk Teachers' Agency, Inc.*, 3 F.2d 7 (8th Cir., 1924).

The rights and duties of the franchisor and franchisee are largely defined by their franchise agreement. Although the parties may initially execute a vague commitment letter, the relationship is precisely defined in the franchise contract. The terms in franchise agreements vary among industries and even between brands within a product market. Most franchise agreements include trademark licenses as well as many of the distribution contract terms discussed throughout this chapter.

The FTC definition classifies several key franchise features into three general groups: control, assistance, and supply. The **control feature** is satisfied when the franchisor exerts significant controls over the franchisee's business operations: business organization, promotional activities, management, marketing plan, or business affairs. Control is an essential feature because the Lanham Act requires a trademark owner to enforce quality-control standards over all who use the trademark. This factor contributes to the success of fast-food franchises because consumers can rely on consistent quality at any restaurant in the system. The **assistance feature** exists when the franchisor provides significant assistance to the franchisee on managerial or operational matters. The **supply feature** is characterized by the franchisee's sale of goods or services supplied by the franchisor, its affiliate, or sourced from a third party designated by the franchisor. Most successful franchises include all these features.

The FTC further classifies franchises into package franchises, product franchises, and business-opportunity franchises. In a **package franchise,** the franchisee must use a uniform business format specified by the franchisor and identified by the trademark. The franchisee usually pays a periodic royalty determined by the level of sales. The franchisee in a **product franchise** distributes goods bearing the franchisor's trademark and produced by the franchisor or under the franchisor's control. Automobile dealers and soft drink bottlers are the best known examples of product franchises. They are usually required to pay an initial fee to purchase the franchise. The franchisor earns additional profits as part of the price of goods distributed through the franchisee (new cars, replacement parts, soft drink concentrate). The **business-opportunity franchise** is a catchall category that includes other franchises in which the franchisor supplies goods to the franchisee, the franchisor secures retail outlets for the franchisee, and a fee is paid.

Franchise Regulation

The regulatory approach to franchising has been decidedly laissez-faire. There is no single comprehensive regulatory scheme, and the parties have the freedom to negotiate varying terms in their franchise agreements. Some franchisors exercise strong controls over their franchisees, but others exercise only weak control. Therefore, as the states and federal governments have gained experience with franchises, they have passed narrow regulations to target specific aspects after abuses are discovered. Franchise regulation generally falls into three major areas: (1) protection of franchisees, (2) protection of customers, and (3) protection of competition and the markets.

Franchises are most successful when the franchisor designs a popular product and business method and then sustains the system's growth by recruiting numerous successful franchisees. For the large, well-known franchises, it is easy to recruit competent franchisees. However, newer, smaller, and unestablished franchises must aggressively market their franchise systems to be successful. Franchisors often use seminars and information packages that describe business prospects to potential franchisees in glowing terms. The failure of many franchises in the late 1960s and early 1970s led to federal disclosure requirements and to state regulations in nearly half the states. Franchisors or brokers dealing in franchises must disclose sufficient information for the prospective purchaser to make an informed decision. This disclosure often includes the name, address, and business experience of the franchisor and its affiliates; its litigation experience; recent financial statements; a copy of the franchise agreement; and a description of all the fees, royalties, or hidden costs necessary to operate the franchise. The antitrust aspects of franchises are discussed in Chapter 12.

ONLINE

State Franchise Laws
**http://www.ftc.gov/
bcp/franchise/
netdiscl.htm**

Franchise Termination

Franchise agreements typically provide for termination of the parties' obligations so that neither is required to continue if the relationship becomes unprofitable or unsuitable. The franchise relationship usually runs for a renewable fixed term but can be terminated "for cause" after notice is given. Most franchisees invest considerable time and money to start and maintain their businesses, but individual franchisees are relatively powerless to modify the termination provisions. Experience with arbitrary terminations by some franchisors has led to litigation and legislation to protect franchisee rights.

Automobile dealer franchisees are protected from bad-faith termination by a federal statute, the **Automobile Dealer Day in Court Act**. This law also prevents automobile manufacturers from threatening dealers with termination unless they accept more cars, parts, or other services from the manufacturer. The **Petroleum Marketing Products Act** gives gas station operators an opportunity to purchase the premises when the franchisor refuses to renew the lease. Several states have passed similar statutes to protect franchisees in other types of business. Absent such statutory protection, some franchisees have been successful convincing courts to limit the franchisor's right to terminate at will. These suits are often based on the UCC's good faith provision. Some courts award damages to the franchisee equal to the out-of-pocket expenses in purchasing the franchise. Other courts have expanded the allowable damages to include the loss of future profits expected in operating the franchise.

PUBLICITY, ENDORSEMENT, OR AFFILIATION

Marketing increasingly claims that relationships among firms and persons mutually enhance their individual brand images. For example, advertisers use the appeal of celebrity endorsement to enhance the desirability of their products. Web sites post trademarked logos of independent firms to enhance each firm's goodwill with the other firm's brand image—cobranding. Independent firms join in strategic alliances to leverage their specific advantages into stronger products. The reputation of search engines and portals improves with more reliable links to useful sites. How do affiliations raise legal or regulatory questions?

Affiliation requires some compliance with consumer protections, privacy, IP, and licensing law. First, the descriptions and actual performance of such affiliations should be accurate to avoid liability for fraud or false advertising. Second, licenses may be needed before the parties begin their public activities and before they create or publicize their relationship. Generally, such licensing may cover interests such as an individual celebrity's right to privacy, copyrights in another firm's content, and trademarks of other firms used by each firm to demonstrate a relationship exists with other firms. Contracts between these participants are often needed to create the affiliation. Third, linking may involve moral rights because the linked site's reputation is at stake. Licenses may also be needed in two key areas: (1) celebrity endorsements and (2) Internet affiliations.

Licensing Celebrity Endorsement

Celebrities have the exclusive right to control the commercial exploitation of their endorsements or personae. This right is based on an inherent property interest derived from the state law of privacy rights, discussed in Chapter 13, called misappropriation or the right of publicity. The publicity right can also be based on two tort theories that an unauthorized endorsement (1) causes damage to the celebrity's reputation or (2) constitutes a misrepresentation. What are the elements of a celebrity's persona that can be protected? Endorsement law protects the celebrity from unauthorized use of various separate elements of the persona: name, likeness (photo, drawing, look-alike), and voice or style (the unique "sound" of Bette Midler's singing voice).[13]

Authorization is needed to use a celebrity's endorsement; New York law makes such an endorsement a crime without written authority. This permission should be granted in a written license by the celebrity or by the estate of a deceased celebrity (in 13 states). Licensing terms should include the duration, the elements authorized, geographic limitations, itemization of products endorsed, compensation, and the celebrity's approval over the particular use (creative control). A license to use a **stock photo** from a photographer does not assure that the photographed celebrity gave permission. A **morals clause** may create grounds for termination if the celebrity's image is tarnished by scandal or illegal activity. Perhaps the celebrity should have a similar right to terminate if the manufacturer or its product line falls into disrepute.

Internet Affiliations: Linking, Framing, and Meta-tags

Affiliations on the Internet have grown rapidly. Web sites link to unaffiliated sites or otherwise use their content. Most are not authorized by the site linked. Does this raise IP infringement or other legal issues? If so, would it be best to secure permission to link or frame, using an authorization by license? Downloading creates a copy of copyrighted expression to the user's RAM and screen and is often printed or saved. Those who post to Web sites know the whole World Wide Web can access their content, so it can be argued that posting material to a Web site by implication grants permission to view. Does any such permission extend to linking, framing, saving, printing, or sending such files to others?

Linking or hypertext links occur when one Web site, the **linking site**, provides a complete uniform resource locator (URL) to another Web site, the **linked site**, to

---

13. *Midler v. Young & Rubicam*, 944 F.2d 909 (1991), *cert.denied* 503 U.S. 951 (1992).

access a document. The link may appear on the linking site's page in its raw form [http://www.thompson.com], or the raw form URL can be embedded within a highlighted word, phrase, title, button, or graphic. Browsers (Netscape Communicator, Microsoft Explorer), Web-authoring tools (FrontPage), viewers (Adobe Acrobat), word processors, and many other computer applications automatically convert URLs directly into clickable links when keyed into a document as it is created or modified. When these Web pages are posted, downloaded, or otherwise distributed (e-mail attachment), they are used by other users to automatically launch the download of material contained at that linked site.

The culture of the Internet expects linking to flourish unhindered by property rights claims by the linked site's owner. Further, it is argued that site owners wishing to block access to unauthorized or unknown outsiders may simply use password protection, cookie technology, or some other authentication scheme to exclude unwanted downloads. Under copyright infringement law, linking is not a reproduction or public display of another's copyrighted expression. Linking simply points the way and saves the user from typing in sometimes long and tedious URLs. However, there is potential liability in linking. For example, if a Web site provides notice or has a user license requiring permission to link, then an unauthorized link might constitute a trespass. The use of a copyrighted graphic or trademarked logo as the link without permission from the IP's owner could constitute infringement. Further, if users are led to believe that the linking site is affiliated or endorsed by the linked site, two other theories of liability may arise: palming off and tortious interference with business, discussed in Chapters 3 and 7.

Deep linking bypasses the home page of a linked site and directly accesses internal pages. Web site owners often want users to pass through shallower pages for various reasons: Users are exposed to banner ads, information is collected, cookies set or retrieved, and the user might make different choices instead. Web site owners might claim that deep linking alters the sequence of pages that users see, which constitutes an unauthorized derivative work infringing the linked site's copyright. As of this writing, no case has held that deep linking is infringement. However, in *Ticketmaster Corp. v. Tickets.com, Inc.,*[14] the trial court dismissed a trespass theory of deep linking but permitted three other claims to go to trial: infringement, palming off, and tortious interference with business. The case was later settled.

Until the legal risks of linking become better settled, both netiquette and careful risk management suggest getting permission to link whenever the linked site demands permission and for deep linking. Deep linking may deprive linked sites from collecting banner ad revenues from advertisers. Linking licenses may include many of the usual licensing terms: grant clause, termination, and duration. They may also include aesthetic and presentation requirements and some sharing of data or ad revenues when collected by the parties. Linking to illegal, terrorist, or pornographic materials may eventually become illegal. For example, both Germany and Japan prohibit some such links.

---

14. 54 U.S.P.Q.2d 1344 (C.D.Cal. 2000).

Framing displays parts of two Web sites simultaneously. Usually the linking site creates a perimeter frame or border, often displaying its logo and other links of its own choosing. Inside the frame is displayed content from the linked site. Some novice users may think there is an affiliation between the sites unless there is conspicuous notice to the contrary. The outer edges of the framed site, including its ads, may be partially blocked by the frame. Alternatively, the framed site may be shrunk to fit inside the frame. This may infringe on the framed site's right to make derivative works. Framing raises the linking site's value by free-riding on the linked site's value. However, experienced users know their browsers permit the framed site to be opened separately in an unframed page.

Meta-tags are hidden html codes in Web pages that ostensibly describe the Web site's content to signal search engines. Meta-tags help users screen for sought-after content or screen out objectionable content (obscenity). Search engines give precedence to Web sites when the search term appears numerous times. Some unscrupulous Web site operators include famous trademarks belonging to others or use inaccurate descriptions in their meta-tags. This practice is arguably fraudulent because these intentionally misdescriptive search terms cause search engines to more prominently display these Web sites when users are looking for other sites, causing users to suffer initial confusion.[15] Web site traffic counters credit such hits to the fraudulent Web site, and some users may stay at the Web sites even if they were searching for other content. Such misuse of meta-tags may cause consumer confusion or dilution that infringes a trademark owner's rights. The fraudulent inflation of Web site hits may also violate the banner advertising contract or constitute false advertising.

LEASING

Many transactions are neither sales nor licenses but occupy a middle ground, leases. A **lease** is a contract granting possession and use of property in exchange for the payment of rent. The owner of the property who sells rights to use the property is the **lessor**. The party acquiring temporary possession and use under the lease is the **lessee**. Leases of real estate (land, buildings) have been a common form of contract for hundreds of years in markets for residences and for business uses such as agriculture, manufacturing or warehouse facilities, and office space. Real estate leases are governed by the common law of real property and various landlord-tenant statutes. Leases of goods are governed by the UCC Article 2A, which has been passed by 49 states (but not Louisiana). Goods leases became quite popular in the twentieth century as their tax and financing advantages became better understood and then were widely accepted. Long experience with unconscionable lease terms led to consumer protections in leasing.

Between the 1950s and the 1980s, many of the original technologies that serve as infrastructure for cyberspace were leased, not purchased. Telecommunications

---

15. See *Brookfield Communications v. West Coast Entertainment Corp.*, 174 F.3d 1036 (9th Cir., 1999).

equipment, mainframe computers and their peripherals, and the software to run them all were leased by the manufacturers or their leasing subsidiaries to both commercial customers and to consumers. The proportion of computers and phone systems under lease dropped dramatically after the AT&T antitrust breakup and after PCs became more commonplace. Since then, most customers purchase their own equipment. One reason that leasing was imposed on customers is that it permitted greater control over the uses of these technologies and arguably legitimized the tying that lessors once commonly required.

Today, leasing of such equipment is not just an interesting phase of business history. Leasing is making a comeback, particularly of PCs to business clients. Web hosting agreements may include the lease of server and storage capacity. In the future, software leasing may reemerge because vendors are attempting to extract higher revenues for the use of their programs. However, a revision of UCC Article IIA that is underway by the National Conference of Commissioners on Uniform State Laws (NCCUSL) could exclude software from leasing in favor of licensing under UCITA.

ONLINE

NCCUSL Web site of uniform laws
http://www.nccusl.org

The leasing of goods under UCC Article 2A essentially mirrors the structure of UCC Article 2 (Sales): both cover transactions in goods. Many contractual elements of sales and leases are similar, and Chapters 8, 9, and 10 have already covered the elements of contract law, such as mutual assent, consideration, defenses, writings, warranties, legality, and performance. Each lease is created in a lease agreement that defines the transfer of rights and possession. It includes the lessee's duties to pay rent and preserve the property leased. The statute of frauds requires a written lease if the total of payments is more than $1,000. A **sublease** provision may permit the lessee to further lease the property to another person, a sublessee, or it might prohibit such activity. **Consumer leases** made by merchant lessors have special protections if the total payments are less than $25,000 and the goods are leased primarily for personal, family, or household use. **Finance leases** are three-party transactions involving the lessee, a lessor who simply finances the lease, and the original supplier of the goods. The lessee's duty to make lease payments to the lessor is independent of the supplier's breach in supplying the goods. This arrangement substantially protects the lessor from loss if the goods are defective and the lessee tries to pressure the supplier by threatening to stop making payments to the lessor. The pending revision of UCC Article 2A would better enable electronic lease contracting, as in other revised articles.

COMPUTER SERVICES AND DEVELOPMENT

Major areas of concern are contracts with outside vendors to provide computer services: the development of software or Web sites, the hosting and delivery of software applications, the hosting of Web sites, and the development of multimedia. Only the largest and most technically savvy firms have the expertise to do all these functions in-house. Most firms developing Internet commerce strategies must manage the technology transfer issues raised by computer service contracts, including ownership and control of IP and information, limitations on their scope of use, and the duration of the relationship.

An important distinction was made in the discussion of mass market licenses under UCITA: Computer services are generally long-term B2B transactions that must be separately negotiated. They are rarely the standard form contracts used in most transactions. Standard forms are only a starting point for the parties to further customize their relationship and the products provided. Negotiations generally begin with the customer's first draft that defines the requirements. The draft is then often communicated in a **request for proposals** (RFP), and one or more candidate firms may respond with a concrete proposal.

Negotiations move smoothly if the client has done some planning beforehand, understands what is needed, and has researched comparable software or Web sites to specify functionality. Preparing proposals is costly and risky. If another bidder wins the contract or the customer withdraws the RFP, there may be no legal basis to bill the customer for the time and expense of developing the proposal. Although proposals are protected by copyright, the bidder's ideas or trade secrets are not protected without an NDA from the customer. Negotiations should result in a written engagement contract, specifically defining the compensation, system requirements, delivery, testing and acceptance of deliverables, ownership, rights to make updates, confidentiality, and warranties on IP, functionality, and scalability.

The creation of IP rights discussed in Chapters 4 through 7 and the licensing of IP rights discussed in this chapter are critical to developing useful terms in both software and Web development contracts. When IP belonging to third parties is used, the burden of obtaining and paying for permission to license that content must be allocated between the developer and the client. The parties should also agree on the ownership of IP created during the development: software, Web sites, and Web site content. Developers want ownership in order to resell the software, information, or content in similar projects for other clients. Also, developers can raise their clients' switching costs by holding ownership, which tends to lock in clients to do most of their future business for maintenance, updates, and upgrades with that developer. By contrast, many clients seek ownership to reduce their switching costs. Clients legitimately hope to prevent the developer from supplying their competitors. If the developer retains ownership, the client usually needs to negotiate the right to update and modify as needed to change the software's functionality or update Web sites.

Software development contracts raise similar issues. Ownership, control, and licensing of the software are the key points of contention. Parties are most satisfied and suffer the least costly surprise when ownership and control are balanced to satisfy both sides' interests. For example, there is considerable development expense in creating an enterprise software package. Software developers must be able to repackage their work for other clients, otherwise they must charge higher fees. Generally, the software developer owns the major functional subroutines, tools, and templates, which can be adapted for other clients' use. Clients must be free to use, modify, and adapt the software efficiently as their business needs evolve. A client will seek to own any new code written to customize the software for that client's particular application. The parties arrive at this balanced split through several stages of negotiations,

first creating a scope for the project in which the client's needs are defined, then iter-
atively adding details to the work plan, and establishing specifications, milestones,
deliverable dates, performance testing, and progress payments.

Web hosting relationships are bundles of services that provide Internet access for
users to the client's content. Web hosts hold the key to the client's success in using
the Web for commercial purposes. The host may agree to obtain domain name registrations, operate sufficient and reliable Internet gateways and server capacity, post
and update clients' Web site content, collect and maintain data (users' private information and transaction information), and administer the transaction processing
needed for e-commerce sites. Another form of hosting involves application service
providers (ASP). ASP relations involve a client's access to software and data, licensed
from a second-party vendor but hosted by a third party, the ASP, using the ASP's
servers and telecommunications facilities. ASP relationships are emerging as an
important business model for e-commerce because the client need not install the software on its computers. The ASP model permits the vendor to use various forms of
compensation, such as flat fees or metered according to usage.

CHAPTER 12
ANTITRUST

Antitrust law is a complex area of regulation that affects strategic planning, business modeling, marketing strategy, pricing, and the conduct of most supply-chain relations with suppliers, competitors, and customers. Antitrust was originally derived from English law that prohibited restraints of trade. It grew to prominence in the United States as the robber barons of the gilded age built huge monopolies. Antitrust analysis cannot be well understood without some familiarity with the economic theory of industrial organization. Economics strongly suggests that when compared with the ideal of perfect competition, monopolies charge higher prices, innovate more slowly, and reduce their output below what the market needs. Repeated experiences with monopolists prove these predictions. Antitrust regulates a wide range of activities involving horizontal relations with competitors, vertical relations with suppliers and customers, and conglomerate relations in other industries.

Antitrust takes on renewed importance as intellectual property (IP) becomes a major source of most firms' value in the future. For example, IP law grants monopoly-like rights to software companies through software copyrights, trade secrets, patents, and trademarks. Microsoft makes the operating systems (Windows) and applications software (Office, Internet browsers) used on 80% to 90% of all personal computers (PCs). Software companies must be compatible with Microsoft's Windows operating system or with its browser, Internet Explorer. Without compatibility, these competitors are nearly locked out of the PC market.

How does society reconcile the monopolies of IP law with the antitrust laws? Each is intended to encourage innovation and efficiency. On one hand, antitrust prohibits monopolization and promotes vigorous, direct rivalry by numerous competitors. On the other hand, IP law grants limited monopolies and gives the patent or copyright holder the power to control or prohibit direct competition. Accommodating these two major bodies of law poses big challenges for the information age. Former Chairman Robert Pitofsky of the Federal Trade Commission (FTC) argues that these laws must be balanced because IP is "now a principal, if not the principal, barrier to new entry in high-tech markets."

FOUNDATIONS OF THE ANTITRUST LAWS

The encouragement of competition is a primary goal of the antitrust laws. Other goals include maintaining liberty, assuring fairness, and providing economic opportunity. The nineteenth-century populists promoted antitrust law as a way to sustain a system of small, independent businesses and preserve the American dream. They thought that further concentration of political and economic power would encourage the growth of power centers, reminiscent of feudalism, that might eventually rival the power of government. Populists considered the diffusion and decentralization of both political and economic power to be necessary conditions for democracy and liberty.

"The Sherman Act was designed to be a comprehensive charter of economic liberty aimed at preserving free and unfettered competition. It rests on the premise that unrestrained interaction of competitive forces will yield the best allocation of our economic resources, the lowest prices, the highest quality, and the greatest material progress."[1] This statement justifies antitrust laws as an incentive to innovate, maintain productive efficiency, and maximize the range and selection of goods. Monopolies are damaging because they limit production, risk poor quality, and empower monopolists to fix prices and exclude competitors. These outcomes directly conflict with the goals promised by competition. Antitrust laws are intended to maintain a competitive environment.

The Microsoft antitrust litigation has focused attention on two important public policy questions going forward. First, in the future, will the world's economy become so dominated by information products that markets for industrial products will become far less relevant? Second, will the economic theory and laws designed for the twentieth-century industrial economy become unsuitable to the evolving marketplace, making the antitrust laws inappropriate for an information economy? This chapter reviews the antitrust laws and gauges their impact on the traditional economy and on IP and the network economy as a means to resolve the question of whether the antitrust laws and the perfect competition model are becoming obsolete or whether a strong economy can be sustained by finding a new balance between strong antitrust values and IP rights.

TRADITIONAL MARKET STRUCTURES

Traditional economic analysis defines five basic market structures: perfect competition, monopoly, oligopoly, monopolistic competition, and monopsony. This analytic model is used to predict the purchasing behaviors of consumers, the pricing and production

---

1. *Northern Pacific Railway Co. v. United States*, 365 U.S. 1 (1958).

behaviors of sellers, and the collusive behaviors of all. Under **perfect competition**, there are a large number of buyers and sellers. No individual firm or consumer has sufficient market power to influence prices or the quantity of production. Perfect competition presumes there are low barriers to entry, uniform products, and perfect information concerning market conditions is shared by all. Antitrust enforcement would be unnecessary if all markets were perfectly competitive. These assumptions are unrealistic in the real world, but perfect competition is useful as a model for economic analysis and as an objective. The securities markets and the markets for gasoline or groceries in larger cities often come close to perfect competition.

Monopoly describes a market dominated by one large seller. Typically, there are no close substitutes for the seller's product. There are usually high **barriers to entry** that make it difficult for other firms to compete. Legal barriers to entry include IP (patents, copyrights, trade secrets), franchises, international trade barriers, and restrictive licenses. Natural barriers to entry include high transportation costs and high capital equipment costs. Some utilities have natural monopolies in their service areas because of the expense to duplicate the power generators or distribution wiring and plumbing. Utilities have been regulated to reduce their monopolistic tendencies. An **oligopoly** is a small number of sellers protected by high barriers to entry. These strong sellers typically have market power to influence prices and quantity. The U.S. domestic steel market was long regarded as an oligopoly: most steel was an interchangeable commodity, and there was little price competition. Prices tend to be higher and output lower in oligopolistic markets than under perfect competition. **Monopolistic competition** involves markets with few sellers offering somewhat substitutable but differentiated products. Examples include automobiles, soft drinks, beer, and PCs. Each producer distinguishes its models in consumers' minds, even though most products are somewhat interchangeable for their basic purposes. Monopolistic competitors possess some market power, are considered slow to innovate, and spend more on marketing than in perfectly competitive markets.

Monopsony exists when a single buyer possesses monopoly buying power. **Oligopsony** exists when a few buyers have market power. For example, the employer in a company town is a monopsonist because, as the predominant buyer of labor, it can affect prices (wages) and set them lower than under perfect competition.

NETWORK EFFECTS AND ANTITRUST

Recall that **network effects** were introduced in Chapter 9 as the main challenge to developing new payment systems. In the antitrust context, network effects are used to criticize traditional **industrial organization economics** as the focus of antitrust law. At the heart of this debate are three key arguments used to oppose antitrust enforcement against firms in the information economy. First, in the future, the information economy will sell ideas and intangibles, and this sector will dominate the whole economy. This argument presumes that the impact of traditional industrial production of physical goods will diminish significantly. Second, it is argued that the information economy is not governed by an industrial age concept, the **law of diminishing returns**, which is based on the scarcity of raw materials. The law of diminishing returns predicts that profitability drops after the production of physical goods expands beyond some point of optimal efficiency. In information businesses, there is an unlimited supply of ideas and intangible assets. They have potentially unlimited **economies of scale** that produce increasing returns as IP or network products are sold to more and more customers.[2] The third argument is that a strong system of IP rights is an adequate substitute as an innovation incentive, so society should abandon antitrust enforcement, particularly in high-technology industries. Such New Age economists believe that society does not long suffer under an IP monopoly because the IP laws provide a strong incentive to develop **substitutes**—new competing technologies that do not directly infringe the monopolist's IP.

These three arguments support a **winner-take-all** system for information products. This results from **positive feedback**, a consumption-side economy of scale produced by the network effects of information products. Information products are most successful if they are allowed a limited-time monopoly to pay back the significant initial R&D expense and technical know-how needed for development. Information products are more valuable to users and producers when they are standardized.

The **first-mover advantage** is also strong for sellers of information products. Sellers have an incentive to enter the market quickly and discount their products. Some even buy their customer base by selling their products below cost to **lock in** a large user base. Thereafter, customers may have high **switching costs**, making it difficult to change vendors or adopt new standards. The seller has a loyal customer base that can be exploited with highly profitable sales throughout the product's useful life. Consider the example of a firm-wide computer network, telephone system, or software purchase. These systems often require training and installation. The costs of switching to competing systems can be so prohibitive that switching occurs only after the assets are fully depreciated or become obsolete.

Some opponents of antitrust enforcement against network industries hope to rely exclusively on the innovation incentive of IP to eventually produce potential competitors. Under this theory, they advocate only a diminished role for antitrust enforcement. The natural behavior and benefits of network industries may produce benefits for society. However, it may be necessary to monitor firms achieving dominance so that innovation by potential competitors is not thwarted. As you become more familiar with antitrust law in this chapter, consider how the traditional antitrust theories could apply to firms in the information economy: monopolization, restraints of trade, and mergers that create monopolies. The application of traditional antitrust theory to IP, to network industries, and to the new economy are discussed throughout this chapter.

THE PRIMARY ANTITRUST LAWS

The U.S. antitrust laws broke new ground by directly regulating restraints of trade and monopolies. The early common law had only indirect prohibitions on covenants not to compete in employment contracts and in sales of businesses, introduced in

---

2. See W. Brian Arthur, Increasing Returns and the New World of Business. *Harvard Business Review*, July–August , 1996.

Chapter 11. The rule of reason, discussed later, is a direct descendent from these principles. The contract law concepts of duress and economic duress underlie other antitrust laws, such as the prohibition on tying arrangements and boycotts. As the industrial revolution progressed, these common law principles were unsuitable to encourage competition sufficiently. Contract law failed to protect the competitive structure of the economy because most customers, competitors, and suppliers of monopolists lacked privity, so there was no enforceable legal remedy. The short-comings of the common law and pressure from populists eventually spawned the federal and state antitrust laws.

SHERMAN ACT

The **Sherman Act** was passed in 1890 as the first major antitrust law. It uses vague and general terms to prohibit anticompetitive devices that restrain trade and erect the barrier of monopoly to any trade or other aspect of interstate commerce. Section 1 of the Sherman Act makes it an unlawful criminal act to enter into a "contract, combination . . . or conspiracy in restraint of trade." Section 2 of the Sherman Act prohibits monopolization by stating that "every person who shall monopolize, or attempt to monopolize, or combine or conspire with any other person or persons, to monopolize any part of the trade of commerce among the several states, or with foreign nations shall be deemed guilty of a felony."

CLAYTON ACT

Initially, the federal courts were quite lenient in their interpretations of the Sherman Act. One early case held that manufacturing was not interstate commerce, so the federal government could not regulate it.[3] Although that view was soon abandoned, it illustrates how the courts' laissez-faire ideology restrained antitrust enforcement. Eventually Congress responded to the mounting criticism in 1914 by passing the **Clayton Act**. It was written in more explicit terms, outlawing specific anticompetitive activities. Whereas the Sherman Act requires proof of completed anticompetitive effects, the Clayton Act can be violated earlier, when anticompetitive tendencies arise from conduct even before competition is damaged. Section 7 of the Clayton Act prohibits interlocking directorates and mergers or stock acquisitions that result in a substantial lessening of competition. Section 3 prohibits tie-in sales, exclusive dealing arrangements, and requirements for contracts that "substantially lessen competition or tend to create a monopoly."

FEDERAL TRADE COMMISSION ACT

The Federal Trade Commission Act was also passed in 1914. It created the FTC and gave the FTC broad powers to enforce the Sherman and Clayton Acts, as well as "unfair methods of competition" and "unfair or deceptive acts or practices."

---

3. *United States v. E.C. Knight Co.*, 156 U.S. 1 (1896).

Practices that are not clearly illegal under other antitrust laws may still be unlawful under the FTC Act. The rule-making power of the FTC permits it to fill in the gaps of the antitrust laws through investigation and enforcement of unfair trade practices. FTC proceedings usually involve an internal hearing held before an administrative law judge. The FTC often resolves such complaints with a **consent decree**, settling charges without an admission or denial. Defendants must usually promise to refrain from the practice in the future. The FTC may also issue **cease and desist orders**, which are stronger than injunctions because the defendant must stop the activity that is an unfair trade practice. Also, the defendant bears the stigma of a repeat offender. The FTC's orders are enforced with contempt citations, fines, and imprisonment. Appeals may be taken to the FTC commissioners and ultimately through the U.S. Court of Appeals and on to the U.S. Supreme Court.

Like many other agencies, the FTC provides guidance and detailed notice of what the FTC considers unfair trade practices. These guidelines sometimes create **safe harbors** for specific conduct; that is, the FTC promises not to prosecute a business that conforms its transactions to the guidelines. However, FTC advisory opinions and guidelines do not have the force of law and may be reinterpreted by the courts. The FTC may also issue specific trade regulation rules that do have the force of law, for example, the FTC's requirement that gasoline retailers post octane numbers on gas pumps. Private parties may also request the FTC to issue an **advisory opinion** regarding the legality of specific proposed conduct.

ADDITIONAL FEDERAL AND STATE ANTITRUST LAWS

Over the years, Congress has strengthened the antitrust laws. In 1936, price discrimination was specifically outlawed by the **Robinson-Patman Act**. In 1950, the **Celler-Kefauver Amendment** closed a loophole by extending the merger prohibition to include corporate acquisitions in which the assets of another firm are purchased. In 1976, the **Hart-Scott-Rodino Antitrust Improvement Act** expanded the DOJ's investigative powers. Hart-Scott-Rodino requires public notice of mergers prior to their completion, and it permits prosecution of antitrust violations by the attorneys general of the states for damages caused to state citizens. The **Tunney Act** was passed after Congress became concerned that the DOJ might settle antitrust suits by favorably approving mergers and monopolization activities conducted by corporations that were substantial campaign contributors. The Tunney Act requires federal district court review of antitrust settlements negotiated between the DOJ and antitrust defendants because of the potential for political influence on the presidential administration.

Most states have antitrust laws that parallel the federal antitrust laws and the FTC Act. Typically, state antitrust laws outlaw particular anticompetitive acts such as restraints of trade, price-fixing, exclusive dealing, and tying. In recent years, several states' attorneys general have cooperated to enforce both their state and federal antitrust laws. The National Association of Attorneys General (NAAG) has coordinated various suits. Business must not be lulled into complacency over antitrust enforcement, even if federal

ONLINE
National Association of Attorneys General
http://www.naag.org

regulators temporarily relax their enforcement activity. State attorneys general and private parties may use state laws as an alternate basis for antitrust litigation, making enforcement less susceptible to lobbying or ideological shifts in Washington.

ANTITRUST ENFORCEMENT

The United States has four basic antitrust law enforcers: the DOJ, the FTC, state attorneys general, and private parties. The DOJ Antitrust Division is the only enforcer with both criminal and civil enforcement powers under the Sherman Act, and the DOJ also has civil enforcement powers under the Clayton Act. The DOJ is directed by the attorney general, a cabinet member who is usually a close ideological confidant of the president. The FTC may bring civil enforcement actions for violations of the Clayton Act and has sole enforcement authority of the FTC Act. The FTC is a quasi-independent regulatory agency headed by five commissioners appointed by the president and confirmed by the Senate. This gives the FTC some political independence from the president and Congress.

Private parties may bring civil damage suits under the Sherman Act or the Clayton Act. A private party may wait to sue until a government agency successfully prosecutes the violator—a good tactic for private plaintiffs because a successful government enforcement action often provides convincing evidence of fault. **Class action** antitrust lawsuits are permissible in certain limited situations, such as when several individuals are harmed in a similar way by the defendant's monopolistic conduct. State attorneys general may sue in their *parens patrie* role—that is, on behalf of their state's consumers or competitors. Congress permitted these broad antitrust enforcement alternatives to promote vigorous enforcement of the antitrust laws.

CRIMINAL PENALTIES

There are substantial penalties to deter anticompetitive conduct. The Sherman Act imposes criminal sanctions on individuals, including fines of up to $100,000, prison sentences of up to three years, or both. Corporations may be fined up to $1 million per occurrence. Criminal convictions require proof of criminal intent, which means that the defendant must have had "knowledge of the probable consequences" of the anticompetitive action. The intent and burden of proof requirements make it difficult to obtain criminal convictions, and the predominant enforcement emphasis is on civil suits. No criminal sanctions are authorized by the Clayton or FTC Acts.

PRIVATE RIGHTS OF ACTION

The Clayton Act grants standing to "any person . . . injured in his business or property by reason of anything forbidden in the anti-trust laws," under either the Sherman Act or the Clayton Act. Private plaintiffs may recover **treble damages** (three times the actual damage sustained), plus litigation costs and reasonable attorneys' fees. Treble damages are similar to punitive damages and they are an incentive to sue. Injured competitors, consumers, suppliers, state attorneys general, and even foreign governments may sue for treble damages, but the plaintiff must be a direct purchaser. Indirect purchasers, those who purchase further down the distribution chain, are not directly injured by the anticompetitive conduct, so they may not bring treble damage claims.[4]

CIVIL REGULATORY REMEDIES

Both the FTC and the Justice Department use enforcement devices to obtain innovative remedies. First, **equitable relief** such as an injunction to prohibit future antitrust violations, is possible. This broad power permits the federal courts to restrain a particular anticompetitive conduct, compel divestiture of subsidiaries, dismember monopolies to create more competitive industries, cancel a merger, order licensing of patents with reasonable royalty payments, and cancel existing contracts. Second, consent decrees permit the government and the defendant to avoid trial by agreeing to a settlement. Typically, the defendant is notified that the regulator will file charges and then voluntarily agrees to cease its anticompetitive actions. Usually the defendant neither admits nor denies any violation of the law, and a court approves the settlement but issues a permanent injunction against future violations. **Consent decrees** avoid costly litigation and appeals. Subsequent damage suits by private plaintiffs may not take advantage of the consent decree to prove the violation; their cases must be proven separately, an added incentive for defendants to accept a consent decree. The FTC is limiting the duration of consent decrees to 20 years, and the DOJ's orders average only about 10 years.

Some settlements and consent decrees are controversial. The Tunney Act requires that a federal court must review settlements to avoid politically inspired collusion and assure that settlements are in the public interest. A federal judge found that the 1995 DOJ settlement with Microsoft was not in the public interest. Microsoft's alleged "vaporware" (premature product announcements that deter consumer purchases of competitive products) and other exclusionary practices were not addressed in the settlement, disappointing competing software companies who alleged that Microsoft restrains trade and monopolizes the software and operating system markets.[5]

INTERNATIONAL ANTITRUST ENFORCEMENT

The Sherman and Clayton acts apply to both domestic and foreign commerce that affects the United States. Some observers argue that U.S. antitrust laws should apply to all foreign firms' anticompetitive practices. The U.S. courts examine several factors before applying U.S. antitrust law to foreign firms' activities. Certain principles of international law restrict antitrust litigation against foreign firms. For example, the **act of state doctrine** and **sovereign immunity** prevent application of U.S. laws if the

---

4. *Illinois Brick Co. v. Illinois*, 431 U.S. 720 (1977).
5. *United States v. Microsoft Corp.* (Civ. No. 94-1564), 1995 W.L. 59580 (D.D.C.).

foreign activity is sponsored by a foreign government. These principles prevented challenges to Japanese firms' collusion because their activities were promoted by MITI, Japan's Ministry of Trade and Industry. **Comity** generally permits a foreign court to refuse enforcement of foreign antitrust laws unless that nation has similar laws. Strong U.S. antitrust enforcement also risks trade retaliation by foreign governments. However, when a foreign firm has assets, affiliates, or operations on U.S. soil, antitrust liability can be enforced.

European Union Laws
http://www.europa.org

Some foreign nations have further impeded U.S. antitrust suits against their home industries with **blocking laws** that prohibit compliance with U.S. pretrial discovery requests. Canada, France, and the UK passed these laws in the 1970s after aggressive U.S. antitrust enforcement against the uranium cartel. For example, it is common for antitrust plaintiffs to request from foreign firms numerous documents crucial to prove their case. Blocking laws often require precompliance notification to the foreign government, enabling foreign regulators to bar compliance with a U.S. production of documents request, effectively frustrating the antitrust suit.

During the twentieth century, most nations have had weaker antitrust enforcement than the United States. Many nations promote domestic monopolies so that they can compete more effectively in international commerce. Many educated people in developing nations are torn between the two extremes of nationalist monopoly and the consumer benefits of competition. On one hand, popular nationalism motivates governments to grant monopolies to strengthen domestic industry. On the other hand, many of these supporters also denounce the inevitable decline in their personal standard of living caused by paying high monopoly prices for domestic products and services. This tension has led to anticompetitive and protectionist laws regulating foreign trade: discriminatory taxes, tariffs, quotas, and excessive inspections. There is often hostility toward foreign competition, particularly large foreign firms. Overall, the efforts of GATT negotiations to reduce international trade barriers parallel antitrust enforcement that targets industry restraints of trade. They are remarkably the same problem at different levels.

The U.S. economy no longer acts in isolation. It is increasingly part of an interconnected global marketplace, with implications for the stringent antitrust enforcement of the past. Excessive enforcement could weaken U.S. competitors, particularly if foreign competitors receive government sponsorship or are permitted to monopolize in their home markets. Many nations subsidize their sole producers of various products for nationalistic pride or perceived self-sufficiency purposes. Some industries may need to consolidate and become larger to gain the economies of scale necessary to effectively compete, or to maintain national security.

Antitrust Enforcement Guidelines for International Operations
http://www.usdoj.gov/ atr/public/guidelines/ internat.htm

ANTITRUST EXEMPTIONS

Antitrust regulation of some industries, such as insurance companies and financial institutions, is the responsibility of other government agencies. To ensure their survival, some industries are permitted to use restraints of trade more freely than would be legal for other industries. For example, IP owners receive government-granted monopoly-like rights. The holders of patents, copyrights, and trademarks are encouraged to innovate by having exclusive rights to exploit the product of their creativity. Congress and the courts have also granted antitrust exemptions to certain industries. These exemptions are narrowly construed under the strict constructionism policy, and there is little flexibility to exempt a new variation of an exempt activity unless it is almost identical to the original.

The Clayton Act specifically exempts nonprofit **agricultural cooperatives** organized to provide mutual assistance to farmers. The **Capper-Volstead Act** extended this exemption to "persons engaged in the production of agricultural products such as farmers, planters, ranchmen, dairymen, or nut and fruit growers." Fishing cooperatives are also exempt. The exemption applies only to "persons engaged in agricultural production" and not to packing houses or to associations involved in both production and distribution. The court's unwillingness to extend this exemption to packing houses illustrates strict constructionism.

The National Labor Relations Act is considered a sufficient regulatory program for labor unions. The antitrust laws do not apply to most labor union activities that pursue their members' welfare. However, the exemption does not protect conspiracies to restrain trade. Labor union activities that provide aid to nonlabor groups or that tend to create monopolies or control marketing are not exempt. For example, labor agreements that require the employer to avoid dealing with a particular supplier or customer may be anticompetitive. Such agreements are enforceable only if they are designed to protect a legitimate labor union interest.

Restraints of trade or monopolizations that result from valid governmental actions are exempt from the Sherman Act under the **state action** exemption.[6] For example, state licensing of liquor stores or firearm sales often creates oligopolies that restrict the number of sellers, an anticompetitive condition. However, these restraints of trade are not illegal if state licensing is for the public's protection. Adequate supervision provided by the state's regulations is considered to justify the exemption. For the state action exemption to apply, there must be a clearly defined state policy permitting or requiring the particular activity or restraint. The exemption does not apply to nongovernmental functions the state supplies by itself. For example, the state action exemption did not protect (1) alleged conspiracies by municipally owned utilities to exclude the services from utilities outside the municipality and (2) a conspiracy between a city's sports stadium and its airport authority to exclude a particular brand of beer sold at both facilities. The city of Boulder, Colorado, violated the Sherman Act by preventing a cable television company from expanding its service territory.[7] Boulder's action in that case was not taken pursuant to a valid and clearly articulated state policy.

Until 1944, the insurance industry was not considered part of interstate commerce, so antitrust regulation of insurance was prohibited. The **McCarran-Ferguson**

---

6. *Parker v. Brown*, 317 U.S. 341 (1943).
7. *Community Communications Co. v. City of Boulder, Colorado*, 455 U.S. 40 (1982).

Act was passed in 1945 to continue this special exemption in states that regulate the insurance industry, such as by setting premium rates, regulating selling and advertising of policies, and the licensing of insurance agents. The insurance industry's exemption does not exempt other activities, except sharing actuarial data. For example, antitrust law would prohibit an insurance company's boycott, coercion, or intimidation of competitors.

Stock exchanges have a limited form of antitrust exemption because they are considered necessary to support the regulatory framework of the securities laws. Bank and other financial institution mergers are exempt from antitrust laws because they are regulated by federal and state agencies, such as the Federal Reserve Board, the Comptroller of the Currency, the Federal Deposit Insurance Corporation, and the Office of Thrift Supervision. The exemption for formerly regulated transportation industries is largely removed now, although there is some uncertainty as to which regulator has jurisdiction. As utility and telecommunication deregulation continues, their exemptions may diminish.

Most **professional sports** involve at least some restrictive actions among club owners, players' representatives, and facility owners (e.g., arenas, stadiums). For example, the limits on "free agency" prohibit players from moving between teams at will. Football, boxing, basketball, and hockey are all subject to antitrust enforcement, but the Supreme Court exempted professional baseball in 1922, 1953, and again in 1972. However, the baseball exemption is probably an aberration inconsistent with other laws.

Groups of businesses may join together to take mutually advantageous **political action** without violating the Sherman Act. The Supreme Court has refused to apply the Sherman Act to bona fide political activities of competitors, even if their objective is noncompetitive legislation, regulations, or administrative action. The **Noerr-Pennington doctrine** is based on two First Amendment rights: freedom of speech and the right to petition the government for redress of grievances.[8] However, a **sham exception** to the Noerr-Pennington doctrine does not exempt intentional efforts to harass a competitor. For example, purposeful interference with potential competitors' access to either the courts or regulatory agencies is not protected under *Noerr*. Conspiracy with a foreign government agency to restrain competition is also not protected. Several other laws create some limited exemptions for certain aspects of export goods, R&D, defense activities, oil marketing, and production joint ventures.

MONOPOLIES

Monopolies are the basic evil addressed by the Sherman Act because monopoly power enables price-fixing, reduction of output, and exclusion of competitors. An illegal monopoly arises when monopoly power is intentionally exercised by acts of monopolization.

---

8. *Eastern Railroad Presidents Conference v. Noerr Motor Freight, Inc.*, 365 U.S. 127 (1961).

MONOPOLY POWER

The central question in most antitrust cases is whether monopoly power exists. The next is whether it is exercised illegally by the defendant. Economists define monopoly power on the basis of the **elasticity of demand**. Perfectly competitive markets are highly elastic: When the price of a product rises, consumers can stretch and substitute purchases of similar products; when the price falls, consumers can quickly shift to purchase that product. The markets for investment securities and certain foodstuffs are highly elastic. There are many substitutes, and most consumers can easily find some alternative.

In an **inelastic market,** consumer demand is relatively unresponsive to small price changes, and consumers cannot easily change their purchases to satisfactory alternatives. Firms in inelastic markets have greater market power that enables them to control prices to a greater extent. An imperfect market is characterized by inelastic demand that gives some degree of market power to monopolists, oligopolists, and monopolistic competitors. Such firms can raise their prices without losing all of the customers because substitute products are not suitably equivalent replacements. The market for patented or copyrighted component parts (microprocessor chips) is often inelastic because buyers cannot easily substitute chips made by other manufacturers. Defining the relevant market is the first step in measuring monopoly power.

Relevant Market

Monopoly is not definable unless some boundary is set on the alleged monopoly in a particular market under analysis. A monopolist's illegal use of market power must exist over (1) an identifiable geographic area and (2) a particular product. The **relevant market** must be defined in cases involving monopolies, mergers, and restraints of trade. It includes all the producers of products or services that are functionally interchangeable and reasonably available to the same pool of consumers.

The first relevant inquiry is a determination of the specific geographic area within which competition is affected. Evidence is presented about consumers' buying patterns to construct a region within which consumers can readily obtain the product or service from any available seller, including the alleged monopolist. The **geographic market** may be local (e.g., city, county, metropolitan area), regional (e.g., state, multiple states), national, or even international. Generally, geographic markets are limited or bounded by the costs of transportation and by the ease with which consumers can gain access to other sellers. Within a particular geographic market, there may also be **submarkets** in which a group of local sellers compete more directly. For example, the shops in a neighborhood commercial area could be a submarket within the broader citywide geographic shopping market. It is often argued that the Internet creates massive, borderless markets for buyers and sellers. However, this may be true only for information transferred over networked computerized telecommunications. Language, cultural, and trade barriers still constrain the cross-border flow of goods and services, even if they are marketed over the Internet.

Next, the **product market** is determined. Consumers' preferences and their willingness to substitute physically different products for the same basic purpose or use are the key factors. The issue is usually whether two products are perceived as reasonably interchangeable or substitutable. To make this determination, courts examine the price, use, and quality of all reasonable substitutes, using the cross-elasticity of demand method of analysis to measure relationships between two possible substitutes. **Cross-elasticity of demand** is defined as the percentage change in the quantity demanded of one product divided by the percentage change of the substitute product's price. When these numbers are large and positive, the two products compared are highly substitutable for each other and should be considered part of the same market (e.g., butter versus margarine). Small positive numbers show some, but imperfect substitutability. Negative cross-elasticities often exist between complementary products. They are not substitutable for each other but might be purchased for use together (e.g., automobiles and tires). Cross-elasticity analysis is not a perfect method of determining product markets because consumers may not be willing to substitute dissimilar products priced at vastly different levels. For example, someone may be willing to ride a bus to work only when it becomes significantly cheaper than commuting by personal automobile.

The relevant market is large if there are many positive cross-elasticities between the monopolist's products and other products. However, if cross-elasticities are low, there may be no reasonable substitutes, and the relevant product market is as small as the market for the alleged monopolist's product. A particular firm's market share in a market with many direct competitors and/or many substitutes is usually small. By contrast, a particular firm's market share is likely to be large if there are few competitors or substitutes. Plaintiffs and enforcement agencies have an incentive to allege that few substitutes exist (low cross-elasticities), and defendants have an incentive to allege that there are many substitutes (high cross-elasticities).

Cross-elasticity analysis has narrowed the product market definition in some cases. For example, professional championship boxing matches are considered a market distinct from other boxing matches. Championship matches are the "cream" of the boxing business, appealing to a broader audience than other boxing matches. A similar analysis could be used to separate the major league baseball market from the minor leagues. Gospel music is considered a market distinct from popular music. A submarket for leasing large IBM mainframes was differentiated from the market for purchasing the same computers.

How do we analyze markets in e-commerce? The same principles apply. The costs of consumers gaining access to other sellers helps determine the geographic market. The cross-elasticity between substitutes determines the product market. The market for information and digital products will be very large if they are easily browsed (located), sold (transaction processed), and delivered over the Internet. Such markets could be expected to extend well beyond national borders if language and currency barriers are low and confidence is good that the transactions will be fully and adequately performed. As for the substitutability of products sold in e-commerce, the range of possibilities is very broad. Standardized goods purchased from various Internet vendors would normally all be part of the same product market. Customized products from different vendors might not be satisfactory substitutes. Different forms of similar goods are substitutable if consumers accept their various forms. For example, antivirus or firewall software can be purchased on a disk at computer stores, via mail or phone order, or directly from Web sites of man-ufacturers or retailers. Such software can also be downloaded in digital format from the vendor, or a subscription could be renewed. Some vendors, such as bookstores sell in parallel channels, through physical retail outlets as well as over the Internet. All these issues must be carefully measured and considered in determining market boundaries in e-commerce.

Market Share

Once the court has defined the relevant product and geographic markets, it must determine the alleged monopolist's market power within that market. Market power is typically measured as **market share**: the percentage of the relevant market the alleged monopolist controls. Measurement requires computing a fraction or per-centage; the fraction's numerator is the defendant's unit sales, and the denominator is the total unit sales of all that product from all vendors. There is no litmus test for determining what market share constitutes a monopoly. Market shares of 90%, 85%, and 75% have been considered monopolies, but shares of 20% or 50% are not usually monopolies. However, in the analysis of mergers, a relatively lower mar-ket share for the merged firms could be sufficient to prohibit the merger.

MONOPOLIZATION

The mere existence of monopoly power does not violate the Sherman Act. Indeed, some industries (e.g., utilities) have been more efficient when operated as a monop-oly. A monopoly becomes illegal when market power is used illegally. This is a **monopolization,** which represents the intentional use of monopoly power to gain an illegal monopoly. The **abuse theory of monopoly** analyzes both the structure of the market and the conduct of the alleged monopolist. A monopoly is illegal if a firm with monopoly power abuses its market power by undertaking purposeful acts to harm competitors and consumers. Market power is not illegal or abusive if it is acquired by historical accident or is obtained or maintained by selling better prod-ucts, using business savvy, or applying superior skill, foresight, and industry.

The types of monopolistic acts that constitute monopolization vary. Whenever a monopolist engages in predatory and coercive conduct in direct violation of the antitrust laws, monopolization intent can be inferred. Acts considered legal in many circumstances may be illegal if the monopolist's market power is employed with monopolistic intent. For example, conduct that is intended to prevent the entry of competitors, such as systematically increasing aluminum production capacity in anticipation of new demand, has been held illegal.[9] In another case, IBM's policy of leasing but never selling computers was considered exclusionary and unlawful.

Predatory Pricing

Predatory pricing, pricing below the producer's marginal cost, may also constitute deliberate and purposeful acts of monopolization. Although predatory pricing results

---

9. *United States v. Aluminum Co. of America*, 148 F.2d 416 (2d Cir., 1945).

in losses on those sales, it often forces competitors out of business. After monopoly is obtained, the monopolist can raise prices to recoup the earlier losses. If a monopolist lowers prices to undercut or restrict the entry of competitors, the intent to monopolize may be inferred. **Marginal cost** is the manufacturer's additional expense to produce one more unit beyond the number produced up to that point. **Average variable cost** is the average of all of the variable expenses for all of the units produced. Some commentators have urged that pricing below average variable cost should be presumed to be predatory pricing. Predatory pricing is monopolistic if it tends to immediately eliminate rivals, thus creating a monopoly. A related tactic is to charge monopoly prices in one geographic or product market and lower prices in the monopolized market to drive out competitors. Discriminatory pricing allows the monopolist to undercut potential competition by taking temporary losses that are made up with profits at other times or in other geographic or product markets.

There may be justifications for predatory pricing. One is to gain a toehold in a market dominated by large rivals. Information products and network industries in e-commerce may try to justify some acts that look like predatory pricing. For example, many sellers take losses on early product sales in hopes of raising switching costs and locking in consumers so higher prices can be charged later. Losses on the early predatory pricing are recouped later when the customer base must purchase more expensive products going forward.

ATTEMPTS TO MONOPOLIZE

The Sherman Act also outlaws **attempts to monopolize**, even if the alleged monopolist is unsuccessful at monopolizing. To prove liability, it must be shown that the defendant employed methods, means, and practices that would, if successful, accomplish monopolization. Even though the defendant fell short of monopolization, nevertheless it approached closely enough to create a dangerous probability of monopolization. The defendant in such cases must be proved to have had the specific intent of excluding competitors through the exercise of monopoly power. The **specific intent** standard for attempts to monopolize requires a higher burden of proof than other monopolization crimes. Nevertheless, intent may be inferred from unfair conduct. For example, inducing others to boycott a competitor's product, using discriminatory pricing, or refusing to deal with a particular customer are all evidence of the specific intent to attempt monopolization. When two or more persons combine their efforts in such acts, their agreement may also constitute a separate crime: **conspiracy to monopolize.**

The monopolization case against Microsoft was called the antitrust trial of the century. Microsoft appealed the trial court decision that follows here, and the U.S. Court of Appeals reversed only the severe "structural" remedies ordered by the trial judge. It then remanded the case back but to a different trial court judge after concluding that the original judge was biased against Microsoft.[10] Soon thereafter, DOJ settled the case with

ONLINE

Microsoft antitrust documents
http://www.usdoj.gov/ atr/cases/ms_index. htm

---

10. *United States v. Microsoft Corp.*, 253 F.3d 34 (D.C.Cir., 2001).

Microsoft, but several holdouts—nine states, private plaintiffs, and the EU antitrust enforcers—continue to pursue antitrust claims against Microsoft on the issues discussed here. As of this writing, the case remains unresolved and is an ongoing and potent political question.

MERGERS

Business combinations involve corporate finance and strategy. They implicate legal areas such as SEC regulations, state corporate law, and antitrust law. Antitrust law poses a difficult question of industrial organization: Will the market structure that results from a merger or an acquisition create an illegal monopoly or otherwise restrain trade?

TYPES OF MERGERS AND BUSINESS COMBINATIONS

Mergers often seem to be the quick and easy expansion method. A **merger** brings together two independent firms, one of which survives, and the other is dissolved. A **consolidation** combines two independent firms; both are terminated and replaced by a newly created combined entity. A **purchase of assets** involves the transfer of an acquired firm's assets to the acquiring firm, neither firm must be dissolved. In an acquisition, a firm acquired by another firm may operate as a separate division or subsidiary. For the purposes of antitrust analysis, all of these transactions are considered mergers.

Early interpretations of the Sherman Act held that mergers destroyed the competition that previously existed between the merged firms. However, this overly restrictive theory would prohibit most mergers simply due to the concentration of power that would result. Eventually the courts refused to use the Sherman Act to restrict mergers so Congress passed §7 of the Clayton Act to specifically prohibit mergers, if they tend to lessen competition.

. . . no person engaged in commerce, or in any activity affecting commerce shall acquire, directly or indirectly, the whole or any part of stock or other share capital . . . [or] . . . the whole or any part of the assets of another person engaged also in commerce or in any activity affecting commerce, where in any line of commerce or in any activity affecting commerce in any section of the country, the effect of such acquisition may be substantially to lessen competition, or tend to create a monopoly.

Section 7 was amended in 1950 by the Celler-Kefauver Act to (1) prohibit non-competitive market structures (e.g., oligopolies, monopolistic competition), (2) encourage internal growth and expansion, and (3) preserve local industrial control and small business viability. Celler-Kefauver also closed a major loophole in the Clayton Act by covering the sale of assets. The amendments apply to all three of the basic merger variations; horizontal mergers between competitors, vertical mergers among suppliers and customers, and conglomerate mergers with firms in other industries.

HORIZONTAL MERGER ANALYSIS

Horizontal mergers are the most basic type and arguably the most harmful to competition. They are combinations of firms that compete at the same level of production in the same industry (see Exhibit 12.1). Merger analysis is very similar to monopoly analysis because the relevant market and market share controlled by the merged firms are determined. Horizontal mergers are challenged when there is increased market dominance after the merger, and a substantial lessening of competition in the relevant market results.

The first step is to determine the **line of commerce**, both the geographic and product markets as introduced previously. Mergers are prohibited when they tend to substantially lessen competition in a particular "section of the country." Markets are defined on a local, regional, or national basis, and submarkets may also exist. The next step examines the relevant product market. Substitute products and their cross-elasticities of demand are identified, and consumers' perceptions of product substitutability are examined. There may also be inquiries into the correlation of price movements between similar products that suggest substitutability. In merger cases, it is necessary to identify all major firms serving a relevant market so that their

Exhibit 12.1 Horizontal Mergers

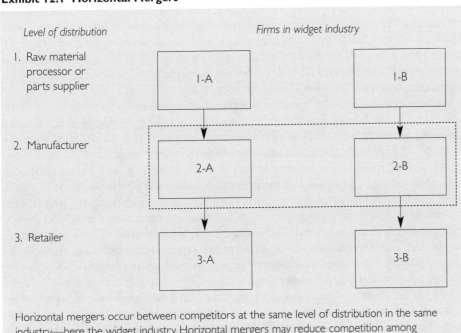

Horizontal mergers occur between competitors at the same level of distribution in the same industry—here the widget industry. Horizontal mergers may reduce competition among competitors, permitting producers to control price, production quantity, quality, and other features (e.g., services).

individual market shares can be computed. Additional firms may be included if they are capable of easily (1) switching to produce the relevant product, (2) reconditioning other products to make them good substitutes for that product, or (3) vertically integrating into the relevant product market. All the merging firms' product lines are considered separately and then aggregated.

ONLINE

FTC-DOJ Horizontal
Merger Guidelines
**http://www.ftc.gov/bc/
docs/horizmer.htm**

The FTC and DOJ have issued merger guidelines that are used to approve or oppose mergers on the basis of **market concentration**, an indication of the potential for exercise of monopoly power. There is greater concentration if there are fewer firms, each with larger market shares. There is less concentration if more firms compete because the market approaches perfect competition.

The **Herfindahl Index** calculates market concentration by *summing the squares of each firm's individual market share*. High Herfindahl numbers result if the market is dominated by monopolists or oligopolists with large market shares. For example, if just one firm in the relevant market had 75% of the market, the Herfindahl Index would be at least $75^2 = 5,625$. By contrast, if 10 firms in the relevant market possessed a market share of 10% each, the Herfindahl Index would be $10^2 + 10^2 + 10^2 + 10^2 + 10^2 + 10^2 + 10^2 + 10^2 + 10^2 + 10^2 = 1,000$. The Herfindahl Index can range from 10,000 for a pure monopoly (100^2) to less than 1 for a perfectly competitive market with near infinite competitors.

The DOJ is unlikely to challenge mergers if the Herfindahl Index remains below 1,000. If the index lies between 1,000 and 1,800, DOJ will challenge a merger that results in an increase of 100 or more Herfindahl points. For index numbers above 1,800, DOJ will challenge a merger that results in an increase of more than 50 points. Markets with Herfindahl indexes greater than 1,800 are considered highly concentrated. The Herfindahl Index does not have the force of law, but DOJ uses it to indicate when prosecution should be undertaken.

The question to be determined is whether a proposed merger would result in the combined firm's having a market share so high that there would be a substantial lessening of competition. Unlike monopolization cases, there is no necessity to prove attempts at predatory conduct or monopolistic acts. Probabilities, not "ephemeral possibilities," must be demonstrated by the party attacking the merger. DOJ considers the competitive impact of most mergers, and most parties will not pursue a merger if DOJ publicly opposes it. Courts prohibit mergers if the newly created firm "controls an undue percentage share" of the relevant market and produces "a significant increase in concentration." In one case, a prohibited merger would have resulted in a combined firm with a 30% market share. In another case, the absorption of a small, aggressive, and innovative firm by Alcoa was prohibited because the merger adversely affected competition.

In *United States v. Von's Grocery Co.*,[11] the Supreme Court upheld a DOJ challenge to a merger between two grocery store chains in the Los Angeles area: Von's and Shopping Bag. The combined sales of the two chains would have been only 7.5% of the metropolitan Los Angeles grocery market. However, the court noted

---

11. 384 U.S. 270 (1966).

that these two firms had experienced tremendous growth and that the "mom and pop" grocery stores were in steady decline. Merger analysis of industry trends toward consolidation may be used to prevent a merger with short-term procompetitive effects but longer-range concentration permitting future collusion. Consider this: Mom-and-pop stores resemble atomized perfect competition, but will they produce the lowest consumer prices?

VERTICAL MERGER ANALYSIS

Vertical mergers combine firms that stand in a supplier-customer relationship along the same chain of distribution (see Exhibit 12.2). **Vertical integration** is an expansion into retail and/or supplier levels along the supply chain. Firms naturally desire control over their customers and suppliers. Vertical mergers enable the resulting firm to squeeze out unintegrated competitors, limit future competition, and erect barriers to entry. Vertically integrated firms tend to exclude competitors from sources of supply or from customers, causing a supply squeeze. Vertically merged firms may also refuse to deal with nonintegrated firms and preferentially allocate products to their own affiliates.

Exhibit 12.2 Vertical Mergers

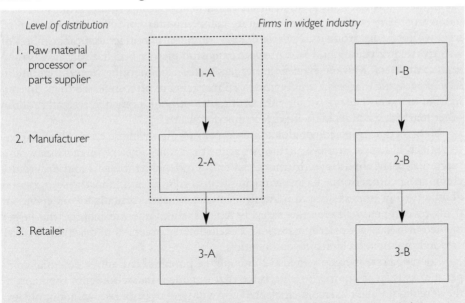

Vertical mergers occur between firms in the same chain of distribution, in the same industry—here the widget industry. Vertical mergers may erect harmful barriers to entry, further industry concentration, and remove the beneficial discipline that comes from active competition at all levels of production.

Vertical merger analysis is similar to horizontal merger analysis. First, the relevant geographic and product markets are determined. Second, the probable effect of the merger on the foreclosure of competition because of the acquisition of excessive market share is analyzed. Third, the courts analyze historical trends toward concentration, the nature and purpose of the merger, and resulting barriers to entry. Because vertical mergers do not immediately result in more concentrated markets, however, this analysis is more difficult.

The potential foreclosure of competition and the resulting barriers to entry by new firms are important factors. A merger is objectionable if potential competitors must thereafter integrate vertically to compete effectively against the merged firm. Challenge of vertical mergers is controversial if the vertical integration makes the industry more efficient, but vertical mergers are challenged when collusion is likely in a highly concentrated **upstream market**—concentration at the supplier level. For example, if suppliers own their retail outlets, then the prices of competing suppliers are apparent when they try to sell to the merged firm's retail outlets. This knowledge can facilitate price-fixing among all suppliers. However, if there are independent and disruptive buyers, then suppliers may be forced to compete for their business.

CONGLOMERATE MERGER ANALYSIS

Conglomerate mergers are all other mergers not classified as horizontal or vertical (Exhibit 12.3). They typically involve acquisition of a firm in another industry or selling other product lines and at any level of production. **Product extension** conglomerate mergers allow a firm to acquire complementary product lines that can be used with existing products. For example, a computer manufacturer's acquisition of a software producer would be a product extension merger because software is used with computers. **Market extension** mergers enable the merging firm to operate in new geographic markets. Totally unrelated mergers are often referred to as **diversification mergers**. They may allow the firm to smooth out its cash flows and profit in other markets when its main market is in a downturn.

Mergers that result in conglomerates appear to involve little or no anticompetitive effect. However, some structuralists argue that conglomerate mergers may reinforce oligopoly conditions, further weakening independent firms and eventually eliminating competition. Large acquiring firms often have financial resources and goodwill from popular brand names that make it more difficult for independent firms to compete or enter the market. After a conglomerate merger, the larger merged firm may use discriminatory and exclusionary practices to discipline smaller competitors, thereby lessening competition.

Conglomerate mergers can also eliminate the **potential entrant** or potential competitor. As long as competitors perceive that outsiders may come into the market, they are disciplined to remain efficient. They will tend to price below monopoly levels, which discourages new entrants. Potential entrants waiting in the wings create an **edge effect** that pressures existing competitors to remain competitive. However, the edge effect is eliminated when a potential entrant simply merges with an existing firm. If, instead of merging, that firm had entered the market **de novo** on its own, competition would increase.

Exhibit 12.3 Conglomerate Mergers

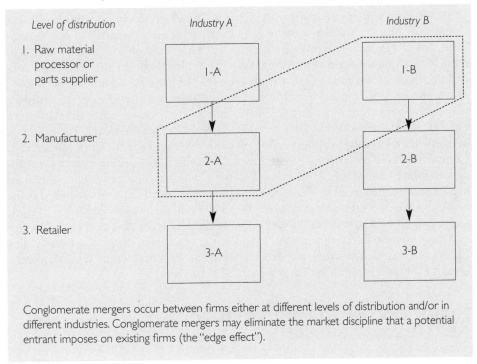

Conglomerate mergers occur between firms either at different levels of distribution and/or in different industries. Conglomerate mergers may eliminate the market discipline that a potential entrant imposes on existing firms (the "edge effect").

Challenging a conglomerate merger is difficult. First, there must be proof that existing competitors perceived and were influenced by the potential entrant. Second, the acquiring firm must have had reasonable means to enter the given market without merging. Third, the number of potential entrants cannot be excessive; otherwise, the elimination of only one would not have any significant impact on competitive discipline. It can be argued that a conglomerate merger between an outsider and the largest or leading seller in a concentrated industry is anticompetitive. The outsider should instead acquire a smaller firm in a **toehold acquisition**, which could preserve competition.

MERGER DEFENSES

A legal challenge to merging firms may be turned away with a **merger defense.** For example, merging firms commonly claim greater efficiency. Another merger justification is the **failing firm defense.** The defendant may argue that one of the merger partners would soon be insolvent, making the merger necessary for the failing firm's survival. For this defense to apply, the failing firm must be unable to reorganize successfully under Chapter 11 of the bankruptcy laws. In addition, the failing firm must have made unsuccessful good faith efforts to find other merger partners that might reduce market concentration. Another defense recognizes that purchases of another corporation's stock solely for investment does not substantially lessen competition.

MERGER ENFORCEMENT PROCEDURES

DOJ antitrust enforcement priorities change when presidential administrations change. Because the attorney general is a cabinet-level officer appointed by the president, the DOJ is likely to pursue the president's antitrust philosophy. By contrast, the FTC is a quasi-independent federal agency not directly under the president's control. Its enforcement may reflect the philosophies of the FTC commissioners, some of whom were appointed during the previous president's term. The courts' attitudes may reflect a third set of priorities. Most mergers are reviewed after submission to the FTC, DOJ, or another agency that closely regulates that industry. For example, mergers in telecommunications are overseen by the Federal Communications Commission (FCC). Premerger negotiations are subject to scrutiny by federal agencies and the press, which affect merger activity by indicating approval or threatening a court challenge. Hart-Scott-Rodino premerger notification is required if the acquiring firm has sales or assets exceeding $100 million and the target has sales or assets exceeding $10 million. Notice is required at least 30 days before the merger and must contain basic information to aid in the evaluation of the acquisition. The EU is becoming stricter when mergers anywhere in the world would lessen competition in EU markets requiring EU review of U.S. mergers.

HORIZONTAL COMBINATIONS, RESTRAINTS OF TRADE

Horizontal restraints of trade can arise when competitors collaborate (see Exhibit 12.4). They are the least justifiable restraints. Adam Smith, the famous laissez-faire economist, strongly urged government to actively ensure competition to counteract the natural tendency of competitors to collude:

> *People in the same trade seldom meet together, even for merriment and diversion, but [that] the conversation ends in a conspiracy against the public, or in some contrivance to raise prices.*

Early Supreme Court interpretations of the Sherman Act were so broad that "every contract, combination . . . or conspiracy in restraint of trade" was condemned. Later cases modified this approach by recognizing that some restraints are reasonable. Two legal tests for restraints developed eventually. The **rule of reason** that emerged from nineteenth-century contract law outlawed only unreasonable restraints. However, the **per se rule** requires a strict interpretation of the Sherman Act's "plain meaning" and leaves little wiggle room for any defense or justification.

RULE OF REASON

Section 1 of the Sherman Act literally prohibits "every contract, combination . . . or conspiracy in restraint of trade." However, if this provision was strictly applied, every contract would be illegal because contracts always restrain trade in some small way. For example, goods or services purchased by one person become unavailable

Exhibit 12.4 Horizontal Restraints of Trade

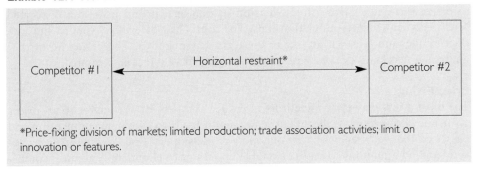

*Price-fixing; division of markets; limited production; trade association activities; limit on innovation or features.

to others, and so the buyer does not purchase them from a competitor. Trade is restrained even more by outputs or requirements contracts, by exclusive dealing or supply contracts, and by covenants not to compete. Yet these restraints can be justified in certain circumstances. The Sherman Act is intended to encourage free markets and should not prohibit reasonable restraints of trade.

The rule of reason permits courts to be more flexible by using a less stringent market share analysis than was used in monopolization or merger cases. The rule of reason developed to prohibit contracts that will reduce competition if they are intended to *unreasonably* restrict competition, if the parties have the power to implement their scheme, and/or if they have a less restrictive alternative to the scheme. In 1918, Justice Brandeis announced the rule of reason analysis in *Chicago Board of Trade v. United States*:[12]

The true test of legality is whether the restraint imposed is such as merely regulates and perhaps thereby promotes competition or whether it is such as may suppress or may even destroy competition. To determine that question, the court must ordinarily consider the facts peculiar to the business to which the restraint is applied; its condition before and after the restraint was imposed; the nature of the restraint and its effect, actual or probable. The history of the restraint, the evil believed to exist, the reason for adopting the particular remedy, the purpose or end sought to be obtained, are all relevant facts.

PER SE VIOLATIONS

Courts have encountered many types of agreements that are almost always unjustifiable. The rule of reason is an inefficient use of judicial and regulatory resources. Some business agreements, such as price-fixing, are designated illegal per se, and so they are never justified. Therefore, the inquiry ends if a per se violation is proven. Trials are shortened and simplified by avoiding unnecessary attempts to justify the

---

12. 246 U.S. 231 (1918).

restraint. The per se rule also provides business managers with clearer guidance. Per se offenses include price-fixing, division of markets, group boycotts, concerted refusals to deal, and tie-in relationships. The courts first determine whether the conduct in question falls within one of these per se categories. Thereafter, no further analysis is necessary because unlawful anticompetitive effect is presumed.

Price-Fixing

The most direct way for competitors to reduce competition is to agree to set prices artificially. **Price-fixing** is illegal per se because it tends to eliminate competition and passes on the inefficiencies of the oligopoly to consumers. Price-fixing is never justified by good intentions to set "reasonable" prices or to eliminate "ruinous" competition. But what constitutes illegal price-fixing? Agreements to fix minimum prices are illegal. For example, at one time state and local bar associations had minimum fee schedules requiring lawyers to charge a minimum price for particular services such as writing a will or drafting a contract. These fee schedules are illegal per se as price-fixing. It is also illegal to set maximum resale prices, even though fixing "low" prices might not seem harmful. Low prices tend to stabilize prices; they drive out competitors and reduce nonprice competition for optional features, improvements, or additional services.

Credit terms are often inseparable from price, so fixing these terms is also illegal per se. In one case, an agreement among beer distributors to eliminate trade credit to retailers was found to be illegal price-fixing as an equivalent to eliminating discounts. Several plywood producers allegedly agreed to charge a uniform freight rate regardless of the source of supply or the destination. This illegal scheme is known as **phantom freight** because it equalized freight charges without considering the actual distance or transportation charges. Phantom freight eliminates competition based on the purchaser's closeness to the source of supply and may also be a form of price discrimination. An agreement among oil companies to buy excess spot market supplies of crude oil was considered a disguised form of price-fixing.[13]

Some restraints of trade involving incidental price-fixing are judged under the rule of reason. Cooperation is sometimes necessary to advance the market. For example, it is impractical for music copyright owners to separately negotiate licensing fees for every performance of their works on television or radio or in public. The rule of reason applied to the blanket fee arrangement with Broadcast Music, Inc. (BMI) or the American Society of Composers, Authors and Publishers (ASCAP). These performing rights organizations (Chapter 13) provide clearinghouse services essential to effective licensing because they actually encourage the licensing and enforcement of music copyrights.[14]

The rule of reason has been used to judge a price-fixing scheme illegal. The National Collegiate Athletic Association (NCAA) negotiated television contracts for all college football games between 1982 and 1985. However, television fees paid to schools were based neither on the size of the viewing audience nor on the popularity of the teams.

---

13. *U.S. v. Socony-Vacume Oil Co., Inc.*, 310 U.S. 150 (1950).
14. *Broadcast Music Inc. v. CBS*, 441 U.S. 1 (1979).

The NCAA contracts with ABC and CBS limited the number of televised games and precluded price negotiation between the networks and the schools. The NCAA scheme was invalid price-fixing under rule of reason analysis because both price and output were restrained, thereby effectively raising television fees above competitive levels with a system unresponsive to viewer demand. The per se rule was inapplicable because some horizontal restraint in athletics is needed to make the product available.[15]

Trade Association Activities

The prohibition against collusion and price-fixing is very strong. Competitors must be careful about their collective activities. For example, competitors' exchange of price information generally makes price-fixing easier. An unreasonable restraint may arise if a trade association acts as a clearinghouse for competitors to exchange price information. Critics of this approach charge that to remain competitive in world markets, competitors should be permitted to "network" by joining together for legitimate purposes that promote their collective success and improve product quality. For example, trade associations regularly engage in activities protected by the First Amendment: political lobbying, public affairs, and distributing information about suppliers and new technologies.

Despite the good intentions of trade associations, some have disguised their price-fixing when distributing price information. In the 1920s, for example, 365 hardwood manufacturers exchanged details of individual sales, production, inventories, and current price lists through their trade association. An expert analyst constantly warned members against overproduction. The plan was found illegal after hardwood prices increased sharply. The paper box industry voluntarily exchanged price quotes that identified transactions with particular customers, so the plan was held illegal because it tended to stabilize prices. By contrast, the maple flooring trade association circulated average costs, freight rates, and past transaction information without identifying individual buyers or sellers. This exchange was not illegal because future prices were never discussed. The exchange of information through trade associations is not illegal if it is not intended to lessen competition. For example, a cement manufacturers' association distributed a list of construction contractors that abused the free delivery of cement, a measure that was justifiable to prevent fraud on the cement manufacturers.

Bidding rings are illegal per se as a form of price-fixing. They have arisen among construction contractors and in some auction markets. For example, contractors could preselect a different winner for each of several successive construction projects. The designated "losers" agree to bid high, and the selected winner rigs its bid to appear as the "lowest." The selected winner's price is typically higher than it would have been under genuine competitive bidding. It was once a common practice in Japan for construction contractors to consult each other before bidding on public works projects, a form of bid-rigging.

Industry self-regulation by trade groups is gaining favor as an alternative to government regulation and costly litigation. Care must be taken to prevent "industry

---

15. *NCAA v. Board of Regents of the University of Oklahoma*, 468 U.S. 85 (1984).

codes of conduct" from becoming disguised methods for collusion or price-fixing. Recall the examples of the National Society of Professional Engineers' prohibition against competitive bidding and the bar associations' minimum fee schedules. The quality control arguments for these trade association activities was weak when compared with their anticompetitive impact. Excessive discipline of a highly competitive member suggests that other members are really suppressing competition—an ironic misuse of a professional association's powers, particularly when rationalized as ethical rules.

Some trade associations limit their membership, which may be procompetitive if membership reflects integrity, quality, or reliability. Trade guilds and the apprenticeship system were once justified on this basis. However, excluding members from practice becomes anticompetitive when it limits the number of competitors or limits access to some valuable facility operated by the trade association. Consider that local real estate associations enhance their members' sales of listed properties by operating multiple listing services. Denying membership or limiting nonmember access to these print or web-based catalogs of real estate offerings reduces competition in commission rates.

B2B–Antitrust Guidelines for Collaborations among Competitors
http://www.ftc.gov/ os/2000/04/ ftcdojguidelines.pdf

Electronic business-to-business (B2B) exchanges (Chapter 8) pose some similar antitrust problems. These on-line auction markets might be tempted to use collusive practices, unfair discipline or outright exclusions of competitive members, and standards-setting activities that risk antitrust enforcement. For example, it could be anticompetitive if some potential members were excluded, a division of markets resulted, the auction operated as a group boycott of particular members, the market's information-reporting system facilitated price signaling or price fixing, or the auction was an attempt to monopolize or a conspiracy to monopolize.

Division of Markets

Competitors may attempt to divide markets so that only certain producers serve particular regions or specified customers. A **division of markets** is illegal per se because it gives the producer an effective monopoly in an assigned market segment. Even if there are other competitors selling in the affected region, the preferred firm has some market power. In one case, a group of independent local grocers formed a group buying chain. Their joint exercise of buying power was illegal because many members were forced to locate their stores in designated territories. This division of markets was not justified by the grocers' intent to compete more effectively against larger chain stores.

Group Boycotts

Individuals are usually free to deal with whomever they please. But when a group of competitors agree to boycott certain individuals or groups, it may be illegal. **Group boycotts** are generally illegal per se, but some courts use the rule of reason. It may be illegal for competing sellers to agree not to sell to a particular customer, reseller, or class of persons. A group of buyers with market power (monopsony or oligopsony) may also be guilty of an illegal boycott if certain sellers are shunned. In one case, an apparel manufacturers' trade association urged its members to boycott any retailers selling pirated designs (e.g., fake designer jeans). In another case, a National Football League rule required a team to compensate the former team of a free agent if the player changed teams. Both actions were illegal concerted refusals to deal. At one time, the American Medical Association had rules of ethics that prohibited doctors from participating in prepaid medical plans or from receiving a salary for practicing medicine. Those rules were illegal because they tended to destroy competition among professional groups. How might such rules affect evolving health care systems like HMOs?

JOINT VENTURES

A **joint venture** is a form of partnership in which two entities (i.e., persons, partnerships, corporations) enter into a limited business activity together. Joint ventures are subject to rule of reason analysis because they are sometimes justifiable, such as when economic efficiency is the purpose and effect. The test is whether the restraint is really necessary to achieve the lawful purpose. The courts balance the joint venture's potential anticompetitive effects against its alleged efficiency. For example, the Associated Press is a cooperative wire service with thousands of members. Access to this service is often critical to effective competition. At one time, the bylaws of the Associated Press contained a veto clause permitting any member to blackball a competitor seeking membership. This arrangement was held illegal under rule of reason because competitors' exclusion from the joint venture posed a substantial barrier to entry for new firms in the newspaper business. A joint ownership of theaters by moviemaking companies was also held illegal because new releases were not freely available to nonmember theaters, substantially lessening competition.

PROOF OF AN ILLEGAL AGREEMENT OR COMBINATION

Participants in an unlawful collusion or restraint of trade are usually very careful to avoid leaving any clear trail of evidence. Their agreements are hidden and off the record, and clandestine tactics such as secret meetings or secret codes might be used. Because the Sherman Act's criminal provisions require proof beyond a reasonable doubt, it is difficult to prove such hidden guilt with direct evidence. Therefore, illegal concerted activity is usually inferred from circumstantial evidence. Many types of business and supply chain contracts are restricted from disclosure to the press or competitors by nondisclosure agreements (NDAs).

Some firms in monopolistic or oligopolistic industries mimic the pricing decisions of an industry leader. This is **conscious parallelism** so there is no overt agreement. In 1939, the Supreme Court stated: "[i]t is enough that, knowing that concerted action was contemplated and invited, the distributors [of feature films] gave their adherence to the scheme and participated in it." This is the *Interstate* formula, which permits proof of an illegal collusive agreement if there is conscious parallelism.[16] The

16. *Interstate Circuit, Inc. v. United States*, 306 U.S. 208 (1939).

more modern formulation of conscious parallelism is more limiting. It recognizes that legal conduct may incorrectly appear to be conscious parallelism. Businesses must often respond quickly to changes in market conditions or to new contract terms offered by their competitors. For example, changes in the price of crude oil often quickly lead to similar changes in the gasoline pump prices charged by independent gasoline retailers. "[T]he crucial question is whether the respondents' conduct . . . stems from an independent decision or from an agreement, tacit or expressed. But, this court has never held that proof of parallel business behavior conclusively establishes agreement."[17]

Section 8 of the Clayton Act outlaws certain **interlocking directorates**—that is, the same person sitting on the board of two competitors. It prohibits any person from "at the same time be[ing] a director in two or more corporations . . . if such corporations are or shall have been theretofore, by virtue of their business and location of operation, competitors, so that the elimination of competition by an agreement between them would constitute a violation of any of the provisions of any of the antitrust laws." A common director between competitors could provide a convenient conduit for collusive communication. Although FTC enforcement is lax, the DOJ is more aggressive, extending the prohibition to firms engaged in "related businesses." For example, it could be unlawful for a single individual to sit on the boards of a computer mainframe manufacturer and a manufacturer of mainframe software.

The interlocking directorate prohibition has exceptions. Interlocking directorates may exist between firms that are in a vertical relationship or in different industries. Suppliers and customers commonly solidify their relationship with common directors. Indirect interlocks are also permissible. For example, a bank employee may legally sit on the boards of two competing industrial firms. A nondirector employee of one firm may sit on the board of a competing firm. These interlocks are actively used in Japanese Keiretsu ("feudal families of firms"). Given the post-Enron trend toward increased director liability, attracting competent, experienced directors can be challenging. Vigorous enforcement of §8 could impair the overall quality of corporate management and directorships. It may also be inconsistent with the closer contacts firms may need to assure total quality and technological compatibility from suppliers and to customers.

VERTICAL RESTRAINTS OF TRADE

Vertical restraints of trade are significantly different from horizontal restraints. Vertical relationships are intended to restrict certain activities along the supply chain between manufacturers, wholesalers, and retailers, despite the impact on consumers. Vertical restraints usually include resale price maintenance, restrictions on territorial or customer access, or restrictions on the freedom to sell competing brands. Vertical restraints may also require the purchase of less desirable goods in order to receive desirable ones. Exhibit 12.5 illustrates vertical restraints.

---

17. *Theatre Enterprises v. Paramount Film Distributor Corp.*, 346 U.S. 537 (1954).

Exhibit 12.5 Vertical Restraints of Trade

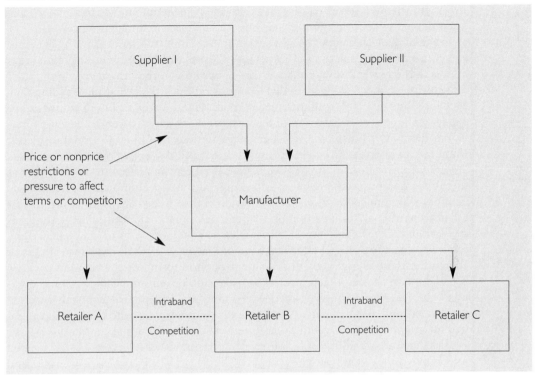

VERTICAL PRICE RESTRAINT: RESALE PRICE MAINTENANCE

The most direct vertical restraint is a manufacturer's **vertical price-fixing**. It requires the retailer to charge consumers a specified retail price, usually a minimum price. However, even a maximum price is considered **resale price maintenance**. Today, the courts apply the rule of reason, and resale price maintenance is no longer a per se violation. Pressures for resale price maintenance sometimes come from retailers. They may secretly request the manufacturer to set minimum prices as a hidden method to achieve horizontal price-fixing. A specified maximum retail price often becomes an unspoken minimum price, and all retailers sell only at that price.

Political pressure from small retailers urged Congress to abandon per se illegality of resale price maintenance. In 1937, the **Miller-Tydings Act** permitted state statutes to legitimize resale price maintenance if required by a manufacturer's supply contract with retailers. After the Great Depression, chain stores proliferated, forcing many small and inefficient retailers and wholesalers out of business. Small businesses insisted that products should be sold at higher and "fairer" prices that allow them a fair rate of return. By the early 1950s, 45 state statutes permitted resale price maintenance agreements. At one point, more than 1,500 manufacturers enforced the fair-trade laws through agreements with retailers that required them to charge at least the "manufacturer's list price." Congress further reinforced these agreements in 1952 with the **McGuire Act**, extending resale price maintenance to retailers that never agreed under **nonsigner provisions**. Resale price maintenance prevented discounting of many consumer goods, such as name-brand clothes, furniture, cameras, and consumer electronics in the 1950s to 1970s. By the 1960s, however, mail order houses in the few states without fair-trade laws eroded the increasingly unpopular resale price maintenance. Eventually, Congress repealed both the Miller-Tydings and McGuire Acts in 1975, again permitting more widespread intrabrand competition.

The failure of resale price maintenance caused manufacturers to develop alternative methods to discipline retailers who refused to observe minimum prices. Manufacturers often initiated a **refusal to deal** with disruptive retailers. In *United States v. Colgate*,[18] the Supreme Court permitted certain refusals to deal as long as there was no contract agreement requiring sales at specific prices. The Colgate Company announced publicly that it would refuse to deal with distributors that failed to participate in its announced resale price maintenance policy. Later cases severely limit *Colgate* but have not overruled it. Today, resale price maintenance and refusals to deal are judged under the rule of reason. A refusal to deal is illegal and coercive if there is any active harassment or monitoring of the retailer's pricing behaviors or if the manufacturer uses a suspension or reinstatement system to discipline retailers. For example, Parke Davis distributed its pharmaceuticals through wholesalers and drug retailers.[19] Its wholesale catalogue announced a refusal to deal with discounters, and its retail prices often included a 50% markup. Parke Davis's wholesalers ceased filling orders for several retailers who advertised discounted prices on Myadek vitamins. The Supreme Court held that Parke Davis went beyond mere announcement of a refusal to deal by implementing an illegal resale price maintenance combination and conspiracy.

VERTICAL NONPRICE RESTRAINTS

Manufacturers, unable to rely on vertical price restraints, often try to impose nonprice restraints to more directly control the free-riding behaviors of retailers. One method prevents retailers from selling to discounters for resale. Another imposes territorial limitations that prohibit retailers from engaging in intrabrand competition. Both devices are vertical nonprice restraints. Although nonprice restraints may have legitimate purposes, they can be used to enforce illegal resale price maintenance.

Exclusive Dealing

The term **exclusive dealership** indicates some sort of restriction in the resale arrangement. **Exclusive** often refers to fashionable or privileged status. However, in antitrust law it has two different meanings. First, the sole right to sell a manufacturer's products within a given region is known as an **exclusive distributorship**. No other dealer in the same region may sell the manufacturer's products. An exclusive distributor

---

18. 250 U.S. 300 (1919).
19. *U.S. v. Parke Davis & Co.*, 362 U.S. 29 (1960).

might also sell competitors' products. Manufacturers generally have wide freedom to pick their retailers or wholesalers, but an exclusive distributorship may not be justified if there are few substitutes for a manufacturer's products. Exclusive distributorships are judged by the rule of reason, though some recent cases hold that abuses within them are illegal per se. For example, it is illegal for one distributor to pressure the manufacturer to terminate sales to the only competing distributor.

The second use of the term *exclusive* relates to **exclusive dealing**—requiring the buyer to resell only the products of a single manufacturer. Exclusive dealing is illegal under §3 of the Clayton Act if it tends to create a monopoly or substantially lessens competition: "shall be unlawful for any person engaged in commerce to lease or make a sale . . . of . . . commodities . . . on the condition, agreement or understanding that the lessee or purchaser thereof shall not use or deal in . . . commodities of a competitor . . . of the lessor or seller, where the effect of such . . . [agreement] may substantially lessen competition or tend to create a monopoly in any line of commerce."

Manufacturers and suppliers cannot generally insist that a retailer refuse to carry a competitor's products. Exclusive dealing contracts are judged by the **quantitative substantiality** test, which presumes exclusive dealing adversely affects competition when it covers a substantial dollar volume. Thus, a violation of §3 of the Clayton Act may occur with a far lower percentage of market control than would be considered a monopoly or merger violation. Recent cases focus more on unit market share rather than dollar volume.

A subtler way to enforce an exclusive dealing arrangement is to rely on the protection of the *Colgate* doctrine by simply refusing to sell to nonexclusive dealers. Manufacturers seeking this protection have replaced exclusive dealing language in their supply contracts with **adequate representation clauses**, which require retailers to make substantial efforts to market the manufacturer's products. Manufacturers can terminate dealers that do not provide advertising, inventory maintenance, service expertise, or sales effort that is specified in their supply contract.

Customer and Territorial Restrictions

Manufacturers' efforts to restrict retailers from selling to particular customers or in specific territories are probably illegal. Arrangements that restrict retailers' sales to a geographic region or that require retailers to sell only to a particular list of customers deny retailers the right to sell to others, so they are illegal. At first, such arrangements were considered illegal per se under the *Schwinn* rule.[20] In 1977, however, this rule was replaced with the rule of reason, now applicable to nearly all vertical nonprice restrictions. The EU has banned territorial restraints in an effort to lower the barriers imposed by its member nations' national borders. Some vertical nonprice restrictions are valid because they enhance interbrand competition. There are two important questions in the analysis of vertical territorial or customer restrictions: (1) Does the restriction tend to limit competition? (2) Are there legitimate economic and business objectives for the restriction?

---

20. *United States v. Arnold Schwinn & Co.*, 388 U.S. 365 (1967).

Vertical nonprice restrictions may be illegal if there is little interbrand competition, if the manufacturer has considerable market power, or if high barriers to entry exist for new producers. GTE Sylvania limited the number of retail franchises within specified geographic territories to strengthen its retail network.[21] Franchised retailers could sell GTE Sylvania products only at locations specified in their supply contracts. Continental was one of Sylvania's most successful retailers in San Francisco. It complained when Sylvania granted a franchise to another local retailer. Sylvania had refused to give Continental a franchise in Sacramento after Continental canceled a large Sylvania order. The U.S. Supreme Court overruled the *Schwinn* per se rule and justified Sylvania's actions by referring to the free rider controversy.

Dealer Terminations

Manufacturers have the freedom to select new dealers or terminate existing dealers for reasons such as performance, breach of contract on key provisions in the distributorship agreement (e.g., adequate representation), and deviation from announced pricing or from the manufacturer's marketing strategy. However, the power to terminate the dealers is not unlimited. Both federal and state laws protect against some types of arbitrary franchise termination, as noted in Chapter 13. Some state laws require manufacturers to exercise "good faith" or limit terminations to "just cause." Many foreign nations provide similar protection for local dealers of foreign-made goods. Dealer terminations are permitted if no concerted action is taken to maintain resale prices. *Monsanto Co. v. Spray-Rite Service Corp.*[22] subjects vertical nonprice restrictions to the rule of reason.

TYING

The Clayton Act generally prohibits tying arrangements. **Tying,** or a tie-in agreement, requires customers to purchase certain commodities or goods. Typically, the seller refuses to sell a desirable **tying product** unless the customer agrees to purchase a less desirable **tied product**. The tie-in relationship coerces buyers to purchase the less desirable product if they want to obtain the more desirable product. This practice ties their main purchases to other purchases of supplementary goods. A tie-in is effective only when the seller has some market power in the desirable or tying product, perhaps resulting from a patent, a secret process, or a uniquely superior product. The Clayton Act prohibits tying only of goods, not services or land sales. However, tying could be illegal under the Sherman Act for markets in real estate, intangibles, and services. Tying is often called a per se violation, but the cases show courts often do thorough rule of reason analysis in tying cases. Recall that the *Microsoft* case discussed the tying offense.

Tying usually arises in one of three types of relationships. First, the tied and tying products are used together in fixed proportions (e.g., nuts and bolts, tires on automobiles). Second, the tied product may be necessary for use with the tying product

---

21. *Continental T.V., Inc. v. GTE Sylvania, Inc.*, 433 U.S. 36 (1977).
22. 465 U.S. 752 (1984).

(e.g., computer cards or peripherals with a computer). Third, the products may be only loosely usable together and may even be used separately (e.g., seed and fertilizer). Three elements must be established before tying is illegal. First, there is an analysis of the relevant market for the tying product and the relevant market for the tied product. It requires evidence of the seller's sale of one product conditioned on the purchase of another. Second, the seller must have sufficient economic or market power to force the tie-in, which may be shown where buyers clearly prefer the seller's tying product. If several buyers agree to a coercive tie-in, the seller may be presumed to have market power. Third, the level of competition restricted in the less desirable tied product must be more than insubstantial. There must be proof of a substantial amount of commerce in the tied product. For example, $500,000 of the salt market and $60,000 of the film market were considered substantial, regardless of the market shares involved.

Justifications for Tying

Tying relationships force buyers to purchase tied products in larger quantities than they would without the tie-in. Otherwise, purchasers could probably obtain the tied product or a substitute more cheaply from other sellers. Tying reduces the buyer's freedom to use the least-cost vendor and permits the tying seller to charge near-monopoly prices for the tied product. Tying unjustifiably expands the seller's near-monopoly in the tying product to the tied product's market and raises entry barriers for potential competitors.

It can be difficult to determine whether there really are two products rather than just one product. For example, both a picture tube and the accompanying television set or an automobile and its built-in radio can be viewed as either separate or single products. The real question here is whether there is a substantial market for the installation of the tied product into the tying product. There is only a replacement and repair market for television picture tubes, but a healthy and competitive installation aftermarket exists for car radios and stereos. Ford has repeatedly tried to tie higher-priced and/or lower-quality car stereos (tied product) to their automobiles (tying product) by making its electrical system technically incompatible with aftermarket stereos. Some automakers permit buyers to delete standard-equipment radios for a credit.

Financing can be seen as an integral part of a product. U.S. Steel (later U.S.X.) insisted on selling high-priced prefabricated homes by providing low-cost loans. Homes and loans are obviously not a single product. Consumers might be willing to pay higher prices for the less desirable prefabricated homes (the tied product) if they receive desirable low-cost loans (the tying product).[23] Today, many automobile and appliance manufacturers use their captive finance companies (e.g., GMAC, FOMOCO Credit, GE Credit) to provide low-cost financing without violating the tying prohibition.

Tying relationships can be justified if they result in economic efficiency. During start-up, new businesses may need to assure the proper functioning of their complex

---

23. *U.S. Steel Corp. v. Fortner Enterprises, Inc.*, 429 U.S. 610 (1977).

products. Once a business has become established, the tying relationship may be no longer justified. For example, a TV antenna manufacturer required the purchase of service contracts with the purchase of its equipment. This tie-in was justified only until the business had become well established. Tying relationships are also justified if the quality of the tied product is higher than that of competitors' similar products. The seller may claim that without the tie-in the goodwill it derives from the tying product will suffer. This argument is not always successful. At one time, IBM required that only the IBM brand of punch cards could be used with its tabulating machines. Although other vendors sold similar punch cards, IBM argued that only the IBM cards could prevent fouling of the machines.[24] Similarly, the Bell System once required its customers to use only Western Electric–brand telephones and switching equipment. In both instances, the alleged low quality of competitors' products was solved by other reasonable means, such as measurable design and performance specifications. Specifications for the thickness and resilience of tabulating cards are sufficient to prevent damage to IBM's machines. Specifications for the electrical characteristics of telephone equipment can be sufficient to prevent damage to the Bell System's equipment. The quality-control argument is weak if the company is well established and specifications can be drawn up to ensure compatibility.

The quality-control justification generally protects the product specifications required in franchise businesses. In *Principe v. McDonald's Corp.*,[25] a form of tying was justified under the quality-control requirements for federal trademark usage under the Lanham Act. McDonald's franchises must pay royalties for the franchise, rent their storefront from a McDonald's affiliate, purchase particular foodstuffs from specified suppliers (e.g., Coke products), and adhere to exacting production quality standards. Tying the storefront lease to the franchise license was found to be a single product rather than two products. Recall that tying Microsoft's browser Explorer to the Windows operating system was a major part of the monopolization case discussed earlier in this chapter. Tying is the major antitrust problem for owners of IP, as discussed next.

ANTITRUST AND INTELLECTUAL PROPERTY RIGHTS

Antitrust and IP use seemingly opposite approaches to achieve consumer welfare. Although both encourage innovation and competition, antitrust disfavors monopolies and market power. By contrast, IP grants monopoly-like property rights to incentivize R&D investment. These two legal regimes must coexist, requiring close scrutiny of IP rights when IP owners go beyond exploitation of their invention or expression to commit anticompetitive acts. The primary antitrust constraint on IP is a corollary of the equitable doctrine **unclean hands** that limits the IP owner's rights when there is an unreasonable extension of the IP right through **misuse**.

---

24. *International Business Machines v. U.S.*, 298 U.S. 131 (1936).
25. 631 F.2d 303 (4th Cir., 1980).

INTELLECTUAL PROPERTY MISUSE

Misuse most typically occurs through tying. A patent holder conditions the grant of patent rights (in a license of a patented process or sale of patented products) to the buyer's purchase of unpatented collateral products or services. Applying the tying analysis, the patent holder must have power in the market for the patented, tying product and then use this power to require the purchase of unpatented, tied products, which has an adverse impact on competition in the tied product's market. Misuse can also arise in other situations: (1) **package licensing** if both the tied and tying products are patented, (2) a customer is forbidden from purchasing other vendors' products that could substitute for the tying product, and (3) a patent or copyright is acquired by fraud. A 1988 statute makes it clear that patent holders may simply refuse to license or use their patent rights. Trademark misuse is unlikely because the imperative to preserve the goodwill of a trademark permits tying to maintain quality control. However, the trademark misuse theory is still possible.

ESSENTIAL FACILITIES DOCTRINE

Some firms control an **essential facility**: an asset indispensable for competition in the market. The moniker "bottleneck monopoly" aptly describes how competition was substantially lessened in *U.S. v. Terminal Railroad Ass'n*.[26] The famous robber baron Jay Gould controlled the railroad tunnels, bridges, terminals, and switching yards around St. Louis, Missouri. In the 1880s, rail transportation was predominant, and much transcontinental traffic was funneled through St. Louis. There were only a few key bridges over the Mississippi. Gould charged discriminatory surcharges (arbitraries) to pass through his St. Louis chokehold, which was deemed an essential facility. Antitrust law required Gould to open up membership in the cartel to outsiders, and the Interstate Commerce Commission provided regulatory oversight thereafter.

There are four factors used in essential facilities cases: (1) a monopolist controls the essential facility, (2) competitors are unable to duplicate the facility, (3) the competitor is denied use of the essential facility, and (4) a parallel facility is infeasible. Several facilities have been deemed essential under the doctrine, including newswire services, stock exchanges, wholesale produce markets, real estate multiple listing services, airline reservation systems, electricity distribution lines, petroleum pipelines, storage facilities, airport terminals, and shipping piers. Many essential facilities cases involve restrictions on competition in B2B markets that harm downstream customers. For example, MCI gained access to the essential facilities of AT&T's local consumer telephone connections and switching system to offer competition in long-distance telephone service.[27]

In some cases, there is no essential facility and therefore no antitrust violation, such as when meaningful competition is emerging. For example, the essential facility doctrine is being argued to allow various ISPs access to broadband, high-speed

---

26. 224 U.S. 383 (1912).
27. *MCI Comm. Corp. v. ATT*, 708 F.2d 1081 (7th Cir., 1982).

Internet lines. Consumer choice in picking some other ISP than the cable or landline phone provider has been limited to the owner of the essential facility. This situation may change as broadband becomes available through parallel cable TV lines, telephone DSL, wireless telephony, and satellite systems. There was no antitrust violation in the Washington Redskins' exclusive access to RFK Stadium that prevented an American Football League team from entering the Washington sports market.[28]

Standards

High-technology products often have characteristics of an essential facility, generally through their standardized operation. **Standards** are agreed-upon specifications for the production or operation of functionally compatible goods and services. Standards are the method by which network industries gain increasing economies of scale as more users adopt products complying with the standards, such as fax machines, telephones, music or video recording and playback devices (HDTV, MP3), computer operating systems, computer file formats (ASCII, HTML), Internet communications using packet technologies, and even rules for playing sports or the attachment of bottle caps. Government agencies, trade associations, and individual firms influence the standardization of products, services, or service providers to improve quality, safety, and interchangeability. It can clearly benefit consumers unless standardization becomes a hidden way to fix prices, thwart innovation, or exclude vigorous competitors. However, **closed standards** are a barrier to entry when they are owned or controlled by a monopolist or a cartel.

Antitrust law scrutinizes the development process and ownership of standards to avoid monopolization. **Proprietary standards** controlled by a single firm or consortium tend to develop more quickly, gaining wide acceptance as **de facto standards**. By contrast, consensus standards are adopted more slowly and may require a government mandate to achieve network effects. Antitrust risks may arise when, in the standards-setting context, the participants discuss prices, market allocations, discrimination in licensing, or exclusion of participants from the process and use of the standards. Standards can erect barriers to entry when proprietary IP underlies the standard. Antitrust may be violated when the standard is not made generally available or when participants in the standard setting prevent the emergence of new technologies based on revised standards.

Standards Setting
Organizations
http://www.ansi.org
http://www.ieee.org

LICENSING AND ANTITRUST

The FTC and DOJ have issued antitrust guidelines for the licensing of intellectual property. They recognize that IP is vulnerable to misappropriation and does not automatically confer market power and that licensing is frequently a procompetitive activity. The guidelines create an **antitrust safety zone** or safe harbor so that the agencies will not challenge a particular IP licensing activity if it satisfies two criteria:

---

28. *Hecht v. Pro-Football, Inc.*, 570 F.2d 982 (D.C.Cir., 1977).

1. The restraint is not facially anticompetitive.
2. The licensor and its licensees collectively account for no more than 20% of each relevant market significantly affected by the restraint.

FTC/DOJ Licensing Guidelines
http://www.usdoj.gov/ atr/public/guidelines/ ipguide.htm

Licenses often impose potentially anticompetitive restrictions of one or more of the following types: exclusivity, exclusive dealing, resale price maintenance, cross-licensing, patent pooling, or extending royalties beyond the patent's term.

PRICE DISCRIMINATION

Price discrimination is a seller's practice of charging different prices to different buyers for goods of like grade and quality. It is illegal under the Robinson-Patman Act if it substantially lessens competition or tends to create a monopoly. The FTC has enforcement powers under Robinson-Patman, and a private right of action exists for competitors or buyers damaged by price discrimination. Price discrimination would be impossible in a perfectly competitive market. Any buyer faced with a higher price than that offered to others would simply buy from another seller. However, few markets are perfectly competitive, and some buyers or sellers usually have some market power.

Robinson-Patman was passed to protect small businesses competing with big chain stores that had oligopsony (buyer's) market power. Critics claim that Robinson-Patman has outlived its economic usefulness. Price discrimination can occur when buyers have imperfect information or are ignorant of the prices paid by other buyers or when some buyers are given secret discounts.

PROOF OF PRICE DISCRIMINATION

To establish a violation of the Robinson-Patman Act, a plaintiff or the FTC must prove six elements: (1) discrimination in price, (2) between two different purchases, (3) affecting interstate commerce, (4) concerning sales of commodities of like grade and quality, (5) causing a substantial lessening of competition or a tendency to create a monopoly, and (6) injury to competitors of the seller or the buyer or to their customers.

The two discriminatory transactions must occur within a contemporaneous time frame; an excessive interval probably reflects changing market conditions. There must be two different sales prices as stated in the contracts of sale. Nonprice differences may also be discriminatory. For example, preferential credit terms given to one buyer but not others are prohibited. Quantity discounts theoretically open to all purchasers but in practice denied to small buyers are also discriminatory.

Robinson-Patman does not apply to intangibles, services, and certain mixed sales of goods and services. It is lawful to discriminate in the price charged for securities, mutual fund shares, patents, licenses, real estate leases, and consulting services. Airfares, rental car rates, and hotel rates are commonly discriminatory. Price discrimination in intangibles or services could conceivably violate the Sherman Act as a restraint of trade or an attempt to monopolize, or it could be an unfair method of competition under the FTC Act.

The goods sold must be of like grade and quality; that is, their physical and chemical composition must be similar. If buyers willingly substitute two seemingly different products as interchangeable, they may be of like grade and quality. Subtle differences in the brand names or labels of two similar products do not usually justify price discrimination if consumers perceive the two products as functionally similar.

COMPETITIVE INJURIES FROM PRICE DISCRIMINATION

Liability for price discrimination arises when any person discriminates or knowingly benefits from discrimination, thereby causing someone else to suffer lost profits or missed business opportunities. The level in the supply chain of the business suffering the injury must be identified. Injuries may occur at the seller's level, the buyer's level, or the level of the customers of the buyer. Price discriminations tending to injure those in competition with the discriminating seller are **primary-line injuries**. Price discriminations a seller makes are **secondary-line injuries** if between two reselling buyers that are competing for the same customers. If two buyers have different costs for the same goods, the buyer paying higher prices suffers because the buyer paying lower prices can pass the savings on to its customers. If Buyer A and Buyer B were in distinct geographic markets, no secondary-line injury would occur because their two sets of customers could not practically choose one seller over the other. A more controversial theory of price discrimination involves injury to the buyer's customers. Theoretically, injury may occur at any level in the supply chain, no matter where price discrimination occurs. A **tertiary-line injury** may occur if customers of the buyers are injured by price discrimination such as when the cost savings are passed on through wholesalers to retailers.

PRICE DISCRIMINATION DEFENSES

Price discrimination is sometimes justified by affirmative defenses. The seller may attempt to show that the competitive effect of differential pricing is trivial so there is no competitive injury. Export sales are exempted because the Robinson-Patman Act applies only to "commodities . . . sold for use, consumption, or resale within the United States." There are also three statutory defenses: changing conditions, cost differential, and meeting the competition in good faith.

The Robinson-Patman Act provides a defense when the market has changed so that prices previously charged are no longer realistic. The **changing conditions** defense provides that "nothing herein shall prevent price changes from time to time in response to changing conditions affecting the marketability of the goods concerned, such as (but not limited to) actual or imminent deterioration of perishable goods, obsolescence of seasonal goods, distress sales under court process, or sales in good faith in discontinuance of business." This defense is confined strictly to temporary situations in which the physical nature of the commodity requires a distress sale. A classic example is the lowering of retail automobile prices on the leftover inventory of the prior model year.

The second defense is differences in selling costs: The **cost differential** defense provides that "nothing herein contained shall prevent differentials which make only due allowance for differences in the cost of manufacture, sale, or delivery resulting from the differing methods or quantities in which such commodities are sold or delivered." In practice, this defense is difficult for sellers to rely on. One problem is that there is no universal definition of costs. Robinson-Patman was designed to prevent predatory pricing in which one producer subsidizes low-priced sales from profits earned elsewhere and later raises prices above competitive levels after competitors are driven from the market. Computation of average variable costs requires an allocation of indirect costs (e.g., overhead), a complex and controversial process. The amount of overhead allotted to each unit in addition to average variable costs varies under different assumptions. The cost differential defense is most often successful when discriminatory pricing is based on legitimate quantity discounts that are due to actual savings in packaging, handling, and transportation costs.

Robinson-Patman also permits a seller to discriminate in price if the lower price "was made in good faith to meet an equally low price of a competitor." The price discriminator must have a reasonable belief that granting the lower price is necessary to win the sale. The lower price must exactly meet, but not beat, the competitor's price. Antitrust has a problem of conflicting goals, evident in satisfying this defense. Communications with competitors concerning price strongly suggests price-fixing. Good faith is crucial to the competition defense because price discrimination and price-fixing enforcement must be harmonized. Sellers may show good faith if they investigate the truth of a buyer's claim that a competitor charges a lower price. For example, some retailers require buyers to bring the competitor's ad or a written estimate to prove the lower price. When the necessity of meeting the price has ceased and market conditions return to normal, the seller must cease discriminatory pricing. Sellers may discriminate only in meeting their own competition and may not discriminate to assist a customer in meeting its competition.

The Robinson-Patman Act applies to both buyers and sellers. It is unlawful for "any person . . . knowingly to induce or receive a discrimination in price." Thus, if the buyer has knowledge that the price it obtained was discriminatory, either the buyer or the seller may be held liable. A buyer inducing price discrimination may take advantage of any defense the seller has.

INDIRECT CONCESSIONS

The Robinson-Patman Act also prohibits price discriminations effected through indirect price concessions. It is unlawful for "any person to pay, grant, or receive any brokerage or allowance in lieu thereof except for services rendered in connection with the sale or purchase of goods." This provision prohibits kickbacks, which are effectively a secret discount. Robinson-Patman also prohibits the seller from discriminating by providing promotional payments, services, or facilities, such as giving only select customers some special assistance, allowance for advertising, or display materials. The disadvantaged buyer need prove only (1) that the promotional service or allowance was provided only to other purchasers or (2) that a competitor was favored in its "business stature." Such services are permissible if triggered at specified dollar volumes or are equally available to all buyers.

Price discrimination may also occur when shippers charge discriminatory freight rates. If the quoted sale prices for two sales are identical but either customer pays more or less than the actual cost of shipment, then there is an indirect price discrimination. There is no discrimination if the buyer pays legitimate freight and delivery charges. However, some informal "delivered price" quotes include freight charges. If all buyers pay the same freight charges, as part of a uniform delivered price, then buyers geographically closer to the seller's plant pay higher freight charges per mile than do buyers located farther away. Equal freight rates charged for unequal delivery distances may constitute phantom freight, an illegal price discrimination. Recall that it can also be a form of price-fixing. Phantom freight is classified as (1) a single basing point system if the freight is actually shipped from another place, (2) zone pricing if the same freight rates are imposed on all customers within a zone, regardless of the distance, or (3) a multiple basing point system if the nearest of several base points of origin governs the freight charge.

THE FUTURE REGULATION OF PRICE DISCRIMINATION

Robinson-Patman is often regarded as a widely violated law. Critics charge it perpetuates inefficient small retailers, reduces price competition, and raises consumer prices to uniform levels. However, many of the international fair-trade laws, particularly the antidumping rules, are essentially price discrimination regulations. Dumping is a foreign firm's practice of selling in another nation's market at prices lower than in that firm's home market. The same policy arguments are made in opposition to both practices: Dumping and price discrimination encourage cross-subsidies that drive out competitors, eventually leaving the discriminator with a monopoly.

Finally, as discussed further in Chapter 14, aggressive marketing strategies in the Internet age may seek to achieve **perfect price discrimination**. As Web site operators learn and purchase private information about their customers, they develop customer profiles or dossiers. Profiling permits a better understanding of customers' intensity of interest in products, services, and information and of customers' wealth. Target marketers can then raise prices for customers who value the products more highly and lower prices for those who do not. Although the impact of Robinson-Patman may continue to decline, pressures will intensify to practice price discrimination, and public policy may focus on these trends.

CHAPTER 13
PRIVACY

Privacy assumed major prominence during the twentieth century. Technological advances have made it progressively easier and cheaper to discover, record, and use **personally identifiable information (PII)**. Society is so crowded that few people can withdraw into isolation, either in our communities or in cyberspace. Humans are social and industrious animals with strong emotional and practical needs to interact. Yet privacy remains an aspiration for most, during at least part of our lives. Accommodating privacy requires an understanding of abstract privacy concepts. Society must then balance each individual's interest in confidentiality and seclusion with some legitimate use of private information for society's protection.

Privacy will probably remain a *balance* between individual interests in secrecy or solitude and society's interests in order and efficiency. Privacy questions arise in many aspects of law enforcement, as well as in business relations. Data about individuals' past conduct, their interests, and future plans are needed to exercise discipline, maintain order, assess risks, and predict future performance, such as in contracts of employment, loans, and insurance. Individuals' privacy rights are limited for public health, national security, and the public's right to know. Such data may also become useful to more precisely market products to the most interested users. The effective use of PII may finally permit marketing efficiencies long promised by economic theory.

It seems natural and rational for individuals to resist revealing their PII. Long experience justifies the fear that exposure of private information makes individuals vulnerable. History reveals that several aspects of privacy interests have been fundamental to civil liberty and essential to individual freedom, autonomy, dignity, and good taste. Privacy issues can be expected to engender strong emotional, even visceral, reactions that can translate into draconian regulatory reactions to suppress what the public perceives as privacy abuses.

This chapter discusses the development of privacy law, its application in traditional transactions, and its adaptation to cyberspace and e-commerce. First, the baseline of existing privacy law and society's expectations are discussed. Second, the concept of privacy is explored because it forms the basis for privacy regulation both in the traditional economy and in cyberspace. Third, the basic architecture of data collection and data management is reviewed to pinpoint the workings of privacy law and policy. Fourth, the economic incentives of private data collection are examined to explain the evolution of current privacy law and predict what new privacy laws will emerge. Finally, existing privacy law is examined from constitutional sources, statutes, and regulations. A comparison is made of privacy laws in key sectors: online, telecommunications, children, financial, workplace, and health care. Law affecting these key sectors is examined from various sources, including international, federal, state, and private self-regulation levels. Society will look to self-regulation and privacy law to resolve the challenges as technologies advance in the collection, archiving, analysis, and distribution of private information.

POLITICAL AND SOCIAL CONTEXT OF PRIVACY

With all the controversy emerging over privacy online and even in traditional contexts, the lack of comprehensive U.S. privacy protection and policies is not surprising. Privacy laws are narrowly drawn to particular industry sectors—the **sectoral approach**. Privacy law is generally enacted only after considerable experience with activities the public views as abusive. This approach is consistent with both laissez-faire economics and the common law approach to lawmaking. As a result:

> *U.S. Privacy Law Protection is a hodge-podge, patch-work of sectoral protections, narrowly construed and derived from constitutional, statutory and regulatory provisions of international, federal and state law.*

The U.S. sectoral approach to privacy is different from the European approach, discussed in a later section examining the European Union's (EU's) **omnibus** method. The essentially comprehensive and uniform EU approach to privacy covers most industries and governments with strong privacy rights. Privacy advocates urge the United States to follow this European approach, but many business and government interests oppose the EU's strong, omnibus privacy rights.

Most people in a free society realize that privacy is a fundamental right, a civil liberty interest essential to individual freedom, autonomy, and dignity. The current intensity of the public's interest in privacy probably arises because technological advances in data collection, storage, integration, and secondary use heighten people's concern about potential abuse of private information. Computerized telecommunications and the perceived value of private data result in the **commoditization of private information,** by transforming private information to a commodity easily shared, traded, sold, and presumably valued. In the words of Sun Microsystem's CEO Scott McNealy, "You have zero privacy anyway. Get over it!"

Private information is subject to **data creep**; that is, data collected for one purpose eventually finds its way to secondary and even tertiary uses. For example, Social Security numbers (**ssn**) were originally intended only for keeping records of payments made through the Federal Insurance Contributions Act (FICA) and retirement benefits paid out from the Social Security system. However, the ssn is now the primary individual information locator for both government and the private sector. Information collected for one limited purpose is inevitably used for other purposes, often without the knowledge or consent of the **subject individual**, the person described by the information. Often, the PII is used to the subject individual's disadvantage to deny a loan, insurance coverage, or a job.

Although the public may never know about *all* the methods and uses for their PII, there is a general unease developing about misuse. Many people are suspicious about requests for their PII when it seems irrelevant to transactions, and e-commerce and e-government may suffer without changes in substantive privacy rights. This impacts the public's perception of privacy practices by both governments and private firms. The American public's attitudes towards privacy are changing; most people are becoming savvier and more careful with their PII. According to Alan F. Westin, a privacy expert and director of the Center for Social and Legal Research, a privacy think tank, the public is segmented into three fairly distinct groups in their privacy attitudes and expectations.[1]

SEGMENTATION OF THE AMERICAN PUBLIC ON PRIVACY ISSUES

- **Privacy fundamentalists** value privacy highly, summarily reject business claims that PII needs are legitimate, advocate that individuals refuse to disclose PII, and seek strong regulation of privacy rights.
- **Privacy pragmatists** balance their personal privacy with societal needs for PII, examine privacy policies and practices, disclose PII when economically rational and appropriate, favor industry self-regulation of privacy (voluntary privacy standards and practices), and support privacy regulation only when self-regulation fails.
- **Privacy unconcerned** are typically indifferent about disclosing PII, trust in the benefits derived from disclosing PII, and are unlikely to support strong privacy rights or regulation.

Studies show that the number of privacy fundamentalists has remained steady throughout the 1990s at about 25% of the population. The number of privacy pragmatists has been growing, from 55% during the early 1990s to 63% by year 2000. The proportion of privacy unconcerned has fallen from 20% down to 12%. These

---

1. Alan F. Westin, Interpretive Essay, in *Public Records and the Responsible Use of Information* (Hackensack, N.J.: Choicepoint, 2000), p. 5.

data probably reflect the growing public awareness of data collection practices and the uses for their PII.

WHAT *IS* PRIVACY?

Privacy is an imprecise yet complex term. In its most general sense, **privacy** refers to several distinct interests, individual expectations, legal rights, and PII data practices. Some synonyms for *privacy* are helpful to gain perspective: seclusion, solitude, retreat from intrusion, intimacy, isolation, secrecy, concealment, and separateness. Consider the formal *Webster's* definition of privacy.

Privacy: withdrawn from company or public view, secrecy, one's private life or personal affairs.

Privacy probably has only one absolute meaning: maintaining secrecy over PII. However, in the business context, privacy has no absolute meaning. Instead, it is a relative term determined by the societal balance between disclosure and secrecy as set forth in public policy by privacy laws and actual practice.

The variety of privacy interests may be better understood through the lens of societal motives. Privacy was one of the American colonists' main hopes in their risky move to the New World. Many colonists sought to leave behind government oppression in their native lands. As detailed later, many U.S. Constitutional freedoms are actually forms of privacy: religious freedom, restrictions on search and seizure, prohibitions against the quartering of soldiers, freedom of speech, freedom of press and association, due process, and equal protection. Under this vision, privacy is a fundamental right necessary to achieve liberty, without interference from government or from powerful private interests. Privacy actually promotes competition, a point clearly made in Chapter 5. When individual or firm activities can be held secret, this private information is actually a form of property if the individual or firm exploits it for economic advantage. Privacy rights are critical to excluding the intrusion of others who might appropriate the property rights in private information. Privacy also seems essential to intimacy.

Privacy is a fundamental and enduring expectation of biblical origins. Consider the story of the Garden of Eden. When Adam and Eve ate of the forbidden fruit, they were condemned to suffer *shame* for their transgressions and feel *modesty* about their bodies. Shame throughout history demonstrates that imperfect human decision making and behavior are inevitable and that humans want to avoid embarrassment. When zones of privacy are plentiful, individuals risk less public contempt and retribution. Shame may be a sufficient consequence for many people to repent and voluntarily correct their own bad habits when motivated by the promise of redemption and the self-satisfaction of virtue. Similarly, modesty serves important societal purposes as another form of privacy. Shyness or prudent dress and appearance probably protect individuals from harmful intrusions by societal predators.

Acquiring, maintaining, and overcoming privacy are all costly pursuits. Privacy is argued to be a benefit earned, inherited, or acquired, either with specific effort or as the result of obscurity and public indifference. Consider the extensive efforts of the rich and famous to obtain seclusion. Many spend heavily on isolated residences, gated communities, private clubs, and security systems to keep the public out. Millionaire recluse Howard Hughes feared disease from physical exposure to common people, so he hid from the public and even from his old friends. However, privacy deteriorates as outsiders expend resources to breach the veil of privacy. Consider the **paparazzi,** freelance photographers who hound the famous for candid and revealing photographs. They overcame the privacy efforts of the late British Princess Diana when they concentrated their efforts to stalk, track and pursue her.

Maintaining privacy in cyberspace is similar. Technological advances in capturing, archiving, processing, and disseminating information can be frustrated with clever but often expensive counter-measures and with privacy regulations. Consider the famous words of Phyllis McGinley, a twentieth-century American poet and essayist:

Who could deny that privacy is a jewel? It has always been the mark of privilege, the distinguishing feature of a truly urbane culture. Out of the cave, the tribal tepee, the pueblo, the community fortress, man emerged to build himself a house of his own with a shelter in it for himself and his diversions. Every age has seen it so. The poor might have to huddle together in cities for need's sake, and the frontiersman cling to his neighbors for the sake of protection. But in each civilization, as it advanced, those who could afford it chose the luxury of a withdrawing-place.[2]

PUBLIC-SECTOR VERSUS PRIVATE-SECTOR

In exploring the boundaries of privacy, distinguishing between the public sector and the private sector is also helpful. This dichotomy is useful for two major reasons. First, public versus private often differentiates the ownership and control of institutions. In a democracy, **public sector** activities are owned and controlled politically— that is, by *all* the public equally, as implemented through various government entities. By contrast, **private sector** enterprises are owned and controlled largely by only *some* individuals or business firms. Private sector ownership is seldom in equal shares; instead, it is most often in varying proportions according to the size of the owner's investments. Second, many fundamental privacy laws, particularly those in the U.S. Constitution and many federal statutes, are aimed at preventing privacy abuses by governments acting in the public sector. Until recently, prohibitions against privacy intrusion by private individuals or private firms were much less pervasive. Concern over private sector intrusions has increased in importance, along with the growth of the Internet.

In part, the traditional notion of privacy underlies the public sector versus private sector distinction, at least in most democratic nations; that is, open records laws expose to public scrutiny much of the inner workings, transactions, and other

2. Phyllis McGinley, A Lost Privilege, in *The Province of the Heart*, New York: Viking (1959).

decisions governments and their agencies make. The public accountability of public sector institutions means that many records are openly disclosed and government meetings are open to press coverage and public attendance. Most of the private sector can keep much more of its activity confidential because the right of privacy is a fundamental component of individual autonomy, liberty, and dignity.

PRIVATELY HELD VERSUS PUBLICLY TRADED

Another use of the public-private distinction relates to the extent that ownership of a business firm is closely held by a few shareholders and is not traded on a national securities exchange—that is, **privately held**. This is distinguished from large "for-profit" private-sector firms that have their securities traded on national exchanges. These are called **publicly traded**, or sometimes simply **public firms**. The securities laws limit the confidentiality of internal information from publicly traded firms. Public firms must generally disclose considerable strategic, financial, and operational information before they may access the public capital markets. This privacy balance favors the role corporate information plays in assuring fair capital markets over an individual firm's interests in concealing information from competitors, suppliers, customers, employees, shareholders, or law enforcement.

PRIVACY VERSUS CONFIDENTIALITY

The similarities and differences between confidentiality and privacy are important to understand. The laws, contracts, and practices used to protect confidential corporate information are somewhat different from those protecting PII. Both situations involve secret information that could be used to the advantage of outsiders and possibly to the disadvantage of the subject. The incentive for secrecy by individuals and firms is also similar: Both seek to avoid misuse of secrets that would disadvantage the subject individual or firm. However, corporate confidentiality and individual privacy are often treated differently (1) because individuals may not be as sophisticated as business firms and (2) because of transaction costs. Privacy law provides more automatic protection of PII because individuals may lack the sophistication and bargaining power to adequately protect themselves. Individual PII is collected in numerous, low-value transactions that are more efficiently regulated through default rules.

Business firms can fend for themselves, and they are expected to recognize the value of particular information. Firms should determine what pieces of information should be kept confidential and then limit information transfers with restrictions in their contracts of employment, supply, consulting, and sales. To minimize transaction costs, firms can develop and impose appropriate restrictions in **form contracts** that precisely define their relations with others. Confidentiality is a fundamental part of all agents' fiduciary duties. The legal methods and protections for corporate confidentiality are discussed in the trade secret section of Chapter 5 and also in the employment and distribution contracts sections of Chapter 11.

Shift in Privacy Focus: From Intrusions by
Government to Include Intrusions by Private Parties

Privacy rights protect individuals from intrusion by government and from intrusion by private parties (other individuals, institutions, business firms). In America, privacy rights initially focused on protection for citizens from the government intrusions suffered during the colonial era. Indeed, much of the law of criminal process affords zones of privacy from oppressive and arbitrary government action. In those days, businesses were small, making it impractical, even futile, for businesses to collect or analyze PII data for large segments of the population.

The focus of privacy concerns shifted as the frontier was tamed and the population density increased, particularly in the cities. During the Industrial Revolution, the focus of privacy began to shift from concern over government intrusion to concern about privacy intrusions from private parties. Concern for the sanctity of private property rights reemerged in the late nineteenth century. In the mid-twentieth century, another wave of privacy concern followed, this time over PII, as consumer credit proliferated and the consumer use of insurance became common. This era resembles much of the current privacy debate. The question again is what PII business should use to make employment decisions, grant or deny credit, underwrite or set premiums for insurance, hone their marketing efforts, adjust pricing, or refuse to sell to particular individuals. High-tech investigatory tools are accessible to individuals and business firms that once were available only to government spies. Employers feel a greater need to monitor employee activities and performance because of the growth in individual autonomy and responsibility. Of course, concern over government privacy intrusion will persist as long as government is large and powerful enough to create a realistic threat of repression and tyranny.

REGULATION OF PRIVATE
DATA MANAGEMENT

In the United States, privacy rights are imposed only *after* disputes show a need to settle competing forces. This is a clash over two important values: (1) individual autonomy and (2) personal experience. Privacy must be compared with ownership of data, the informational meaning given that data, and the intangible intellectual property right to use this knowledge or sell it as a service. The controversy over privacy regulation is essentially a struggle to resolve these often conflicting claims when society finds it appropriate to intervene by setting policies for the benefit of individuals and society. For example, this conflict is settled in favor of individual privacy interests when restrictions are placed on data collection or use, such as the financial and health care information privacy restrictions discussed later. By contrast, the balance can also favor the rights to use and own observations and perceptions; examples include broadening law enforcement investigatory powers and the protectability of corporate information and data as trade secrets.

BASIC MECHANICS OF MODERN PRIVATE DATA ACTIVITIES

The basic structure of data management activities shows how and where privacy regulations will be focused. The privacy balance is reconciled by restrictions placed at several major choke points along the sequence of events typical to the data management process. Most of these regulatory approaches are *preventive*; they seek to deter the intrusion. However, if prevention fails, damage suits are a *curative* solution for past, unprevented privacy violations. No privacy regulation could long be effective without a clear, technical understanding of data management practices. New techniques could be developed to circumvent weak restrictions. Privacy regulation can encourage or limit particular activities at each or any stage during data management.

There are three basic steps in the data management of PII: (1) collection, (2) analysis, and (3) use. These steps can be further broken down into additional discrete segments. Consider the flow and processing of PII in Exhibit 13.1.

Data Acquisition

The first step in PII data management is collection, or **data acquisition**, the observation of some activity, followed by collecting and coding into data storage. In cyberspace, much observed information is captured as it flows through telecommunications wires, along the airwaves, within networks, or at particular Web sites. Information **capture** generally refers to the interception and storage of data during its creation, entry, discovery, detection, or transmission by an interception device installed somewhere en route. For example, in traditional commerce, information is directly observed and captured as transactions are recorded. Vendors and delivery services must make reports of consumer purchases, loan payments or defaults must be recorded by lenders, an insured's careful or risky acts are highly relevant data routinely gathered by insurers for underwriting, and employers must record and analyze employee activities as they accomplish job-related goals or engage in misconduct. In the on-line world, Web sites are visited, hot links are clicked, queries are answered with PII data, cookie data is available to servers from user's PCs as electronic probes read data files, and numerous other types of activities become more readily observable. This on-line data is captured when electronic records are made.

The **right to learn** from our direct experience generally permits us to observe, record, and remember these data. Although not expressly stated in the U.S. Constitution, the right to learn can be inferred from First Amendment speech and association. Learning is more than a right; it is a duty in some contexts, from the obligation to attend school to various regulatory duties to collect, analyze, disclose, and act upon business-related information. The right to learn is clearly critical to people's growth and development because learning underlies nearly all progress.

From this perspective, privacy regulation intercedes only as an exception to learning when the balance favors individual privacy or commercial confidentiality. Some privacy laws prohibit even the observation or recording of some data. For example, a common law privacy right restricts outsider intrusion upon the seclusion

Exhibit 13.1 PII Distribution Chain of Custody and Data Management Sequence

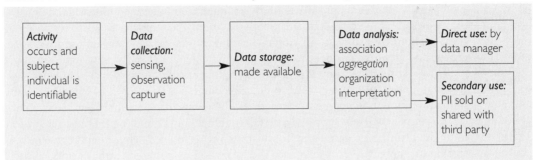

of others, criminal and tortious trespass laws forbid entry into the sanctity of another's property, it is generally illegal for voyeurs or Peeping Toms to use surreptitious means to visually observe others, and some forms of employer monitoring are restricted. With some law enforcement exceptions, wiretap laws prohibit listening to landline or wireless telephone transmissions, and it is generally illegal to intercept computerized telecommunications (e.g., e-mail, file attachments). In the future, further prohibitions on direct observation seem likely, such as restrictions on the monitoring of children's activities, unauthorized decryption, prohibitions on taking human tissue samples for genetic testing, and the unauthorized interception of financial transactions. In all these activities, public policy views the collection of these data as unduly intrusive because it violates intimacy, solitude, and modesty or gives the observer an unfair advantage over the subject individual.

Information Analysis
The second step in the sequence of data management is the organization and analysis of the data to create information useful for some purpose. Before computerized telecommunications and storage, most data was transcribed by hand into paper databases. For example, the primary function of double-entry accounting systems was to create a discipline for handwritten bookkeeping entries. The use of simultaneous debit and credit entries permitted systematic organization of accounting records that reduced errors, permitted correct classification of items, and allowed reconciliation—the subsequent inspection for quality control purposes. Similarly, analysis of PII must also follow systematic handling and pragmatic evaluation before valid conclusions can be drawn.

As data collection and organization have become mechanized, these activities are termed **data warehousing**. The impromptu analysis of this data in real time is often called **data mining**. Innovative methods of analysis of huge databases can reveal important and useful relationships, but not all firms are capable of effective information analysis. Often the PII captured is disclosed to third-party firms that specialize in gathering PII from several sources to provide analysis for clients. The verb **aggregate** (suffix pronounced -*gate*) is often used to describe the process of combining PII about one or more individuals from multiple sources. An **aggregator** is a database manager who usually combines partial bits of PII data about an identified individual from several sources. When collected and properly organized, these data form a profile or dossier about that subject individual that is useful in making marketing, insurance, credit, and employment decisions.

Contrast this activity with the adjective form of the same word: *aggregate* (suffix pronounced *-git*). When used to describe databases composed of PII about many individuals, the term *aggregate data* generally means that personal identifiers are not captured or have been stripped away. Therefore, no PII can be linked to a subject individual from aggregate data. To illustrate the difference between aggregate (adjective) and aggregate (verb), consider the following example of traffic counts. Vehicle traffic can be counted using detector loops embedded in the pavement without identifying drivers or their license plates. This "aggregate data" of traffic volume is used to plan for new traffic signals or to maintain highways. By contrast, this highway planning could also be based on data from highway video cameras that can identify each car's license plate. An aggregator could combine this information with PII data from wireless calls and credit card purchases made en route to profile the continuing whereabouts of each subject individual caught traveling on that highway.

Data analysts often "drill down" into large accumulations of data to draw conclusions that are useful to their own decision making or useful when further disclosed to their clients. Key to these efforts are evolving methods of data organization, structuring, filtering, aggregation, association, and analysis. Nearly all conclusions are based on theories and conjecture or on generalizations from empirical testing. Of course, some forms of analysis are based on faulty assumptions, erroneous calculations, or premature generalizations (e.g., junk science). For example, law enforcement is generally prohibited from interpreting lie detector evidence to disprove an alibi. In the future, other restrictions may prohibit the use of some data analysis methods. For example, employers and health care providers may be prohibited from using genetic testing of human tissue samples to infer predisposition to disease. Health insurers and employers resist extending coverage to individuals if they or their families have the potential to require high-cost medical treatment. Employers might try to avoid hiring people or fire them if genetic propensity to disease or dishonesty is discovered. Privacy advocates believe that genetic testing should not be used in these ways until there is very strong and reliable scientific consensus connecting particular genetic markers with these undesirable predispositions.

Use of Knowledge

Data are collected and analyzed to give them value. This value is realized as knowledge is used. This is the third stage in the sequence of data management. Without the promise of some economic gain when resources are expended to produce knowledge, then only intellectual curiosity would motivate the collection and analysis of data. High-quality information is presumed in economic theory, but it is only common sense that valuable and accurate knowledge is too often a scarce commodity. Most people have personal experience with an underinformed transaction that confirms this point. Data are collected and information produced for **direct use** by the data manager or for **secondary use** when sold to clients, shared with partner firms, or bartered in return for other information.

This focus on the third stage of data management serves at least two important purposes. First, by prohibiting particular uses of information, use-restriction policies recognize that collection and analysis of PII can often be inevitable. The greatest injury to the subject individual comes with use of PII. The incentive to improve decision making with information is so strong that some firms inevitably learn PII, despite restrictions on collection and analysis. Use restrictions are nearly the last resort because they are intended to prevent the privacy intrusion from actually causing injury to the subject individual. A second reason to focus on use restrictions is that data management is similar to other industries. When information moves from acquisition, through analysis, to ultimate use, these activities are actually a *chain of distribution*. It illustrates that there is value in information; there is value added by intermediate services (e.g., compilation, selection, customization, interpretation), and there are markets for knowledge that is useful to consumers of information.

However, if the "handlers" of PII are regulated under privacy law, this focus shifts from a chain of distribution to a *chain of custody*. Custody recognizes that subject individuals have rights in their own information and that privacy regulation constrains the activities of these PII handlers during the three basic stages of collection, analysis, and use. It also implies that firms involved in data management have general custodial duties of reasonable care, safeguarding, and sometimes even more specific statutory duties. A chain of custody approach suggests that privacy regulation could restrict the transfer, transmission, communication, or receipt of PII. A focus on information handling recognizes the vulnerability of flowing data and reinforces the handler's responsibilities to the subject individual regarding security. It could also be used to more directly control intermediaries and purchasers.

Privacy rights cast as restrictions on use are also quite common. Consider some of the following examples: (1) In underwriting or setting premiums for automobile insurance, the insurer is often prohibited from considering moving violations after a few years pass; (2) potential creditors are forbidden from considering an individual's former bankruptcy in making credit decisions after several years pass; (3) financial and health care privacy rules may require that the subject individual give consent before the release or sale of private data; and (4) law enforcement is prohibited from using a confession to prove guilt unless Miranda warnings were given.

NATURE OF PRIVACY RIGHTS

Privacy is a fragmented, sectoral assortment of "rights" found in international law, constitutions, federal statutes and regulations, state statutes and regulations, common law, and private contracts. Why is privacy noted in so many sources? What is the impact of all this diversity? First, privacy should not be viewed as simple or monolithic because privacy law is a balance among several often competing complex interests. Second, privacy rights may occupy niches in almost all of the major fields of law: constitutional protections, criminal law, tort law, contract rights, and technical requirements from regulations. Some scholars even advocate a property rights vision for private information,[3] based on the opinion that privacy rights are classified as torts but really function more like a part of property law.[4] It is also possible to extend the law of trade secrets, insider trading, and database protections to recognize that "information is property,"[5] thus PPI is also property.

When privacy rights are included within a major field of law, this classification has some significant impact: procedurally, substantively, and remedially. Generally, constitutional rights are so fundamental that they cannot be waived or eliminated by contract. Penalties under the criminal law are generally perceived as more severe than other prohibitions or remedies. Although individuals injured by privacy violations may press for criminal charges, criminal prosecutions are generally discretionary matters within the powers of government prosecutors, who must make resource allocation decisions on whether to seek indictments or prosecute privacy crimes. Violations of privacy regulations are generally enforced by regulators (e.g., FTC, SEC, HHS) and not by injured individuals or by local prosecutors. Regulatory enforcement is generally initiated when proposed or approved by the agency's leadership. Some agencies have independence from the executive administration of the governor at the state level or from the president at the federal level (e.g., FTC). However, the enforcement policies of most other regulators are subject to political influence, such as the emphasis given particular types of crimes prosecuted by the U.S. attorney general or by cabinet-level departments. For example, enforcement priorities for violations of health care information privacy regulations under the Health Insurance Portability and Accountability Act (HIPPA) rules discussed later are within the discretion of the Department of Health and Human Services (HHS). HHS must conform its regulatory enforcement policies to the current president's priorities.[6]

The objective of U.S. civil law is generally not preventative but curative because it compensates victims. When private rights of action for money damages exist, these suits are initiated by the injured individuals and not by prosecutors or regulators. Criminal violations do not always carry an automatic private right of action for the victim to recover damages, although some do exist (e.g., assault, battery). A potential consequence of tort reform may be that privacy rights classified as torts are weakened. In a few instances, federal laws have been passed to enforce Constitutional rights that include tort remedies for damages, such as in the civil rights area.[7] Property rights in private information could conceivably be treated like torts: private rights of action initiated by the subject individual, damages recoverable including other remedies, and perhaps some special constitutional protections extended (e.g., no takings under Fifth Amendment). Privacy policies of Web sites and business firms may be treated as contract duties, giving Web site visitors certain rights to sue for breach of contract. Then privacy policies probably would be enforceable if the contract is properly formed, and such contracts would be

---

3. Lawrence Lessig, The Architecture of Privacy, *Vanderbilt Journal of Entertainment Law and Practice* 1 (1999) 56.
4. Richard A. Posner, *The Economics of Justice* (Cambridge, Mass.: Harvard University Press, 1981), chapters 9 and 10.
5. *Carpenter v. United States*, 108 S.Ct. 316, 321 (1987).
6. Exec. Order No. 12,498.
7. Civil Rights Act of 1871, 42 U.S.C. §1983.

subjected to the performance rules of contract law. It seems unlikely that punitive damages for breach of privacy would be recoverable under contract law.

Finally, the burden of proof in most civil private rights of action (e.g., tort, contract, property rights) is preponderance of the evidence, a relatively low threshold. The preponderance standard makes it easier for plaintiffs to prove a case than it is for a prosecutor to prove criminal guilt. Criminal law generally requires proof beyond a reasonable doubt. In some regulatory actions, the burden of proof is clear and convincing evidence, a standard somewhere between the civil and criminal extremes. Exhibit 13.2 illustrates some of the potential differences in privacy rights, depending on the field of law from which they originate.

LAW AND ECONOMICS OF PRIVATE INFORMATION

Plotting the intersection between information economics and privacy law helps to predict the likely conduct of individuals and data managers. The economics of privacy is complex, as is the range of privacy interests. The incentives and behaviors of the players will change as society struggles to balance personal rights of privacy against society's needs for PII. Three basic principles are fundamental to the economic analysis of privacy: (1) Markets function best with complete information, (2) information is costly and often incomplete, and (3) information often defies exclusive control, making it difficult to maintain secrecy, control its use, or prevent misappropriation.

Under the perfect competition model, perfect information is presumed. Many economists assume that sufficient information is always freely available to inform all parties when they make contracts. With perfect information and rational action by contracting parties, economists predict that efficient markets will result: Market prices correctly assess asset values when well-informed parties bargain for their transactions. As transactions are completed, an information signal communicates the

Exhibit 13.2 Fields of Law That Include Privacy Rights

Field of Law	Enforced by	Remedies
Constitutional protection	Subject individual, prosecutor or attorney general, regulatory agency	Money damages, injunction
Tort rights	Subject individual	Money damages, injunction
Contract duties	Subject individual	Money damages, injunction, delete information
Regulatory requirements	Regulatory agency	Civil penalties, delete information
Criminal prohibitions	Prosecutor or attorney general	Fines, imprisonment, delete or deny use of information
Property rights	Subject individual	Money damages, injunction, delete information

preferences of consumers. Thus, consumer demand attracts optimal investment to produce products and services, using the most promising technologies and businesses. By contrast, lack of demand diverts investment away from less promising alternatives. In sum, many economists presume that the information that parties need to bargain, including the transaction data about their completed contracts, is widely available to guide what Adam Smith called the "invisible hand" optimally for society.

Although neoclassical economics traditionally presumed that information is complete, increasingly some economists admit the existence of market anomalies, a form of market failure where information is imperfect and this leads to market inefficiencies. The imperfection of information explains why so many resources are spent to collect and improve the quality of information. Imperfect information is often regulated where there has been a history of secrecy that society eventually discovers to be harmful (e.g., corporate financial reporting, toxic chemical disclosures, Megan's laws governing whereabouts of sex offenders).

Information is seemingly inexhaustible: The original copy usually persists even if numerous copies are made. However, inexhaustibility is only an illusion because it is difficult to make a profit from information without maintaining exclusive control over it. After information is published or otherwise becomes available to competitors or suppliers, its value to the owner steadily erodes. When these two factors combine, this pithy observation is often made: Information wants to be free. That is, there are strong pressures to learn or share information, and information is vulnerable to unauthorized communication and even unlawful misappropriation.

After information is revealed, it cannot be withdrawn. Important information will become widely known. When analogized to intellectual property (IP), information almost defies exclusive possession. Information is not like tangible property: Tangibles can be possessed by only one person at a time. By contrast, unauthorized copies of information can proliferate even without the rightful owner knowing that copies were made, who has these copies, or for what purpose the copies are used. Consider how profit-making opportunities are siphoned off from the rightful owner of data, software, music, or video when illegal copies are obtained by serious potential buyers. The rightful owner is deprived of all the marginal revenue from those who would have paid for a copy. The effect is similar for private information. Others who use PII concerning a subject individual deprive the subject individual of the power to control whether their PII may be used or how it will be used. When other people trade in a subject individual's information, this activity siphons off the individual's opportunity to receive its value.

This analysis illustrates the basic economic conundrum of private information: Who should capture the value of a subject individual's information, the **intruder** or the subject individual? Advocates of database rights argue that experience belongs to each person and that the finder of information should become the owner. Without such incentives, highly valuable information will be lost, and the result will be less economic efficiency, a bad outcome for society. By contrast, privacy advocates seek limitations on database property rights because PII is a product of each subject individual's right of self-expression (thought, action, ingenuity). Society cannot accommodate both these extreme positions. A balance must be drawn; adjustments are needed to accommodate societal interests in efficient markets, justice, and social order while still indulging individual liberty and autonomy and incentivizing other forms of well-being derived from privacy.

Drawing the Privacy "Balance"

This chapter repeatedly describes privacy as a balance between each individual's rights and society's rights set within the context of our long cultural and legal history. However, there is not much practical guidance on how that balance is drawn because there is really no deterministic or formulaic balancing method. Instead, balancing is a compromise resulting from social, economic, and political pressures. Experience with repeated privacy intrusions from government or private entities leads society to evaluate two major factors: (1) the usefulness to society of the type of information acquired in the intrusion and (2) the repugnance of such intrusions. This balance has inspired various social pressures and legal responses. The extent of privacy protection depends on existing mores and society's legitimate needs for information to function properly. Society then chooses either to permit such intrusions, to regulate them, or to prohibit them.

Richard A. Posner, the noted professor of law and economics, Seventh Circuit federal appeals court judge, and influential writer, suggests this balancing can be conceptualized by using an adaptation of Judge Learned Hand's formula for tort liability.[8] Applied generally to privacy, Judge Learned Hand's model might help solve privacy problems by balancing three factors.[9] First, society must consider the probability (P) that particular types of intrusions will discover critically useful information. Second, society should consider the costs of the intrusion (B), both in collecting the data and in damage to the subject individual from the loss of privacy. Third, the model requires a determination of the losses (L) suffered by society (e.g., other individuals, other firms) if the information is *not* discovered. Hand's formula would support privacy protection when intrusion costs are greater than the likely losses ($B > P * L$). It would permit the intrusion when the likely losses are greater than the costs of intrusion ($B < P * L$). Of course, it is difficult to operationalize this model because it requires probability, cost, and loss valuations that are arbitrary, are difficult to estimate, or defy quantification. Nevertheless, the legislative process for privacy law probably makes rough approximations of these factors.

Arguments *against* Strong Privacy Rights

The most potent argument economists advance against strong privacy rights stems from the drive to achieve economic efficiency. Markets are less prone to failure when all parties are relatively well informed. Data are needed to evaluate the subject matter of transactions as well as the counterparty *before* contracts are negotiated. Strong privacy rights restrict the potential availability of highly relevant information

---

8. Richard A. Posner, *Economic Analysis of Law*, 3d ed. (Boston: Little Brown, 1986), chapter 29.
9. *United States v. Carroll Towing Co.*, 159 F.2d 169, 173 (2d Cir., 1947).

potentially leading to **adverse selection**; that is, when underinformed contracting parties are ignorant of critical information, they cannot effectively evaluate the transaction or the counterparty's ability to perform satisfactorily. This lack of information leads to bad decision making. For example, consider the underwriting of risks by an insurance company or a creditor's decision to make a loan. If prospective insureds can hide information about their health risks or their dangerous driving records, the insurer will suffer losses that could have been prevented if PII were used. Eventually, insurers must charge higher premiums to all customers to stay profitable. Similarly, the solvency of lenders is endangered and the cost of credit rises for all borrowers if loan applicants keep secret their previous loan defaults.

Richard Posner calls such "bad information" about someone's reputation **deservedly discrediting information.**[10] This approach creates an important distinction in PII between favorable information about an individual—"good information"—and disfavorable information about an individual—"bad information." Those opposing strong privacy rights argue that information showing the subject individual in a bad light should be made available because it helps society better assess the risk that these individuals might breach their contracts. Firms have obligations to their shareholders and to their employees to investigate new recruits and monitor employees. Of course, contract law encourages candor about many matters: The laws of fraud and misrepresentation, as well as disclosure regulations, protect innocent parties when the counterparty provides material misinformation and sometimes when key information is withheld.

Economists generally believe that efficiency is enhanced when an activity is provided by the party who has the lowest cost of performing. This is the concept of the **least cost provider.** It suggests that subject individuals should reveal all their relevant PII. Thereby, society would spend less in the aggregate on investigations, data collection, and analysis. Curiously, economists also believe that developing new markets whenever possible is usually a good thing. If subject individuals regularly and cheaply revealed discrediting information, they would slow the development of new markets in PII.

The mass customization of products and the advertising needed to attract such sales requires significant PII. Many economists now argue that consumers will find more precisely targeted marketing to be much more advantageous than traditional marketing. For example, strong privacy laws could stifle a reduction in inefficient junk mailings or the annoyance of irrelevant telemarketing calls. Weak privacy protections enable the construction of personal profiles, clickstream dossiers, and digital silhouettes that could reveal individual interests, purchasing habits, characteristics, and judgments that could enable sellers to predict future interests and buying habits. Therefore, to achieve this optimal marketing system, the public must not insist on strong privacy rights.

Some sellers apparently have another objective in assuring weak privacy protections: **perfect price discrimination.** Classical economics has never adequately solved a major problem: variable pricing of goods or services according to each individual

---

10. Richard A. Posner, *Economic Analysis of Law*, 2d ed. (Boston: Little Brown, 1986), p. 545.

customer's utility function. More precise customer ranking would permit sellers to charge more to rich individuals or those who take pride in owning superior technologies. Simultaneously, consumers of moderate means would pay lower prices, closer to what they could afford. Discriminatory pricing would permit sellers to maintain economies of scale by producing larger quantities while avoiding the lower profitability of conventional, single-tier pricing.[11] Some observers predict an opposite result from data warehousing of consumer PII.[12] They point to the mounting experience with banks and their credit card divisions that charge higher fees to unprofitable customers while giving special discounts to their "best," most profitable customers. PII can also lock in customers, a major objective of customer loyalty programs (e.g., frequent flyer, grocery bonus member programs). Of course, both discriminatory pricing systems could succeed if consumers accept these practices.

Most consumers are unlikely to willingly tolerate price discrimination, particularly if revealing their PII could cost them more for goods or services. Many people would condemn the favoritism of lower prices for some and the punitive exploitation of higher prices for others. Chapter 12 discusses the Robinson-Patman Act, an antitrust law that prohibits many forms of price discrimination. However, it applies to only the markets for goods. Nevertheless, consumers are forced to tolerate some price discrimination in a few areas. Price discrimination is not generally illegal in services. Price discrimination occurs frequently in goods that have new technology; the early adopters pay off the R&D costs, allowing later purchasers to pay less once economies of scale are achieved.

In the service sector, price discrimination regularly occurs. Consider travel services: lodging, airfares, and vehicle rentals that are often priced higher for customers seeking convenience, last-minute bookings, or first-class accommodations. Discounts are readily available for those consumers who can tolerate some uncertainty or inconvenience (e.g., Saturday night stayover, weekend rates, return vehicles to the same location). Some toll roads and public transit systems use **congestion pricing** by charging higher prices during rush hour because the market will bear it and it encourages carpooling and public transit.

PII profiles permit deep knowledge about consumers that may be particularly useful to sellers of luxury goods. Such sellers can choose not to sell to customers considered inappropriate to the maintenance of their luxury reputation. For example, a seller of luxury-class automobiles might try to maintain brand image by refusing to make sales to consumers that PII databases classify as not among the "executive class." Sales outside this "target demographic" group might depreciate the brand's desirability among their target group of loyal customers. Critics compare this practice with **redlining**, a discriminatory technique of refusing home mortgage lending in neighborhoods with particular demographic or criminal activity profiles.

Several organizations are likely to fight strong privacy protections. The U.S. Chamber of Commerce and many other trade associations can be expected to

11. Soon-Yong Choi, Dale O. Stahl, & Andrew B. Whinston, *The Economics of Electronic Commerce* (Indianapolis: Macmillan Technical Publishing, 1997), chapter 8.
12. Marcia Stepanek, Weblining, *Business Week* (April 3, 2000), EB 26–34.

protect their members' access to PII as long as the data seems useful. The credit bureau industry—including Equifax, TransUnion, Experian, and TRW—has a substantial business that could be adversely affected if privacy rights were strengthened. Another segment of the PII data industry is ramping up: aggregators who facilitate the collection, archiving, and warehousing of PII, notably DoubleClick, Acxiom, Naviant Technologies, and HotData. These organizations and firms can be expected to engage in data warehousing activities both inside cyberspace and from sources in traditional commerce.

Law enforcement at all levels (local, state, federal, regulatory, self-regulation) is highly conscious of the useful insights possible from PII data warehousing. The law enforcement community was one of the original focal points for strong privacy rights. Indeed, the most powerful Constitutional rights to privacy were generally directed at the long history of intrusion by government agents. The law enforcement community may better understand the potential for negative political and public relations implications because they have long negative experience with too publicly advocating weak privacy.

Arguments *for* Strong Privacy Rights

Privacy advocates make economic arguments in favor of strong privacy protections that challenge the arguments just discussed. Proponents of strong privacy protections maintain there are market failures in PII data management practices. These generally relate to the incentives of the data management industry as well as the discipline exerted by the market and by law on that industry. First, the data manager "gains the full benefit of using the information in its own marketing or in the fee it receives when it sells information to third parties."[13] This is related to the observation made in the previous section that PII is useful because it so often informs better decision making.

The second economic reason supporting strong privacy rights is that while the subject individual may suffer injury when their PII is disclosed (e.g., bad information), the data manager disclosing the information does not suffer any injury. Indeed, PII helps the data manager or its clients reject contracting with subject individuals or change the terms of their contracts. Third, the data management industry generally does not fully reveal all PII dossier details to the subject individual. Similarly, subjects are generally unaware of the use of their data or the identity of the purchaser and even the identity of the collector. All this secrecy in collection and use of PII means the subject individuals cannot effectively monitor the use of their data. Subject individuals have difficulty in correcting erroneous data or explaining the context of accurate data. Of course, the customers purchasing erroneous data might eventually gain enough experience to discipline the data manager for poor product or service quality. However, the subject individual has the stronger and

---

13. Peter P. Swire and Robert E. Litan, *None of Your Business: World Data Flows, Electronic Commerce, and the European Privacy Directive* (Washington, D.C.: Brookings Institution Press, 1998).

more immediate incentive to assure accuracy, which is precisely why subject individuals have "access rights" under the Fair Credit Reporting Act, discussed later, to view their credit histories and correct errors after an adverse credit decision is made.

Finally, there are many potential terms regarding the handling of each individual's PII and thus far little bargaining between data managers and subject individuals over them. Competition within the data management industry is only beginning, so there is little market discipline to even offer competitive terms or negotiate unique terms. Most data managers refuse to bargain over individual terms of privacy policies, partly because bargaining costs are high relative to the small value of most PII. In sum, the data management industry can capture most of the benefits of PII, yet it bears little responsibility for the data until required to do so by competitive market conditions or privacy regulations.

The property rights approach to PII recognizes that individuals have ownership and control rights over their PII. An individual's information is a form of currency belonging to the subject individual that can be useful in bargaining with business firms. Subject individuals lose some of this advantage when their PII is first revealed. However, further sale and disclosure of the subject individual's PII decreases its value to the subject individual unless privacy policies or privacy rights restrict resale or secondary use. Individuals are unlikely to overcome the market power of the data management industry, particularly in that the industry has an incentive to hide its activities and generally most subjects remain ignorant of how their PII is used.

In the future, **digital rights management** systems, somewhat like the systems coming into use to deter and track on-line copyright infringement, could be adapted to PII collection, aggregation, use, and resale. Such systems attach hidden data along with the primary data (text, music, images, video, PII). For example, **metatags** and **digital watermarks** are hidden data of this type, used to identify and track sources and then enforce restrictions. A **digital privacy rights management** system could include a profile of the subject individual's privacy preferences. This information could accompany digital copies of their PII records to enforce restrictions on the collection and use of their PII. Electronic agents may also implement these privacy restrictions and keep records about secondary uses. Privacy advocacy organizations such as the Electronic Privacy Information Center (EPIC.org) can be expected to advocate stronger privacy rights for PII of subject individuals.

ONLINE

The Electronic Privacy
Information Center (EPIC)
http://www.epic.org

For example, privacy issues arise when PII can pinpoint the time, location, and activities of travelers through intelligent transportation systems (ITS), which generally include smart cars and highways plus the application of high-technology, computer, and telecommunications systems to improve transportation safety, reduce congestion and adverse environmental impacts, and provide better traveler information and logistics management. These **location-referencing** technologies such as electronic toll tags for bridges, tunnels, and turnpikes; wireless phones; global positioning systems (GPS); traffic video; global information systems (GIS); telematics; and other emerging technologies create the field of mobile commerce.

DEVELOPMENT OF FAIR INFORMATION PRACTICE PRINCIPLES

Underlying many contemporary privacy laws and privacy policies are five key **fair information practices** that had their origins in a 1973 advisory committee report to the U.S. Department of Health, Education and Welfare, *Records, Computers and the Rights of Citizens*. The advisory committee's recommendations have had a lasting impact, influencing the work of modern privacy task forces. They have been adopted in numerous privacy statutes, regulations, and privacy policies discussed here.

The first fair information practice principle is **notice**. Subject individuals should be given notice and have a clear awareness whenever an entity's PII capture practices might affect that individual. Before any information is collected, the subject individual must be given reasonably adequate, conspicuous, and comprehensible notification of the data capture practices. Notice is necessary before the subject individual can make an informed choice regarding the data capture. Notice enables individuals to take measures to protect their privacy. The notice should identify all details needed to permit informed choice. At a minimum, this information should include (1) who is collecting the data, (2) who will receive the data, (3) how the data will be used, (4) what data is collected, (5) what means, methods, or mechanisms will collect the data, (6) whether the data to be collected is required for access to a Web site or required for initiating a relationship with the collector, and (7) a description of the quality and security controls used. Other terms may also become important with further sophistication of PII capture methods and as subject individuals begin to see how their PII is used.

The second principle of fair information practice is **choice**. The subject individual must be given a choice as to whether and how their PII is collected. Choice must be made by the subject as a clear and intentional manifestation of consent. The consent should extend to primary uses of the information necessary for the immediate transaction or purpose. Additionally, consent must address any *secondary uses* of the PII, those uses beyond the immediate needs in the current transaction. Consent for secondary use should address the collector's expected future use, as well as any transfer of the PII for use by others. An **opt-out** consent requires the subject individual to take a clear and affirmative act to *prevent* collection and use of PII. By contrast, an **opt-in** form of consent requires the subject individual to take a clear and affirmative act to *permit* collection and use of PII Collector. Opt out versus opt in is detailed later. As parties become more sophisticated, the consent should become more complex than a simple, binary yes or no. As the terms of privacy become more complicated, the form of consent should also allow subject individuals to tailor the nature of their PII use.

The third principle of fair information practice is **access**. The subject individual must be given timely, accurate, and inexpensive access to review their file: the PII archived about themselves. Long experience with credit bureaus and with other databases shows that errors too often occur in such databases that are disadvantageous to the subject individual. Participation by the subject individual is essential to both the accuracy and the legitimacy of PII information in databases. The subject individual has the strongest incentive to review and assure accuracy of the data. When errors are discovered, there should be a simple and effective method to contest and correct inaccurate data.

The fourth principle of fair information practice is **security**. There are two major custodial duties for the owners and operators of PII databases: quality control and safeguarding. The PII collector must continually take reasonable steps to assure the accuracy of PII. Also, the PII database operator must take precautions, including careful maintenance of administrative and technical security measures to prevent unauthorized access, destruction, misuse, or unauthorized disclosure of PII.

The fifth principle of fair information practice is **enforcement**. The PII collection and database management process must have mechanisms to enforce the privacy practices, including self-regulation or legal protections such as private rights of action for redress and/or regulatory enforcement. The implementation of these fair information practices is evident in the following sections of this chapter and summarized in Exhibit 13.3.

EFFECTING CHOICE: OPT IN VERSUS OPT OUT

Consumer choice can be achieved in various ways. Both voluntary privacy policies and several new privacy laws require a form of choice. Some laws relate primarily to Internet activities, and other laws apply more broadly to data collection online and off line. Notice and consent in traditional commerce can be made expressly in

Exhibit 13.3 Fair Information Practice Principles

Fair Information Practice Principle	Explanation of Fair Information Practice Principles
Notice/awareness	Subject individuals should be given notice of an entity's practices before any information is collected from them by identifying details about the data collection, security, and uses.
Choice/consent	Subject individual has choice on whether and how PII is collected. Consent might be manifested with an *opt out* (an affirmative act *preventing* PII collection and/or use) or an *opt in* (an affirmative act *permitting* collection and/or use).
Access/participation	Subject individual can gain timely and inexpensive access to review PII about themselves. A simple and effective method should exist to contest and correct inaccurate data.
Integrity/security	Collector takes reasonable steps to assure accuracy of PII, as well as administrative and technical security measures to prevent unauthorized access or disclosure, destruction, or misuse of PII.
Enforcement/redress	Mechanisms exist to enforce privacy practices, including self-regulation, private rights of action, and criminal or regulatory enforcement.

written contracts or inferred from conversations or conduct. However, for low-stakes transactions and in much activity online (e.g., e-commerce) there may be only one practical method for consumer privacy notice and consent: on-line access to notice of privacy policies and click-through consent. As discussed previously, some-day it may be possible for firms using electronic agents to implement a digital pri-vacy rights management system. Electronic agents could conceivably negotiate and enforce restrictions on the collection and use of PII automatically. However, until these technologies become reliable and commonplace, most consumer privacy con-sent will be made through simple click-through choices. Most U.S. privacy consents in use today are opt-out systems. However, there is a trend to use the European-style opt-in system.

Generally, a privacy consent system is either opt-out or opt-in. Opt-out systems require the consumer to make an affirmative act that *denies* authorization for the collection and/or use of PII. They contrast with other systems using the opt-in approach, in which an affirmative act *grants* authorization to collect and/or use PII. Opt out is supported by many business firms and by data managers. Opt out is likely to provide an immediate increase in the value of PII databases. An opt-out default permits collection and use, unless and until consumers take the trouble to opt out, meaning that the group of consumers from whom data can be collected legally starts out very large, nearly the whole population. Thereafter, as individuals exercise their choice to withdraw by opting out, the number of subject individuals eventually declines. This decline will happen slowly if it is difficult to exercise the option, the option process is unclear, or individuals do not think their PII is used to their disad-vantage. Of course, if the option is easily exercised or individuals quickly learn that their PII is being misused, then the rate of opting out would rise. Therefore, data managers have an incentive to make it more difficult to opt out, with confusing pri-vacy notices or lengthy and complex opt-out procedures. In sum, an opt-out form of privacy consent is more desirable for data managers because initially the population participating is large and the decline in its size is slow, depending on several factors largely within the data manager's control. Exhibit 13.3 illustrates this point.

Contrast opt-out procedures with opt-in procedures. Opt in poses serious dis-advantages to data managers: They cannot collect PII until and unless the subject individual consents. When opt in is used or required, data managers have an incen-tive to make it easy, quick, and simple for consumers to choose to participate. The default number of individuals participating necessarily starts at zero. All growth in participation depends on several factors: Consumers perceive that they benefit by sharing their PII, opting in is simple, or access to many Internet sites is blocked unless they share PII. Therefore, Web sites and other firms hoping to collect PII must work hard to lure participation. Additionally, the mere existence of opt-in rights strongly suggests that individuals have property rights in their PII. This concept makes database maintenance more problematic than under opt-out conditions because the collector's rights are subject to stronger consumer privacy protections. Exhibit 13.4 illustrates the contrast between opt out and opt in.

Currently, many U.S. privacy laws favor self-regulation and businesses' right to build and use PII databases under opt out. However, there is a shift underway from

Exhibit 13.4 Proportion of Participants: Opt-in versus Opt-out Consents

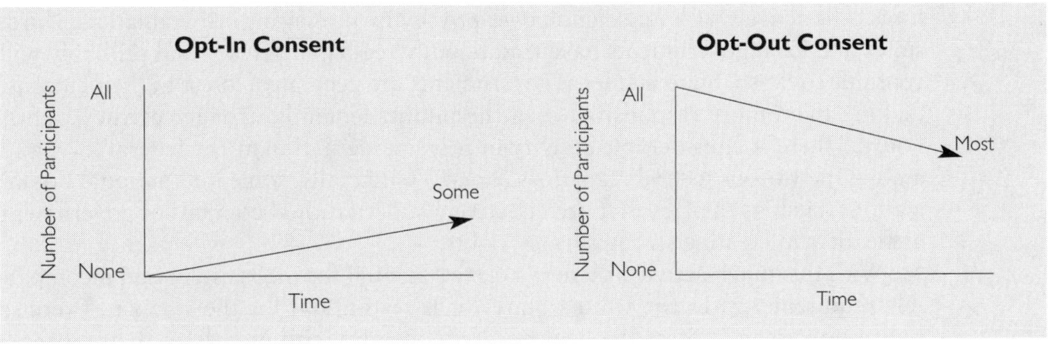

opt out to opt in. First, certain aspects of health care and children's on-line privacy in the United States may become opt in. Second, the EU's privacy data directive, an opt-in regime, is becoming influential. Third, opt in is being adopted by many progressive Internet sites and will probably be advocated persistently by privacy fundamentalists. Finally, some observers argue that Web sites or firms use opt in only when the subject individual is purchasing goods or services. If competing sellers can divert sales with greater privacy protections, businesses may find it necessary to use the more privacy-conscious opt-in procedure. These observers then argue that opt out should still be appropriate for Web sites offering free content. As discussed in Chapter 8, this view presumes the individual's PII is payment to gain access to content on the data collector's site. Therefore, for free Web site access, providing PII is price of Web site admission and the PII data constitute contractual consideration. Under this theory, opt-in regulations could constitute a taking of private property.

JURISDICTION OVER PRIVACY PRACTICES

Jurisdiction is a key question in privacy, much as it has been in other areas where activities span state and national boarders. Increasingly, many jurisdictions are enacting privacy protection regulations. Many nations, notably member states of the EU, the United States, and Canada, have passed privacy legislation in recent years that affect both traditional commerce and Internet activities. During 2000, nearly 1,000 pieces of proposed legislation were introduced in the United States. Although few were enacted, many new privacy laws should be expected over the next few years.

Other institutions are competing to seize jurisdiction and regulate privacy. First, privacy-conscious individuals should take responsibility for their own privacy by carefully reviewing privacy policies, pursuing every opportunity to limit others' use of their PII, keeping up-to-date on privacy matters, and monitoring the use of their PII to control misuse. Many individuals can also participate in the formulation of privacy regulations. Second, many industries, trade associations, and their member firms now actively seek jurisdiction over privacy by promoting self-regulation. Third, states and local governments have traditionally regulated privacy and probably will continue to do so. State and local governments are generally closest to their citizens, making them more responsive when the public demands stronger privacy rights. Fourth, there is considerable activity in privacy regulation at the federal level and among the various federal regulators (e.g., FTC). Finally, some international organizations, such as the EU, that are effectively supranational councils of government are leaders in creating strong privacy rights.

With this much activity, there is a clear potential for inconsistent and incompatible requirements. In the United States, it is traditional for the states to exercise **police powers** to protect the health, safety, welfare, and morals of their citizens. Clearly, the creation and strengthening of privacy rights are within state police powers, particularly when privacy is conceived as protecting property rights in PII, avoiding intrusions from societal predators, or preventing contacts that endanger health, safety, or morals. Conflicts between the privacy regulations from various jurisdictions seem inevitable. Traditional jurisdictional conflicts arise when on-line or traditional commerce involves consumers in one jurisdiction and either the product or service vendor or the data manager in another jurisdiction. For example, does the law of the subject individual's residence apply when PII is collected by an Internet site owned by a firm from another state or nation? Generally, the principles of jurisdiction discussed in Chapter 1 apply.

Traditionally in the United States and to some extent in the EU, when such conflicts become intolerable, there are three possible resolutions. First, the Constitutional framers enumerated particular powers to be exercised only by the federal government (e.g., international relations, defense, foreign and interstate commerce). Second, the states have been quite successful in drafting and adopting uniform laws when inconsistent state laws would needlessly raise transactions costs (e.g., commercial law). Third, federal law can preempt state law if the potential for inconsistent state law very significantly deters progress.

EU PERSONAL DATA PROTECTION DIRECTIVE

In the past, many European people suffered at the hands of many tyrannical governments (e.g., feudal lords, Nazis, Fascists and Communists) that used PII to oppress and punish dissenters. It is not surprising that this experience led the EU to become a model for strong privacy rights. EU privacy rights span all industries and all EU nations. The flow of private data is severely restricted across borders. The **EU Personal Data Protection Directive** was enacted by the EU Parliament in 1995. EU directives like this one require all the **member states** (European nations) to enact national laws consistent with the directive. A majority of EU nations have now done so. The term used in the EU Directive for PII is **personal data,** which includes any information relating to an identifiable person. The directive regulates the **processing** of personal data, which includes operations performed on personal data either by automated or manual means and personal data that becomes part of a **filing system.**

Data managers and their clients are called **data controllers**, which gives them various duties concerning processing of personal data.

Substantive articles (sections) of the EU Directive parallel the Fair Information Practice Principles, but the EU adds some other detailed privacy concepts. First, Articles 10 and 11 provide for notice and awareness, called **data controller identification**, which includes the collector's identity, the purposes for data processing, and other information needed to assure fair and lawful processing. Second, Article 7 requires **legitimacy of data processing**, a less restrictive concept than consent because it includes other circumstances that may justify data collection. Generally, personal information may be processed only if there is unambiguous consent, essentially an opt-in system. However, processing is also lawful without consent for other reasons, such as when processing is necessary: (i) to perform a contract or protect the interests of the data subject (subject individual), (ii) to comply with legal obligations of the subject or controller, (iii) for the controller to exercise its legitimate rights so long as the data subject's fundamental rights are not violated, and (iv) for the public interest. A unique opt-out provision exists for data subjects to avoid automated processing that evaluates personal aspects of the data subject or that would otherwise have a significant effect on the data subject. For example, the opt out would apply if a decision to extend credit would be made by computer or electronic agents using defined creditworthiness criteria (e.g., earnings, credit histories).

Articles 12 and 14 of the EU Directive give the data subject rights similar to the third principle, access. Subjects have the right to confirm that there is processing of data concerning them, including the purpose, categories of data, and recipients receiving the personal data. The data subject has **objection rights** to prevent use of data in direct marketing. When the data is incomplete or inaccurate, the data subject has the right to rectify or correct and to erase or block to data processing. The EU Directive has several provisions addressing data integrity and security. Article 6 requires the personal data to be accurate and current and to be retained as PII no longer than necessary. This provision appears to permit longer retention and use of aggregate data stripped of personal identifiers. Article 17 requires the data collector to use technical and organizational security and integrity measures to avoid data loss, unlawful destruction, or unauthorized access, alternation, or disclosure. Articles 22, 23, and 24 provide that the national laws of the EU member nations are the primary source for enforcement and redress. However, a private right of damages for the data subject is specifically required in suits against the responsible data controller.

In addition to provisions paralleling the five Fair Information Practice Principles, there are some additional rights. Use restrictions under Article 6 require fair and lawful data processing and only for the use originally collected. Data collected must be adequate, relevant, and not excessive, considering the authorized purpose for processing. Article 8 creates a class of **highly sensitive data** that receive greater protection, including ethnic or racial demographics; opinions or beliefs based on political, religious, or philosophical views; health or sex life information; and membership in unions. For example, cross-border data flows cannot be permitted by member states unless adequately safeguarded in the destination nation.

EU Safe Harbor

Article 25 of the EU Personal Data Protection Directive prohibits member nations from permitting any transfer of personal data to some other nation that does not provide an *adequate level of protection* to privacy matters. Adequacy is assessed from all the circumstances, including (i) nature of the data, (ii) purpose and duration of the proposed processing, (iii) nation where data originates, (iv) nation of final destination, and (v) privacy laws, professional rules, and security measures in the final destination nation. EU member nations should evaluate these factors whenever data transfers to non-EU nations are contemplated by an EU data collector. The guidelines envision that the EU will keep **white lists** that publicize which non-EU nations have been evaluated and provide an adequate level of protection.

Transfer of data to nations not certified as providing adequate protection may still be possible. However, EU nations are expected to more carefully examine proposed data transfers to such nations. The relevant factors about the proposed transfer include whether the data transfer would involve highly sensitive data, the potential for financial loss (e.g., Internet credit card payment), personal safety risks (e.g., PII showing subject's location), data are intended for decision making significantly affecting a data subject, repetitive transfers of mass volumes of data, and covert or clandestine practices to collect data (e.g., Internet browser cookies). Permission to transfer PII satisfying one or more of these factors would be less likely to be granted.

The U.S. Department of Commerce negotiated a **safe harbor** with the European Commission to recognize when U.S. privacy protection meets the adequacy standard. The safe harbor specifies adequate PII data-handling methods and practices that, if carefully followed, will shield U.S. firms from EU legal action for privacy violations. The safe harbor may become very important for U.S. and multinational businesses doing business inside and outside EU nations. For example, any severe restriction on personal data flows from an EU nation to the United States could prove difficult for those firms with personnel information (e.g., skills databases, employment history, benefits) or client information in industries like insurance, consulting, banking, and auditing. Unfortunately, the EU Parliament voted to reject this safe harbor. Nevertheless, the EU Commission overrode the rejection and formally recognizes that U.S. firms complying with the safe harbor will be deemed as providing adequate protection.

Adequacy can be demonstrated with self-certification showing that a firm's privacy policies meet the safe harbor requirements. Additionally a U.S. regulator in that firm's industry must serve as a forum for appeals. Each U.S. firm must submit an annual letter to the U.S. Commerce Department self-certifying its compliance with the safe harbor either through participation in a self-regulatory privacy program or by using its own privacy policy. Updates are found on the U.S. Commerce Department Web site.

The self-regulatory regime must provide a dispute-resolution system to investigate and resolve individual complaints. It must also have procedures for verifying compliance and provide a remedy for problems arising out of a failure to comply. Examples include the seal programs discussed as self-regulation. Additionally, an appeal process must be available through a federal or state regulator that must have authority to remedy the U.S. firm's failure to comply with the firm's self-regulation by bringing action under a federal or state law that prohibits unfair and deceptive acts. A self-regulatory regime must assure compliance with seven personal data protection principles (listed in Exhibit 13.5). that closely resemble the Fair Information Practice Principles and the EU Directive.

CONSTITUTIONAL BASIS FOR PRIVACY RIGHTS

Several provisions of the U.S. Constitution create or affect privacy rights for individuals in their homes and in their other activities. Most are derived from the Bill of Rights and other Constitutional amendments. Some provisions explicitly protect privacy, and other protections are inferred from broader principles. However, a few provisions actually limit privacy rights. The U.S. Constitution is the supreme law so its privacy principles are very strong and cannot be overridden by federal, state, or local law. Exhibit 13.6 summarizes these Constitutional rights applicable to privacy rights.

Exhibit 13.5 EU Safe Harbor Principles

Principle	Explanation of EU Safe Harbor Principle
Notice	Must notify individuals about the purposes for data collection and use, provide contact information for inquiries or complaints, list which third parties will receive the information, and explain the choices and means offered to limit use and disclosure.
Choice	Opt out if their PII will be disclosed or used outside the original purposes for collection. Opt in for highly sensitive information.
Onward transfer	Transfer of personal data to third-party agents must bind the third party to the safe harbor, assure that the third party is subject to the directive or have a contract with such third party requiring at least the same level of privacy protection as required by the relevant principles.
Access	Individuals must have access to PII held by an organization to permit correction, amendment, or deletion if inaccurate unless such access would be excessively burdensome or expensive compared with the risks to the individual's privacy.
Security	Must take reasonable precautions to protect PII from loss, misuse, and unauthorized access, disclosure, alteration, and destruction.
Data integrity	PII must be relevant for the purposes to be used. Must take reasonable steps to ensure that data are reliable for the intended use, accurate, complete, and current.
Enforcement	There must be readily available and affordable independent recourse mechanisms to investigate and resolve complaints and disputes, with damages awardable where provided by law; procedures verifying commitments to adhere to implementation of the safe harbor principles; and obligations to remedy failures to comply with the principles. Sanctions must be sufficiently rigorous to ensure compliance. Safe harbor benefits are no longer assured for failure to provide annual self-certification letters.

Exhibit 13.6 Constitutional Provisions Affecting Privacy

Constitutional Provision	Rights Protected	Impact on Privacy
First Amendment	Freedoms of speech, religion, press, assembly, petitions	Privacy of literature, entertainment, ideas, absorbed political and religious beliefs, worship practices, group membership; but permits observation and learning.
Third Amendment	No quartering of soldiers	Protection from military's physical intrusion and surveillance into the home.
Fourth Amendment	No unlawful search and seizure; warrants, subpoenas, or court orders are required	Protection from unreasonable search of persons, homes, papers, or effects without warrant based on probable cause; secrecy of communications and correspondence.
Fifth Amendment	No double jeopardy; no self-incrimination; due process (federal); no uncompensated taking of private property	Protects from repeated legal process, forced revelation of information, enhances autonomy; but protects from federal action taking ownership of observation and knowledge acquired about others' private activities.
Sixth Amendment	Trials in the public record, confront witnesses	Prevents secrecy of trials; permits intrusion into witnesses' solitude to require testimony, and cross-examination opens up witnesses' past and conduct to scrutiny.
Ninth Amendment	Enumeration of rights in Constitution does not deny the people other rights	Basis to infer privacy rights, even though not expressly stated in Constitution.
Tenth Amendment	Reserves power of government to the states or to the people	Basis to infer state authority to enact privacy laws and to the people to protect their privacy.
Fourteenth Amendment	Due process (states); privileges and immunities; equal protection of the laws	Basis to withhold or limit access to information, freedom of personal choice; but protects from state action taking ownership of observation and knowledge acquired about others' private activities.

The Fourth, Fifth, and Ninth Amendments have been most influential. The 1965 case of *Griswold v. Connecticut*[14] became the foundation for a **zone of privacy** for individuals.[15] Later cases reserve this zone whenever there is a **reasonable expectation of privacy**:

- Subject individual exhibits actual expectation of privacy.
- Society recognizes that the expectation of privacy is reasonable.

The Fourth Amendment restricts government from capturing information where there is a reasonable expectation of privacy. It forms the basis for prohibitions against wiretapping, electronic eavesdropping, disclosure of prescription drug records,[16] and

14. 381 U.S. 479 (1965), holding unconstitutional a Connecticut statute outlawing use and advice on using birth control devices as an intrusion into zone of privacy.
15. Samuel Warren and Louis Brandeis, The Right to Privacy, *Harvard Law Review* 4 (1890), 193.
16. *Whalen v. Roe*, 429 U.S. 589, 599 (1977).

the right to reproductive freedom. *Katz v. U.S.*[17] is an early electronic eavesdropping case illustrating how society's expectations expand the zone of privacy to a public place. This case found that individuals may have a reasonable expectation of privacy even when talking in a public phone booth. Law enforcement did not use direct wire-tapping but installed a listening device mounted outside a phone booth. The lack of visual privacy in a glass-walled phone booth does not forfeit the aural privacy of the enclosed space. One possible implication for cyberspace may be that unencrypted communications, if too easily intercepted, may not exhibit a sufficient privacy expectation to be protected.

One of the most controversial Supreme Court cases of modern times is a privacy case. *Roe v. Wade* chronicles the development of the Constitutional basis for privacy as a **fundamental right**, creating the right to an abortion.

Constitutional protection is lost when the information is given to another person. After private information flows into commerce, there is an "assumption of risk" that Constitutional privacy protection is lost by the subject individual. For example, there is no Constitutional expectation of privacy in bank records, phone numbers dialed, trash container contents left at curbside, or activities subject to aerial observation from aircraft. Nevertheless, other state and federal privacy laws may protect some of these activities.

The Fifth Amendment self-incrimination privilege limits *how* government can capture incriminating information, such as in police interrogation or tax returns. However, this right does not protect the contents of papers of any kind because record keeping is not a compelled act of self-incrimination. This raises an important distinction: The Fifth Amendment protects mental thoughts but not physical manifestations. This may be the reason that courts increasingly find that physical examinations and samples are not protected by the Fifth Amendment. For example, individuals accused of criminal activity are not protected by the Fifth Amendment from requirements to submit samples of fingerprints, voiceprints, tissue for DNA testing, blood, urine, or hair follicles.

It will be interesting to see how these rules will adapt to electronic records and security methods in cyberspace. Consider a critical distinction made in *Doe v. United States*. The defendant was "forced to surrender a key to a strongbox containing incriminating documents, but not to reveal the combination to his wall safe" or to force him to actually use the combination he knew would open the safe.[18] In the electronic and cyberspace world, passwords or software keys are needed to access files on computer hard drives, retrieve files from network storage, access e-mail accounts, or restore encrypted files. Such protection may not be available for an employee who is hiding information on systems owned by her or his employer.

PRIVACY IN LITIGATION, REGULATION, AND LAW ENFORCEMENT

Recall the discussion of litigation and trial process in Chapter 1. The Fourth Amendment provides business with the greatest protection from unfair criminal

---

17. 389 U.S. 347 (1967).
18. *Doe v. United States*, 487 U.S. 201 (1988).

or regulatory investigations. Fourth Amendment protection generally arises before a criminal defendant is indicted or before a civil administrative case is filed. Both natural persons and corporations are protected from unreasonable searches and seizures. In all types of cases, after suit has been filed, all parties, including defendants, prosecutors, private litigants, and administrative agencies, may use discovery to obtain information from the opposing side to help prove its case. **Discovery** devices include written **interrogatories** to question opposing parties and **depositions** to orally question witnesses. A **production of documents** request permits the examination of private files. Before suit is filed, investigators may get information from various sources: investigators, required reports, on-site inspections, and subpoenas. After assessing this information, the plaintiff, prosecutor, or agency enforcement division may decide whether there is sufficient evidence to sue or prosecute.

Many other nations prohibit such expansive discovery in noncriminal cases. In most civil law nations of Europe and Latin America, the criminal judges also serve as the prosecutor, which gives them very broad **inquisitorial** powers of discovery. However, civil plaintiffs do not share these rights to obtain documents from opposing parties. It can be very difficult to prove wrongdoing in such nations because of their strong secrecy norms.

Statutes require the keeping of many records for the public's benefit, so they are considered **public records** with no right to privacy. Administrative agencies may share with other agencies any nonprivileged evidence they gather. For example, federal agencies may generally refer investigative files to the Justice Department (DOJ) for criminal prosecution. The FTC may inform the DOJ about information it discovers about privacy violations, which could lead to DOJ criminal charges.

Administrative agencies are created by **enabling legislation** that empowers the agency to act and often authorizes the agency to subpoena witnesses and documents. Criminal prosecutors generally have similar powers once a criminal indictment is issued. **Subpoenas** require pretrial and trial testimony from witnesses. A *subpoena duces tecum* requires the production of documents. Regulatory agencies may not abuse the subpoena power for ulterior motives. For example, agencies may not harass businesses by issuing excessive subpoenas, and they may not publicly disclose trade secrets and other private matters examined under subpoena. Administrative subpoenas are not self-executing. This is a limitation to discourage agencies from exceeding their subpoena powers. The recipient of an administrative subpoena may validly refuse to testify or to produce the documents requested until ordered to do so by a court.

An agency must justify a subpoena before a court will order enforcement. Four fairness standards, established in *United States v. Powell*,[19] require the agency to prove that its investigation is legitimate and that the information it seeks is relevant. The subpoena recipient can be ordered to comply if the agency satisfies the *Powell* criteria.

---

19. *United States v. Powell*, 379 U.S. 48 (1964).

> ### *United States v. Powell* **Subpoena Enforcement Standards**
> 1. Agency has a *legitimate purpose* to investigate.
> 2. Inquiry must be *relevant* to that legitimate purpose.
> 3. Agency may *not* already have the requested information *in its possession*.
> 4. Agency must *follow* its own *administrative procedures* in issuing the subpoena.

The protection of witnesses from compelled self-incrimination constitutes one of the best known aspects of the Fifth Amendment. By "pleading the Fifth," witnesses may refrain from giving evidence that might tend to show their own guilt. However, documents that are required to be kept for governmental purposes are not privileged. The Fifth Amendment constrains the investigatory activities of administrative agencies, prosecutors, police, and Congressional committees. It protects the most intimate and private thoughts of those accused of wrongdoing. An important limitation on the protection against self-incrimination has developed. That protection is a personal right, so it protects only a natural person from whom testimony is sought. Therefore, corporations and other business entities do not receive protection against incriminating evidence taken from an employee's testimony in matters involving the corporation. Employees may assert the privilege of protection against self-incrimination to protect only their personal privacy interests. The privilege does not protect the employer from incrimination.

In many instances, evidence that incriminates one party is in the hands of someone else. For example, an ISP may hold subscriber's e-mail and file attachments on its server. Accountants or attorneys often hold tax or litigation documents for their clients. When government officials seek this information, the clients may try to plead the Fifth to keep the information secret. This argument usually fails because the privilege is testimonial, so it protects only verbal and not documentary evidence. Several statutes remove the privilege if the person receives immunity from prosecution.

PRIVILEGED COMMUNICATIONS

Other types of evidentiary privileges can be used to keep information private. Most are based on state common law and not directly on Constitutional provisions. These privileges usually protect the accused from the release of confidential information known by close associates. Such associates include spouses, attorneys, priests or ministers, doctor-patient, and accountant-client (in about 20 states but not in federal cases). These privileges have developed around the relationships among these persons to encourage frank and open disclosure and to foster the relationships. The attorney-client privilege may be available to keep information secret if (1) information passes (2) from client to practicing attorney (3) in confidence, (4) not from some other source, and (5) for the purpose of receiving professional advice. Attorneys can generally communicate confidentially by using e-mail or intranet schemes if their clients consent after being informed of the risks of interception.

In the corporate context, there are additional requirements to gain the secrecy benefits of the attorney–corporate client privilege: (1) The employee must be or dered to communicate to the attorney (2) about information gained within the employee's duties (3) that is not immediately available to upper management. The Supreme Court has observed that the potential for expanding the attorney-client privilege to idle communications is too great. Unprivileged idle communications are those not made in confidence or not seeking legal advice. Additionally, the strict privilege requirements enumerated here are designed to prevent misuse of the privilege. Communications with corporate attorneys should not be made intentionally to shield information if the purpose is not primarily for the attorney's professional advice.

SEARCH AND SEIZURE

Some agencies have the authority to search private areas of personal or business premises without a warrant. These privacy intrusions may be illegal as unreasonable searches or seizures unless certain conditions are met. A few industries have a long history of close and pervasive regulation and cannot reasonably expect total privacy. For example, in the sales of firearms, liquor, food, and drugs, the public's interest in safety outweighs the individual businesses' right to privacy. Also, in emergency situations, where consent is given, or where the regulated activities are in open and plain view, agencies may conduct surprise inspections even without a search warrant. Law enforcement cannot open mail without the recipient's consent or a search warrant. However, transactional information on the outside of the envelope, called **mail covers**, is not private. Postcard correspondence also seems vulnerable.

In almost all other situations, regulators must obtain a warrant from a federal magistrate before searching employees, premises, and paper or computer files. The warrant should be issued only on the agency's showing of **administrative probable cause**. Three factors can form the basis for the grant of an **ex parte warrant** when the target is not present at the hearing: (1) "specific evidence of existing violations," (2), employee complaints, or (3) "reasonable legislative or administrative standards" (i.e., random, regular, and routine inspections, reinspections, or follow-up inspections). The surprise element may be necessary to avoid destruction of evidence, intimidation of witnesses, or correction of the violation.

PRIVACY UNDER FEDERAL FREEDOM OF INFORMATION AND STATE OPEN RECORDS LAWS

The investigatory powers of government permit the collection of considerable private information. The **Freedom of Information Act (FOIA)** and **state open records laws** were passed because regulatory agencies were widely believed to operate in a cloud of secrecy. To make government more responsive to the public will, these laws now require federal and state governments to disclose most information contained in government files. Government must disclose information whenever a specific request is made by nearly anyone: individuals, public interest groups, research scholars, journalists, and even foreigners. There is thus very little privacy for PII or corporate information held by regulators. However, every president since George Washington has claimed a constitutional right to an **executive privilege**, exempting sensitive information from public disclosure. Today, there can still be some privacy

Exhibit 13.7 FOIA Exemptions

- National defense, national security, or foreign policy matters designated by presidential executive order
- Agency's internal personnel rules and practices
- Exemptions required by other statutes
- Trade secrets and commercial or financial information that is privileged or confidential concerning regulated entities, but only in the agencies' discretion
- Internal deliberative process in interagency or intra-agency memoranda or letters
- Agency personnel or medical files
- Investigatory files compiled for law enforcement purposes
- Bank secrecy condition reports of financial institutions
- Geological and geophysical information concerning oil and gas wells

covering information in government hands under FOIA and most state open records laws, which provide a few specific statutory exemptions to disclosure (Exhibit 13.7).

All reasonably well-described requests for records from whatever internal agency source must be disclosed. Under amendments made in the **Electronic Freedom of Information Act (eFOIA)** of 1996, the same standards apply to both "hard-copy" and electronic files. Thus, e-mail, letters, and notes must be accessible, and the same FOIA exemptions apply to electronic records. The agency must publish an on-line index and provide on-line reading rooms where those documents likely to be requested frequently are made available. The agency may charge reasonable fees for document search and photocopying, although many agencies regularly decline to charge fees in the public interest. An appeal may be made to the agency's head when a lower echelon official withholds disclosure. These appeals must be processed within 20 working days. When agencies do not provide information, a complaint can be made to the U.S. District Court to seek an injunction. Courts may issue contempt citations against agency personnel for refusing to comply with court-ordered disclosure.

The selective release of information by agencies may represent an abuse of its discretion. If an agency publicly discloses or leaks information, a private entity's trade secrets may be lost, destroying a competitive advantage. An agency that threatens disclosure of confidential information to force settlement or compliance is clearly abusing its discretion. In such cases, the information supplier may sue for a **protective order** prohibiting disclosure. The Justice Department may prosecute disclosures that are illegal under the Trade Secrets Act. However, such issues are not ripe for adjudication until after the disclosure is made, and the damage may already be done. In the alternative, regulated entities may seek judicial review of an agency's decision to release information. Unfortunately, an agency might not notify the suppliers of information until after the secret is already disclosed. Initially, the **Privacy Act of 1974** appeared to block federal agencies from disclosing PII from their files without the consent of the subject individual. However, a 1984 amendment makes it clear that unless exempt under FOIA or another law (e.g., IRS records) PII must be disclosed in a FOIA request.

PRIVACY RIGHTS UNDER STATE LAW

A few states have constitutional provisions explicitly directed to protect privacy. Alabama, California, and Florida have broad privacy rights for individuals that prohibit government intrusion; a few are listed as inalienable rights. Some other states, including Pennsylvania, Colorado, and New Jersey, interpret their constitutional search and seizure provisions more broadly than the Fourth Amendment. For example, in some states, people can keep their banking records secret, and other states give people the right to keep secret the telephone numbers they dial. However, state constitutions are not the major source of privacy rights. State privacy law most often comes from state statutes and the common law. State privacy statutes are discussed later, in sections covering privacy in various specific contexts (e.g., online, children, financial, health, employment, telecommunications).

This section reviews the four major common law privacy rights: (1) intrusion upon seclusion, (2) public disclosure of private facts, (3) false light, and (4) misappropriation. These rights were first organized into four distinct categories by the eminent tort law scholar, William L. Prosser.[20] Today, most exist in some form in all 50 states, largely by common law precedent and now enshrined in the *Restatement of the Law Second, Torts*. A few states have codified them into statutory provisions. Generally, these privacy torts offer remedies of money damages or an injunction to halt the privacy intrusion when a subject individual's privacy is violated.

INTRUSION UPON SECLUSION

Section 652B of the *Restatement of the Law Second, Torts* is the most common form of the **intrusion** tort that protects the sanctity of the "right to be let alone." It is defined by §652B as arising when another person:

> *intentionally intrudes, physically or otherwise, upon the solitude or seclusion of another or his private affairs or concerns . . . if the intrusion would be highly offensive to a reasonable person.*

A subject individual must prove three elements to obtain a remedy based on the tort of intrusion: (1) The intruder intended to intrude, (2) there was a reasonable expectation of privacy under the circumstances, and (3) the intrusion is substantial and therefore highly offensive to a reasonable person.

First, like other intentional torts, the intrusion cannot be accidental or unknown by the intruder. Although there is no requirement that the subject individual knows of the intrusion when it happened, the intruder must have known of the acts taken that caused the intrusion. For example, it might not be wrongful to read an e-mail or file attachment mistakenly sent to your e-mail client (computer program) if you reasonably believed the message was intended for you. However, a hacker's knowing use of a "sniffer" program to read files from another person's computer or while files are in transit over the network would clearly show an intent to intrude.

---

20. William L. Prosser, Privacy, *California Law Review* 48 (1960), 383.

The second element of intrusion considers the surrounding circumstances. In what contexts does society recognize that activities include a reasonable expectation of privacy? Most people expect that their activities at home hold a reasonable expectation for privacy. However, the expectation of privacy might be lost when an activity is done in clear and plain view by a passer-by. Typically, the inquiry focuses on whether the situation is open to view or closed to intrusion without the use of mechanical or electronic surveillance techniques. For example, activities visible on a public street, viewable in public areas of a private building, or easily monitored with standard radio receivers generally offer no expectation of privacy. These situations contrast with the intruder making an "informational breaking and entering" into spaces typically closed to casual view.

Although the tort of intrusion does not protect any particular "place," it does protect persons in particular types of places that society believes people should reasonably expect not to be under surveillance. An intrusion can occur when there is a physical trespass into private space, such as tapping telephones, opening mail, intercepting Internet communications, or using secret cameras or listening devices to surveil inside a home, personal vehicle, or office. However, an intrusion can be unreasonable even without a physical trespass. Trespass is a separate but related and sometimes overlapping tort. It is also a crime. Trespass involves an intentional, physical entry into another's real estate or the physical interference with another person's personal property. Trespass protects the exclusive right to use real property (e.g., land and buildings) or personal property (e.g., computer).

The third requirement is for the intrusion to be highly offensive to a reasonable person. This element assesses the seriousness of the intrusion, and some courts may require the intrusion to be outrageous. It is not a subjective test that simply asks whether the subject individual is offended, which should be presumed if a suit is brought. Instead, it is an objective test using the mythical person of ordinary sensibilities. It is probably often satisfied by the jury's collective sensibilities or by the judge's estimation of society's revulsion with the seriousness of the intrusion.

There is no requirement that an intrusion be published (disclosed to others); the wrongful activity is in the mere surveillance. All three of the other privacy torts and many other privacy rights prohibit particular uses of private data, such as publication or disclosure. The intrusion tort simply focuses on the earlier actions that intrude and not on the actual use of information discovered thereby. Although publication might be protected expression under the First Amendment if the story is newsworthy, "The First Amendment is not a license to trespass, to steal, or to intrude by electronic means into the precincts of another's home or office."[21] Subject individuals who give permission or consent to the intrusion cannot complain. Similarly, there is generally no wrongful intrusion claim for activities conducted in public view. However, the consent must be examined carefully, as an intruder gaining admittance under false pretenses would probably not have genuine consent. For example, it could be an intrusion or trespass for a Web site to access a user's hard drive to read cookies or other data without specific consent.

---

21. *Dietemann v. Time, Inc.*, 449 F.2d 245 (9th Cir., 1971).

PUBLIC DISCLOSURE OF PRIVATE FACTS

Section 652D of the *Restatement of the Law Second, Torts* has been called an extension of the tort of defamation. It prohibits only highly offensive and broad-based disclosures of highly embarrassing and **private facts** that are not newsworthy, when someone:

> *gives publicity to a matter concerning the private life of another . . . [if it] (a) would be highly offensive to a reasonable person, and (b) is not of legitimate concern to the public.*

The subject individual whose private facts are revealed is seldom successful. Courts must balance the media's First Amendment rights to exercise news judgment in determining the public's interest in the facts. Factors likely to excuse the publicity include (1) a long time passing between the events and the publicity, (2) the publicity is not simply tastelessly pandering, (3) society has a legitimate interest in the information, and (4) the impact is not shockingly harmful to the subject individual.

The publicity must be made to such a large group of the **public at large** that it would probably become public knowledge. Nevertheless, some cases find a violation if the main audience includes the subject individual's coworkers, family, neighbors, or members of her or his church or clubs. The facts must have been private before the wrongdoing, so publicity of information already in the public domain, information obtained legally, or information that was a matter of public record are not actionable. Community standards of what is "highly offensive to a reasonable person" are used to evaluate whether the publicity shocks the ordinary sense of decency or propriety. This privacy right has been most clearly applicable to the traditional news media (e.g., print, radio, TV), particularly to the tabloid, scandal, and gossip press. However, it may expand to include persons not a regular part of the press. For example, new forms of mass communication (e.g., Web site postings, chat rooms, bulletin boards) and databases of personal information (medical and credit histories) may become involved. These database matters are discussed later.

FALSE LIGHT

Section 652E of the *Restatement of the Law Second, Torts* provides for another privacy tort that closely resembles defamation. The **false light** tort prohibits making a false connection between a person and illegal, immoral, or embarrassing activity that causes injury to the subject individual. This tort is similar to private facts discussed previously. False light is triggered whenever someone gives:

> *publicity to a matter concerning another that places the other before the public in a false light . . . (a) . . . highly offensive to a reasonable person and (b) the actor had knowledge or acted in reckless disregard as to the falsity . . . and false light in which the other would be placed.*

It would be a false light violation to attribute to a subject individual false statements, authorship, or political views. Fictional dramatizations of identifiable, often famous people can be actionable under the false light tort if they falsely depict relationships, dialogue, thoughts, or activities. The elements include intentionally or recklessly making a connection between the subject individual and the untrue description. For example, a preliminary finding of false light was made in a magazine's publication of nude beach photographs of Brad Pitt with a former girlfriend because it implied his consent to the publication.[22]

In recent years, activity resembling false light has been recognizable in cyberspace. For example, Web sites falsely connect individuals to activities, and e-mail attachments often circulate that falsely depict famous people in caricatures or photographs modified to be insulting or falsely showing the subject individual in untrue or compromising situations. Some states now refuse to recognize the false light tort. Nevertheless, it may emerge as an important constraint on unreasonable personal attacks in e-mail and on Web sites.

MISAPPROPRIATION

The fourth traditional state common law privacy right is found in the *Restatement of the Law Second, Torts* in §652C. This **right of publicity** subjects to liability anyone who:

> *appropriates to his own use or benefit the name or likeness of another . . . to advertise the defendant's business or product, or for some similar purpose.*[23]

This privacy tort resembles a property right in one's own personality because it protects the subject individual's right to control the commercial exploitation of her or his own personal endorsement. As a practical matter, only celebrities have much commercial potential in their endorsement and public reputation. The right is also known as the **appropriation right** because it resembles the misappropriation right in IP law. The tort's impact is illustrated in a case enjoining the publication of a frontal nude drawing of Muhammed Ali, the famous heavyweight prizefighter:

> *The distinctive aspect of this common law right of publicity is that it recognizes the commercial value of the picture or representation of a prominent person or performer and protects his proprietary interest in the profitability of his public reputation or persona.*[24]

Although the media is a for-profit industry, it is not generally liable for misappropriation when pursuing its primary purpose of news gathering and reporting. Even parodies of famous public figures do not generally trigger misappropriation liability as long as the stories are newsworthy. This illustrates the **incidental use** doctrine, which uses the First Amendment to permit news reporting on a celebrity or even when the media touts its own accomplishments. Web posting of Howard Stern's nude buttocks was a protected incidental use because the Web site was devoted to his

---

22. *Pitt v. Playgirl*, 178 BC 503 (Cal.Sup.Ct., 1977).
23. *Restatement of the Law Second, Torts* in §652C and comment b.
24. *Ali v. Playgirl, Inc.*, 447 F.Supp. 723 (S.D.N.Y., 1978).

candidacy for the New York governorship.[25] However, the First Amendment defense has its limits when a media organization appropriates the celebrity's entire perform-ance, act, or exhibition under the pretext of news reporting.

The potential for misappropriation liability in on-line activity seems considerable. The migration of news services as well as audio and video entertainment to the Internet suggest that precedents from the traditional media will apply to on-line activity. For example, celebrity **look-alike** and **sound-alike** advertising is vulnerable to liability. Jacqueline Kennedy Onassis and Woody Allen won judgments against advertisers that used look-alike models. Bette Midler won damages against an ad agency for using a convincing impersonation of her voice, sung by her former back-up singer.[26]

The states differ on whether the misappropriation right survives the celebrity's death. For example, in some cases the celebrity's heirs can continue to enforce the property right for many years, up to 50 years in California. In other states, the right terminates at death, putting the celebrity's persona into the public domain for use by anyone. Finally, a few states permit suits by heirs only if the celebrity's persona was commercially exploited prior to death.

ELECTRONIC PRIVACY: COMPUTER, INTERNET, AND TELECOMMUNICATIONS

Much of the contemporary concern over privacy focuses on how greatly the Internet expands the amount of PII that can be captured, analyzed, and transferred onward. On-line privacy concerns may become the main focus for the privacy debate as more businesses use the Internet for record keeping and as they exploit the value of PII from on-line databases. The regulation of on-line privacy will probably involve applications of federal and state laws originally designed to regulate telephone pri-vacy, computer security, and secrecy of entertainment preferences. This section dis-cusses the convergence of various privacy laws in the on-line environment, including the special treatment of children's privacy. E-mail privacy is discussed later, in the employment privacy section.

PROFILING

Currently, the major objective in collecting clickstream and on-line behavior data is to permit the emerging network advertising industry to target banner advertisements to Web users. Targeting is intended to reduce marketing expenses and raise sales. Through the use of cookies, **Web bugs**,[27] and other emerging technologies, Web site operators and third-party firms can track Web users' browsing habits and product

---

25. *Stern v. Delphi Internet Services Corp.* 626 N.Y.S.2d 694 (N.Y.Sup.Ct., 1995).

26. *Midler v. Young & Rubicam*, 944 F.2d 909 (1991), *cert. denied* 503 U.S. 951 (1992).

27. Web bugs are tiny graphic image files embedded in a Web page, generally the same color as the background on which they are displayed, invisible to the naked eye, and detectable only by looking at the page's source code. The Web bug sends back considerable data to its home server: computer's IP address, the URL of the viewed page, the time of view-ing, the type of browser used, and the identification number of any cookie previously placed by that server.

interests. This PII is organized into dossiers that provide profiling services to advertisers, Web sites, and data aggregators. Sometimes the data are non-PII; the user is not identified by name, but the targeting of ads is still possible. The FTC's *Online Profiling: A Report to Congress* describes **profiling**:

[M]any of the banner ads displayed on Web pages are not selected and delivered by the Web site visited by a consumer, but by network advertising companies that manage and provide advertising for numerous unrelated Web sites. In general, these network advertising companies do not merely supply banner ads; they also gather data about the consumers who view their ads. Although the information gathered by network advertisers is often anonymous (i.e., the profiles are linked to the identification number of the advertising network's cookie on the consumer's computer rather than the name of a specific person), in some cases, the profiles derived from tracking consumers' activities on the Web are linked or merged with personally identifiable information. This consumer data can also be combined with data on the consumer's offline purchases, or information collected directly from consumers through surveys and registration forms.[28]

Inferences are drawn from these profiles in an attempt to predict consumer purchasing habits and tastes. This practice permits automatic, split-second decisions to deliver particular ads targeted to each different consumer's specific interests.

Cookies are small files that Web sites cause to be saved on a Web user's hard drive. They contain **values**, alphanumeric expressions that are sometimes encrypted as well as coded. Few users know when cookies are in use or how to interpret them. Cookie files are generally less than 4 Kb in size, up to the equivalent of a full typed page of characters. They typically identify the Web site URL (content) once visited, include a set date and an expiration date, often many years in the future. Cookies are usually sent back to the originating Web site or to a third party, such as DoubleClick, which supplies Web site tracking services. Some cookies are temporary; session cookies are deleted when the browser program closes because they are useful only during that session. For example, a cookie can prove a user is registered with rightful access to a secure Web site after the initial logon. It is argued that cookies are harmless to users' computers and cannot spread viruses, but this may not remain true. Also, cookies raise questions of trespass; few users grant permission to set cookies. For example, German law requires users' consent because setting cookies is considered an invasion of another's computer.[29]

ONLINE

Cookie demonstration
**http://www.privacy.
net/track/**

The FTC has taken the lead among all regulators in overseeing on-line privacy policies. The FTC has no general authority to prescribe privacy policies, require their posting, or assure compliance by Web sites or their partners. However, as discussed in later sections, the FTC has authority over privacy in both consumer finance and children's on-line activities. Nevertheless, the FTC Act gives the agency authority to prohibit unfair methods of competition and unfair or deceptive trade practices.

---

28. See http://www.ftc.gov/os/2000/07/onlineprofiling.htm.
29. Cookies are explained in detail at http://www.cookiecentral.com/.

UNSOLICITED COMMERCIAL E-MAIL: SPAM

Spam is an emerging area of privacy that resembles the intrusion tort because it arguably violates the right to be left alone. **Spam** is the e-mail version of mass distributions of direct marketing solicitations traditionally achieved by flyer, junk mail, or telemarketing calls. Spam may also be called **unsolicited commercial e-mail** (UCE). The rise in UCE volume and the controversy suggest that this marketing tool can be cost-effective. Indeed, there are low marginal costs to the sender of spam who expands an e-mail recipient list. However, consumers are responding negatively to these unwanted, annoying, and time-wasting solicitations. Spammers free-ride on the computer and communications capacity of ISPs,[30] which forces ISPs to add expensive Web servers, technicians, and bandwidth to accommodate the growing volume of spam. An ISP unable to handle spam could suffer a tarnished reputation when spam overloads crash their servers. Spam is triggering both litigation and legislation. Antispam laws that focus on fraud, trespass, hacking, or infringement are most likely valid. However, there may be Constitutional problems because the First Amendment freedom of speech and press and the commercial speech doctrine may protect some forms of spam. Also, the commerce clause may prohibit state antispam laws if they unduly burden interstate commerce.

Four federal laws can probably be adapted to prohibit some aspects of spam. First, the **Telephone Consumer Protection Act (TCPA)** regulates several phone telemarketing activities: (1) it prohibits automated dialing systems that charge the call to the receiving landline or wireless phone, (2) it prohibits fax flooding (unsolicited ads sent by fax), and (3) it gives consumers the right to be removed from telemarketing lists. The TCPA could be applied to e-mail spam, probably with recognition that phone, cable, and wireless networks are converging. Second, the **Computer Fraud and Abuse Act (CFAA)** provides for civil and criminal penalties for unauthorized access or molestation of protected computer systems. Spam is likely unlawful under CFAA provisions prohibiting intrusions into a protected computer system: (1) intentional access that causes damage; (2) sending commands, data, or software that causes damage; or (3) intentional fraudulent access to obtain something of value. At least two CFAA cases involved spam: *Hotmail v. Van$ Money Pie, Inc.*[31] (transmission of false e-mail addresses, resulting in a denial of service) and *AOL v. LCGM, Inc.*[32] (extraction of e-mail accounts to evade ISPs' spam-blocking software). The third federal law is **FTC Act §5**, prohibiting unfair and deceptive trade practices, which could apply to fraudulent, unsolicited e-mail spam. ReverseAuction.com settled FTC §5 charges that it violated an agreement with eBay by harvesting e-mail addresses and spamming e-mail recipients with the deceptive subject line "will EXPIRE soon."[33] Fourth, spam misrepresenting the sender's identity may violate the federal trademark law, the **Lanham Act,** for false designation of origin.

---

30. *Report to the Federal Trade Commission of the Ad-Hoc Working Group on Unsolicited Commercial Email* (July 1998) at http://www.cdt.org/spam.
31. 47 U.S.P.Q.2d (BNA) 1020 (N.D.Cal., 1998).
32. 46 F.Supp.2d 444 (E.D.Va., 1998).
33. *In re ReverseAuction.com* (Civ. Action No. 000032); see http://www.ftc.gov/opa/2000/01/reverse4.htm.

The states are cracking down on spam, although most state laws apply only to spam originating from within their state or destined into their states. One California law requires spam to include return addresses or toll-free numbers in the first message line so the recipient can opt out and get off the list. The subject line must include ADV to indicate the message is an ad. The Nevada law was the nation's first opt-out spam law. Another California law requires spammers to comply with ISPs' privacy policies and makes it criminal to falsify or impersonate the domain name of the spam sender, a form of **technical fraud**. The Washington and Virginia laws also prohibit this form of technical fraud. The law in Maryland criminalizes harassing or obscene e-mail.

Constitutional law and tort law are also important to the spam controversy. In *Cyber Promotions, Inc. v. AOL, Inc.*,[34] the ISP refused to deliver nearly 2 million UCE ads daily that Cyber Promotions attempted to send. In its refusal, AOL did not violate Cyber Promotions' First Amendment rights. Given that there are other communications channels available for ads, the AOL decision does not amount to state action blocking free speech. Spam may not always be advertising; sometimes it is political speech or just vindictive. Intel won an injunction against a former employee who sent 30,000 e-mails on six occasions to all Intel employees discussing the work environment. The spam constituted a trespass to chattels because the employee evaded Intel's e-mail controls. Consider the damage to Intel: If each employee spent an average of two minutes reading each of the six e-mails, the firm lost more than 1,000 hours of employee productivity.

TELECOMMUNICATIONS

Wiretapping, the interception and recording of telephone calls during transmission, is a major privacy intrusion. Under authority of the search and seizure provision of the Fourth Amendment, Congress passed the federal wiretap statute in 1968 as part of the **Omnibus Crime Patrol and Safe Streets Act**. Government, private parties, and employers are generally prohibited from wiretapping or recording oral communications. Exceptions permit wiretapping with either party's consent, employer monitoring "in the ordinary course of business" after notification of employees, national security and foreign intelligence matters, and for law enforcement under a court order. Unauthorized wiretapping carries criminal penalties. Evidence obtained from an unauthorized wiretap is *not* admissible at trial, and any further evidence discovered by leads obtained from an unauthorized wiretap is also inadmissible under the **fruit of the poisonous tree doctrine**.

Wiretapping warrants can be issued only by a judge upon the showing of probable cause when law enforcement demonstrates a reasonable probability that the wiretap will capture conversations related to criminal activity. These proceedings are **ex parte**; that is, the subject of the wiretap is not present, and the court must supervise the wiretapping. Clearly, the subject individual should not even know of the wiretap; otherwise, any information useful to the investigation is unlikely to be spoken over that phone line. Other laws may prohibit placing listening devices in homes or

---

34. 948 F.Supp. 436 (E.D.Pa. 1996).

offices to capture one side or all of phone conversations. For example, the FCC has a **phone rule** that prohibits the media from recording a phone call for broadcast without first notifying the caller of the recording.

The original federal wiretap law applied only to voice communications and not to the transmission or storage of computerized communications. As a result, Congress amended the wiretap law with the **Electronic Communications Privacy Act (ECPA)** in 1986 to expand the wiretapping provisions to wireless telephony (cellular) and e-mail communications. The ECPA has criminal penalties and civil remedies, including punitive damages. The ECPA prohibits unauthorized interception or disclosure of **electronic communications**, defined as:

> *any transfer of signs, signals, writing, images, sounds, data or intelligence of any nature transmitted in whole or part by wire, radio, electromagnetic, photoelectric or photooptical system.*

Therefore, the ECPA covers communications via pager, cellular and wireless telephony, browser requests, Internet downloads, chat room traffic, voice mail, and e-mails (including attachments) when transmitted by common carriers in interstate commerce. ISPs are prohibited from disclosing these to outsiders. There are prohibitions against **unlawful access to stored communications**—that is, probing into computer storage, such as RAM or disk drives, for information in source or destination computers or during transit while the communication in temporary intermediary storage such as on a server.

Exceptions under the ECPA allow some interception or access. An **intranet** or in-house system is not covered, and the wiretap exceptions mentioned previously also apply under the ECPA. An ISP can monitor its subscribers' electronic communications as necessary to provide ISP services (quality control) or protect the ISP's rights or property. **Parties to a communication** may collect, analyze, and disclose electronic communications. This provision presumably would permit a Web site's profiling activities about its visitors. Prior consent by either the sender or the recipient is a defense. However, it is uncertain whether the mere posting of a monitoring policy would suffice, without a clear consent using something like a click-wrap. Law enforcement must obtain a warrant to intercept transmissions or access information in storage. However, an ISP may disclose evidence of criminal activity it discovers if the monitoring is permitted by an exception.

Wireless devices are proliferating: cell phones, wireless Web connections, personal data assistants (PDAs), and intelligent transportation systems (ITS, in-vehicle information and toll payment systems). Some systems come equipped with global positioning system (GPS) capability that can determine location by triangulating from satellite signals. Another technology is increasingly used: Cellular service providers can use signal strength, triangulation, and other technologies to pinpoint the user's location within only a few meters. The **Wireless Communications and Public Safety Act of 1999 (WCPSA)** requires wireless carriers (cell phone companies) to capture location data of 911 emergency calls (E911) made by cell phones. This should help in the dispatch of emergency assistance (e.g., police, fire, ambulance, HazMat teams) more quickly and precisely than the haphazard experience of many emergency control centers. Although 911 calls are easily located by using caller ID systems on landlines, cellular E911 callers often cannot accurately describe their location, delaying the emergency response. For example, automated crash notification systems like GM's OnStar provide pinpoint location data.

Privacy fundamentalists are concerned that mobile location referencing could lead to constant monitoring of individuals' location and movements, with grave potential for privacy intrusions. As a result, the WCPSA added "location" to the list of **customer proprietary network information (CPNI)** that must be kept private by a telephone carrier. CPNI is now defined as:

> *information that relates to the quantity, technical configuration, type, destination,* location, *and amount of use of a telecommunications service subscribed to by any customer.*

CPNI may be used for emergency and billing purposes, but the customer must opt in to any resale of CPNI to third parties for marketing purposes. For example, electronic coupons could appear on a cell phone or PDA whenever the customer passed by the particular retailer accepting the coupon.

Two federal laws protect the privacy of video viewing habits. The **Cable Communications Policy Act of 1984 (CCPA)** requires that subscribers to cable TV services consent before PII is captured through the cable system, such as pay-per-view purchases or regular viewing habits. The CCPA prohibits disclosure of such PII and requires annual disclosures to subscribers about PII policies and their capture practices. Subscribers must have access to inspect and correct such records. PII about video rental and purchase habits was restricted by the **Video Privacy Protection Act of 1988 (VPPA)**. The VPPA is also known as the Bork bill because PII about Supreme Court nominee Robert Bork's viewing habits may have influenced his Senate confirmation. The VPPA requires a customer's consent before disclosing PII about video purchase or rental habits. The CCPA and VPPA could be applied to video entertainment delivery over the Internet.

CHILDREN'S ON-LINE PRIVACY

Congress passed the **Children's On-line Privacy Protection Act (COPPA)**, encouraged by the FTC's 1998 report criticizing self-regulation as ineffective.[35] COPPA charged the FTC to issue implementing regulations resembling the Fair Information Practices, which became effective in April 2000. PII of children under age 13 generally cannot be collected, used, or disclosed onward unless notice and opt-in parental consent is given. Web sites targeting children or Web sites that actually know they collect PII from children must comply. PII under COPPA includes first or last name, e-mail address, phone number, home address, ssn, product preferences, or personal interests when collected online. Notice must indicate what PII is collected and how it will be used or disclosed. The notice must also recite the COPPA requirements and detail **parental refusal rights,** a form of continuing opt out.

---

35. *Privacy Online: A Report to Congress* (June, 1998); see http://www.ftc.gov/reports/privacy3/index.htm.

Verifiable parental consent, an opt in, is COPPA's key feature. It is defined as:

reasonable efforts to ensure that before personal information is collected from a child, a parent of the child receives notice of the operator's information practices and consents to those practices.[36]

Initially, the FTC used a *sliding scale* to judge the sufficiency of consent, depending on how the operator uses the child's personal information. A less rigorous method of consent was required for PII used for internal purposes, such as parental e-mail and follow-up. However, a more reliable method of consent is required if the PII was disclosed onward to others because this raises the danger to children (e.g., credit card, postal mail, digital signature). New consent is required if the Web site materially changes its PII practices.

COPPA rules require access: Parents must be able to verify what PII has been collected and may revoke their consent and require the Web site to delete all PII collected. After revocation, the Web site may terminate the child's future Web site privileges. Parental consent is not required in a few instances, such as acquisition of an e-mail address for the child's one-time inquiry or the parent's name or e-mail address for consent purposes. Web sites are prohibited from refusing to permit participation to a child who does not provide additional PII that is unnecessary to participate (e.g., contest requirement to provide parent's credit card number). COPPA has substantive requirements for the content and format of children's privacy policies. At this writing, the FTC is certifying safe harbors: self-regulatory programs that will oversee industry guidelines to provide incentives and independently assess compliance.

FINANCIAL PRIVACY

Financial privacy has assumed major importance for many years. The United States probably has more experience with federal regulation of privacy in the reporting of credit histories than with privacy regulation in any other sector. Creditworthiness is judged by a **credit history**, data archived about a debtor's timely payments or payment defaults. This information is sold as consumer reports to lenders, insurers, prospective employers, and others to infer character and general reputation. Many people insist this information is relevant to decisions in employment, bonding, and insurance underwriting. Financial PII, or personally identifiable financial information (PIFI), about most individuals is increasingly available from confidential credit records and from publicly available court filings, mortgage records, personal property liens, and other sources. PIFI based on transaction history directly with a creditor is **experience information,** and information from all other sources is **nonexperience information**.

The principal piece of financial privacy legislation is the 1970 **Fair Credit Reporting Act (FCRA)**. It is intended to assure fairness in credit reports without

---

36. *How to Comply with the Children's Online Privacy Protection Rule: A Guide from the FTC, Direct Marketing Assn. and the Internet Alliance* (June 2000); see http://www.ftc.gov/bcp/conline/pubs/buspubs/coppa.htm.

unduly burdening the credit reporting system. More recently, financial privacy has taken on new urgency. Considerable PIFI has migrated onto computerized databases and may become accessible through telecommunications. The merger of financial institutions seems to promise the combination of each formerly separate firm's incomplete data into larger, comprehensive, and more valuable PIFI databases. New financial privacy concerns have led to the passage of various state financial privacy laws and the federal privacy provisions of **Gramm-Leach-Bliley Act (GLB)** in 1999. This section discusses how compliance with both laws is necessary under contemporary regulation.

FAIR CREDIT REPORTING ACT

A "good credit rating" is essential to get access to credit to finance a car, home, or business. The debtor has ultimate responsibility for good credit through personal discipline: by exercising restraint in borrowing, budgeting wisely, and making timely payments. Hundreds of small credit reporting agencies (credit bureaus) and a few huge financial information service firms (Equifax, TransUnion, Experian, TRW) sell creditworthiness reporting services to lenders, insurers, and prospective employers. These services include the investigation, archiving and reporting of PIFI concerning debtors. **Consumer reports,** also known as credit histories, are compiled from lender reports about the promptness and fullness of installment repayments on loans and credit cards. Credit reporting agencies also collect information about the reputation and character of debtors. The FCRA provides debtors with access to their credit histories on a limited basis, permitting them to correct mistakes in these reports. FCRA also requires the removal of obsolete information. For example, bankruptcies more than 14 years old and bad debt information more than 7 years old may not be included in a consumer report.

Any entity in interstate commerce that is regularly engaged in the collection or evaluation of consumer credit information provided to third parties must comply with the FCRA. Reports concerning transactions between the consumer and the reporter are not regulated. Credit reporting agencies must verify the accuracy of the information. If a consumer disputes information in an agency's files, whether or not that information has yet been reported, the agency must reinvestigate unless the consumer's dispute is frivolous. If the objectionable information is not deleted, consumers are entitled to include a brief statement of their version of the dispute. For example, if two consumers have the same name, but with different spellings (e.g., Johnson vs. Johnsen), an inaccurate report might be made. Either is permitted to include a statement in the files concerning this potential confusion. If adverse information on a consumer is not deleted from an agency's files, all reports on that consumer sent out from the agency must include the consumer's statement or an accurate abstract of it. The consumer may insist that the statement be given to anyone who received the adverse information within the prior two years for employment purposes or within the prior six months for other purposes.

The customers of credit reporting agencies are usually potential creditors, insurers, or employers. However, these users must have legitimate purposes to request a report. Reports may be legitimately supplied pursuant to a court order, on written request of the consumer, or to any entity reasonably expected to use the reports in making decisions on such matters as (1) the granting of consumer credit, (2) the issuance of insurance policies, (3) employment, (4) the granting of governmental licenses, or (5) other legitimate purposes. Many lenders request potential borrowers to give written authorization before credit histories are purchased.

There are strong principles of enforcement under FCRA and under some states' common law, as well as remedies for unconscionable conduct in credit investigations. The FTC may designate particular activities of violators as unfair and deceptive trade practices or issue cease and desist orders. Users who obtain information from credit reporting agencies under false pretenses may be criminally liable. For example, falsification of the prospective debtor's authorization for request of credit information is a federal crime, called pretexting. Credit reporting agencies that knowingly provide information for illegitimate purposes may also be held criminally liable, with fines of up to $5,000 and/or imprisonment for up to one year. Agencies that willfully or negligently violate the act may have civil liability for actual damages, reasonable attorney's fees, and court costs. Punitive damages may be assessed for willful violations.

Enforcement is also used to motivate PIFI security. Credit reporting agencies may be held liable for negligence if they do not install and maintain reasonable procedures to ensure the accuracy of reports and supply the reports only for legitimate purposes. A damaged consumer may also use the common law torts of defamation and invasion of privacy. Users, credit reporting agencies, and those who supply inaccurate information to credit reporting agencies may be held liable for damages if the information is false or violates the common law or other privacy rights. In the early 1990s, evidence surfaced that sloppy procedures at some credit reporting agencies showed individuals' records full of inaccuracies, causing damage to their prospects for credit, insurance, licenses, and employment. The FTC and 19 states' attorneys general settled charges with TRW based on allegations it sold sensitive data to junk mailers, permitted errors to recur, and inadequately investigated customer complaints. This settlement pressures other credit reporting agencies to adopt similar protections or risk further federal financial privacy regulation like the Gramm-Leach-Bliley Act.

GRAMM-LEACH-BLILEY ACT

The Gramm-Leach-Bliley Act (GLB, the Financial Modernization Act of 1999) was primarily intended to break down the separation between the three major sectors of financial services: commercial banking, investment banking, and insurance. GLB repealed a New Deal–era law—the Glass-Steagall Act—permitting a form of **universal banking** prevalent in most other industrialized nations. GLB signals an inevitable consolidation of financial service firms. It permits the merging firms to combine their separate financial PII into huge new databases containing customers' banking, brokerage, and insurance information. GLB required the major federal regulators of financial services to coordinate new privacy regulations to restrict the onward transfer of financial PII outside these affiliating firms. GLB requires security measures, notice, and opt-out consent.

Substantially identical GLB regulations have been issued by the FDIC, SEC, FTC, Federal Reserve Board, Office of Thrift Supervision, and Comptroller of the Currency. Each agency regulates a separate part of the financial services business. The precise definition of the **financial institutions** subject to the GLB financial privacy rules is unclear. Eventually, any firm regularly engaged in financial transactions could become subject to the GLB financial privacy rules. Initially, the financial service businesses regulated under GLB privacy rules include securities brokers, banks, thrifts, credit unions, check cashing services, retailers issuing credit cards, appraisers, vehicle lessors, check printers, tax preparers, investment advisers, mortgage brokers, trust services, and credit counselors. GLB authorizes the states to regulate privacy in the gap of federal regulation over the insurance industry, and states may enact stronger PIFI protections than does GLB.

GLB financial privacy applies whenever a customer inquires about or obtains a financial product for personal, family, or household purposes. GLB also applies to the resulting transaction data. Whether the financial PII is collected online or by traditional means is irrelevant. The PII can be collected either directly from the subject individual or from third parties. Financial institutions must develop privacy policies and notify customers when accounts are opened and annually thereafter. An opt-out consent must be offered for the customer to prevent onward transfer of financial PII. The exercise of opt-out must be reasonable: E-mail, Web site forms, checkoffs on paper forms, and toll-free numbers are probably reasonable but not requiring each customer to initiate the opt out by writing a letter. Before GLB, banks could sell their customers' "transactions and experience" financial PII data to third parties. Now, such sales are permissible only after adequate notice and as long as customers choose not to opt out. GLB further restricts third parties from redisclosing some of the PIFI they receive from a financial institution.

GLB does not require financial institutions to notify customers exactly how their financial PII will be used. Instead, GLB requires that the notice simply describe general categories of financial PII collected and disclosed and to whom it is disclosed. GLB does not require that customers have access to their financial PII. Financial PII may be shared freely and without any consent privilege among related affiliates of the financial services firm, such as a broker, bank, or insurer controlled by the same holding company. GLB critics expect that privacy bills will be introduced to close this loophole.

HEALTH CARE PRIVACY

Health care information may include a wide variety of diagnostic and treatment PII. These data often show the subject individual's former and present health condition (e.g., test results for blood pressure, HIV, biopsy). Such PII informs predictions about the physical condition and future health care costs of subject individuals and their families. Physicians cannot render effective diagnosis and treatment without much of the test data and prior record of treatments and responses. Health insurers must have truthful treatment information to accurately and efficiently make health care payments. These are immediate uses of health care information needed for the rendering of essential health care services, called **uses and disclosures for treatment, payment, and operations**.

Privacy fundamentalists warn that secondary uses of these data, called **uses and disclosures other than for treatment, payment, and operations**, are less valid. These secondary uses might include such things as a determination of those who should not be hired, insured, or treated. Most people would find public disclosure of such sensitive data repulsive. Imagine video replays of embarrassing surgery or public revelation of medical treatment history. Such exposure would be among the most basic attacks on human dignity. Indeed, the confidentiality of doctor-patient relations is among the most sacred of societal mores. The theory underlying confidential relationship privileges is that loss of this privacy through disclosure by PII databases will deter patients from seeking necessary medical treatment. Therefore, health care privacy is a fundamental human precept found in many state and federal laws. Of course, we all benefit from medical research that identifies cures or alleviates suffering. Secondary use of health care information is essential to the progress of medical science.

Congress passed the Health Insurance Portability and Accountability Act (HIPPA) in 1996 to permit freer movement of employees among the different health care insurance plans of different employers. HIPPA also restricts disclosure of health care PII by the medical profession, hospitals, health insurers, employers, and health care intermediaries. The health care PII issues were so contentious that it took nearly four years after HIPPA's passage for the Department of Health and Human Services (HHS) to finally issue the HIPPA privacy regulations in December 2000. These rules are extremely detailed and potentially costly to implement. HHS used estimates for implementation costs that ranged from $5 billion to $17 billion annually, with $9 billion to $21 billion in annual benefits. As with most potentially costly regulatory programs, the industry estimated the costs will be higher and the benefits lower.

HIPPA defines health care–related PII as **protected health information (PHI)** and restricts the data management and disclosure activities of several **covered entities**, including health care providers, plans, clearinghouses, HMOs, Preferred Provider Organizations (PPOs), and their affiliates. Oral, written, and electronic PHI are all covered. The general rule is that patients must give prior written consent—opt in—before PHI can be used for treatment or can be disclosed for other uses. The forms of consent are different in various contexts and are subject to highly technical requirements. It appears that covered entities in the health care industry can decline to provide services or payments unless patients give consent, except for emergency medical services. Patients have notice, access, and correction rights and may demand an accounting of disclosures made (date, recipient, brief description of PHI). Exceptions were created for obvious purposes: emergency treatments, imminent threats to public health, and some law enforcement and judicial uses. Conflicting state laws are largely preempted. The HIPPA regulations are being phased in until full implementation in 2004. There are strong security and enforcement provisions. For example, violations are punishable by civil and *criminal* penalties. At this writing a rule proposal from HHS would eliminate the consent requirement.

EMPLOYMENT AND WORKPLACE PRIVACY

Employers increasingly use tests and gather other PII to predict the performance of new hires and monitor existing employees. References and PII from former employers seem relevant. Information about individuals' lifestyles, habits, use of substances, and past behaviors could conceivably have a bearing on their honesty and prospects. However, many people view tests and background checks as excessive intrusion. Some tests have questionable validity (e.g., polygraph) on account of scientifically fallacious theories or slipshod testing procedures. The employment privacy controversy illustrates a growing tension between employers' stated needs and rights advocated by employees.

Many employers require interviewees to take batteries of tests, including psychological, medical, drug, intelligence, and skills tests. Psychological testing may reveal an applicant's work ethic, criminal tendencies, ability to work with others, performance under stress, and aptitude for leadership. Intelligence and skills tests can reveal knowledge and ability to perform necessary job tasks. Medical tests may reveal that the predisposition of an applicant or immediate family to certain diseases could require expensive treatment. For example, mandatory HIV testing for the AIDS virus is a controversial procedure disapproved by some courts.[37] Some employers may try to administer genetic testing, hoping to predict an applicant's honesty, criminal tendencies, or future burden for health care expense. The administration, management, and use of PII based on intrusive tests raise contentious public policy, legal, and privacy issues.

SUBSTANCE ABUSE

Employees' abuse of certain substances can adversely affect performance, productivity, health, and workplace safety. For example, tobacco use is strongly linked to lung cancer and emphysema. Whereas workplace smoking bans and hiring bans on smokers are probably legal, firing smokers may not be legitimate. Thousands of local ordinances and employer work rules regulate smoking. Similarly, alcohol and drug abuse can be directly related to jobsite accidents and public safety, as well as employees' diminished capacity and productivity. Many large firms have drug testing programs for prospective new hires, usually performed through urinalysis or the assay of hair samples.

Some firms monitor employee drug use. Drug testing poses numerous legal issues. Policies covering unionized employees must be negotiated with the union because testing is a term or condition of employment. Random drug testing of existing employees may not be permissible, with some exceptions for federal employees where there is "reasonable suspicion" or "probable cause" that drug abuse has impaired the employee's job performance. The justification for drug testing is clearest when the employee's job affects public safety, such as operators of dangerous

---

37. *Glover v. Easter Nebraska Community Office of Retardation*, 686 F.Supp. 243 (D.Neb. 1988).

equipment, transportation workers, pilots, train engineers, air traffic controllers, and bus drivers. The Drug-Free Workplace Act of 1988 requires private contractors supplying the federal government to establish and enforce drug-free policies, although the act requires neither drug testing nor rehabilitation services.

FEDERAL LIE DETECTOR PROHIBITIONS

The **Employee Polygraph Protection Act** prohibits most employers' use of lie detectors without a reasonable suspicion of losses caused by employees. A lie detector test may be conducted if the employer provides a written statement showing a reasonable suspicion that the employee had access to damaged or missing material and was involved in the matter. The questions must relate only to the alleged misconduct and may not be the only basis for an employee's dismissal. Employers may not retaliate against employees who refuse to take a lie detector test. Violators are subject to liability for punitive damages, civil fines, and attorney's fees. Some exemptions exist for governments, government defense contractors, drug producers, and security protection companies. The unreliability of polygraph PII makes the results generally inadmissible to prove guilt in a criminal trial.

WORKPLACE SURVEILLANCE AND E-MAIL PRIVACY

Workplace surveillance is nothing new. Laziness, disloyalty, and mistrust long have inspired close supervision. However, technological advances enable new and creative forms of secret surveillance. Many employers are expanding their privacy intrusions, which severely limits each employee's expectations of zones of privacy in the workplace.[38] Indeed, the business necessity exceptions to prohibitions on workplace wiretapping and on-line surveillance provide employers with a fairly strong basis for surveillance. On-line surveillance is generally permissible if the employer owns the networks and computers. The use of cameras and listening devices is also increasing.

These realities must be balanced with the widespread encouragement employees receive to explore the Internet generally or e-commerce sites specifically and to use computerized communications to achieve the firm's efficiency and competitiveness goals. Only recently have many employees acquired broadband Internet and high-speed e-mail access at their homes. Workplace access has been the predominant medium for most employees' on-line activity. There is an ongoing tension between two major forces. On one hand, there are workplace rules prohibiting unauthorized use of employer facilities (phone, e-mail, Internet) and the employer's increasing legal risks for employees' unlawful activities. On the other hand, employees apparently will make inevitable use of the employer facilities for at least some personal purposes. Lax enforcement of these policies expose employers to considerable liability (copyright infringement, pornography, defamation, privacy violations, discrimination). Legislation may be proposed to specifically prohibit harassing, obscene, or abusive e-mail. Overly stringent policies risk both absenteeism and employees

---

38. *Smyth v. Pillsbury Co.*, 914 F.Supp. 97 (E.D.Pa. 1996).

inevitably finding work-arounds, such as moving their on-line activities to personal wireless devices (pagers, cell phones, wireless Internet).

Employers generally lay claim to ownership of internal workplace computers, networks, and other communications facilities, which allows the employer to (1) maintain confidentiality of trade secrets and (2) prohibit personal uses of employer assets, often justifying closer surveillance. Any lingering doubts are eliminated with workplace rules. Employees must bind themselves to restrictions, often with a separate part of their employment contract, as introduced in Chapter 13. Privacy policies that are clearly communicated and rigorously followed reduce liability risks for the employer. It seems unlikely that wiretapping laws will protect the workplace privacy of employees. The ECPA's exceptions for workplace notice support the employer's surveillance of e-mail and Internet activity. However, smaller firms using public e-mail systems may risk liability under the ECPA for unlawful interception.

Yet, many people still mistakenly believe that e-mail and on-line activity are evanescent, remain unrecorded, are not intercepted, and can be easily disowned. Anonymous remailers can forward e-mail messages with the sender's identity stripped. However, as the world discovered in the Microsoft antitrust litigation, confidential and damaging e-mail from Bill Gates concerning competitive strategies is very difficult to erase. Both electronic and print copies too often proliferate. In litigation, it is now routine to subpoena print and electronic records during pretrial discovery. It may take some time for Internet newcomers and even seasoned e-mail users to recognize the permanence of their too often frank, hostile, or incriminating e-mails, as well as other records of their workplace Internet activities. Employer policies generally extend to prohibit unauthorized sharing of user IDs and passwords to access the firm's computers, either at the workplace or remotely by computer. By contrast, home e-mail and Internet activities are much more likely to maintain some protection under privacy law.

PRIVACY AND SELF-REGULATION

The United States will probably continue to try to supervise privacy policy with self-regulation rather than government regulation or private rights of action. The pioneers who developed the Internet generally despise legal regulation and often insist that the Internet can never be regulated. This position is becoming untenable and unrealistic. Nevertheless, many "netizens" are proponents of **netiquette**, an unofficial form of self-regulation that emphasizes courtesy, respect, and self-restraint. The success of netiquette should probably unclog bandwidth and avert over-regulation. Self-regulation enhances trust that may also avert more stringent regulation. Many firms realize the costly stakes if privacy policies are not forthcoming. Increasingly, firms' privacy efforts are more serious, and **chief privacy officers** are taking re sponsibility for compliance and coordinating the diverse, sectoral privacy problems for employee PII, financial PII, health care PHI, and their on-line presence. Self-regulation may be essential for firms dealing with the EU.

Industry may be able to avert more stringent privacy regulation with more objective self-regulation that is supplemented by industry associations and third parties.

Trade associations traditionally have served to mediate disputes with outsiders. When such programs build the trust of outsiders and prove to be objective, they can win the support of regulators and even the public.[39] For example, the Direct Marketing Association has created privacy guidelines and works closely with the FTC to assure compliance with the COPPA privacy regulations. Another approach is for independent third parties to establish guidelines and provide some verification that firms are compliant. For example, the Better Business Bureau has established BBBOnline, a code of on-line business practices and dispute resolution through arbitration. It is a form of **seal program** that is intended to raise the public's expectation of trust in the fairness of on-line privacy practices. The TRUSTe program is similar. The stakes are enormous: If self-regulation of privacy practices fails, more stringent legislation seems inevitable.

O N L I N E

http://www.truste.org
http://www.
bbbonline.org

Of course, effective self-regulation begins inside each firm. Privacy issues must be taken seriously and commitment made by the firm's leadership. Privacy policy making and enforcement should be an important organizational goal, perhaps managed by high-ranking form officer. Privacy policy making and implementation must be seen as important and revised as privacy developments unfold. Periodic privacy audits may be appropriate to assure that compliance and privacy practices are current. Most firms will have at least some employees who need privacy training to comply with privacy policies, privacy law, and society's evolving privacy expectations. Recall that the United States negotiated a safe harbor from the EU Data Directive that relies on self-regulatory programs.

---

39. *Self-Regulation and Privacy Online: A Report to Congress* (FTC, July 1999); see http://www.ftc.gov/os/1999/9907/pt071399.htm.

CHAPTER 14
INTERNET REGULATION

Before the Internet, individual and mass communications were made individually and in mass using face-to-face methods, print, and electronic means (mostly phone and broadcast). Freedom to communicate is an essential right given in the Bill of Rights; the First Amendment assures freedom of speech, press, and assembly. As discussed in Chapter 2, these freedoms are not limited to political expression but are also important for the proper functioning of commerce and the self-expression needed for true liberty.

Internet growth continues to suffer, at least in part, because of opposing visions of regulation. Early Internet adopters embraced a laissez-faire attitude. In their view, the Internet was a borderless new cyberspace that could not be tamed by traditional government means. The history of government political processes shows they are usually limited to influencing physical, geographic space. This Internet libertarianism truly reawakened the eighteenth- and nineteenth-century laissez-faire spirit on which much of America's public policies were originally built.

The Internet eventually encountered difficulties much like the nineteenth-century westward expansion that temporarily produced the Wild West. The prevailing conception of the role of law and order in this new space is changing. Now governments all over the world are trying to rein in abuses (hacking, fraud, stalking, theft, espionage, vandalism) that have become widespread. Nevertheless, cyberspace libertarians continued to argue that Internet regulation is impossible and largely ineffective.

Eventually, the defense of Internet laissez-faire shifted to another perspective: cost-benefit analysis. Cyberspace libertarians now argue that regulation will mute the efficiency and freedoms seemingly possible in unfettered cyberspace. They claim that governments will never understand cyberspace and too readily impose restrictions that dampen innovation and prevent e-commerce from achieving its efficiency and productivity promises. They perceive government to be largely incompetent and ignorant of the issues and capabilities of the Internet. Further, government enforcement will probably remain underfunded and unable to regulate as effectively as it has in traditional areas. Government regulators are unlikely to remain current in the technical capabilities necessary for effective and efficient regulation. From this standpoint, industry should embrace self-regulation as a means to achieve society's goals and avoid the draconian overregulation that too often follows scandal or catastrophe.

Many aspects of Internet regulation are covered elsewhere in this handbook. For example, criminal and tort liability, gambling and obscenity, the creation and defense of intellectual property rights, commercial law processes and safeguards, privacy, and monopolies were discussed in preceding chapters. This chapter discusses several remaining areas of Internet regulation: consumer protection, taxes, and telecommunications. First, the conceptual basis for regulation is presented. This theoretical framework developed during the industrialization of the nineteenth and twentieth centuries. Now, many aspects are adapting to cyberspace and e-commerce. Second, consumer protection, largely administered by the Federal Trade Commission (FTC) and the states, is discussed. Third, the highly controversial problem of Internet taxation is covered. Finally, the regulation of e-commerce infrastructure—telecommunications—is discussed.

CONCEPTUAL BASIS FOR BUSINESS REGULATION

Traditional business and e-commerce are both regulated by local, state, federal, and international governmental authorities. In addition, there is a trend toward private regulation by professional associations and self-regulatory organizations (SROs). This was not always so. Before the New Deal era, U.S. Supreme Court interpretations reinforced the historical U.S. preference for public policy decision making largely by the free market. This philosophy was founded on the colonists' contempt for the British crown's authoritarian rule and the economic restraint imposed by British mercantilism. Indeed, the Constitutional framers designed the Bill of Rights with broad social, political, and economic freedoms to encourage free markets and other libertarian fundamentals. These laissez-faire principles have limited the role of government in the economy and thereby minimized governmental intrusion on business. Even today, U.S. economic freedom stands in stark contrast to the pervasive intrusion of other governments into their national economies. Government decision making has historically prevailed throughout the world's developed and developing economies at most times in history. Provisions of the U.S. Constitution illustrate this preference. The contracts clause prohibited states from legislating to impair the obligations of contracts. Regulation can diminish the value of private property, so regulation is generally limited by the economic due process concept.

Adam Smith probably makes the best-known statement of this laissez-faire preference in his 1776 publication *The Wealth of Nations*. The "invisible hand" of capitalism is implemented through self-interest that "naturally" drives the market to optimize social welfare. Private property incentivizes risk and innovation as long as actors can retain the fruits of their effort (profits). Competition disciplines the participants to become efficient. New competitors are attracted when any endeavor makes abnormally high profits. The primary economic questions are answered with allocative efficiency: what is produced, how is it produced, who receives that production, and how production changes or maintains flexibility. Curiously, Adam Smith was a career British bureaucrat.

Adam Smith's model makes some assumptions similar to those in the perfect competition model: (1) There are numerous rational buyers and sellers in all markets, (2) all have perfect information, (3) no barriers restrict the entry of new firms into markets, (4) only standardized products are sold, and (5) no participant has market power (e.g., no monopoly power). The market "clears" for quantities and at prices that form an equilibrium. Adam Smith believed that government intrusion into such free markets was "unnatural." Therefore, there is only limited justification for government intervention. Smith saw only three legitimate governmental roles: (1) national defense, (2) administration of justice to preserve property rights and facilitate enforcement of transactions, and (3) establish public works or other public goods that are valuable throughout society but that private enterprise might neglect (e.g., roads, dams, parks). This section discusses some of the traditional market failure arguments and the regulatory programs that grew up to cure them.

MARKET FAILURES

Considerable real-world experience illustrates that Adam Smith had a simplistic view of markets. His assumptions seldom hold true in the real world, and markets often do not behave as predicted. Sometimes market inefficiencies or market failures occur. Market failures harm society's welfare because there is an injurious side to self-interest. For example, the side effects of pollution are often hidden, eventually harming society. Critics often justify government intervention to correct market failures through the tool of regulation. Some critics of a free market argue that competitive market systems cannot adequately address social problems. Therefore, the public's policy preferences are also focused through pluralistic democracy. Public consensus brings pressure through government to distribute income more equitably, conserve natural resources, eliminate discrimination, pursue nationalistic goals, and stabilize economic volatility.

Monopoly Power

The perfect competition model can allocate scarce resources efficiently only when no seller possesses monopoly power and no buyer possesses monopsony power. Monopolies are the antithesis of perfect competition. A monopolist has power to set high prices, reduce the quantity produced, and be slow to innovate. The result is an artificial equilibrium that gives the monopolist high monopoly profits and society a lower level of products. There is a dead-weight loss that transfers wealth from society to the monopolist. Monopolists can reinforce their monopoly power by thwarting competition—for example, by raising barriers to entry with patents, high fixed costs, or trade barriers.

Opponents of monopoly argue that regulatory policies should limit monopoly power and force the market back toward the benefits of competition. For example, antitrust laws are designed to correct for the market failure of monopolies. The "free trade" movement among nations serves a similar purpose. Trade barriers erect monopolistic barriers to entering foreign markets. They tend to preserve market power for each nation's domestic producers at the expense of more perfect competition.

In another form of monopolization, one or a few sellers supply less of scarce commodities than the market demands. The seller(s) can earn windfall profits that trigger political pressures to regulate or tax them if no particular skill or ingenuity was involved and the windfall profits are very large. For example, regulation may impose windfall profit taxes to transfer the windfall back to society from producers. After the Arab oil embargo raised energy prices nearly 20-fold during the 1970s, Congress regulated oil and gas pricing and taxed the oil industry's windfall profits. A similar theory leads to rationing scarce commodities during wartime and to price controls to control inflation. President Nixon imposed such a price control program in the early 1970s. Cornering a market in commodities by buying or tying up all the available supply is illegal under the commodities laws.

Monopsony is buyers' market power that creates unequal bargaining power. This problem is significant in the labor markets. Most employees have a weak bargaining position because they are dispersed and unconnected as individuals. Large employers thus have a monopsony—more accurately, oligopsony—power, to buy services. Employers' inherent bargaining advantage was particularly evident during the early industrial revolution. The inevitable reaction was the unionization movement, and it also inspired the more severe backlash of socialism and communism.

Natural Monopolies and Destructive Competition

An area of particular importance to e-commerce is natural monopolies. **Natural monopolies** are believed inevitable in some industries because monopoly is occasionally more efficient than competition. The theory is that industries with declining long-run average costs provide cheaper products with a monopoly than is possible with direct competition. For example, recall the discussion of network economics in Chapter 9. It seems foolish to have numerous competing utilities serving the same customers, each with duplicate physical distribution systems, such as electric wires or pipes for water, natural gas, or sewers. Utilities have high fixed costs to establish their generation capacity; to pay for the expenses of generation, pumping, and transport; and to create and maintain their distribution networks of miles of wires or pipe. These are natural monopolies like the winner-take-all philosophy underlying network industries today.

At the turn of the twentieth century, the fledgling electric power industry became a natural monopoly after experience with another market failure, **destructive competition**. Rampant price-cutting between competing electric utilities led to selling below cost. Eventually, most went bankrupt, leaving the lone survivor as an unregulated monopoly. Every state and most foreign nations adopted public utility rate regulation to permit the economies of scale that utilities need, along with avoiding costly duplication of their network capacities. Another example of destructive competition periodically plagues the U.S. airline industry. After deregulation in 1980, the airlines had more capacity than demand, so they began a period of destructive competition. Several U.S. airlines eventually went bankrupt.

Destructive competition causes an inefficient waste of societal resources. Competition in a natural monopoly requires competitors to duplicate their networks. None can offer prices as low as could a single monopolist. Therefore, the regulatory response is for government to grant an exclusive franchise creating the legal monopoly for each utility. State public utility commissions regulate prices and profits to avert the natural monopolist's tendency to raise price and cut output.

Natural monopolies are not perpetual. Over time, technology can eliminate the cost advantages of a natural monopoly. For example, deregulation of long-distance telephone service, local cellular phone service, and cable television occurred after competition became a more efficient way to discipline these markets than regulation. Also, the railroad's natural monopoly eventually disappeared as pipelines, motor transport, and airlines became more acceptable, reliable, and cost-effective.

Externalities

The pursuit of self-interest through competitive markets often produces side effects that affect others—negatively and positively. **Externalities** are by-products of an individual's economic activities that can impose costs and/or bestow benefits on others. Externalities are a form of market failure that economists define as any cost or benefit transfer of the activity that is not bargained for in the contractual exchange.

Pollution is a classic negative externality. Consider the manufacturing process that produces wastewater dumped into rivers and particulate and toxic gases released into the air. What are the manufacturer's natural incentives to control pollution? Abatement equipment is costly, and outsiders may be unable to discover or prove the pollution's source. If the polluter externalizes these costs on the environment, pollution harms the public. Polluters are **free riders** because others actually bear the costs of pollution in cleanup, disease, and lost productivity. Free markets encourage pollution when it is difficult to detect or the damage manifests slowly, such as a latent disease. Free riders take advantage by shifting the cleanup costs component of their production costs on to society as a disease or lower living standards.

As the pollution example suggests, many externalities are eventually discovered, triggering political pressure for regulation. Regulation and tax policies can address the market's failure to discipline the producers of negative externalities. Public policy sometimes encourages **positive externalities**, which are beneficial effects of economic activity. For example, many states and local governments use tax and industrial incentives to attract new industry that benefits local merchants, employment, the surrounding community, and the tax base for local governments.

There are critics of using externalities to justify regulation. Ronald Coase has suggested that bystanders may already be compensated for externalities through cheaper land purchases or higher wages for employees in dangerous industries. The costs of controlling externalities should be weighed against the benefits expected before society implements any costly regulatory policy.

Public Goods

Markets sometimes fail to provide certain types of goods or services. **Public goods** are the prime example, so government often provides them. Public goods are nonrival and typically underproduced by competitive forces. The additional or marginal cost of providing more public goods to an additional person is usually small. Also, it is difficult to exclude people from consuming them. For example, private enterprise is unlikely to provide the sea navigational assistance of a lighthouse. Ship owners, consumers, and suppliers share the benefit of safe and reliable trade, so government supplies lighthouse safety services. In general, government provides tax-financed public goods or regulation to cure the market's failure to supply them.

Garrett Hardin's famous narrative on the **Tragedy of the Commons** illustrates the public goods problem. Consider the capacity problem of the U.S. open range in the late 1800s. Each cattle rancher expanded his herd in order to raise his income. The public open range appeared to be in limitless supply, and feeding cattle there seemed costless. However, the range could not feed all the cattle as the number of ranchers and their herds grew. Eventually the forage grass was stripped away and did not regenerate, ranchers' herds were malnourished, and many cattle died off, bankrupting ranchers. Hardin commented, "Ruin is the destination toward which all men rush, each pursuing his own best interest in a society that believes in the freedom of the commons. Freedom in a commons brings ruin to all." Advocates of laissez-faire economics and libertarianism cite this "Tragedy" to justify converting public lands into private property and hold that individual ranchers are not likely to overgraze if they must personally bear the negative "wealth effects" of overusing land they own.

Can this same analysis be applied beyond land to other common things? How could air and water resources be cordoned off? Are these "commons" subject to a similar tragic destruction? Critics of pollution argue that air and water are public goods that must be regulated to avoid the "Tragedy." This debate reinforces the significance of distinguishing between private and public goods. Society has experimented with privatizing several previously public goods: (1) police and fire protection, (2) roads and turnpikes, (3) mail service, and (4) utilities. The governments of many nations still own their telephone service. There are few "pure" public goods because most goods and services have some aspect of rivalry or excludability. The "goods" listed in Exhibit 14.1 are often cited as public goods. Each has been "under-produced" by private enterprise at some time in history, so they became the subject of regulation or public financing.

Asymmetric Information

Free market economists predict the market will operate efficiently when buyers and sellers are well informed. Transactions entered without key information about the value of the products or the reliability of the other party may lead to **adverse selection**. Information is costly in the real world. Many market participants have

Exhibit 14.1 Potential Public Goods

Grain elevators	Airports	National defense	Waterworks
Docks and wharves	Train stations	Justice system	Utilities
Parks, public lands	Bus terminals	Public education	Public sanitation
Public markets	Roads and streets	Basic research	Fireworks displays
Locks and dams	Harbors	Public universities	Emergency service
Scenic views	Public broadcasting	Law enforcement	Mail services
Communications	Industrial policy	Civil defense	Public airwaves
Internet			

limited ability to effectively process the information they acquire. Further, parties have an incentive to hide critical information. For example, employees often have incomplete information about workplace hazards or pollution. With better information, employees might demand higher wages, bargain for safety and health protections, or pressure politicians for enhanced safety regulations. Imperfect information is the reality of most markets. Political pressures for disclosure regulations result, such as the food and drug labeling laws and the securities and franchising laws. These regulations seek to improve information and avoid adverse selection.

EVALUATING REGULATORY JUSTIFICATIONS

Regulatory programs usually result from social and political pressures to cure market failure. Such regulatory programs are always evaluated by value judgments about the **fairness** or the redistribution of income, but regulation can also be evaluated by economic analysis. **Economic efficiency** is cited to justify regulations that arguably reduce the waste of societal resources for a given level of economic activity. **Pareto optimality** is another measure of regulatory success. Under this model, a regulation or any other action produces optimal efficiency when it causes society, as a whole, to become better off, while no one is made worse off. Pareto efficiency is used to protect some faction of the economy from carrying the whole burden of the change.

Few regulatory programs are based on a single justification. Sometimes the market failure explanation is weak, but the political pressures are strong and persistent. In other instances, a regulatory program may be rationalized as correcting multiple market failures. For example, product liability laws attempt to correct the market's failure to supply consumers with more perfect information about products. Product liability laws can be explained as a method to prevent manufacturers from externalizing their costs of defective design or negligent production techniques.

The regulatory programs discussed throughout this book should be evaluated with market failure criteria. Pressures to regulate e-commerce and the Internet should also be subjected to these analyses. Consider the major regulatory issues of cyberspace mentioned in this and previous chapters: obscenity, privacy, monopolization, law enforcement, Internet communications infrastructure, and the expansion of intellectual property rights. Each area should be examined under this law and by economics analysis to aid public policy making and guide regulators to make effective and least costly regulations.

CONSUMER PROTECTION

Before the 1930s, there was little comprehensive consumer protection regulation. Only the common law contract and tort principles of misrepresentation, warranty, and interference with economic relations provided any legal protection. However, they were insufficient, and Congress expanded the regulatory powers of the **Federal Trade Commission (FTC)** in 1938. The FTC directs much of its energy toward product marketing, where evidence has mounted that some sellers take advantage of unsophisticated buyers and fail to admit their products' shortcomings. As some industries became known for their abusive practices, pressures to legislate eventually addressed these abuses. This section examines the FTC's consumer protection regulatory powers over deceptive advertising and unfair and deceptive trade practices.

THE FEDERAL TRADE COMMISSION

The FTC is an independent regulatory agency with five commissioners appointed by the president and confirmed by the Senate. There must be political balance on the FTC, with no more than three members from any one political party. The FTC is entrusted by Congress to promote a competitive business environment. Originally created to enforce the antitrust laws in 1914 under the FTC Act (discussed in Chapter 12), the FTC has had consumer protection authority since the Wheeler-Lea Act of 1938. The FTC's powers in consumer finance under the Truth in Lending and Consumer Credit Protection Act were discussed in Chapter 13.

There is considerable overlap between the FTC's consumer protection function and its powers to promote competition. The FTC fosters competition by monitoring business practices and setting policies for consumer protection such as prohibiting practices found to be deceptive that might divert sales from honest competitors. Deceptive advertisements distort consumers' information, making their purchasing decisions inferior. Therefore, deceptive advertising undermines the goals of perfect competition. The FTC's interpretation of this mission undergoes change as the political makeup of the commissioners changes. For example, the FTC's vigorous industrywide enforcement of the 1960s and 1970s gave way to a restrained case-by-case approach in the 1980s, and then stricter enforcement returned in the mid-1990s.

The FTC also has the power to prosecute violations of §5 of the FTC Act, which prohibits unfair methods of competition and unfair or deceptive trade practices. The courts have interpreted trade practices to be *unfair* if they offend established public policy and are immoral, unethical, oppressive, unscrupulous, or apt to substantially injure consumers. FTC interpretations may be different from those of the courts, reflecting the prevailing ideology of the FTC and the judiciary. Trade practices are usually found "deceptive" if they *tend to deceive* the consumer, even if no actual deception is proved.

FTC Powers

The FTC exercises several powers that facilitate enforcement of the consumer protection laws. The FTC defines unfair and deceptive trade practices by issuing **trade regulation rules,** which have the force of law. These rules prohibit deceptive activity in one or more industries. For example, there are trade regulation rules that address abuses in door-to-door sales, bait-and-switch sales tactics, direct marketing schemes, and used car sales. The FTC also may issue **advisory opinions** to individual firms seeking to avoid charges of unfair or deceptive trade practices in their proposed activities. More comprehensive advice is sometimes available through **industry guides** that address the trade practices of an entire industry. FTC advisory opinions and industry guides do not bind the courts, but there is often deference to the FTC's expertise. Of course, these policy statements may be amended later by the FTC itself. Influential members of President George W. Bush's administration have actively sought to stop federal agencies from issuing such guidelines as part of a deregulation effort originally started in the 1980s by his father, George H. W. Bush, then vice president under Ronald Reagan.

Some industries are exempt from FTC regulation if they are regulated by another federal, state, or local agency (e.g., public utilities, securities). A few industries, such as food and consumer credit, are regulated by both the FTC and another agency. For example, the FTC and the Food and Drug Administration (FDA) have overlapping jurisdiction over food labeling and food ads. The two agencies are beginning to cooperate to avoid costly and conflicting regulations. The FTC can share its investigatory files with other agencies such as the Justice Department to trigger a criminal prosecution.

FTC Consumer Protection Remedies

FTC investigations and enforcement actions are initiated after consumers, business competitors, administrative agencies, or Congress complains. The FTC also initiates its own investigations. The FTC's Bureau of Consumer Protection monitors consumer sales practices to obtain evidence of potential violations. The FTC may then conduct an investigation and gather sufficient evidence to bring an enforcement action. The FTC may issue **cease and desist orders** or settle charges with a **consent decree,** without going to trial, in which the defendants agree to eliminate the deception.

The FTC may also issue an **affirmative disclosure order** requiring an offender to provide information in future ads. A **corrective advertising order** may be issued to require new ads to correct past misleading ads. A **multiple product order** prohibits future deceptive advertising by a firm with a history of false advertising in selling any of its products. The FTC has also successfully sought rescission of contracts, returns of property, refunds of the purchase price, and damage payments to consumers. In one case, the FTC settled charges of false ad claims by requiring a health product retailer to fund health research.

If the business under investigation disputes the charges, an administrative hearing may be held before an administrative law judge (ALJ). Appeals from the ALJ's decision go to the FTC commissioners. Appeals then go to the U.S. Circuit Courts of Appeals for judicial review. Violators of FTC regulations or cease and desist orders may be fined up to $10,000 per violation per day. Although the FTC's powers are generally intended to be preventive, the power to fine can add up. For example, Reader's Digest was fined $7.75 million for violating an FTC order.[1] However, a 1994 report indicated that since 1980 the FTC had collected only about one-third of the nearly $363 million in fines for advertising or marketing fraud it has levied on 187 companies.

ADVERTISING REGULATION

The advertising of consumer products has contributed to the tremendous industrial expansion of the twentieth century. A legitimate function of advertising is to inform consumers and eliminate information asymmetries. However, advertising and promotional activities are less legitimate when the advertising is deceptive, false, or misleading. The U.S. Constitution protects free speech against government censorship unless the censorship is very closely related to a compelling governmental purpose, such as the prevention of fraud, defamation, riots, or subversive activities. Although political speech is given the greatest protection, **commercial speech** such as advertising is well protected. Information is essential to the efficient operation of markets. Advertising can be regulated under the common law and by the FTC for consumer protection purposes.

Regulation addresses advertising in all its traditional forms as well as many new forms. Consumer protections discussed in this chapter apply to print, electronic media, billboard, TV, and radio forms, as well as to newer forms such as ads on commercial Web sites, banner ads, bulletin boards, chat sites, e-mail, and spam ads. Some aspects of advertising regulation are adapted to the special circumstances of the Internet.

Common Law Remedies

The common law remedies for victims of deceptive advertising are generally ineffective. For example, a seller's advertisement is seldom treated as an offer. If the product's actual specifications, its price at the store, or its characteristics as delivered differ from the advertised specifications, there is no breach of contract because no enforceable contract had been made. Warranty liability may arise from advertising and other language in the sales materials or contract. Warranties may also become the basis for a consumer's complaint about deception.

The tort of deceit or fraud may exist if an advertiser knowingly makes material misrepresentations of fact on which an injured purchaser justifiably relies. Protection of trademarks and trade names exists under both common law and federal statutes. If an advertiser makes untrue statements in comparing its goods with the goods of a competitor, the defamed competitor may sue for trade libel, slander, or disparagement, as discussed in Chapter 7.

---

1. *United States v. Reader' Digest Ass'n, Inc.*, 662 F.2d 995 (3d Cir.1981).

Deceptive Advertising

Congress found the common law remedies were ineffective to protect consumers so it passed the Wheeler-Lea Act in 1938 to deal with **deceptive advertising**. The FTC is authorized to prosecute unfair or deceptive trade practices in advertising. To measure deception, the FTC uses a deception policy that requires assessment of ads by the total impression created in the consumer's mind. To be deceptive, an ad must make a *misrepresentation or omission* in its communication to consumers. The misleading statement need have only a capacity to mislead consumers about some *material* aspect of the product. This test is interpreted by using a hypothetical "typical ordinary consumer . . . who is acting reasonably under the circumstances." It is not necessary to prove either that the advertiser intended to deceive or that actual deception occurred. However, the deceptiveness must be so strong that a reasonable person, not just a gullible one, would be deceived. Courts have admitted survey evidence to show how a reasonable consumer might interpret an ad.

False or Unsubstantiated Claims

Ads are deceptive if patently false or if the claims are not supported by a reasonable basis in scientific evidence. Demonstrations must accurately depict the performance of the product advertised and illustrate some relevant or meaningful product attribute. Test results that create an impression of the product's superiority must be based on studies or surveys conducted scientifically. This means that clinical tests must be well controlled and use reasonable statistical inference. This is the **prior substantiation** rule: It requires that the evidence used in an ad must be gathered *before* the ads are run. FTC enforcement can require advertisers to submit substantiation.

Product performance claims about composition, durability, capacity, or endurance under adverse conditions must be true. For example, a dishwasher retailer was ordered to cease and desist from claiming that no prewashing was necessary.[2] Numerous sellers of nutritional and health products have been ordered to stop advertising false or unsubstantiated health improvement claims. Kraft was ordered to discontinue ads falsely suggesting its cheese slices had the same calcium content as five ounces of milk. Haagen-Dazs agreed to refrain from advertising that its frozen yogurt bars were 98% fat free because several flavors allegedly contained more than 2% fat, some averaging 8 to 12 grams of fat per serving.[3] The FTC prohibited Stouffer Foods from falsely advertising that Lean Cuisine was low in sodium.[4] The FTC order required Stouffer to compare its sodium content to established public guidelines for "low-sodium" and FDA "recommended daily allowances (RDA)." Now these are called "daily values."

Green Ads and Eco-Labeling

The so-called green ads targeting environmentally conscious consumers are susceptible to abuse. Ad claims such as "recyclable" or "biodegradable" are not well

---

2. *Sears, Roebuck & Co., v. FTC*, 676 F.2d 385 (9th Cir., 1982).
3. *In re Haagen-Dazs Co. Inc.*, FTC File 942-3028 (Nov. 7, 1994).
4. *Stouffer Foods Corp.*, FTC Docket 9250 (Aug. 6, 1993).

defined and subject to abuse because many consumers are swayed by the desire to satisfy their environmental responsibilities. The FTC worked with the EPA to issue voluntary environmental advertising guidelines in 1992, which were revised in 1998 and are now published in *Complying with the Environmental Marketing Guides*. For example, products labeled "recycled" must be made from 100% recycled materials; otherwise, it should state an accurate proportion of recycled material.

The green guidelines urge that claims be true and not meaningless. They discourage exaggerated environmental benefits of advertised products, and claims must be specific and substantiated like any other ad claim. In one FTC case, the manufacturer of a spray product was ordered to stop claiming it was environmentally safe because it contained an ozone depleting propellant. The manufacturer of a gasoline additive was ordered to stop claiming fuel economy improvements of "up to 15%" without significant evidence that actual consumers could regularly achieve such performance. There have been various experiments with **eco-labeling**, voluntary and mandatory. For example, some firms eco-label, touting environmental benefits of their products. In some other instances, governments have mandated eco-labeling requirements that would require products sold to follow particular environmental processes. They can erect trade barriers if the products are from nations that do not follow the eco-standards.

FTC Environmental
Marketing Compliance
**http://www.ftc.gov/
bcp/conline/pubs/
buspubs/greenguides.
htm**

Consumers in many nations have nationalistic pride that encourages them to purchase domestic products. For example, the South Koreans are actively discouraged from buying "luxury goods" produced abroad. Many U.S. manufacturers and retailers encourage consumers to "Buy American" or claim their goods are made in the USA. This has raised questions about the "domestic content" of goods. Wal-Mart's "Made in the USA" advertising program was subjected to national TV criticism after discovery that much of its apparel was foreign-made. Other products, such as sneakers and computers, touted as made in America are often just assembled in the United States from foreign-made components.

Most automobiles made by the Big Three U.S. manufacturers have at least some foreign content, and many are assembled in Canada or Mexico. The U.S. law requires window stickers on all new cars citing the precise "North American Content." There are similar domestic content labeling laws for apparel. The increasing globalization of the market may eventually curtail such claims unless more laws are passed that arbitrarily set some minimum measure for the "domestic value added" of goods with foreign content that would then permit ads claiming "Made in the USA." Other nations have similar domestic content laws.

FTC's domestic content
guidelines
**http://www.ftc.gov/os/
statutes/usajump.htm**

Puffing

Puffing is the seller's opinion or generalized commendation of value. Puffing is not a misrepresentation under contract law, nor does it form the basis for an express warranty. Puffing in ads is *not* generally considered deceptive by the FTC unless accompanied by more concrete but false statements about the product's characteristics or performance. Obviously false and exaggerated ad claims may not be illegal as puffing if reasonable consumers could easily see that a statement such as "faster than lightning" is an exaggeration.

Mockups

A **mockup** is a false demonstration to improve the appearance or effect of an ad. The mockup is deceptive if the viewer believes it represents the real thing. A mockup that fails to disclose important facts or clearly acknowledge that the demonstration is not genuine is an unfair or deceptive practice. For example, Volvo has an enviable and deserved reputation for safety. Its ad agency chose to tout the structural integrity and crashworthiness of Volvo cars in a staged mockup of a car-crushing event. The ad showed a Volvo surviving uncrushed as it was driven over by "big-wheel" four-wheel-drive vehicles in an arena while other brands were quickly and easily crushed. Volvo's ad agency could have cited extensive valid scientific evidence of Volvo's safety. However, the agency decided the repeated trials necessary to adequately catch the event on film would eventually crush even the Volvo. Later Volvo fired the ad agency when it was discovered the Volvo in the film was extensively reinforced to survive the many film "takes" necessary to shoot a successful commercial. This ad was a mockup because viewers were led to believe the Volvo in the ad was standard.

Colgate-Palmolive used a series of one-minute commercials allegedly showing that the use of Rapid Shave would enable a razor to "cut right through this tough, dry sandpaper." Actually, a mockup of loose sand applied to Plexiglas was used. Real sandpaper would require 80 minutes of soaking with shaving cream to soften enough to be shaved as shown. The U.S. Supreme Court acknowledged the FTC's expertise in determining the deceptiveness of ads and held: "We think it inconceivable that the ingenious advertising world would be unable to conform to the FTC's insistence that the public be not misinformed."[5]

Omissions and Half-Truths

Advertisers must also refrain from deception by disguising it with some truth that omits facts necessary for clarification. An **omission** or **half-truth** is deceptive if more information is necessary to keep the ad from being misleading. For example, the selective use of data, comments, or conclusions from scientific studies may be deceptive half-truths. The FTC ordered P. Lorillard to stop advertising that Old Gold cigarettes were lower in tar and nicotine than the six leading brands because the differences were statistically negligible. The ads cited selective data from a *Reader's Digest* article concluding Old Gold's lower tar and nicotine content was not meaningful for smokers' health. Only the article's most favorable portion was extracted. The more negative conclusion was omitted, creating an "entirely false and misleading impression" in the ad about the article's content and Old Gold's health impact.[6]

In some ads, a false impression is created about the seller's credentials, which is also a misleading omission.[7] For example, persons falsely appearing to be scientists

---

5. *FTC v. Colgate-Palmolive Co.*, 380 U.S. 374 (1965).
6. *P. Lorillard v. FTC*, 186 F.2d 52 (4th Cir., 1950).
7. *Erickson v. FTC*, 272 F.2d 385 (7th Cir., 1959).

or medical doctors are misleading half-truths. Misleading health claims can emerge from literal truths that withhold other important information. For example, the ad for a water purification device claimed to remove several contaminants but failed to mention it added another potentially hazardous chemical. Food ads claiming health benefits such as reduced heart disease from a product's low-fat or low-cholesterol content are misleading if they contain high sodium content, which is directly connected to heart disease.

Endorsements

The FTC has issued several guidelines for endorsements. Endorsements by sports figures, celebrities, or experts, such as those found in shaving, beer, and medical insurance commercials, should reflect the actual opinions of these people. An advertiser may use such an endorsement only while the celebrity actually uses the product. Ads appearing to be the endorsements of consumers must use actual consumers and not actors. By contrast, fictional dramatizations without endorsements may use unknown actors. When fictional, the actor need not have a heartfelt positive opinion of the product or actually use the product. Many responsible advertisers use disclaimers indicating the commercial is a fictional dramatization, although some such disclaimers are in small type or run across the TV or computer screen too fast for careful detection. False endorsements may trigger liability for fraud for the advertiser and for the celebrity.

Corrective Advertisements

When an advertiser makes misstatements in advertisements, the FTC assumes that the misconception may be durable, remaining in the consumer's mind for some time. Only further advertising of a similar magnitude, duration, and creativity can correct such "resilient" false impressions. In some cases, a court-approved consent decree requires the advertiser to conduct **corrective advertising** or **counteradvertising** to rebut the misleading claims of prior ads. The FTC has used corrective advertising orders since the well-known Listerine case, in which Warner-Lambert was ordered to conduct $10 million of new ads correcting its former claims that Listerine killed millions of "germs." The germs Listerine eliminated did not cause colds, even though reasonable consumers might interpret this from the ads. The FTC's power to order a corrective ad was upheld on appeal; the required ads stated: "Contrary to our prior advertising, Listerine will not help prevent colds or sore throats or lessen their severity."[8] Another manufacturer was ordered to run corrective ads for a year, admitting its products were not superior insulation to regular glass storm windows. In another case, Novartis claimed its product Doan's Pills were particularly effective against back pain and contained an ingredient not found in other over-the-counter analgesics. While literally true, the FTC found that consumers would mistakenly believe the product was superior to its competitors. Corrective ads were ordered and affirmed by the Court of Appeals.[9] The FTC's corrective ad standard appears in Exhibit 14.2.

---

8. *Warner-Lambert Co. v. FTC*, 562 F.2d 749 (D.C. Cir. 1977).
9. *Novartis Corp. v. FTC*, 223 F.3d 783 (D.C.Cir. 2000).

Exhibit 14.2 Corrective Advertising Standard

[I]f a deceptive advertisement has played a substantial role in creating or reinforcing in the public's mind a false and material belief that lives on after the false advertising ceases, there is clear and continuing injury to competition and to the consuming public as consumers continue to make purchasing decisions based on the false belief. Since this belief cannot be averted by merely requiring respondent to cease disseminating the advertisement, we may appropriately order respondent to take affirmative action designed to terminate the otherwise ill effects of the advertisement.

Comparative Ads and the Lanham Act

The FTC favors the recent trend toward scientifically verifiable comparative advertising because it encourages competition. The "Pepsi Challenge" blind taste tests were conducted over decades, using large random samples and performed nationwide by independent testing agents. Therefore, there is strong scientific validity to such consumer preference comparisons. However, not all comparative ads are as rigorous. Invalid comparisons may be false and deceptive, exposing the advertiser to damages under the common law tort of trade disparagement and for lost profits under §43(a) of the Lanham Act (federal trademark law). The disparaged competitor may sue if the comparison makes false or misleading statements of fact or misrepresentations about the nature, characteristics, geographic origin, or quality of a competitor's products, services, or commercial activities. The false statement must have a tendency to deceive a substantial segment of the intended audience, it must influence purchasing decisions, and it must be likely to injure the disparaged trademarked product.

Comparative ad cases under the Lanham Act illustrate that a false advertiser is subject to suit even if the competitor's precise product is not directly identified in the ad. It is enough if the advertiser misleads consumers about important features, such as a false statement about a computer monitor's compatibility with a new video standard.[10]

Packaging and Labeling

Congress has passed numerous consumer protection laws directly regulating product packaging and labeling. Generally, the law requires accuracy in labels. The **Fair Packaging and Labeling Act of 1966** provides for general labeling requirements. As increased packaging obscures the consumer's actual view of the product, accurate label descriptions become important for product evaluation. Labels must (1) identify the product; (2) identify the name and address of the manufacturer, packer, or distributor; and (3) list the quantity and serving size in a specific manner.

FTC rules require particular labeling of numerous diverse products. For example, accurate octane numbers must appear on gasoline pumps. There are numerous

---

10. *Princeton Graphics v. NEC Home Electronics*, 732 F.Supp. 1258 (S.D.N.Y. 1990).

additional federal and state labeling laws regulating wool products, cigarettes, flammable fabrics, textiles, poisons, food, drugs, and cosmetics. Many of these laws empower various agencies to regulate labeling or deceptive practices.

Internet and On-line Ad Regulation

The FTC issued guidelines in 2000 reaffirming that its advertising regulations apply to deceptive marketing online. These guidelines largely emphasize the principles discussed previously, applying them to on-line marketing. The FTC's ad rules apply to all advertising media, including the Internet. Key terms must be disclosed in a clear and conspicuous manner, and on-line customers often do not see everything on a full Web page. They may not click through or find disclaimer language that generally benefits the marketer. Therefore, forthright disclosure is even more critical online. Disclosures must be placed close to the web page areas where most consumers will view them, not in tiny type on another page. The type size must be large enough to be readily seen, moving features in the ad must not distract from the disclosure message, and disclosures unlikely to be readily seen may need to be repeated or made in multimedia (audio, video, text) to assure communication.

FTC Dot Com Disclosure
Guidance
**http://www.ftc.gov/
bcp/conline/pubs/
buspubs/dotcom/
index.html**

Web site designers may be held liable for unfair and deceptive ads. Since on-line ads have proliferated, the FTC has brought hundreds of enforcement actions against Web sites for violation of the ad rules. Examples include pyramid sales schemes, credit and investment scams, unfair auctions, health care swindles, Web site hijacking, and unauthorized credit card transactions.

TRADE REGULATION RULES AND DECEPTIVE TRADE PRACTICES

The FTC may use the notice and comment rule-making procedure to issue consumer protection regulations. The FTC's proposed regulations are first published in the *Federal Register*, which permits affected parties to comment. Comments can influence the FTC to change the final rule. The following sections discuss some of the more significant FTC trade regulation rules issued under §18 of the FTC Act and as deceptive practices challenged under §5. One such rule was discussed in Chapter 9, the FTC's **holder in due course disclosure rule**, issued in 1976, which suspends the HDC rule from the UCC for individual consumer purchases or leases of goods and services. This rule requires that any consumer credit contract must contain a bold-face clause permitting the consumer to stop paying on debts if the seller committed fraud or breached the contract or if the goods are defective.

Bait and Switch

Some sellers stock a limited supply of inexpensive "loss leader" merchandise as "bait" to lure potential buyers into the store, hoping that sales personnel can "switch" them into purchasing products with higher profit margins. This **bait-and-**

switch tactic violates FTC guidelines if a salesperson refuses to show the cheaper merchandise, represents that the bait will be out of stock for a long time, holds an inadequate supply of the bait, or is following instructions to actively switch customers to alternative goods. For example, it is illegal to hold insufficient inventory of an inexpensive color TV advertised and then instruct salespeople to encourage buyers to switch to more expensive models. Ads for cheap eyeglass frames often result in purchases of more expensive "designer" frames.

Direct Marketing and Mail Order

The FTC promulgated a 30-day rule in 1975 for telephone and mail order. The rule prohibits sellers from soliciting orders unless the goods can be shipped within 30 days after receiving a prepaid order. Sellers cannot sit on orders, must clearly state expected shipping dates, and must ship promptly. If there are unanticipated delays, the seller may (1) cancel orders and refund payments or (2) notify consumers of the delay and provide an option of shipment or cancellation. High-quality mail order retailers wait until after shipment to charge customers' credit cards, notify customers of their order's status, and remind customers of their alternatives. Many states impose similar mail order rules. In 1993, the rule was extended to include orders transmitted by computer, fax, or other means using telephone lines. A U.S. Postal Service rule makes unsolicited merchandise sent by mail a gift to the recipient and a penalty to the sender.

Door-to-Door Sales

The FTC imposes a **cooling-off period** for door-to-door sales that gives consumers an opportunity to reassess purchases for three days following sales over $25. The rule counteracts the high-pressure tactics often used to sell such merchandise as vacuum cleaners and encyclopedias. Door-to-door sales contracts must warn the buyer that the cancellation right exists and provide a cancellation form. Several types of sales are exempt: real estate, insurance, securities or commodities from a registered broker, and most sales solicited by the buyer. Some state laws also apply to door-to-door sales, including those exempt under the FTC rule.

Telemarketing

The "boiler room" technique used in high-pressure securities marketing moved into the consumer market as telemarketing expenses dropped and database mining for private information made target marketing feasible (see Chapter 13). **Telemarketing** consists of several marketing techniques: unsolicited sales calls, fax contacts, and even toll-free inquiries or orders initiated by consumers. Telemarketing can impose costs on consumers because the calls divert consumer time (during the dinner hour), tie up the recipient's line, and consume the consumer's fax capacity and consumables (paper, ink). Spam e-mail was discussed in Chapter 13.

Congress passed two laws to address consumer dissatisfaction with the annoyance of telemarketing. First, the **Telephone Consumer Protection Act of 1991**, discussed later, authorizes the Federal Communications Commission (FCC) to regulate telemarketing.

The TCPA prohibits automatic dialing systems and prerecorded messages. The call recipient must be able to effectively disconnect by hanging up. Senders must get permission before sending fax ads. The TCPA gives consumers a private right of action in state court against telemarketers for the greater of their actual damages or $500 for each violation. Marketers have been generally unsuccessful at challenging the TCPA on First Amendment grounds, as discussed later. Second, the **Telemarketing and Consumer Fraud and Abuse Act of 1994** empowers the FTC to regulate the content of telemarketing calls. The FTC has rulemaking authority and may enforce this law against telemarketers. In 1995, the FTC promulgated its telemarketing sales rule that requires several disclosures by telemarketers: The caller must identify himself or herself and the product offered, the recipient must be informed the call is for sales purposes, misrepresentation is prohibited, the total cost of the product and special contractual terms must be disclosed, and calls may be made only after 8 A.M. and before 9 P.M. Many state telemarketing laws are even more stringent. This rule is inapplicable to transactions made entirely using the Internet. Several key industries are exempt: financial institutions, telecommunications carriers, airlines, and nonprofits. The FTC may seek injunctions and civil penalties up to $10,000 per violation.

Other Trade Regulations

There are several other FTC trade regulation rules. A used car rule requires a window sticker or buyer's guide on used cars clearly stating the warranties, whether the car is sold "as is," estimated repair costs after the sale, suggesting an independent mechanical inspection, and reminding consumers that the dealer's oral promises are difficult to prove. The insulation rule requires standardized testing and disclosure of home insulation "R-value" to facilitate comparison-shopping. The funeral rule recognizes consumers are seldom careful comparison shoppers at the time of a loved one's death. It requires itemized price lists and provides consumer information about various funeral services in the FTC Funeral Guide. Other rules have addressed unfair and deceptive trade practices in the following industries: correspondence schools, hearing aid sales, automobile repairs and estimates, entertainment clubs, health spas, dance studios, insurance, and home improvement. Medical services are under investigation at this writing. For example, there is evidence that excessive and often unnecessary hysterectomies are performed.

Pay-per-call services, such as 900 numbers, charge the caller's phone bill largely for "information services" provided by the call recipient. Some considerable abuses, particularly dial-a-porn targeting youth, caused the FTC to impose a **900-Number Rule**. The call recipient must identify herself or himself and the cost of the call early in the call to give the caller an opportunity to hang up without incurring a charge. Further, 900 services may not target children under 12 unless for bona fide educational services, and contests or sweepstakes must disclose additional information.

The FTC's early cases focused mostly on "deceptive" trade practices. Increasingly, it also focuses on unfairness, originally defined as immoral, unethical, oppressive, or unscrupulous activity that violates fairness and causes substantial consumer injury. Later refinements to *unfairness* include conduct causing substantial and unavoidable consumer injury not outweighed by consumer benefits or the competition.

STATE LAWS PROHIBITING UNFAIR COMPETITION

States have legislation paralleling the FTC Act, the so-called **Mini-FTC Acts**. These laws typically empower the state attorney general or a special administrative agency to enforce prohibitions against unfair and deceptive trade practices and unfair methods of competition. Several states permit private rights of action by damaged consumers for damages, treble damages, punitive damages, attorney's fees, injunctions, rescission of contracts, and class action suits. State attorneys general may seek injunctions, restitution, civil penalties, criminal punishment, and other remedies. One of the most notable developments in the 1980s was the coordination of enforcement efforts by various states' attorneys general through their National Association of Attorneys General organization. Various other state statutes regulate particular aspects of consumer fraud, such as lemon laws, door-to-door sales, and use of plain English in insurance contracts. Business must remain aware of this expanding area of federal and state consumer protection.

INTERNET TAXATION

"The power to tax is the power to destroy."[11] This famous quote illustrates the pervasiveness of power held by the federal, state, and local government. Most U.S. taxes are levied on retail transactions, property, and income. Many other nations have huge social benefit programs funded by high-level consumption and income taxes. By contrast, a major impetus for U.S. independence from England was strong feelings about the fairness and scope of the tax system (e.g., Boston Tea Party).

There is widespread concern that the states and local taxing authorities may specifically target new taxes to e-commerce and Internet access. Opponents are concerned that such new taxes create uncertainties, and inconsistencies among them could stifle e-commerce development. This tax controversy is really part of the Constitutional question over the connection between a governmental unit and a particular regulated activity. It is the classic issue of jurisdiction constrained by Constitutional principles, as introduced in Chapters 1 and 2, and e-commerce increases the opportunities for tax avoidance, making e-commerce taxation hotly controversial. This section explores the Constitutional and definitional difficulties in applying traditional taxes to e-commerce. Particular emphasis is given to the multi-jurisdictional aspects of taxation and potential new forms of taxation.

COMPLEXITY OF TAXATION OF E-COMMERCE

Tax compliance is a highly complex matter consuming the full-time attention of legions of accountants and lawyers. Individuals and businesses must be constantly aware of their tax liability, and this is much more than the annual income tax ritual. Internet activity poses some tax definitional questions and reopens some strong controversies

---

11. *McCulloch v. Maryland*, 17 U.S. 316 (1819) (Chief Justice Marshall's oft quoted passage).

over taxation. Taxation of traditional commerce and e-commerce can occur in numerous ways, and the various levels and units of government should be expected to use existing taxes aggressively, as well as search for new forms of tax on nearly any identifiable aspect of Internet use. In the United States, much more than in most other nations, the forms of tax and its scope are constrained by two major institutions: the U.S. Constitution and the political legitimacy of particular taxes and the government programs they fund.

Types of Taxes

There are three basic forms of taxation. First, income taxes are levied on individuals, corporations, and other business entities by municipalities, states, and the federal government. Taxable income is generally defined as gross receipts net of allowable expense deductions. There is considerable complexity, particularly in the federal income tax, over the treatment of different types of income, such as salary, business profits, capital gains, royalties, and rents. Also important are choices among accounting treatments used to determine deductions, such as amortization, depreciation, ordinary and necessary expenses, and capitalization.

Property taxes are levied on the owners or lessees of property, usually levied on one day each year—tax day. Real estate taxes levied by school districts, counties, municipalities, and states are the primary method of financing public education. Personal property taxes on vehicles and intangibles taxes on investment securities are additional examples. Some states levy severance taxes on mining and petroleum extraction.

Taxes on transactions are also quite common. States and municipalities levy sales and use taxes, mostly on consumer purchases. State and federal taxes are levied on the sale of fuels to fund road building and maintenance. There are state and federal taxes on sales of alcohol, tobacco, and firearms, as well as excise taxes on certain luxury goods. Transfer taxes are levied on real estate and securities transactions. Most forms of taxes that yield significant revenue can be classified as income, property, or transaction. There are also a few additional types of tax that combine some aspects of these three main types of tax, such as the estate, gift, and inheritance taxes and tariffs on international trade.

Several existing forms of tax either already apply or could be made to apply to Internet activity. Most centrally, e-commerce produces income that can be taxed by the federal government. However, the imposition of state or local income taxes could be more problematic for particular Internet businesses that have uncertain "tax domiciles." Property taxes may be less significant for e-commerce than for traditional bricks-and-mortar industries. For example, virtual businesses with few major facilities and just-in-time inventories may have few assets to tax. However, such pure-play dot.coms are probably less significant today than are the hybrid businesses with both traditional and e-commerce presence. These converging firms have property tax liabilities that are already well established.

The most controversial e-commerce taxes are sales and use taxes on purchases made over the Internet. Sales taxes are transaction taxes applicable generally to consumer sales of most goods. Several major classifications of exemptions vary widely by state. For example, groceries and clothing are exempt in Pennsylvania and New Jersey, and most states exempt newspapers and some services. States have been generally unsuccessful in requiring out-of-state vendors to collect and remit their sales or use taxes. This traditionally left a major loophole for phone and mail order businesses that now appears similarly significant for out-of-state e-commerce firms. Businesses that sell at a distance or directly to consumers from out of state do not generally collect or remit sales and use taxes. However, distance sellers generally must charge separately for shipping and handling. This difference creates a distinct "advantage" for distance sellers when the goods are small, light, and high value. The advantage diminishes when the goods are bulky, heavy, and low value. For example, local retailers generally do not charge shipping and handling but must collect and remit sales tax. Mail, phone, and Internet businesses generally charge shipping and handling but do not collect and remit sales and use taxes. Mail, phone, and Internet sellers have an advantage for certain products such as small and expensive electronics and jewelry.

Several other taxes affect e-commerce. The federal telecommunications tax is a form of excise tax that was traditionally levied only on "luxury" items. Increasingly, excise taxes cover items generally considered "quasi-necessities." State and local sales tax may also apply to telecommunication services. Sometimes local property taxes are levied at higher rates on some types of business, such as service industries or utilities. Perhaps the utility's natural monopoly gives it the market power to pass its taxes through to customers. In some states, there are fees paid to government to acquire and maintain rights of way for utility connections (phone, CATV). Much of the controversy leading to the Internet Tax Freedom Act (ITFA) is based in concerns over new forms of tax primarily targeting Internet use. For example, before passage of the ITFA, a few states and local governments imposed Internet access taxes, which are essentially sales or excise taxes. Another tax proposal is the bit tax—a tax levied for each bit of data transferred. The bit tax causes great anxiety because it varies largely with the amount of use and taxes large files most heavily (streaming video, audio, images). The value-added tax (VAT), a common form of consumption tax in most other nations, is discussed later.

ONLINE

Internet tax challenges
**http://www.nasbo.org/
publications/9604/quiz
.html**
**http://www.nga.org/
nga/salestax**

STATE TAXATION OF INTERSTATE BUSINESS

States may impose burdens on interstate commerce by taxing out-of-state businesses. Taxation is justifiable if the out-of-state business has some connection, local operations, or **nexus** with the taxing state. The nexus is a valid basis for taxation because all residents and nonresidents should pay for their use of governmental benefits, including the protection of the state's laws, police, fire department, and courts, as well as use of its public facilities, such as the direct use of roads or the indirect use of parks or schools by employees. **Use taxes**, as a substitute for sales tax, can be legitimately levied on out-of-state mail order sales if the purchaser resides within the taxing state and the retailer actively solicits orders by mail or phone order.

The collection and remittance of taxes typically occur at points that are most efficient and effective for compliance. For example, income and sales taxes are largely collected and remitted to the state by employers and sellers, respectively. However, the states have been unsuccessful in overcoming due process and commerce clause barriers to imposing collection and remittance duties on out-of-state vendors that have no nexus with the taxing state. This means that some taxes must be collected from individuals, a more costly and less effective process. Use tax collections are much like the difficulty of withholding income taxes on income from nonsalary sources. Both use taxes on self-employment income require a self-reporting honor system. A series of cases on state taxation of interstate commerce has left the states with few good options for collection and remittance of use taxes.

In *National Bellas Hess v. Illinois Dept. of Revenue*,[12] the U.S. Supreme Court held that Illinois could not force a Missouri mail order seller to collect Illinois use tax. Bellas Hess had no facilities within Illinois. Constitutional principles for imposing tax collection and remittance duties on out-of-state businesses were established in *Complete Auto Transit v. Brady*.[13] A sufficient nexus exists to impose these duties when (1) the activity taxed has substantial nexus to the taxing state, (2) the tax is apportioned fairly, (3) the tax does not discriminate against interstate commerce, and (4) the tax fairly relates to services provided by the taxing state.

Sufficient nexus with the taxing state is the key issue in use tax collection cases. Nexus is the same issue discussed in Chapter 1 for jurisdiction purposes. A preponderance of the following factors is used to identify when a firm has sufficient nexus with a taxing state for the state to impose duties to collect and remit without unduly burdening interstate commerce. Most important, a nexus exists when the firm has a substantial physical presence in the state. Physical presence can arise when it has offices, warehouses, and physical inventories within the taxing state. These may be owned or rented spaces. Presence may arise if the firm has sales staff calling on clients in the state, the firm attends trade shows there, uses a Web server in the taxing state, licenses software in the state, or hires agents in the state. For example, out-of-state mail order businesses are generally immune from collecting sales and use taxes in a state where they have neither agents nor physical facilities and contact customers only via phone, mail, delivery carrier, and/or the Internet. However, if the retailer has a single mall or outlet store in the state, a sufficient nexus exists, and the taxing state can require collection and remittance of sales and use taxes. All states have taxing authorities, usually their departments of revenue. These agencies supply use tax forms to customers who purchase taxable goods out-of-state. It is the purchaser's responsibility to pay use taxes.

INTERNET TAX FREEDOM ACT

Throughout the late 1990s, political forces supported continued freedom of e-commerce from new taxes and new compliance burdens. The *Framework* asserted that no new taxes should be imposed on Internet commerce but any Internet taxes should be consistent with the established principles, should avoid inconsistent tax jurisdictions and

---

12. 386 U.S. 753 (1967).
13. 430 U.S. 274 (1977).

double taxation, and should be simple to administer and easy to understand. Several important principles were established. First, Internet taxes should neither distort nor hinder commerce. No tax system should discriminate among types of commerce, nor should it create incentives that will change the nature or location of transactions. Second, the tax system should be simple and transparent, capable of capturing most appropriate revenues, and with burdens of record keeping minimized. Third, the system should accommodate various tax systems in use. Fourth, adaptation of existing taxation concepts and principles is desirable. The *Framework* urges states and local governments to cooperate and develop a uniform approach to e-commerce taxation.

Congress acted on the *Framework* with passage in 1998 of the **Internet Tax Freedom Act (ITFA)**. The ITFA places a temporary moratorium on new application of existing taxes or on the imposition of any new taxes on the Internet. The ITFA did not disturb sales and use and Internet access taxes existing when the act was passed. ITFA appointed a multidisciplinary commission to study and recommend revisions to the labyrinth of different taxes imposed at nearly every level of government. The **Advisory Commission on Electronic Commerce (ACEC)** was chaired by former Virginia Governor James Gilmore. There was no broad consensus in its findings to Congress due in May 2000, so Congress extended the moratorium for another three years.

ONLINE

Commission on Electronic Commerce (ACEC)
http://www. ecommerce commission.org/about .htm

Partisans in the Internet taxation controversy propose solutions that fall into three major groupings. First, there are still Internet advocates who argue that all taxes should be eliminated because they stifle growth in Internet commerce. This position has had some success in creating gridlock but seems unlikely to prevail in the long run. Second, a group advocating tax simplification hopes to achieve a permanent reduction of tax categories applicable to all aspects of Internet use. This proposal holds great promise for efficiency, but many interests can be expected to oppose it. For example, states are likely to resist eliminating their unique tax subjects or methods, and tax preparation professionals probably prefer the complexity of the status quo. A third group seeks to simplify and standardize taxation mechanisms: forms, exemptions, rates, remittance responsibility, and audit procedures, a view with great promise if Congress endorses it.

The Internet and computerization reduce the burden of multijurisdictional complexity. Spreadsheets or other computer programs can much more easily accommodate the various rates and exemptions of all U.S. jurisdictions and any revisions. Complexity is no longer a good excuse for tax simplification or elimination, given that technology now exists to manage the calculation, collection, and remittance of varying taxes. Many of the arguments against state taxation of interstate or international transactions simply are no longer valid. However, reconciling the parochial and historical interests to achieve harmonization of Internet taxation may be a monumental political achievement.

INTERNATIONAL TAXATION

Just like the U.S. municipalities and states, many nations are looking to the Internet for new sources of revenue, particularly for the rather considerable social welfare programs in Europe and Canada. Some are trying to levy taxes and/or tariffs on global e-com-merce. The United States is working through the World Trade Organization (WTO) to declare the Internet a tariff-free environment when used to deliver products or services. However, the prospects for success are limited. Already the EU is seeking to force U.S. phone, mail, and Internet sellers to collect and remit their VAT taxes.

Value-Added Taxes (VAT)

The **value-added tax** (VAT) is an enormously successful tax in most industrialized nations. VAT is a hidden tax that is seldom enumerated on sales invoices. VAT is most often a huge tax applied to the value added at each point along the supply chain. VAT ranges from 15% in Luxembourg to 25% in Sweden and Denmark. VAT is owed by a manufacturer on the difference between the cost of raw materials or component parts and the sale price of finished goods. Similarly, VAT is owed by the wholesaler and retailer on their markup. Therefore, large VAT amounts are collected and remitted all along the supply chain. VAT is a major source of funding for social programs in most other industrialized nations. Of course, VAT makes the cost of comparable goods much higher in those nations than in the United States. By con-trast, sales and use taxes are consumption taxes that are highly visible, and taxpay-ers are always cognizant of their tax burden.

The EU has a complex system to account for and remit VAT for goods sold within EU nations and in cross-border transactions. Usually, the nation with VAT taxing authority is the nation of origin of the product. VAT becomes more prob-lematic when the products sold are intangible, such as software, information, or other digital or "virtual goods." When the products are digital, EU nations suffer a problem similar to the collection of interstate use tax discussed previously. Non-EU nations cannot be compelled to collect VAT on deliveries into the EU from outside the EU. The EU proposes to require all non-EU sellers to "domesticate" by register-ing to do business with at least one EU nation that would give tax nexus and require VAT collection and remittance duties. The EU may try to impose VAT collection and remittance duties on U.S. sellers of digital products.

TELECOMMUNICATIONS REGULATION

E-commerce must use communications networks to carry the electronic messages that negotiate, conclude, and perform contracts. This communications infrastructure includes several evolving technologies and sectors of the telecommunications indus-try. Historically, two major regulatory programs address communications: (1) fed-eral regulation of broadcast and telephone service and (2) state or local regulation of utilities. Much of telecommunications regulation has changed because of the **Telecommunications Act of 1996**. This law partially deregulates the industry, and it encourages competition in various services. This section discusses these regulatory methods as traditionally used for communications infrastructure, the impact of their deregulation, and the prospects for this type of regulation on new services in the converging telecommunications technologies.

REGULATORY FRAMEWORK FOR TELECOMMUNICATIONS

The states have regulated public utilities since the turn-of-the-twentieth-century experience with destructive competition. Under this theory of regulation, utilities are seen as natural monopolies because competition would be inefficient and create duplicate networks. As introduced earlier, the states responded to destructive competition and the resulting natural monopolies by regulating public utilities. The states qualify competent utility firms, grant monopoly-like franchises to provide service in a defined geographic region, require service to all customers, and fix each utility firm's prices by using rate-of-return regulation on their invested capital. Franchise regulation covers various utilities: water, electricity, sewers, natural gas, phone, and cable television (CATV). Utilities are generally viewed as necessities of life (heat in winter), so much of utility regulation concerns assuring all customers access at fair prices (rates).

Although the federal government has also regulated utilities (energy, power), the most enduring federal regulation concerns telecommunications. Regulation of the radio spectrum began in 1910, when radio was expected to have only military and emergency applications. The **radio spectrum** is a limited and scarce public resource. All the available frequencies must be shared by broadcast and communication by radio, TV, wireless, and two-way radio. Only so many users can use the radio spectrum before interference degrades quality. By 1927, Congress created the Federal Radio Commission, assuming that the airwaves are a form of public good. Use of the public airwaves by firms is a privilege that carries public duties.

Although technology continues to expand the capacity of the existing radio spectrum, the increase in users strains this scarce public resource. For example, consider that a decade ago few people used cellular service. Today, many people have landlines at home and work as well as cellular service. This increased usage strains the available phone numbers and the public airwave capacity, as calls and Internet usage shift to wireless. The Communications Act of 1934 created the **Federal Communications Commission (FCC)** to maximize effective use of this scarce telecommunications capacity. The radio spectrum is a scarce resource used for radio and TV broadcasts, wireless telecommunications (portables, cellular, PCS), two-way radio (CB, ham, walkie-talkie, emergency, military), radar, weapons guidance systems, and many promising future uses.

ONLINE

The radio spectrum can be viewed at **htp://www.jsc.mil/ images/speccht.jpg** or **http://www.ntia.doc. gov/osmhome/ allochrt.pdf**

During the twentieth century, regulation by local municipalities, the states, and the FCC has varied as technology has broadened the range of available services and firms have developed new business models. Congress borrowed heavily from the Interstate Commerce Commission's regulation of transportation as it designated telephone firms as common carriers. **Common carriers** offer communication services (telephony, telegraphy) for hire to the public; common carriers have special duties in the public interest.

Telecommunications regulatory programs address five basic objectives. First, regulators limit the firms that may provide telecommunications services. Firms are licensed or allotted franchise territories when these firms qualify as responsible telecommunications providers. Second, the structure of ownership and corporate affiliation among media and telecommunications firms is regulated to capture the benefits of competition when possible and to avert the disadvantages of monopolies and complex corporate affiliations. Third, the prices charged customers by telecommunications firms with natural monopolies are controlled under rate regulation. Fourth, the technologies and technical methods used by telecommunications firms are regulated to achieve standardization and reduce interference. Finally, regulators occasionally exert some control over content. **Content** is the objectives, substance, meaning, and style of the communication's subject matter. Content regulation is sometimes influenced directly but is also influenced indirectly by telecommunications regulation of entry, structure, and rates. The First Amendment constrains content regulation by the states and the FCC.

FEDERAL COMMUNICATIONS COMMISSION

The FCC is a quasi-independent federal agency charged with regulating interstate and international communications by radio, TV, wire, satellite, and cable. The FCC is directed by five commissioners appointed by the president with Senate confirmation for five-year terms. One of the commissioners is designated by the president to serve as chairperson. The FCC must have political balance; no more than three commissioners may be from the same political party. The FCC's jurisdiction over **communications** includes "transmissions of writings, signs, signals, pictures and sounds of all kinds." This includes analog and digital data and all the infrastructure and apparatus used in such transmissions.

The FCC has six operating bureaus and ten staff offices. Among the most important here is the **International Bureau**, with responsibility for satellite and international matters. The **Media Bureau** regulates AM and FM radio and television broadcast stations, as well as multipoint distribution (i.e., cable and satellite) and instructional television fixed services. The **Wireless Telecommunications Bureau** oversees cellular and PCS phones, pagers, and two-way radios and regulates use of the radio spectrum. The **Wireline Competition Bureau** oversees regulation of telephone companies that provide interstate telecommunications services over wire-based transmission facilities (corded and cordless phones). The **Office of Engineering and Technology** allocates spectrum for nongovernment use in cooperation with the Departments of Commerce and Defense and provides the FCC with expert advice on many technical issues (electrical engineering, computer science).

FCC Rule-Making and Enforcement Powers

The FCC's rule-making powers span its regulatory programs in broadcast and telecommunications. The FCC has had some difficulties when new technologies create new businesses outside the FCC's traditional regulatory spheres. For example, CATV was not clearly broadcast TV, nor was it common carriage. Although the FCC could assert some jurisdiction over CATV, the FCC's powers were limited until Congress expressly broadened the FCC's authority over CATV. The Internet and other new technologies are raising similar difficulties for the FCC. For example,

Internet telephony, broadband carried over wireless, CATV, or DSL phone lines, and other **enhanced telecommunications services** continue to raise questions of the FCC's power to regulate entry, rates, competition, technical standards, and content.

STATE AND LOCAL REGULATORS

State and local regulation of telecommunications has generally followed the public utility regulation model. Various regulatory agencies seek to qualify entry by licensing only one or a few firms to become natural monopolies that will exclusively serve a geographic area. Both phone service and CATV rates have been regulated by state and local regulators. However, two forces are reducing the regulatory powers of state and local governments over telecommunications. First, the deregulation movement in the 1980s significantly reduced the power of states and municipalities to regulate monthly cable fees except for basic cable. There is continuing controversy over inflation in CATV rates. CATV rate rises outpace inflation, yet the CATV industry argues that video sales and rentals, video game consoles, movie theaters, and broadcast TV provide sufficient competition so that rates should be completely deregulated. Second, programming and phone service can be delivered using new technologies, and these are introducing some competition (e.g., Internet or CATV telephony, video downloads). The deregulation movement, FCC preemption, and competition from other technologies all suggest that state and local telecommunication regulation will continue to decline.

LICENSING AND ENTRY

A basic function of telecommunications regulation in broadcast and telephony is to create legal barriers to entry. Only firms qualified to do business are given a license or granted operating authority under a franchise. Qualification scrutinizes various factors believed to lead to successful service: which firms are financially sound and which firms are most likely to serve the **public interest**. Over the years, many factors have been used to define public interest, some of which overlap with content regulation; these factors include avoiding indecency, maintaining political balance, maintaining a balanced range of programming (talk, music, news, public affairs), and avoiding excessive commercialization, among others. All these factors are constrained by the First Amendment's freedom of expression. Licensees are qualified by examination of their technical capability to provide the services (transmitters, wiring, trained operators); they must be of good character, free of criminal convictions, have no substantial foreign ownership, and not be guilty of misrepresentations made to regulators.

Access
An important part of telecommunications regulation is **access**, also known as universal service. Telecommunications firms may become common carriers, many with natural monopoly franchises or broadcast over the public airwaves. In exchange for this privilege, telecommunications firms must provide their services to everyone at

reasonable rates. The access principle is at the heart of several well-recognized telecommunications issues: public access CATV channels, equal time in political campaign advertising, and scheduling of neighborhood CATV wiring and rollout. Access is the main issue in the **digital divide**—the difficulty some people experience in accessing the Internet because of their income, lack of broadband in their neighborhood, inappropriate Web site design for people with disabilities, and similar issues.

Access is a two-way street. Web site owners also argue they should not be denied access to post and maintain Web sites to conduct e-commerce or to speak freely over the Internet. In the Internet world, access by suppliers or telecommunications firms is less the traditional issue of radio spectrum scarcity than it is of financial resources and quality performance of these firms. As licensing and other legal barriers to entry decline in importance for telecommunications, access may emerge as a bigger social issue.

STRUCTURAL REGULATION

Structural regulation is an issue related to entry qualification for the firms providing telecommunications services. Structural regulation seeks to prevent monopolies from controlling the major sources of media and communications. Monopolies in telecommunications are undesirable because monopolists who own the infrastructure could slant programming, particularly the news, and influence political questions or provide favoritism to affiliated businesses. The famous antitrust case that resulted in the breakup of the Bell System in 1980 is a dramatic example of antitrust theory applied to the structure of the telecommunications industry.

In recent years, the FCC has relaxed some of its structural regulations. Most of these prevented firms from owning all the major media outlets (radio, TV, newspaper) in metropolitan areas and prohibited affiliated firms from owning more than five TV stations. Structural regulation is an indirect form of content regulation. Competition is used to assure diverse programming and reasonable access by and to various societal factions. Structural regulation was the major issue in the simplification of ownership and control in the electric utility industry after implementation of the Public Utility Holding Company Act of 1935. Such matters are still problematic. For example, the complex affiliation structure of Enron was a major problem leading to its bankruptcy. Enron was an energy company that operated a large pipeline network, traded in energy futures and derivatives, and "dabbled" in broadband telecommunications.

REGULATION OF RATES

Rate regulation is the mechanism intended to balance the public interest with the natural monopoly aspects of network industries. It is too inefficient for several utilities to serve the same customers with duplicate service networks and generation capacities. Public utility commissions and the FCC conduct rate regulation because natural monopolies are more efficient but monopolists are not trusted to treat customers fairly. In the twentieth century, a very extensive experience by the FCC and state utility regulators developed. These adversarial proceedings examined financial measures to set the maximum rates that a utility can charge. Even the deregulation and competition movement in electricity does not convince that rate regulation is passé. Indeed, California's electricity deregulation experience in 2001 and allegations that energy trading firms manipulated wholesale and retail electricity prices suggest that rate regulation is not a dead letter. Periodically, phone and CATV rates have been subject to rate regulation.

TECHNOLOGY AND STANDARDS

Recall the discussion of network industries in Chapters 9 and 11. Telecommunications is the classic network industry because it becomes more valuable as more users participate and there are many technical specifications needed to permit interoperability by all participants. Another major function of telecommunications regulation has been to identify technical specifications needed for interoperability and then establish them as standards. The FCC both sets and recognizes standards so the networks can operate. For example, precise electronic signaling methods must be used in broadcast and telephony so that equipment will work and can be efficiently produced (e.g., phones, ringer equivalency, NTSC, TVs, radios, switches, transmitters, cabling, modems). Technical specifications are also needed so that licensees are confined to use only their limited portion of the radio spectrum. For example, the location and power of broadcast transmitters is important for TV, radio, and cellular services. These limitations help assure adequate signal delivery within the coverage area without creating interference for other rightful users of the radio spectrum.

TELECOMMUNICATIONS REGULATION AND E-COMMERCE

Going forward, telecommunications will continue to be the crucial infrastructure for effective e-commerce. Whether firms implementing EDI use dedicated systems or consumers connect to the Internet via landline or wireless common carriers, this infrastructure is the key component. Telecommunications is historically a closely regulated industry, treated largely like a utility. New technologies replacing old methods and deregulation are two strong forces that may limit the growth of telecommunication regulation. However, the **convergence** of technologies continually raises new questions of consumer protection, competition, and content regulation. For example, the emerging use of the Internet to bypass long-distance telephone carriers illustrates that traditional classification of these infrastructure systems or the business models of telecommunications firms is subject to abrupt change. Many of these issues have been covered in this chapter and elsewhere in this handbook.

INDEX

525